MARVEL MASTERWORKS

PRESENTS

THE Fantastic Four

VOLUME 10

COLLECTING

THE FANTASTIC FOUR NOS. 94-104

& FANTASTIC FOUR: THE LOST ADVENTURE

STAN LEE • JACK KIRBY

WITH JOHN ROMITA

Collection Editor
Cory Sedlmeier

Book Design
Nickel DesignWorks

SVP of Print & Digital Publishing Sales
David Gabriel

Editor in Chief
Axel Alonso

Chief Creative Officer
Joe Quesada

Publisher
Dan Buckley

Executive Producer
Alan Fine

MARVEL MASTERWORKS: THE FANTASTIC FOUR VOL. 10. Contains
material originally published in magazine form as FANTASTIC FOUR #94-
104 and FANTASTIC FOUR: THE LOST ADVENTURE #1. First printing 2014.
ISBN# 978-0-7851-8839-1. Published by MARVEL WORLDWIDE, INC., a
subsidiary of MARVEL ENTERTAINMENT, LLC. OFFICE OF PUBLICATION:
135 West 50th Street, New York, NY 10020. Copyright © 1970, 2007 and
2014 Marvel Characters, Inc. All rights reserved. All characters featured in
this issue and the distinctive names and likenesses thereof, and all related
indicia are trademarks of Marvel Characters, Inc. No similarity between
any of the names, characters, persons, and/or institutions in this magazine
with those of any living or dead person or institution is intended, and any
such similarity which may exist is purely coincidental. **Printed in the
U.S.A.** ALAN FINE, EVP - Office of the President, Marvel Worldwide, Inc. and
EVP & CMO Marvel Characters B.V.; DAN BUCKLEY, Publisher & President -
Print, Animation & Digital Divisions; JOE QUESADA, Chief Creative Officer;
TOM BREVOORT, SVP of Publishing; DAVID BOGART, SVP of Operations
& Procurement, Publishing; C.B. CEBULSKI, SVP of Creator & Content
Development; DAVID GABRIEL, SVP of Print & Digital Publishing Sales;
JIM O'KEEFE, VP of Operations & Logistics; DAN CARR, Executive Director
of Publishing Technology; SUSAN CRESPI, Editorial Operations Manager;
ALEX MORALES, Publishing Operations Manager; STAN LEE, Chairman
Emeritus. For information regarding advertising in Marvel Comics or on
Marvel.com, please contact Niza Disla, Director of Marvel Partnerships,
at ndisla@marvel.com. For Marvel subscription inquiries, please call 800-
217-9158. **Manufactured between 1/3/2014 and 2/10/2014 by R.R.
DONNELLEY, INC., SALEM, VA, USA.**

10 9 8 7 6 5 4 3 2 1

MARVEL MASTERWORKS
CREDITS

THE
FANTASTIC FOUR
NOS. 94-104 & FANTASTIC FOUR: THE LOST ADVENTURE

Writer: **Stan Lee**

Pencilers: **Jack Kirby** (Nos. 94-102; *The Lost Adventure*)
John Romita (Nos. 103, 104)
Ron Frenz (*The Lost Adventure*)

Inkers: Joe Sinnott (Nos. 94, 95, 98-102; *The Lost Adventure*)
Frank Giacoia (Nos. 96, 97)
John Verpoorten (Nos. 103, 104)

Letterers: Sam Rosen (Nos. 94, 96, 97, 100, 103)
Art Simek (Nos. 95, 98, 99, 101, 102, 104)
Dave Lanphear (*The Lost Adventure*)

Collection Cover Art: Jack Kirby & Richard Isanove

Color & Art Reconstruction: Michael Kelleher & Kellustration

Special Thanks: Tom Brevoort, Tony Fornaro, Lisa Kirby, Ralph Macchio, John Morrow, Barry Pearl & Paul Shiple

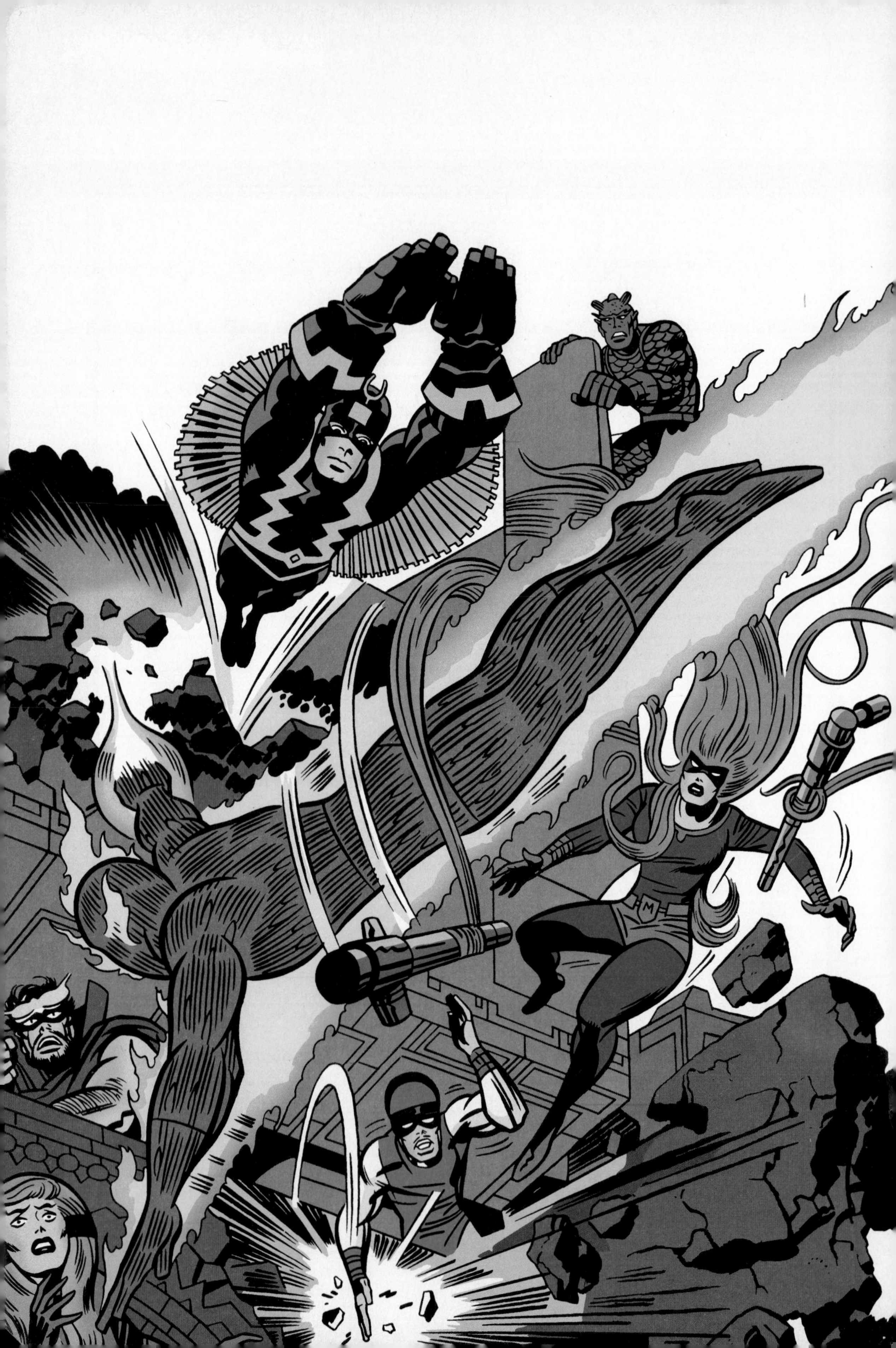

MARVEL MASTERWORKS
CONTENTS

INTRODUCTION
BY STAN LEE

Hi, Heroes!

Well, this is it! This is the one I've been looking forward to—and dreading, at the same time.

Looking forward because we're finally in double digits. I mean, can you imagine, it's the tenth edition of the good ol' FF Masterworks. Hey, that's gotta be some sort of comic book record, right?

But, I've also been dreading it because it completes my run with Jack. Issue #102 was when Jack reluctantly decided it was time to let someone else play in the *Fantastic Four* playground while he went on to other projects. But we both knew it would be fun to see if any other team could beat our unbroken record for a string of more than 100 consecutive issues.

And I've just gotta say it. They weren't just over 100 normal comic book issues. No way! I've just reread most of the stories and, even though it'll sound swell-headed, I've gotta tell you—they're as good or better than any comic books before or after! I'll admit I'm prejudiced, but I dare you to read these strips and tell me I'm wrong!

Speaking of the strips themselves, the FF is probably the only comic book in which two of the main characters get married and then have a baby who becomes part of the ongoing legend. Yep, in issue 94 you're gonna meet Franklin Benjamin Richards, and you'd better not go kootchy-kootchy-koo around him because super hero kids don't dig that kind'a stuff.

Y'know, my own daughter was growing up about the time that baby Franklin made his appearance, so writing about Reed and Sue's little baby took on an extra dramatic meaning for me.

But let me give you a small inkling about the great stuff that you're gonna find on the pages ahead. (I know the writer isn't supposed to say how great the stories are, but hey, let's face it, I happen to be my biggest fan!)

Right off, you're gonna meet Agatha Harkness, the most mysterious babysitter of all time. Then, to add some additional excitement, the Frightful Four decide to drop in for some deadly fun and games.

The next few issues, starting with the Mad Thinker and his Androids of Death, gave Jack and me a chance to return to the grand and gory days of our old monster strips. No matter what else we might have produced, we always had a warm spot in our mixed-up little hearts for mad scientists and macabre monsters.

Then, once we got The Monster from the Lost Lagoon out of the way, it seemed like a good idea to take our burgeoning band of bantering heroes to the moon. After all, I figured it would be easier for Jolly Jack to draw some simple moonscapes than the usual elaborate and exotic backgrounds for which he was justly famous. Face it, even the King deserved a break now and then.

Y'know, Jack and I tried to keep our strip as topical as possible. So what could be more natural than to have the FF try to save the Apollo 11 moon mission. Once again, ol' Kirby's artwork was so great that I got airsick just lookin' at it!

I've always thought that one of the great things about the Fantastic Four is the way they introduced other new characters who were so exciting, so colorful, so interesting that they really deserved to be in books of their own. Right at the head of that luminous list is the uncanny Inhumans. Man, how I loved those guys! Just between us, I never understood why the powers that be at mighty Marvel didn't give Black Bolt and his somewhat peculiar playmates a book of their own as soon as they saw how magnificently Jack drew them—especially after the ton of fan mail came pouring in. But, there's always tomorrow.

I can't wait till you get to issue #100! If you think it was easy getting all those super-villains in one story, you're dead wrong. But, if you think it was fun, go to the head of the class. Just between us, I always marveled (my favorite word!) at how Jack could remember all the characters he had drawn over the years. I had trouble even recalling their names, but he remembered every little feature and costume and weapon and intricate detail of each and every one of them. I sometimes suspected that he hadn't really designed them at all—for all I knew, he had a big barn in back of his house where he kept them all locked up until he needed them to pose for him!

And how about our three-part epic beginning with ish #102, which pits the fighting FF against two of literature's all-time greatest characters, the Sub-Mariner and Magneto! Of course, since we always try to give Comicdom Assembled its money's worth, we even included a guest appearance by President Richard Nixon. I was sure he'd give Marvel some sort of award for that, but I guess he was just too busy to read that issue. Oh well, it was his loss.

I'm sure the sharp-eyed among you noticed something odd. The last two issues, #s 103 and 104, were drawn by Jazzy Johnny Romita. You can see why he too has become a comic book legend when you realize that it's hard to tell that there's a different artist on the strip. Any time he had to pinch-hit for another artist, he could do it so magnificently that the reader couldn't even tell the difference except for the fact that I always insisted that every strip bear the name of the artist who drew it. We may not always have pleased every reader with every story, but we always did our best to level with our fans. You see, we're fans, also, so we know how you feel.

Well, I really feel kind'a sad about ending this intro, because the FF means so much to me. As you probably know, they were the first of the mighty Marvel pantheon of comic book Masterworks. They set the pace, they set the style and made it all begin. Truly, there'll always be new, terrific super heroes coming along, but there'll never be another Fantastic Four—and you can take that to the bank!

EXCELSIOR!

Stan Lee

2006

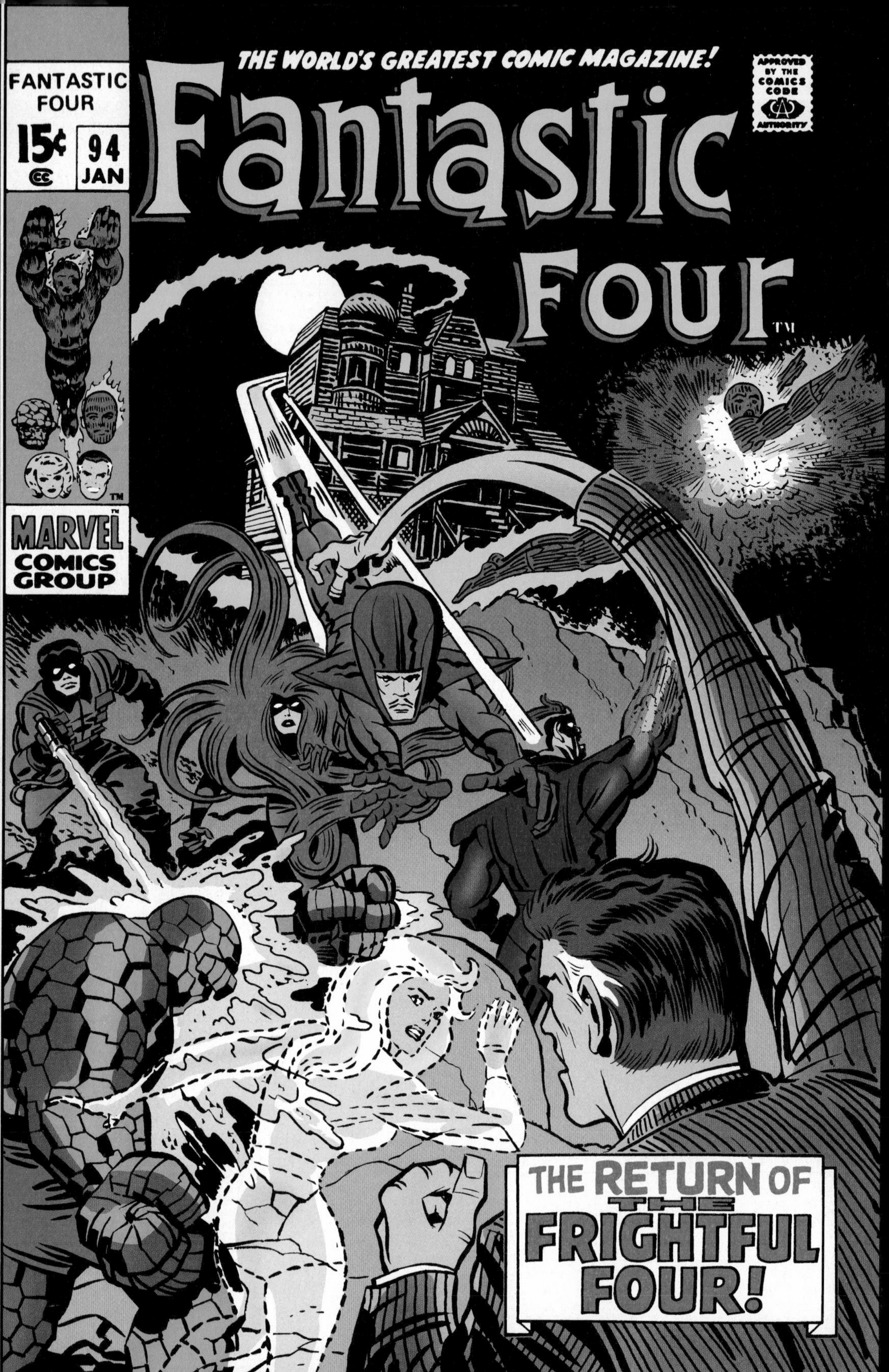
FANTASTIC FOUR
15¢
94 JAN
THE WORLD'S GREATEST COMIC MAGAZINE!
APPROVED BY THE COMICS CODE AUTHORITY
Fantastic Four
MARVEL COMICS GROUP
THE RETURN OF THE FRIGHTFUL FOUR!

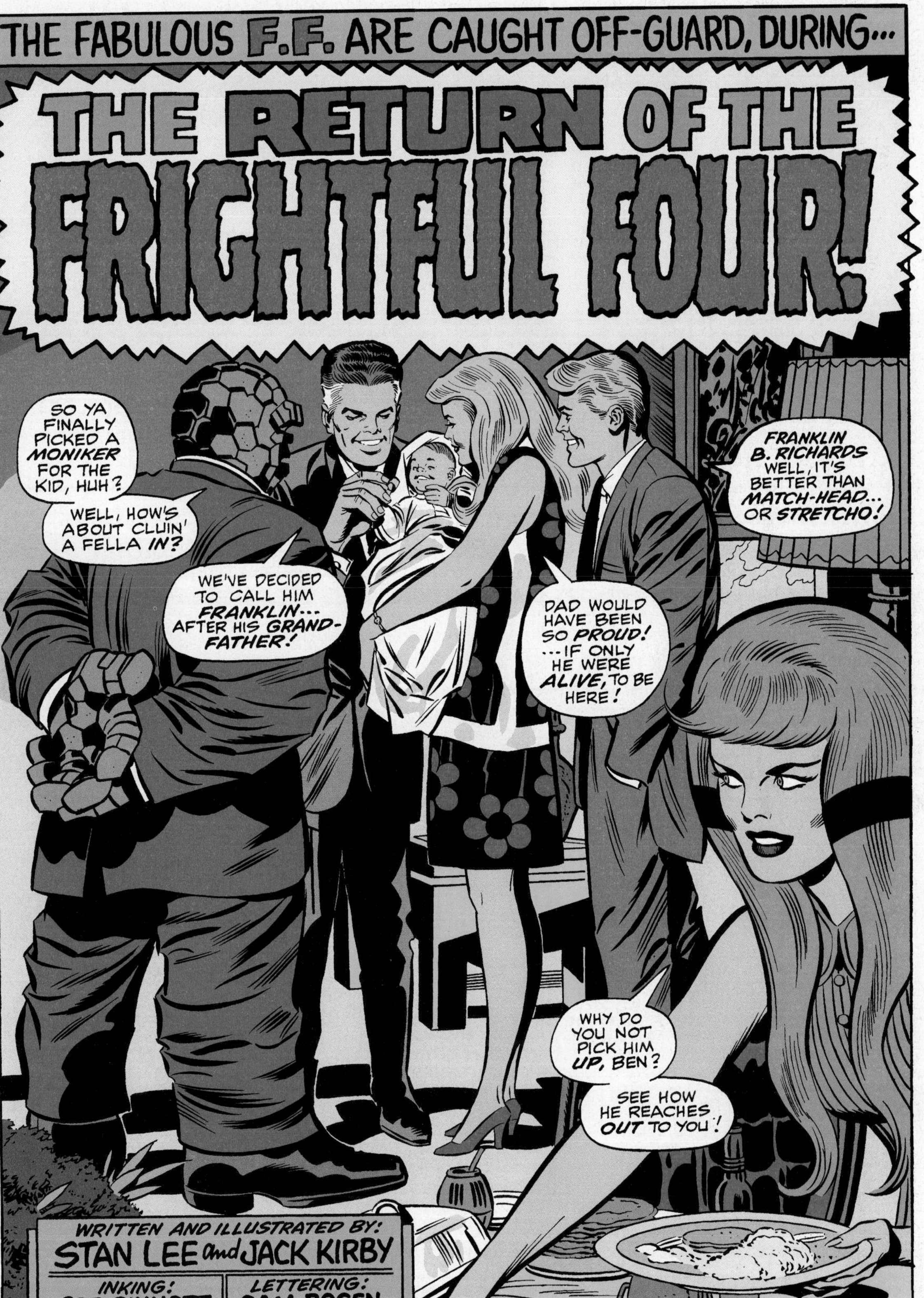

THE FABULOUS F.F. ARE CAUGHT OFF-GUARD, DURING...
THE RETURN OF THE FRIGHTFUL FOUR!
SO YA FINALLY PICKED A MONIKER FOR THE KID, HUH?
WELL, HOW'S ABOUT CLUIN' A FELLA IN?
WE'VE DECIDED TO CALL HIM FRANKLIN... AFTER HIS GRAND-FATHER!
DAD WOULD HAVE BEEN SO PROUD! ...IF ONLY HE WERE ALIVE, TO BE HERE!
FRANKLIN B. RICHARDS WELL, IT'S BETTER THAN MATCH-HEAD... OR STRETCHO!
WHY DO YOU NOT PICK HIM UP, BEN?
SEE HOW HE REACHES OUT TO YOU!
WRITTEN AND ILLUSTRATED BY: STAN LEE and JACK KIRBY
INKING: JOE SINNOTT
LETTERING: SAM ROSEN

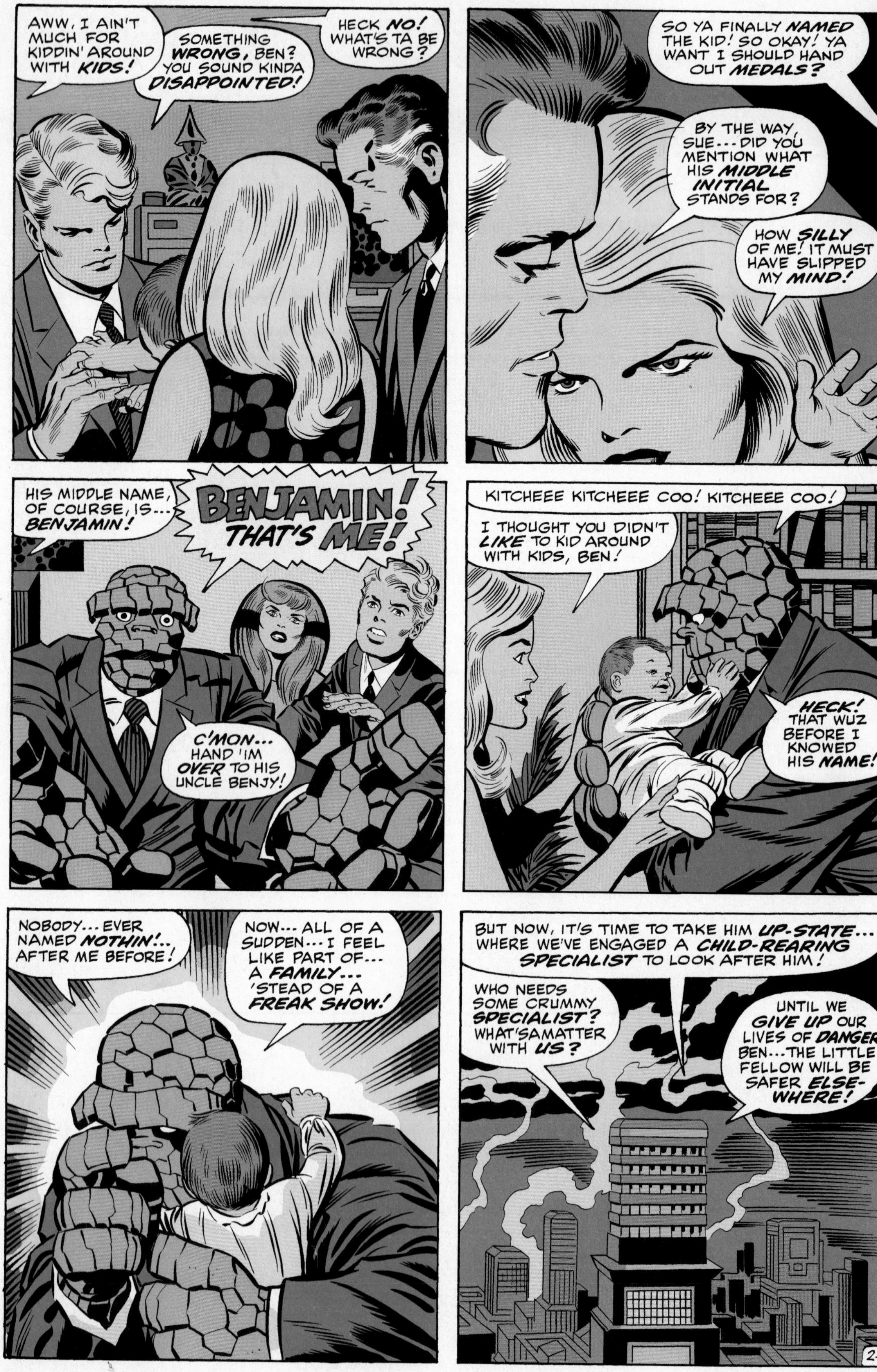
AWW, I AIN'T MUCH FOR KIDDIN' AROUND WITH KIDS!
SOMETHING WRONG, BEN? YOU SOUND KINDA DISAPPOINTED!
HECK NO! WHAT'S TA BE WRONG?
SO YA FINALLY NAMED THE KID! SO OKAY! YA WANT I SHOULD HAND OUT MEDALS?
BY THE WAY, SUE... DID YOU MENTION WHAT HIS MIDDLE INITIAL STANDS FOR?
HOW SILLY OF ME! IT MUST HAVE SLIPPED MY MIND!
HIS MIDDLE NAME, OF COURSE, IS... BENJAMIN!
BENJAMIN! THAT'S ME!
C'MON... HAND 'IM OVER TO HIS UNCLE BENJY!
KITCHEEE KITCHEEE COO! KITCHEEE COO!
I THOUGHT YOU DIDN'T LIKE TO KID AROUND WITH KIDS, BEN!
HECK! THAT WUZ BEFORE I KNOWED HIS NAME!
NOBODY... EVER NAMED NOTHIN'... AFTER ME BEFORE!
NOW... ALL OF A SUDDEN... I FEEL LIKE PART OF... A FAMILY... 'STEAD OF A FREAK SHOW!
BUT NOW, IT'S TIME TO TAKE HIM UP-STATE... WHERE WE'VE ENGAGED A CHILD-REARING SPECIALIST TO LOOK AFTER HIM!
WHO NEEDS SOME CRUMMY SPECIALIST? WHAT'SAMATTER WITH US?
UNTIL WE GIVE UP OUR LIVES OF DANGER, BEN... THE LITTLE FELLOW WILL BE SAFER ELSE-WHERE!
2.

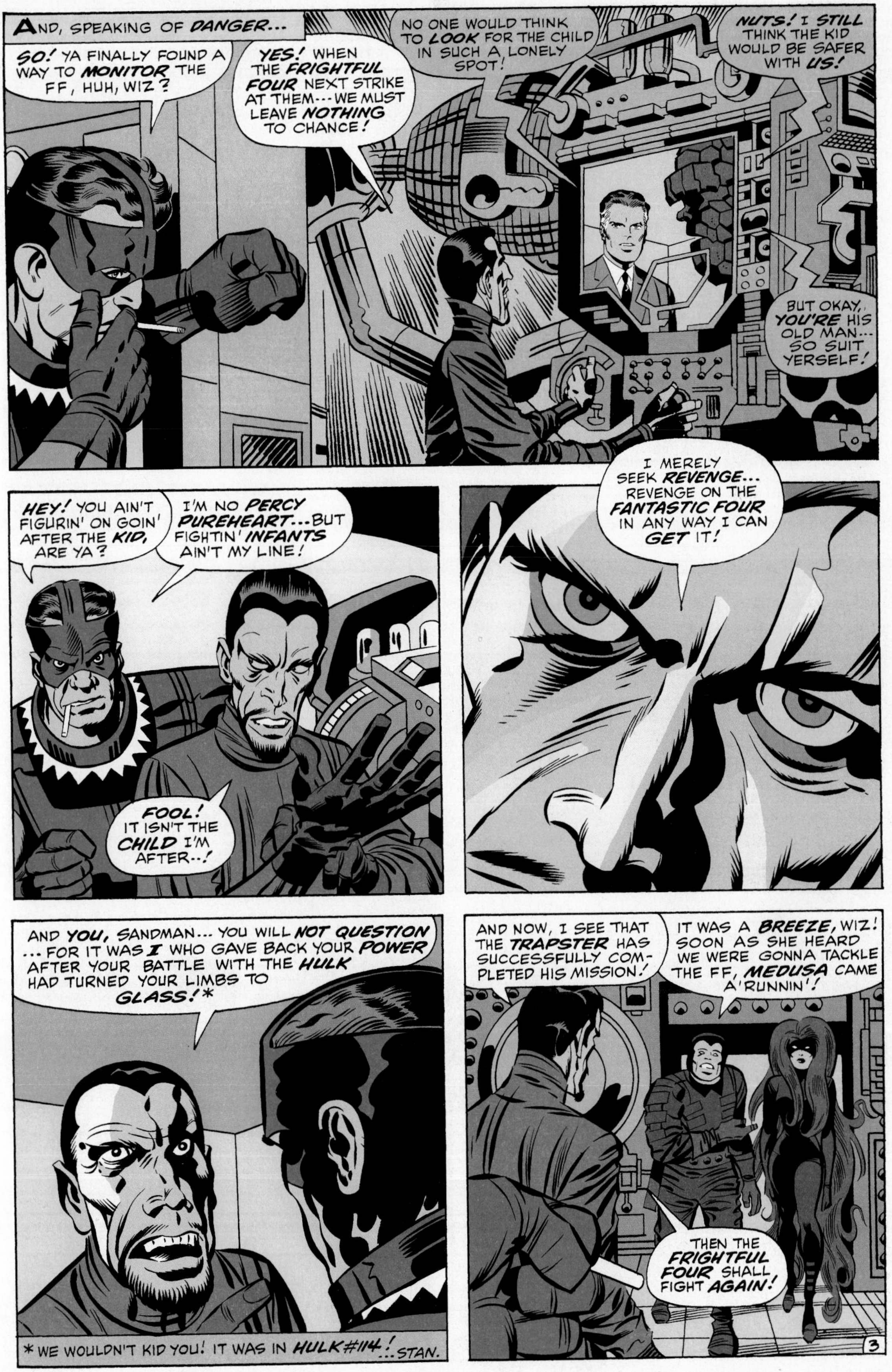

AND, SPEAKING OF DANGER...
SO! YA FINALLY FOUND A WAY TO MONITOR THE FF, HUH, WIZ?
YES! WHEN THE FRIGHTFUL FOUR NEXT STRIKE AT THEM--- WE MUST LEAVE NOTHING TO CHANCE!
NO ONE WOULD THINK TO LOOK FOR THE CHILD IN SUCH A LONELY SPOT!
NUTS! I STILL THINK THE KID WOULD BE SAFER WITH US!
BUT OKAY, YOU'RE HIS OLD MAN... SO SUIT YERSELF!
HEY! YOU AIN'T FIGURIN' ON GOIN' AFTER THE KID, ARE YA?
I'M NO PERCY PUREHEART... BUT FIGHTIN' INFANTS AIN'T MY LINE!
FOOL! IT ISN'T THE CHILD I'M AFTER..!
I MERELY SEEK REVENGE... REVENGE ON THE FANTASTIC FOUR IN ANY WAY I CAN GET IT!
AND YOU, SANDMAN... YOU WILL NOT QUESTION ... FOR IT WAS I WHO GAVE BACK YOUR POWER AFTER YOUR BATTLE WITH THE HULK HAD TURNED YOUR LIMBS TO GLASS! *
* WE WOULDN'T KID YOU! IT WAS IN HULK #114! ...STAN.
AND NOW, I SEE THAT THE TRAPSTER HAS SUCCESSFULLY COMPLETED HIS MISSION!
IT WAS A BREEZE, WIZ! SOON AS SHE HEARD WE WERE GONNA TACKLE THE FF, MEDUSA CAME A'RUNNIN'!
THEN THE FRIGHTFUL FOUR SHALL FIGHT AGAIN!
3

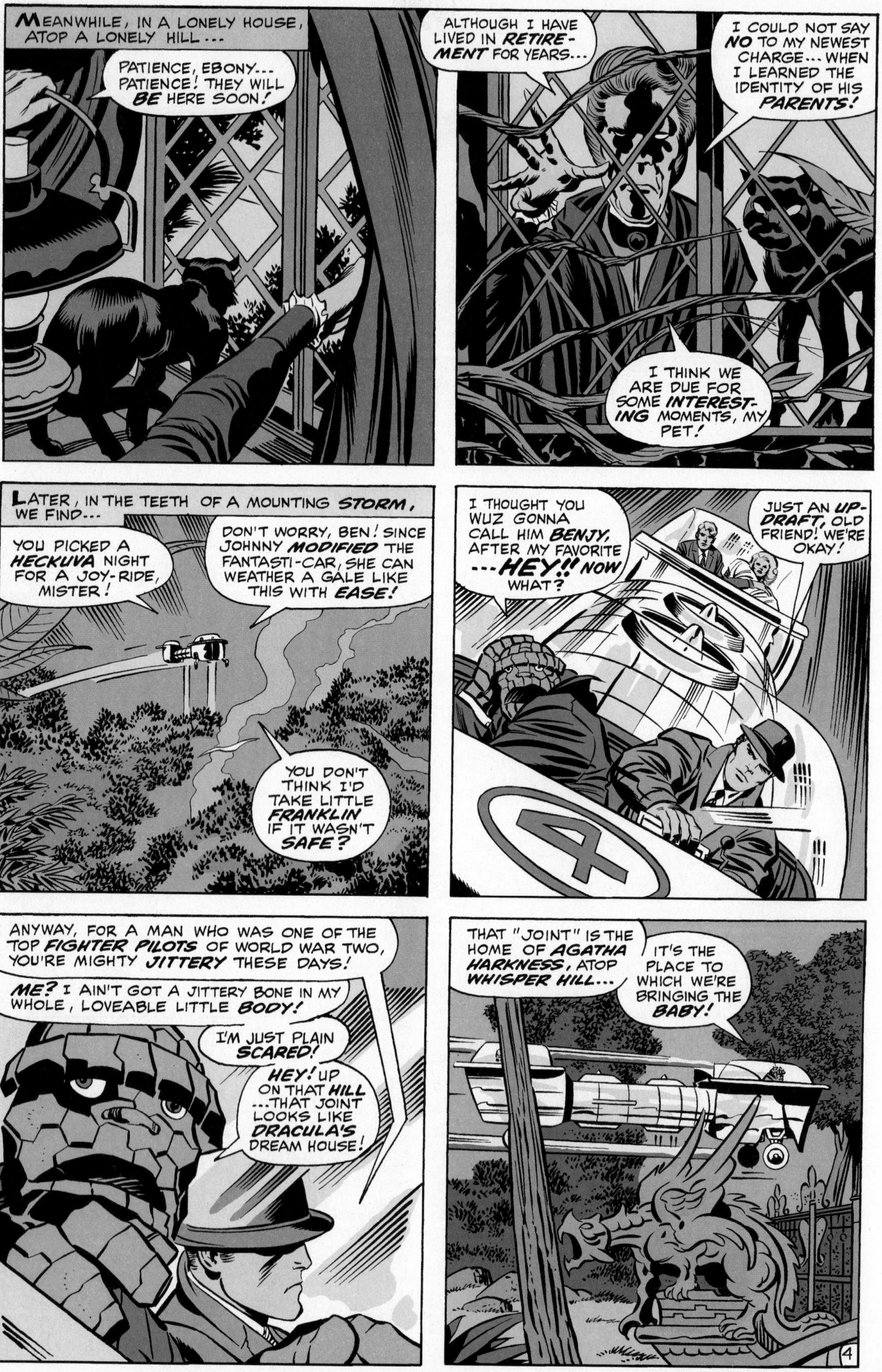
MEANWHILE, IN A LONELY HOUSE, ATOP A LONELY HILL...
PATIENCE, EBONY... PATIENCE! THEY WILL BE HERE SOON!
ALTHOUGH I HAVE LIVED IN RETIREMENT FOR YEARS...
I COULD NOT SAY NO TO MY NEWEST CHARGE... WHEN I LEARNED THE IDENTITY OF HIS PARENTS!
I THINK WE ARE DUE FOR SOME INTERESTING MOMENTS, MY PET!
LATER, IN THE TEETH OF A MOUNTING STORM, WE FIND...
YOU PICKED A HECKUVA NIGHT FOR A JOY-RIDE, MISTER!
DON'T WORRY, BEN! SINCE JOHNNY MODIFIED THE FANTASTI-CAR, SHE CAN WEATHER A GALE LIKE THIS WITH EASE!
YOU DON'T THINK I'D TAKE LITTLE FRANKLIN IF IT WASN'T SAFE?
I THOUGHT YOU WUZ GONNA CALL HIM BENJY, AFTER MY FAVORITE ---HEY!! NOW WHAT?
JUST AN UP-DRAFT, OLD FRIEND! WE'RE OKAY!
ANYWAY, FOR A MAN WHO WAS ONE OF THE TOP FIGHTER PILOTS OF WORLD WAR TWO, YOU'RE MIGHTY JITTERY THESE DAYS!
ME? I AIN'T GOT A JITTERY BONE IN MY WHOLE, LOVEABLE LITTLE BODY!
I'M JUST PLAIN SCARED!
HEY! UP ON THAT HILL ...THAT JOINT LOOKS LIKE DRACULA'S DREAM HOUSE!
THAT "JOINT" IS THE HOME OF AGATHA HARKNESS, ATOP WHISPER HILL...
IT'S THE PLACE TO WHICH WE'RE BRINGING THE BABY!
4

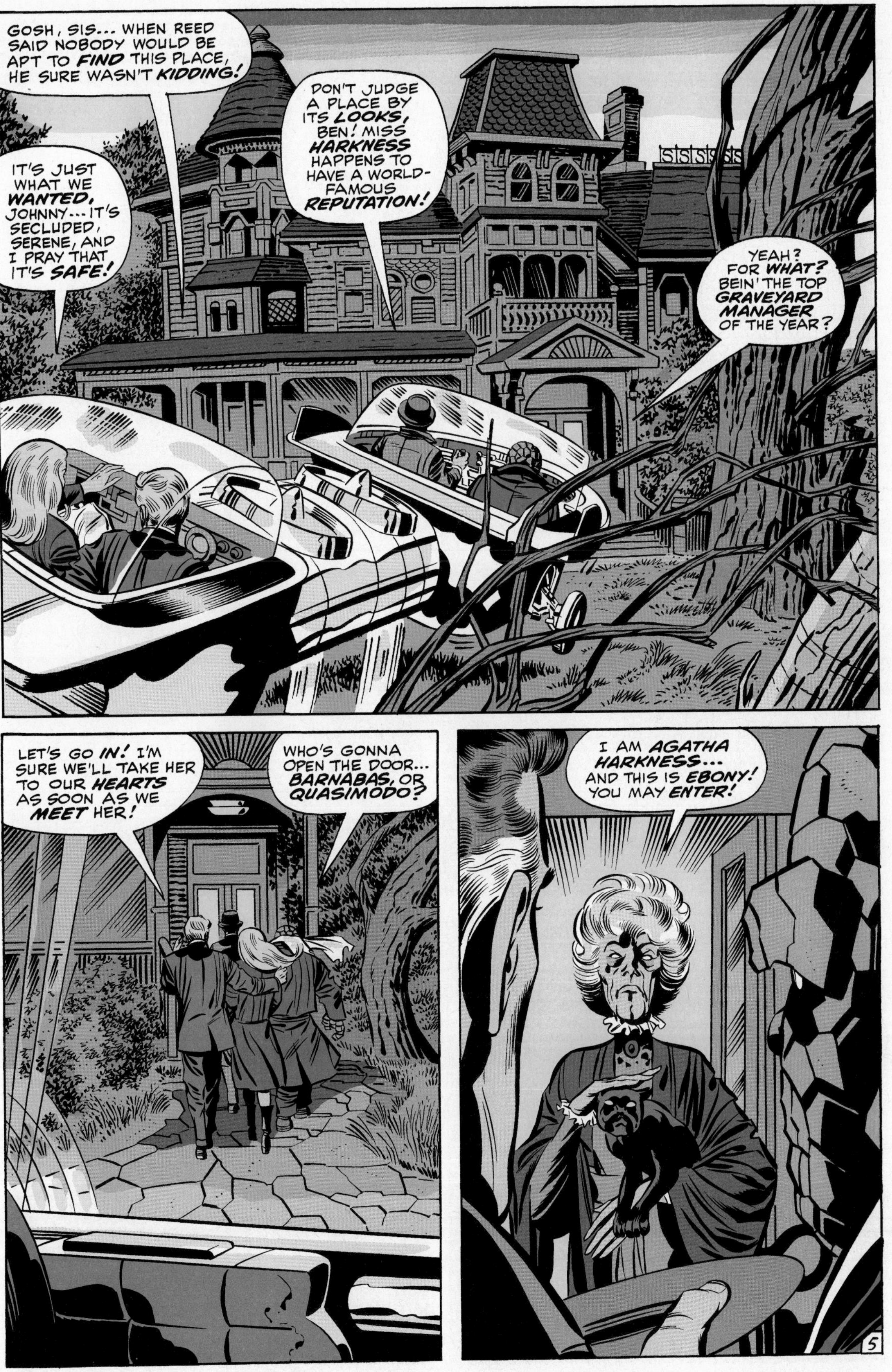
GOSH, SIS... WHEN REED SAID NOBODY WOULD BE APT TO FIND THIS PLACE, HE SURE WASN'T KIDDING!
IT'S JUST WHAT WE WANTED, JOHNNY... IT'S SECLUDED, SERENE, AND I PRAY THAT IT'S SAFE!
DON'T JUDGE A PLACE BY ITS LOOKS, BEN! MISS HARKNESS HAPPENS TO HAVE A WORLD-FAMOUS REPUTATION!
YEAH? FOR WHAT? BEIN' THE TOP GRAVEYARD MANAGER OF THE YEAR?
LET'S GO IN! I'M SURE WE'LL TAKE HER TO OUR HEARTS AS SOON AS WE MEET HER!
WHO'S GONNA OPEN THE DOOR... BARNABAS, OR QUASIMODO?
I AM AGATHA HARKNESS... AND THIS IS EBONY! YOU MAY ENTER!
5

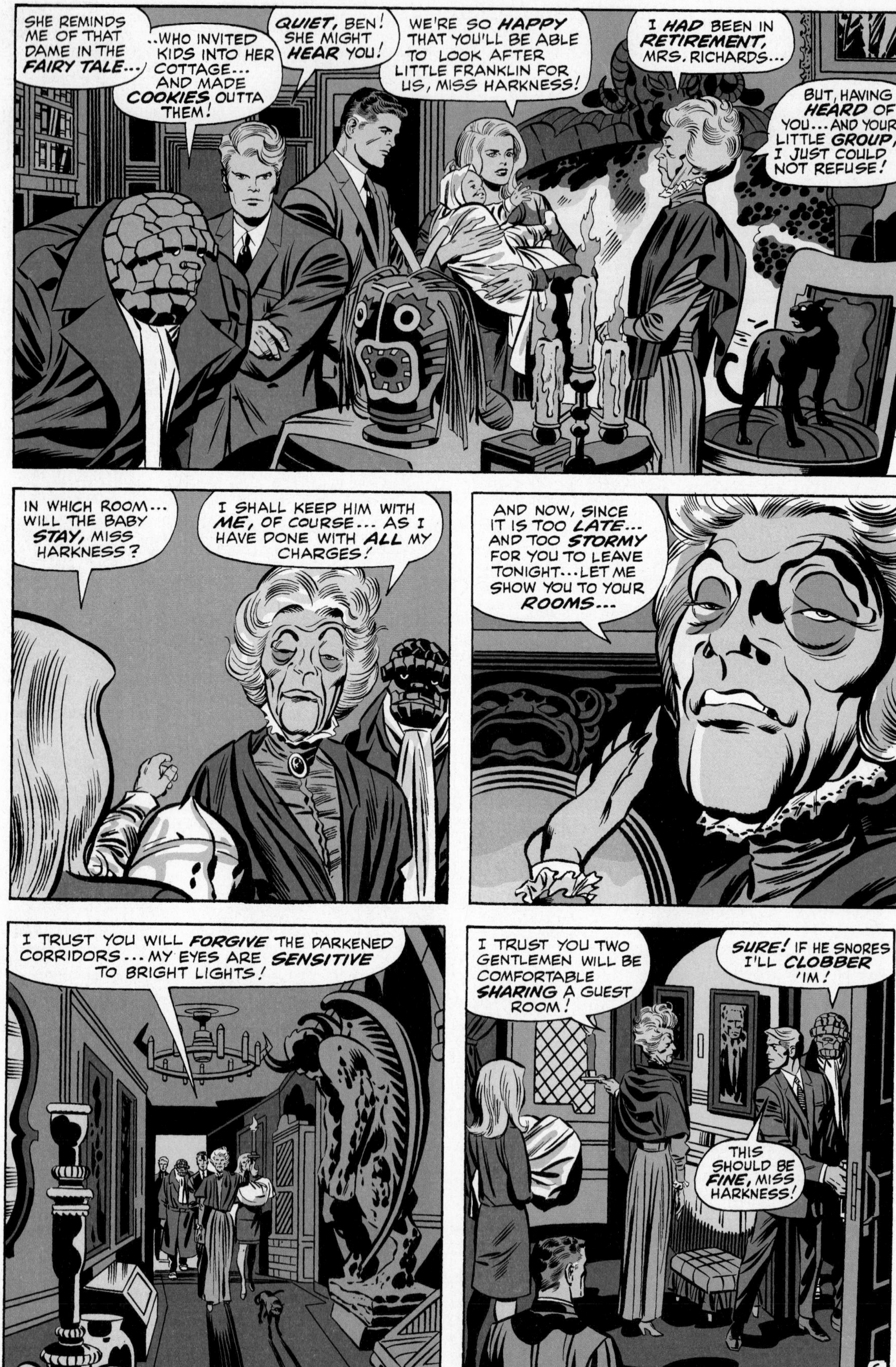
SHE REMINDS ME OF THAT DAME IN THE FAIRY TALE...
..WHO INVITED KIDS INTO HER COTTAGE... AND MADE COOKIES OUTTA THEM!
QUIET, BEN! SHE MIGHT HEAR YOU!
WE'RE SO HAPPY THAT YOU'LL BE ABLE TO LOOK AFTER LITTLE FRANKLIN FOR US, MISS HARKNESS!
I HAD BEEN IN RETIREMENT, MRS. RICHARDS...
BUT, HAVING HEARD OF YOU... AND YOUR LITTLE GROUP, I JUST COULD NOT REFUSE!
IN WHICH ROOM... WILL THE BABY STAY, MISS HARKNESS?
I SHALL KEEP HIM WITH ME, OF COURSE... AS I HAVE DONE WITH ALL MY CHARGES!
AND NOW, SINCE IT IS TOO LATE... AND TOO STORMY FOR YOU TO LEAVE TONIGHT... LET ME SHOW YOU TO YOUR ROOMS...
I TRUST YOU WILL FORGIVE THE DARKENED CORRIDORS... MY EYES ARE SENSITIVE TO BRIGHT LIGHTS!
I TRUST YOU TWO GENTLEMEN WILL BE COMFORTABLE SHARING A GUEST ROOM!
SURE! IF HE SNORES I'LL CLOBBER 'IM!
THIS SHOULD BE FINE, MISS HARKNESS!
6

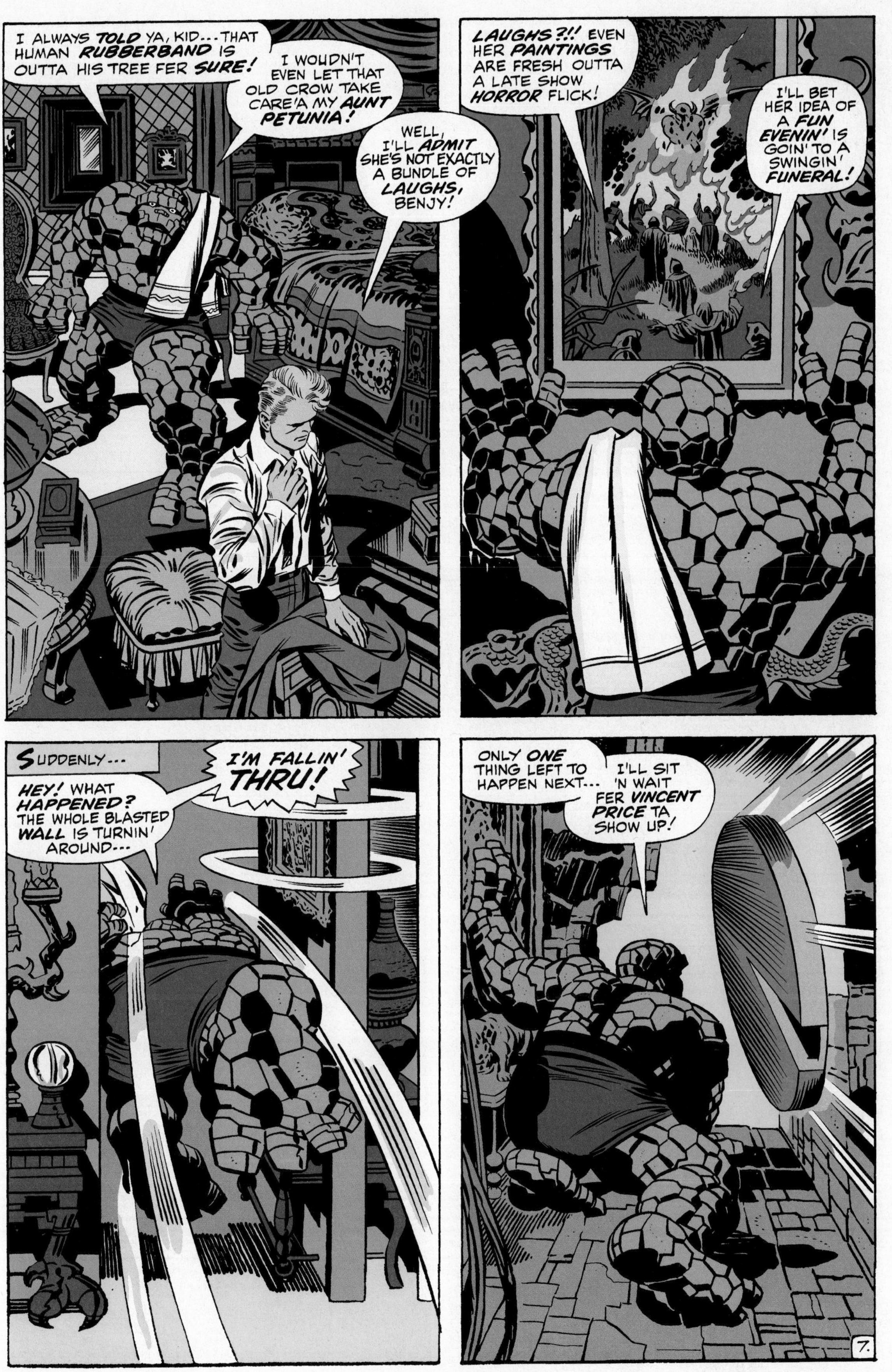
I ALWAYS TOLD YA, KID... THAT HUMAN RUBBERBAND IS OUTTA HIS TREE FER SURE!
I WOULDN'T EVEN LET THAT OLD CROW TAKE CARE'A MY AUNT PETUNIA!
WELL, I'LL ADMIT SHE'S NOT EXACTLY A BUNDLE OF LAUGHS, BENJY!
LAUGHS?!! EVEN HER PAINTINGS ARE FRESH OUTTA A LATE SHOW HORROR FLICK!
I'LL BET HER IDEA OF A FUN EVENIN' IS GOIN' TO A SWINGIN' FUNERAL!
SUDDENLY...
HEY! WHAT HAPPENED? THE WHOLE BLASTED WALL IS TURNIN' AROUND...
I'M FALLIN' THRU!
ONLY ONE THING LEFT TO HAPPEN NEXT...
I'LL SIT 'N WAIT FER VINCENT PRICE TA SHOW UP!
7.

YEOW!

SOMETHIN' HIT MY *BACK*...STICKIN' TO IT...PUSHIN' ME *UP*...TO THE *CEILIN'!*

CAN'T EVEN *REACH* BACK THERE---TO GIT IT *OFF!*

WHAT AM I SUPPOSED TA DO *NOW?*

MERELY *REMAIN* THERE... HELPLESS AND INEFFECTUAL... BECAUSE OF MY *ANTI-GRAV DISC!*

I GOTTA *HAND* IT TO YA, *WIZ!* YOU GOT 'IM *FIRST* CRACK OUTTA THE *BOX!*

NOW THERE'S ONLY *THREE* MORE TO GO!

THE *WIZARD*... AND *SAND-MAN!* I SHOULDA *GUESSED!*

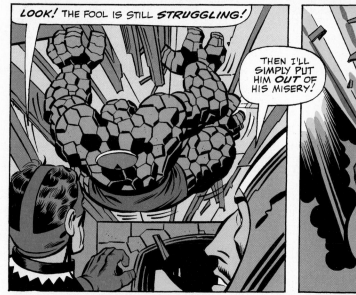

LOOK! THE FOOL IS STILL *STRUGGLING!*

THEN I'LL SIMPLY PUT HIM *OUT* OF HIS MISERY!

A *DOUBLE-INTENSITY* BLAST FROM MY *POWER GLOVE* SHOULD DO THE TRICK!

BULL'S EYE!

8

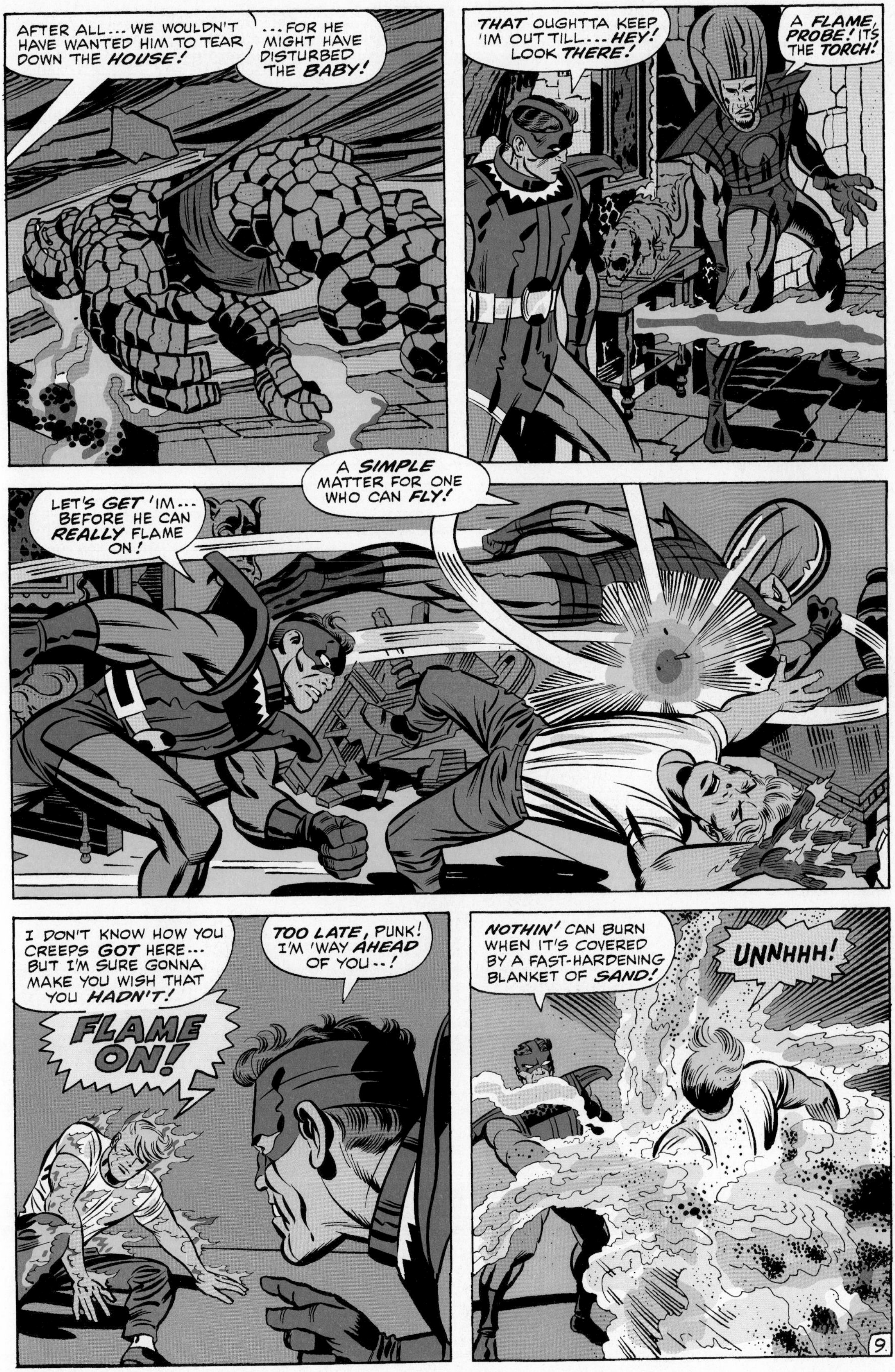
AFTER ALL... WE WOULDN'T HAVE WANTED HIM TO TEAR DOWN THE HOUSE!
...FOR HE MIGHT HAVE DISTURBED THE BABY!
THAT OUGHTTA KEEP 'IM OUT TILL... HEY! LOOK THERE!
A FLAME, PROBE! IT'S THE TORCH!
LET'S GET 'IM... BEFORE HE CAN REALLY FLAME ON!
A SIMPLE MATTER FOR ONE WHO CAN FLY!
I DON'T KNOW HOW YOU CREEPS GOT HERE... BUT I'M SURE GONNA MAKE YOU WISH THAT YOU HADN'T!
FLAME ON!
TOO LATE, PUNK! I'M 'WAY AHEAD OF YOU--!
NOTHIN' CAN BURN WHEN IT'S COVERED BY A FAST-HARDENING BLANKET OF SAND!
UNNHHH!
9

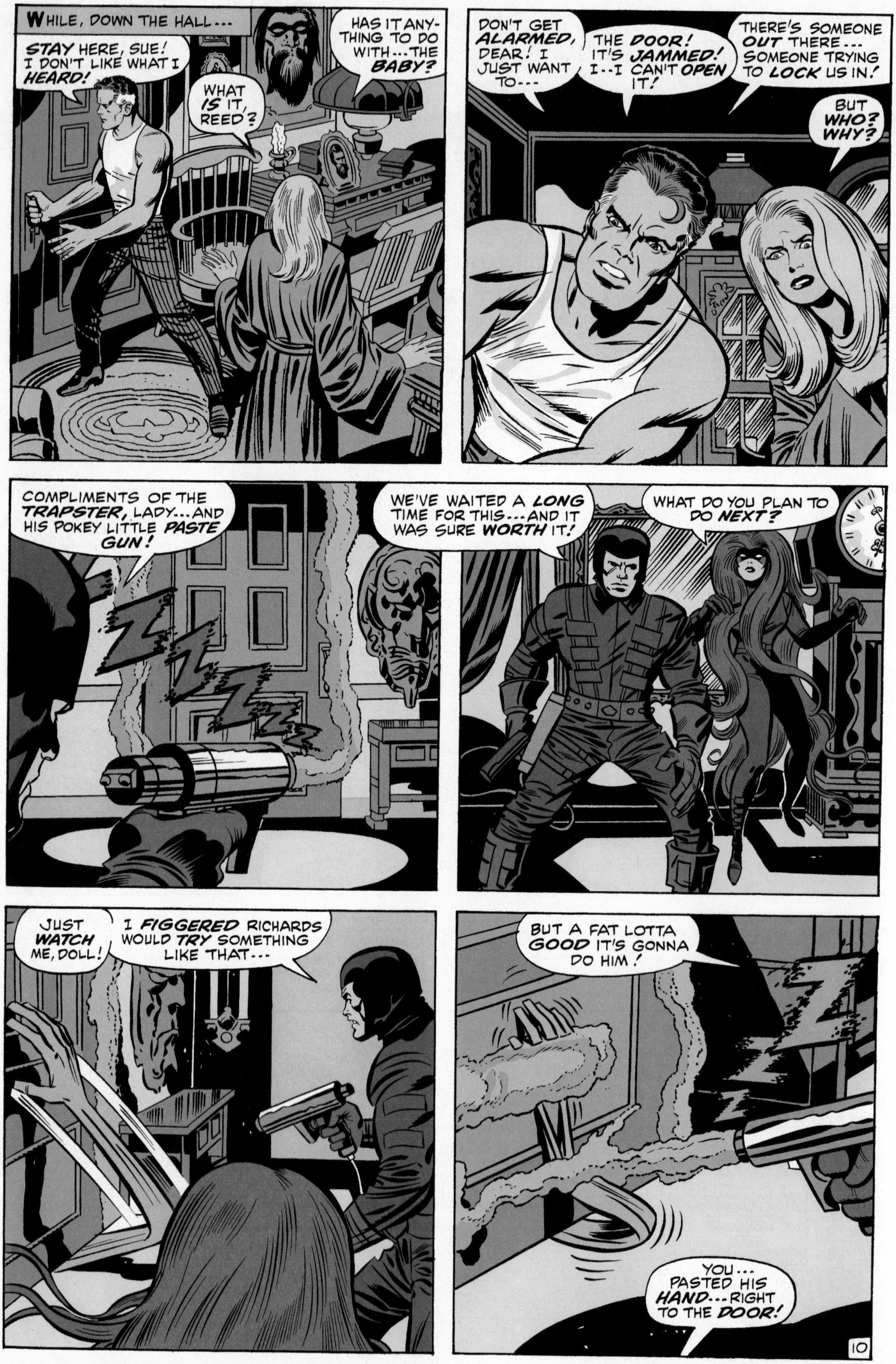

WHILE, DOWN THE HALL...
STAY HERE, SUE! I DON'T LIKE WHAT I HEARD!
WHAT IS IT, REED?
HAS IT ANYTHING TO DO WITH... THE BABY?
DON'T GET ALARMED, DEAR! I JUST WANT TO---
THE DOOR! IT'S JAMMED! I--I CAN'T OPEN IT!
THERE'S SOMEONE OUT THERE--- SOMEONE TRYING TO LOCK US IN!
BUT WHO? WHY?
COMPLIMENTS OF THE TRAPSTER, LADY... AND HIS POKEY LITTLE PASTE GUN!
WE'VE WAITED A LONG TIME FOR THIS---AND IT WAS SURE WORTH IT!
WHAT DO YOU PLAN TO DO NEXT?
JUST WATCH ME, DOLL!
I FIGGERED RICHARDS WOULD TRY SOMETHING LIKE THAT---
BUT A FAT LOTTA GOOD IT'S GONNA DO HIM!
YOU... PASTED HIS HAND... RIGHT TO THE DOOR!
10

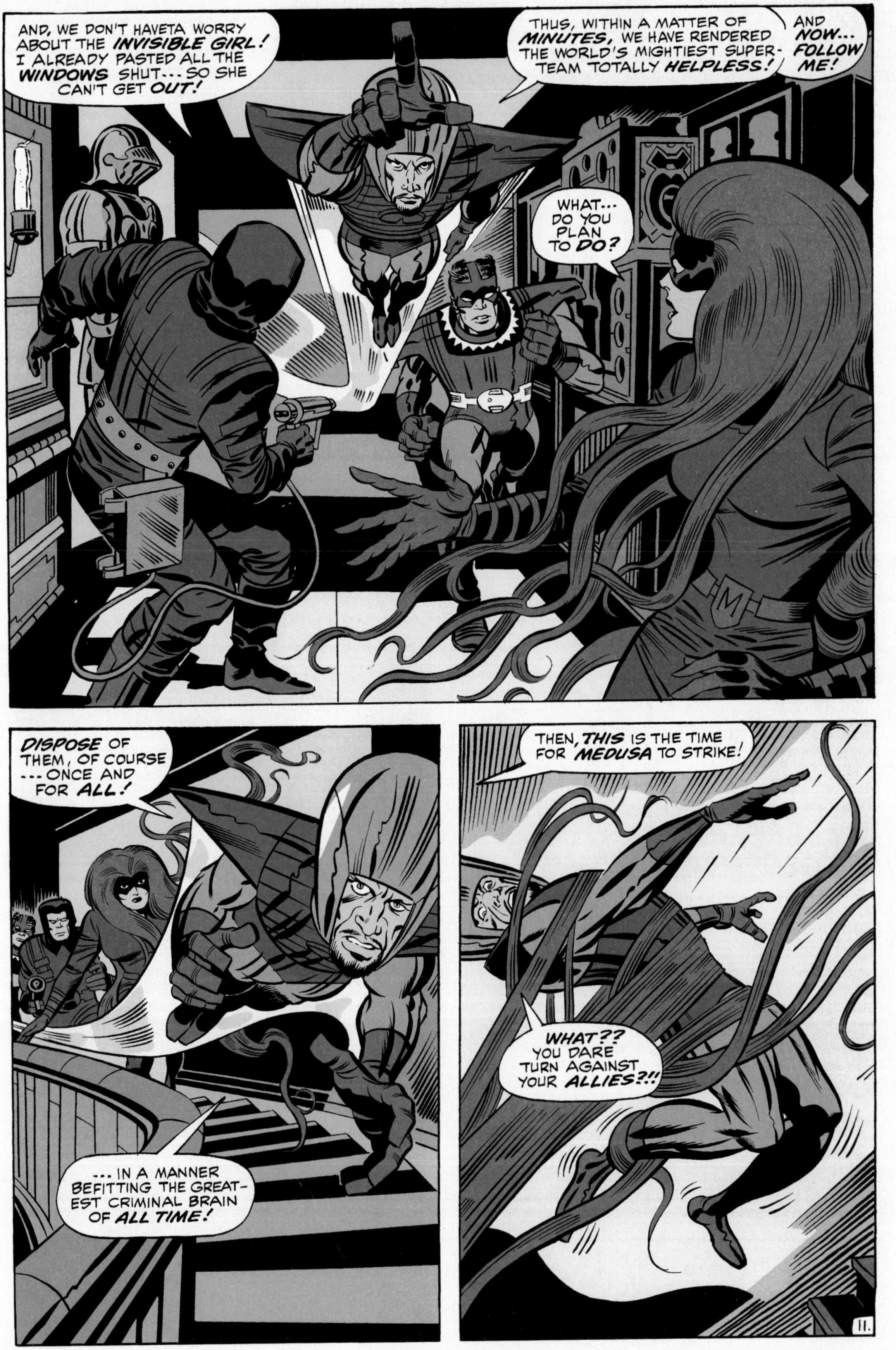
AND, WE DON'T HAVETA WORRY ABOUT THE INVISIBLE GIRL! I ALREADY PASTED ALL THE WINDOWS SHUT... SO SHE CAN'T GET OUT!
THUS, WITHIN A MATTER OF MINUTES, WE HAVE RENDERED THE WORLD'S MIGHTIEST SUPER-TEAM TOTALLY HELPLESS!
AND NOW... FOLLOW ME!
WHAT... DO YOU PLAN TO DO?
DISPOSE OF THEM, OF COURSE --- ONCE AND FOR ALL!
...IN A MANNER BEFITTING THE GREATEST CRIMINAL BRAIN OF ALL TIME!
THEN, THIS IS THE TIME FOR MEDUSA TO STRIKE!
WHAT?? YOU DARE TURN AGAINST YOUR ALLIES?!!
11.

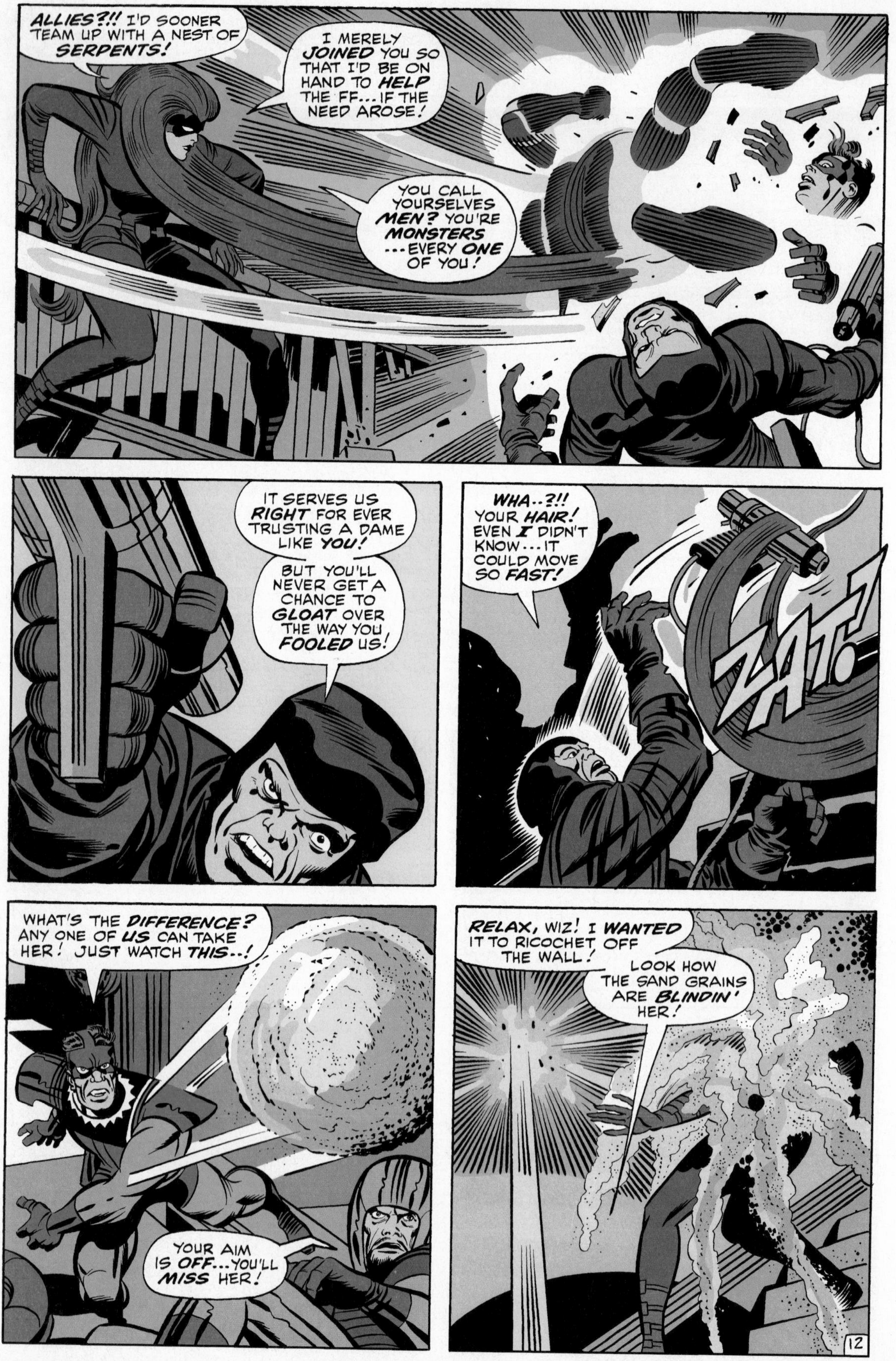
ALLIES?!! I'D SOONER TEAM UP WITH A NEST OF SERPENTS!
I MERELY JOINED YOU SO THAT I'D BE ON HAND TO HELP THE FF... IF THE NEED AROSE!
YOU CALL YOURSELVES MEN? YOU'RE MONSTERS --- EVERY ONE OF YOU!
IT SERVES US RIGHT FOR EVER TRUSTING A DAME LIKE YOU!
BUT YOU'LL NEVER GET A CHANCE TO GLOAT OVER THE WAY YOU FOOLED US!
WHA..?!! YOUR HAIR! EVEN I DIDN'T KNOW... IT COULD MOVE SO FAST!
ZZAT!
WHAT'S THE DIFFERENCE? ANY ONE OF US CAN TAKE HER! JUST WATCH THIS..!
YOUR AIM IS OFF... YOU'LL MISS HER!
RELAX, WIZ! I WANTED IT TO RICOCHET OFF THE WALL!
LOOK HOW THE SAND GRAINS ARE BLINDIN' HER!
12

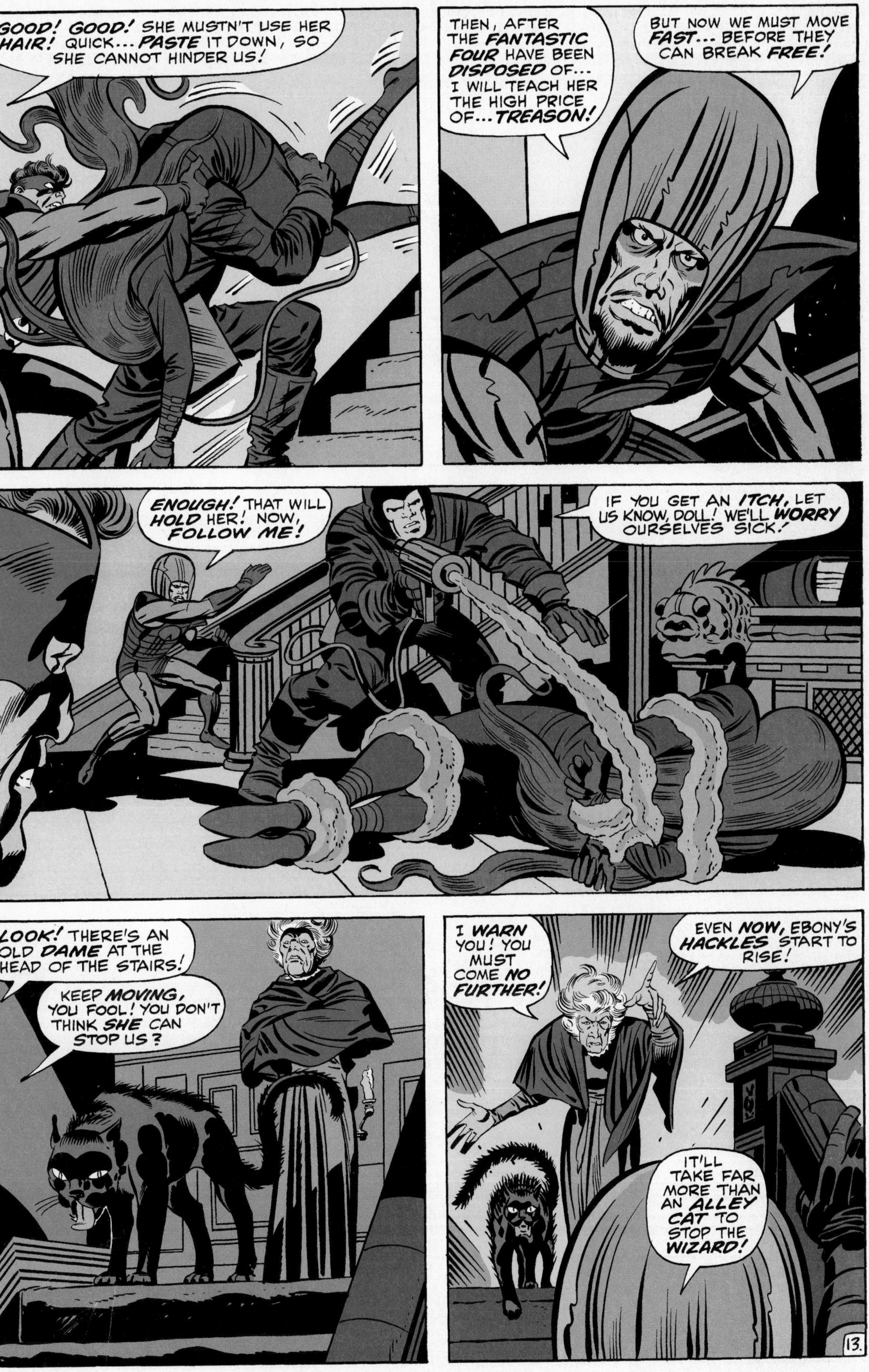
GOOD! GOOD! SHE MUSTN'T USE HER HAIR! QUICK... PASTE IT DOWN, SO SHE CANNOT HINDER US!
THEN, AFTER THE FANTASTIC FOUR HAVE BEEN DISPOSED OF... I WILL TEACH HER THE HIGH PRICE OF... TREASON!
BUT NOW WE MUST MOVE FAST... BEFORE THEY CAN BREAK FREE!
ENOUGH! THAT WILL HOLD HER! NOW, FOLLOW ME!
IF YOU GET AN ITCH, LET US KNOW, DOLL! WE'LL WORRY OURSELVES SICK!
LOOK! THERE'S AN OLD DAME AT THE HEAD OF THE STAIRS!
KEEP MOVING, YOU FOOL! YOU DON'T THINK SHE CAN STOP US?
I WARN YOU! YOU MUST COME NO FURTHER!
EVEN NOW, EBONY'S HACKLES START TO RISE!
IT'LL TAKE FAR MORE THAN AN ALLEY CAT TO STOP THE WIZARD!
13.

AH, BUT EBONY *IS...*

FAR, FAR *MORE...*

THAN JUST AN *ALLEY CAT!*

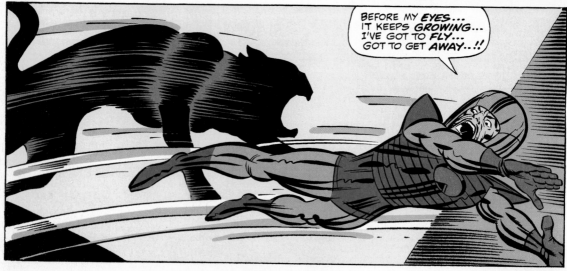

BEFORE MY *EYES...* IT KEEPS *GROWING...* I'VE GOT TO *FLY...* GOT TO GET *AWAY..!!*

KRASH!

THERE'S NO *ESCAPING* IT--- NO MATTER WHERE I *GO!!*

14

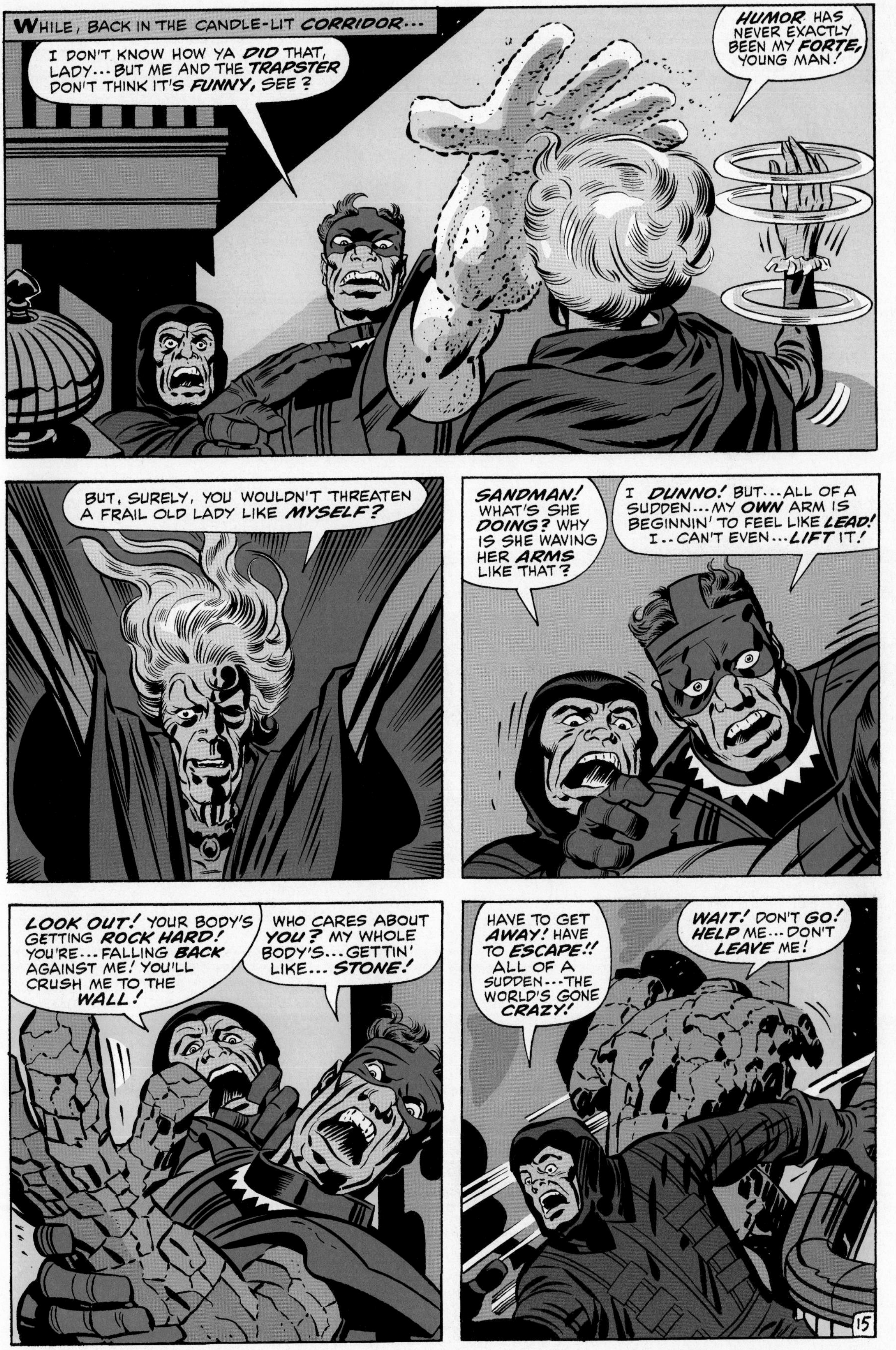
WHILE, BACK IN THE CANDLE-LIT CORRIDOR...
I DON'T KNOW HOW YA DID THAT, LADY... BUT ME AND THE TRAPSTER DON'T THINK IT'S FUNNY, SEE?
HUMOR HAS NEVER EXACTLY BEEN MY FORTE, YOUNG MAN!
BUT, SURELY, YOU WOULDN'T THREATEN A FRAIL OLD LADY LIKE MYSELF?
SANDMAN! WHAT'S SHE DOING? WHY IS SHE WAVING HER ARMS LIKE THAT?
I DUNNO! BUT... ALL OF A SUDDEN... MY OWN ARM IS BEGINNIN' TO FEEL LIKE LEAD! I.. CAN'T EVEN... LIFT IT!
LOOK OUT! YOUR BODY'S GETTING ROCK HARD! YOU'RE... FALLING BACK AGAINST ME! YOU'LL CRUSH ME TO THE WALL!
WHO CARES ABOUT YOU? MY WHOLE BODY'S... GETTIN' LIKE... STONE!
HAVE TO GET AWAY! HAVE TO ESCAPE!! ALL OF A SUDDEN--THE WORLD'S GONE CRAZY!
WAIT! DON'T GO! HELP ME... DON'T LEAVE ME!
15

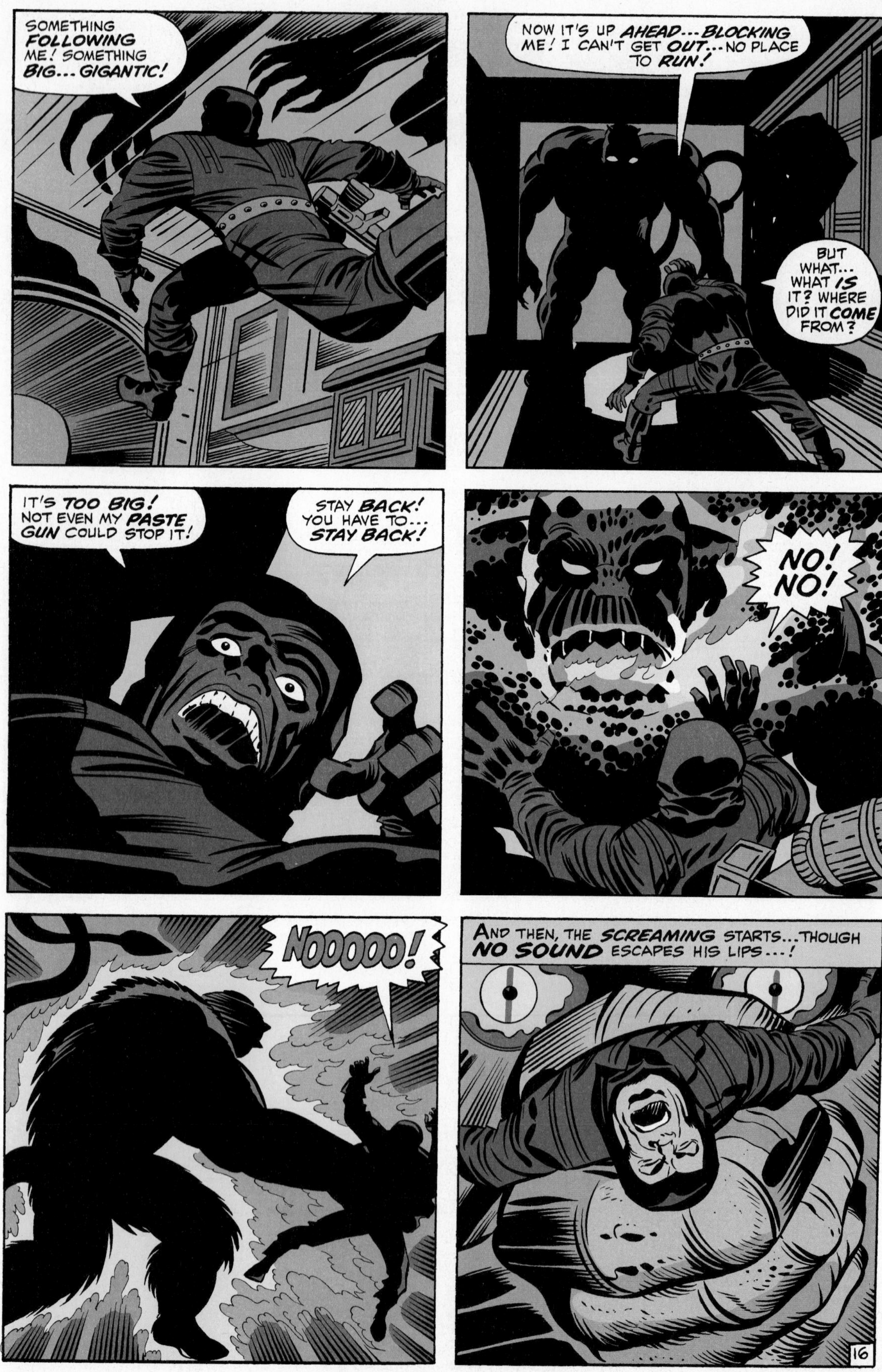

SOMETHING FOLLOWING ME! SOMETHING BIG... GIGANTIC!
NOW IT'S UP AHEAD... BLOCKING ME! I CAN'T GET OUT... NO PLACE TO RUN!
BUT WHAT... WHAT IS IT? WHERE DID IT COME FROM?
IT'S TOO BIG! NOT EVEN MY PASTE GUN COULD STOP IT!
STAY BACK! YOU HAVE TO... STAY BACK!
NO! NO!
NOOOOO!
AND THEN, THE SCREAMING STARTS... THOUGH NO SOUND ESCAPES HIS LIPS...!
16

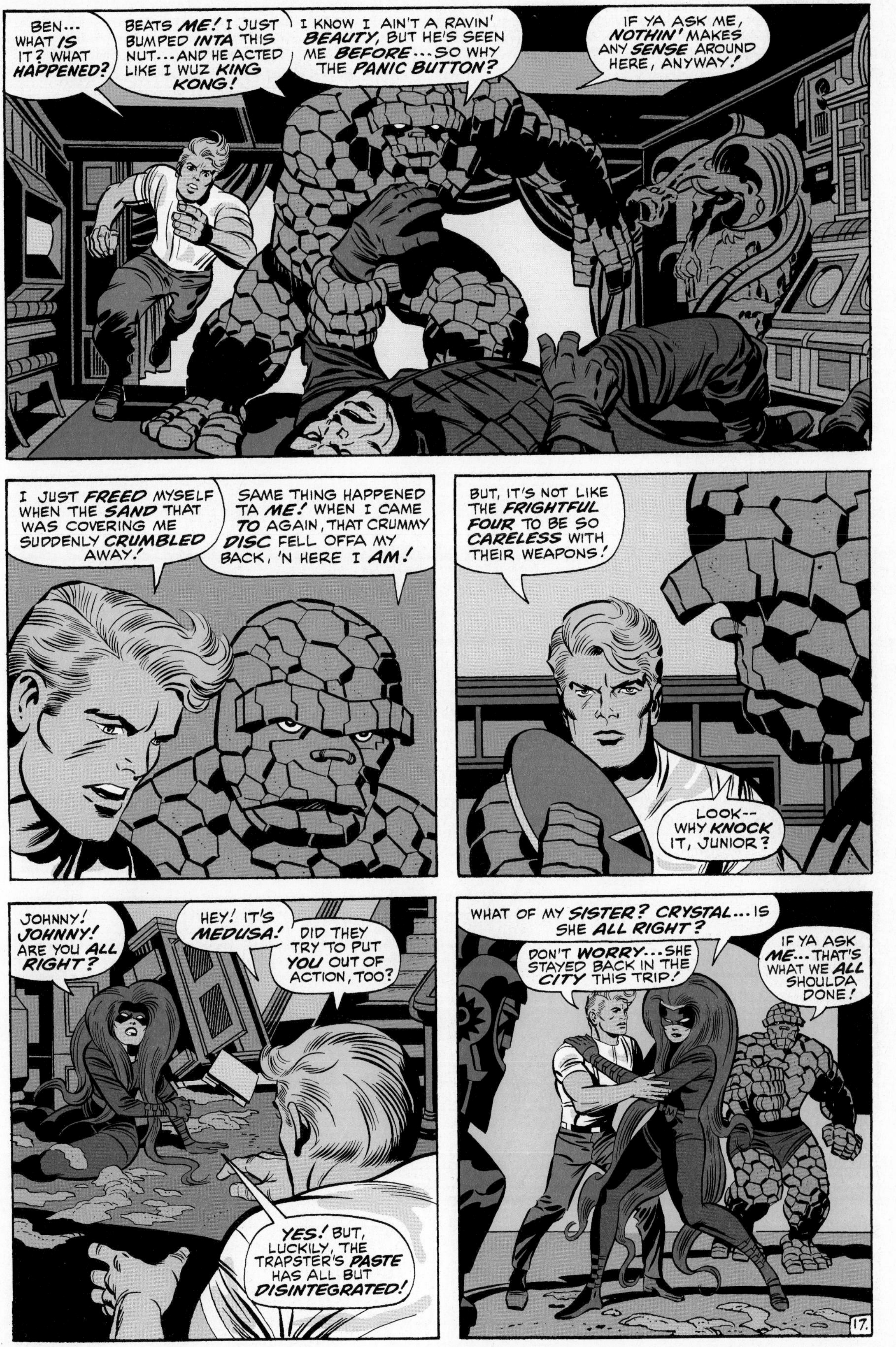

BEN... WHAT IS IT? WHAT HAPPENED?
BEATS ME! I JUST BUMPED INTA THIS NUT...AND HE ACTED LIKE I WUZ KING KONG!
I KNOW I AIN'T A RAVIN' BEAUTY, BUT HE'S SEEN ME BEFORE...SO WHY THE PANIC BUTTON?
IF YA ASK ME, NOTHIN' MAKES ANY SENSE AROUND HERE, ANYWAY!
I JUST FREED MYSELF WHEN THE SAND THAT WAS COVERING ME SUDDENLY CRUMBLED AWAY!
SAME THING HAPPENED TA ME! WHEN I CAME TO AGAIN, THAT CRUMMY DISC FELL OFFA MY BACK, 'N HERE I AM!
BUT, IT'S NOT LIKE THE FRIGHTFUL FOUR TO BE SO CARELESS WITH THEIR WEAPONS!
LOOK-- WHY KNOCK IT, JUNIOR?
JOHNNY! JOHNNY! ARE YOU ALL RIGHT?
HEY! IT'S MEDUSA!
DID THEY TRY TO PUT YOU OUT OF ACTION, TOO?
YES! BUT, LUCKILY, THE TRAPSTER'S PASTE HAS ALL BUT DISINTEGRATED!
WHAT OF MY SISTER? CRYSTAL...IS SHE ALL RIGHT?
DON'T WORRY...SHE STAYED BACK IN THE CITY THIS TRIP!
IF YA ASK ME...THAT'S WHAT WE ALL SHOULDA DONE!
17.

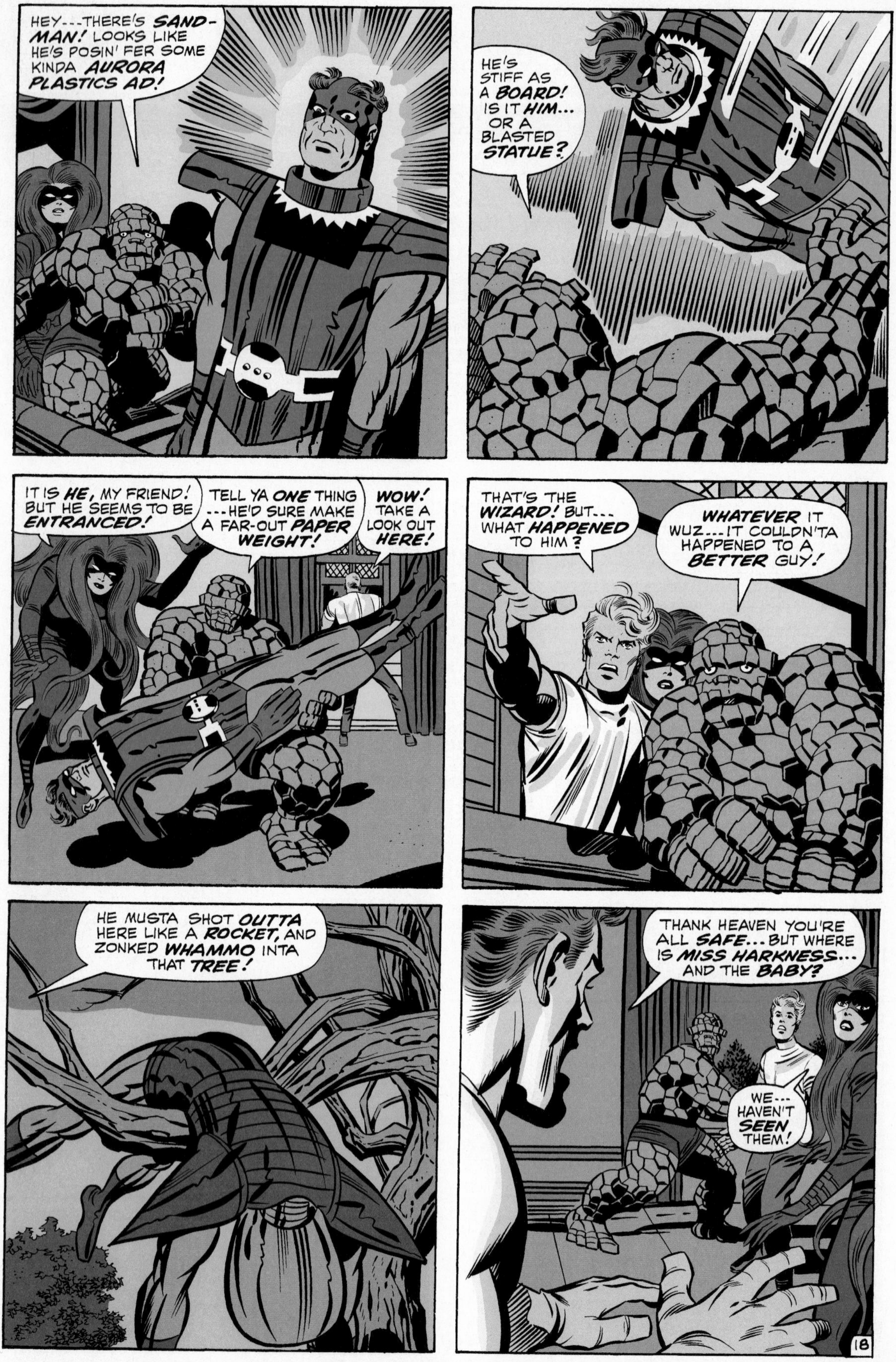

HEY---THERE'S SANDMAN! LOOKS LIKE HE'S POSIN' FER SOME KINDA AURORA PLASTICS AD!
HE'S STIFF AS A BOARD! IS IT HIM... OR A BLASTED STATUE?
IT IS HE, MY FRIEND! BUT HE SEEMS TO BE ENTRANCED!
TELL YA ONE THING ---HE'D SURE MAKE A FAR-OUT PAPER WEIGHT!
WOW! TAKE A LOOK OUT HERE!
THAT'S THE WIZARD! BUT--- WHAT HAPPENED TO HIM?
WHATEVER IT WUZ---IT COULDN'TA HAPPENED TO A BETTER GUY!
HE MUSTA SHOT OUTTA HERE LIKE A ROCKET, AND ZONKED WHAMMO INTA THAT TREE!
THANK HEAVEN YOU'RE ALL SAFE... BUT WHERE IS MISS HARKNESS... AND THE BABY?
WE--- HAVEN'T SEEN THEM!
18

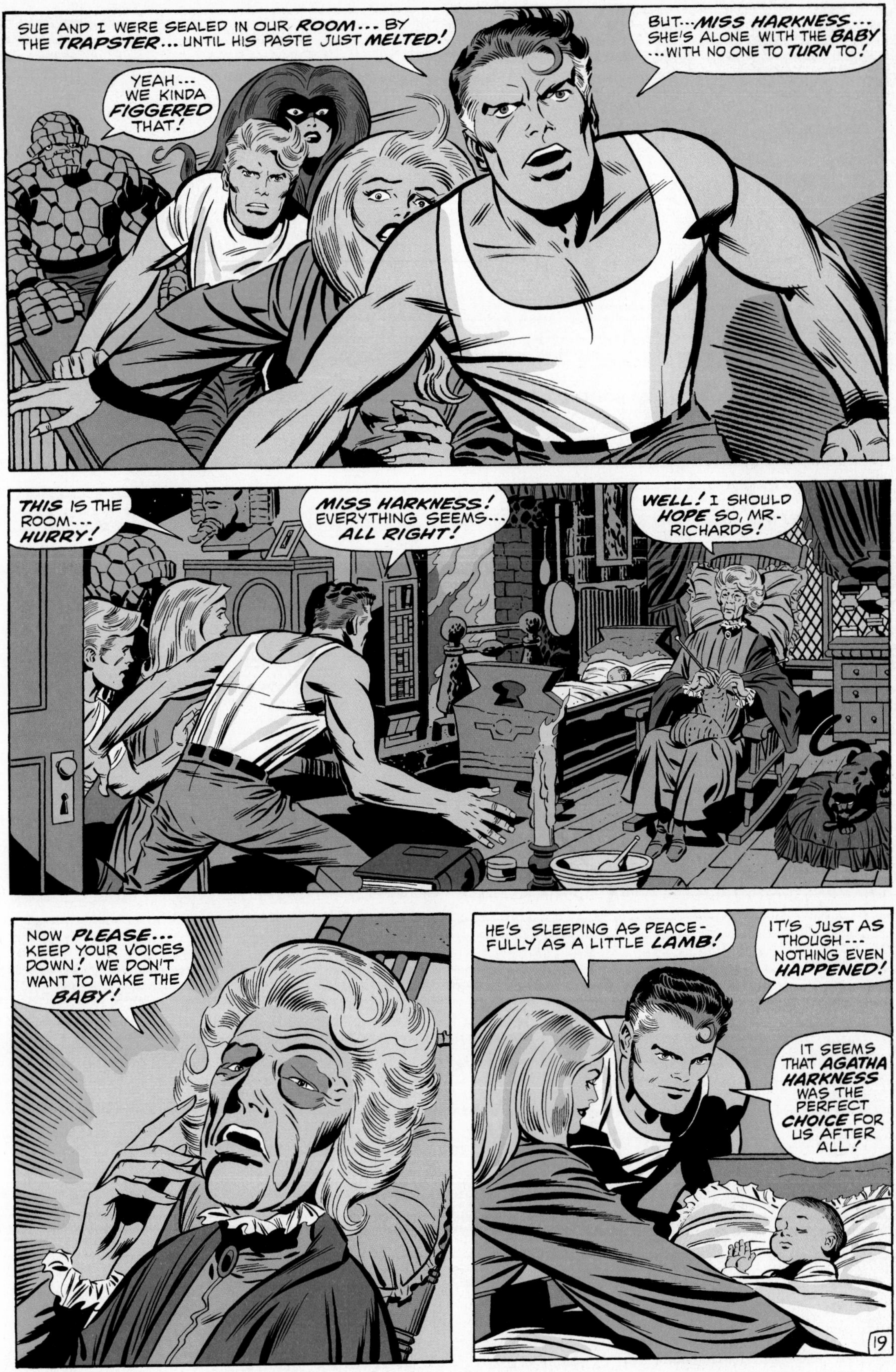
SUE AND I WERE SEALED IN OUR ROOM... BY THE TRAPSTER... UNTIL HIS PASTE JUST MELTED!
YEAH--- WE KINDA FIGGERED THAT!
BUT...MISS HARKNESS... SHE'S ALONE WITH THE BABY ...WITH NO ONE TO TURN TO!
THIS IS THE ROOM--- HURRY!
MISS HARKNESS! EVERYTHING SEEMS... ALL RIGHT!
WELL! I SHOULD HOPE SO, MR. RICHARDS!
NOW PLEASE... KEEP YOUR VOICES DOWN! WE DON'T WANT TO WAKE THE BABY!
HE'S SLEEPING AS PEACE-FULLY AS A LITTLE LAMB!
IT'S JUST AS THOUGH--- NOTHING EVEN HAPPENED!
IT SEEMS THAT AGATHA HARKNESS WAS THE PERFECT CHOICE FOR US AFTER ALL!
19

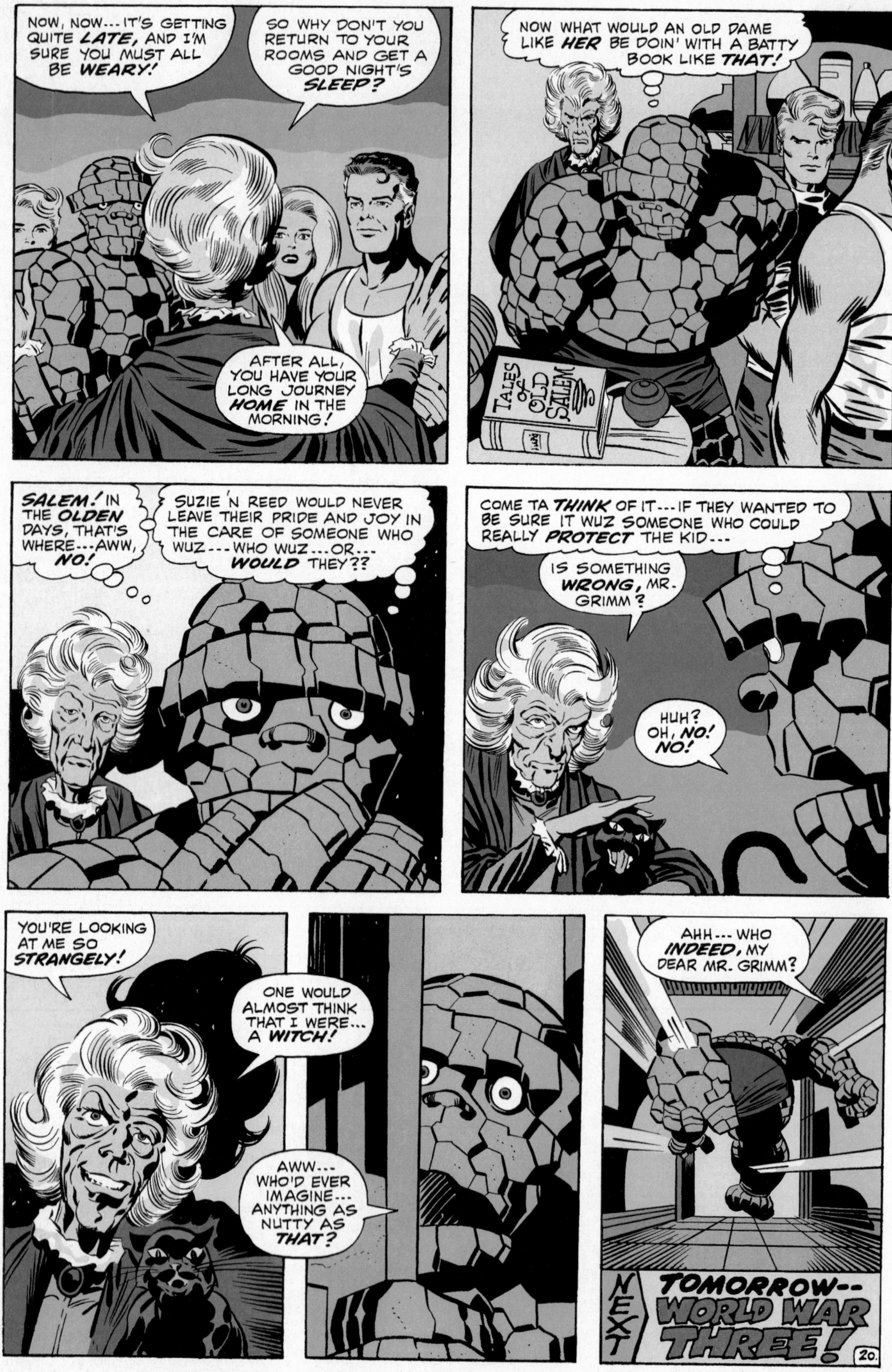
NOW, NOW--- IT'S GETTING QUITE LATE, AND I'M SURE YOU MUST ALL BE WEARY!
SO WHY DON'T YOU RETURN TO YOUR ROOMS AND GET A GOOD NIGHT'S SLEEP?
AFTER ALL, YOU HAVE YOUR LONG JOURNEY HOME IN THE MORNING!
NOW WHAT WOULD AN OLD DAME LIKE HER BE DOIN' WITH A BATTY BOOK LIKE THAT!
TALES OF OLD SALEM
SALEM! IN THE OLDEN DAYS, THAT'S WHERE---AWW, NO!
SUZIE 'N REED WOULD NEVER LEAVE THEIR PRIDE AND JOY IN THE CARE OF SOMEONE WHO WUZ---WHO WUZ---OR--- WOULD THEY??
COME TA THINK OF IT---IF THEY WANTED TO BE SURE IT WUZ SOMEONE WHO COULD REALLY PROTECT THE KID---
IS SOMETHING WRONG, MR. GRIMM?
HUH? OH, NO! NO!
YOU'RE LOOKING AT ME SO STRANGELY!
ONE WOULD ALMOST THINK THAT I WERE... A WITCH!
AWW--- WHO'D EVER IMAGINE--- ANYTHING AS NUTTY AS THAT?
AHH--- WHO INDEED, MY DEAR MR. GRIMM?
NEXT
TOMORROW-- WORLD WAR THREE!
20.

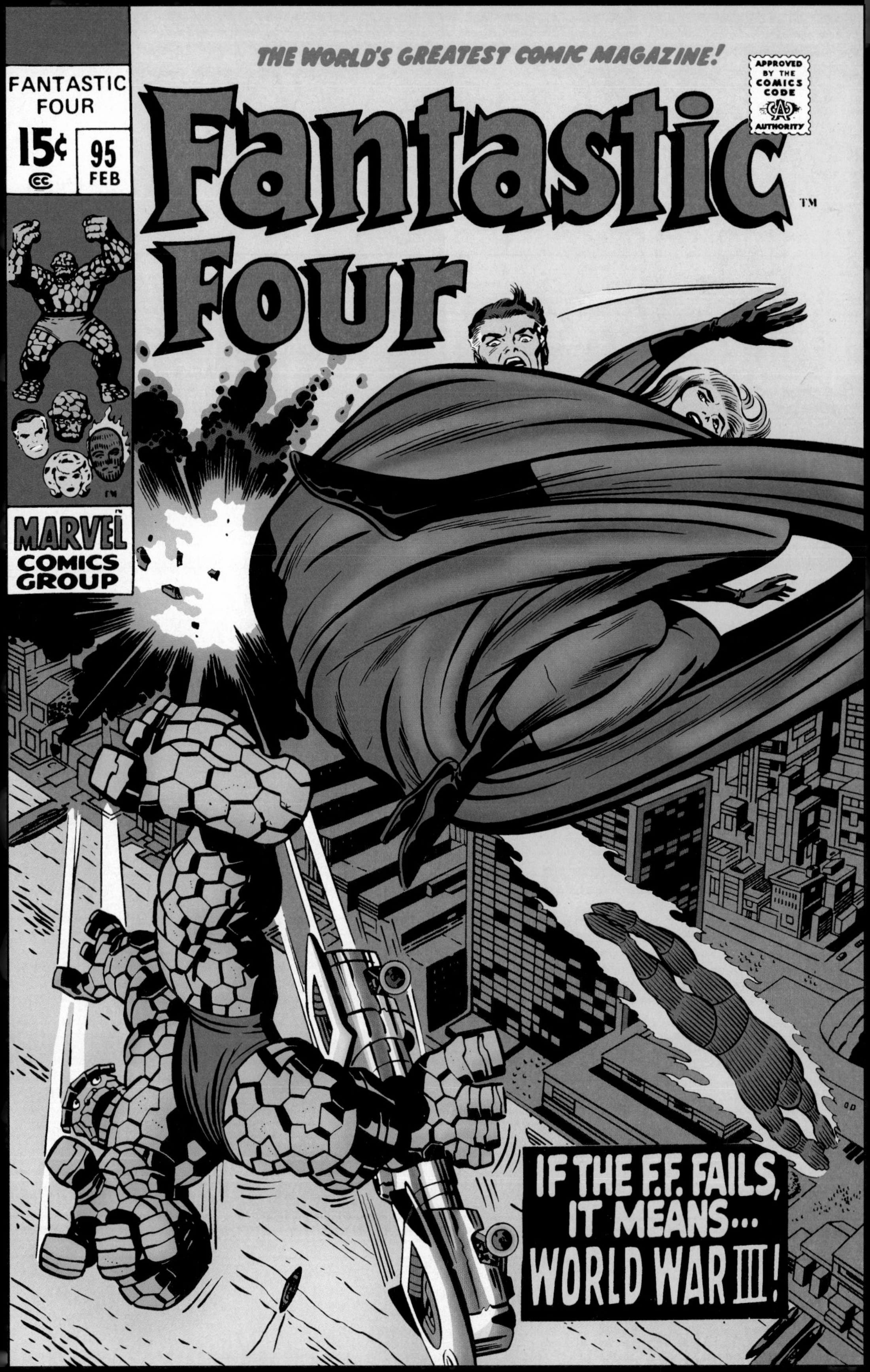
THE WORLD'S GREATEST COMIC MAGAZINE!
APPROVED BY THE COMICS CODE AUTHORITY
FANTASTIC FOUR
15¢
95 FEB
Fantastic Four
MARVEL COMICS GROUP
IF THE F.F. FAILS, IT MEANS... WORLD WAR III!

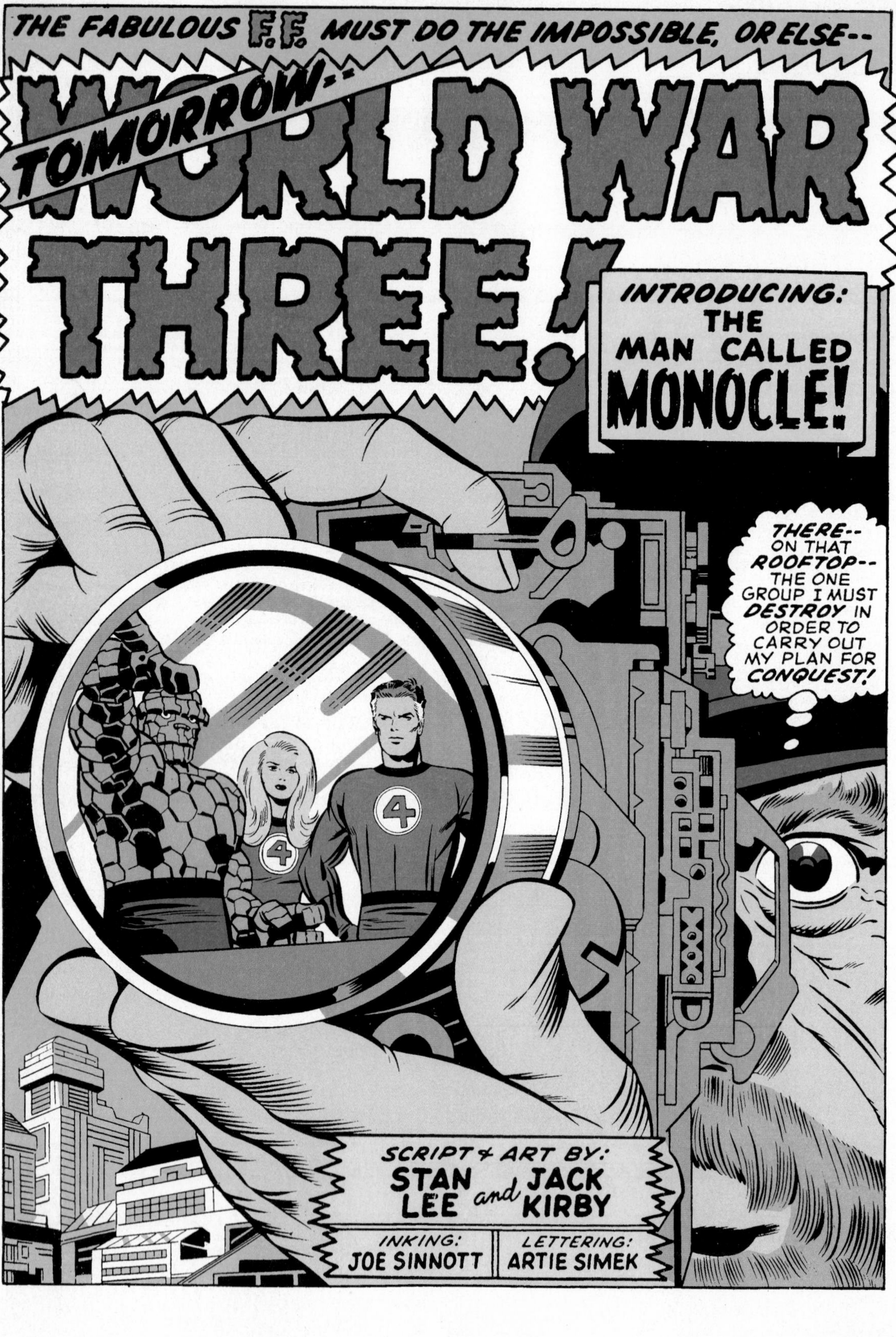
THE FABULOUS F.F. MUST DO THE IMPOSSIBLE, OR ELSE--
TOMORROW-- WORLD WAR THREE!
INTRODUCING: THE MAN CALLED MONOCLE!
THERE-- ON THAT ROOFTOP-- THE ONE GROUP I MUST DESTROY IN ORDER TO CARRY OUT MY PLAN FOR CONQUEST!
SCRIPT & ART BY: STAN LEE and JACK KIRBY
INKING: JOE SINNOTT
LETTERING: ARTIE SIMEK

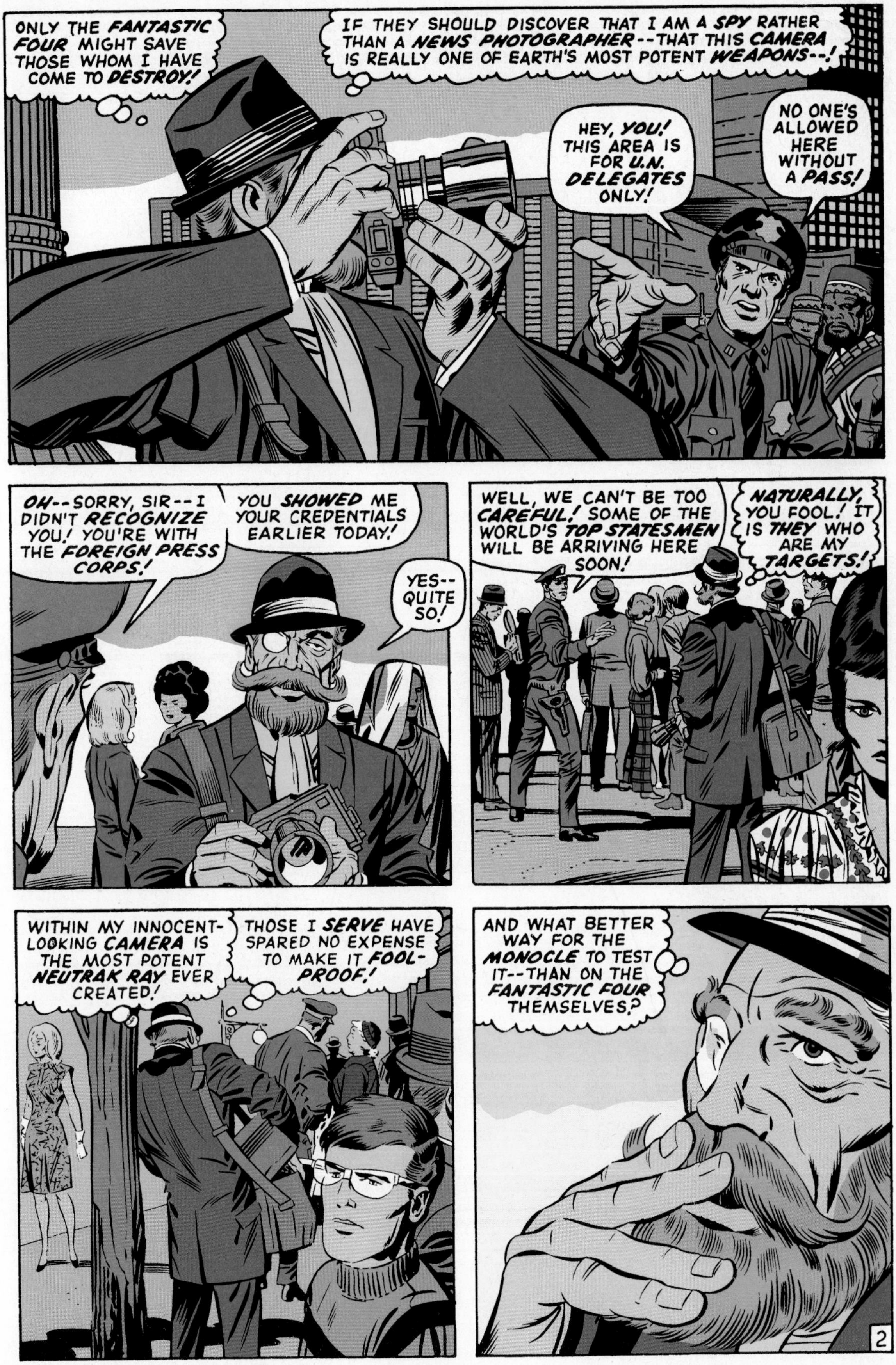
ONLY THE FANTASTIC FOUR MIGHT SAVE THOSE WHOM I HAVE COME TO DESTROY!
IF THEY SHOULD DISCOVER THAT I AM A SPY RATHER THAN A NEWS PHOTOGRAPHER--THAT THIS CAMERA IS REALLY ONE OF EARTH'S MOST POTENT WEAPONS--!
HEY, YOU! THIS AREA IS FOR U.N. DELEGATES ONLY!
NO ONE'S ALLOWED HERE WITHOUT A PASS!
OH--SORRY, SIR--I DIDN'T RECOGNIZE YOU! YOU'RE WITH THE FOREIGN PRESS CORPS!
YOU SHOWED ME YOUR CREDENTIALS EARLIER TODAY!
YES--QUITE SO!
WELL, WE CAN'T BE TOO CAREFUL! SOME OF THE WORLD'S TOP STATESMEN WILL BE ARRIVING HERE SOON!
NATURALLY, YOU FOOL! IT IS THEY WHO ARE MY TARGETS!
WITHIN MY INNOCENT-LOOKING CAMERA IS THE MOST POTENT NEUTRAK RAY EVER CREATED!
THOSE I SERVE HAVE SPARED NO EXPENSE TO MAKE IT FOOL-PROOF!
AND WHAT BETTER WAY FOR THE MONOCLE TO TEST IT--THAN ON THE FANTASTIC FOUR THEMSELVES?
2

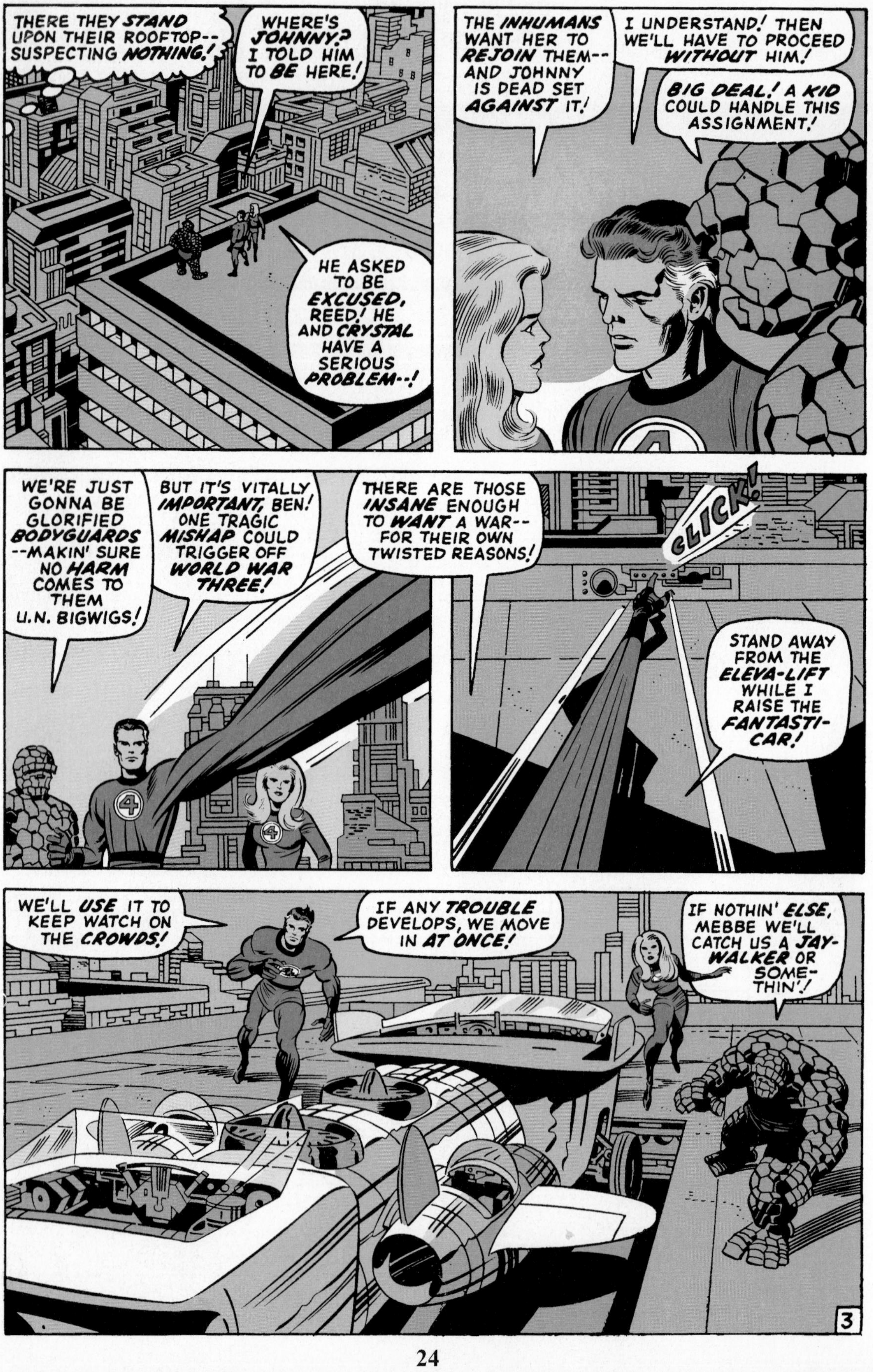
THERE THEY STAND UPON THEIR ROOFTOP-- SUSPECTING NOTHING!
WHERE'S JOHNNY? I TOLD HIM TO BE HERE!
HE ASKED TO BE EXCUSED, REED! HE AND CRYSTAL HAVE A SERIOUS PROBLEM--!
THE INHUMANS WANT HER TO REJOIN THEM-- AND JOHNNY IS DEAD SET AGAINST IT!
I UNDERSTAND! THEN WE'LL HAVE TO PROCEED WITHOUT HIM!
BIG DEAL! A KID COULD HANDLE THIS ASSIGNMENT!
WE'RE JUST GONNA BE GLORIFIED BODYGUARDS --MAKIN' SURE NO HARM COMES TO THEM U.N. BIGWIGS!
BUT IT'S VITALLY IMPORTANT, BEN! ONE TRAGIC MISHAP COULD TRIGGER OFF WORLD WAR THREE!
THERE ARE THOSE INSANE ENOUGH TO WANT A WAR-- FOR THEIR OWN TWISTED REASONS!
CLICK!
STAND AWAY FROM THE ELEVA-LIFT WHILE I RAISE THE FANTASTI-CAR!
WE'LL USE IT TO KEEP WATCH ON THE CROWDS!
IF ANY TROUBLE DEVELOPS, WE MOVE IN AT ONCE!
IF NOTHIN' ELSE, MEBBE WE'LL CATCH US A JAY-WALKER OR SOME-THIN'!
3

WHY ARE ALL THEM FANCY-PANTS AT THE *U.N.* TODAY, ANYWAY?

THEY'RE WORRIED ABOUT THOSE *FLARE-UPS* IN THE *MID-EAST,* BEN! IT CAN BE A *FUSE* THAT MAY IGNITE A *HOLOCAUST!*

KNOW SOMETHIN'? I'M SORRY I *ASKED!*

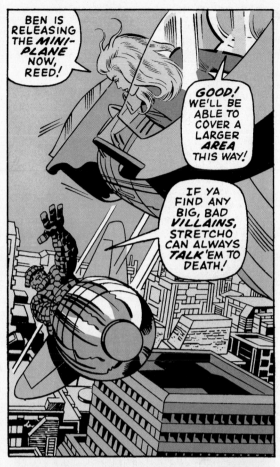

BEN IS RELEASING THE *MINI-PLANE* NOW, REED!

GOOD! WE'LL BE ABLE TO COVER A LARGER *AREA* THIS WAY!

IF YA FIND ANY *BIG, BAD VILLAINS,* STRETCHO CAN ALWAYS *TALK* 'EM TO DEATH!

THIS KINDA JOB CAN BE REAL *DANGEROUS--* ON ACCOUNTA THE CRUMMY *AIR POLLUTION!*

WHAT DO YOU EXPECT TO *FIND* UP HERE, DEAR?

YOUR GUESS IS AS GOOD AS *MINE,* HONEY--

BUT, THERE COULD BE ANY SORT OF *MURDERER* OR *MADMAN* IN THE TEEMING CROWDS BELOW--

NOW--WHILE THEY CRUISE OVER THE CITY-- THIS IS MY CHANCE TO *DESTROY* THEM!

AND THEN-- MY *PRIME* TARGET-- THE *U.N.* ITSELF!

4

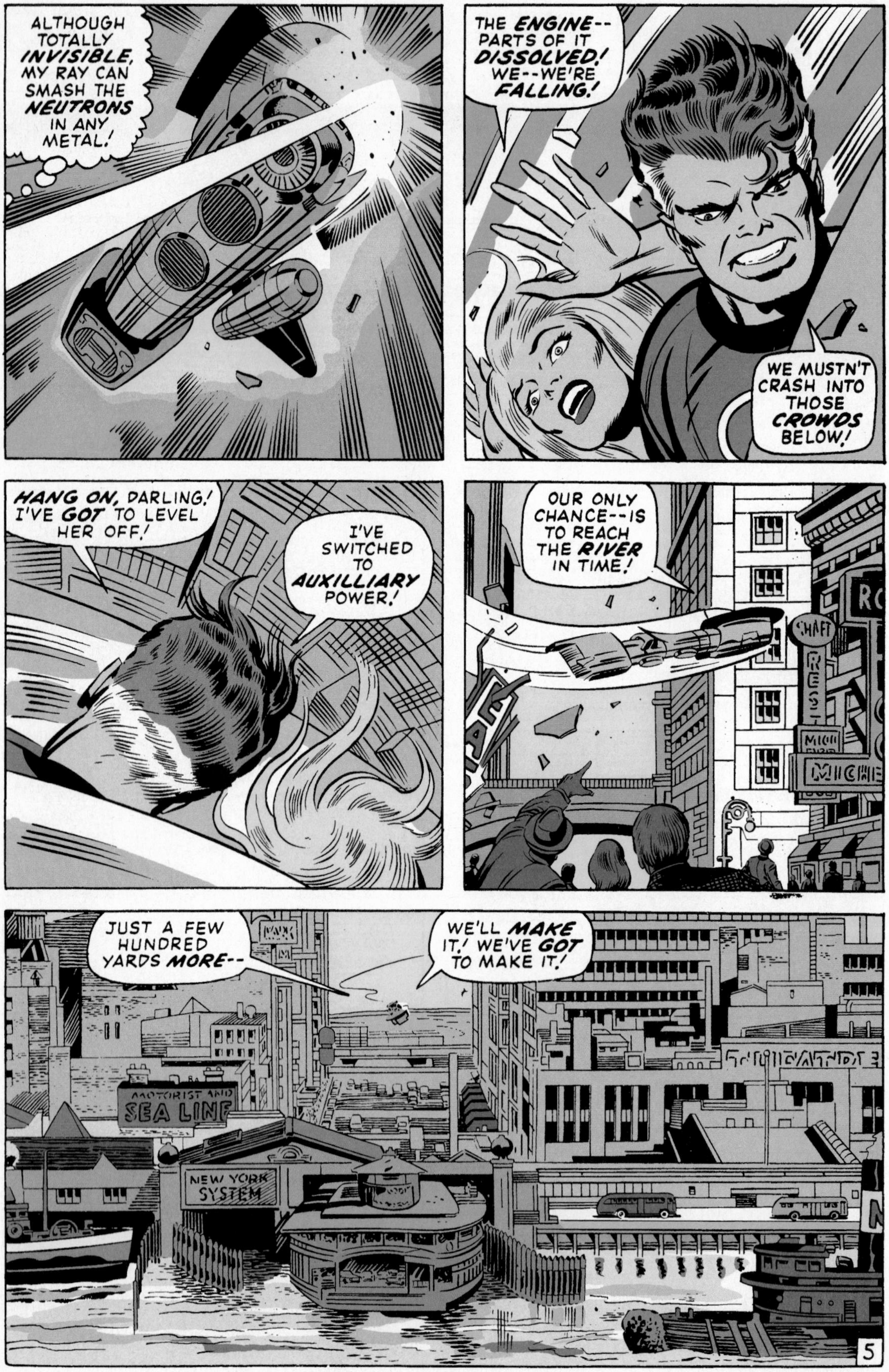
ALTHOUGH TOTALLY INVISIBLE, MY RAY CAN SMASH THE NEUTRONS IN ANY METAL!
THE ENGINE-- PARTS OF IT DISSOLVED! WE--WE'RE FALLING!
WE MUSTN'T CRASH INTO THOSE CROWDS BELOW!
HANG ON, DARLING! I'VE GOT TO LEVEL HER OFF!
I'VE SWITCHED TO AUXILLIARY POWER!
OUR ONLY CHANCE--IS TO REACH THE RIVER IN TIME!
JUST A FEW HUNDRED YARDS MORE--
WE'LL MAKE IT! WE'VE GOT TO MAKE IT!
NEW YORK SYSTEM
5

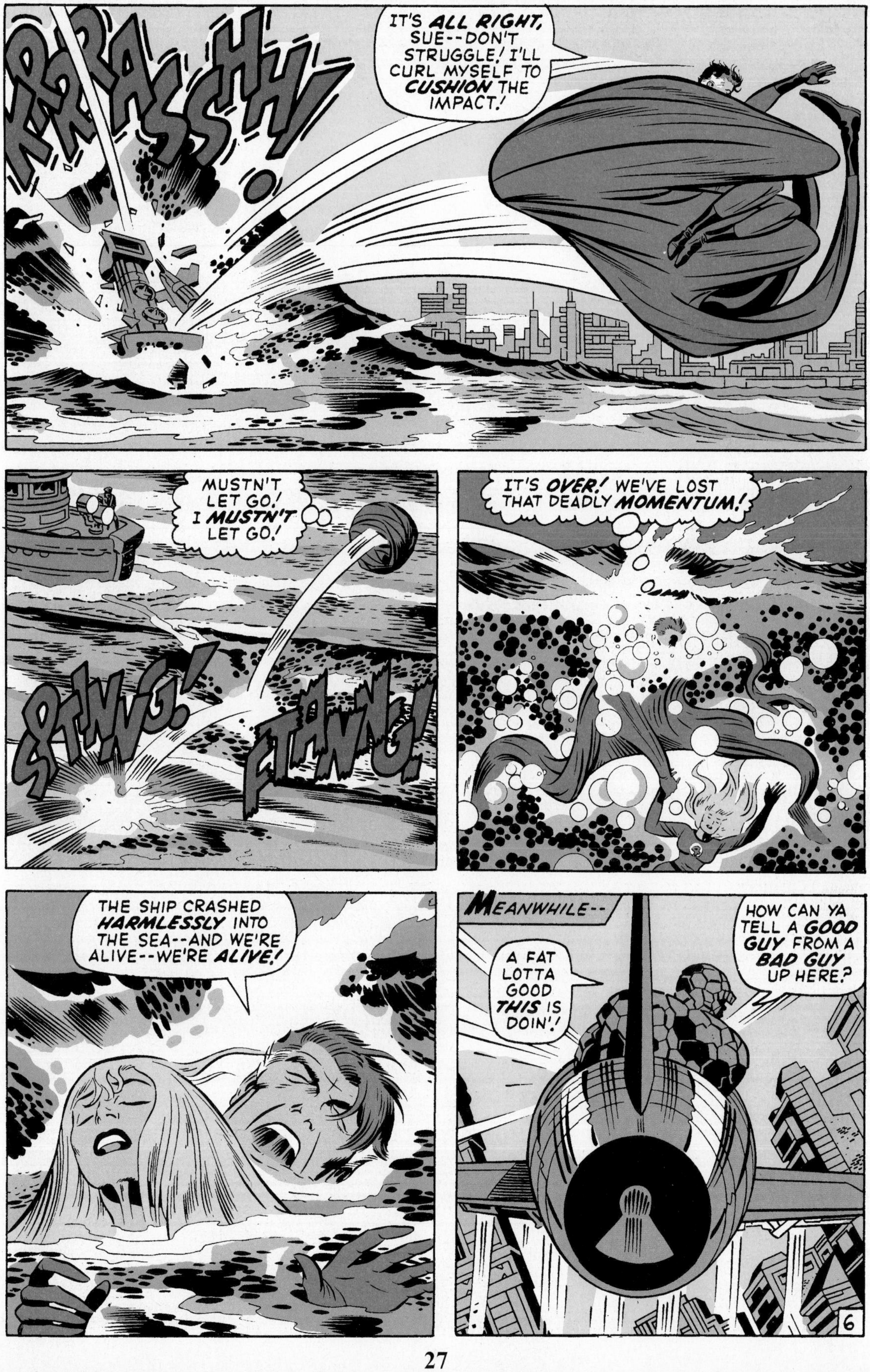

KRRRASSHH!
IT'S ALL RIGHT, SUE--DON'T STRUGGLE! I'LL CURL MYSELF TO CUSHION THE IMPACT!
MUSTN'T LET GO! I MUSTN'T LET GO!
SPTANG!
KTANNG!
IT'S OVER! WE'VE LOST THAT DEADLY MOMENTUM!
THE SHIP CRASHED HARMLESSLY INTO THE SEA--AND WE'RE ALIVE--WE'RE ALIVE!
MEANWHILE--
HOW CAN YA TELL A GOOD GUY FROM A BAD GUY UP HERE?
A FAT LOTTA GOOD THIS IS DOIN'!
6

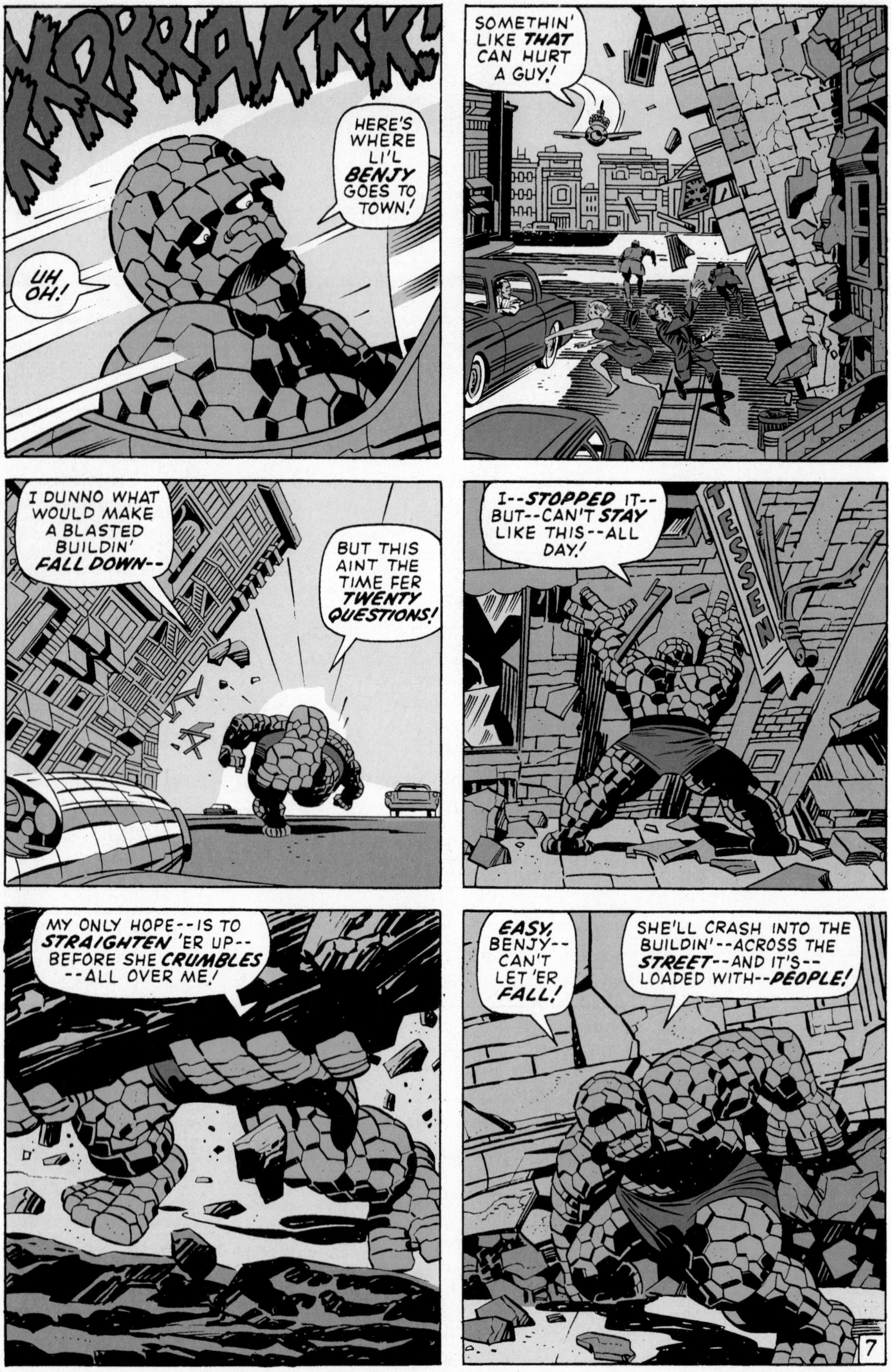
KRRAKKK!
HERE'S WHERE LI'L BENJY GOES TO TOWN.!
UH OH!
SOMETHIN' LIKE THAT CAN HURT A GUY!
I DUNNO WHAT WOULD MAKE A BLASTED BUILDIN' FALL DOWN--
BUT THIS AINT THE TIME FER TWENTY QUESTIONS!
I--STOPPED IT--BUT--CAN'T STAY LIKE THIS--ALL DAY!
TESSEN
MY ONLY HOPE--IS TO STRAIGHTEN 'ER UP--BEFORE SHE CRUMBLES--ALL OVER ME!
EASY, BENJY--CAN'T LET 'ER FALL!
SHE'LL CRASH INTO THE BUILDIN'--ACROSS THE STREET--AND IT'S--LOADED WITH--PEOPLE!
7

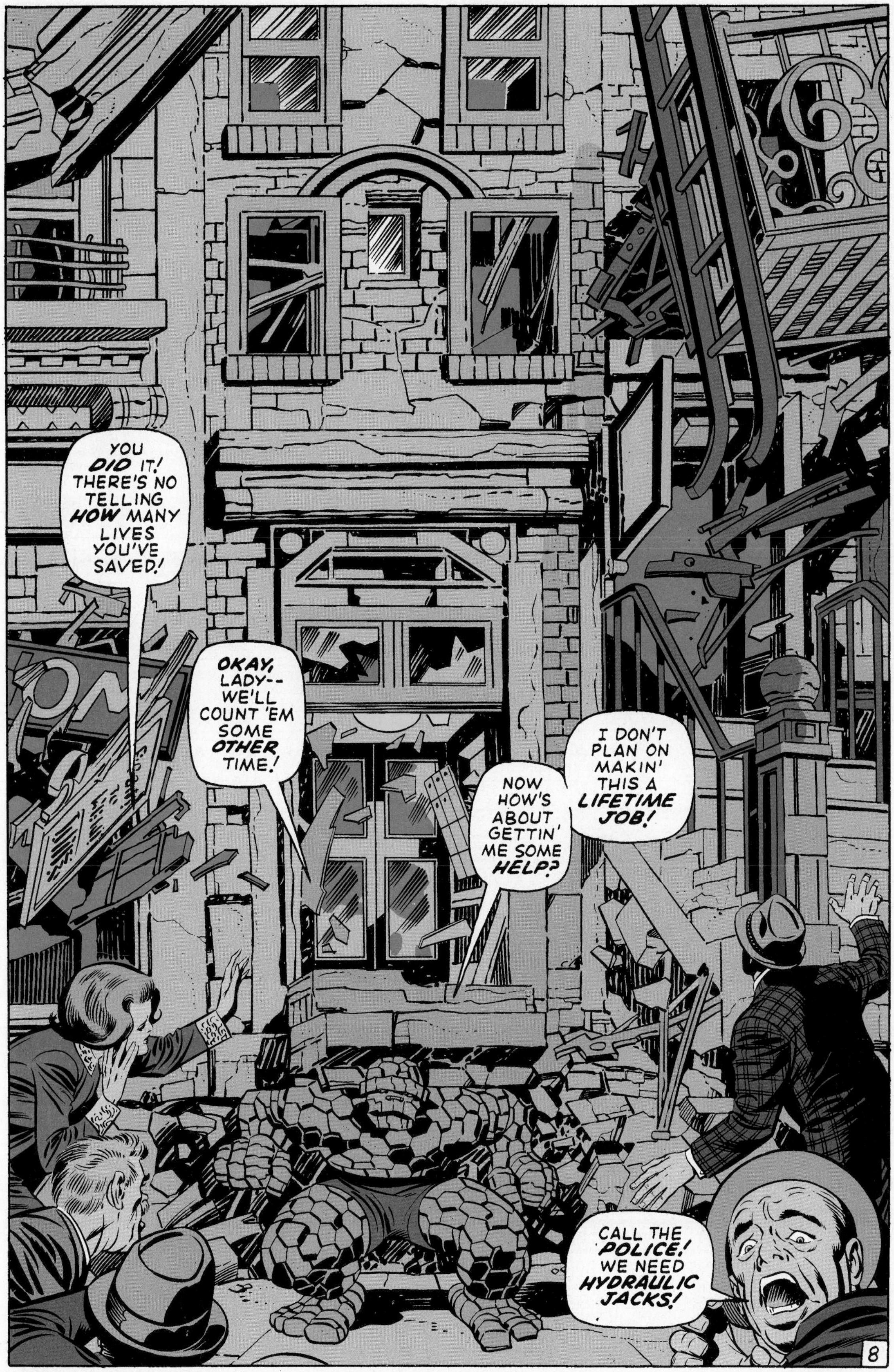
YOU DID IT! THERE'S NO TELLING HOW MANY LIVES YOU'VE SAVED!
OKAY, LADY-- WE'LL COUNT 'EM SOME OTHER TIME!
NOW HOW'S ABOUT GETTIN' ME SOME HELP?
I DON'T PLAN ON MAKIN' THIS A LIFETIME JOB!
CALL THE POLICE! WE NEED HYDRAULIC JACKS!
8

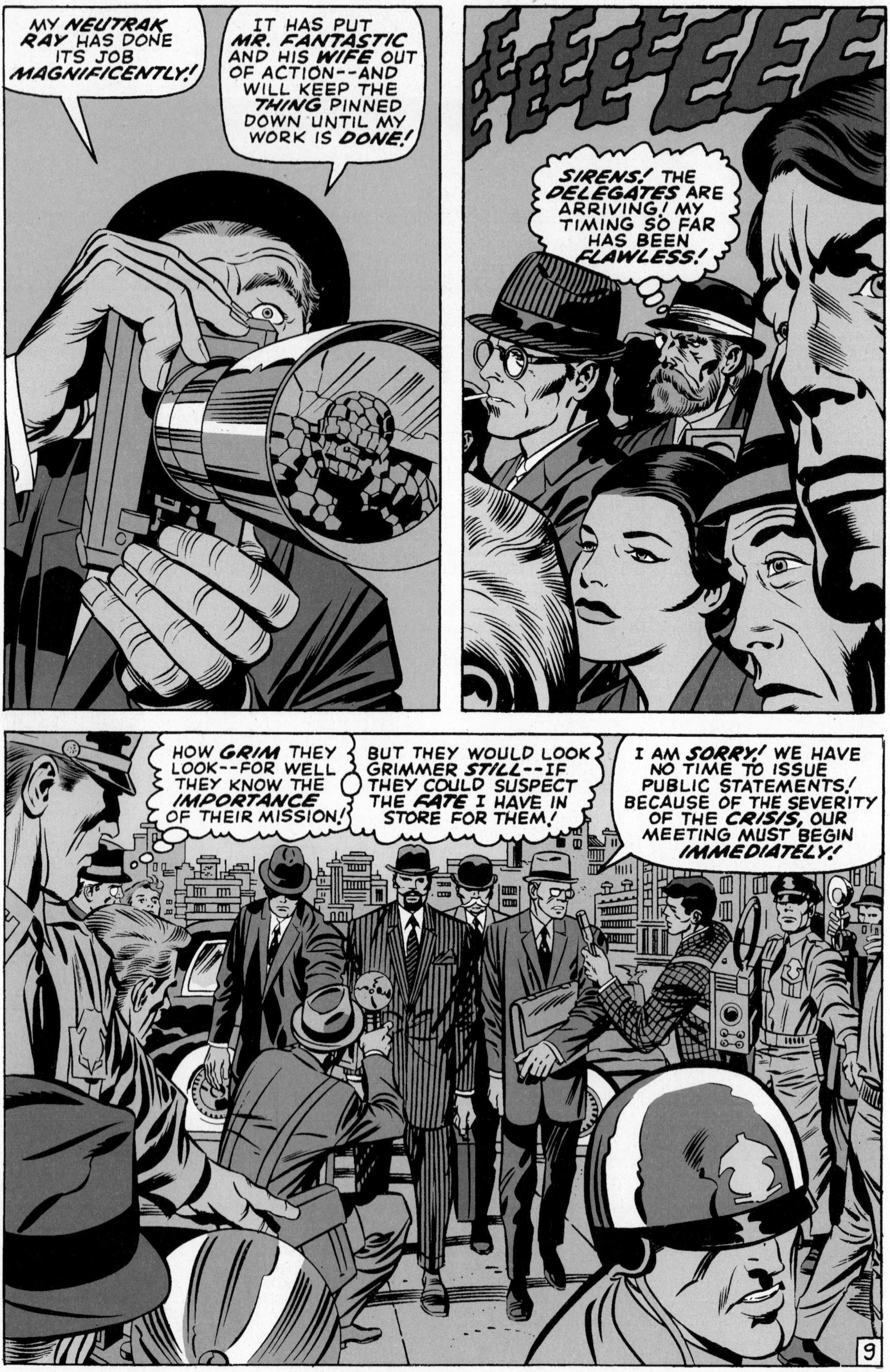
MY NEUTRAK RAY HAS DONE ITS JOB MAGNIFICENTLY!
IT HAS PUT MR. FANTASTIC AND HIS WIFE OUT OF ACTION--AND WILL KEEP THE THING PINNED DOWN UNTIL MY WORK IS DONE!
EEEEEEEEEE
SIRENS! THE DELEGATES ARE ARRIVING! MY TIMING SO FAR HAS BEEN FLAWLESS!
HOW GRIM THEY LOOK--FOR WELL THEY KNOW THE IMPORTANCE OF THEIR MISSION!
BUT THEY WOULD LOOK GRIMMER STILL--IF THEY COULD SUSPECT THE FATE I HAVE IN STORE FOR THEM!
I AM SORRY! WE HAVE NO TIME TO ISSUE PUBLIC STATEMENTS! BECAUSE OF THE SEVERITY OF THE CRISIS, OUR MEETING MUST BEGIN IMMEDIATELY!
9

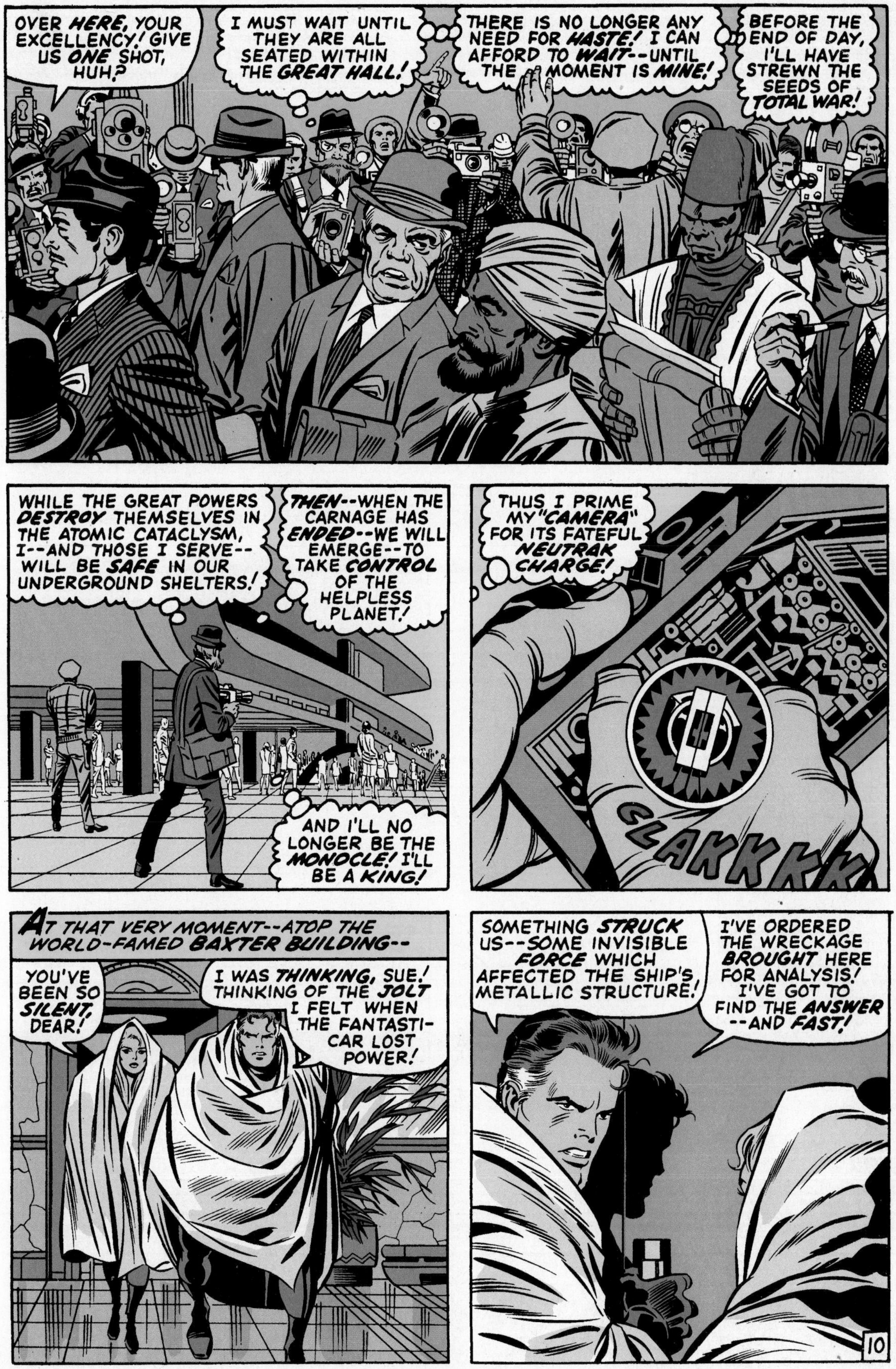
OVER HERE, YOUR EXCELLENCY! GIVE US ONE SHOT, HUH?
I MUST WAIT UNTIL THEY ARE ALL SEATED WITHIN THE GREAT HALL!
THERE IS NO LONGER ANY NEED FOR HASTE! I CAN AFFORD TO WAIT--UNTIL THE MOMENT IS MINE!
BEFORE THE END OF DAY, I'LL HAVE STREWN THE SEEDS OF TOTAL WAR!
WHILE THE GREAT POWERS DESTROY THEMSELVES IN THE ATOMIC CATACLYSM, I--AND THOSE I SERVE--WILL BE SAFE IN OUR UNDERGROUND SHELTERS!
THEN--WHEN THE CARNAGE HAS ENDED--WE WILL EMERGE--TO TAKE CONTROL OF THE HELPLESS PLANET!
AND I'LL NO LONGER BE THE MONOCLE! I'LL BE A KING!
THUS I PRIME MY "CAMERA" FOR ITS FATEFUL NEUTRAK CHARGE!
CLAKKKK
AT THAT VERY MOMENT--ATOP THE WORLD-FAMED BAXTER BUILDING--
YOU'VE BEEN SO SILENT, DEAR!
I WAS THINKING, SUE! THINKING OF THE JOLT I FELT WHEN THE FANTASTI-CAR LOST POWER!
SOMETHING STRUCK US--SOME INVISIBLE FORCE WHICH AFFECTED THE SHIP'S METALLIC STRUCTURE!
I'VE ORDERED THE WRECKAGE BROUGHT HERE FOR ANALYSIS! I'VE GOT TO FIND THE ANSWER --AND FAST!
10

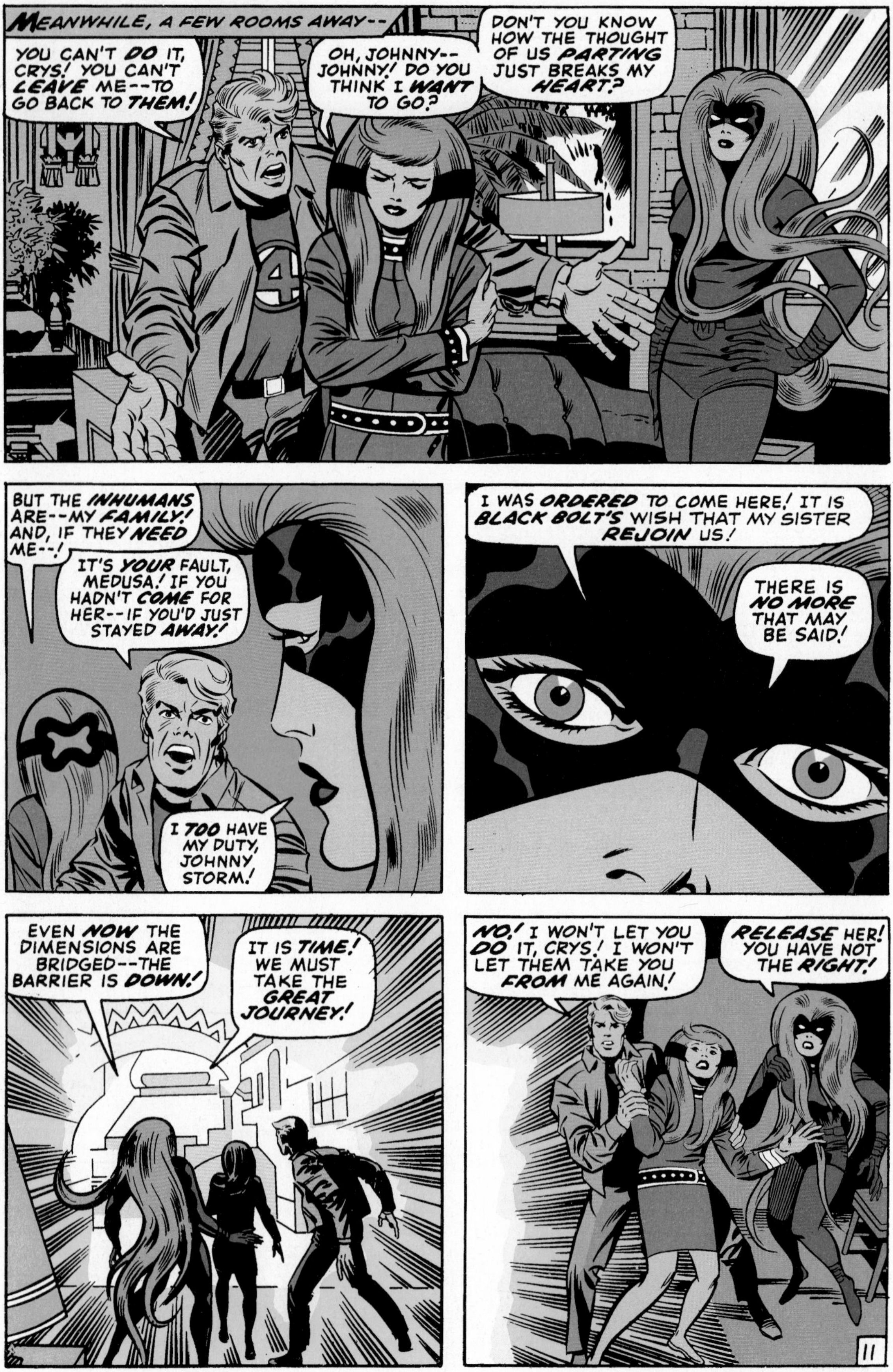
MEANWHILE, A FEW ROOMS AWAY--
YOU CAN'T DO IT, CRYS! YOU CAN'T LEAVE ME--TO GO BACK TO THEM!
OH, JOHNNY--JOHNNY! DO YOU THINK I WANT TO GO?
DON'T YOU KNOW HOW THE THOUGHT OF US PARTING JUST BREAKS MY HEART?
BUT THE INHUMANS ARE--MY FAMILY! AND, IF THEY NEED ME--!
IT'S YOUR FAULT, MEDUSA! IF YOU HADN'T COME FOR HER--IF YOU'D JUST STAYED AWAY!
I TOO HAVE MY DUTY, JOHNNY STORM!
I WAS ORDERED TO COME HERE! IT IS BLACK BOLT'S WISH THAT MY SISTER REJOIN US!
THERE IS NO MORE THAT MAY BE SAID!
EVEN NOW THE DIMENSIONS ARE BRIDGED--THE BARRIER IS DOWN!
IT IS TIME! WE MUST TAKE THE GREAT JOURNEY!
NO! I WON'T LET YOU DO IT, CRYS! I WON'T LET THEM TAKE YOU FROM ME AGAIN!
RELEASE HER! YOU HAVE NOT THE RIGHT!
11

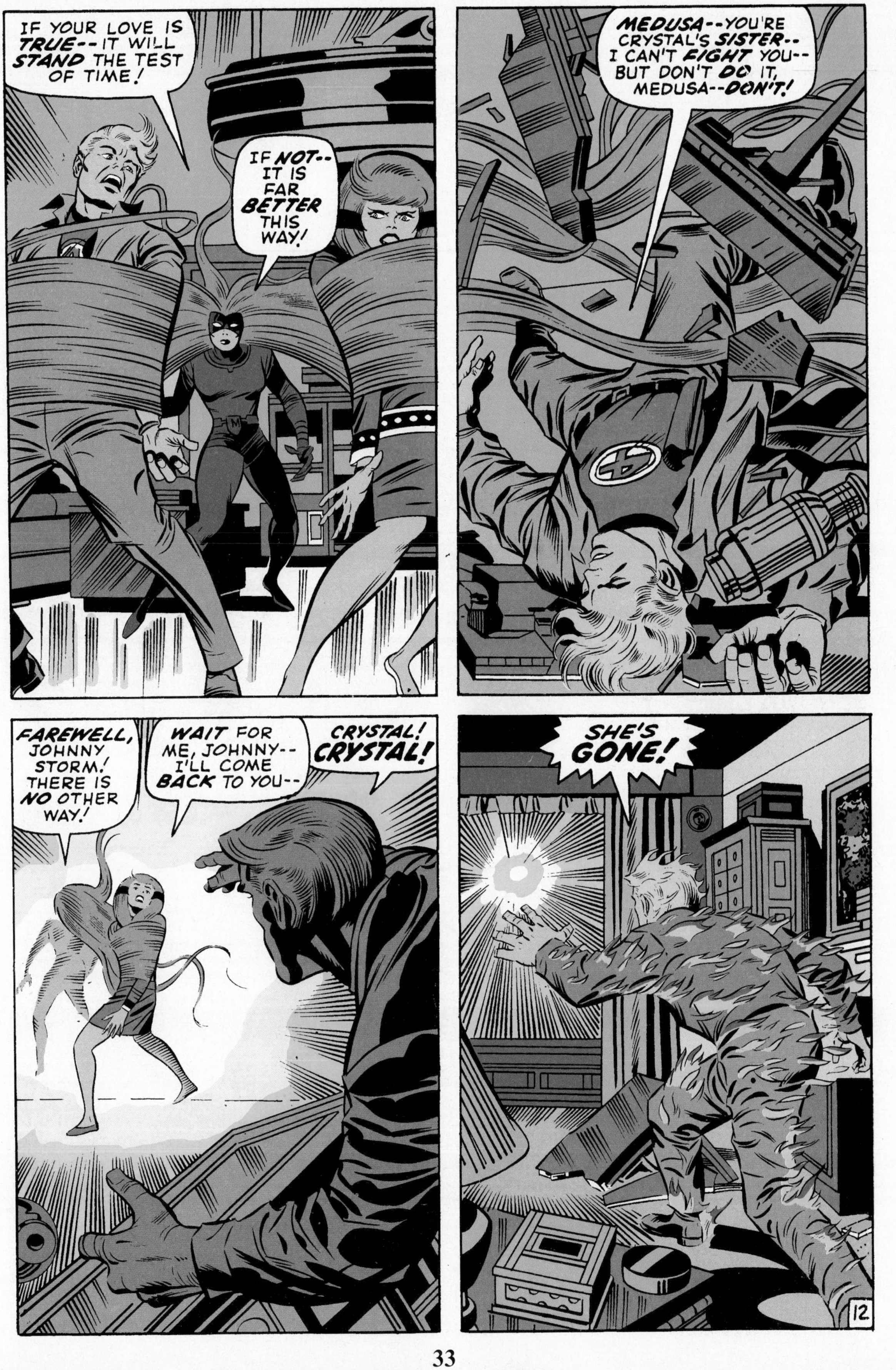
IF YOUR LOVE IS TRUE-- IT WILL STAND THE TEST OF TIME!
IF NOT-- IT IS FAR BETTER THIS WAY!
MEDUSA--YOU'RE CRYSTAL'S SISTER-- I CAN'T FIGHT YOU-- BUT DON'T DO IT, MEDUSA--DON'T!
FAREWELL, JOHNNY STORM! THERE IS NO OTHER WAY!
WAIT FOR ME, JOHNNY-- I'LL COME BACK TO YOU--
CRYSTAL! CRYSTAL!
SHE'S GONE!
12

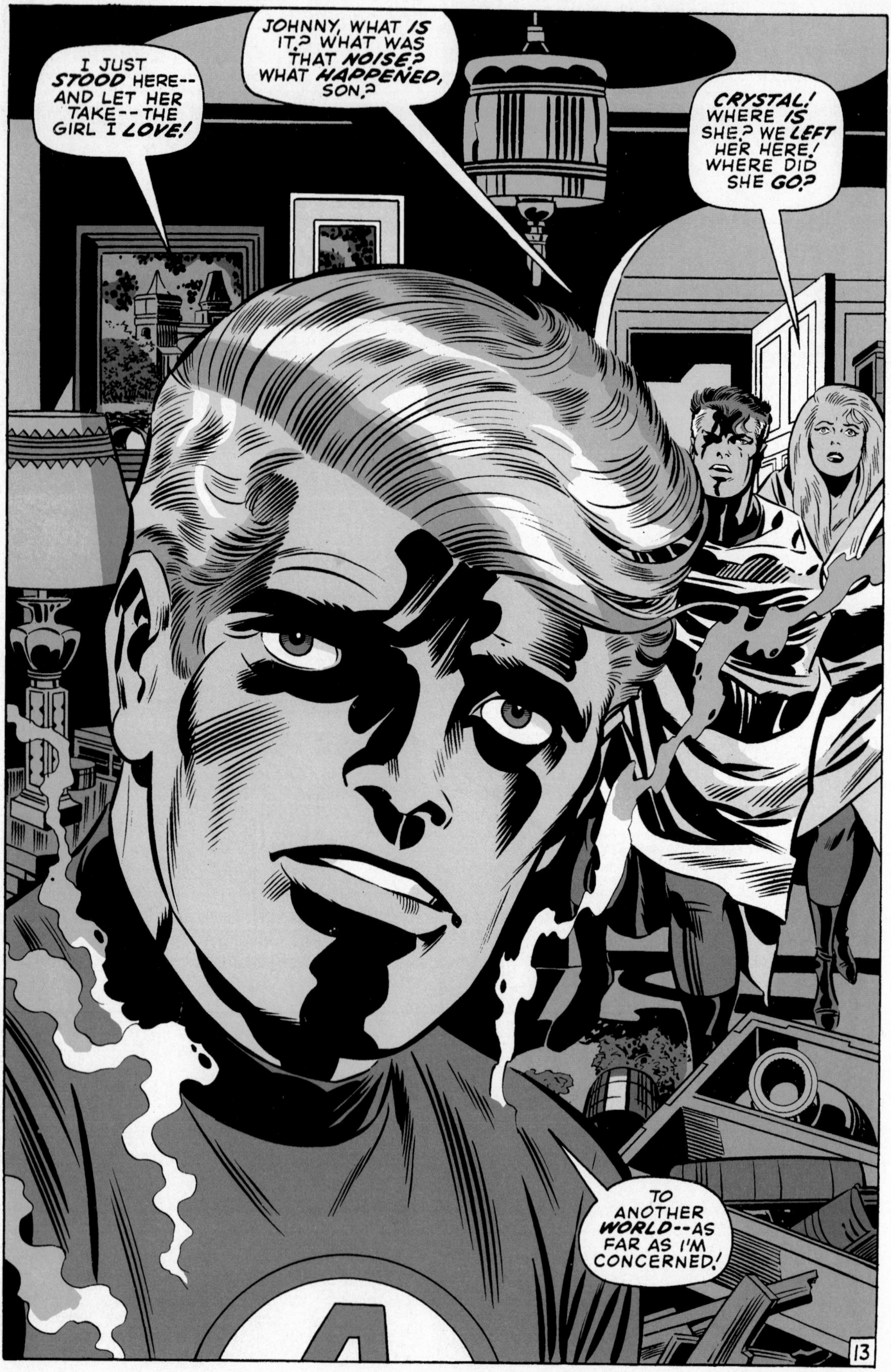
I JUST STOOD HERE--AND LET HER TAKE--THE GIRL I LOVE!
JOHNNY, WHAT IS IT? WHAT WAS THAT NOISE? WHAT HAPPENED, SON?
CRYSTAL! WHERE IS SHE? WE LEFT HER HERE! WHERE DID SHE GO?
TO ANOTHER WORLD--AS FAR AS I'M CONCERNED!
13

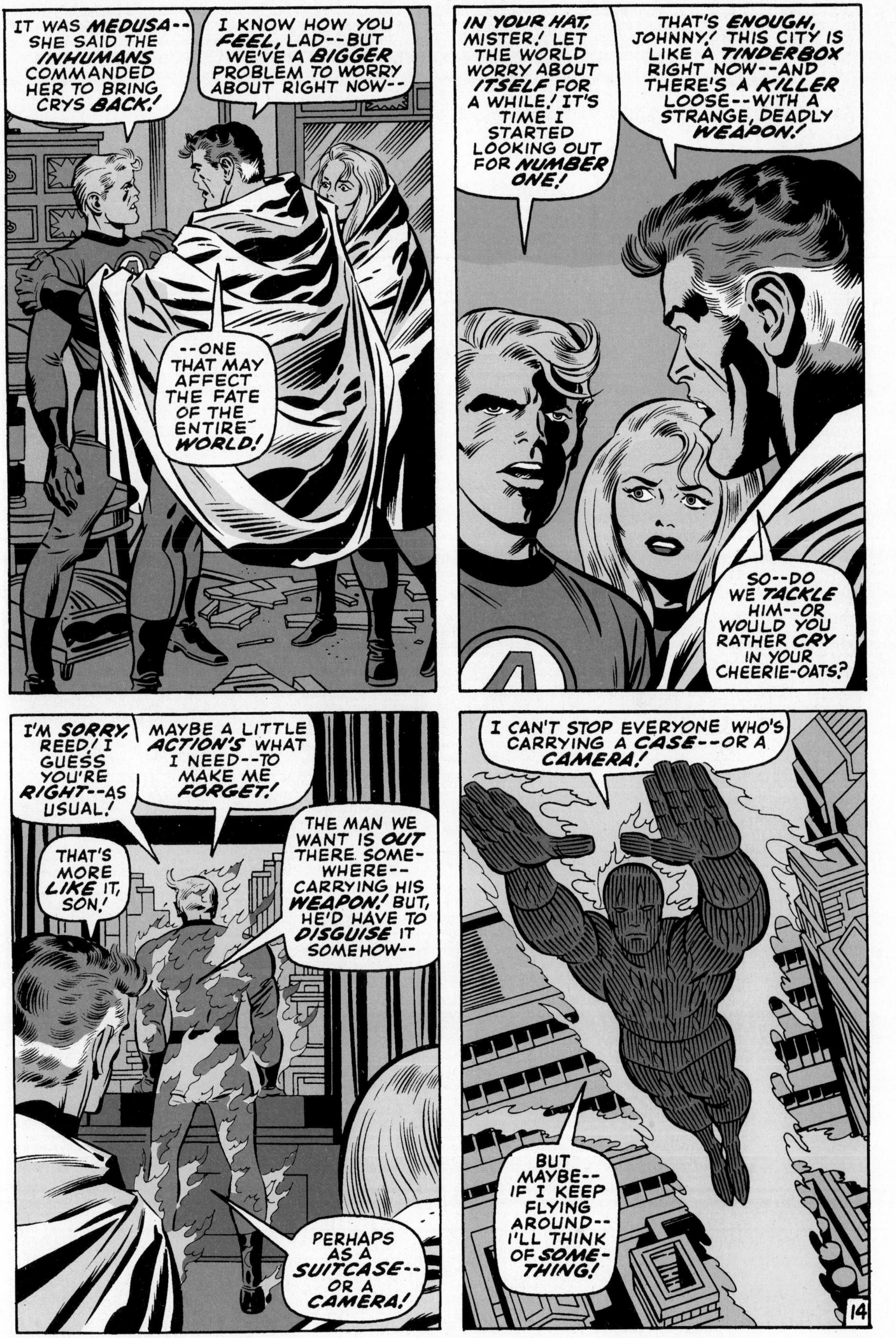
IT WAS MEDUSA--SHE SAID THE INHUMANS COMMANDED HER TO BRING CRYS BACK!
I KNOW HOW YOU FEEL, LAD--BUT WE'VE A BIGGER PROBLEM TO WORRY ABOUT RIGHT NOW--
--ONE THAT MAY AFFECT THE FATE OF THE ENTIRE WORLD!
IN YOUR HAT, MISTER! LET THE WORLD WORRY ABOUT ITSELF FOR A WHILE! IT'S TIME I STARTED LOOKING OUT FOR NUMBER ONE!
THAT'S ENOUGH, JOHNNY! THIS CITY IS LIKE A TINDERBOX RIGHT NOW--AND THERE'S A KILLER LOOSE--WITH A STRANGE, DEADLY WEAPON!
SO--DO WE TACKLE HIM--OR WOULD YOU RATHER CRY IN YOUR CHEERIE-OATS?
I'M SORRY, REED! I GUESS YOU'RE RIGHT--AS USUAL!
MAYBE A LITTLE ACTION'S WHAT I NEED--TO MAKE ME FORGET!
THAT'S MORE LIKE IT, SON!
THE MAN WE WANT IS OUT THERE SOME-WHERE--CARRYING HIS WEAPON! BUT, HE'D HAVE TO DISGUISE IT SOMEHOW--
PERHAPS AS A SUITCASE--OR A CAMERA!
I CAN'T STOP EVERYONE WHO'S CARRYING A CASE--OR A CAMERA!
BUT MAYBE--IF I KEEP FLYING AROUND--I'LL THINK OF SOME-THING!
14

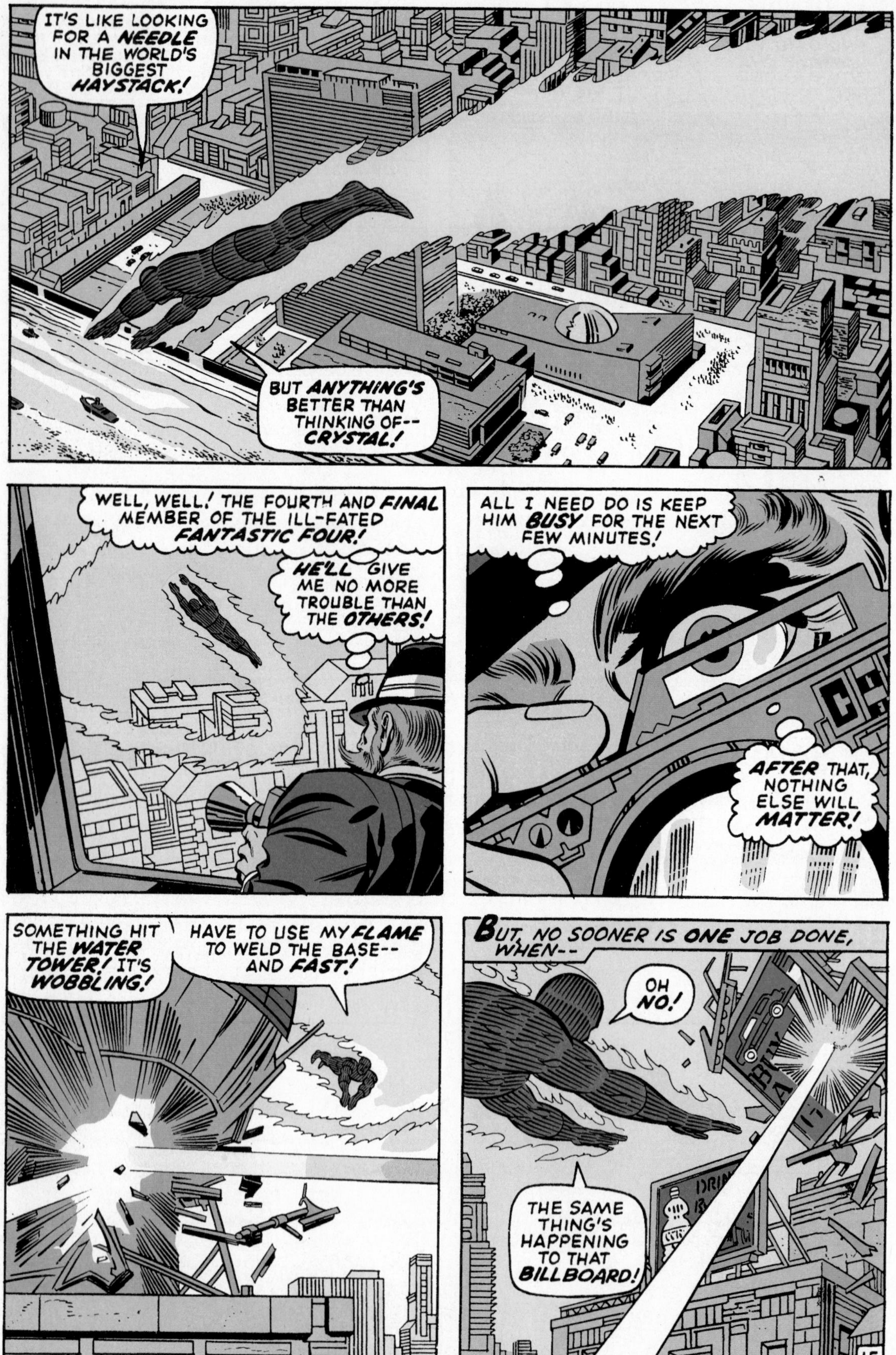
IT'S LIKE LOOKING FOR A NEEDLE IN THE WORLD'S BIGGEST HAYSTACK!
BUT ANYTHING'S BETTER THAN THINKING OF-- CRYSTAL!
WELL, WELL! THE FOURTH AND FINAL MEMBER OF THE ILL-FATED FANTASTIC FOUR!
HE'LL GIVE ME NO MORE TROUBLE THAN THE OTHERS!
ALL I NEED DO IS KEEP HIM BUSY FOR THE NEXT FEW MINUTES!
AFTER THAT, NOTHING ELSE WILL MATTER!
SOMETHING HIT THE WATER TOWER! IT'S WOBBLING!
HAVE TO USE MY FLAME TO WELD THE BASE-- AND FAST!
BUT, NO SOONER IS ONE JOB DONE, WHEN--
OH NO!
THE SAME THING'S HAPPENING TO THAT BILLBOARD!
15

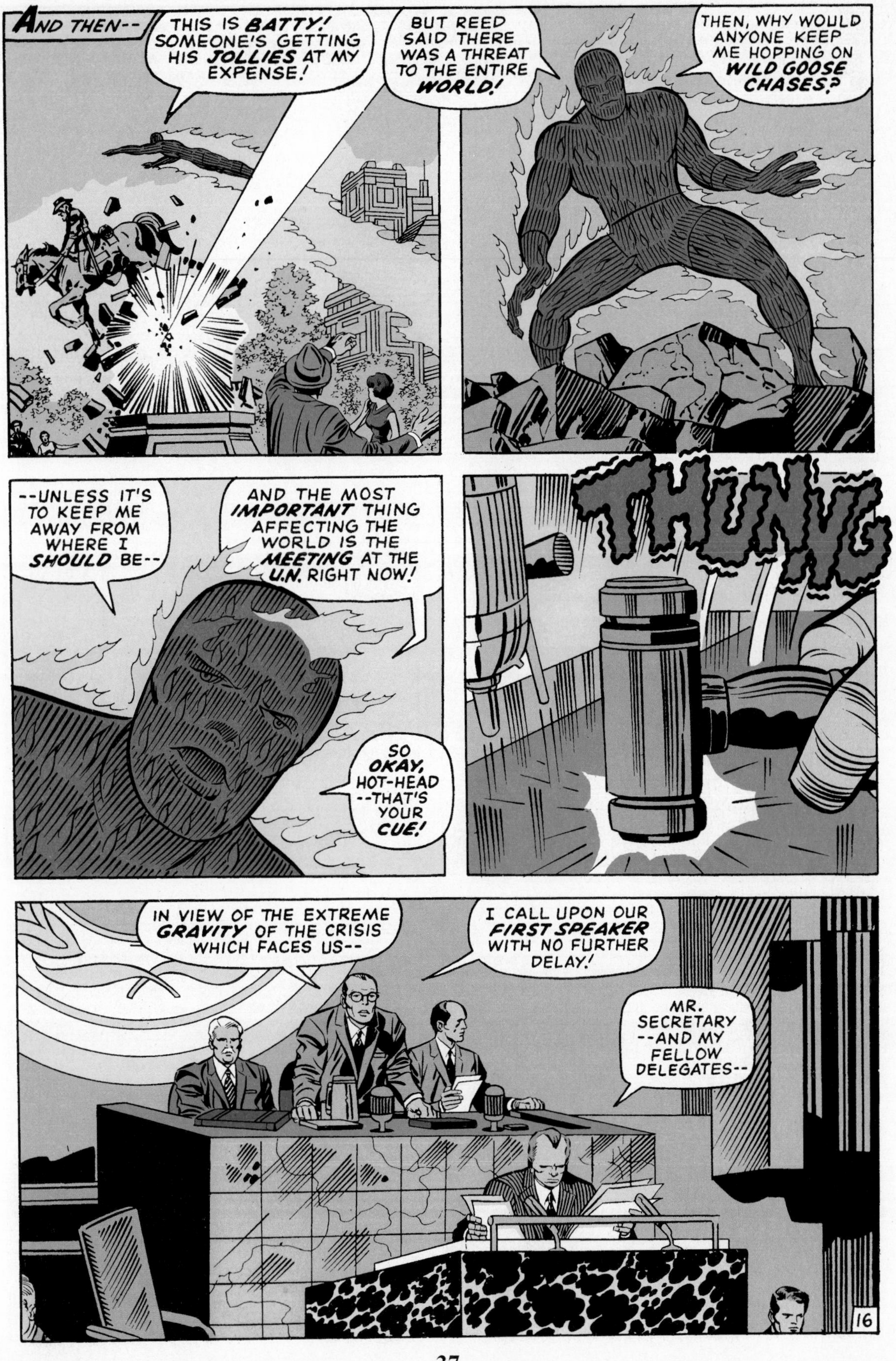
AND THEN--
THIS IS BATTY! SOMEONE'S GETTING HIS JOLLIES AT MY EXPENSE!
BUT REED SAID THERE WAS A THREAT TO THE ENTIRE WORLD!
THEN, WHY WOULD ANYONE KEEP ME HOPPING ON WILD GOOSE CHASES?
--UNLESS IT'S TO KEEP ME AWAY FROM WHERE I SHOULD BE--
AND THE MOST IMPORTANT THING AFFECTING THE WORLD IS THE MEETING AT THE U.N. RIGHT NOW!
SO OKAY, HOT-HEAD --THAT'S YOUR CUE!
THUNG
IN VIEW OF THE EXTREME GRAVITY OF THE CRISIS WHICH FACES US--
I CALL UPON OUR FIRST SPEAKER WITH NO FURTHER DELAY!
MR. SECRETARY --AND MY FELLOW DELEGATES--
16

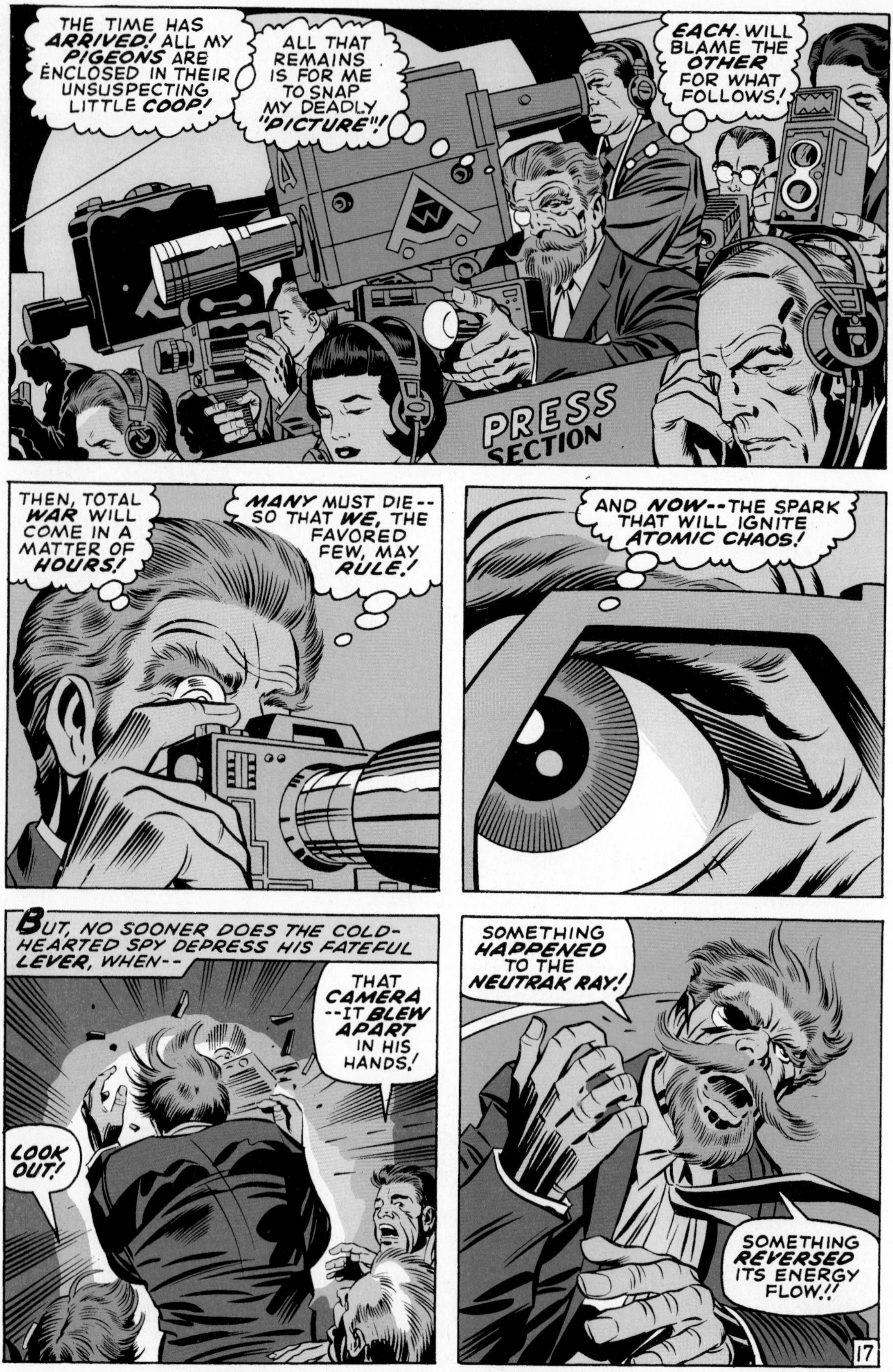

THE TIME HAS ARRIVED! ALL MY PIGEONS ARE ENCLOSED IN THEIR UNSUSPECTING LITTLE COOP!
ALL THAT REMAINS IS FOR ME TO SNAP MY DEADLY "PICTURE"!
EACH WILL BLAME THE OTHER FOR WHAT FOLLOWS!
PRESS SECTION
THEN, TOTAL WAR WILL COME IN A MATTER OF HOURS!
MANY MUST DIE-- SO THAT WE, THE FAVORED FEW, MAY RULE!
AND NOW--THE SPARK THAT WILL IGNITE ATOMIC CHAOS!
BUT, NO SOONER DOES THE COLD-HEARTED SPY DEPRESS HIS FATEFUL LEVER, WHEN--
THAT CAMERA --IT BLEW APART IN HIS HANDS!
LOOK OUT!
SOMETHING HAPPENED TO THE NEUTRAK RAY!
SOMETHING REVERSED ITS ENERGY FLOW!!
17

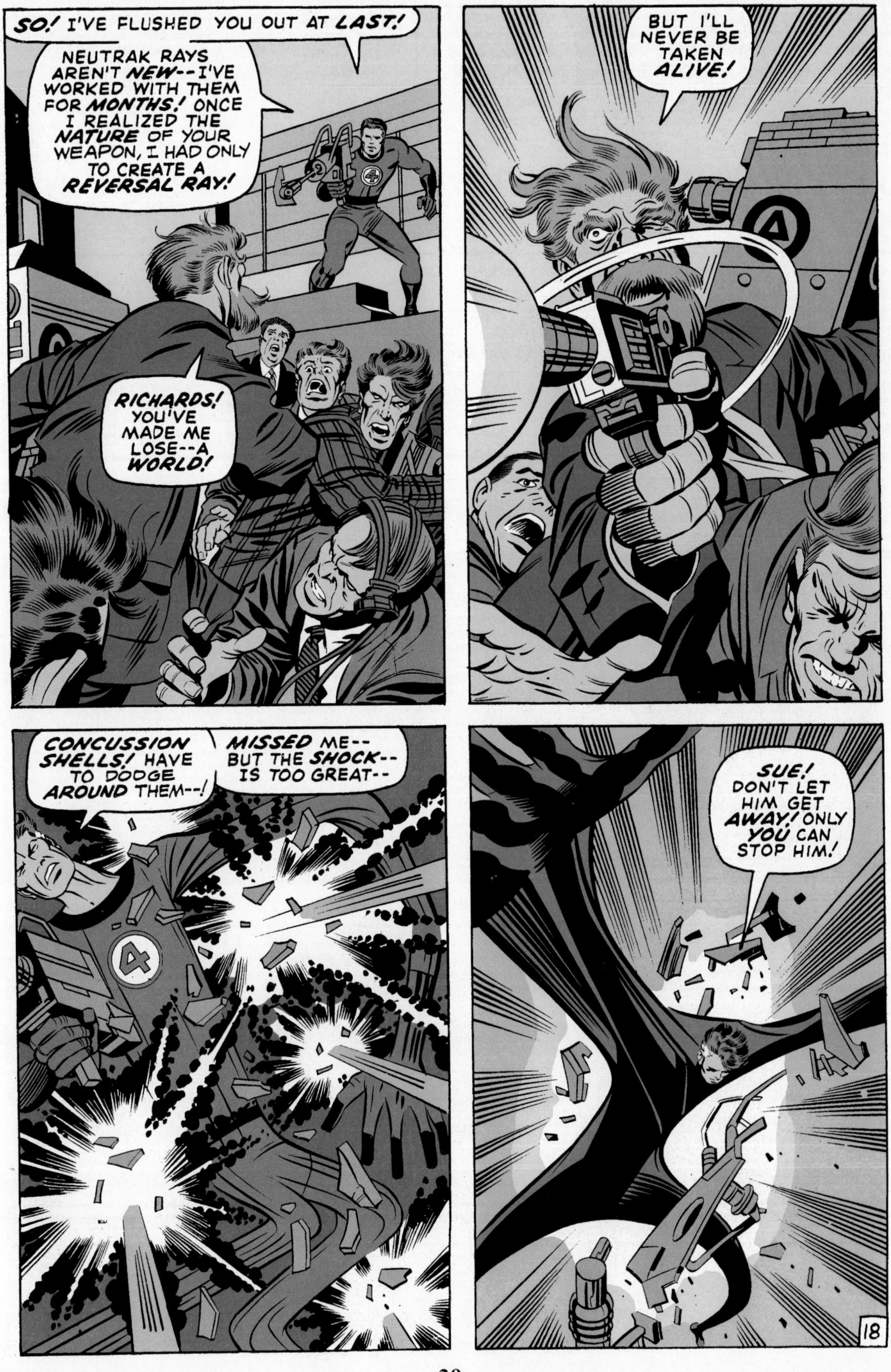
SO! I'VE FLUSHED YOU OUT AT LAST!
NEUTRAK RAYS AREN'T NEW--I'VE WORKED WITH THEM FOR MONTHS! ONCE I REALIZED THE NATURE OF YOUR WEAPON, I HAD ONLY TO CREATE A REVERSAL RAY!
RICHARDS! YOU'VE MADE ME LOSE--A WORLD!
BUT I'LL NEVER BE TAKEN ALIVE!
CONCUSSION SHELLS! HAVE TO DODGE AROUND THEM--!
MISSED ME-- BUT THE SHOCK-- IS TOO GREAT--
SUE! DON'T LET HIM GET AWAY! ONLY YOU CAN STOP HIM!
18

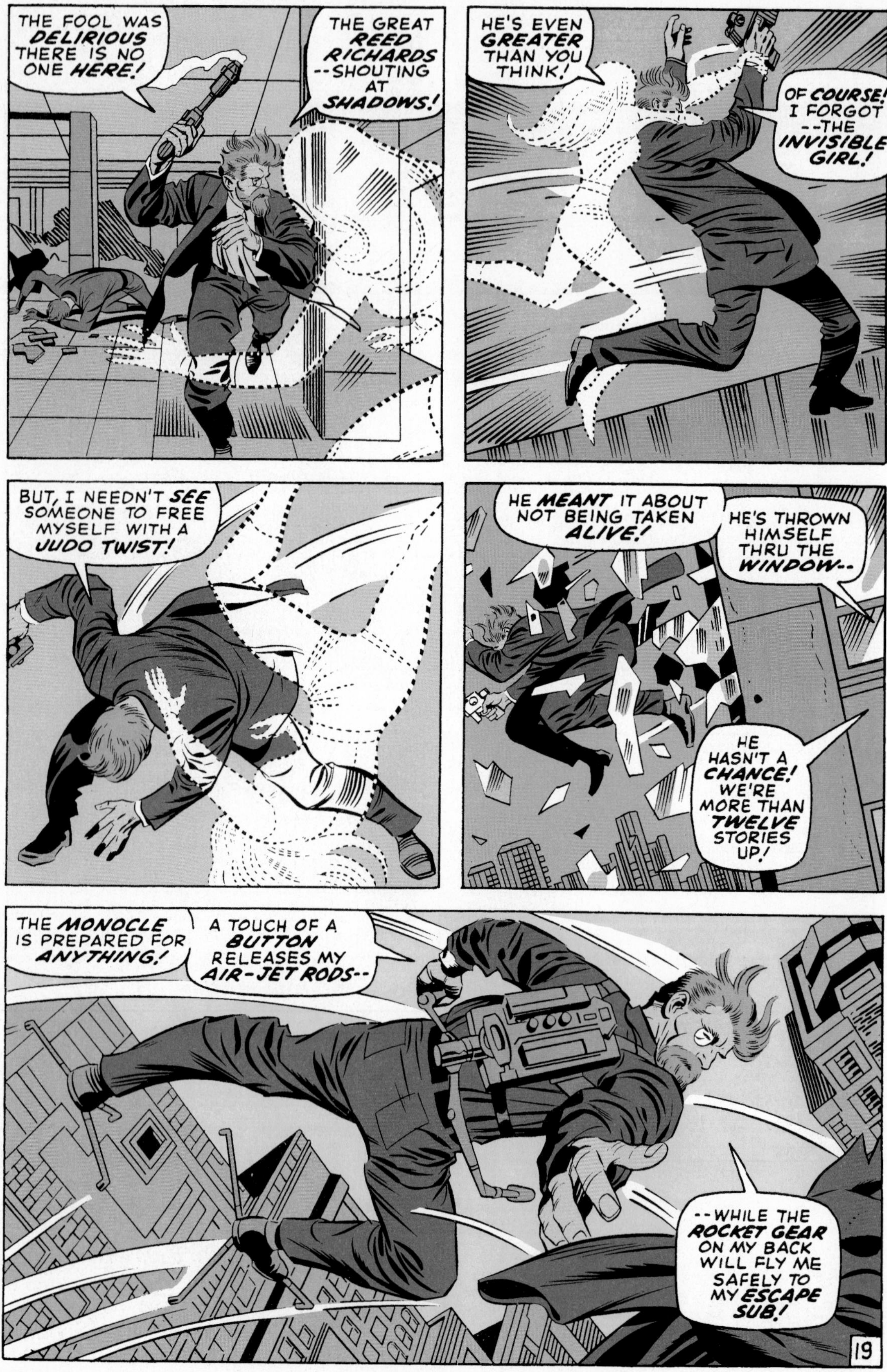
THE FOOL WAS DELIRIOUS THERE IS NO ONE HERE!
THE GREAT REED RICHARDS --SHOUTING AT SHADOWS!
HE'S EVEN GREATER THAN YOU THINK!
OF COURSE! I FORGOT --THE INVISIBLE GIRL!
BUT, I NEEDN'T SEE SOMEONE TO FREE MYSELF WITH A JUDO TWIST!
HE MEANT IT ABOUT NOT BEING TAKEN ALIVE!
HE'S THROWN HIMSELF THRU THE WINDOW--
HE HASN'T A CHANCE! WE'RE MORE THAN TWELVE STORIES UP!
THE MONOCLE IS PREPARED FOR ANYTHING!
A TOUCH OF A BUTTON RELEASES MY AIR-JET RODS--
--WHILE THE ROCKET GEAR ON MY BACK WILL FLY ME SAFELY TO MY ESCAPE SUB!
19

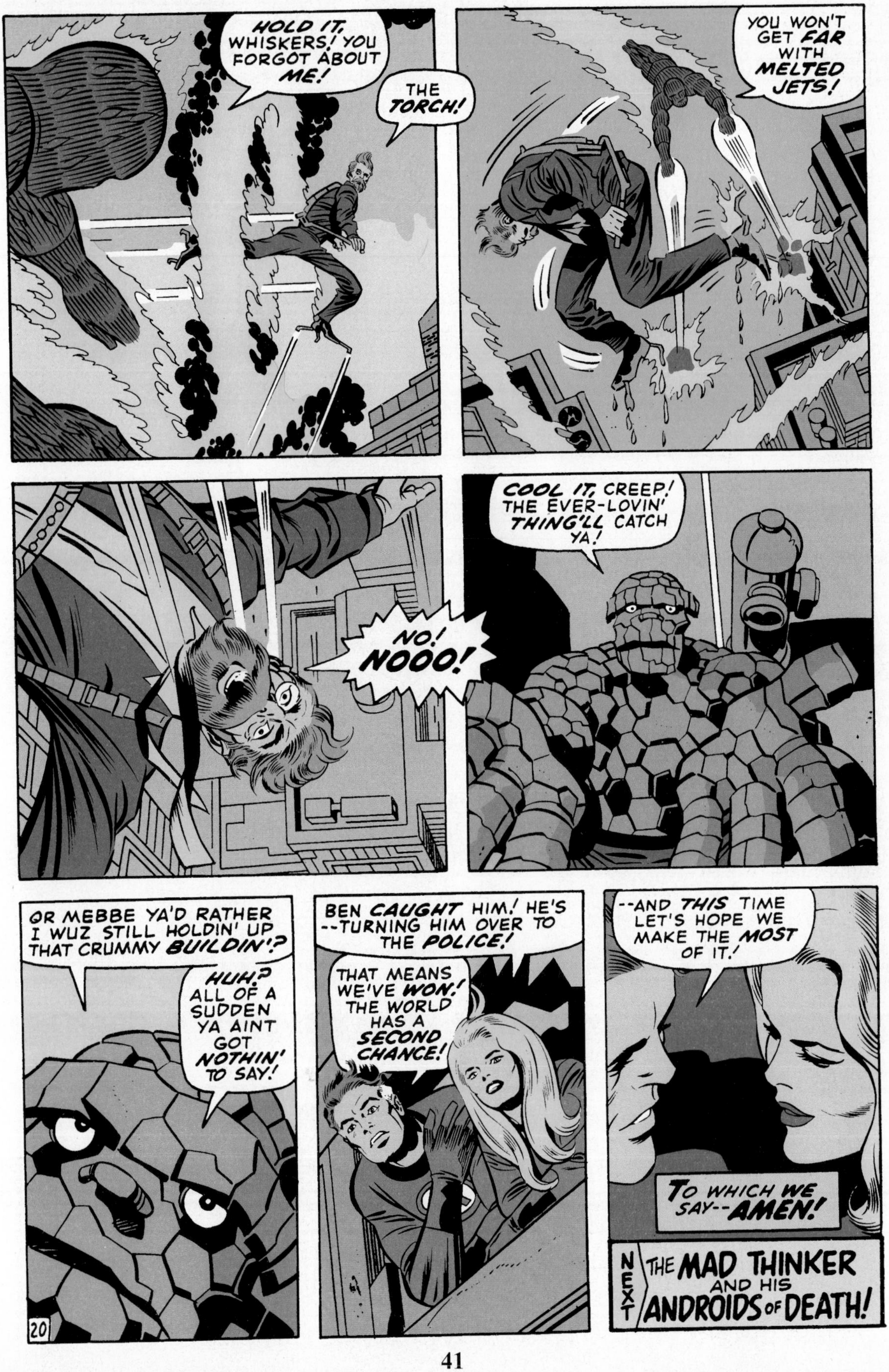
HOLD IT, WHISKERS! YOU FORGOT ABOUT ME!
THE TORCH!
YOU WON'T GET FAR WITH MELTED JETS!
NO! NOOO!
COOL IT, CREEP! THE EVER-LOVIN' THING'LL CATCH YA!
OR MEBBE YA'D RATHER I WUZ STILL HOLDIN' UP THAT CRUMMY BUILDIN'?
HUH? ALL OF A SUDDEN YA AINT GOT NOTHIN' TO SAY!
20
BEN CAUGHT HIM! HE'S --TURNING HIM OVER TO THE POLICE!
THAT MEANS WE'VE WON! THE WORLD HAS A SECOND CHANCE!
--AND THIS TIME LET'S HOPE WE MAKE THE MOST OF IT!
TO WHICH WE SAY--AMEN!
NEXT THE MAD THINKER AND HIS ANDROIDS OF DEATH!

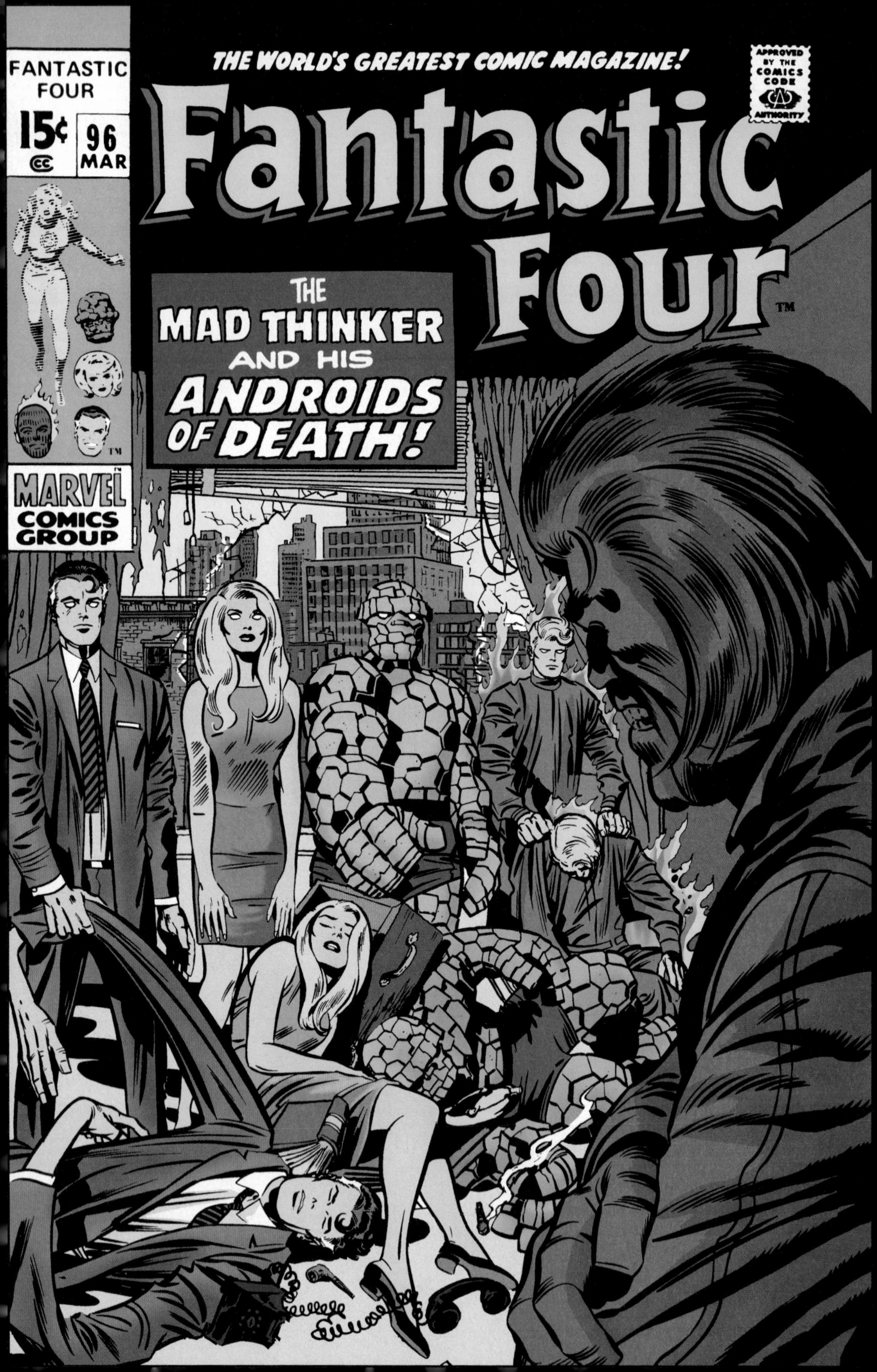

THE WORLD'S GREATEST COMIC MAGAZINE!
FANTASTIC FOUR
15¢
96
MAR
APPROVED BY THE COMICS CODE AUTHORITY
Fantastic Four
THE MAD THINKER AND HIS ANDROIDS OF DEATH!
MARVEL COMICS GROUP

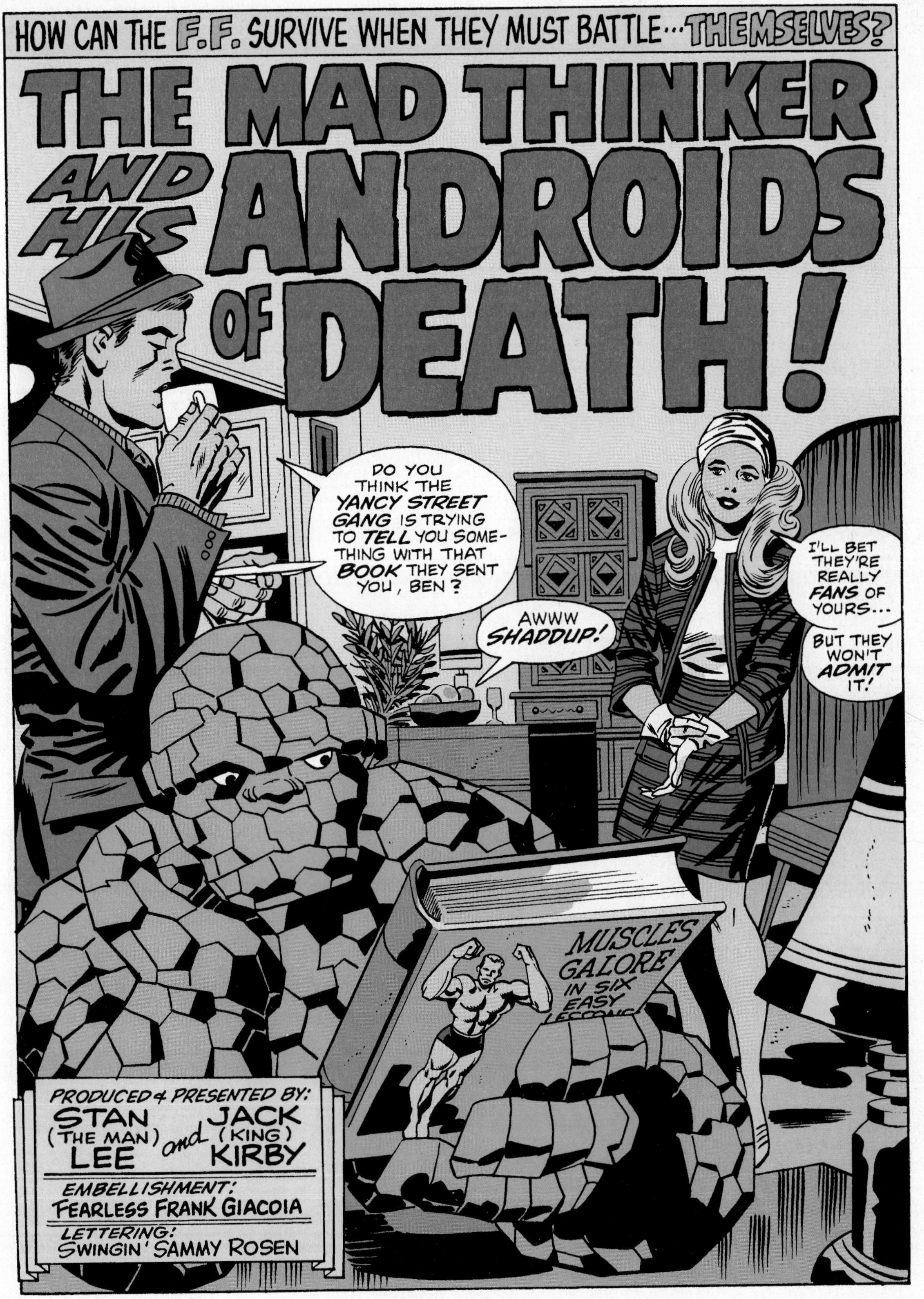
HOW CAN THE F.F. SURVIVE WHEN THEY MUST BATTLE... THEMSELVES?
THE MAD THINKER AND HIS ANDROIDS OF DEATH!
DO YOU THINK THE YANCY STREET GANG IS TRYING TO TELL YOU SOMETHING WITH THAT BOOK THEY SENT YOU, BEN?
AWWW SHADDUP!
I'LL BET THEY'RE REALLY FANS OF YOURS...
BUT THEY WON'T ADMIT IT!
MUSCLES GALORE IN SIX EASY
PRODUCED & PRESENTED BY: STAN (THE MAN) LEE and JACK (KING) KIRBY
EMBELLISHMENT: FEARLESS FRANK GIACOIA
LETTERING: SWINGIN' SAMMY ROSEN

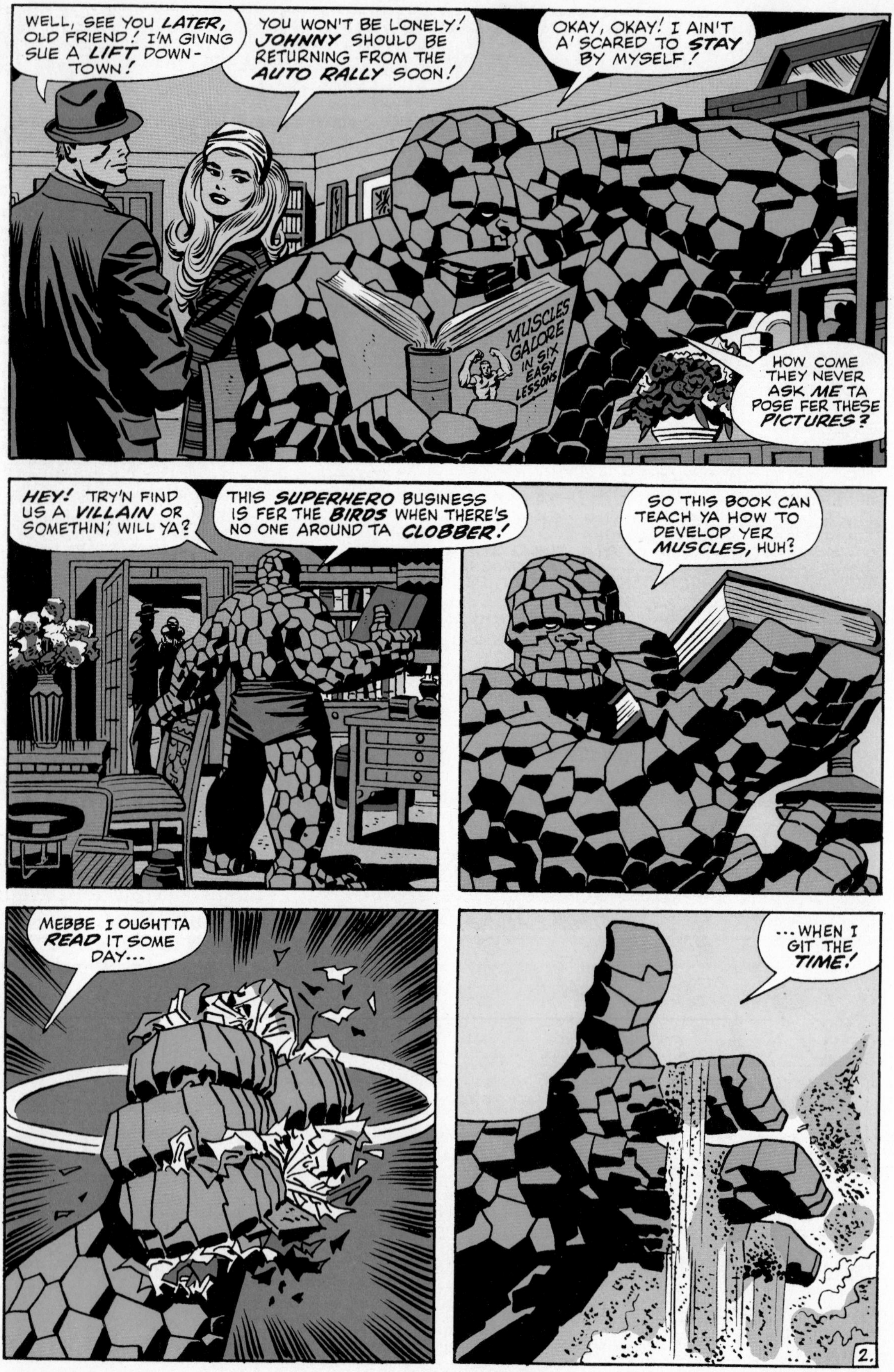
WELL, SEE YOU LATER, OLD FRIEND! I'M GIVING SUE A LIFT DOWN-TOWN!
YOU WON'T BE LONELY! JOHNNY SHOULD BE RETURNING FROM THE AUTO RALLY SOON!
OKAY, OKAY! I AIN'T A' SCARED TO STAY BY MYSELF!
MUSCLES GALORE IN SIX EASY LESSONS
HOW COME THEY NEVER ASK ME TA POSE FER THESE PICTURES?
HEY! TRY'N FIND US A VILLAIN OR SOMETHIN', WILL YA?
THIS SUPERHERO BUSINESS IS FER THE BIRDS WHEN THERE'S NO ONE AROUND TA CLOBBER!
SO THIS BOOK CAN TEACH YA HOW TO DEVELOP YER MUSCLES, HUH?
MEBBE I OUGHTTA READ IT SOME DAY...
...WHEN I GIT THE TIME!
2.

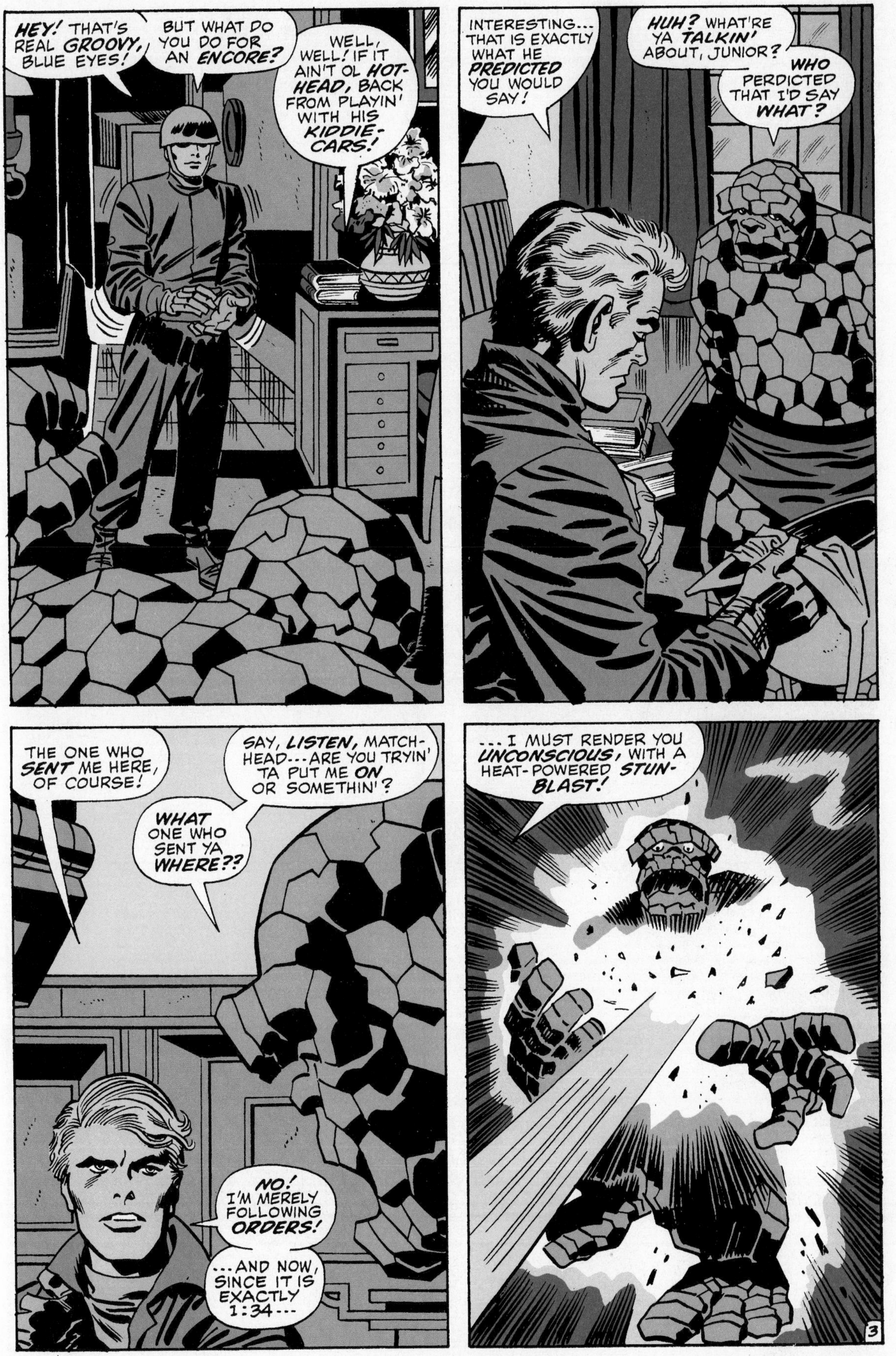
HEY! THAT'S REAL GROOVY, BLUE EYES!
BUT WHAT DO YOU DO FOR AN ENCORE?
WELL, WELL! IF IT AIN'T OL HOT-HEAD, BACK FROM PLAYIN' WITH HIS KIDDIE-CARS!
INTERESTING... THAT IS EXACTLY WHAT HE PREDICTED YOU WOULD SAY!
HUH? WHAT'RE YA TALKIN' ABOUT, JUNIOR?
WHO PERDICTED THAT I'D SAY WHAT?
THE ONE WHO SENT ME HERE, OF COURSE!
SAY, LISTEN, MATCH-HEAD---ARE YOU TRYIN' TA PUT ME ON OR SOMETHIN'?
WHAT ONE WHO SENT YA WHERE??
NO! I'M MERELY FOLLOWING ORDERS!
...AND NOW, SINCE IT IS EXACTLY 1:34---
...I MUST RENDER YOU UNCONSCIOUS, WITH A HEAT-POWERED STUN-BLAST!
3

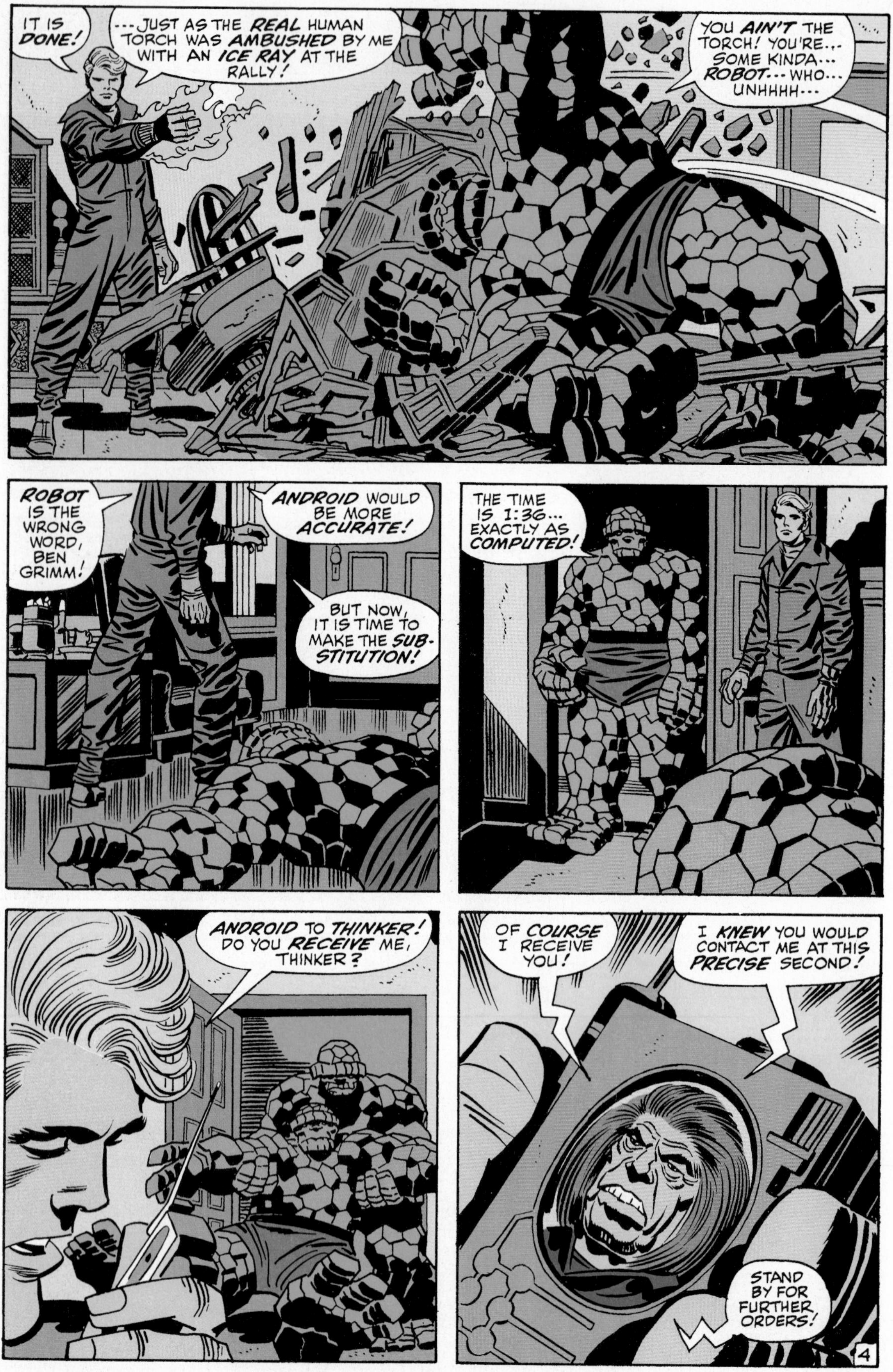
IT IS DONE!
...JUST AS THE REAL HUMAN TORCH WAS AMBUSHED BY ME WITH AN ICE RAY AT THE RALLY!
YOU AIN'T THE TORCH! YOU'RE... SOME KINDA... ROBOT... WHO... UNHHHH...
ROBOT IS THE WRONG WORD, BEN GRIMM!
ANDROID WOULD BE MORE ACCURATE!
BUT NOW, IT IS TIME TO MAKE THE SUB-STITUTION!
THE TIME IS 1:36... EXACTLY AS COMPUTED!
ANDROID TO THINKER! DO YOU RECEIVE ME, THINKER?
OF COURSE I RECEIVE YOU!
I KNEW YOU WOULD CONTACT ME AT THIS PRECISE SECOND!
STAND BY FOR FURTHER ORDERS!
4

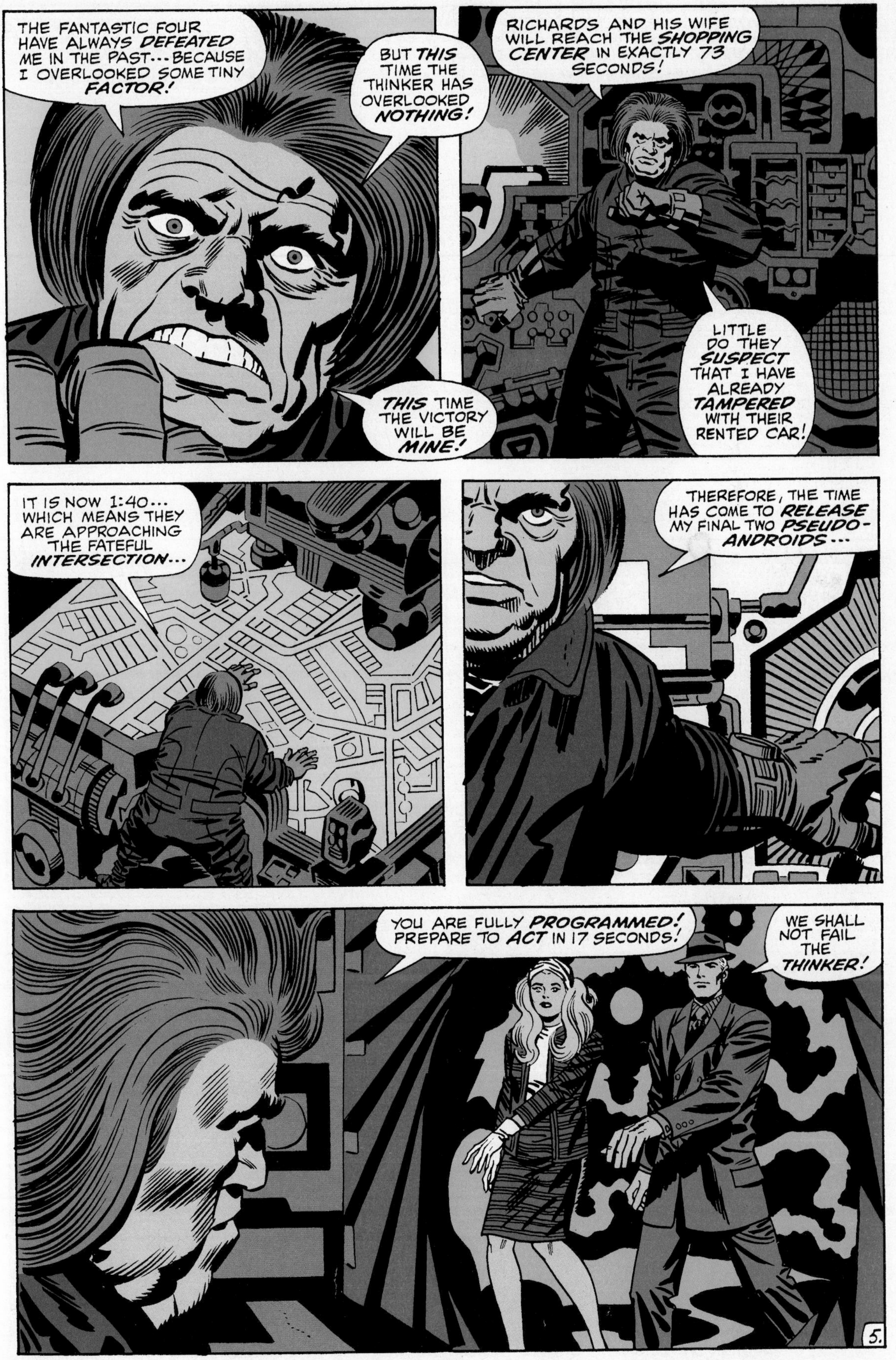
THE FANTASTIC FOUR HAVE ALWAYS DEFEATED ME IN THE PAST...BECAUSE I OVERLOOKED SOME TINY FACTOR!
BUT THIS TIME THE THINKER HAS OVERLOOKED NOTHING!
THIS TIME THE VICTORY WILL BE MINE!
RICHARDS AND HIS WIFE WILL REACH THE SHOPPING CENTER IN EXACTLY 73 SECONDS!
LITTLE DO THEY SUSPECT THAT I HAVE ALREADY TAMPERED WITH THEIR RENTED CAR!
IT IS NOW 1:40... WHICH MEANS THEY ARE APPROACHING THE FATEFUL INTERSECTION...
THEREFORE, THE TIME HAS COME TO RELEASE MY FINAL TWO PSEUDO-ANDROIDS...
YOU ARE FULLY PROGRAMMED! PREPARE TO ACT IN 17 SECONDS!
WE SHALL NOT FAIL THE THINKER!
5.

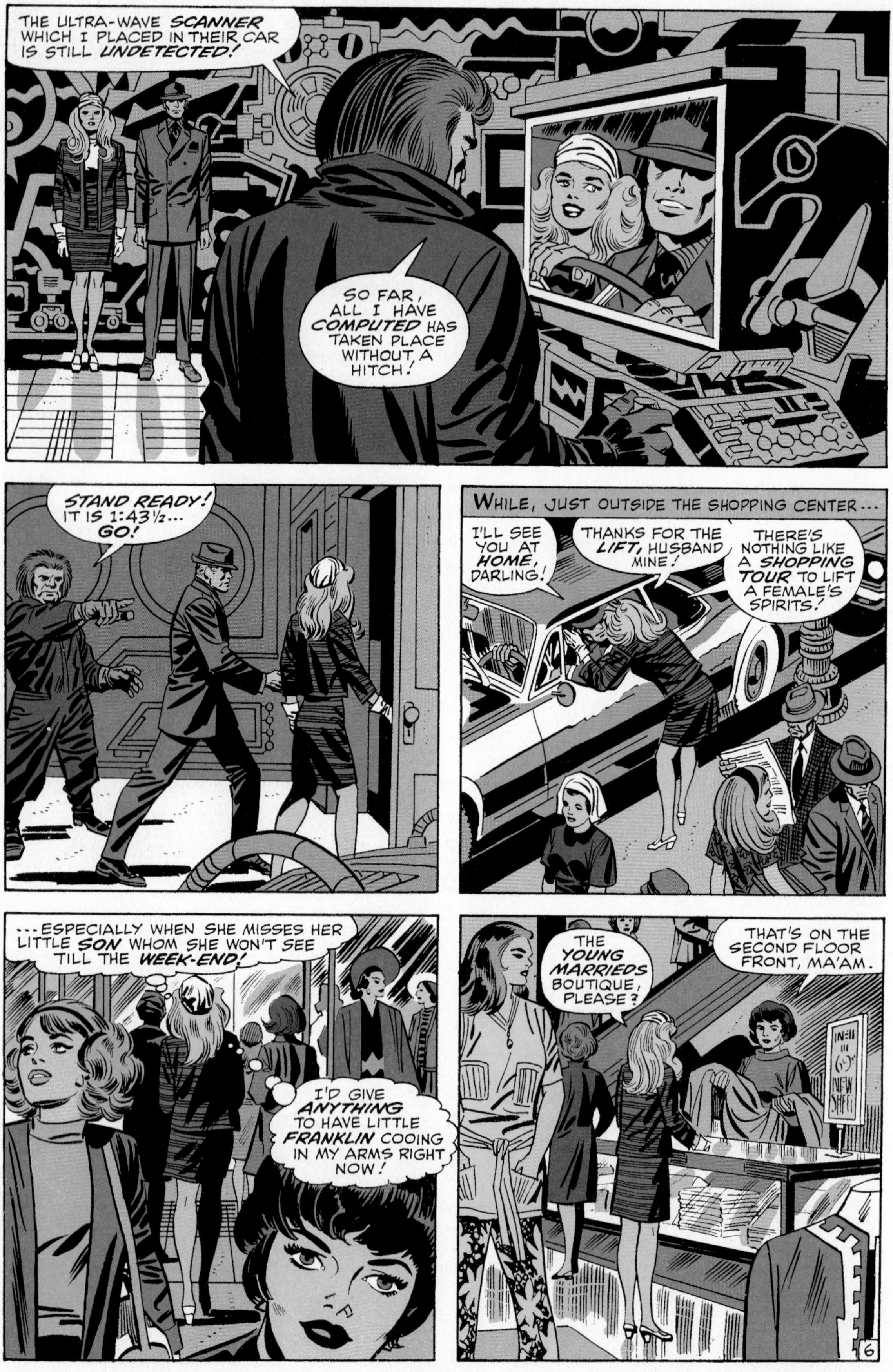
THE ULTRA-WAVE SCANNER WHICH I PLACED IN THEIR CAR IS STILL UNDETECTED!
SO FAR, ALL I HAVE COMPUTED HAS TAKEN PLACE WITHOUT A HITCH!
STAND READY! IT IS 1:43½... GO!
WHILE, JUST OUTSIDE THE SHOPPING CENTER...
I'LL SEE YOU AT HOME, DARLING!
THANKS FOR THE LIFT, HUSBAND MINE!
THERE'S NOTHING LIKE A SHOPPING TOUR TO LIFT A FEMALE'S SPIRITS!
...ESPECIALLY WHEN SHE MISSES HER LITTLE SON WHOM SHE WON'T SEE TILL THE WEEK-END!
I'D GIVE ANYTHING TO HAVE LITTLE FRANKLIN COOING IN MY ARMS RIGHT NOW!
THE YOUNG MARRIEDS BOUTIQUE, PLEASE?
THAT'S ON THE SECOND FLOOR FRONT, MA'AM.
6

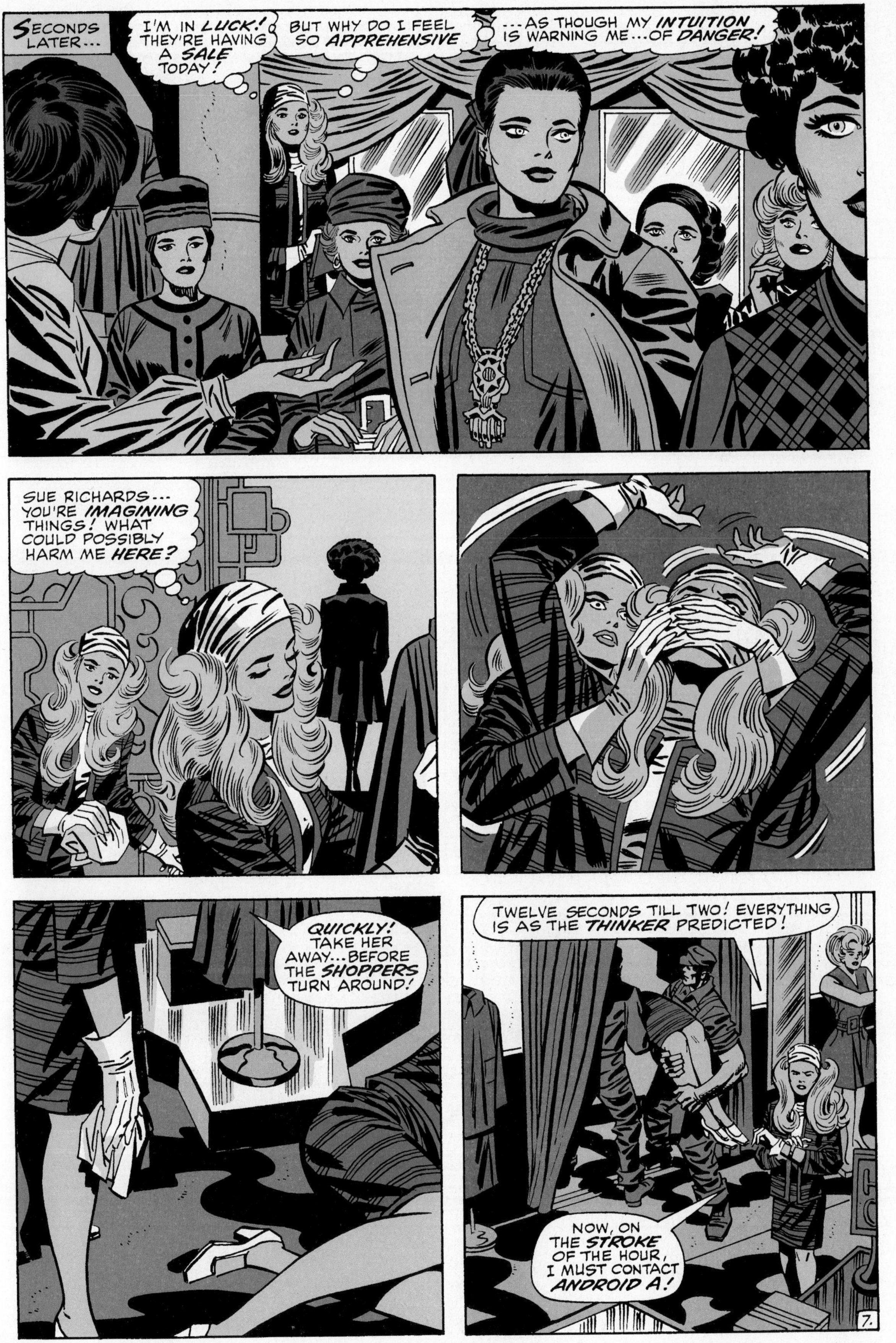
SECONDS LATER...
I'M IN LUCK! THEY'RE HAVING A SALE TODAY!
BUT WHY DO I FEEL SO APPREHENSIVE
...AS THOUGH MY INTUITION IS WARNING ME...OF DANGER!
SUE RICHARDS... YOU'RE IMAGINING THINGS! WHAT COULD POSSIBLY HARM ME HERE?
QUICKLY! TAKE HER AWAY...BEFORE THE SHOPPERS TURN AROUND!
TWELVE SECONDS TILL TWO! EVERYTHING IS AS THE THINKER PREDICTED!
NOW, ON THE STROKE OF THE HOUR, I MUST CONTACT ANDROID A!
7.

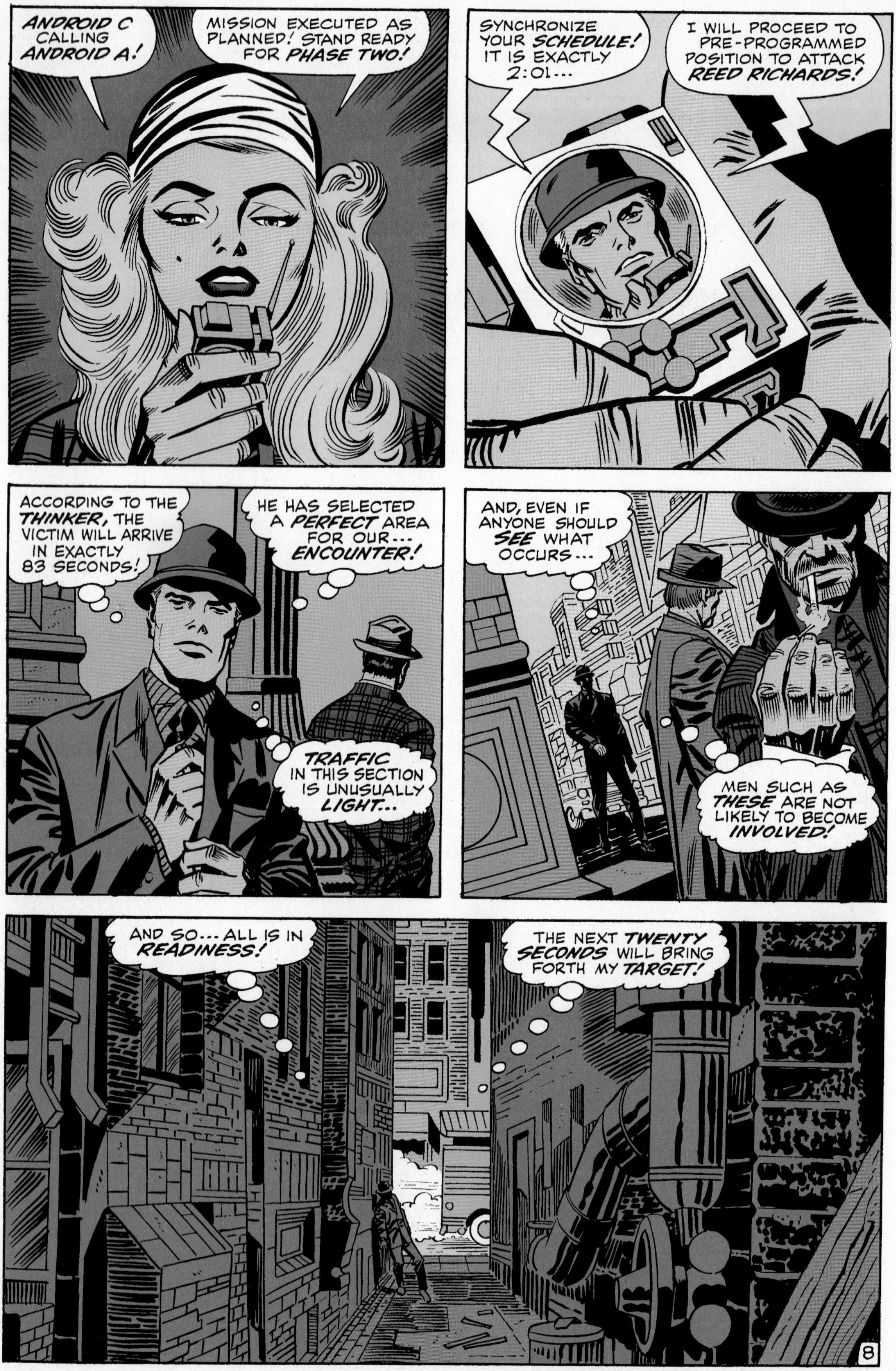
ANDROID C CALLING ANDROID A!
MISSION EXECUTED AS PLANNED! STAND READY FOR PHASE TWO!
SYNCHRONIZE YOUR SCHEDULE! IT IS EXACTLY 2:01...
I WILL PROCEED TO PRE-PROGRAMMED POSITION TO ATTACK REED RICHARDS!
ACCORDING TO THE THINKER, THE VICTIM WILL ARRIVE IN EXACTLY 83 SECONDS!
HE HAS SELECTED A PERFECT AREA FOR OUR... ENCOUNTER!
TRAFFIC IN THIS SECTION IS UNUSUALLY LIGHT...
AND, EVEN IF ANYONE SHOULD SEE WHAT OCCURS...
MEN SUCH AS THESE ARE NOT LIKELY TO BECOME INVOLVED!
AND SO... ALL IS IN READINESS!
THE NEXT TWENTY SECONDS WILL BRING FORTH MY TARGET!
8

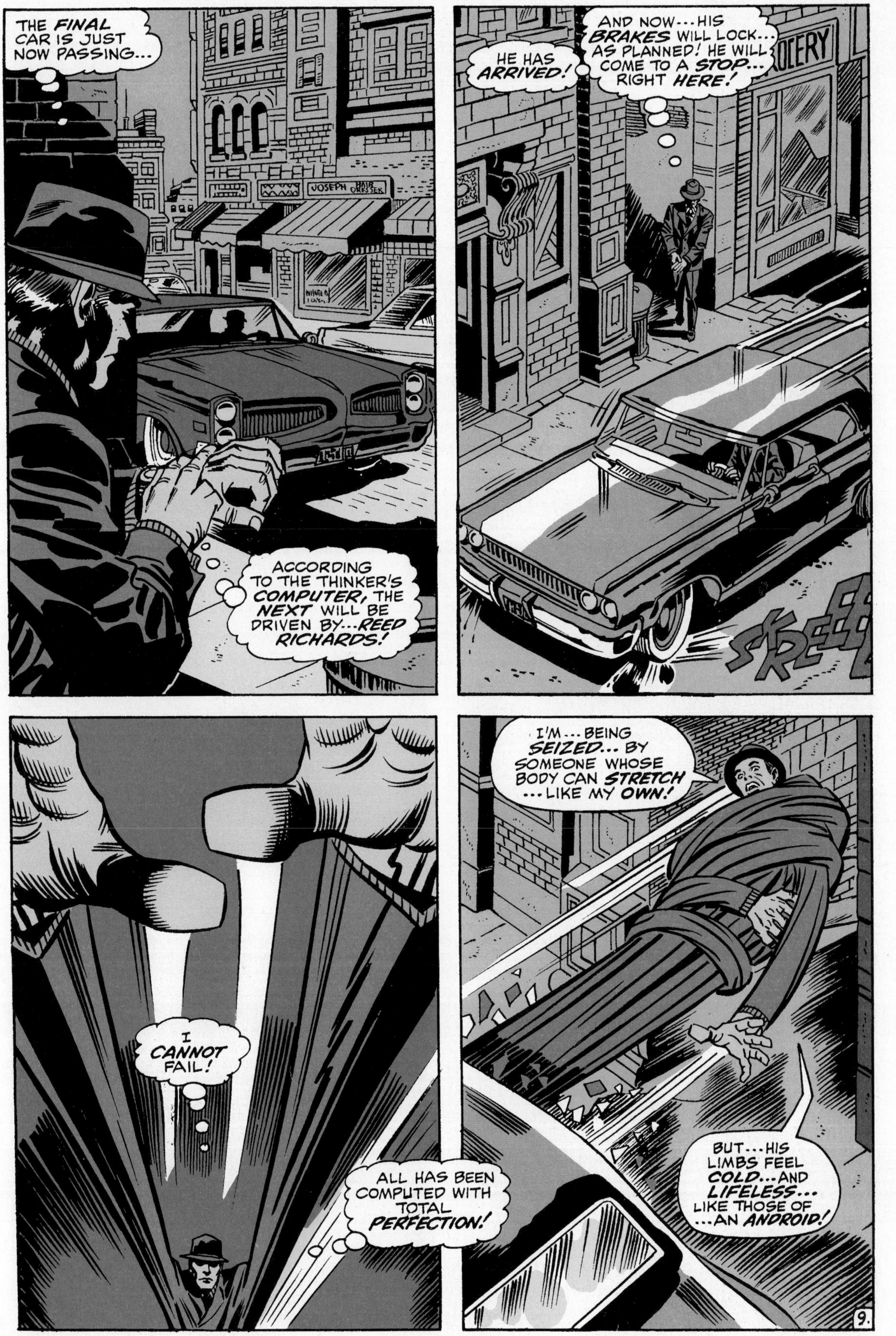
THE FINAL CAR IS JUST NOW PASSING...
ACCORDING TO THE THINKER'S COMPUTER, THE NEXT WILL BE DRIVEN BY...REED RICHARDS!
HE HAS ARRIVED!
AND NOW...HIS BRAKES WILL LOCK... AS PLANNED! HE WILL COME TO A STOP... RIGHT HERE!
SKREEE
I CANNOT FAIL!
ALL HAS BEEN COMPUTED WITH TOTAL PERFECTION!
I'M...BEING SEIZED... BY SOMEONE WHOSE BODY CAN STRETCH ...LIKE MY OWN!
BUT...HIS LIMBS FEEL COLD...AND LIFELESS... LIKE THOSE OF ...AN ANDROID!
9.

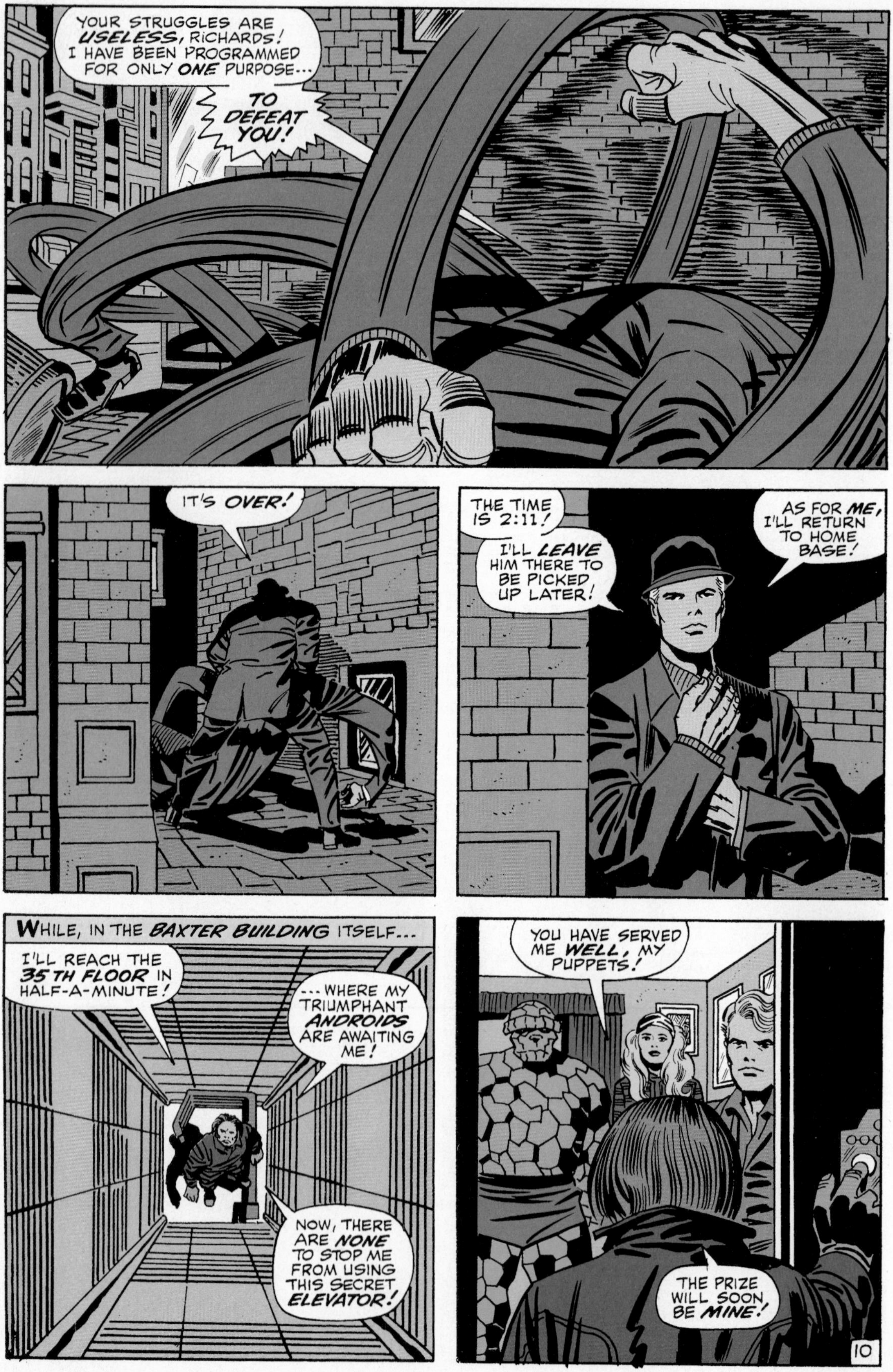
YOUR STRUGGLES ARE USELESS, RICHARDS! I HAVE BEEN PROGRAMMED FOR ONLY ONE PURPOSE...
TO DEFEAT YOU!
IT'S OVER!
THE TIME IS 2:11!
I'LL LEAVE HIM THERE TO BE PICKED UP LATER!
AS FOR ME, I'LL RETURN TO HOME BASE!
WHILE, IN THE BAXTER BUILDING ITSELF...
I'LL REACH THE 35TH FLOOR IN HALF-A-MINUTE!
...WHERE MY TRIUMPHANT ANDROIDS ARE AWAITING ME!
NOW, THERE ARE NONE TO STOP ME FROM USING THIS SECRET ELEVATOR!
YOU HAVE SERVED ME WELL, MY PUPPETS!
THE PRIZE WILL SOON BE MINE!
10

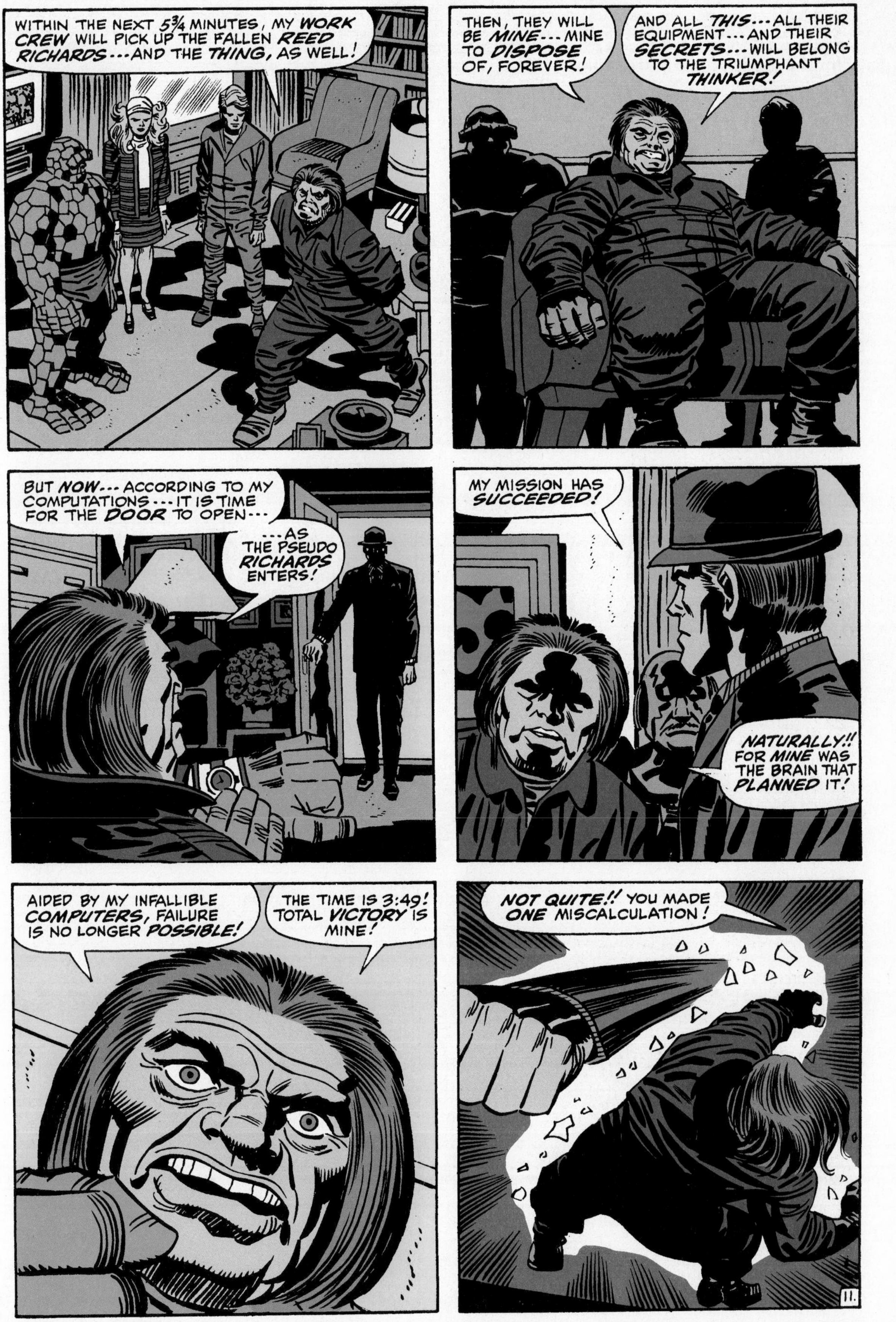

WITHIN THE NEXT 5¾ MINUTES, MY WORK CREW WILL PICK UP THE FALLEN REED RICHARDS --- AND THE THING, AS WELL!
THEN, THEY WILL BE MINE --- MINE TO DISPOSE OF, FOREVER!
AND ALL THIS --- ALL THEIR EQUIPMENT --- AND THEIR SECRETS --- WILL BELONG TO THE TRIUMPHANT THINKER!
BUT NOW --- ACCORDING TO MY COMPUTATIONS --- IT IS TIME FOR THE DOOR TO OPEN ---
--- AS THE PSEUDO RICHARDS ENTERS!
MY MISSION HAS SUCCEEDED!
NATURALLY!! FOR MINE WAS THE BRAIN THAT PLANNED IT!
AIDED BY MY INFALLIBLE COMPUTERS, FAILURE IS NO LONGER POSSIBLE!
THE TIME IS 3:49! TOTAL VICTORY IS MINE!
NOT QUITE!! YOU MADE ONE MISCALCULATION!
11.

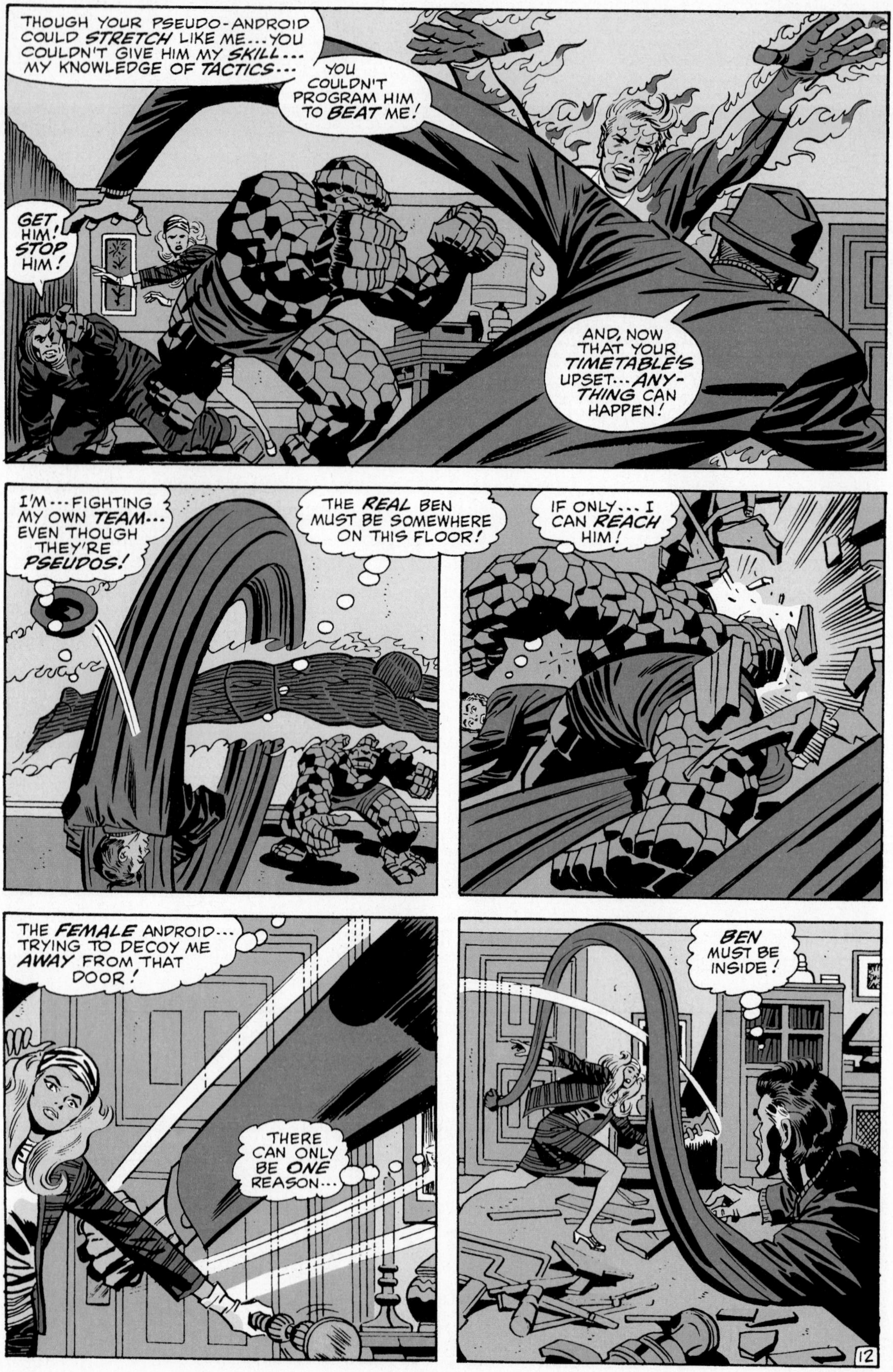
THOUGH YOUR PSEUDO-ANDROID COULD STRETCH LIKE ME... YOU COULDN'T GIVE HIM MY SKILL... MY KNOWLEDGE OF TACTICS...
YOU COULDN'T PROGRAM HIM TO BEAT ME!
GET HIM! STOP HIM!
AND, NOW THAT YOUR TIMETABLE'S UPSET... ANYTHING CAN HAPPEN!
I'M... FIGHTING MY OWN TEAM... EVEN THOUGH THEY'RE PSEUDOS!
THE REAL BEN MUST BE SOMEWHERE ON THIS FLOOR!
IF ONLY... I CAN REACH HIM!
THE FEMALE ANDROID... TRYING TO DECOY ME AWAY FROM THAT DOOR!
THERE CAN ONLY BE ONE REASON...
BEN MUST BE INSIDE!
12

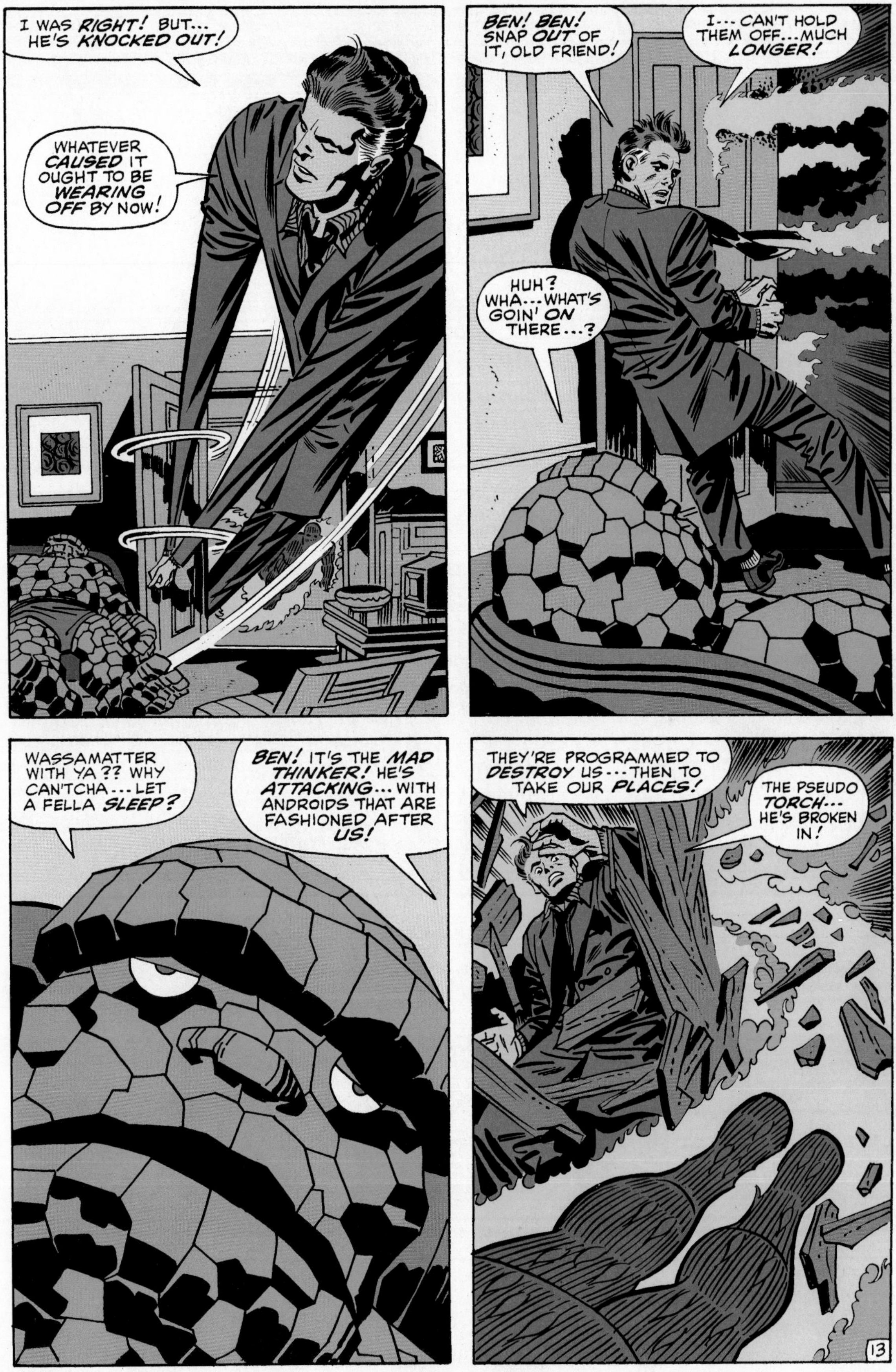
I WAS RIGHT! BUT... HE'S KNOCKED OUT!
WHATEVER CAUSED IT OUGHT TO BE WEARING OFF BY NOW!
BEN! BEN! SNAP OUT OF IT, OLD FRIEND!
I... CAN'T HOLD THEM OFF... MUCH LONGER!
HUH? WHA... WHAT'S GOIN' ON THERE...?
WASSAMATTER WITH YA?? WHY CAN'TCHA... LET A FELLA SLEEP?
BEN! IT'S THE MAD THINKER! HE'S ATTACKING... WITH ANDROIDS THAT ARE FASHIONED AFTER US!
THEY'RE PROGRAMMED TO DESTROY US... THEN TO TAKE OUR PLACES!
THE PSEUDO TORCH... HE'S BROKEN IN!
13

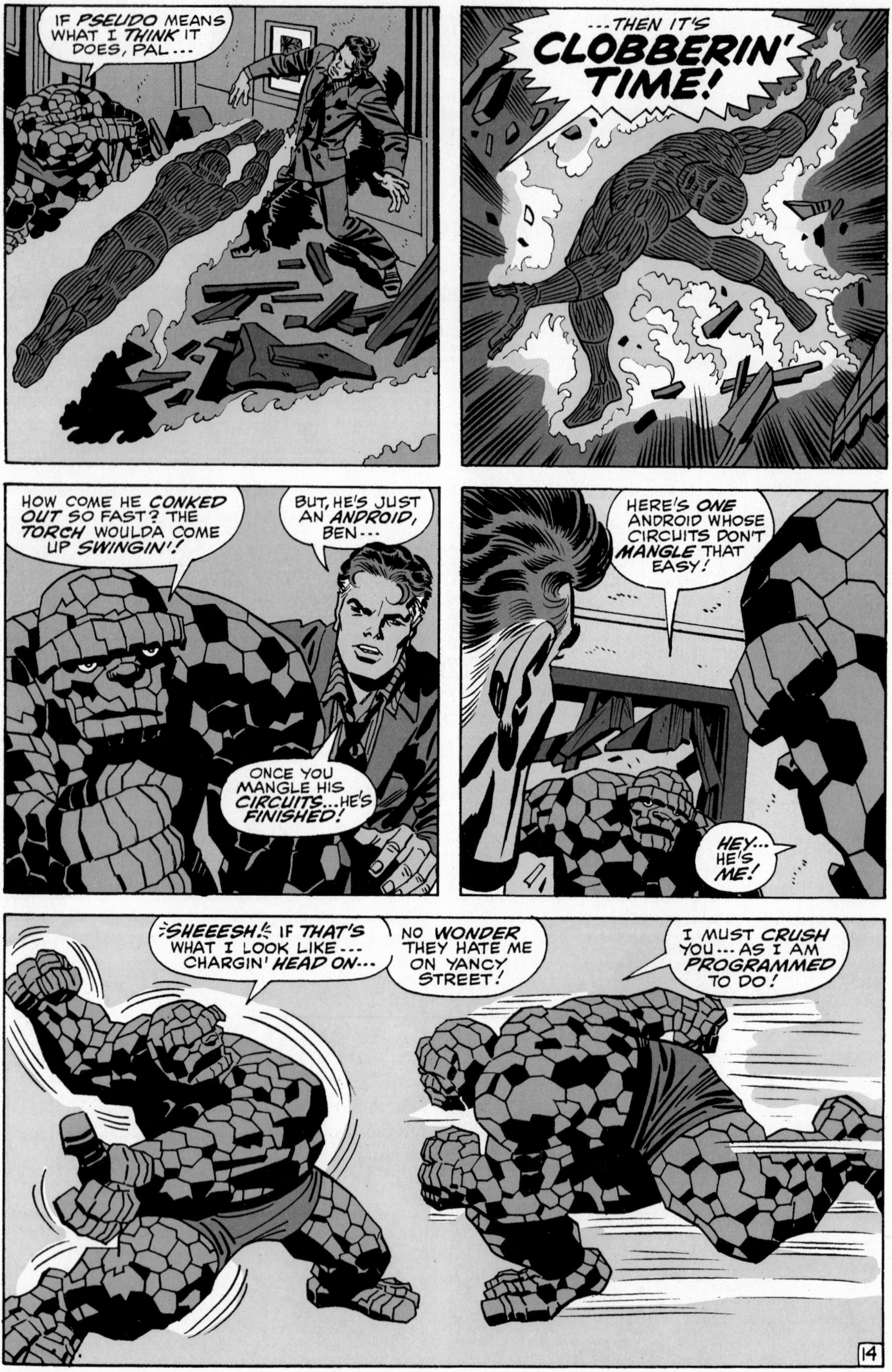
IF PSEUDO MEANS WHAT I THINK IT DOES, PAL---
---THEN IT'S CLOBBERIN' TIME!
HOW COME HE CONKED OUT SO FAST? THE TORCH WOULDA COME UP SWINGIN'!
BUT, HE'S JUST AN ANDROID, BEN---
ONCE YOU MANGLE HIS CIRCUITS...HE'S FINISHED!
HERE'S ONE ANDROID WHOSE CIRCUITS DON'T MANGLE THAT EASY!
HEY... HE'S ME!
SHEEESH! IF THAT'S WHAT I LOOK LIKE--- CHARGIN' HEAD ON---
NO WONDER THEY HATE ME ON YANCY STREET!
I MUST CRUSH YOU--- AS I AM PROGRAMMED TO DO!
14

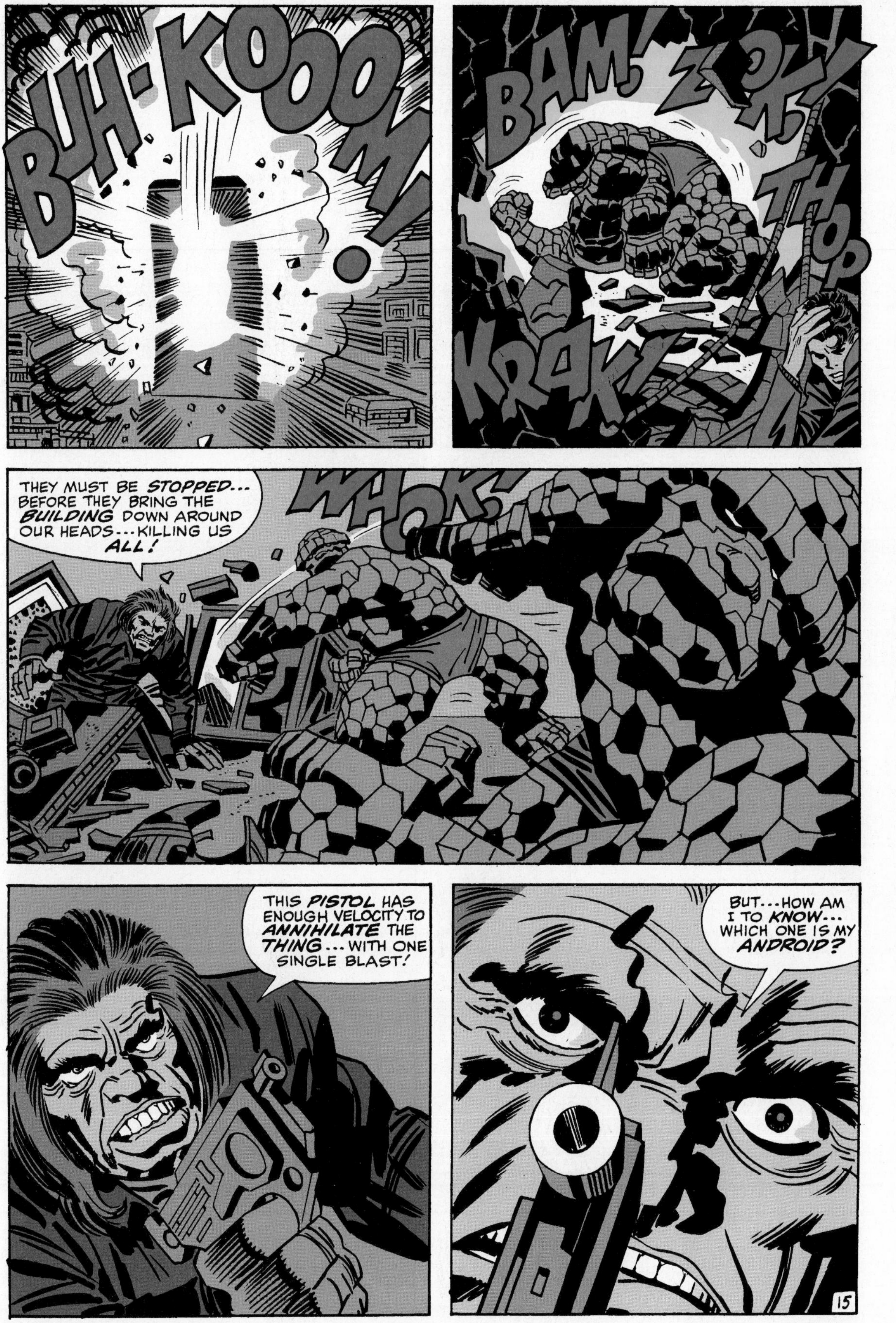
BUH-KOOOM!
BAM! ZOK! THOP
KRAK!
WHOK!
THEY MUST BE STOPPED... BEFORE THEY BRING THE BUILDING DOWN AROUND OUR HEADS... KILLING US ALL!
THIS PISTOL HAS ENOUGH VELOCITY TO ANNIHILATE THE THING... WITH ONE SINGLE BLAST!
BUT... HOW AM I TO KNOW... WHICH ONE IS MY ANDROID?
15

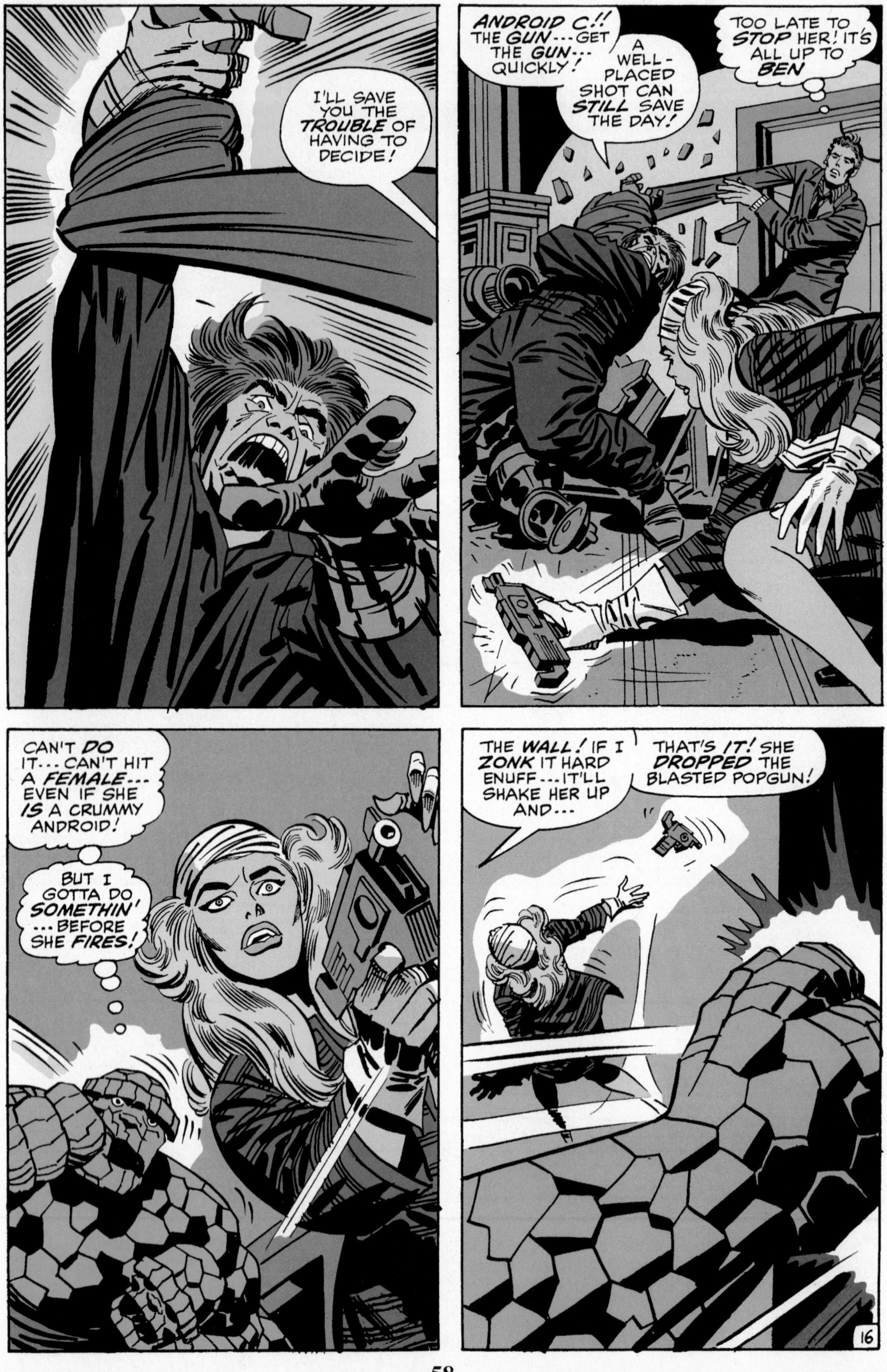
I'LL SAVE YOU THE TROUBLE OF HAVING TO DECIDE!
ANDROID C.!! THE GUN... GET THE GUN... QUICKLY!
A WELL-PLACED SHOT CAN STILL SAVE THE DAY!
TOO LATE TO STOP HER! IT'S ALL UP TO BEN
CAN'T DO IT... CAN'T HIT A FEMALE... EVEN IF SHE IS A CRUMMY ANDROID!
BUT I GOTTA DO SOMETHIN' ...BEFORE SHE FIRES!
THE WALL! IF I ZONK IT HARD ENUFF...IT'LL SHAKE HER UP AND...
THAT'S IT! SHE DROPPED THE BLASTED POPGUN!
16

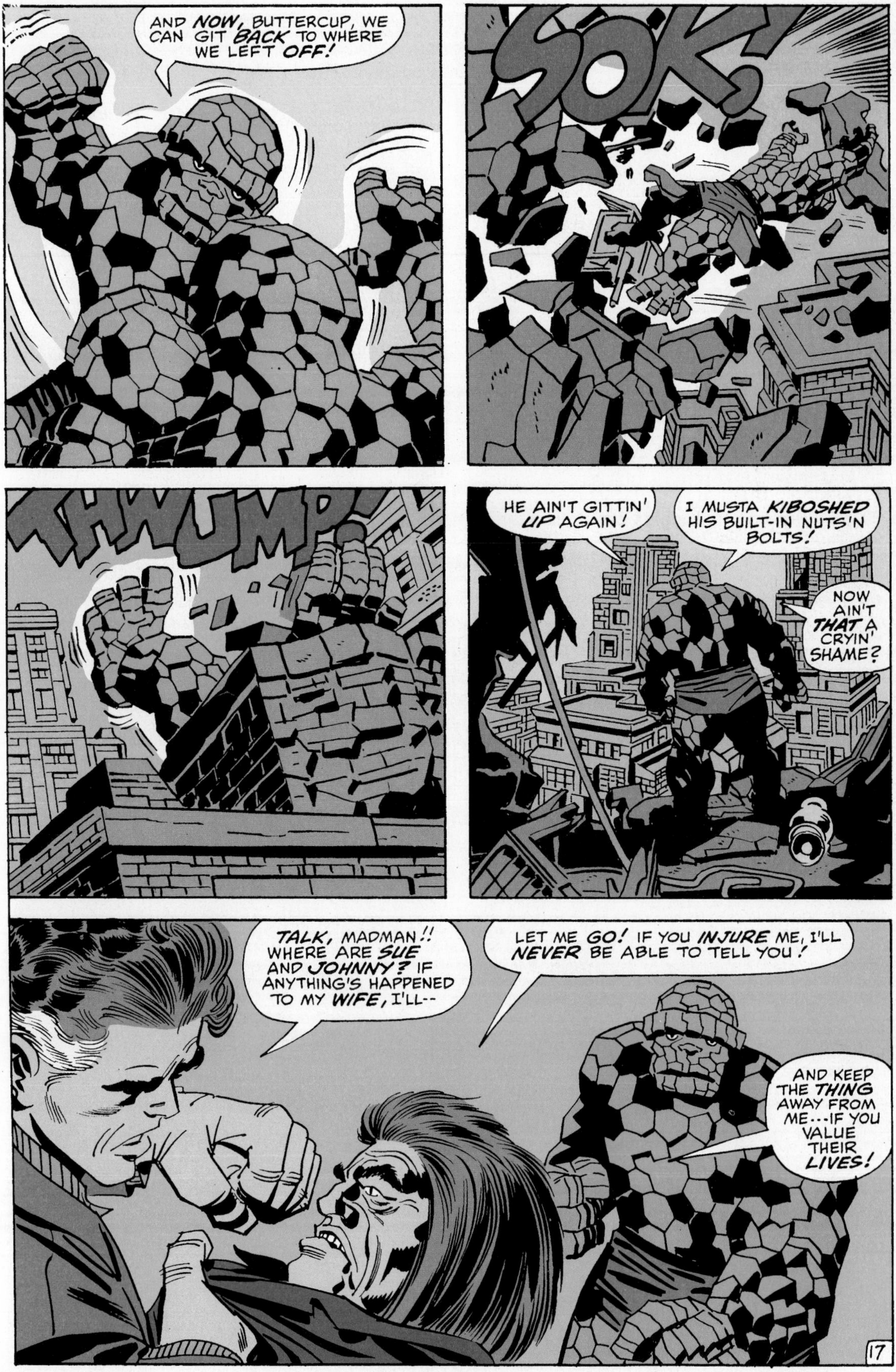
AND NOW, BUTTERCUP, WE CAN GIT BACK TO WHERE WE LEFT OFF!
SOK!
THWUMP!
HE AIN'T GITTIN' UP AGAIN!
I MUSTA KIBOSHED HIS BUILT-IN NUTS'N BOLTS!
NOW AIN'T THAT A CRYIN' SHAME?
TALK, MADMAN!! WHERE ARE SUE AND JOHNNY? IF ANYTHING'S HAPPENED TO MY WIFE, I'LL--
LET ME GO! IF YOU INJURE ME, I'LL NEVER BE ABLE TO TELL YOU!
AND KEEP THE THING AWAY FROM ME---IF YOU VALUE THEIR LIVES!
17

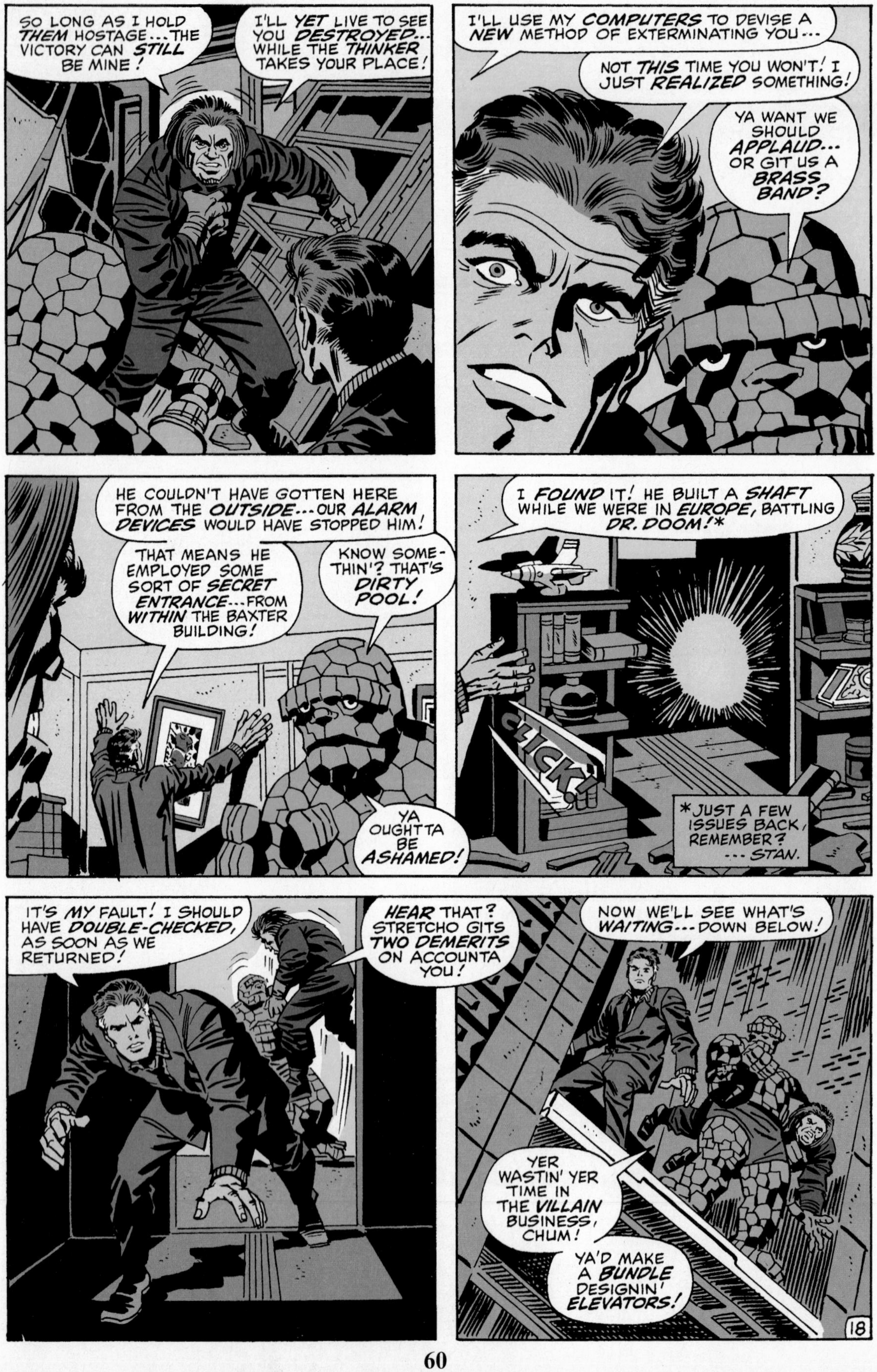
SO LONG AS I HOLD THEM HOSTAGE... THE VICTORY CAN STILL BE MINE!
I'LL YET LIVE TO SEE YOU DESTROYED... WHILE THE THINKER TAKES YOUR PLACE!
I'LL USE MY COMPUTERS TO DEVISE A NEW METHOD OF EXTERMINATING YOU...
NOT THIS TIME YOU WON'T! I JUST REALIZED SOMETHING!
YA WANT WE SHOULD APPLAUD... OR GIT US A BRASS BAND?
HE COULDN'T HAVE GOTTEN HERE FROM THE OUTSIDE... OUR ALARM DEVICES WOULD HAVE STOPPED HIM!
THAT MEANS HE EMPLOYED SOME SORT OF SECRET ENTRANCE... FROM WITHIN THE BAXTER BUILDING!
KNOW SOME-THIN'? THAT'S DIRTY POOL!
YA OUGHTTA BE ASHAMED!
I FOUND IT! HE BUILT A SHAFT WHILE WE WERE IN EUROPE, BATTLING DR. DOOM!*
CLICK!
*JUST A FEW ISSUES BACK, REMEMBER? ---STAN.
IT'S MY FAULT! I SHOULD HAVE DOUBLE-CHECKED, AS SOON AS WE RETURNED!
HEAR THAT? STRETCHO GITS TWO DEMERITS ON ACCOUNTA YOU!
NOW WE'LL SEE WHAT'S WAITING--- DOWN BELOW!
YER WASTIN' YER TIME IN THE VILLAIN BUSINESS, CHUM!
YA'D MAKE A BUNDLE DESIGNIN' ELEVATORS!
18

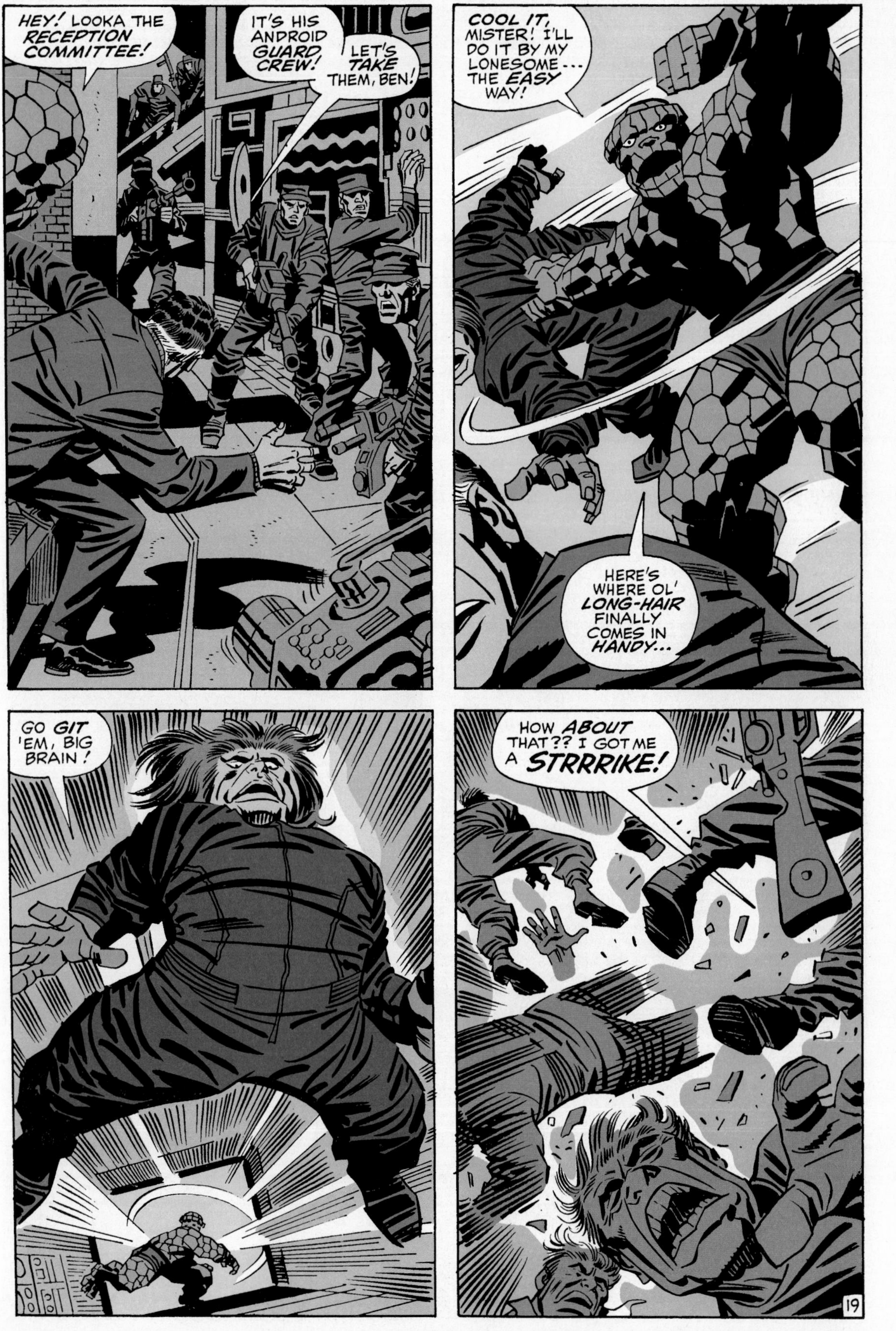
HEY! LOOKA THE RECEPTION COMMITTEE!
IT'S HIS ANDROID GUARD CREW!
LET'S TAKE THEM, BEN!
COOL IT, MISTER! I'LL DO IT BY MY LONESOME--- THE EASY WAY!
HERE'S WHERE OL' LONG-HAIR FINALLY COMES IN HANDY...
GO GIT 'EM, BIG BRAIN!
HOW ABOUT THAT?? I GOT ME A STRRRIKE!
19

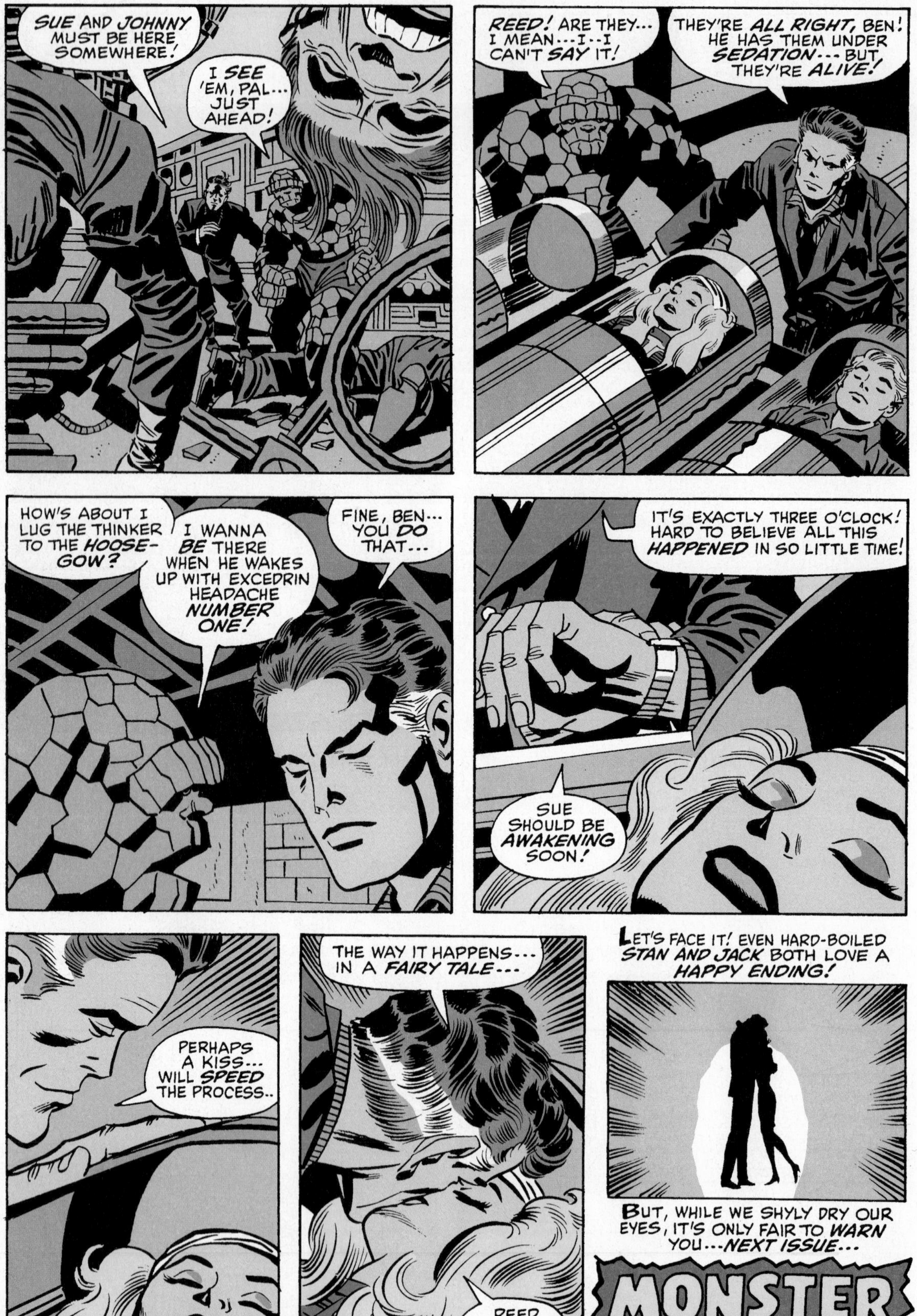
SUE AND JOHNNY MUST BE HERE SOMEWHERE!
I SEE 'EM, PAL... JUST AHEAD!
REED! ARE THEY... I MEAN---I--I CAN'T SAY IT!
THEY'RE ALL RIGHT, BEN! HE HAS THEM UNDER SEDATION--- BUT, THEY'RE ALIVE!
HOW'S ABOUT I LUG THE THINKER TO THE HOOSE-GOW?
I WANNA BE THERE WHEN HE WAKES UP WITH EXCEDRIN HEADACHE NUMBER ONE!
FINE, BEN... YOU DO THAT---
IT'S EXACTLY THREE O'CLOCK! HARD TO BELIEVE ALL THIS HAPPENED IN SO LITTLE TIME!
SUE SHOULD BE AWAKENING SOON!
PERHAPS A KISS... WILL SPEED THE PROCESS..
20
THE WAY IT HAPPENS--- IN A FAIRY TALE---
REED ...MY DARLING...
LET'S FACE IT! EVEN HARD-BOILED STAN AND JACK BOTH LOVE A HAPPY ENDING!
BUT, WHILE WE SHYLY DRY OUR EYES, IT'S ONLY FAIR TO WARN YOU---NEXT ISSUE---
MONSTER FROM THE LOST LAGOON!

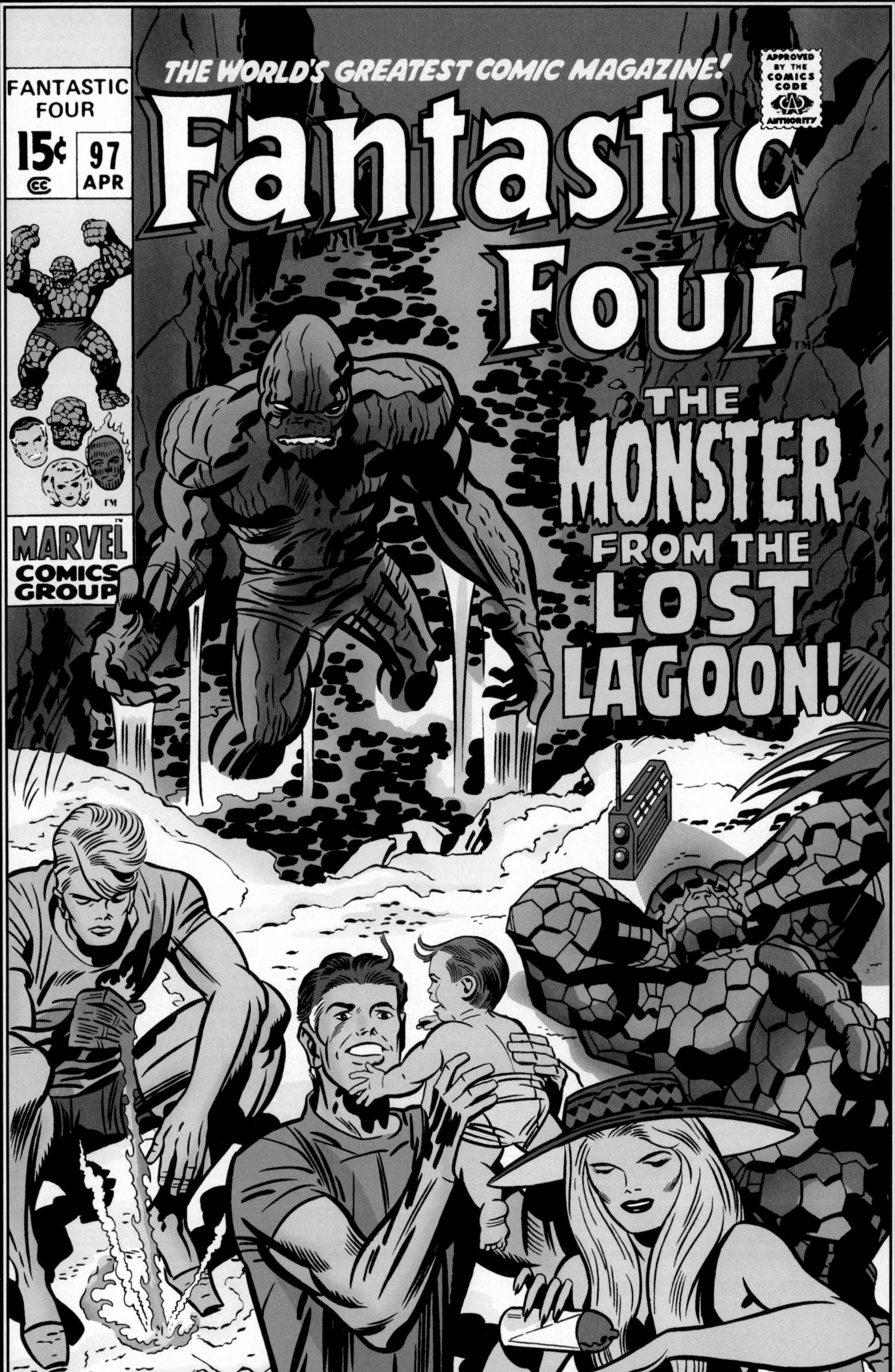

THE WORLD'S GREATEST COMIC MAGAZINE!
FANTASTIC FOUR
15¢ 97 APR
Fantastic Four
APPROVED BY THE COMICS CODE AUTHORITY
MARVEL COMICS GROUP
THE MONSTER FROM THE LOST LAGOON!

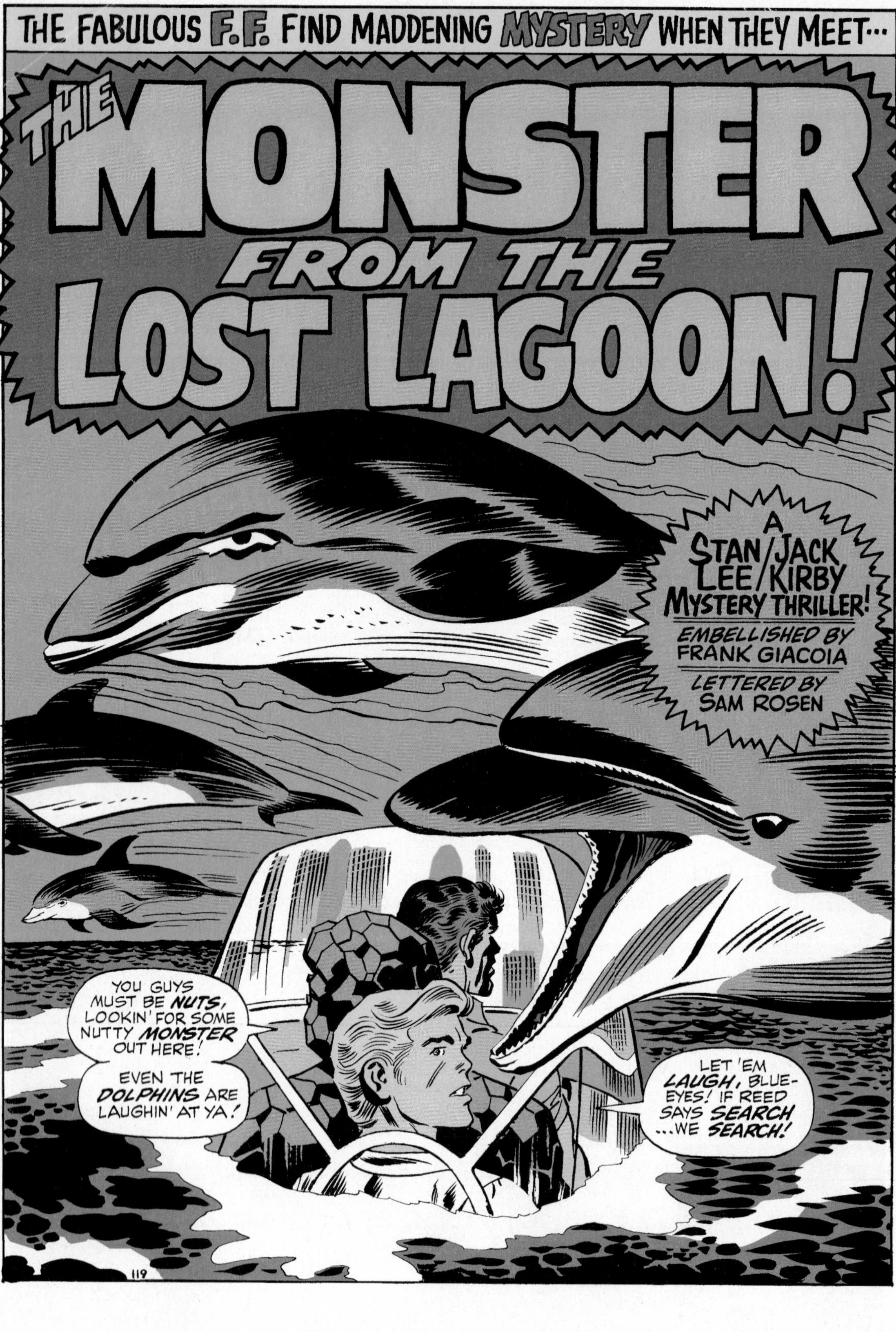
THE FABULOUS F.F. FIND MADDENING MYSTERY WHEN THEY MEET...
THE MONSTER FROM THE LOST LAGOON!
A STAN LEE/JACK KIRBY MYSTERY THRILLER!
EMBELLISHED BY FRANK GIACOIA
LETTERED BY SAM ROSEN
YOU GUYS MUST BE NUTS, LOOKIN' FOR SOME NUTTY MONSTER OUT HERE!
EVEN THE DOLPHINS ARE LAUGHIN' AT YA!
LET 'EM LAUGH, BLUE-EYES! IF REED SAYS SEARCH ...WE SEARCH!
119

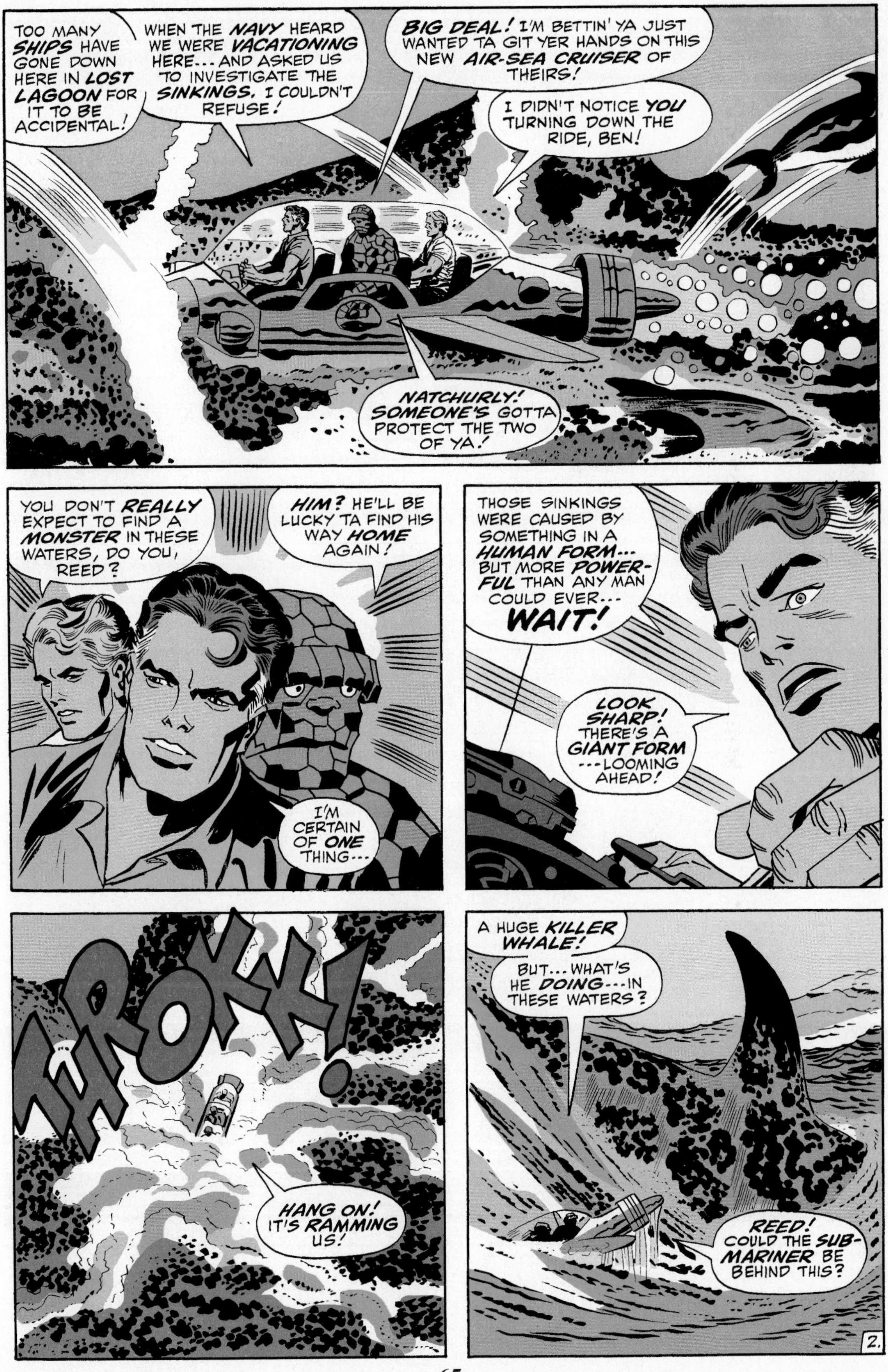
TOO MANY SHIPS HAVE GONE DOWN HERE IN LOST LAGOON FOR IT TO BE ACCIDENTAL!
WHEN THE NAVY HEARD WE WERE VACATIONING HERE... AND ASKED US TO INVESTIGATE THE SINKINGS, I COULDN'T REFUSE!
BIG DEAL! I'M BETTIN' YA JUST WANTED TA GIT YER HANDS ON THIS NEW AIR-SEA CRUISER OF THEIRS!
I DIDN'T NOTICE YOU TURNING DOWN THE RIDE, BEN!
NATCHURLY! SOMEONE'S GOTTA PROTECT THE TWO OF YA!
YOU DON'T REALLY EXPECT TO FIND A MONSTER IN THESE WATERS, DO YOU, REED?
HIM? HE'LL BE LUCKY TA FIND HIS WAY HOME AGAIN!
I'M CERTAIN OF ONE THING---
THOSE SINKINGS WERE CAUSED BY SOMETHING IN A HUMAN FORM... BUT MORE POWERFUL THAN ANY MAN COULD EVER--- WAIT!
LOOK SHARP! THERE'S A GIANT FORM ---LOOMING AHEAD!
THROKK!
HANG ON! IT'S RAMMING US!
A HUGE KILLER WHALE!
BUT... WHAT'S HE DOING---IN THESE WATERS?
REED! COULD THE SUB-MARINER BE BEHIND THIS?
2.

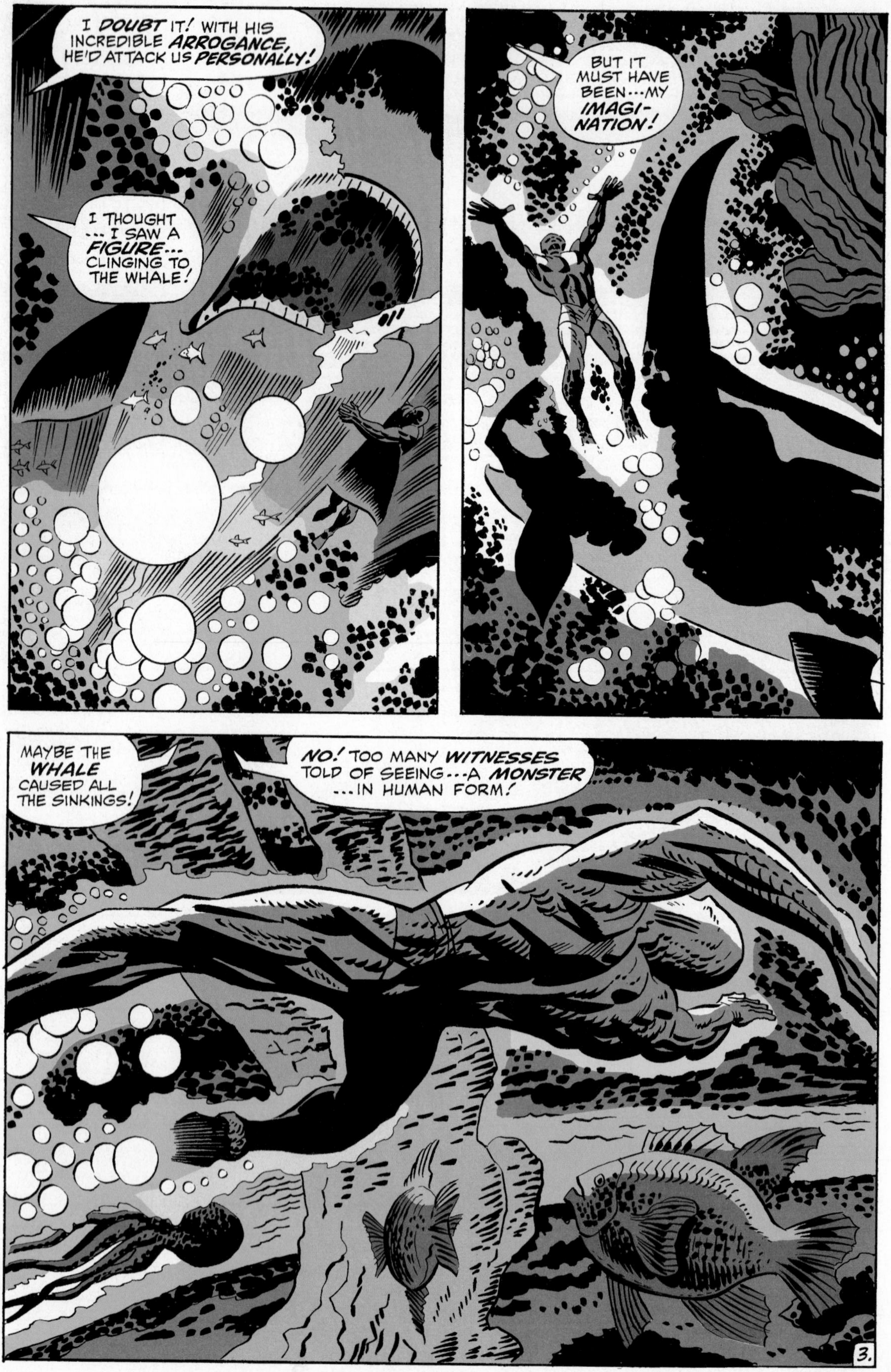
I DOUBT IT! WITH HIS INCREDIBLE ARROGANCE, HE'D ATTACK US PERSONALLY!
I THOUGHT ... I SAW A FIGURE... CLINGING TO THE WHALE!
BUT IT MUST HAVE BEEN---MY IMAGI-NATION!
MAYBE THE WHALE CAUSED ALL THE SINKINGS!
NO! TOO MANY WITNESSES TOLD OF SEEING---A MONSTER ---IN HUMAN FORM!
3.

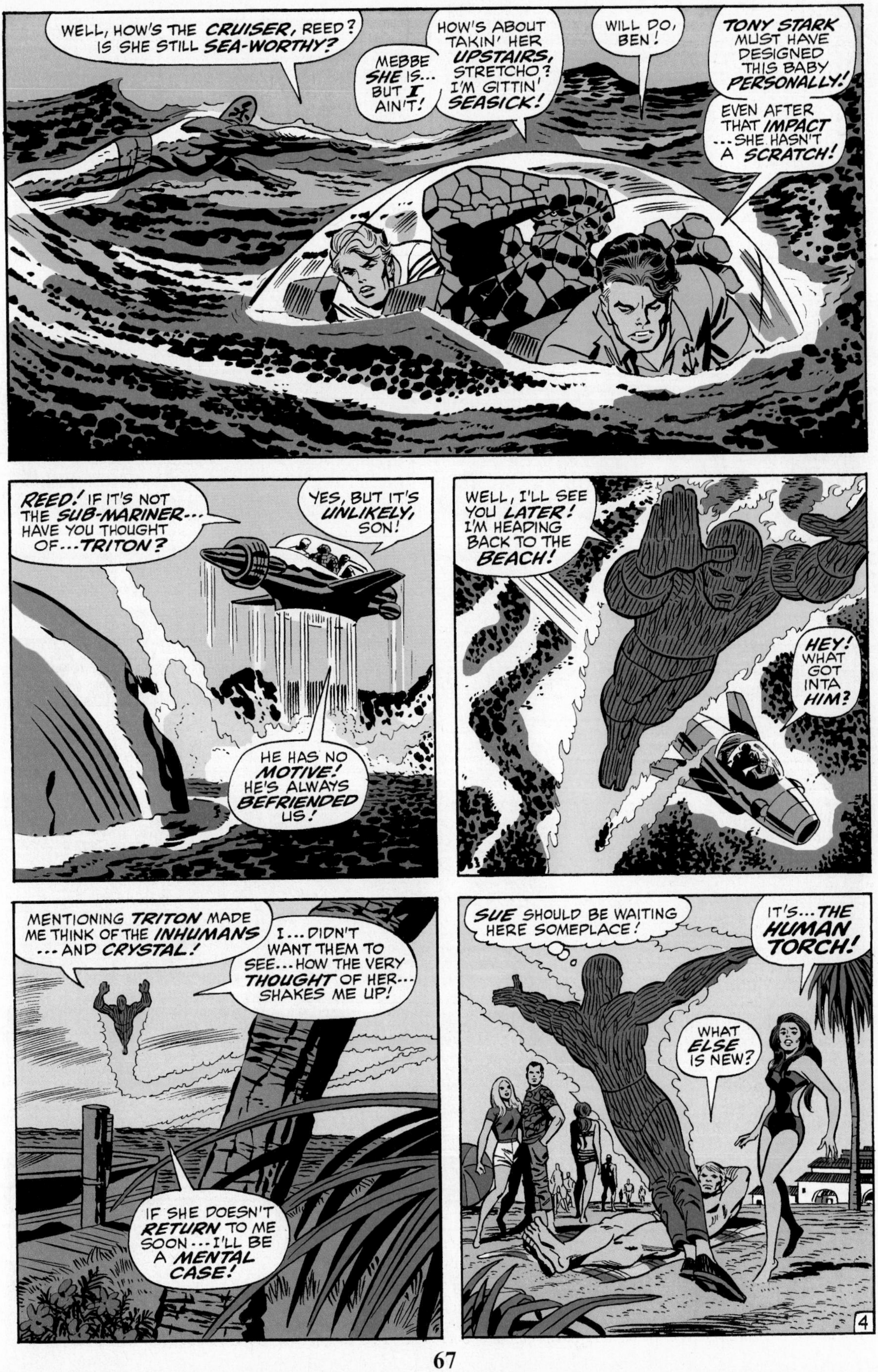
WELL, HOW'S THE CRUISER, REED? IS SHE STILL SEA-WORTHY?
MEBBE SHE IS... BUT I AIN'T!
HOW'S ABOUT TAKIN' HER UPSTAIRS, STRETCHO? I'M GITTIN' SEASICK!
WILL DO, BEN!
TONY STARK MUST HAVE DESIGNED THIS BABY PERSONALLY!
EVEN AFTER THAT IMPACT ...SHE HASN'T A SCRATCH!
REED! IF IT'S NOT THE SUB-MARINER... HAVE YOU THOUGHT OF...TRITON?
YES, BUT IT'S UNLIKELY, SON!
HE HAS NO MOTIVE! HE'S ALWAYS BEFRIENDED US!
WELL, I'LL SEE YOU LATER! I'M HEADING BACK TO THE BEACH!
HEY! WHAT GOT INTA HIM?
MENTIONING TRITON MADE ME THINK OF THE INHUMANS ...AND CRYSTAL!
I...DIDN'T WANT THEM TO SEE...HOW THE VERY THOUGHT OF HER... SHAKES ME UP!
IF SHE DOESN'T RETURN TO ME SOON...I'LL BE A MENTAL CASE!
SUE SHOULD BE WAITING HERE SOMEPLACE!
IT'S...THE HUMAN TORCH!
WHAT ELSE IS NEW?
4

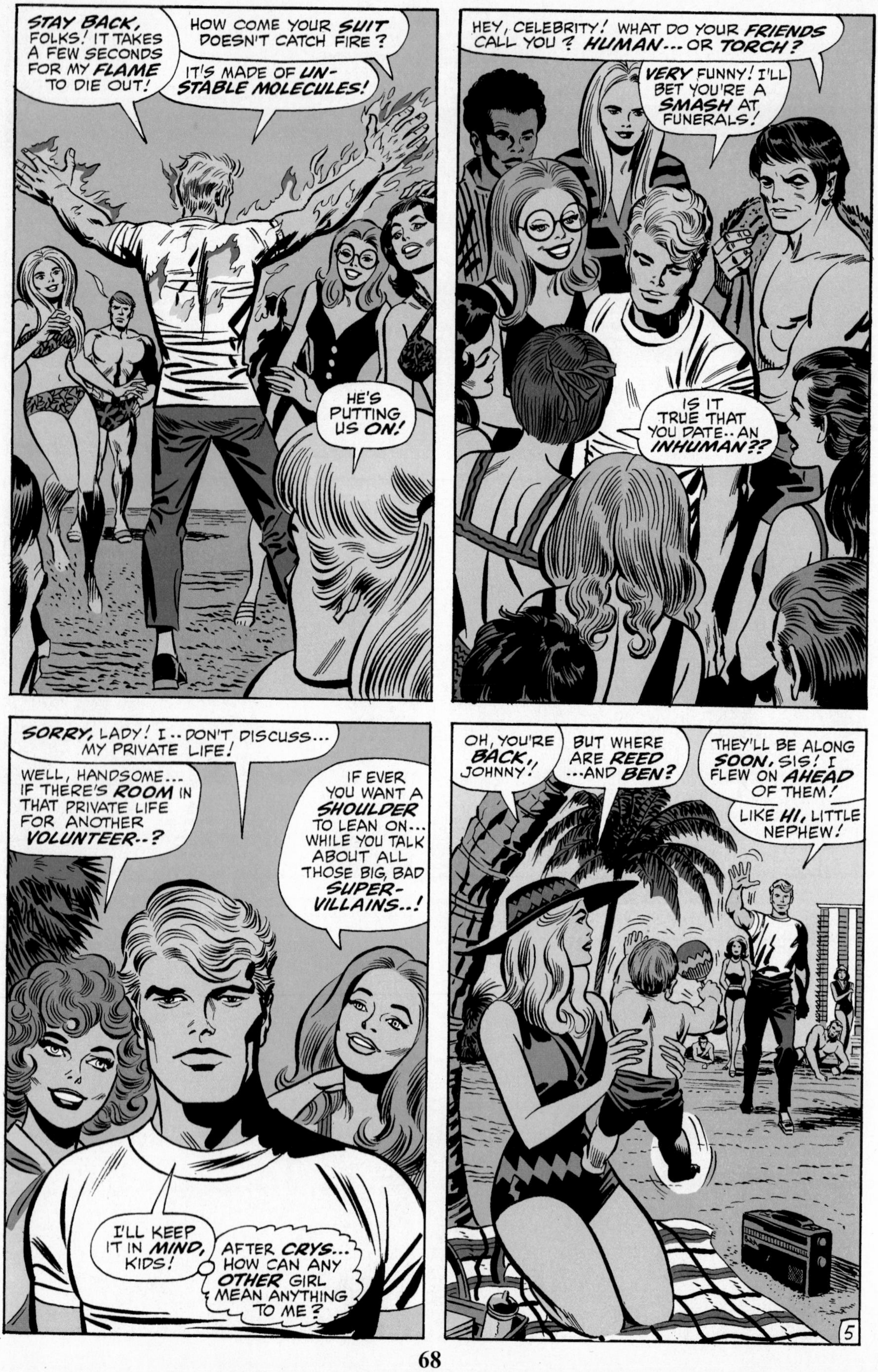
STAY BACK, FOLKS! IT TAKES A FEW SECONDS FOR MY FLAME TO DIE OUT!
HOW COME YOUR SUIT DOESN'T CATCH FIRE?
IT'S MADE OF UNSTABLE MOLECULES!
HE'S PUTTING US ON!
HEY, CELEBRITY! WHAT DO YOUR FRIENDS CALL YOU? HUMAN... OR TORCH?
VERY FUNNY! I'LL BET YOU'RE A SMASH AT FUNERALS!
IS IT TRUE THAT YOU DATE.. AN INHUMAN??
SORRY, LADY! I.. DON'T DISCUSS... MY PRIVATE LIFE!
WELL, HANDSOME... IF THERE'S ROOM IN THAT PRIVATE LIFE FOR ANOTHER VOLUNTEER--?
IF EVER YOU WANT A SHOULDER TO LEAN ON... WHILE YOU TALK ABOUT ALL THOSE BIG, BAD SUPER-VILLAINS..!
I'LL KEEP IT IN MIND, KIDS!
AFTER CRYS... HOW CAN ANY OTHER GIRL MEAN ANYTHING TO ME?
OH, YOU'RE BACK, JOHNNY!
BUT WHERE ARE REED ...AND BEN?
THEY'LL BE ALONG SOON, SIS! I FLEW ON AHEAD OF THEM!
LIKE HI, LITTLE NEPHEW!
5

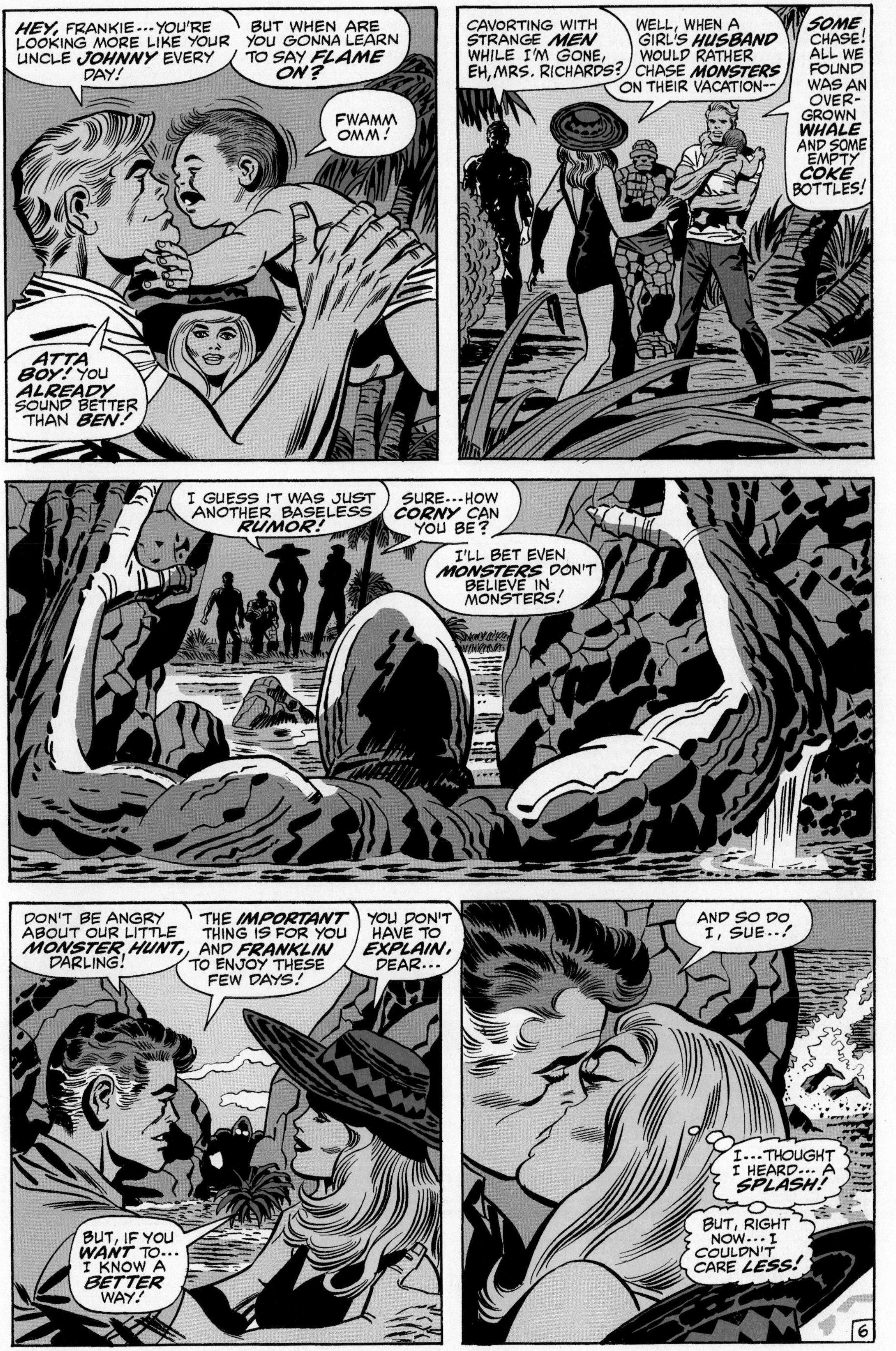
HEY, FRANKIE---YOU'RE LOOKING MORE LIKE YOUR UNCLE JOHNNY EVERY DAY!
BUT WHEN ARE YOU GONNA LEARN TO SAY FLAME ON?
FWAMM OMM!
ATTA BOY! YOU ALREADY SOUND BETTER THAN BEN!
CAVORTING WITH STRANGE MEN WHILE I'M GONE, EH, MRS. RICHARDS?
WELL, WHEN A GIRL'S HUSBAND WOULD RATHER CHASE MONSTERS ON THEIR VACATION--
SOME CHASE! ALL WE FOUND WAS AN OVER-GROWN WHALE AND SOME EMPTY COKE BOTTLES!
I GUESS IT WAS JUST ANOTHER BASELESS RUMOR!
SURE---HOW CORNY CAN YOU BE?
I'LL BET EVEN MONSTERS DON'T BELIEVE IN MONSTERS!
DON'T BE ANGRY ABOUT OUR LITTLE MONSTER HUNT, DARLING!
THE IMPORTANT THING IS FOR YOU AND FRANKLIN TO ENJOY THESE FEW DAYS!
YOU DON'T HAVE TO EXPLAIN, DEAR...
BUT, IF YOU WANT TO... I KNOW A BETTER WAY!
AND SO DO I, SUE..!
I---THOUGHT I HEARD--- A SPLASH!
BUT, RIGHT NOW--- I COULDN'T CARE LESS!
6

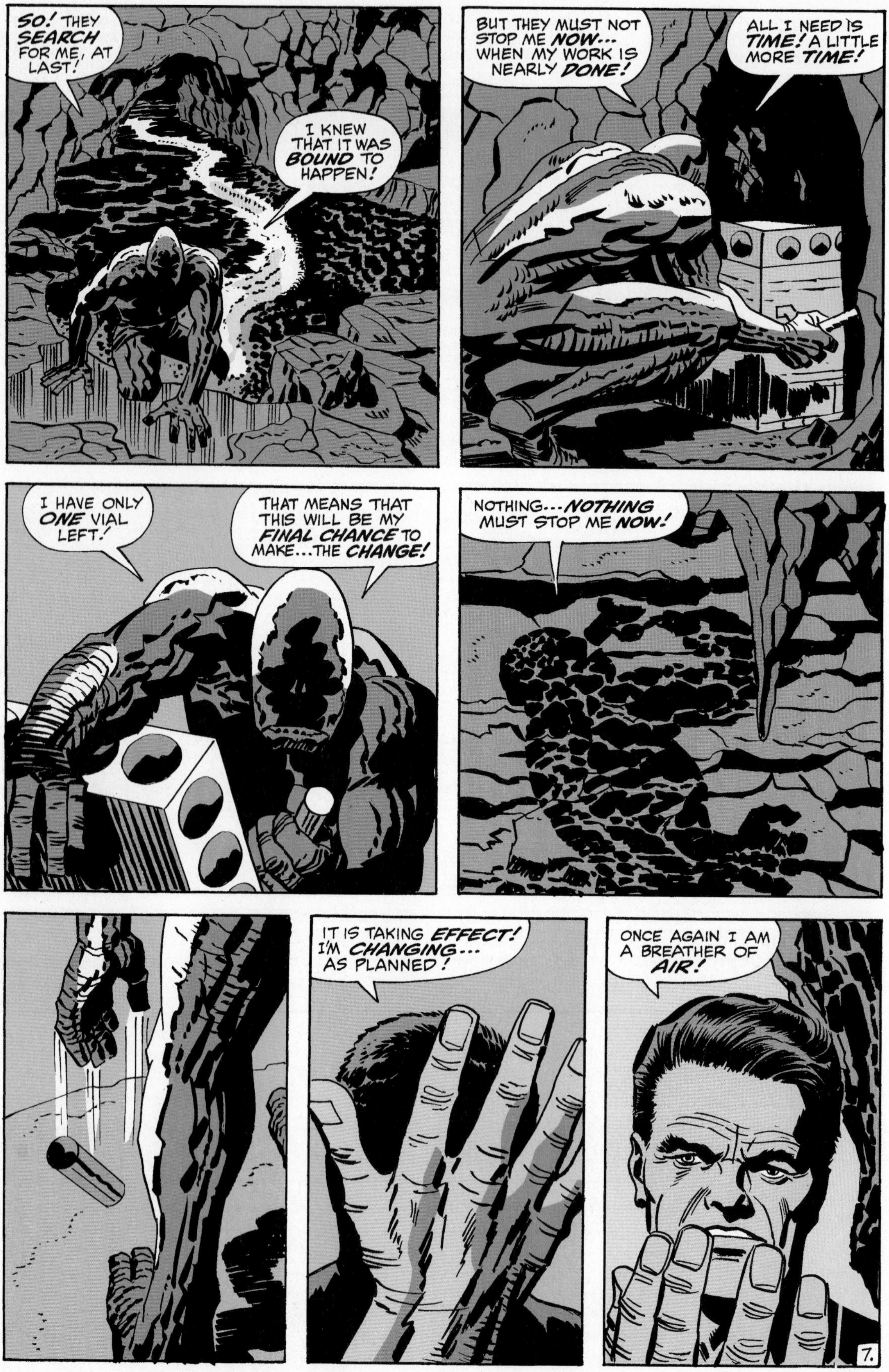

SO! THEY SEARCH FOR ME, AT LAST!
I KNEW THAT IT WAS BOUND TO HAPPEN!
BUT THEY MUST NOT STOP ME NOW... WHEN MY WORK IS NEARLY DONE!
ALL I NEED IS TIME! A LITTLE MORE TIME!
I HAVE ONLY ONE VIAL LEFT!
THAT MEANS THAT THIS WILL BE MY FINAL CHANCE TO MAKE...THE CHANGE!
NOTHING...NOTHING MUST STOP ME NOW!
IT IS TAKING EFFECT! I'M CHANGING... AS PLANNED!
ONCE AGAIN I AM A BREATHER OF AIR!
7.

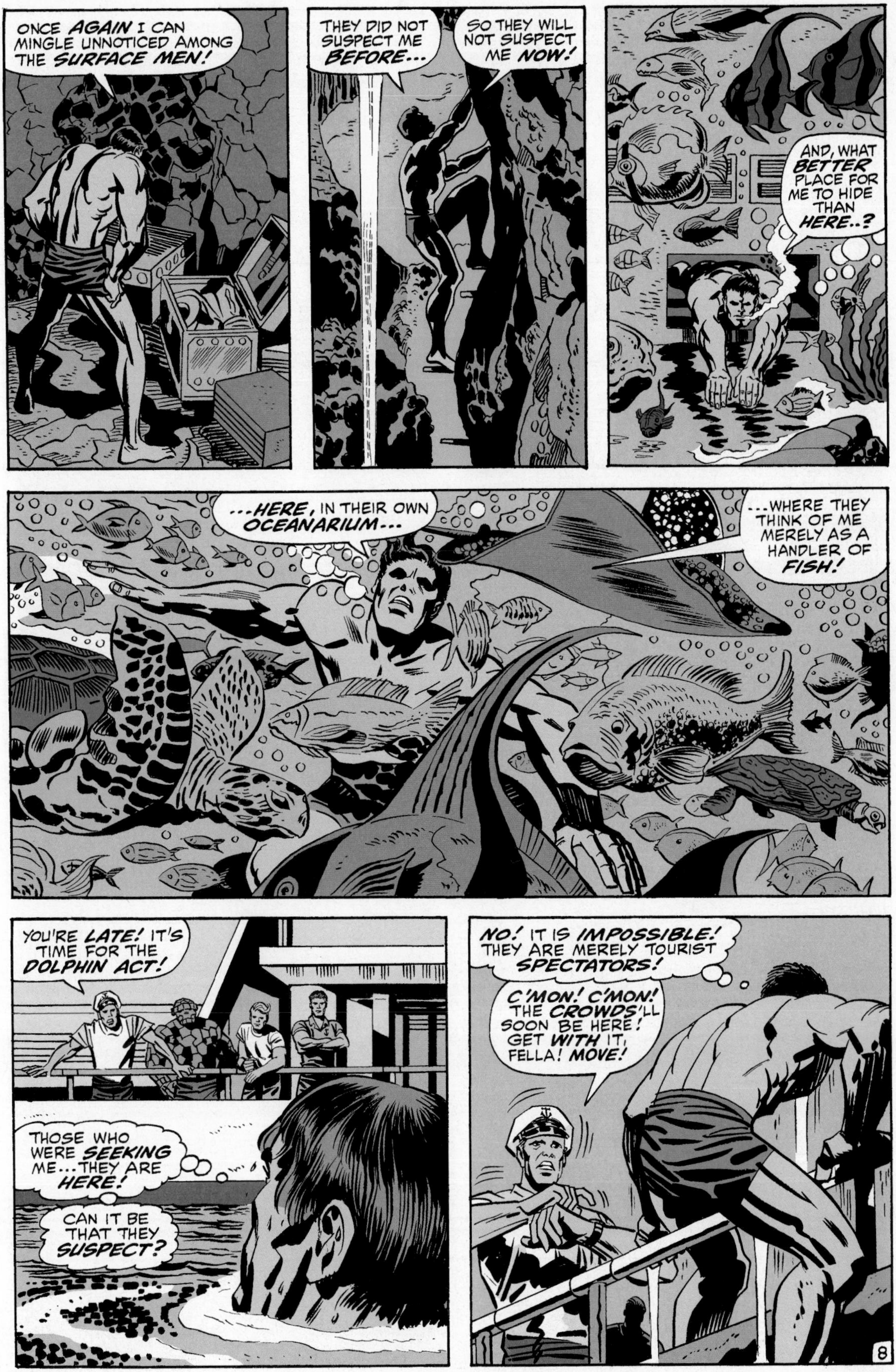

ONCE AGAIN I CAN MINGLE UNNOTICED AMONG THE SURFACE MEN!
THEY DID NOT SUSPECT ME BEFORE...
SO THEY WILL NOT SUSPECT ME NOW!
AND, WHAT BETTER PLACE FOR ME TO HIDE THAN HERE..?
...HERE, IN THEIR OWN OCEANARIUM...
...WHERE THEY THINK OF ME MERELY AS A HANDLER OF FISH!
YOU'RE LATE! IT'S TIME FOR THE DOLPHIN ACT!
THOSE WHO WERE SEEKING ME...THEY ARE HERE!
CAN IT BE THAT THEY SUSPECT?
NO! IT IS IMPOSSIBLE! THEY ARE MERELY TOURIST SPECTATORS!
C'MON! C'MON! THE CROWDS'LL SOON BE HERE! GET WITH IT, FELLA! MOVE!
8

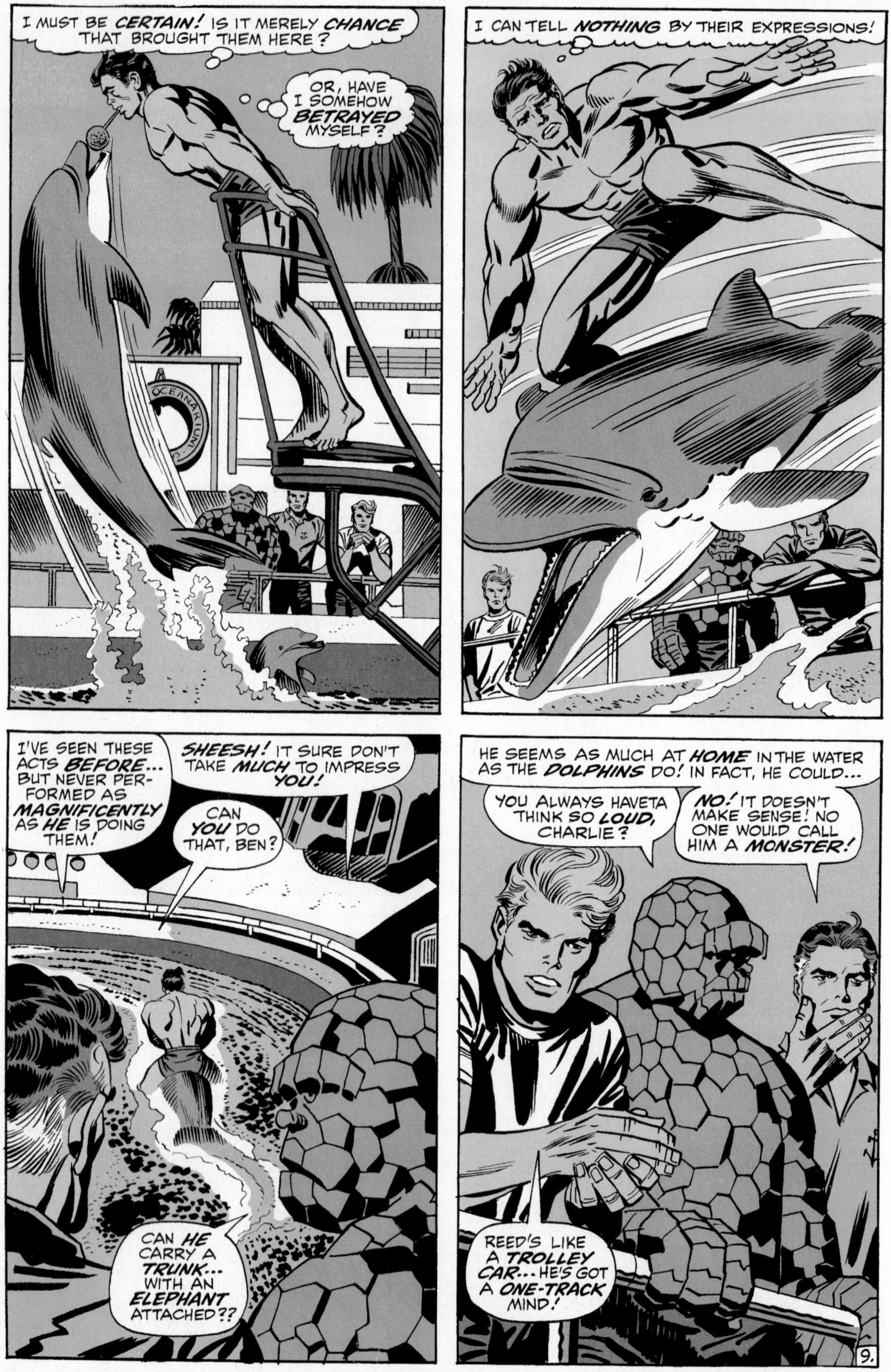

I MUST BE CERTAIN! IS IT MERELY CHANCE THAT BROUGHT THEM HERE?
OR, HAVE I SOMEHOW BETRAYED MYSELF?
OCEANARIUM
I CAN TELL NOTHING BY THEIR EXPRESSIONS!
I'VE SEEN THESE ACTS BEFORE... BUT NEVER PERFORMED AS MAGNIFICENTLY AS HE IS DOING THEM!
SHEESH! IT SURE DON'T TAKE MUCH TO IMPRESS YOU!
CAN YOU DO THAT, BEN?
CAN HE CARRY A TRUNK... WITH AN ELEPHANT ATTACHED??
HE SEEMS AS MUCH AT HOME IN THE WATER AS THE DOLPHINS DO! IN FACT, HE COULD...
YOU ALWAYS HAVETA THINK SO LOUD, CHARLIE?
NO! IT DOESN'T MAKE SENSE! NO ONE WOULD CALL HIM A MONSTER!
REED'S LIKE A TROLLEY CAR... HE'S GOT A ONE-TRACK MIND!
9.

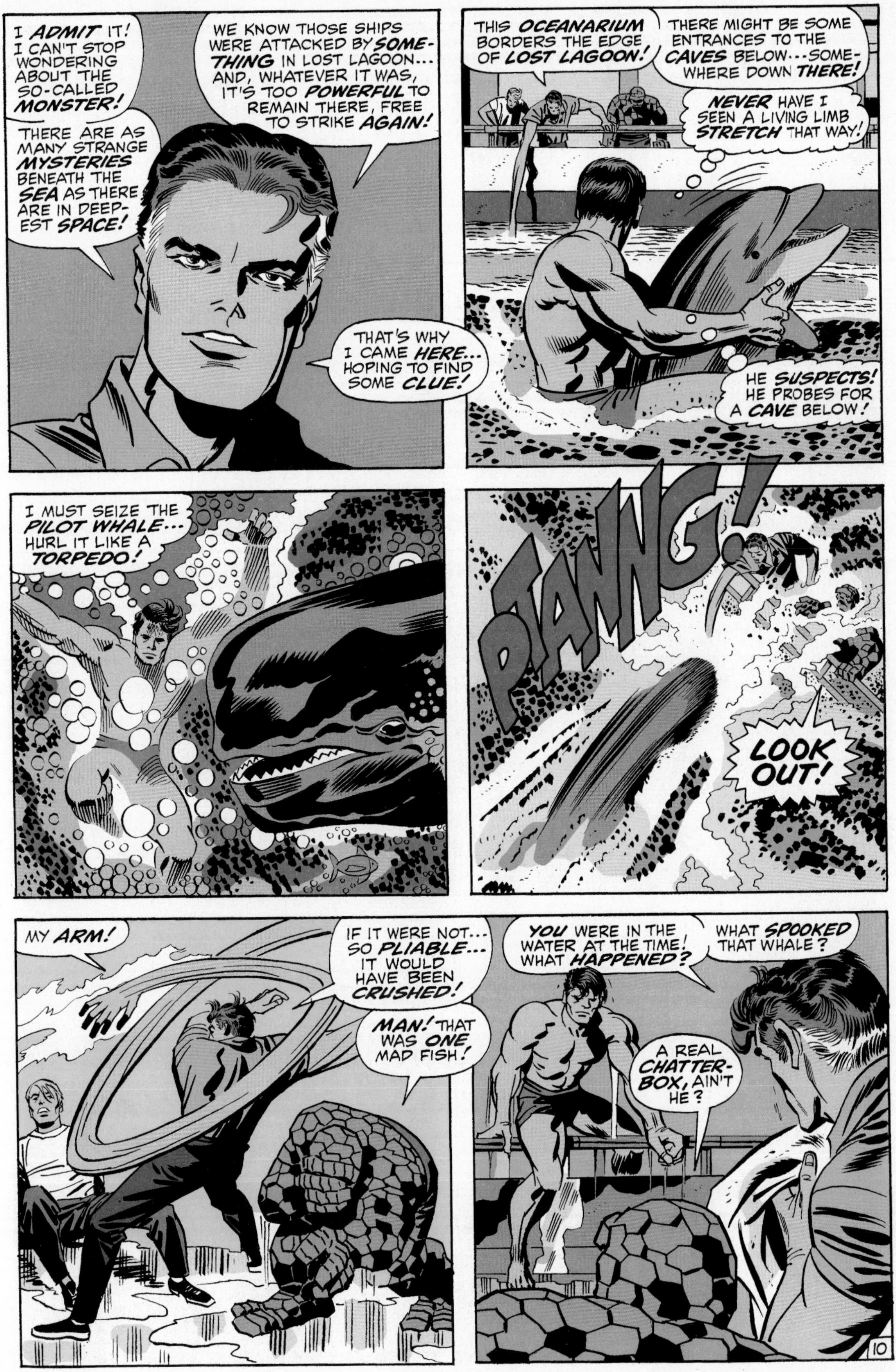

I ADMIT IT! I CAN'T STOP WONDERING ABOUT THE SO-CALLED MONSTER!
THERE ARE AS MANY STRANGE MYSTERIES BENEATH THE SEA AS THERE ARE IN DEEPEST SPACE!
WE KNOW THOSE SHIPS WERE ATTACKED BY SOMETHING IN LOST LAGOON... AND, WHATEVER IT WAS, IT'S TOO POWERFUL TO REMAIN THERE, FREE TO STRIKE AGAIN!
THAT'S WHY I CAME HERE... HOPING TO FIND SOME CLUE!
THIS OCEANARIUM BORDERS THE EDGE OF LOST LAGOON!
THERE MIGHT BE SOME ENTRANCES TO THE CAVES BELOW...SOMEWHERE DOWN THERE!
NEVER HAVE I SEEN A LIVING LIMB STRETCH THAT WAY!
HE SUSPECTS! HE PROBES FOR A CAVE BELOW!
I MUST SEIZE THE PILOT WHALE... HURL IT LIKE A TORPEDO!
PTANNG!
LOOK OUT!
MY ARM!
IF IT WERE NOT... SO PLIABLE... IT WOULD HAVE BEEN CRUSHED!
MAN! THAT WAS ONE MAD FISH!
YOU WERE IN THE WATER AT THE TIME! WHAT HAPPENED?
WHAT SPOOKED THAT WHALE?
A REAL CHATTER-BOX, AIN'T HE?
10

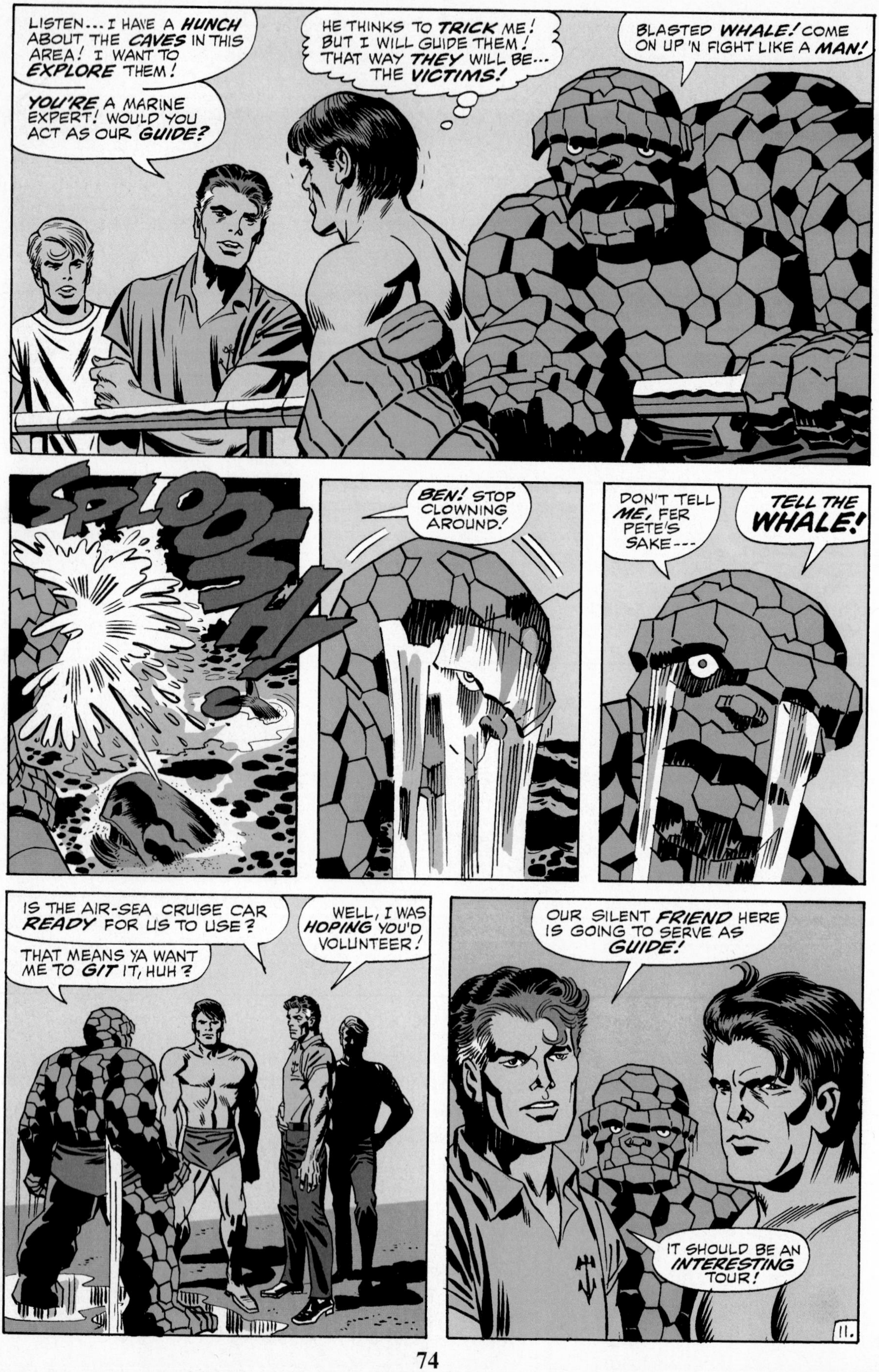
LISTEN... I HAVE A HUNCH ABOUT THE CAVES IN THIS AREA! I WANT TO EXPLORE THEM!
YOU'RE A MARINE EXPERT! WOULD YOU ACT AS OUR GUIDE?
HE THINKS TO TRICK ME! BUT I WILL GUIDE THEM! THAT WAY THEY WILL BE... THE VICTIMS!
BLASTED WHALE! COME ON UP 'N FIGHT LIKE A MAN!
SPLOOSH
BEN! STOP CLOWNING AROUND!
DON'T TELL ME, FER PETE'S SAKE---
TELL THE WHALE!
IS THE AIR-SEA CRUISE CAR READY FOR US TO USE?
THAT MEANS YA WANT ME TO GIT IT, HUH?
WELL, I WAS HOPING YOU'D VOLUNTEER!
OUR SILENT FRIEND HERE IS GOING TO SERVE AS GUIDE!
IT SHOULD BE AN INTERESTING TOUR!
11.

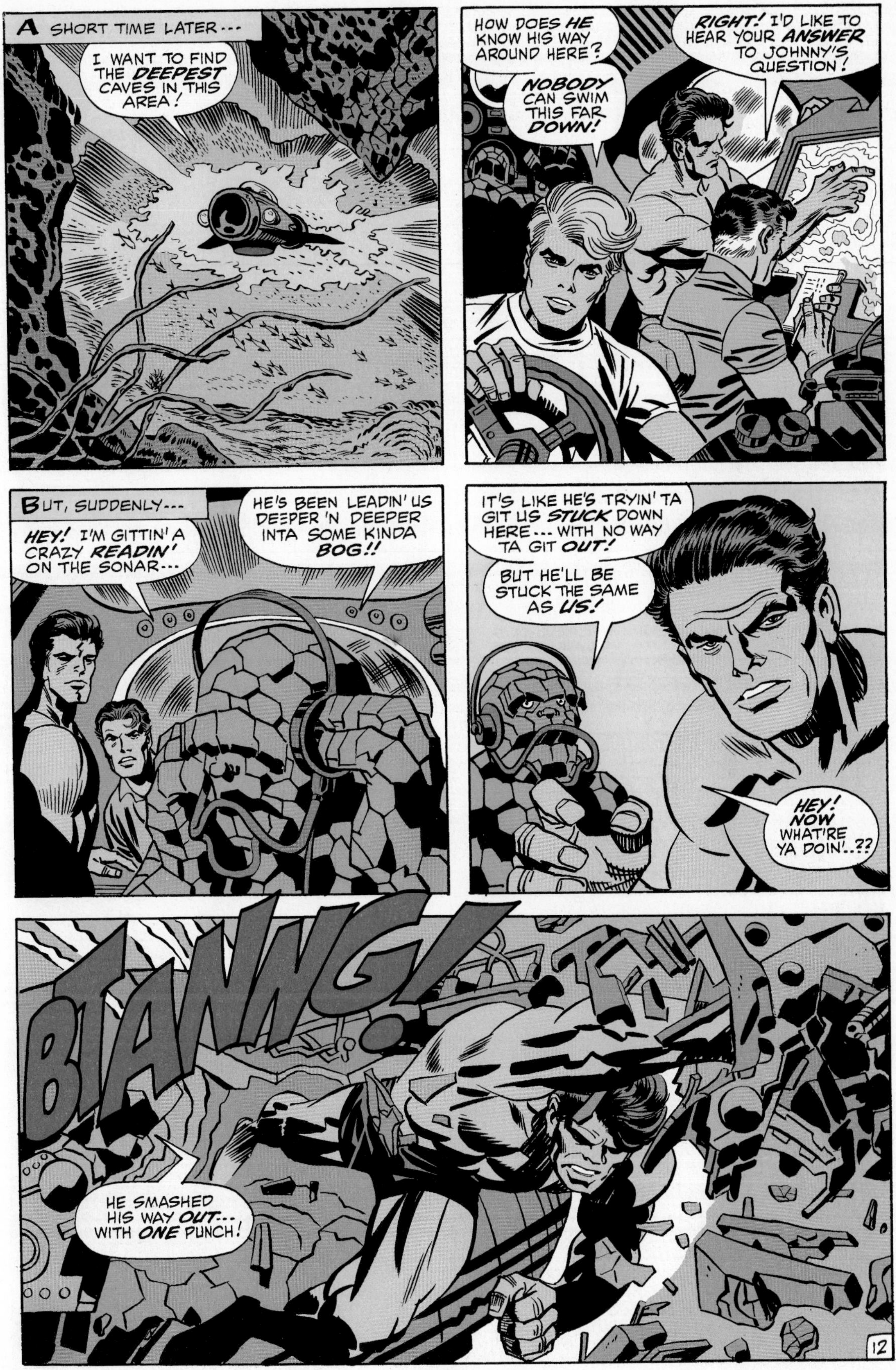
A SHORT TIME LATER---
I WANT TO FIND THE DEEPEST CAVES IN THIS AREA!
HOW DOES HE KNOW HIS WAY AROUND HERE?
NOBODY CAN SWIM THIS FAR DOWN!
RIGHT! I'D LIKE TO HEAR YOUR ANSWER TO JOHNNY'S QUESTION!
BUT, SUDDENLY---
HEY! I'M GITTIN' A CRAZY READIN' ON THE SONAR---
HE'S BEEN LEADIN' US DEEPER 'N DEEPER INTA SOME KINDA BOG!!
IT'S LIKE HE'S TRYIN' TA GIT US STUCK DOWN HERE--- WITH NO WAY TA GIT OUT!
BUT HE'LL BE STUCK THE SAME AS US!
HEY! NOW WHAT'RE YA DOIN'..??
BTANNG!
HE SMASHED HIS WAY OUT--- WITH ONE PUNCH!
12

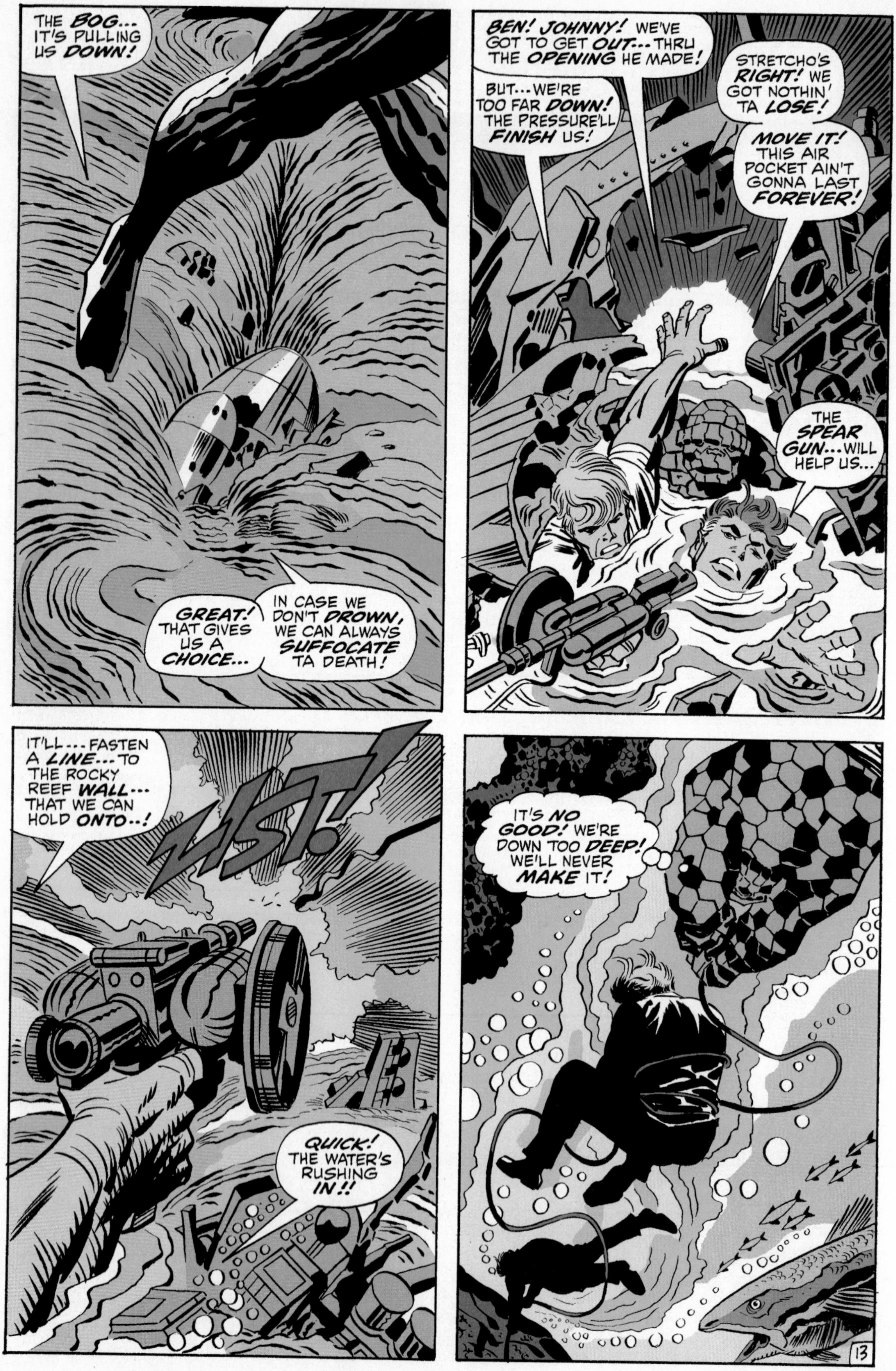
THE BOG... IT'S PULLING US DOWN!
GREAT! THAT GIVES US A CHOICE...
IN CASE WE DON'T DROWN, WE CAN ALWAYS SUFFOCATE TA DEATH!
BEN! JOHNNY! WE'VE GOT TO GET OUT--THRU THE OPENING HE MADE!
BUT...WE'RE TOO FAR DOWN! THE PRESSURE'LL FINISH US!
STRETCHO'S RIGHT! WE GOT NOTHIN' TA LOSE!
MOVE IT! THIS AIR POCKET AIN'T GONNA LAST FOREVER!
THE SPEAR GUN...WILL HELP US...
IT'LL...FASTEN A LINE...TO THE ROCKY REEF WALL...THAT WE CAN HOLD ONTO..!
VVST!
QUICK! THE WATER'S RUSHING IN!!
IT'S NO GOOD! WE'RE DOWN TOO DEEP! WE'LL NEVER MAKE IT!
13

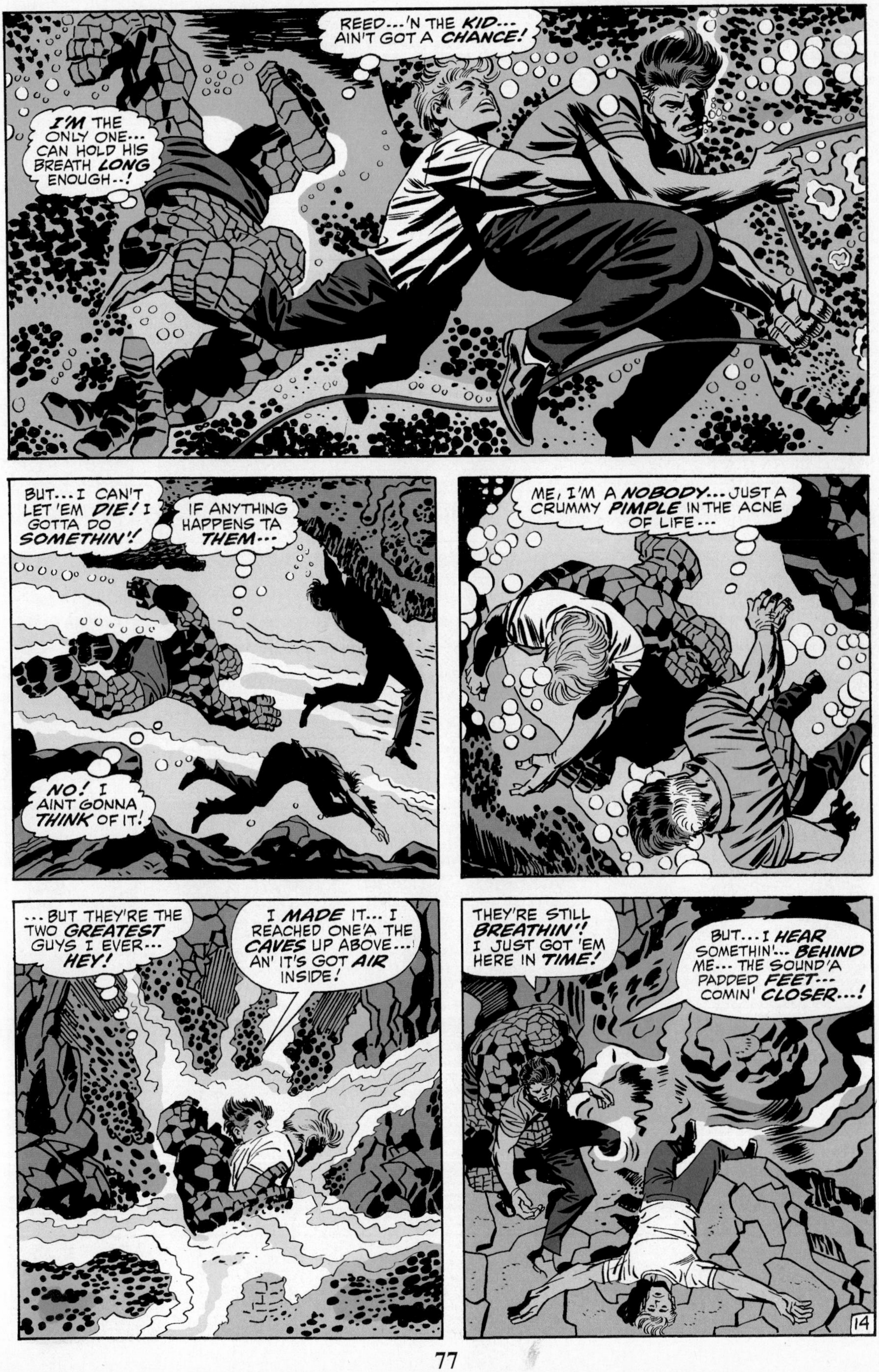
REED...'N THE KID... AIN'T GOT A CHANCE!
I'M THE ONLY ONE... CAN HOLD HIS BREATH LONG ENOUGH..!
BUT... I CAN'T LET 'EM DIE! I GOTTA DO SOMETHIN'!
IF ANYTHING HAPPENS TA THEM...
NO! I AINT GONNA THINK OF IT!
ME, I'M A NOBODY... JUST A CRUMMY PIMPLE IN THE ACNE OF LIFE...
...BUT THEY'RE THE TWO GREATEST GUYS I EVER... HEY!
I MADE IT... I REACHED ONE'A THE CAVES UP ABOVE...! AN' IT'S GOT AIR INSIDE!
THEY'RE STILL BREATHIN'! I JUST GOT 'EM HERE IN TIME!
BUT... I HEAR SOMETHIN'... BEHIND ME... THE SOUND'A PADDED FEET... COMIN' CLOSER...!
14

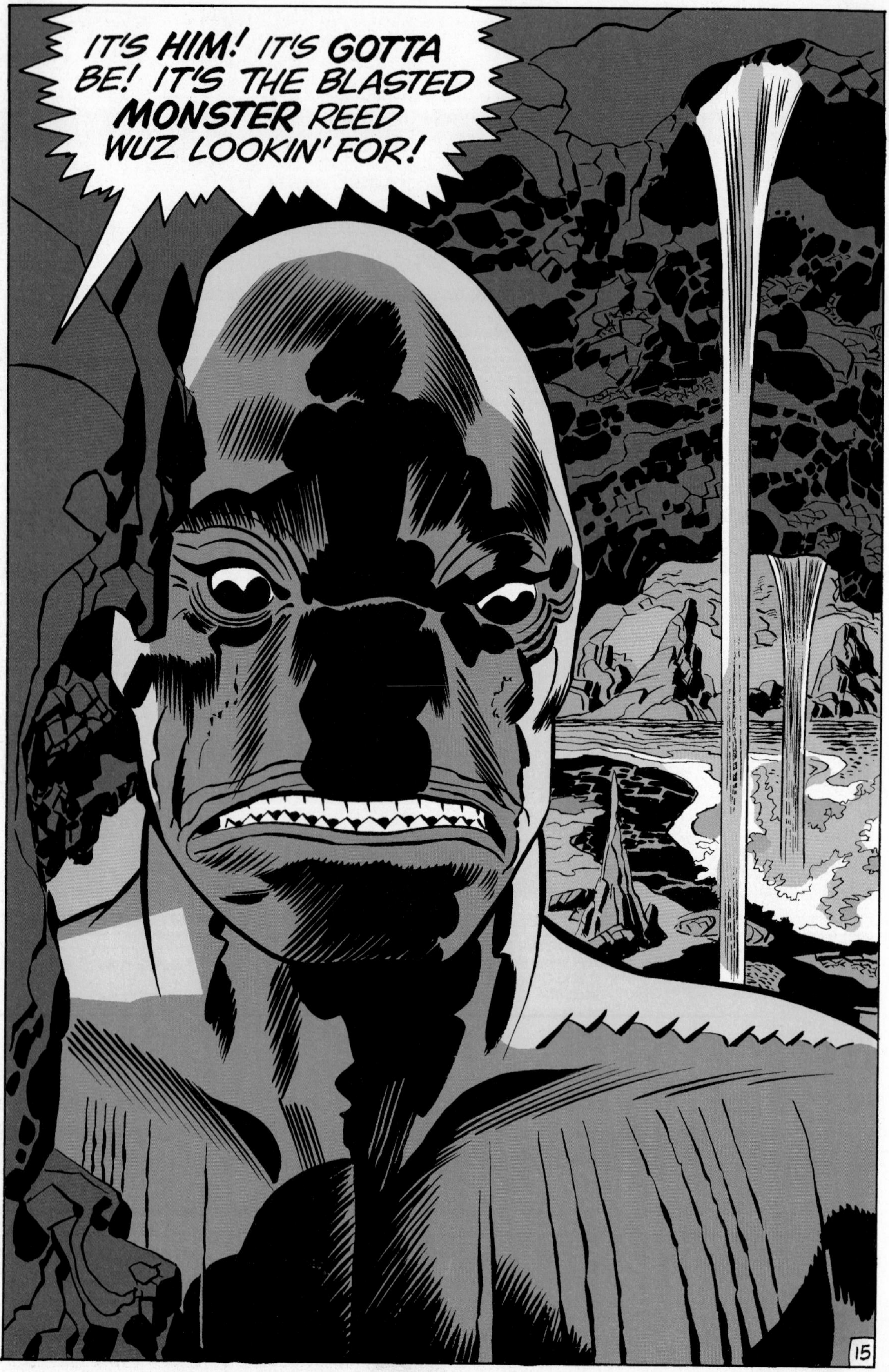
IT'S HIM! IT'S GOTTA BE! IT'S THE BLASTED MONSTER REED WUZ LOOKIN' FOR!
15

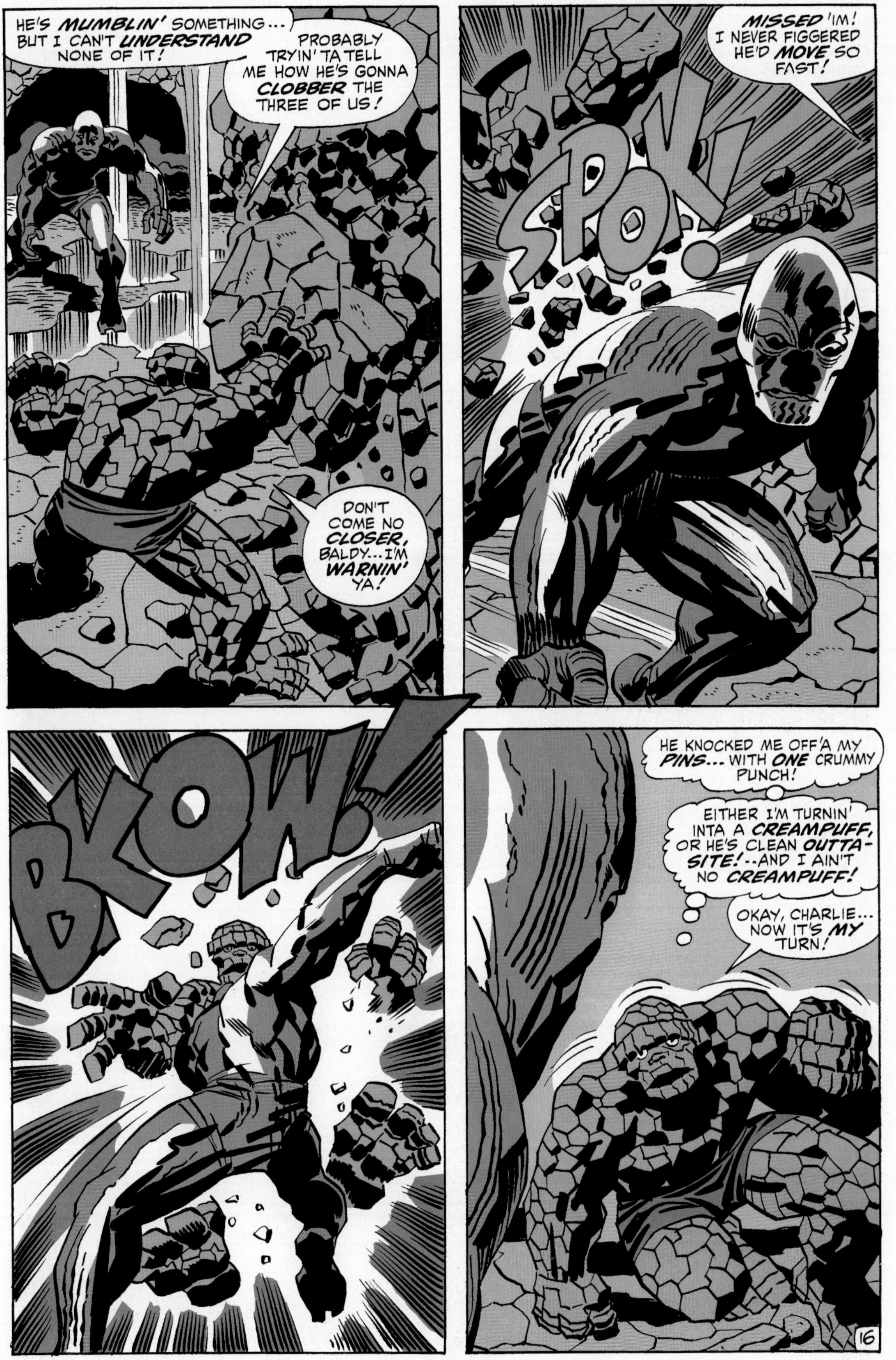

HE'S MUMBLIN' SOMETHING... BUT I CAN'T UNDERSTAND NONE OF IT!
PROBABLY TRYIN' TA TELL ME HOW HE'S GONNA CLOBBER THE THREE OF US!
DON'T COME NO CLOSER, BALDY...I'M WARNIN' YA!
MISSED 'IM! I NEVER FIGGERED HE'D MOVE SO FAST!
SPOK!
BKOW!
HE KNOCKED ME OFF'A MY PINS... WITH ONE CRUMMY PUNCH!
EITHER I'M TURNIN' INTA A CREAMPUFF, OR HE'S CLEAN OUTTA-SITE!..AND I AIN'T NO CREAMPUFF!
OKAY, CHARLIE... NOW IT'S MY TURN!
16

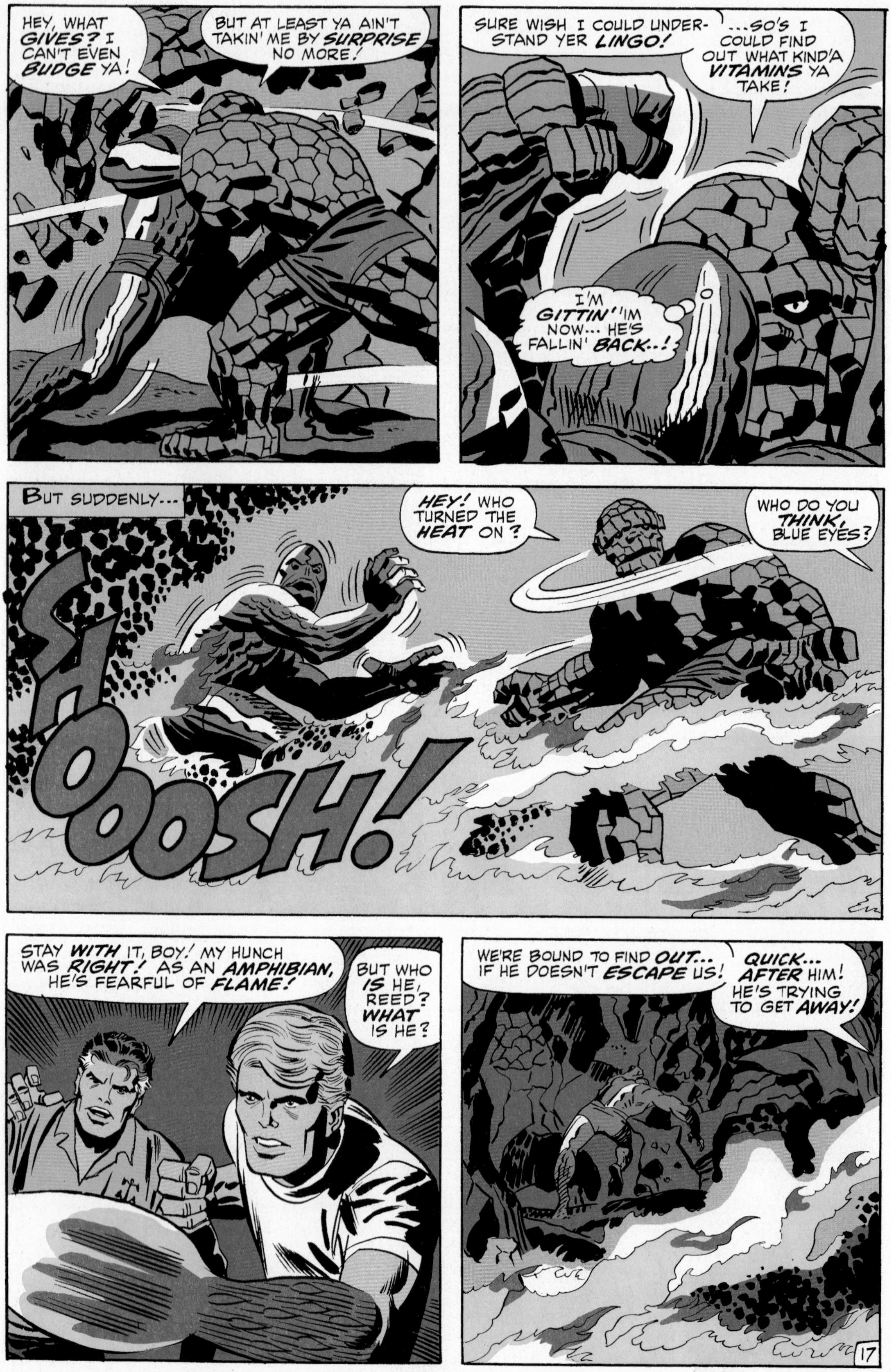
HEY, WHAT GIVES? I CAN'T EVEN BUDGE YA!
BUT AT LEAST YA AIN'T TAKIN' ME BY SURPRISE NO MORE!
SURE WISH I COULD UNDER-STAND YER LINGO!
...SO'S I COULD FIND OUT WHAT KIND'A VITAMINS YA TAKE!
I'M GITTIN' 'IM NOW... HE'S FALLIN' BACK..!
BUT SUDDENLY...
HEY! WHO TURNED THE HEAT ON?
WHO DO YOU THINK, BLUE EYES?
SHOOOOSH!
STAY WITH IT, BOY! MY HUNCH WAS RIGHT! AS AN AMPHIBIAN, HE'S FEARFUL OF FLAME!
BUT WHO IS HE, REED? WHAT IS HE?
WE'RE BOUND TO FIND OUT... IF HE DOESN'T ESCAPE US!
QUICK... AFTER HIM! HE'S TRYING TO GET AWAY!
17

CAREFUL...HE MIGHT BE IN LEAGUE WITH OUR *GUIDE*...IT COULD BE A *TRAP!*

REED...WHAT IF HE'S FROM SOME STRANGE, UNDERSEA *RACE?*

YA MEAN THE OLD "THEY'RE GONNA TAKE OVER THE WORLD" *TRICK?* HOW CORNY CAN YA *BE?*

HEY...WE *LOST* HIM! HE COULD HAVE TAKEN ANY OF A *DOZEN* DIFFERENT PASSAGES!

KEEP YER *DIAPERS* ON, KID! OL' *BASHFUL BENJY*'LL DIG 'IM OUT!

KTHOOOM!

ONE PUNCH'LL CRACK THESE WALLS LIKE A *EGGSHELL!*

IT *WORKED*, BEN! THE CAVE IS *LEVELLING OFF* AHEAD OF US!

HOW COME YA ALWAYS GOTTA *TELL* US WHAT WE CAN SEE FER *OURSELVES?*

YOU IN LOVE WITH YER *VOICE*, OR SOMETHIN'?

LOOK! THERE HE *IS*...!

BUT...I NEVER EXPECTED TA SEE...NOTHIN' LIKE *THAT!*

REED! WHAT DOES IT *MEAN?*

18

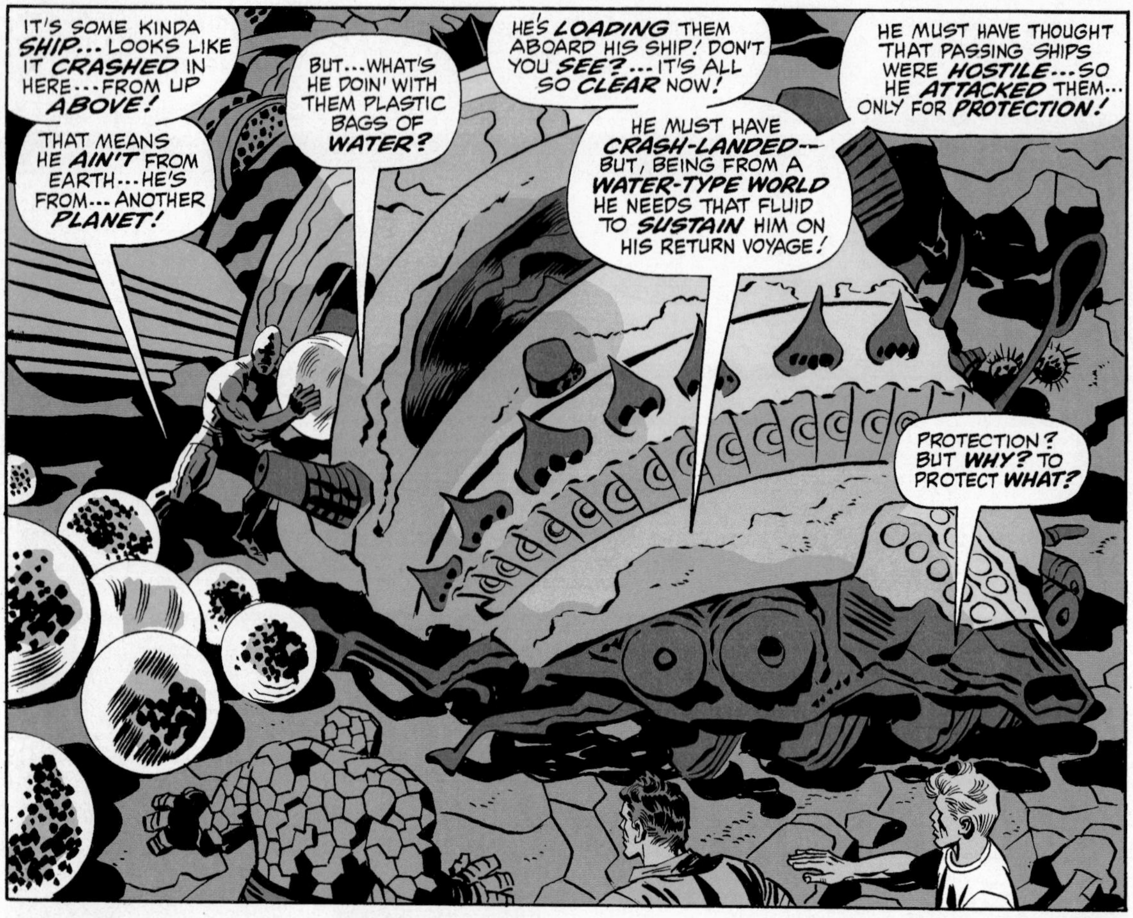
IT'S SOME KINDA SHIP... LOOKS LIKE IT CRASHED IN HERE... FROM UP ABOVE!
THAT MEANS HE AIN'T FROM EARTH... HE'S FROM... ANOTHER PLANET!
BUT... WHAT'S HE DOIN' WITH THEM PLASTIC BAGS OF WATER?
HE'S LOADING THEM ABOARD HIS SHIP! DON'T YOU SEE?... IT'S ALL SO CLEAR NOW!
HE MUST HAVE CRASH-LANDED-- BUT, BEING FROM A WATER-TYPE WORLD HE NEEDS THAT FLUID TO SUSTAIN HIM ON HIS RETURN VOYAGE!
HE MUST HAVE THOUGHT THAT PASSING SHIPS WERE HOSTILE... SO HE ATTACKED THEM... ONLY FOR PROTECTION!
PROTECTION? BUT WHY? TO PROTECT WHAT?

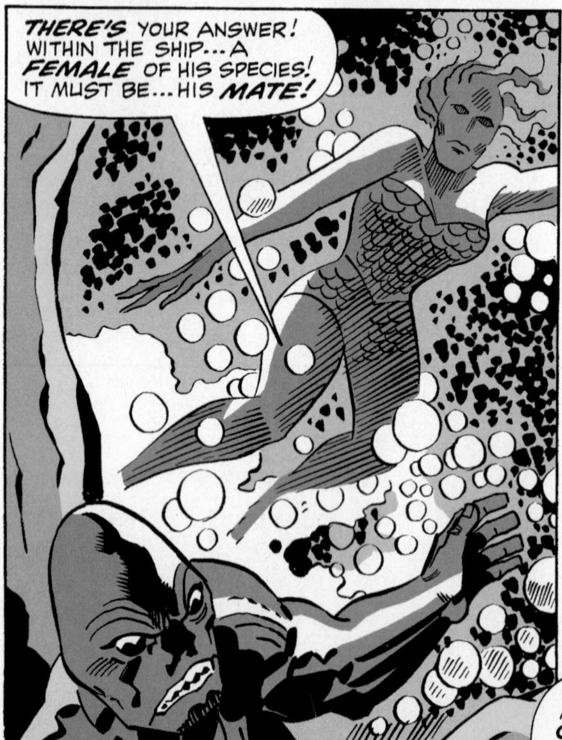
THERE'S YOUR ANSWER! WITHIN THE SHIP... A FEMALE OF HIS SPECIES! IT MUST BE... HIS MATE!

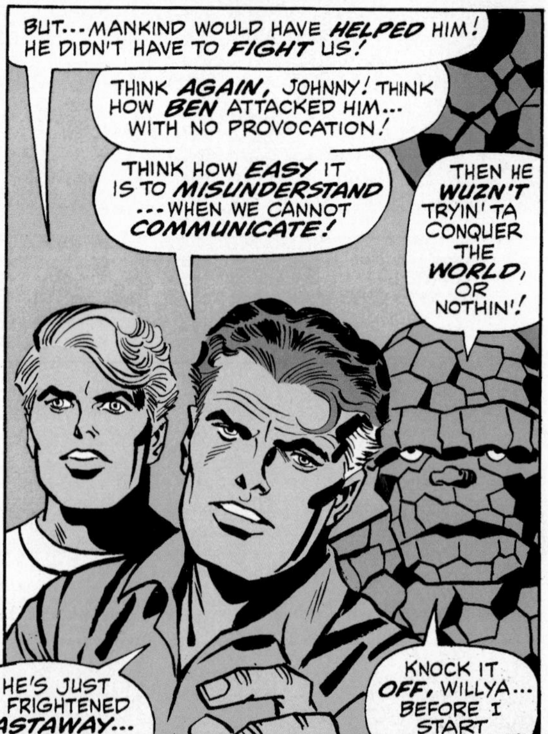
BUT... MANKIND WOULD HAVE HELPED HIM! HE DIDN'T HAVE TO FIGHT US!
THINK AGAIN, JOHNNY! THINK HOW BEN ATTACKED HIM... WITH NO PROVOCATION!
THINK HOW EASY IT IS TO MISUNDERSTAND ... WHEN WE CANNOT COMMUNICATE!
THEN HE WUZN'T TRYIN' TA CONQUER THE WORLD, OR NOTHIN'!
HE'S JUST A FRIGHTENED CASTAWAY... ON A SAVAGE WORLD!
KNOCK IT OFF, WILLYA... BEFORE I START BAWLIN'!
19.

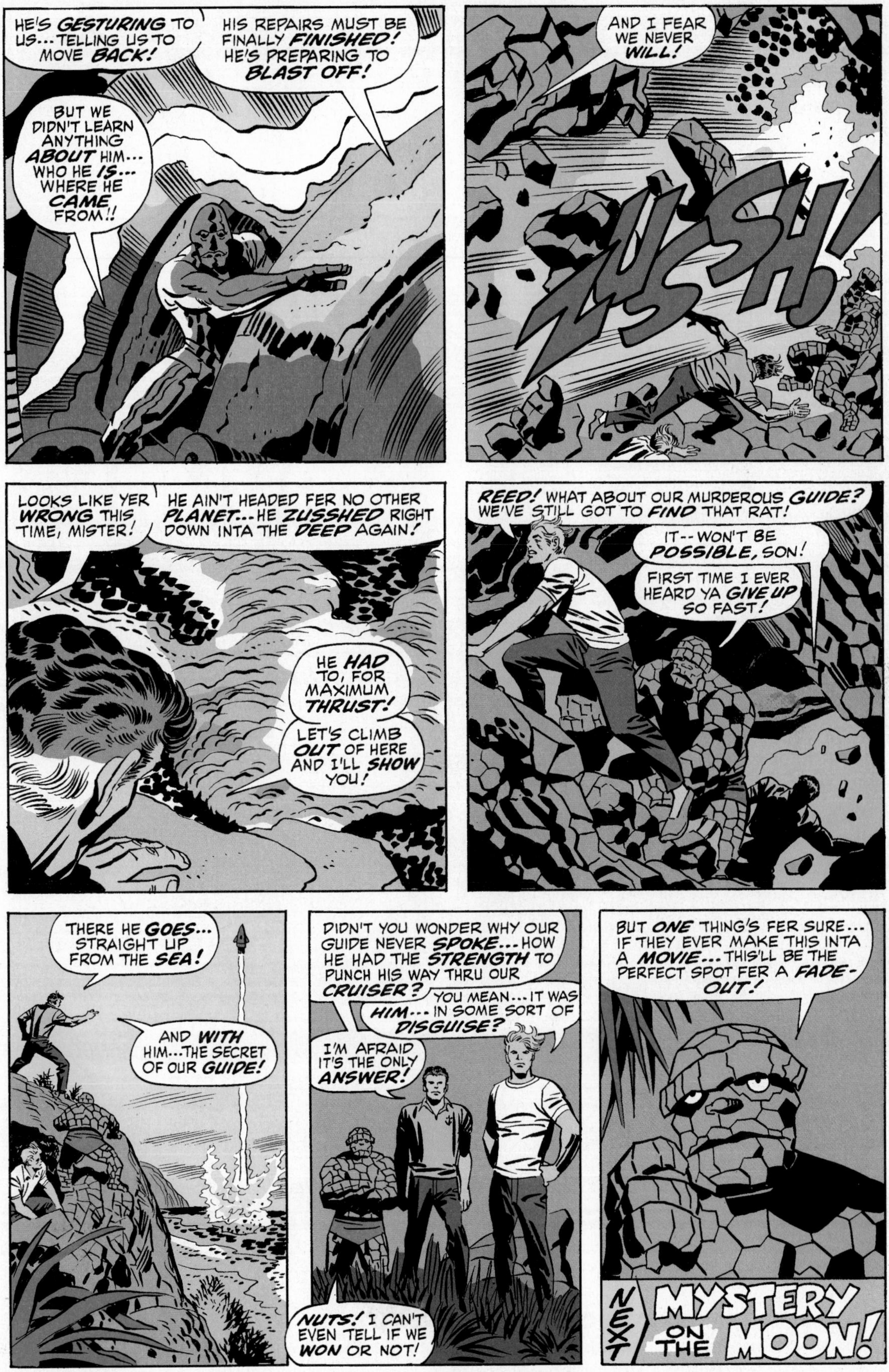
HE'S GESTURING TO US... TELLING US TO MOVE BACK!
HIS REPAIRS MUST BE FINALLY FINISHED! HE'S PREPARING TO BLAST OFF!
BUT WE DIDN'T LEARN ANYTHING ABOUT HIM... WHO HE IS... WHERE HE CAME FROM!!
AND I FEAR WE NEVER WILL!
ZUSSH!
LOOKS LIKE YER WRONG THIS TIME, MISTER!
HE AIN'T HEADED FER NO OTHER PLANET... HE ZUSSHED RIGHT DOWN INTA THE DEEP AGAIN!
HE HAD TO, FOR MAXIMUM THRUST!
LET'S CLIMB OUT OF HERE AND I'LL SHOW YOU!
REED! WHAT ABOUT OUR MURDEROUS GUIDE? WE'VE STILL GOT TO FIND THAT RAT!
IT--WON'T BE POSSIBLE, SON!
FIRST TIME I EVER HEARD YA GIVE UP SO FAST!
THERE HE GOES... STRAIGHT UP FROM THE SEA!
AND WITH HIM...THE SECRET OF OUR GUIDE!
DIDN'T YOU WONDER WHY OUR GUIDE NEVER SPOKE... HOW HE HAD THE STRENGTH TO PUNCH HIS WAY THRU OUR CRUISER?
YOU MEAN... IT WAS HIM... IN SOME SORT OF DISGUISE?
I'M AFRAID IT'S THE ONLY ANSWER!
NUTS! I CAN'T EVEN TELL IF WE WON OR NOT!
BUT ONE THING'S FER SURE... IF THEY EVER MAKE THIS INTA A MOVIE... THIS'LL BE THE PERFECT SPOT FER A FADE-OUT!
NEXT MYSTERY ON THE MOON!

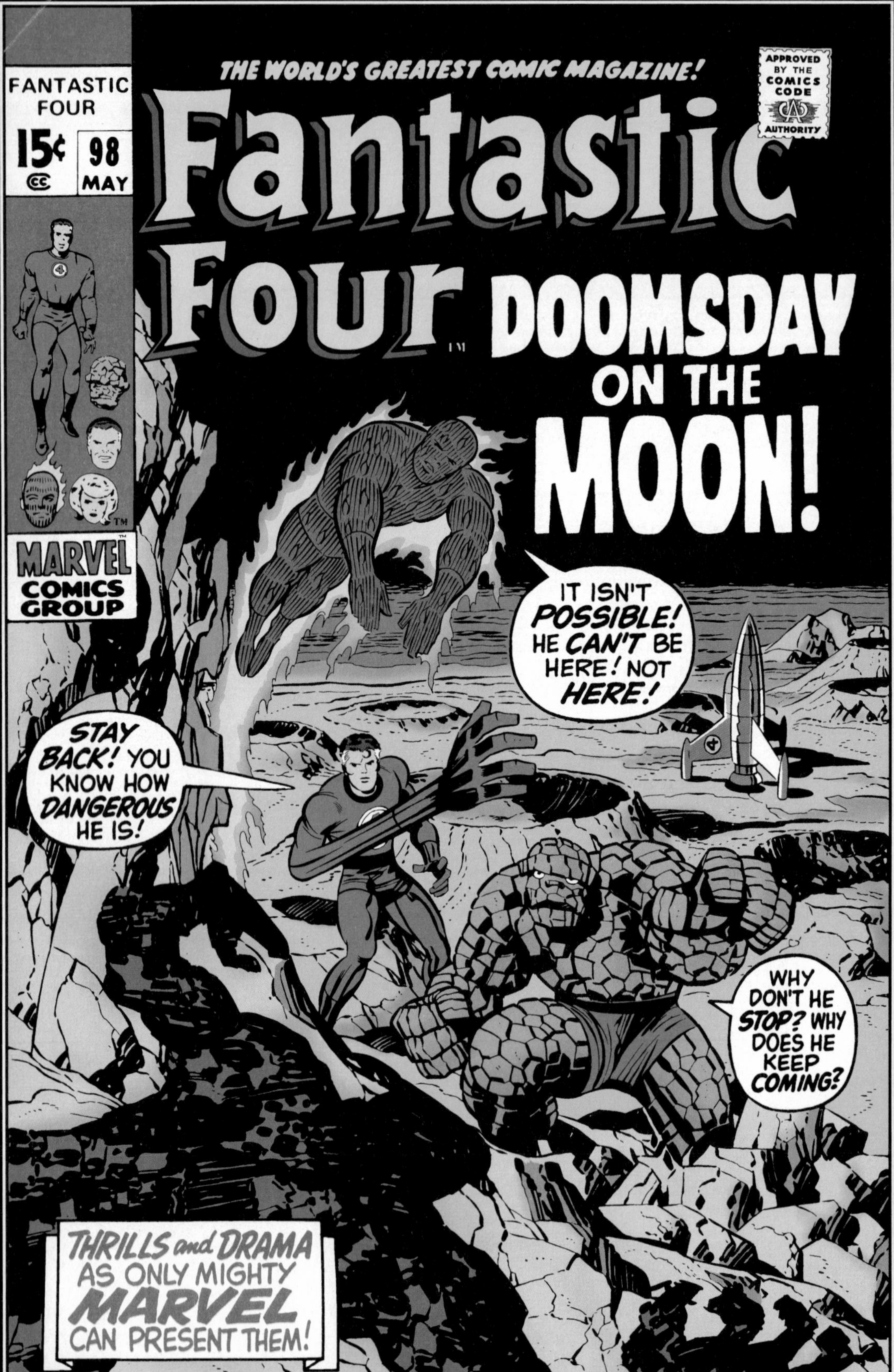
THE WORLD'S GREATEST COMIC MAGAZINE!
FANTASTIC FOUR
15¢
98
MAY
APPROVED BY THE COMICS CODE AUTHORITY
Fantastic Four
DOOMSDAY ON THE MOON!
MARVEL COMICS GROUP
IT ISN'T POSSIBLE! HE CAN'T BE HERE! NOT HERE!
STAY BACK! YOU KNOW HOW DANGEROUS HE IS!
WHY DON'T HE STOP? WHY DOES HE KEEP COMING?
THRILLS and DRAMA AS ONLY MIGHTY MARVEL CAN PRESENT THEM!

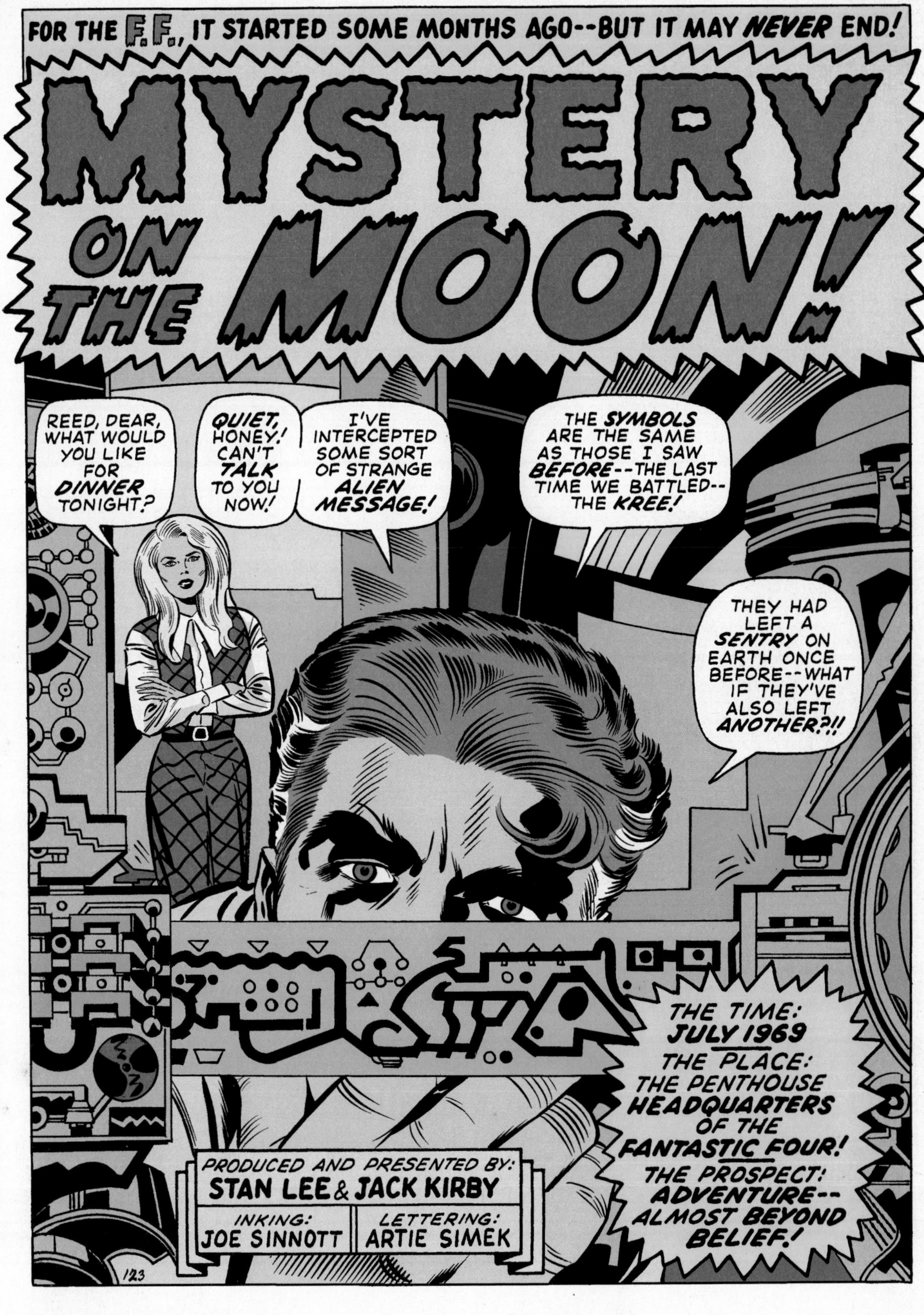
FOR THE F.F., IT STARTED SOME MONTHS AGO--BUT IT MAY NEVER END!
MYSTERY ON THE MOON!
REED, DEAR, WHAT WOULD YOU LIKE FOR DINNER TONIGHT?
QUIET, HONEY! CAN'T TALK TO YOU NOW!
I'VE INTERCEPTED SOME SORT OF STRANGE ALIEN MESSAGE!
THE SYMBOLS ARE THE SAME AS THOSE I SAW BEFORE--THE LAST TIME WE BATTLED--THE KREE!
THEY HAD LEFT A SENTRY ON EARTH ONCE BEFORE--WHAT IF THEY'VE ALSO LEFT ANOTHER?!!
THE TIME: JULY 1969 THE PLACE: THE PENTHOUSE HEADQUARTERS OF THE FANTASTIC FOUR! THE PROSPECT: ADVENTURE--ALMOST BEYOND BELIEF!
PRODUCED AND PRESENTED BY: STAN LEE & JACK KIRBY
INKING: JOE SINNOTT
LETTERING: ARTIE SIMEK
123

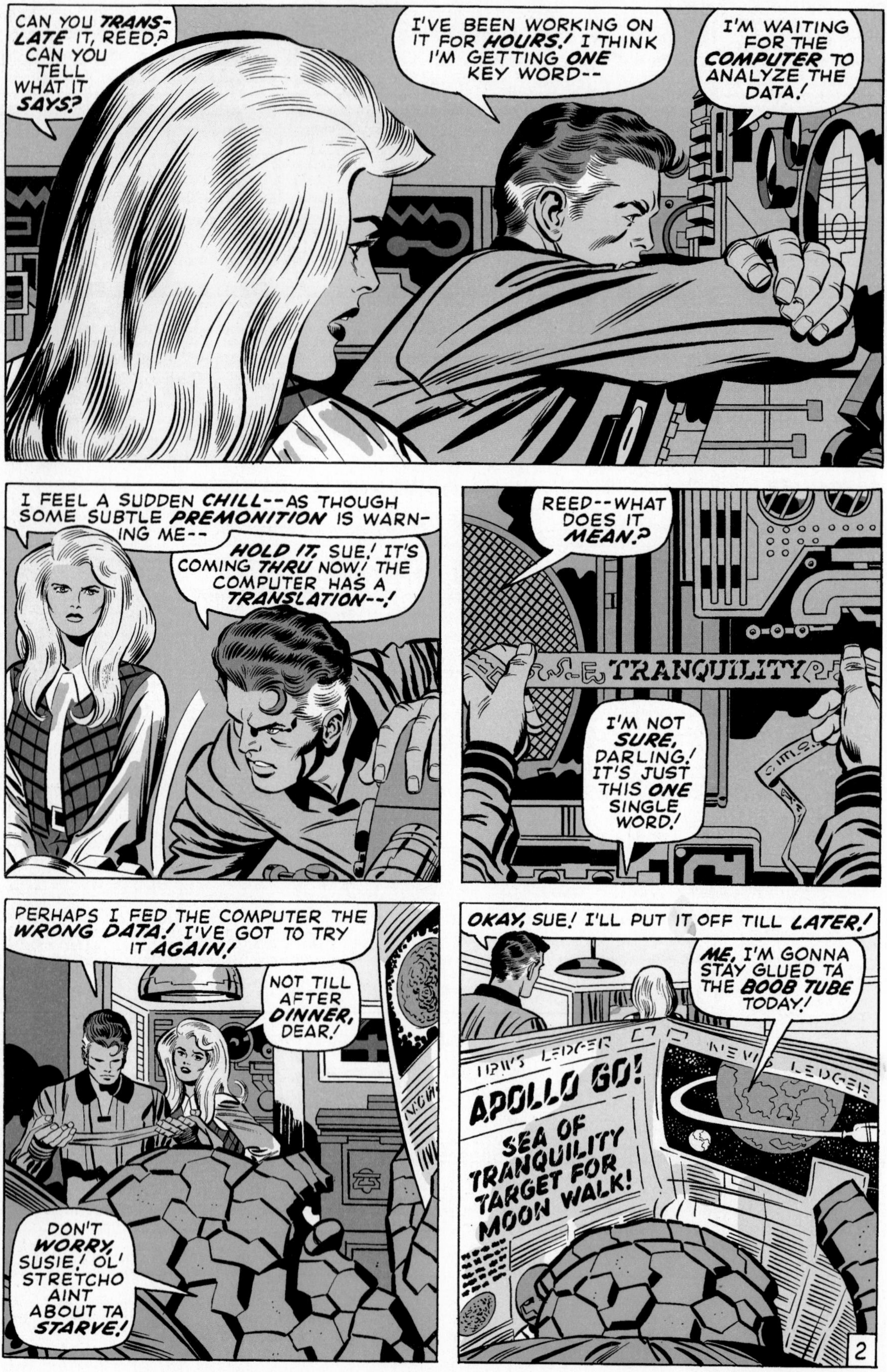
CAN YOU TRANSLATE IT, REED? CAN YOU TELL WHAT IT SAYS?
I'VE BEEN WORKING ON IT FOR HOURS! I THINK I'M GETTING ONE KEY WORD--
I'M WAITING FOR THE COMPUTER TO ANALYZE THE DATA!
I FEEL A SUDDEN CHILL--AS THOUGH SOME SUBTLE PREMONITION IS WARNING ME--
HOLD IT, SUE! IT'S COMING THRU NOW! THE COMPUTER HAS A TRANSLATION--!
REED--WHAT DOES IT MEAN?
TRANQUILITY
I'M NOT SURE, DARLING! IT'S JUST THIS ONE SINGLE WORD!
PERHAPS I FED THE COMPUTER THE WRONG DATA! I'VE GOT TO TRY IT AGAIN!
NOT TILL AFTER DINNER, DEAR!
DON'T WORRY, SUSIE! OL' STRETCHO AINT ABOUT TA STARVE!
OKAY, SUE! I'LL PUT IT OFF TILL LATER!
ME, I'M GONNA STAY GLUED TA THE BOOB TUBE TODAY!
NEWS LEDGER
APOLLO GO!
SEA OF TRANQUILITY TARGET FOR MOON WALK!
2

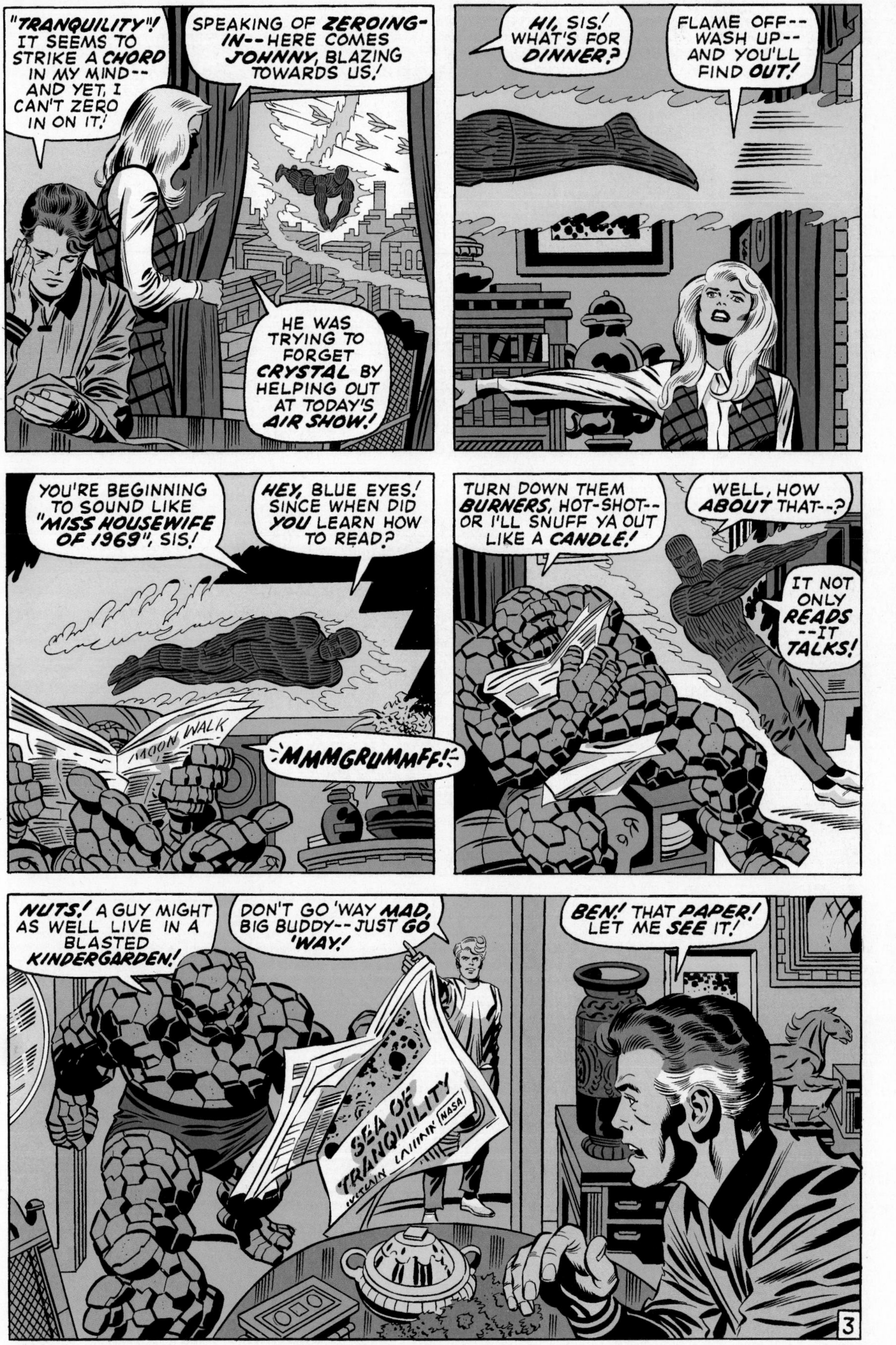
"TRANQUILITY"! IT SEEMS TO STRIKE A CHORD IN MY MIND-- AND YET, I CAN'T ZERO IN ON IT!
SPEAKING OF ZEROING-IN--HERE COMES JOHNNY, BLAZING TOWARDS US!
HE WAS TRYING TO FORGET CRYSTAL BY HELPING OUT AT TODAY'S AIR SHOW!
HI, SIS! WHAT'S FOR DINNER?
FLAME OFF-- WASH UP-- AND YOU'LL FIND OUT!
YOU'RE BEGINNING TO SOUND LIKE "MISS HOUSEWIFE OF 1969", SIS!
HEY, BLUE EYES! SINCE WHEN DID YOU LEARN HOW TO READ?
MOON WALK
MMMGRUMMFF!
TURN DOWN THEM BURNERS, HOT-SHOT-- OR I'LL SNUFF YA OUT LIKE A CANDLE!
WELL, HOW ABOUT THAT--?
IT NOT ONLY READS --IT TALKS!
NUTS! A GUY MIGHT AS WELL LIVE IN A BLASTED KINDERGARDEN!
DON'T GO 'WAY MAD, BIG BUDDY-- JUST GO 'WAY!
BEN! THAT PAPER! LET ME SEE IT!
SEA OF TRANQUILITY
NASA
3

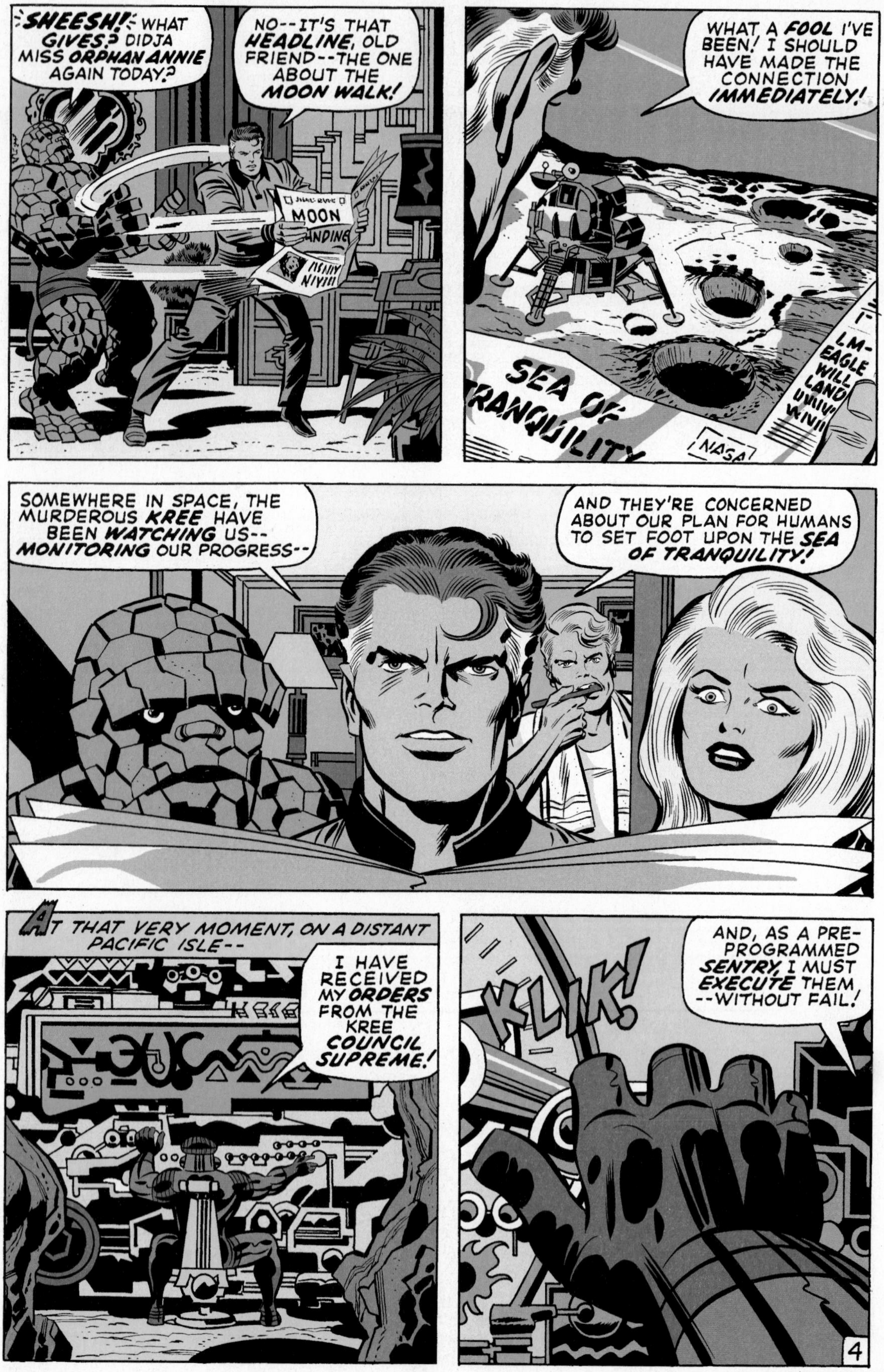
SHEESH! WHAT GIVES? DIDJA MISS ORPHAN ANNIE AGAIN TODAY?
NO--IT'S THAT HEADLINE, OLD FRIEND--THE ONE ABOUT THE MOON WALK!
MOON
WHAT A FOOL I'VE BEEN! I SHOULD HAVE MADE THE CONNECTION IMMEDIATELY!
SEA OF TRANQUILITY
LM-EAGLE WILL LAND
NASA
SOMEWHERE IN SPACE, THE MURDEROUS KREE HAVE BEEN WATCHING US--MONITORING OUR PROGRESS--
AND THEY'RE CONCERNED ABOUT OUR PLAN FOR HUMANS TO SET FOOT UPON THE SEA OF TRANQUILITY!
AT THAT VERY MOMENT, ON A DISTANT PACIFIC ISLE--
I HAVE RECEIVED MY ORDERS FROM THE KREE COUNCIL SUPREME!
KLIK!
AND, AS A PRE-PROGRAMMED SENTRY, I MUST EXECUTE THEM --WITHOUT FAIL!
4

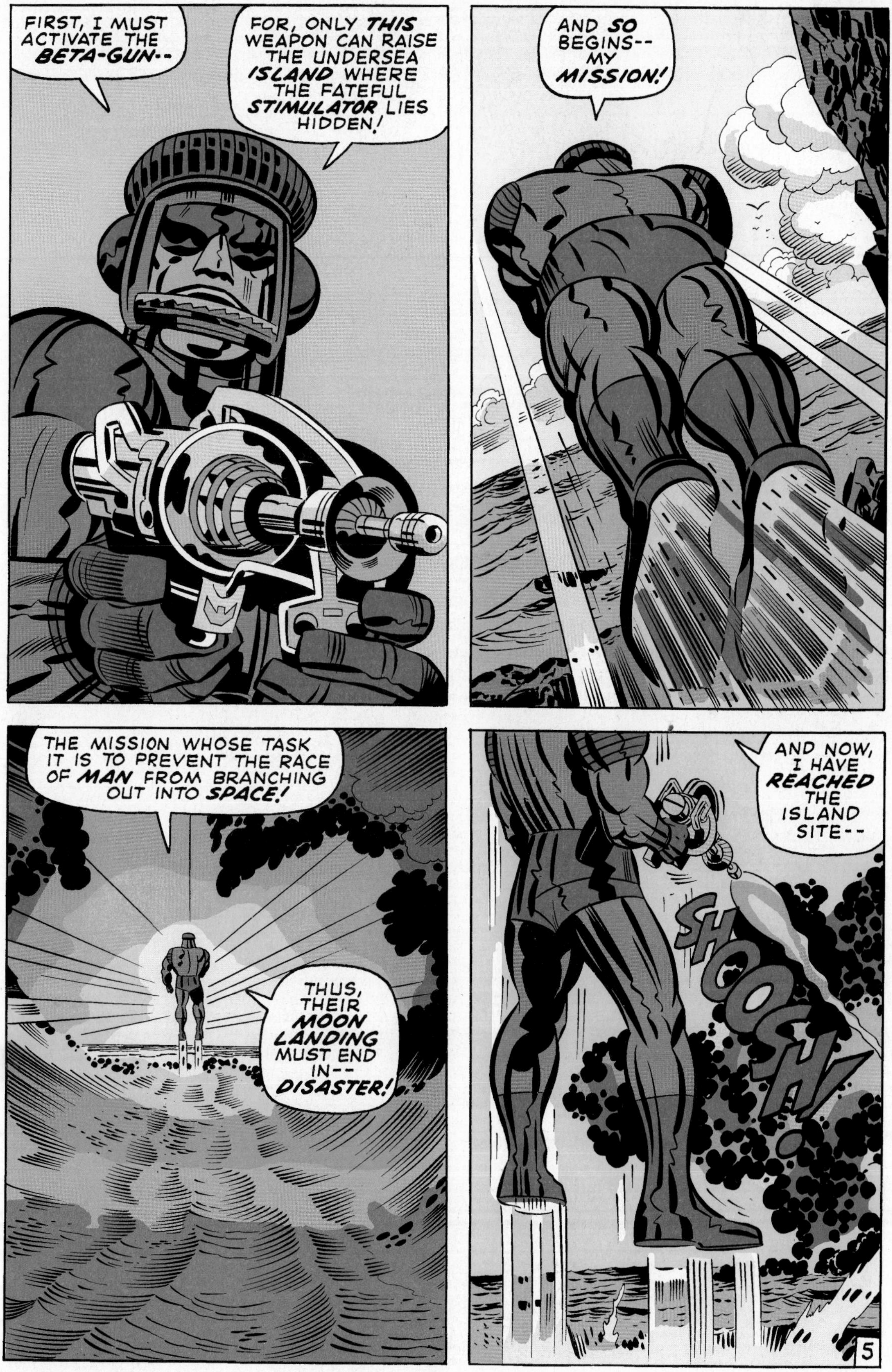

FIRST, I MUST ACTIVATE THE BETA-GUN--
FOR, ONLY THIS WEAPON CAN RAISE THE UNDERSEA ISLAND WHERE THE FATEFUL STIMULATOR LIES HIDDEN!
AND SO BEGINS-- MY MISSION!
THE MISSION WHOSE TASK IT IS TO PREVENT THE RACE OF MAN FROM BRANCHING OUT INTO SPACE!
THUS, THEIR MOON LANDING MUST END IN-- DISASTER!
AND NOW, I HAVE REACHED THE ISLAND SITE--
SHOOOM!
5

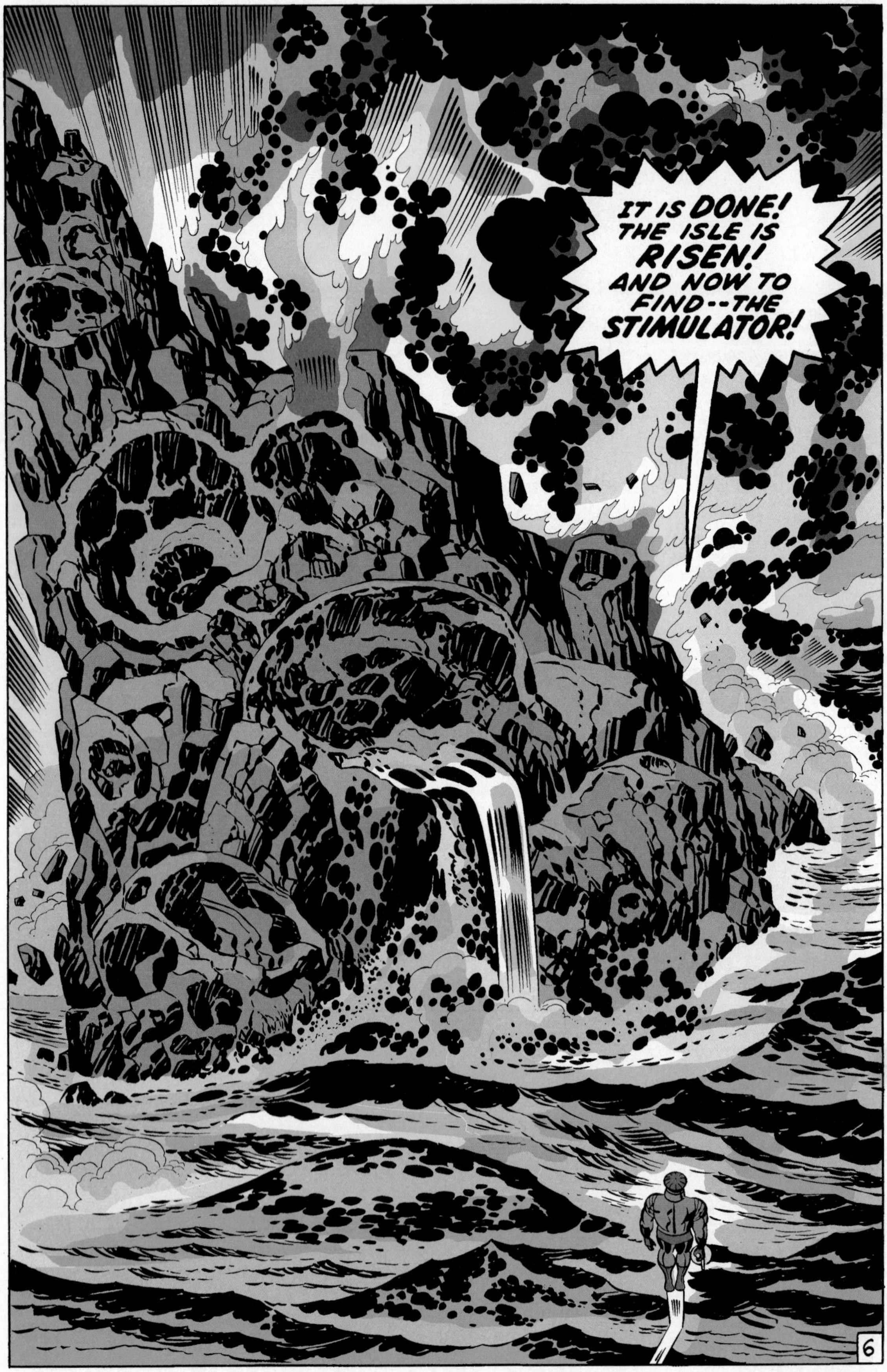
IT IS DONE! THE ISLE IS RISEN! AND NOW TO FIND--THE STIMULATOR!
6

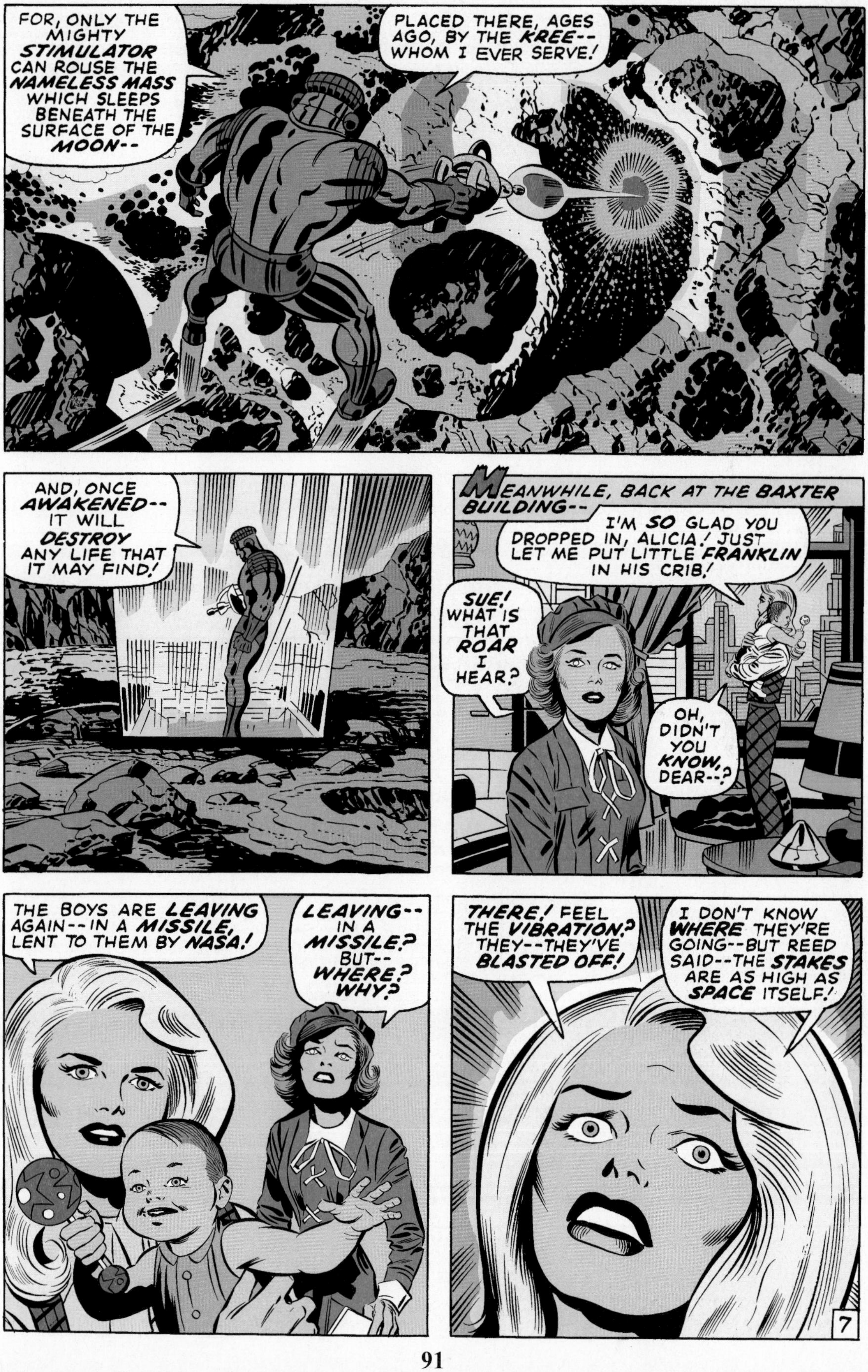
FOR, ONLY THE MIGHTY STIMULATOR CAN ROUSE THE NAMELESS MASS WHICH SLEEPS BENEATH THE SURFACE OF THE MOON--
PLACED THERE, AGES AGO, BY THE KREE-- WHOM I EVER SERVE!
AND, ONCE AWAKENED-- IT WILL DESTROY ANY LIFE THAT IT MAY FIND!
MEANWHILE, BACK AT THE BAXTER BUILDING--
I'M SO GLAD YOU DROPPED IN, ALICIA! JUST LET ME PUT LITTLE FRANKLIN IN HIS CRIB!
SUE! WHAT IS THAT ROAR I HEAR?
OH, DIDN'T YOU KNOW, DEAR--?
THE BOYS ARE LEAVING AGAIN--IN A MISSILE, LENT TO THEM BY NASA!
LEAVING-- IN A MISSILE? BUT-- WHERE? WHY?
THERE! FEEL THE VIBRATION? THEY--THEY'VE BLASTED OFF!
I DON'T KNOW WHERE THEY'RE GOING--BUT REED SAID--THE STAKES ARE AS HIGH AS SPACE ITSELF!
7

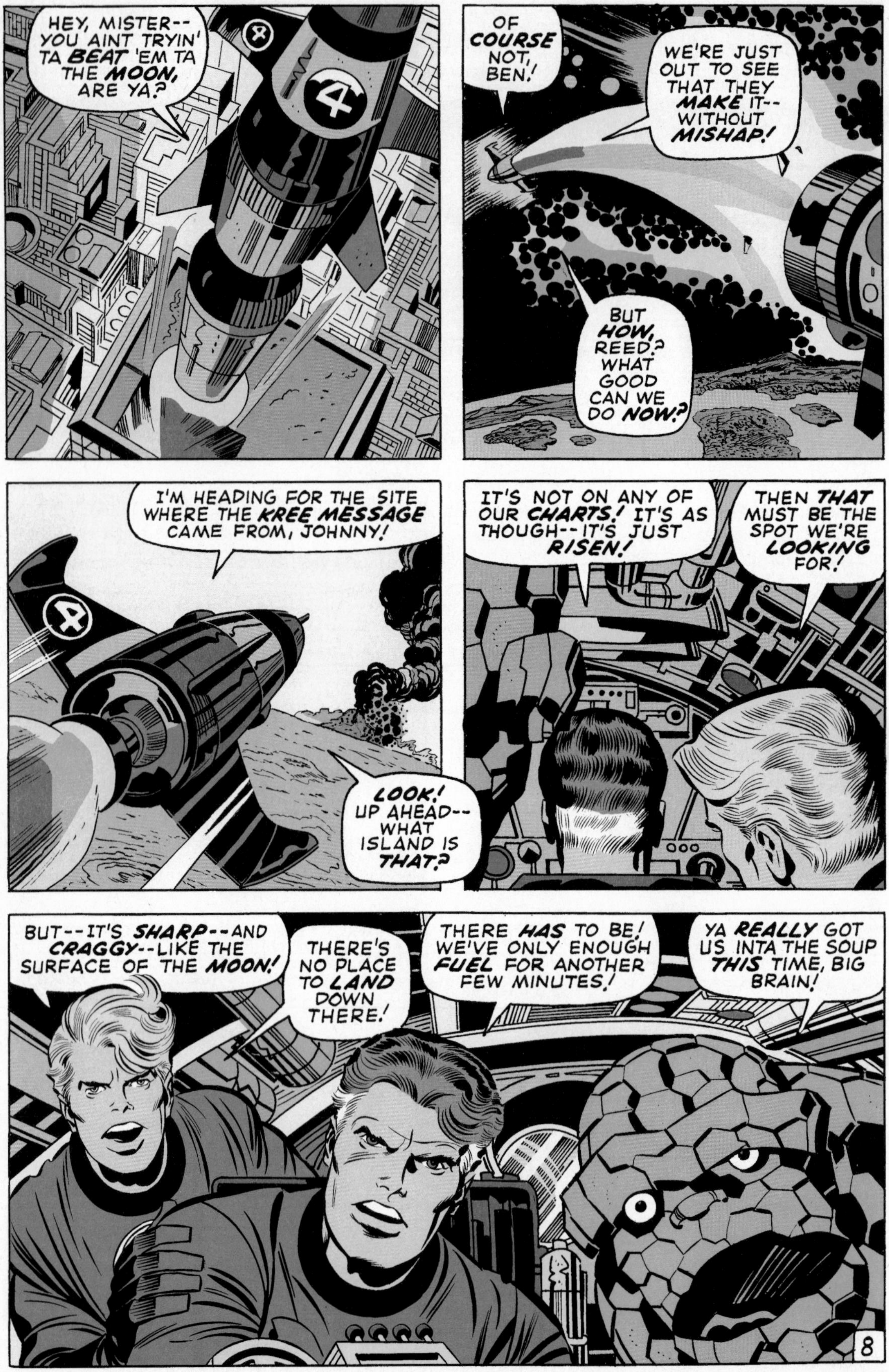
HEY, MISTER-- YOU AINT TRYIN' TA BEAT 'EM TA THE MOON, ARE YA?
OF COURSE NOT, BEN.!
WE'RE JUST OUT TO SEE THAT THEY MAKE IT-- WITHOUT MISHAP!
BUT HOW, REED? WHAT GOOD CAN WE DO NOW?
I'M HEADING FOR THE SITE WHERE THE KREE MESSAGE CAME FROM, JOHNNY!
LOOK! UP AHEAD-- WHAT ISLAND IS THAT?
IT'S NOT ON ANY OF OUR CHARTS! IT'S AS THOUGH-- IT'S JUST RISEN!
THEN THAT MUST BE THE SPOT WE'RE LOOKING FOR!
BUT--IT'S SHARP--AND CRAGGY--LIKE THE SURFACE OF THE MOON!
THERE'S NO PLACE TO LAND DOWN THERE!
THERE HAS TO BE! WE'VE ONLY ENOUGH FUEL FOR ANOTHER FEW MINUTES!
YA REALLY GOT US INTA THE SOUP THIS TIME, BIG BRAIN!
8

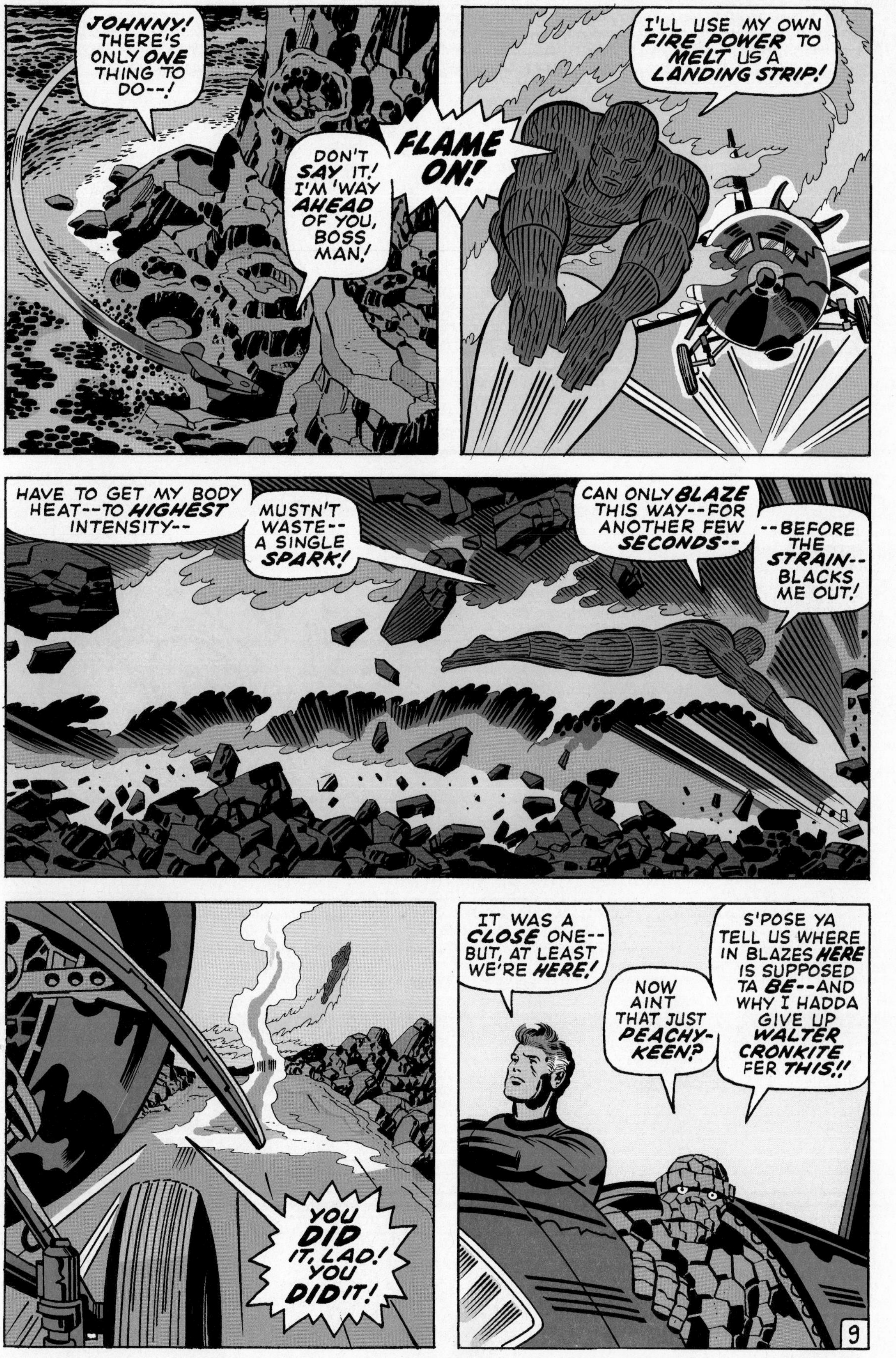
JOHNNY! THERE'S ONLY ONE THING TO DO--!
DON'T SAY IT! I'M 'WAY AHEAD OF YOU, BOSS MAN!
FLAME ON!
I'LL USE MY OWN FIRE POWER TO MELT US A LANDING STRIP!
HAVE TO GET MY BODY HEAT--TO HIGHEST INTENSITY--
MUSTN'T WASTE-- A SINGLE SPARK!
CAN ONLY BLAZE THIS WAY--FOR ANOTHER FEW SECONDS--
--BEFORE THE STRAIN-- BLACKS ME OUT!
YOU DID IT, LAD! YOU DID IT!
IT WAS A CLOSE ONE-- BUT, AT LEAST WE'RE HERE!
NOW AINT THAT JUST PEACHY-KEEN?
S'POSE YA TELL US WHERE IN BLAZES HERE IS SUPPOSED TA BE--AND WHY I HADDA GIVE UP WALTER CRONKITE FER THIS!!
9

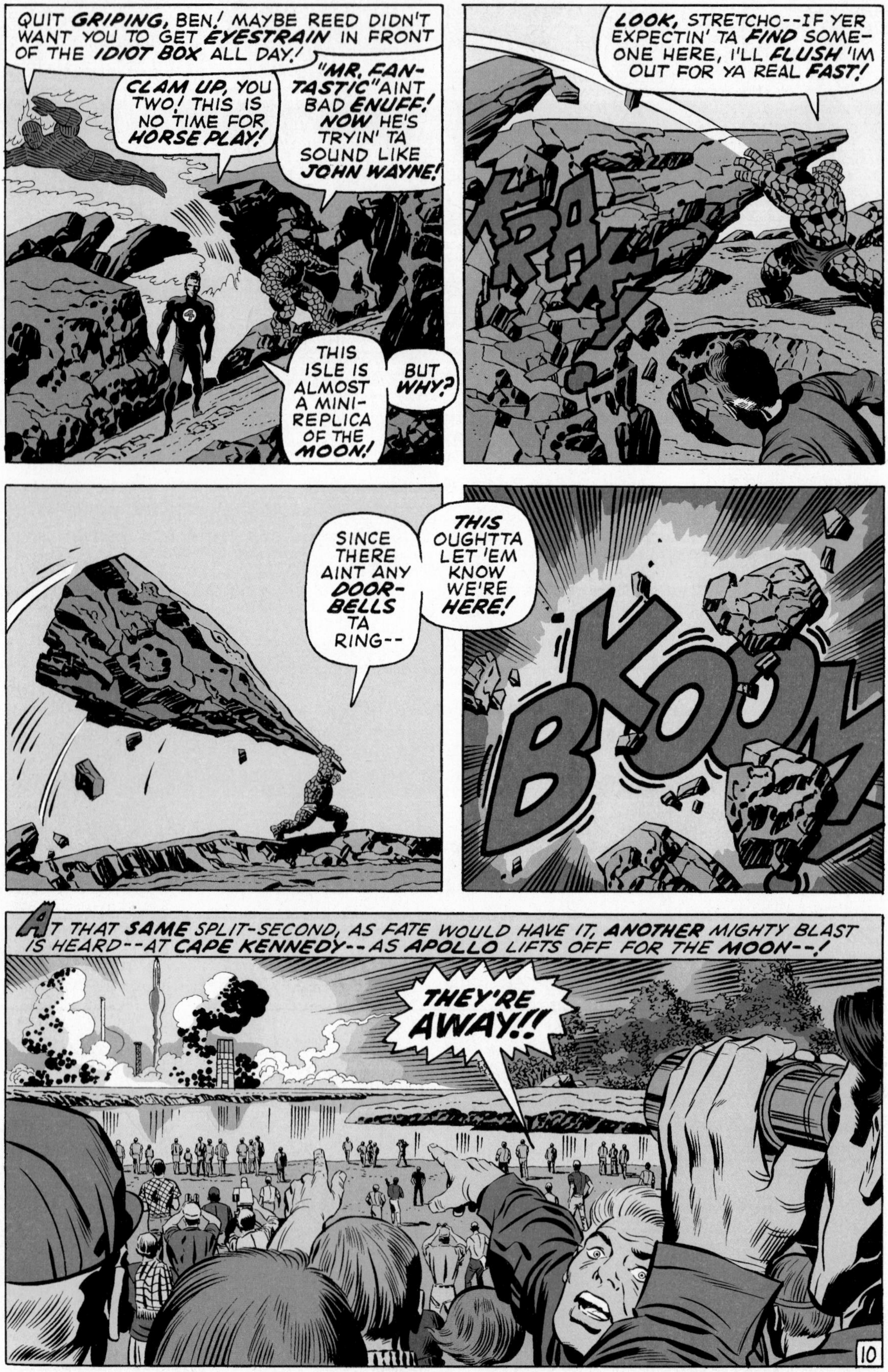
QUIT GRIPING, BEN! MAYBE REED DIDN'T WANT YOU TO GET EYESTRAIN IN FRONT OF THE IDIOT BOX ALL DAY!
CLAM UP, YOU TWO! THIS IS NO TIME FOR HORSE PLAY!
"MR. FANTASTIC" AINT BAD ENUFF! NOW HE'S TRYIN' TA SOUND LIKE JOHN WAYNE!
THIS ISLE IS ALMOST A MINI-REPLICA OF THE MOON!
BUT WHY?
LOOK, STRETCHO--IF YER EXPECTIN' TA FIND SOMEONE HERE, I'LL FLUSH 'IM OUT FOR YA REAL FAST!
KRAK
SINCE THERE AINT ANY DOOR-BELLS TA RING--
THIS OUGHTTA LET 'EM KNOW WE'RE HERE!
BKOOM
AT THAT SAME SPLIT-SECOND, AS FATE WOULD HAVE IT, ANOTHER MIGHTY BLAST IS HEARD--AT CAPE KENNEDY--AS APOLLO LIFTS OFF FOR THE MOON--!
THEY'RE AWAY!!
10

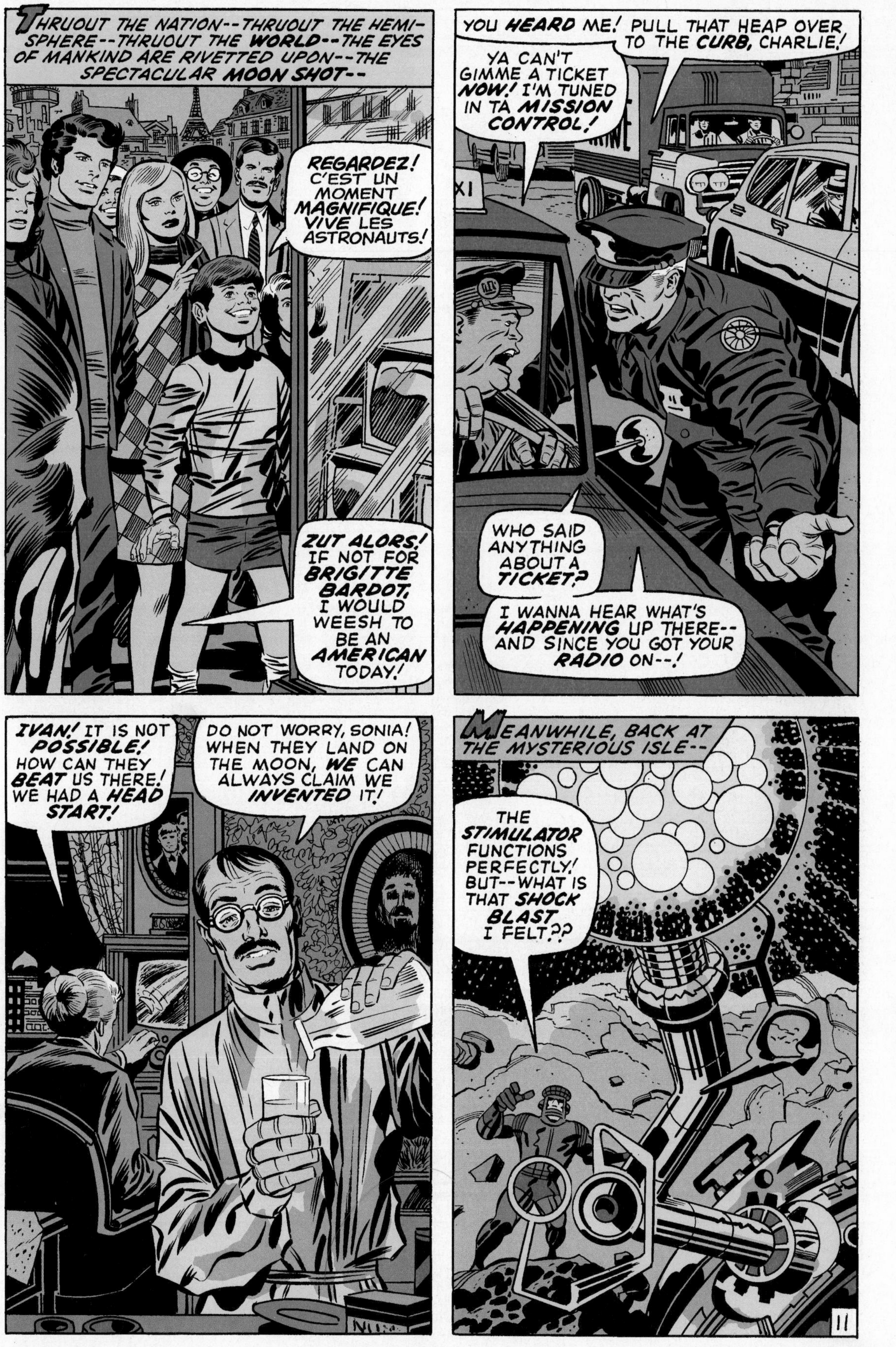
THRUOUT THE NATION--THRUOUT THE HEMISPHERE--THRUOUT THE WORLD--THE EYES OF MANKIND ARE RIVETTED UPON--THE SPECTACULAR MOON SHOT--
REGARDEZ! C'EST UN MOMENT MAGNIFIQUE! VIVE LES ASTRONAUTS!
ZUT ALORS! IF NOT FOR BRIGITTE BARDOT, I WOULD WEESH TO BE AN AMERICAN TODAY!
YOU HEARD ME! PULL THAT HEAP OVER TO THE CURB, CHARLIE!
YA CAN'T GIMME A TICKET NOW! I'M TUNED IN TA MISSION CONTROL!
WHO SAID ANYTHING ABOUT A TICKET?
I WANNA HEAR WHAT'S HAPPENING UP THERE--AND SINCE YOU GOT YOUR RADIO ON--!
IVAN! IT IS NOT POSSIBLE! HOW CAN THEY BEAT US THERE! WE HAD A HEAD START!
DO NOT WORRY, SONIA! WHEN THEY LAND ON THE MOON, WE CAN ALWAYS CLAIM WE INVENTED IT!
MEANWHILE, BACK AT THE MYSTERIOUS ISLE--
THE STIMULATOR FUNCTIONS PERFECTLY! BUT--WHAT IS THAT SHOCK BLAST I FELT??
11

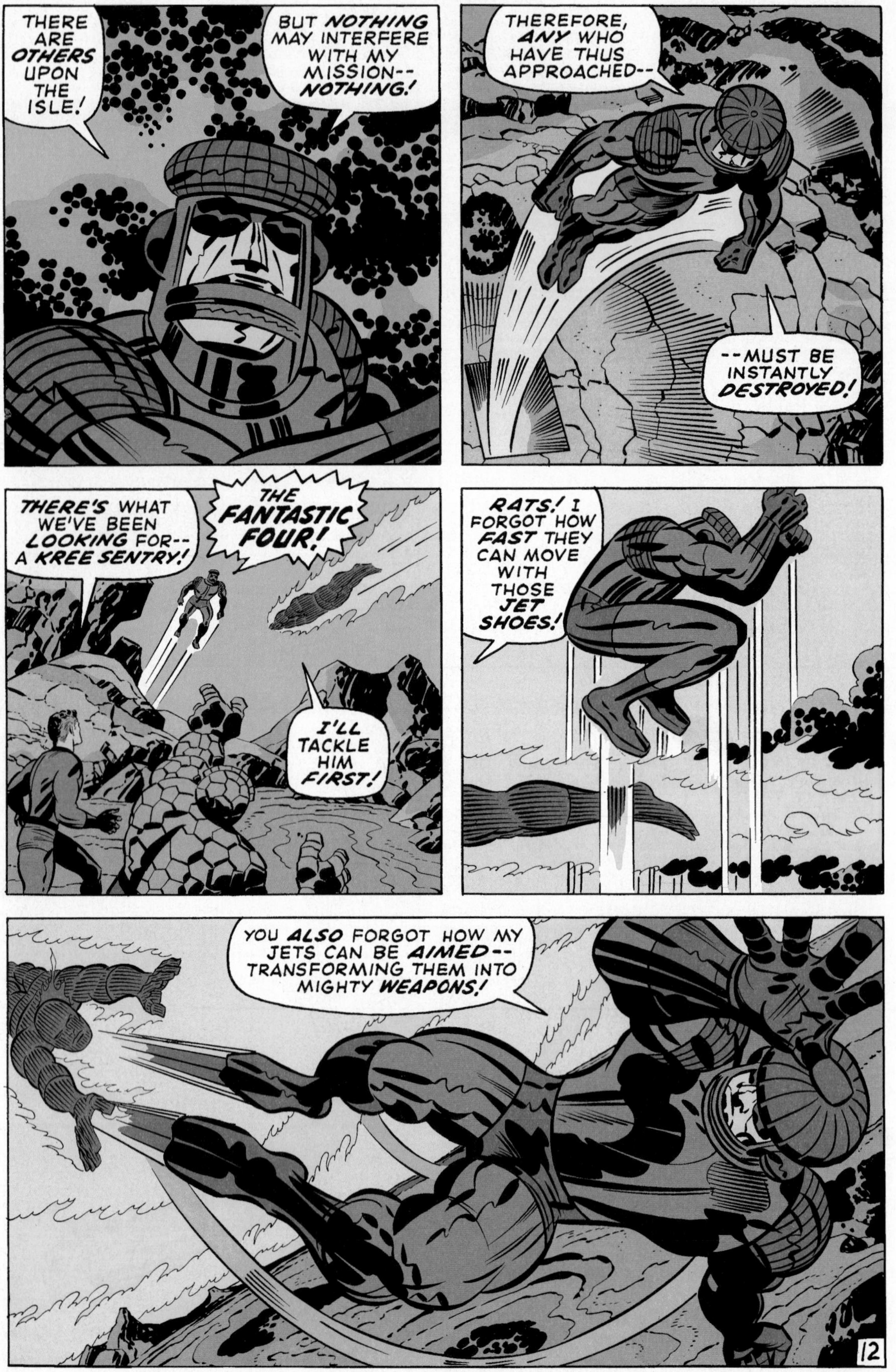
THERE ARE OTHERS UPON THE ISLE!
BUT NOTHING MAY INTERFERE WITH MY MISSION-- NOTHING!
THEREFORE, ANY WHO HAVE THUS APPROACHED--
--MUST BE INSTANTLY DESTROYED!
THERE'S WHAT WE'VE BEEN LOOKING FOR-- A KREE SENTRY!
THE FANTASTIC FOUR!
I'LL TACKLE HIM FIRST!
RATS! I FORGOT HOW FAST THEY CAN MOVE WITH THOSE JET SHOES!
YOU ALSO FORGOT HOW MY JETS CAN BE AIMED-- TRANSFORMING THEM INTO MIGHTY WEAPONS!
12

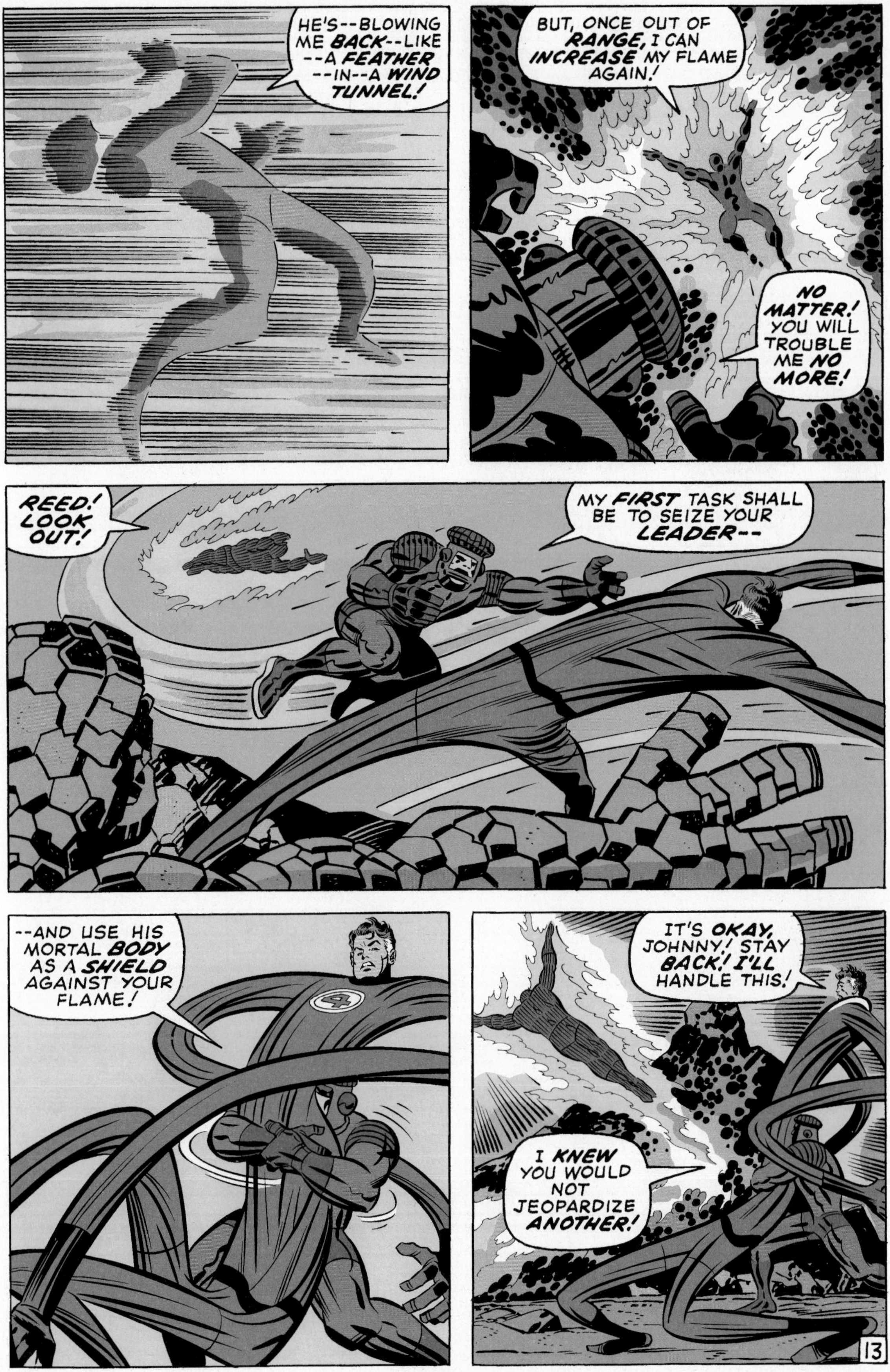
HE'S--BLOWING ME BACK--LIKE --A FEATHER --IN--A WIND TUNNEL!
BUT, ONCE OUT OF RANGE, I CAN INCREASE MY FLAME AGAIN!
NO MATTER! YOU WILL TROUBLE ME NO MORE!
REED! LOOK OUT!
MY FIRST TASK SHALL BE TO SEIZE YOUR LEADER--
--AND USE HIS MORTAL BODY AS A SHIELD AGAINST YOUR FLAME!
IT'S OKAY, JOHNNY! STAY BACK! I'LL HANDLE THIS!
I KNEW YOU WOULD NOT JEOPARDIZE ANOTHER!
13

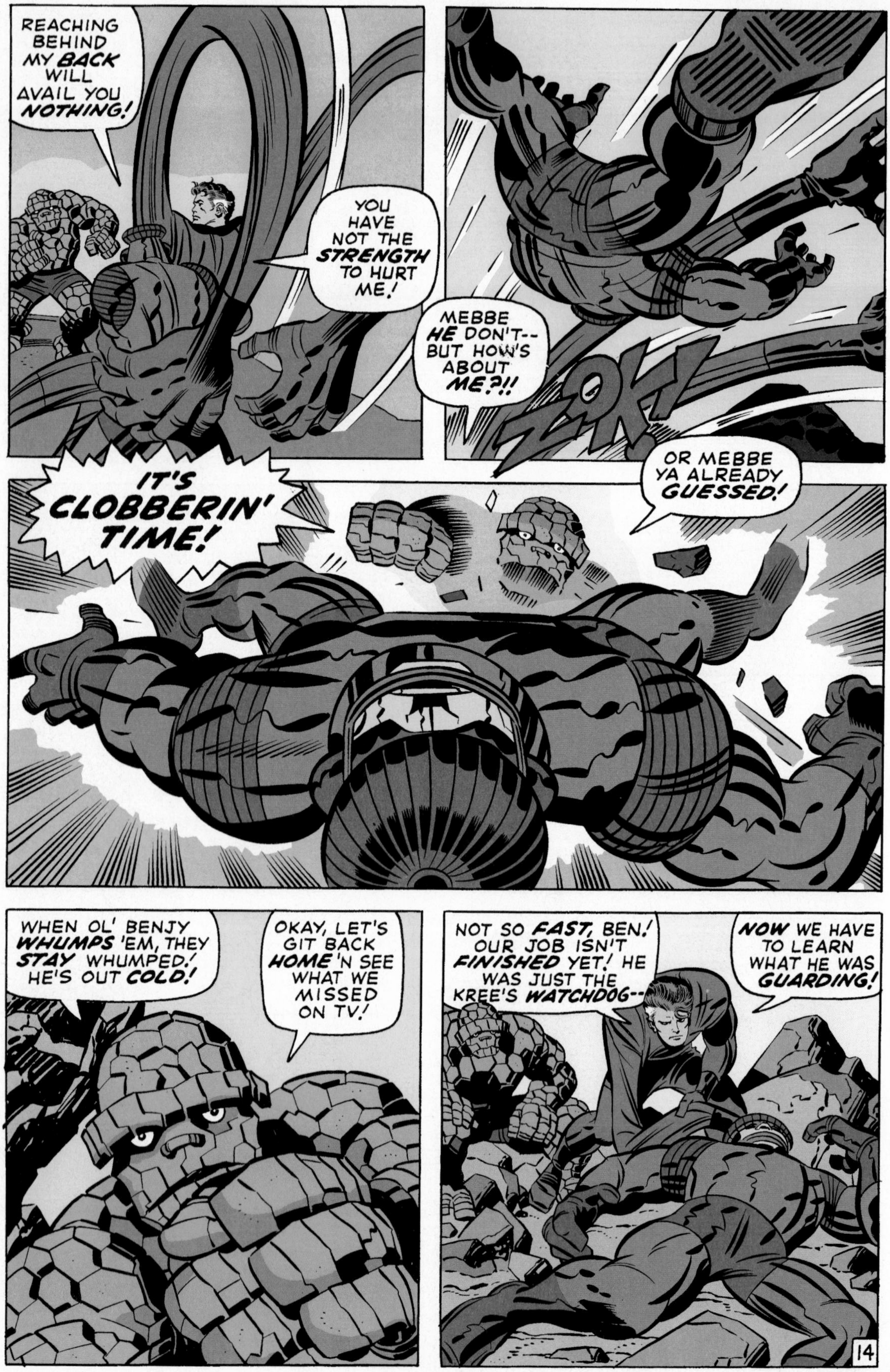
REACHING BEHIND MY BACK WILL AVAIL YOU NOTHING!
YOU HAVE NOT THE STRENGTH TO HURT ME!
MEBBE HE DON'T-- BUT HOW'S ABOUT ME?!!
ZZOK!
IT'S CLOBBERIN' TIME!
OR MEBBE YA ALREADY GUESSED!
WHEN OL' BENJY WHUMPS 'EM, THEY STAY WHUMPED! HE'S OUT COLD!
OKAY, LET'S GIT BACK HOME 'N SEE WHAT WE MISSED ON TV!
NOT SO FAST, BEN! OUR JOB ISN'T FINISHED YET! HE WAS JUST THE KREE'S WATCHDOG--
NOW WE HAVE TO LEARN WHAT HE WAS GUARDING!
14

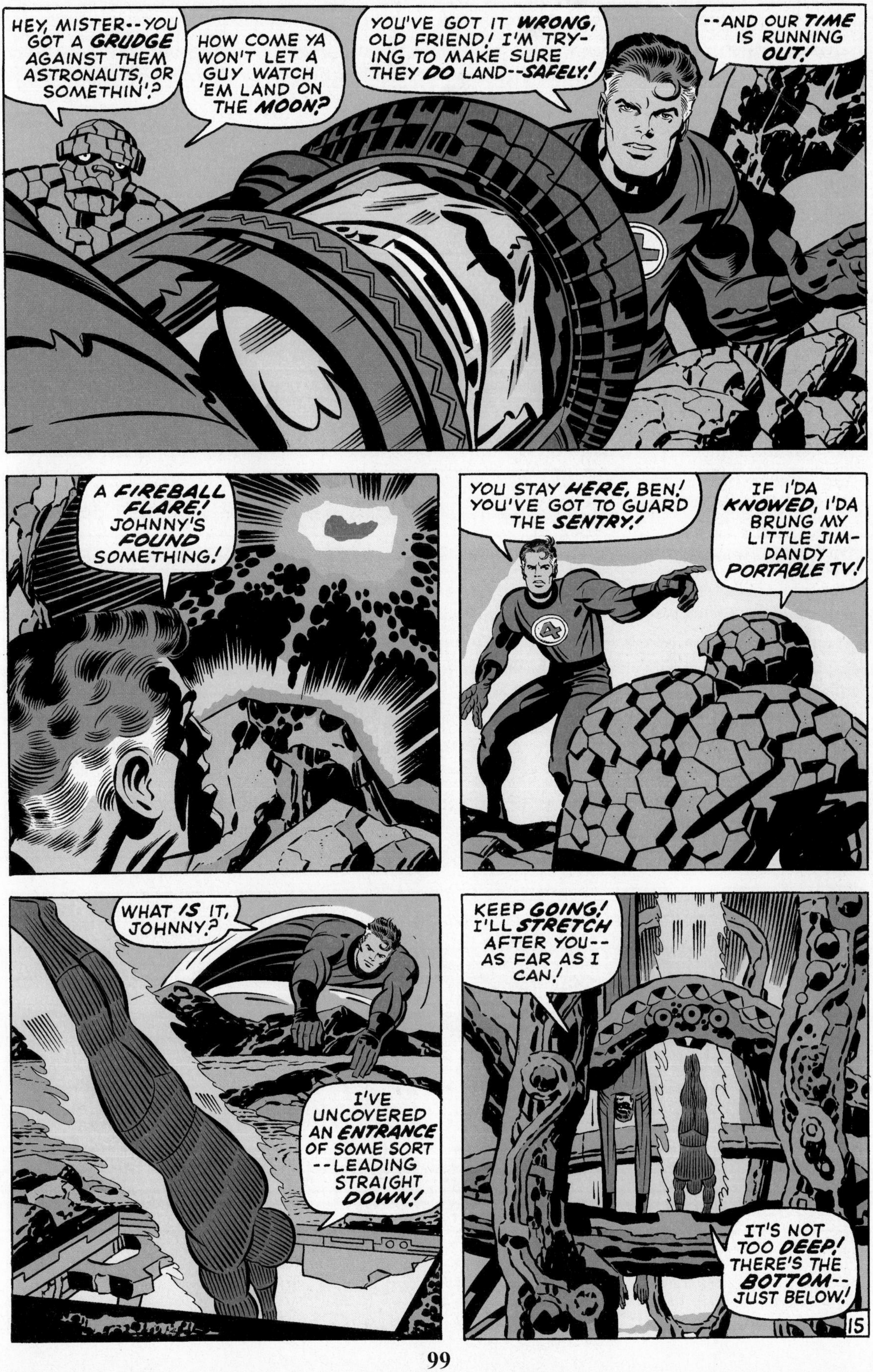
HEY, MISTER--YOU GOT A GRUDGE AGAINST THEM ASTRONAUTS, OR SOMETHIN'?
HOW COME YA WON'T LET A GUY WATCH 'EM LAND ON THE MOON?
YOU'VE GOT IT WRONG, OLD FRIEND! I'M TRYING TO MAKE SURE THEY DO LAND--SAFELY!
--AND OUR TIME IS RUNNING OUT!
A FIREBALL FLARE! JOHNNY'S FOUND SOMETHING!
YOU STAY HERE, BEN! YOU'VE GOT TO GUARD THE SENTRY!
IF I'DA KNOWED, I'DA BRUNG MY LITTLE JIM-DANDY PORTABLE TV!
WHAT IS IT, JOHNNY?
I'VE UNCOVERED AN ENTRANCE OF SOME SORT --LEADING STRAIGHT DOWN!
KEEP GOING! I'LL STRETCH AFTER YOU--AS FAR AS I CAN!
IT'S NOT TOO DEEP! THERE'S THE BOTTOM--JUST BELOW!
15

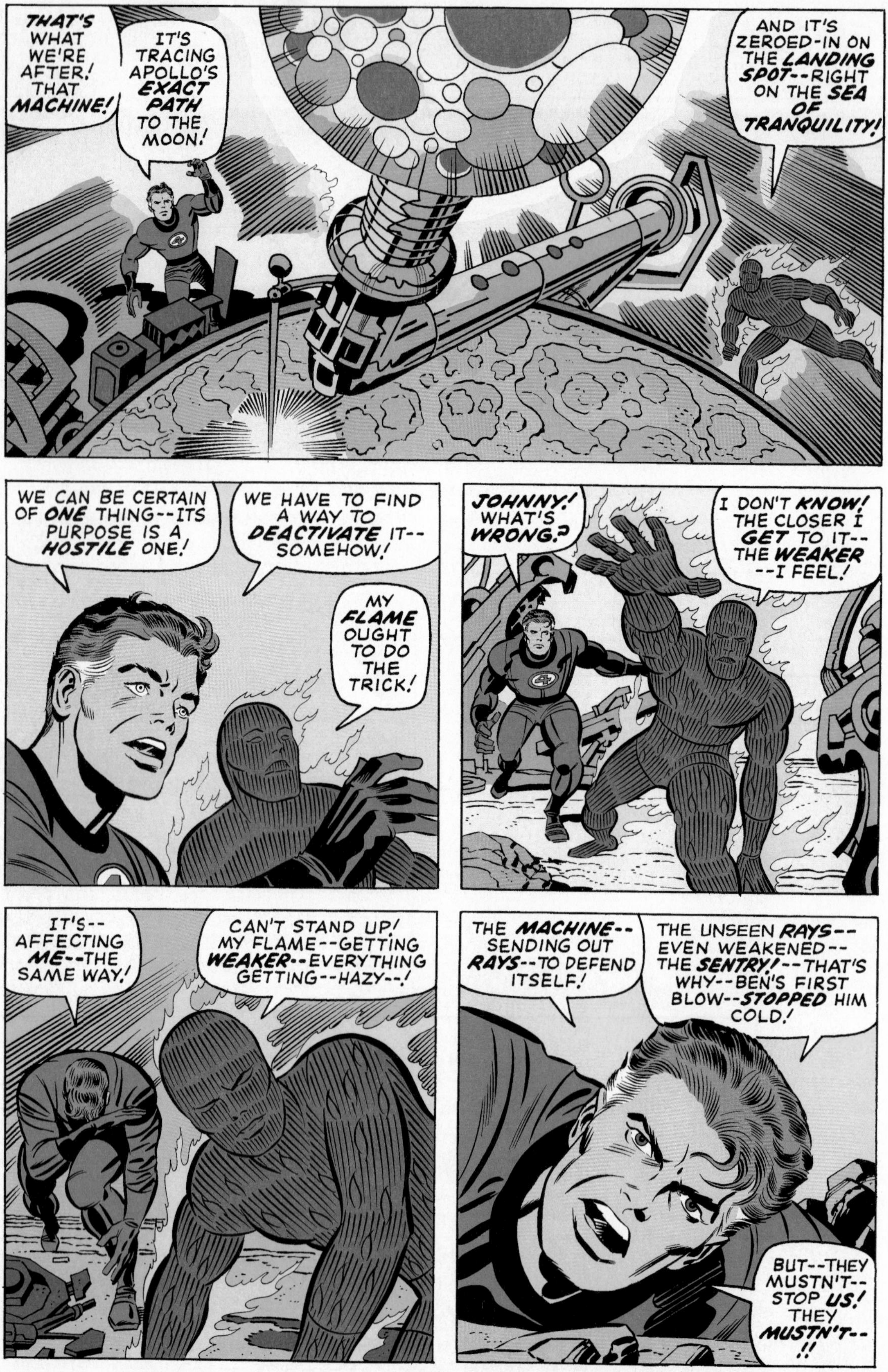
THAT'S WHAT WE'RE AFTER! THAT MACHINE!
IT'S TRACING APOLLO'S EXACT PATH TO THE MOON!
AND IT'S ZEROED-IN ON THE LANDING SPOT--RIGHT ON THE SEA OF TRANQUILITY!
WE CAN BE CERTAIN OF ONE THING--ITS PURPOSE IS A HOSTILE ONE!
WE HAVE TO FIND A WAY TO DEACTIVATE IT--SOMEHOW!
MY FLAME OUGHT TO DO THE TRICK!
JOHNNY! WHAT'S WRONG?
I DON'T KNOW! THE CLOSER I GET TO IT--THE WEAKER--I FEEL!
IT'S--AFFECTING ME--THE SAME WAY!
CAN'T STAND UP! MY FLAME--GETTING WEAKER--EVERYTHING GETTING--HAZY--!
THE MACHINE--SENDING OUT RAYS--TO DEFEND ITSELF!
THE UNSEEN RAYS--EVEN WEAKENED--THE SENTRY!--THAT'S WHY--BEN'S FIRST BLOW--STOPPED HIM COLD!
BUT--THEY MUSTN'T--STOP US! THEY MUSTN'T--!!

EVEN AS REED RICHARDS CRIES OUT-- ABOVE THE CRATERS OF THE MOON APOLLO'S LUNAR MODULE PREPARES FOR LANDING--

BUT, BENEATH THE BARREN, CRAGGY SURFACE, A DEADLY NAMELESS MASS STIRS ITSELF AT LAST--

SILENTLY, EFFORTLESSLY, IT SLITHERS BELOW THE MODULE--WAITING FOR THE FATEFUL MOMENT WHEN ITS VICTIM LANDS ABOVE--!

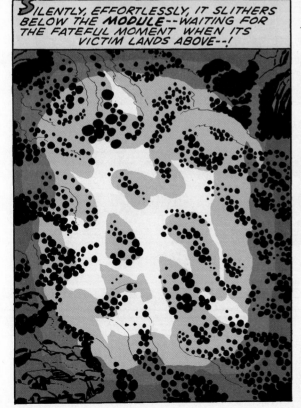

LANDING PROBE DOWN! 200 FEET! 100 FEET--!

17

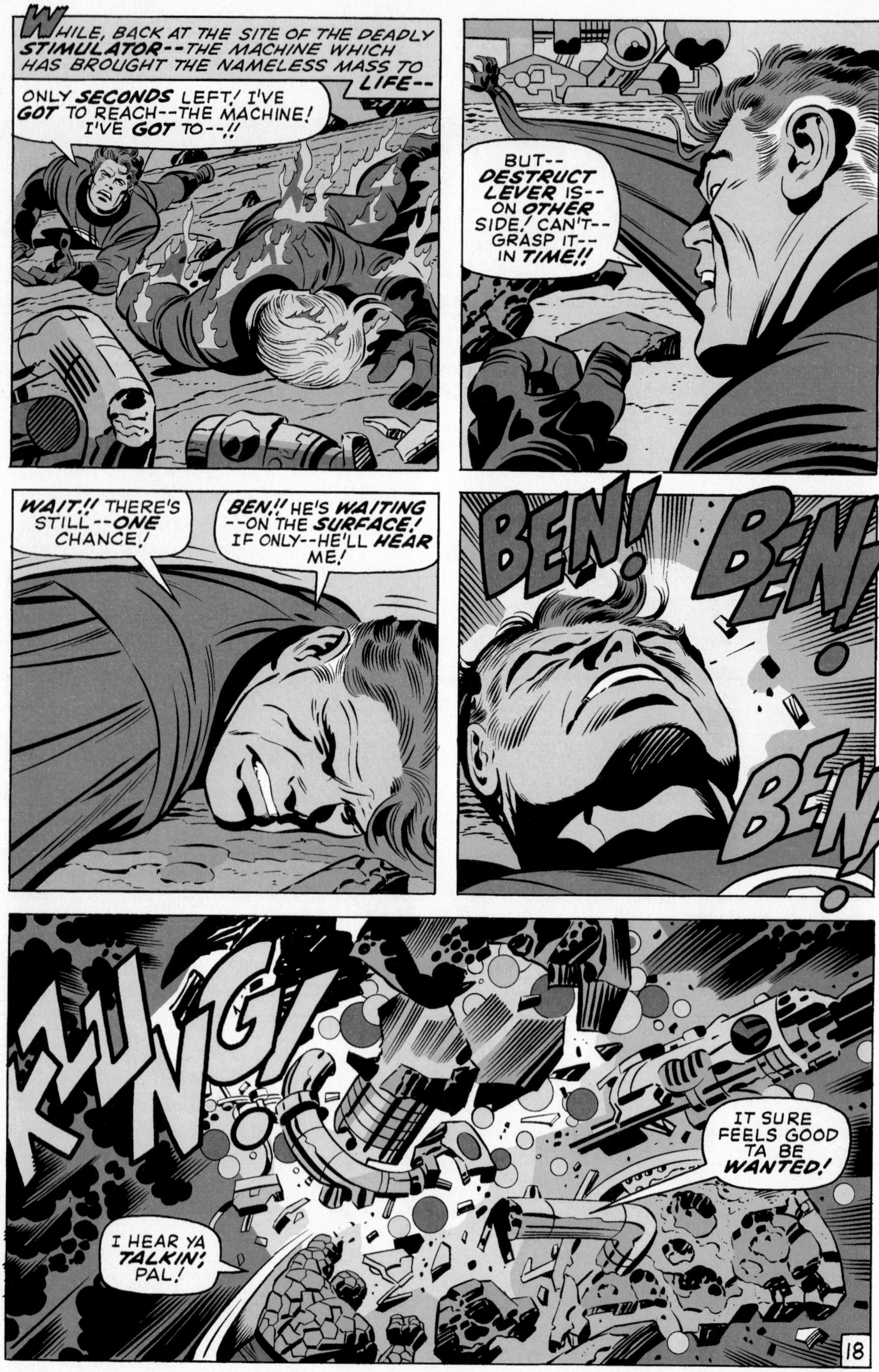
WHILE, BACK AT THE SITE OF THE DEADLY STIMULATOR--THE MACHINE WHICH HAS BROUGHT THE NAMELESS MASS TO LIFE--
ONLY SECONDS LEFT! I'VE GOT TO REACH--THE MACHINE! I'VE GOT TO--!!
BUT-- DESTRUCT LEVER IS-- ON OTHER SIDE! CAN'T-- GRASP IT-- IN TIME!!
WAIT!! THERE'S STILL --ONE CHANCE!
BEN!! HE'S WAITING --ON THE SURFACE! IF ONLY--HE'LL HEAR ME!
BEN! BEN! BEN!
KLUNG!
IT SURE FEELS GOOD TA BE WANTED!
I HEAR YA TALKIN', PAL!
18

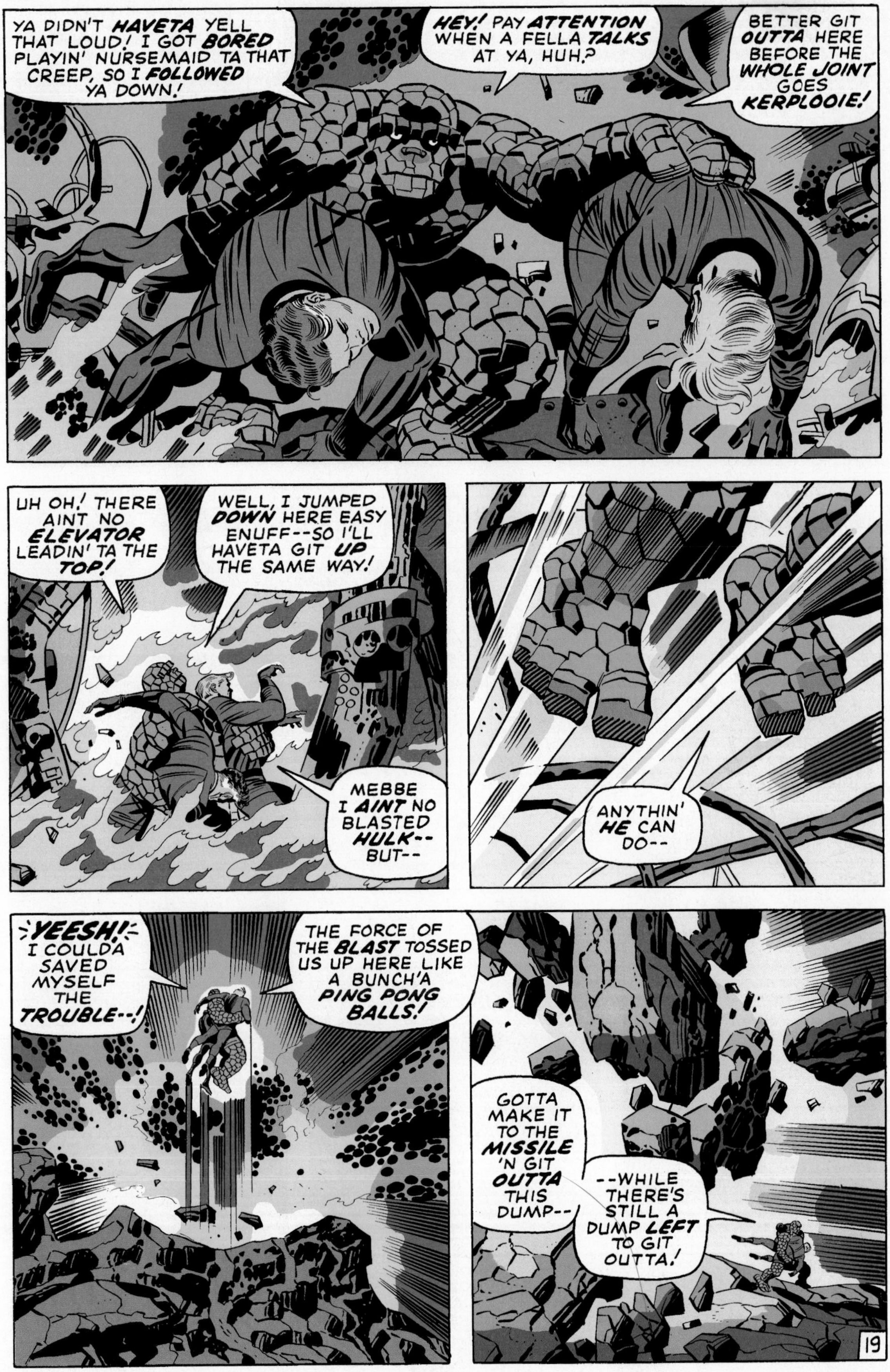
YA DIDN'T HAVETA YELL THAT LOUD! I GOT BORED PLAYIN' NURSEMAID TA THAT CREEP, SO I FOLLOWED YA DOWN!
HEY! PAY ATTENTION WHEN A FELLA TALKS AT YA, HUH?
BETTER GIT OUTTA HERE BEFORE THE WHOLE JOINT GOES KERPLOOIE!
UH OH! THERE AINT NO ELEVATOR LEADIN' TA THE TOP!
WELL, I JUMPED DOWN HERE EASY ENUFF--SO I'LL HAVETA GIT UP THE SAME WAY!
MEBBE I AINT NO BLASTED HULK--BUT--
ANYTHIN' HE CAN DO--
YEESH! I COULDA SAVED MYSELF THE TROUBLE--!
THE FORCE OF THE BLAST TOSSED US UP HERE LIKE A BUNCH'A PING PONG BALLS!
GOTTA MAKE IT TO THE MISSILE 'N GIT OUTTA THIS DUMP--
--WHILE THERE'S STILL A DUMP LEFT TO GIT OUTTA!
19

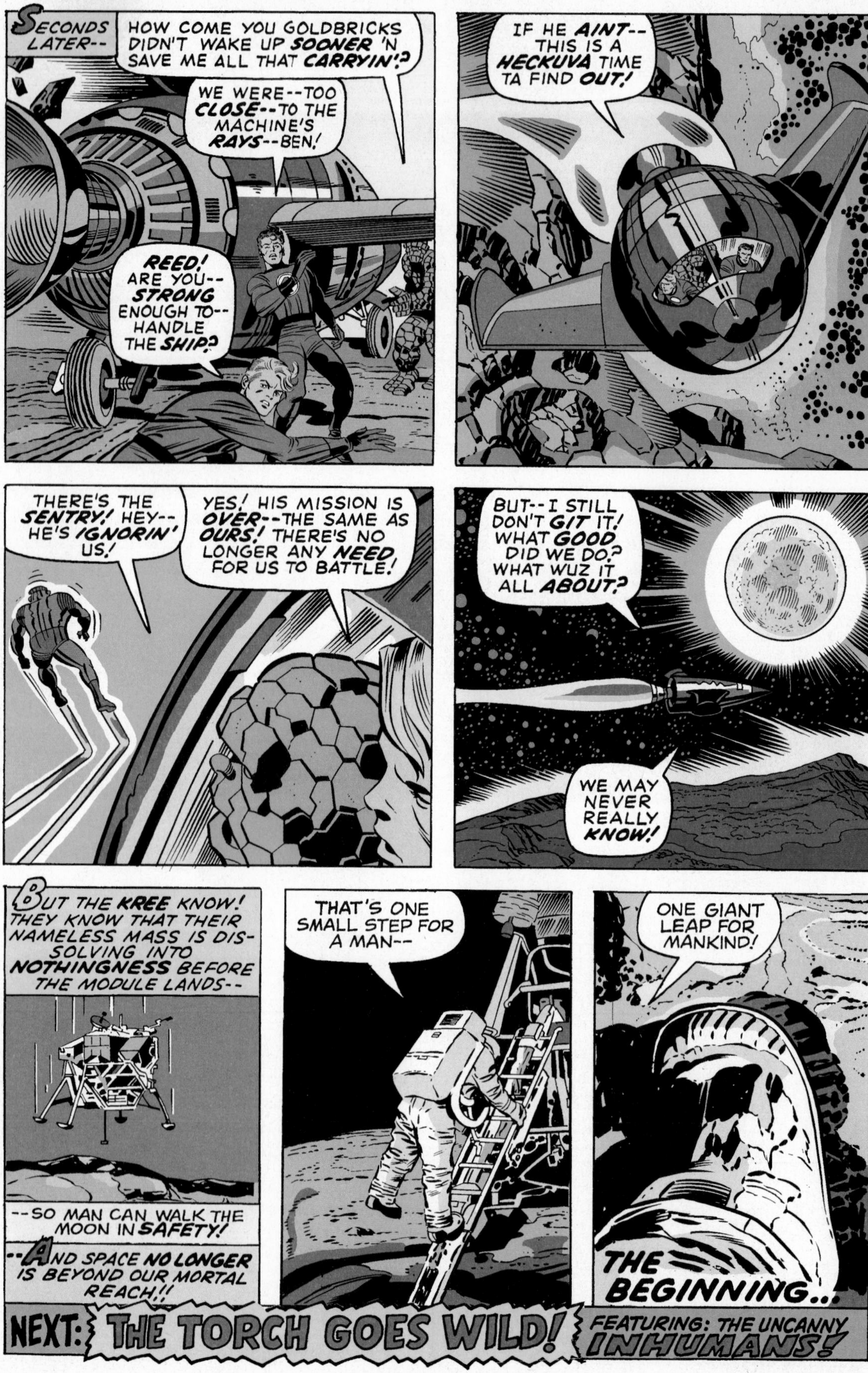
SECONDS LATER--
HOW COME YOU GOLDBRICKS DIDN'T WAKE UP SOONER 'N SAVE ME ALL THAT CARRYIN'?
WE WERE--TOO CLOSE--TO THE MACHINE'S RAYS--BEN!
REED! ARE YOU--STRONG ENOUGH TO--HANDLE THE SHIP?
IF HE AINT--THIS IS A HECKUVA TIME TA FIND OUT!
THERE'S THE SENTRY! HEY--HE'S IGNORIN' US!
YES! HIS MISSION IS OVER--THE SAME AS OURS! THERE'S NO LONGER ANY NEED FOR US TO BATTLE!
BUT--I STILL DON'T GIT IT! WHAT GOOD DID WE DO? WHAT WUZ IT ALL ABOUT?
WE MAY NEVER REALLY KNOW!
BUT THE KREE KNOW! THEY KNOW THAT THEIR NAMELESS MASS IS DISSOLVING INTO NOTHINGNESS BEFORE THE MODULE LANDS--
--SO MAN CAN WALK THE MOON IN SAFETY!
--AND SPACE NO LONGER IS BEYOND OUR MORTAL REACH!!
THAT'S ONE SMALL STEP FOR A MAN--
ONE GIANT LEAP FOR MANKIND!
THE BEGINNING...
NEXT: THE TORCH GOES WILD! FEATURING: THE UNCANNY INHUMANS!

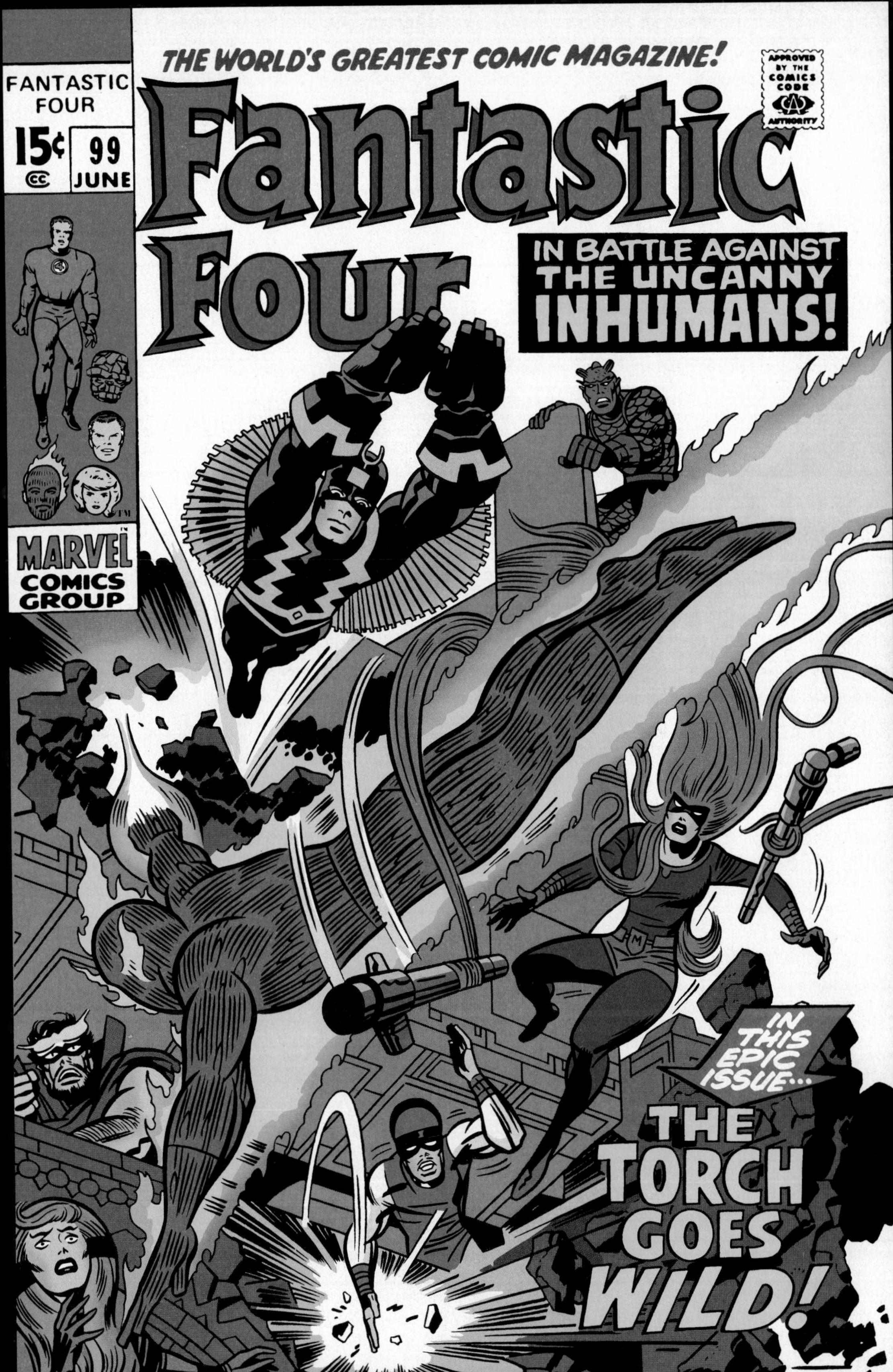

THE WORLD'S GREATEST COMIC MAGAZINE!
APPROVED BY THE COMICS CODE CA AUTHORITY
FANTASTIC FOUR
15¢
99
JUNE
Fantastic Four
IN BATTLE AGAINST THE UNCANNY INHUMANS!
MARVEL COMICS GROUP
IN THIS EPIC ISSUE...
THE TORCH GOES WILD!

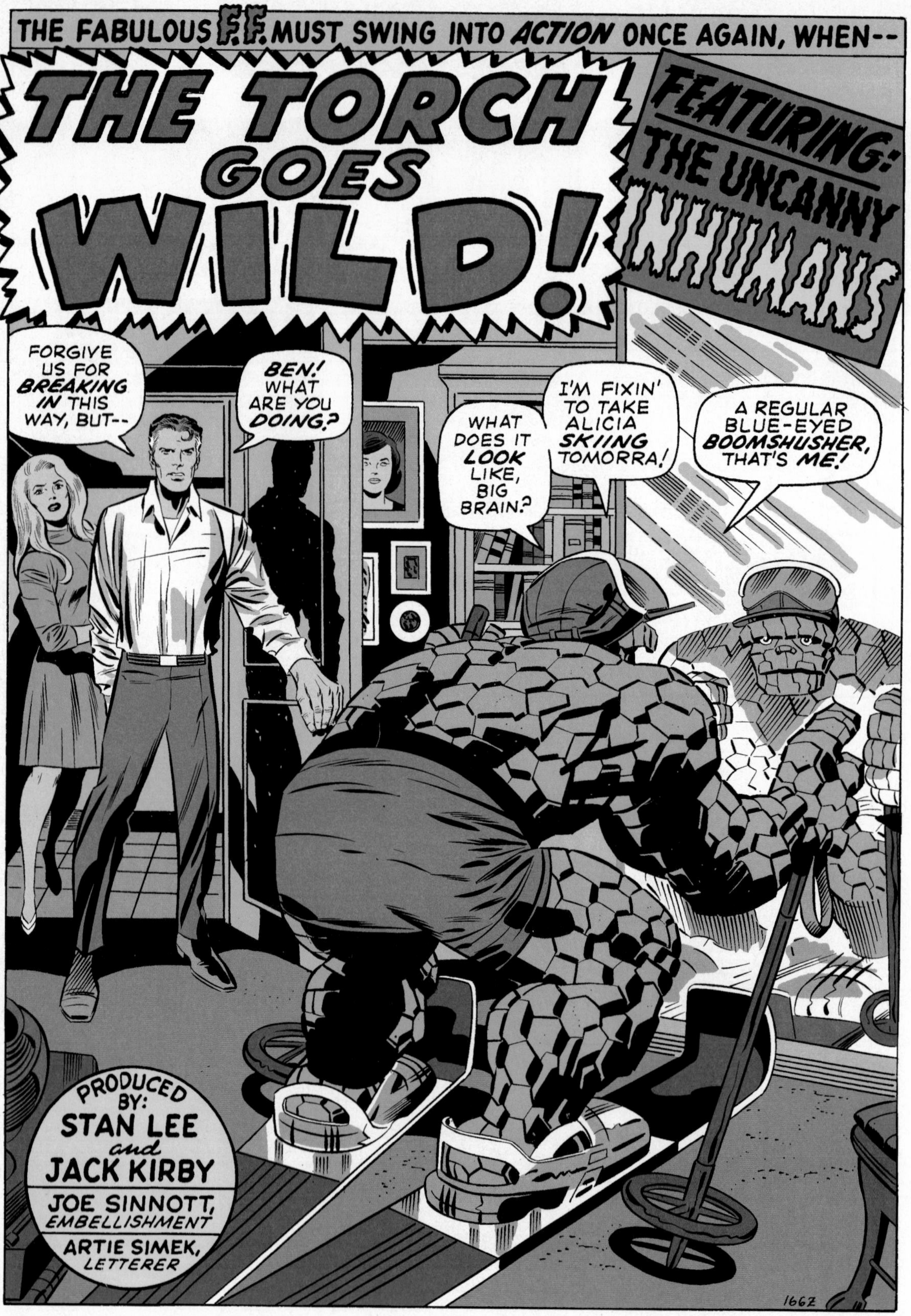
THE FABULOUS F.F. MUST SWING INTO ACTION ONCE AGAIN, WHEN--
THE TORCH GOES WILD!
FEATURING: THE UNCANNY INHUMANS
FORGIVE US FOR BREAKING IN THIS WAY, BUT--
BEN! WHAT ARE YOU DOING?
WHAT DOES IT LOOK LIKE, BIG BRAIN?
I'M FIXIN' TO TAKE ALICIA SKIING TOMORRA!
A REGULAR BLUE-EYED BOOMSHUSHER, THAT'S ME!
PRODUCED BY: STAN LEE and JACK KIRBY
JOE SINNOTT, EMBELLISHMENT
ARTIE SIMEK, LETTERER
1662

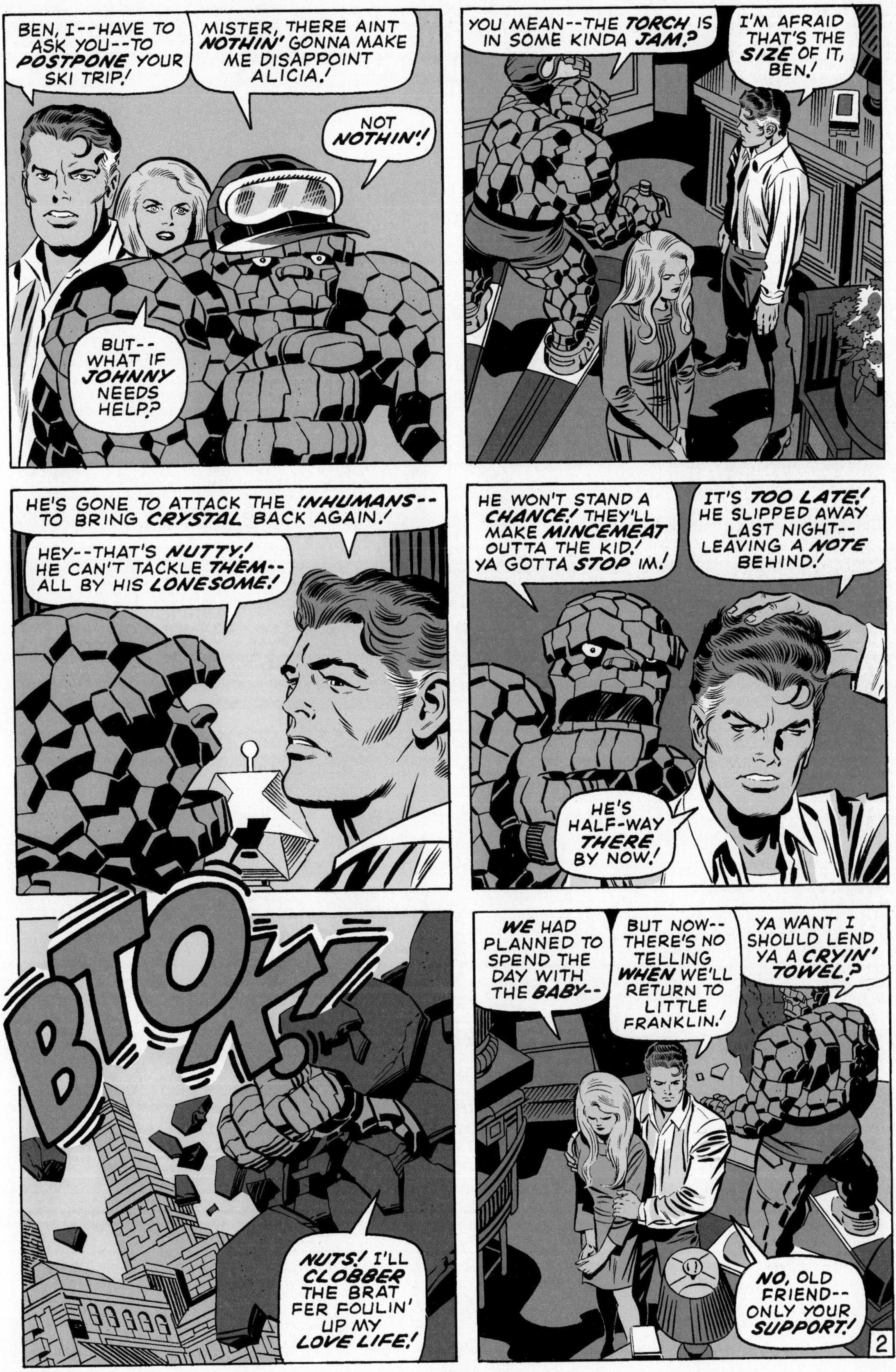

BEN, I--HAVE TO ASK YOU--TO POSTPONE YOUR SKI TRIP!
MISTER, THERE AINT NOTHIN' GONNA MAKE ME DISAPPOINT ALICIA!
NOT NOTHIN'!
BUT--WHAT IF JOHNNY NEEDS HELP?
YOU MEAN--THE TORCH IS IN SOME KINDA JAM?
I'M AFRAID THAT'S THE SIZE OF IT, BEN!
HE'S GONE TO ATTACK THE INHUMANS--TO BRING CRYSTAL BACK AGAIN!
HEY--THAT'S NUTTY! HE CAN'T TACKLE THEM--ALL BY HIS LONESOME!
HE WON'T STAND A CHANCE! THEY'LL MAKE MINCEMEAT OUTTA THE KID! YA GOTTA STOP IM!
IT'S TOO LATE! HE SLIPPED AWAY LAST NIGHT--LEAVING A NOTE BEHIND!
HE'S HALF-WAY THERE BY NOW!
BTOK!
NUTS! I'LL CLOBBER THE BRAT FER FOULIN' UP MY LOVE LIFE!
WE HAD PLANNED TO SPEND THE DAY WITH THE BABY--
BUT NOW--THERE'S NO TELLING WHEN WE'LL RETURN TO LITTLE FRANKLIN!
YA WANT I SHOULD LEND YA A CRYIN' TOWEL?
NO, OLD FRIEND--ONLY YOUR SUPPORT!
2

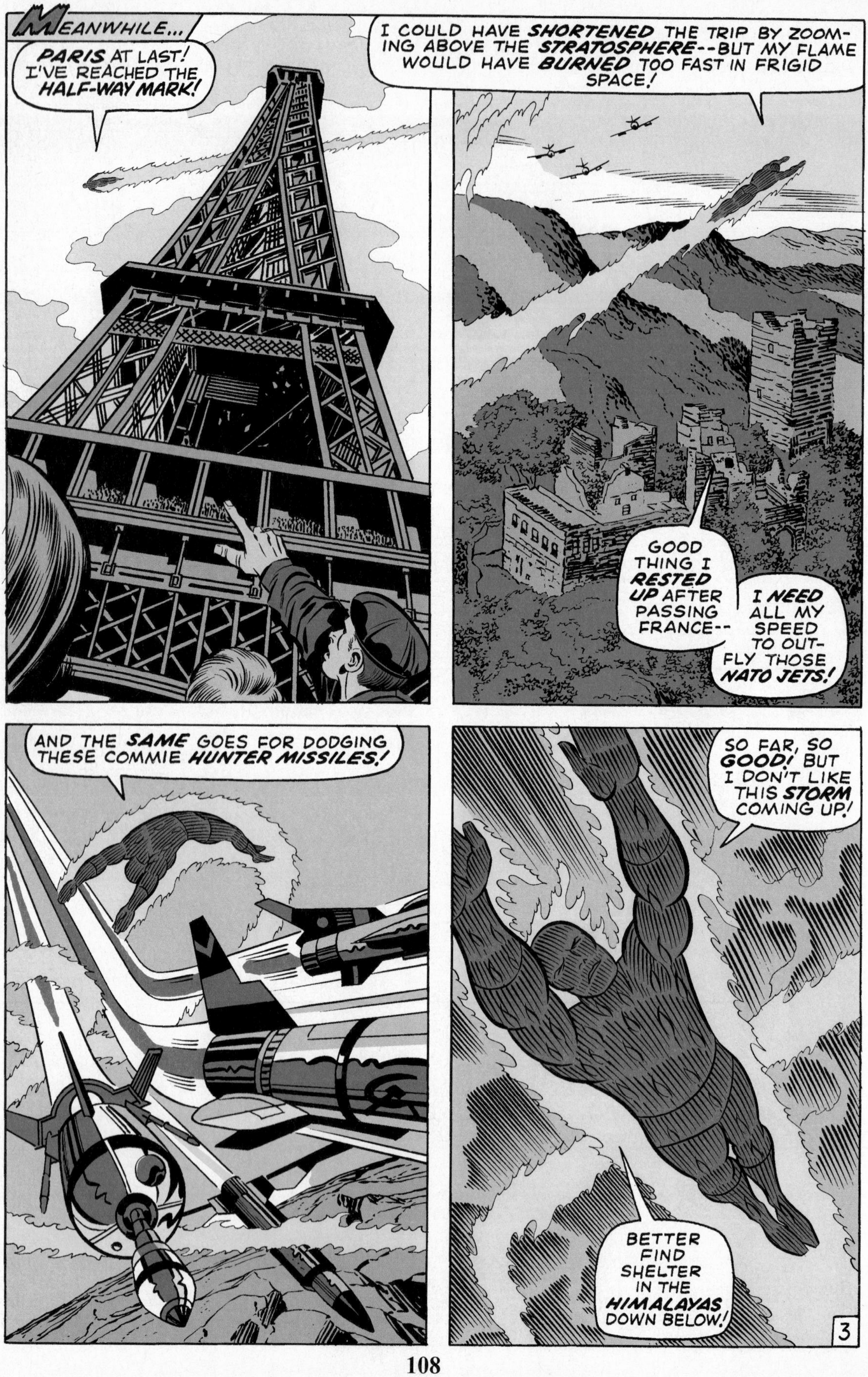
MEANWHILE...
PARIS AT LAST! I'VE REACHED THE HALF-WAY MARK!
I COULD HAVE SHORTENED THE TRIP BY ZOOMING ABOVE THE STRATOSPHERE--BUT MY FLAME WOULD HAVE BURNED TOO FAST IN FRIGID SPACE!
GOOD THING I RESTED UP AFTER PASSING FRANCE--
I NEED ALL MY SPEED TO OUT-FLY THOSE NATO JETS!
AND THE SAME GOES FOR DODGING THESE COMMIE HUNTER MISSILES!
SO FAR, SO GOOD! BUT I DON'T LIKE THIS STORM COMING UP!
BETTER FIND SHELTER IN THE HIMALAYAS DOWN BELOW!
3

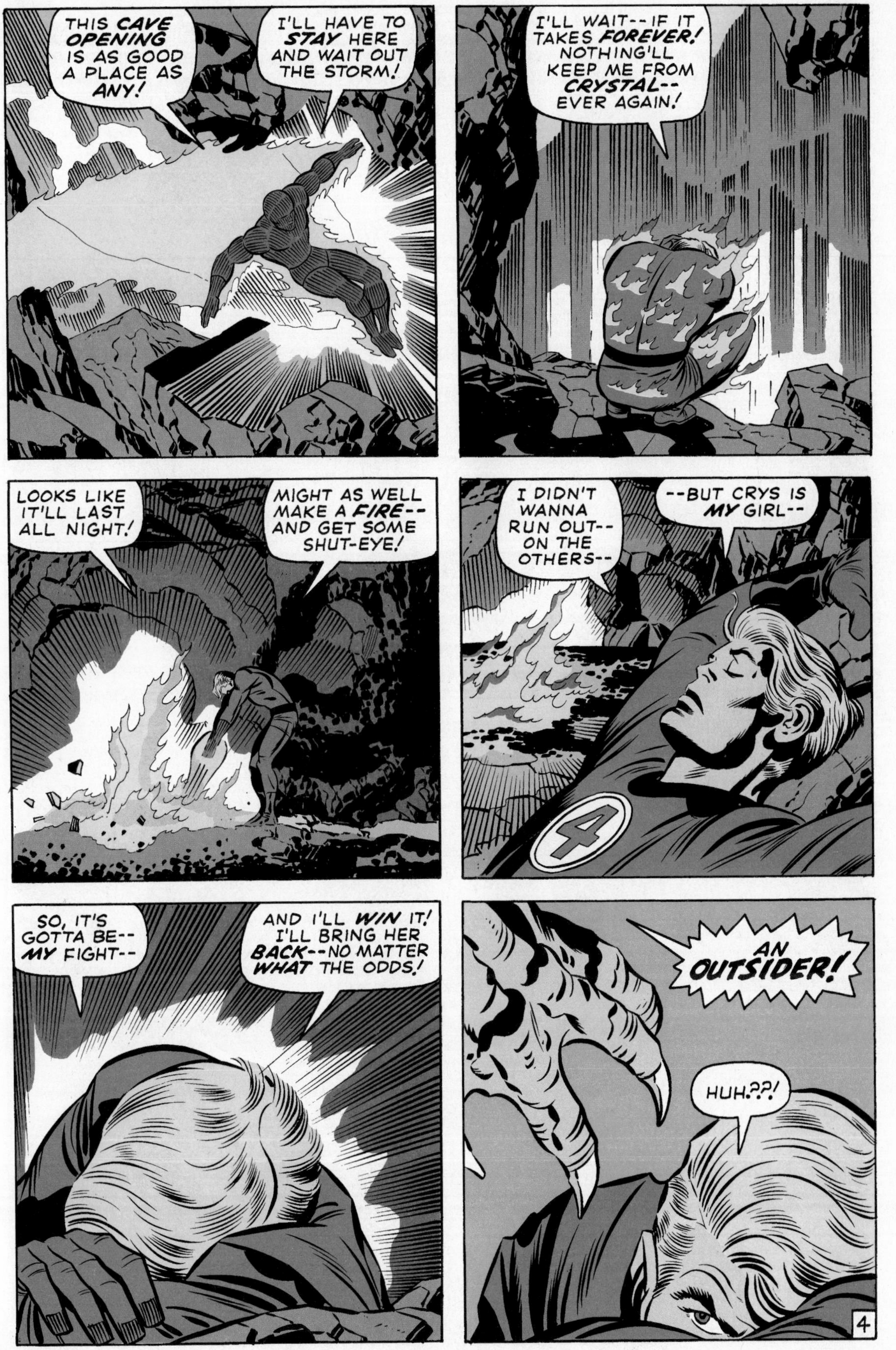
THIS CAVE OPENING IS AS GOOD A PLACE AS ANY!
I'LL HAVE TO STAY HERE AND WAIT OUT THE STORM!
I'LL WAIT--IF IT TAKES FOREVER! NOTHING'LL KEEP ME FROM CRYSTAL--EVER AGAIN!
LOOKS LIKE IT'LL LAST ALL NIGHT!
MIGHT AS WELL MAKE A FIRE--AND GET SOME SHUT-EYE!
I DIDN'T WANNA RUN OUT--ON THE OTHERS--
--BUT CRYS IS MY GIRL--
SO, IT'S GOTTA BE--MY FIGHT--
AND I'LL WIN IT! I'LL BRING HER BACK--NO MATTER WHAT THE ODDS!
AN OUTSIDER!
HUH.??!
4

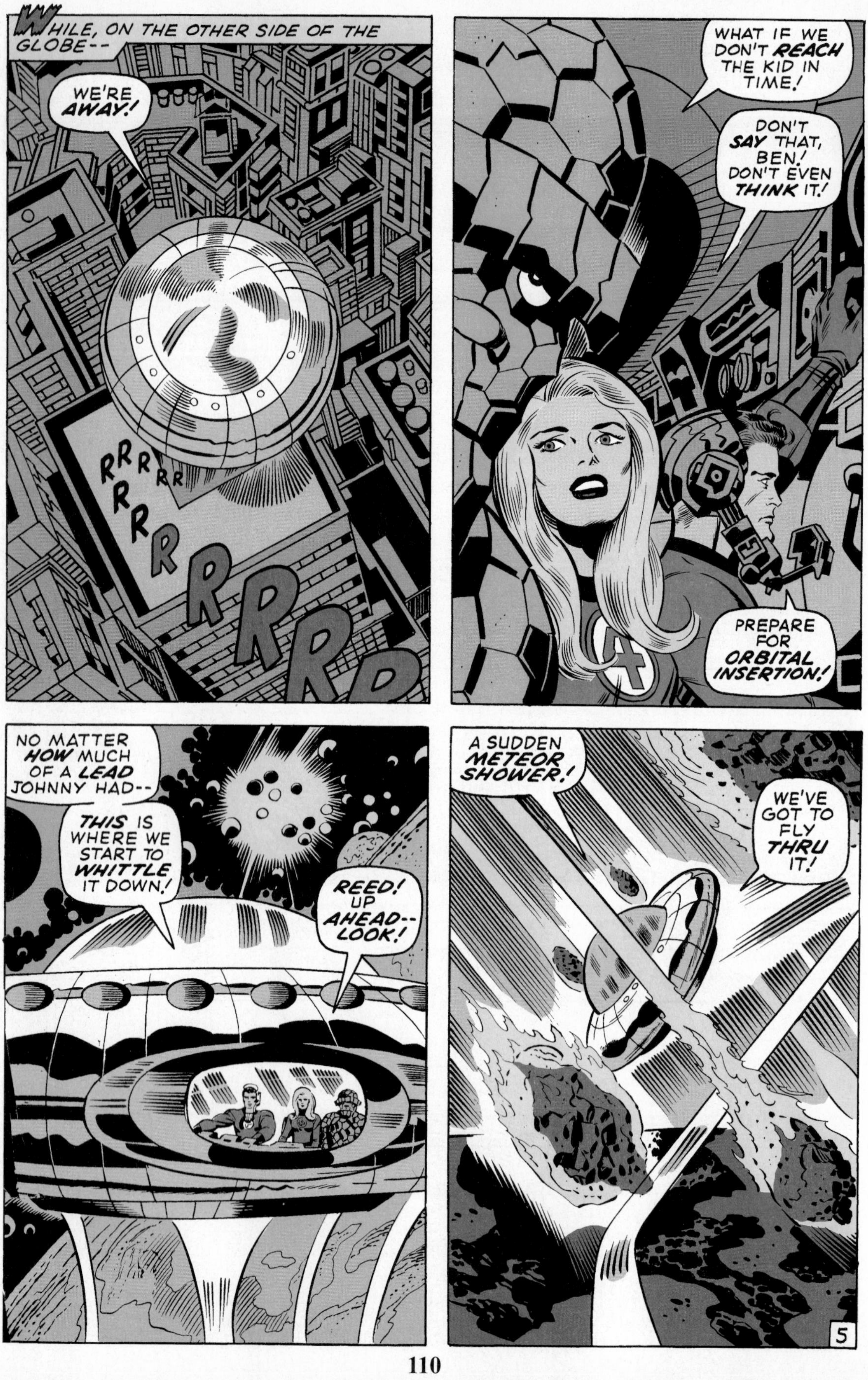
WHILE, ON THE OTHER SIDE OF THE GLOBE--
WE'RE AWAY!
RRRRRRRRRRRRR
WHAT IF WE DON'T REACH THE KID IN TIME!
DON'T SAY THAT, BEN! DON'T EVEN THINK IT!
PREPARE FOR ORBITAL INSERTION!
NO MATTER HOW MUCH OF A LEAD JOHNNY HAD--
THIS IS WHERE WE START TO WHITTLE IT DOWN!
REED! UP AHEAD-- LOOK!
A SUDDEN METEOR SHOWER!
WE'VE GOT TO FLY THRU IT!
5

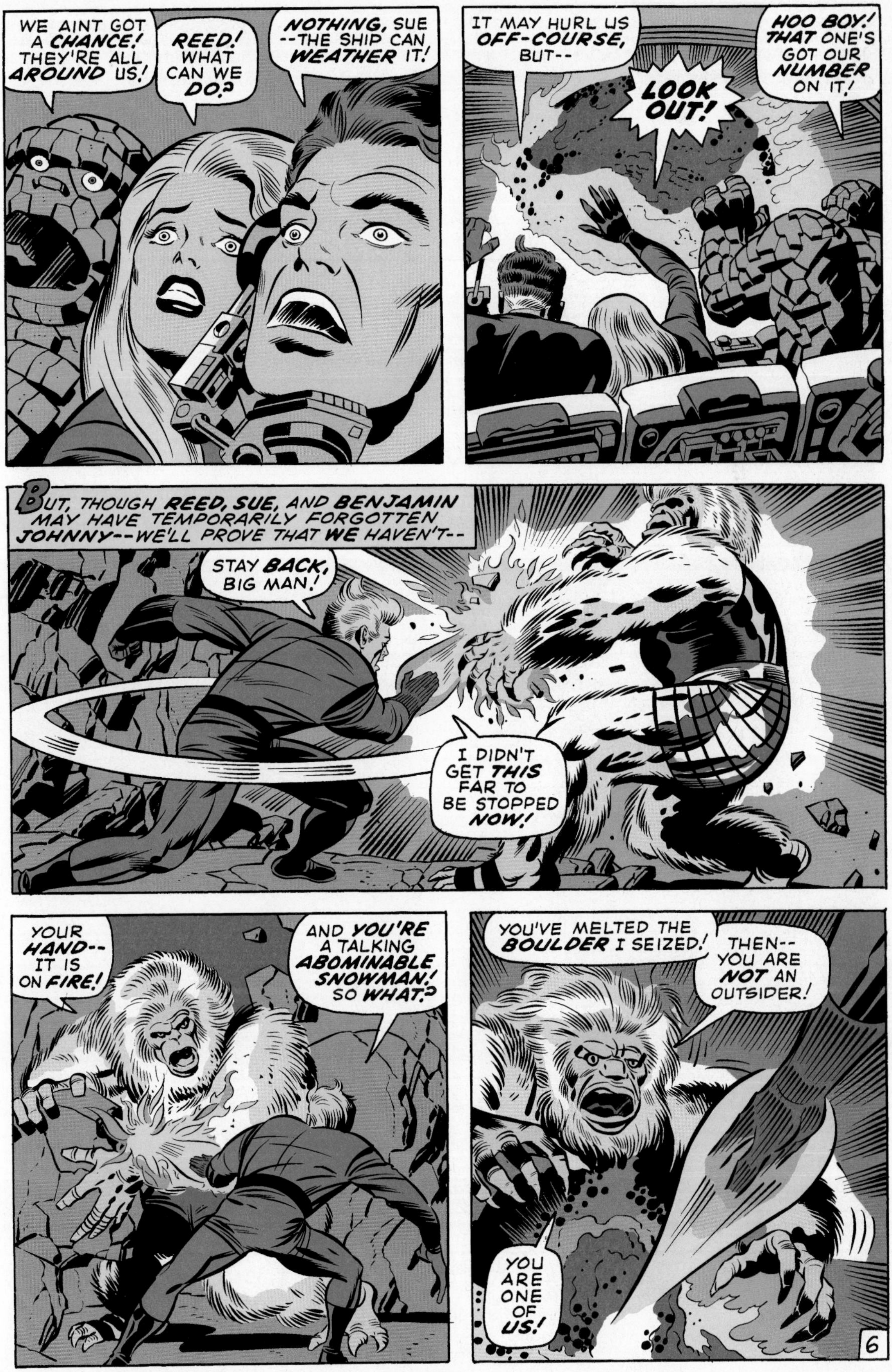

WE AINT GOT A CHANCE! THEY'RE ALL AROUND US!
REED! WHAT CAN WE DO?
NOTHING, SUE --THE SHIP CAN WEATHER IT!
IT MAY HURL US OFF-COURSE, BUT--
LOOK OUT!
HOO BOY! THAT ONE'S GOT OUR NUMBER ON IT!
BUT, THOUGH REED, SUE, AND BENJAMIN MAY HAVE TEMPORARILY FORGOTTEN JOHNNY--WE'LL PROVE THAT WE HAVEN'T--
STAY BACK, BIG MAN!
I DIDN'T GET THIS FAR TO BE STOPPED NOW!
YOUR HAND-- IT IS ON FIRE!
AND YOU'RE A TALKING ABOMINABLE SNOWMAN! SO WHAT?
YOU'VE MELTED THE BOULDER I SEIZED!
THEN-- YOU ARE NOT AN OUTSIDER!
YOU ARE ONE OF US!
6

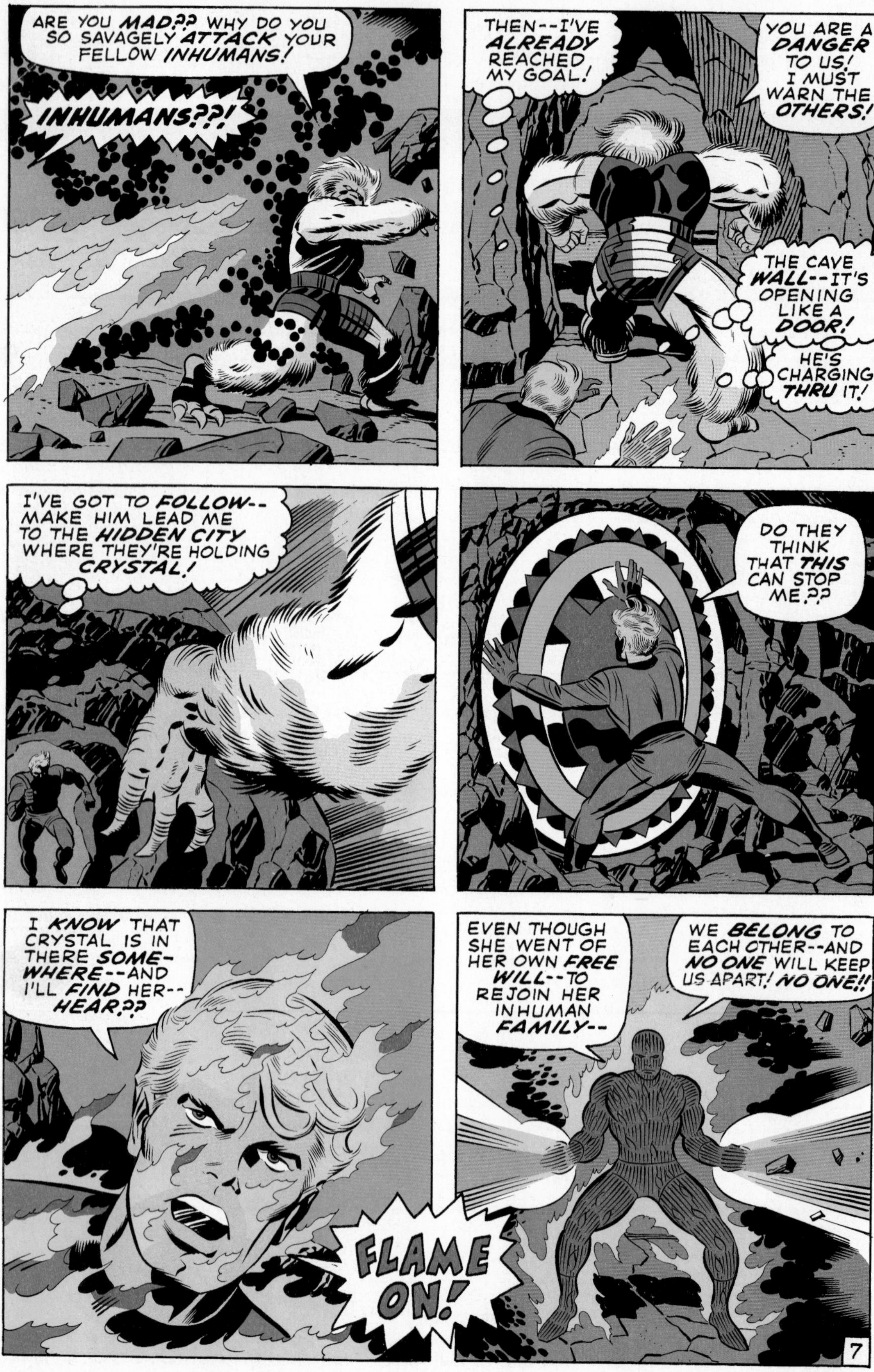
ARE YOU MAD?? WHY DO YOU SO SAVAGELY ATTACK YOUR FELLOW INHUMANS!
INHUMANS??!
THEN--I'VE ALREADY REACHED MY GOAL!
YOU ARE A DANGER TO US! I MUST WARN THE OTHERS!
THE CAVE WALL--IT'S OPENING LIKE A DOOR!
HE'S CHARGING THRU IT!
I'VE GOT TO FOLLOW--MAKE HIM LEAD ME TO THE HIDDEN CITY WHERE THEY'RE HOLDING CRYSTAL!
DO THEY THINK THAT THIS CAN STOP ME??
I KNOW THAT CRYSTAL IS IN THERE SOME-WHERE--AND I'LL FIND HER--HEAR??
FLAME ON!
EVEN THOUGH SHE WENT OF HER OWN FREE WILL--TO REJOIN HER INHUMAN FAMILY--
WE BELONG TO EACH OTHER--AND NO ONE WILL KEEP US APART! NO ONE!!
7

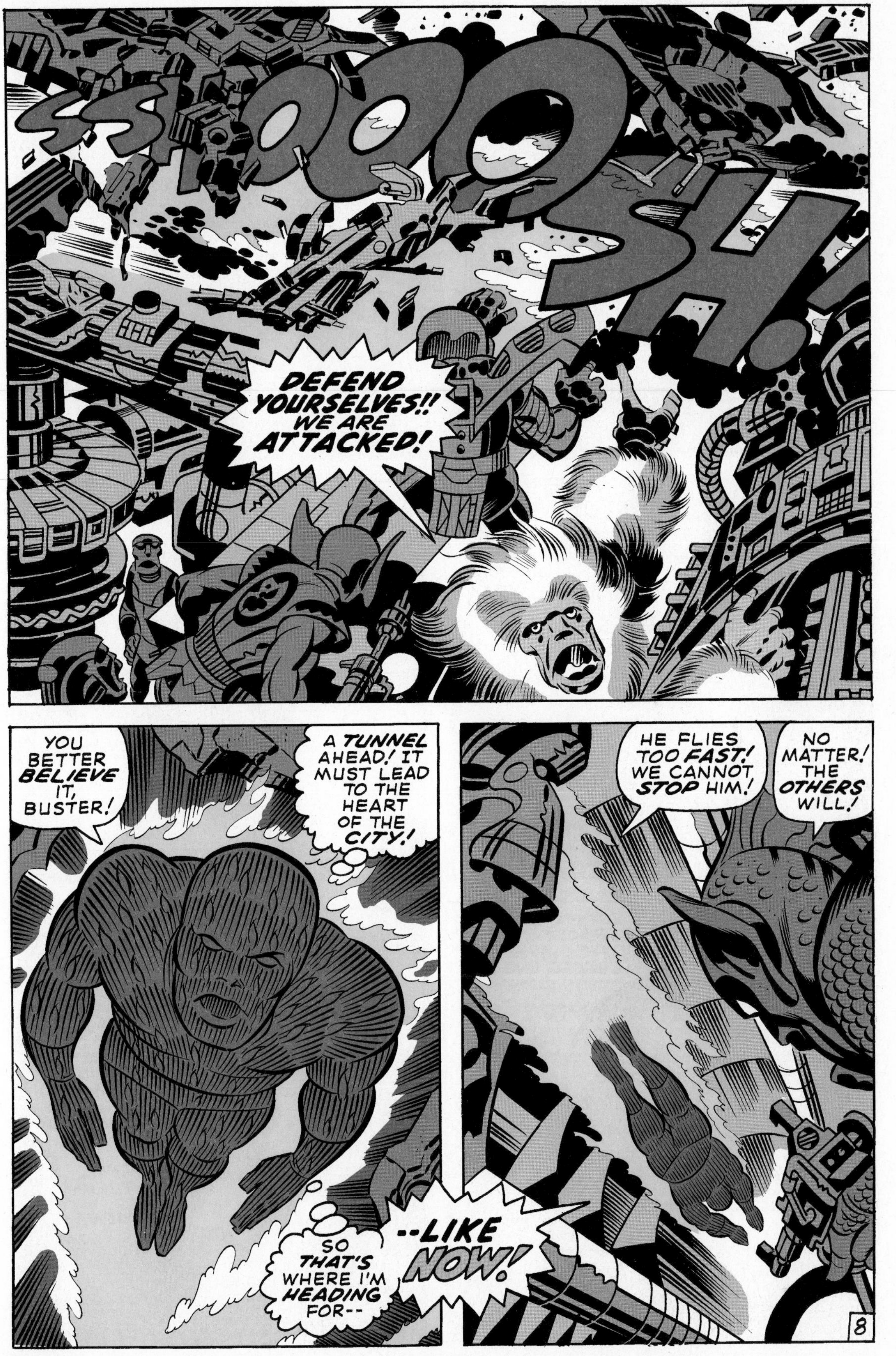
SSHOOOOSH!!
DEFEND YOURSELVES!! WE ARE ATTACKED!
YOU BETTER BELIEVE IT, BUSTER!
A TUNNEL AHEAD! IT MUST LEAD TO THE HEART OF THE CITY!
HE FLIES TOO FAST! WE CANNOT STOP HIM!
NO MATTER! THE OTHERS WILL!
SO THAT'S WHERE I'M HEADING FOR--
--LIKE NOW!
8

MADE IT! BUT THEY'VE SOUNDED THE ALARM!

THEY'RE COMING AFTER ME--FROM EVERY-WHERE!

HE'S--TRYING TO--SMOTHER MY FLAME--!

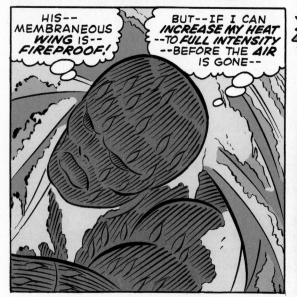

HIS--MEMBRANEOUS WING IS--FIREPROOF!

BUT--IF I CAN INCREASE MY HEAT --TO FULL INTENSITY --BEFORE THE AIR IS GONE--

IT WORKED!

FIRE-PROOF OR NOT, MY FLAME WEAKENED HIM!

NOW IT'S MY TURN-- TO ATTACK!

9

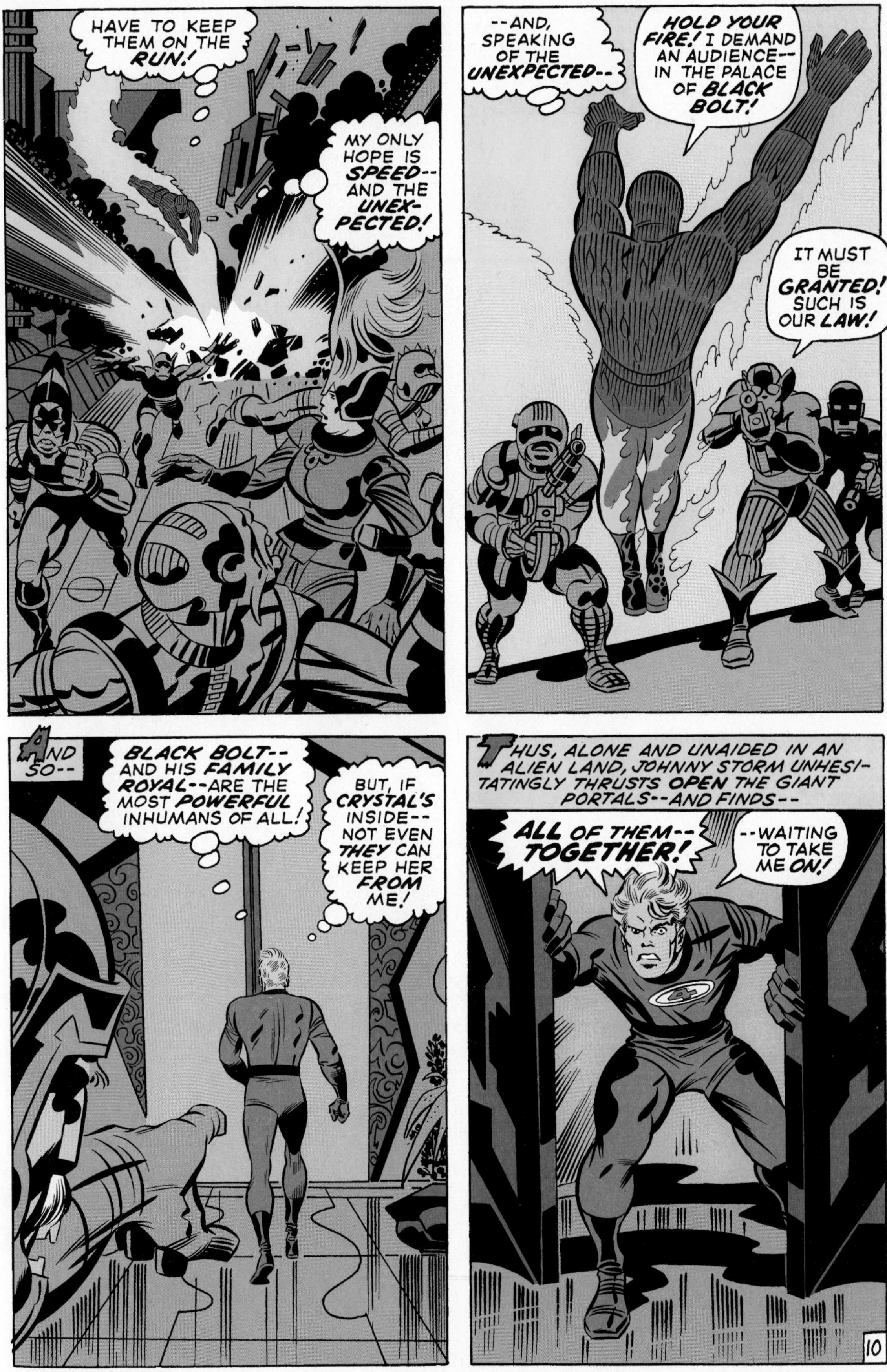
HAVE TO KEEP THEM ON THE RUN!
MY ONLY HOPE IS SPEED-- AND THE UNEXPECTED!
--AND, SPEAKING OF THE UNEXPECTED--
HOLD YOUR FIRE! I DEMAND AN AUDIENCE-- IN THE PALACE OF BLACK BOLT!
IT MUST BE GRANTED! SUCH IS OUR LAW!
AND SO--
BLACK BOLT-- AND HIS FAMILY ROYAL--ARE THE MOST POWERFUL INHUMANS OF ALL!
BUT, IF CRYSTAL'S INSIDE-- NOT EVEN THEY CAN KEEP HER FROM ME!
THUS, ALONE AND UNAIDED IN AN ALIEN LAND, JOHNNY STORM UNHESITATINGLY THRUSTS OPEN THE GIANT PORTALS--AND FINDS--
ALL OF THEM-- TOGETHER!
--WAITING TO TAKE ME ON!
10

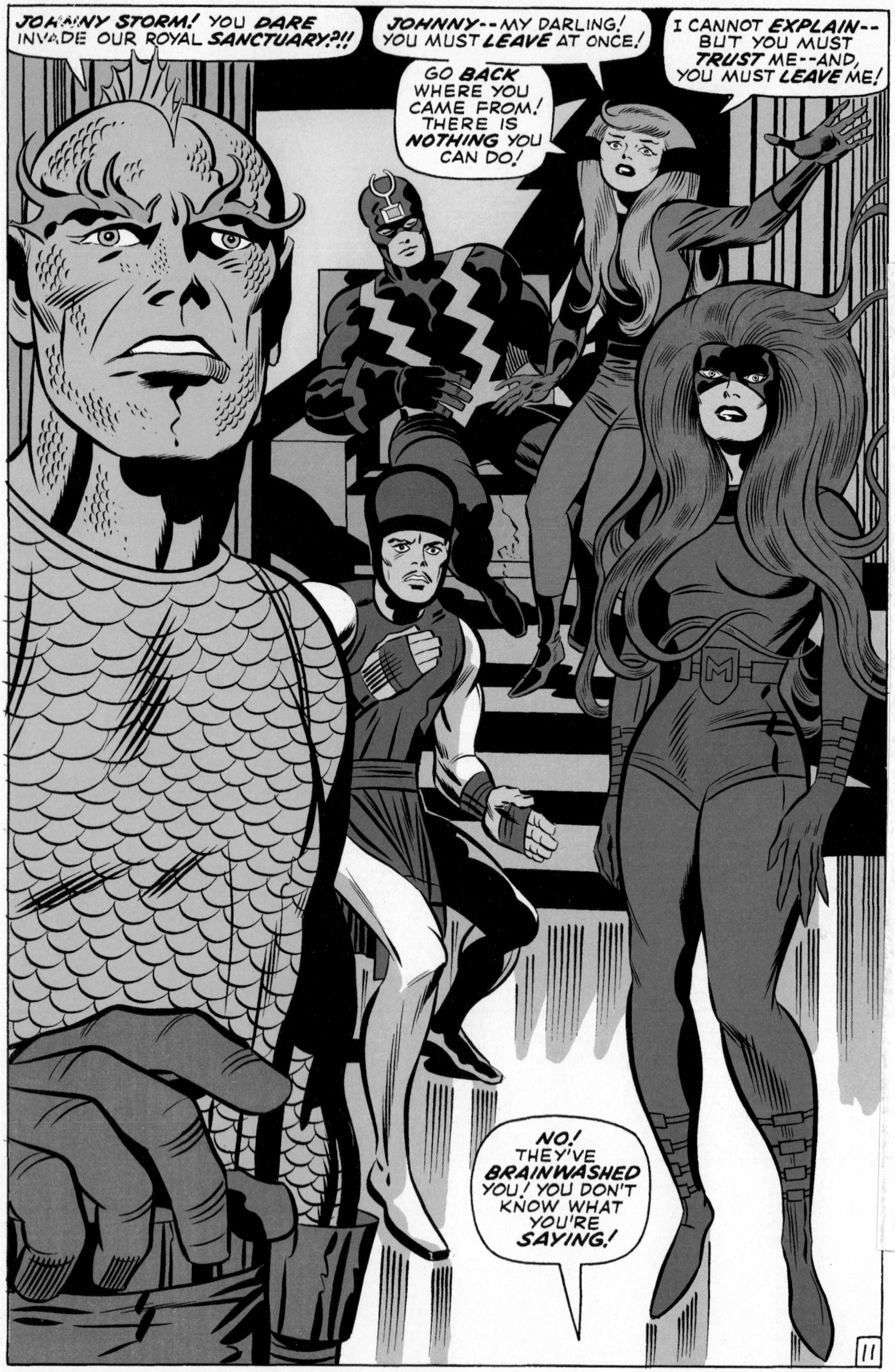
JOHNNY STORM! YOU DARE INVADE OUR ROYAL SANCTUARY?!!
JOHNNY--MY DARLING! YOU MUST LEAVE AT ONCE!
GO BACK WHERE YOU CAME FROM! THERE IS NOTHING YOU CAN DO!
I CANNOT EXPLAIN--BUT YOU MUST TRUST ME--AND, YOU MUST LEAVE ME!
NO! THEY'VE BRAINWASHED YOU! YOU DON'T KNOW WHAT YOU'RE SAYING!
11

STAND ASIDE! DON'T FORCE ME TO *FLAME ON!*

HALT! NONE MAY THREATEN THE THRONE OF *BLACK BOLT!*

TO *BLAZES* WITH BLACK BOLT--*AND* HIS THRONE! IT'S *CRYSTAL* I WANT.!!

NO, JOHNNY--*NO!* YOU DON'T KNOW WHAT WHAT YOU'RE *DOING!!*

BETTER LUCK *NEXT* TIME, KARNAK!

I'VE BEEN TAUGHT BY *EXPERTS!*

ZZZZT!

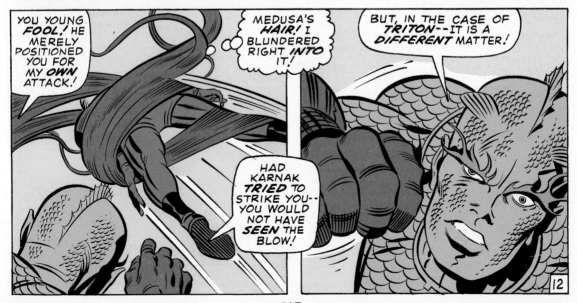

YOU YOUNG *FOOL!* HE MERELY POSITIONED YOU FOR MY *OWN* ATTACK!

MEDUSA'S *HAIR!* I BLUNDERED RIGHT *INTO* IT!

BUT, IN THE CASE OF *TRITON*--IT IS A *DIFFERENT* MATTER!

HAD KARNAK *TRIED* TO STRIKE YOU-- YOU WOULD NOT HAVE *SEEN* THE BLOW!

12

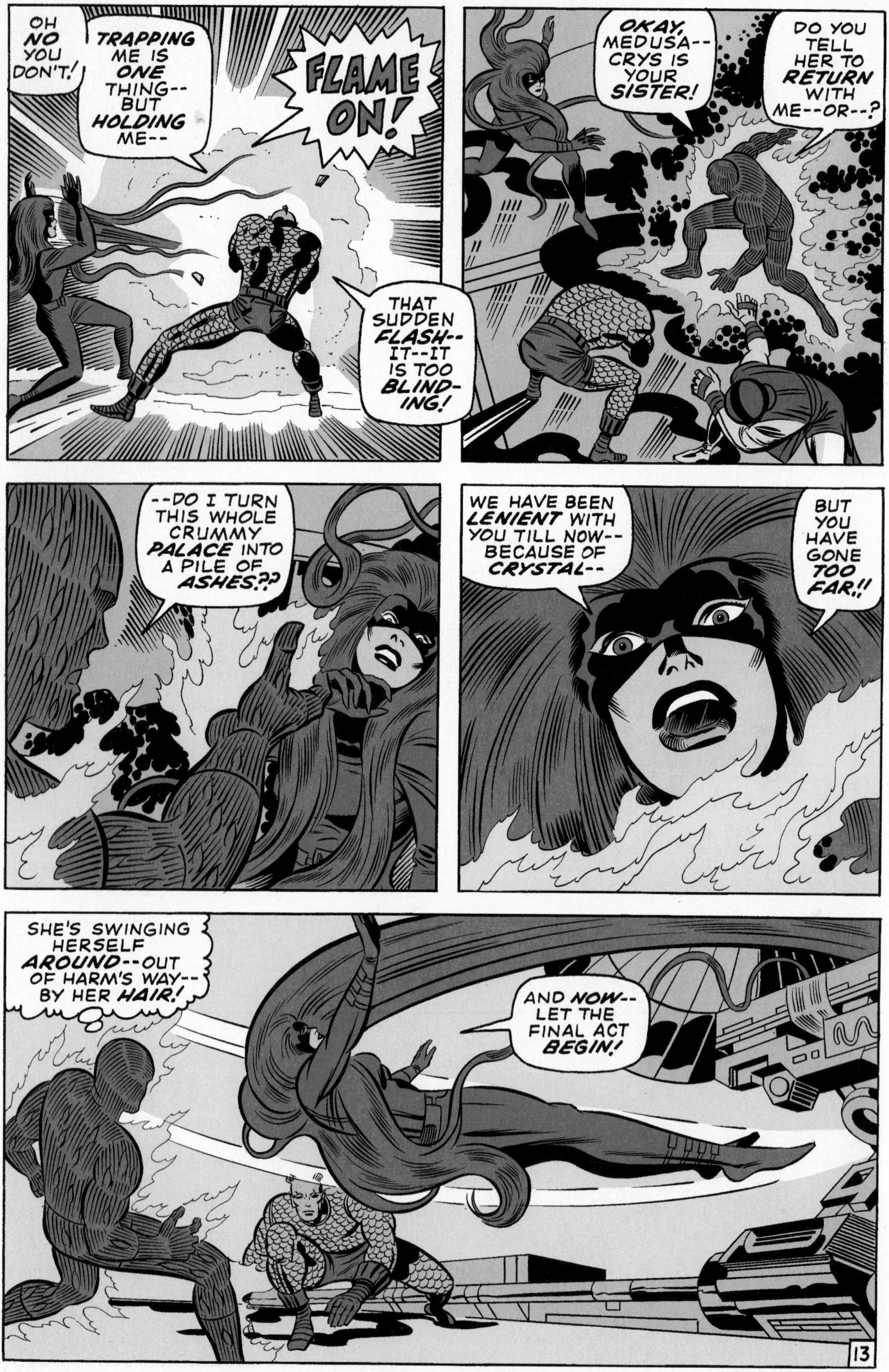
OH NO YOU DON'T!
TRAPPING ME IS ONE THING-- BUT HOLDING ME--
FLAME ON!
THAT SUDDEN FLASH-- IT--IT IS TOO BLINDING!
OKAY, MEDUSA-- CRYS IS YOUR SISTER!
DO YOU TELL HER TO RETURN WITH ME--OR--?
--DO I TURN THIS WHOLE CRUMMY PALACE INTO A PILE OF ASHES??
WE HAVE BEEN LENIENT WITH YOU TILL NOW-- BECAUSE OF CRYSTAL--
BUT YOU HAVE GONE TOO FAR!!
SHE'S SWINGING HERSELF AROUND--OUT OF HARM'S WAY-- BY HER HAIR!
AND NOW-- LET THE FINAL ACT BEGIN!
13

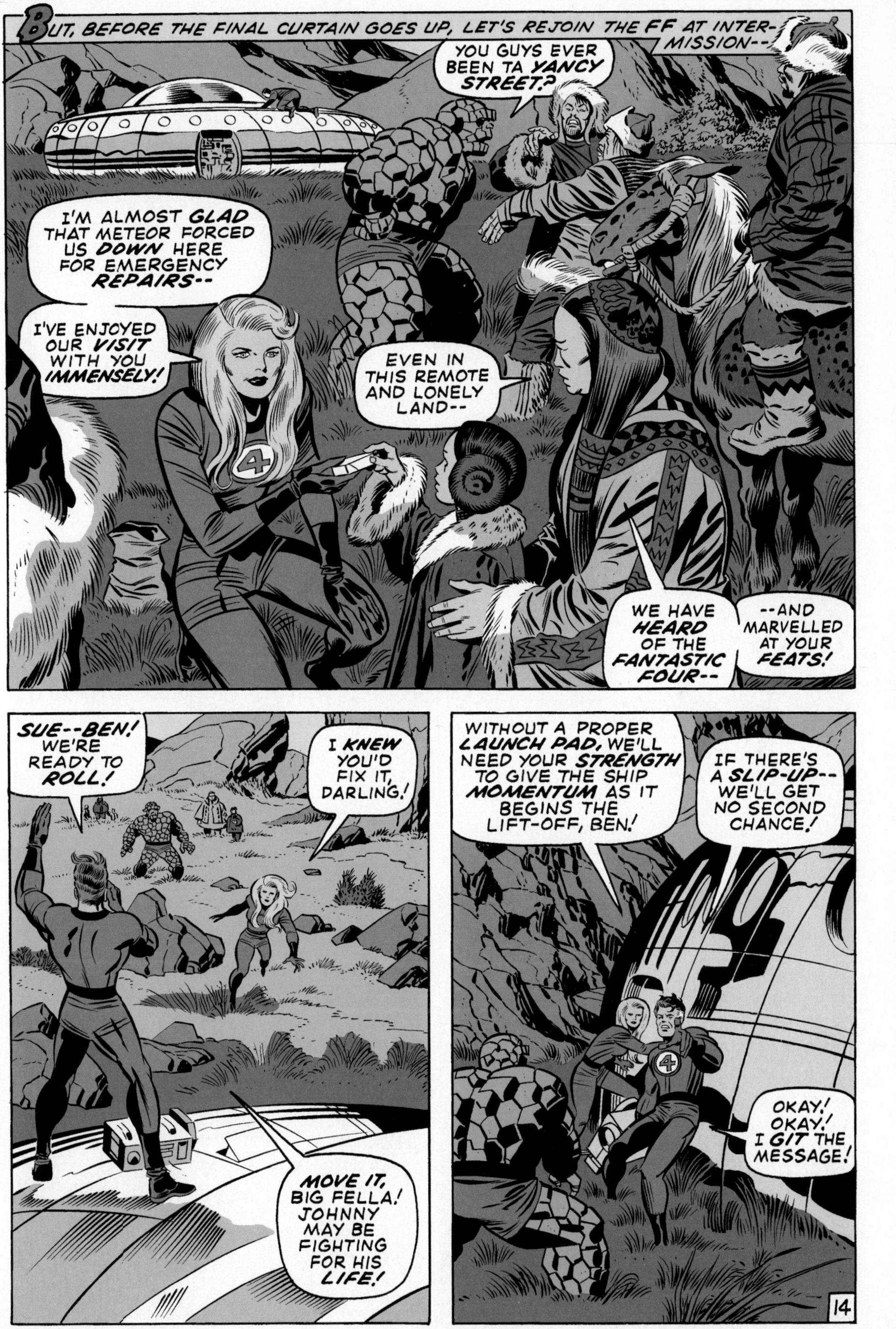

BUT, BEFORE THE FINAL CURTAIN GOES UP, LET'S REJOIN THE FF AT INTER-MISSION--
YOU GUYS EVER BEEN TA YANCY STREET?
I'M ALMOST GLAD THAT METEOR FORCED US DOWN HERE FOR EMERGENCY REPAIRS--
I'VE ENJOYED OUR VISIT WITH YOU IMMENSELY!
EVEN IN THIS REMOTE AND LONELY LAND--
WE HAVE HEARD OF THE FANTASTIC FOUR--
--AND MARVELLED AT YOUR FEATS!
SUE--BEN! WE'RE READY TO ROLL!
I KNEW YOU'D FIX IT, DARLING!
MOVE IT, BIG FELLA! JOHNNY MAY BE FIGHTING FOR HIS LIFE!
WITHOUT A PROPER LAUNCH PAD, WE'LL NEED YOUR STRENGTH TO GIVE THE SHIP MOMENTUM AS IT BEGINS THE LIFT-OFF, BEN!
IF THERE'S A SLIP-UP-- WE'LL GET NO SECOND CHANCE!
OKAY! OKAY! I GIT THE MESSAGE!
14

GOOD OLD BEN! FOR ALL HIS GRUMBLING, HE'S NEVER *FAILED* US!

BUT WILL HE BE ABLE TO DO WHAT'S NEEDED *NOW?*

JUST YOU *WATCH* HIM, HONEY!

OKAY, BEN-- THIS IS *IT!*

HEY! I JUST THOUGHT--

WHAT ABOUT *ME?*

WE WOULDN'T *FORGET* YOU, OLD FRIEND!

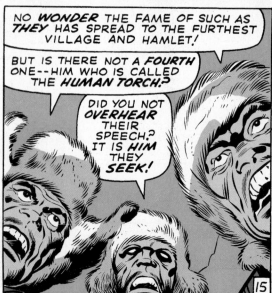

NO *WONDER* THE FAME OF SUCH AS *THEY* HAS SPREAD TO THE FURTHEST VILLAGE AND HAMLET!

BUT IS THERE NOT A *FOURTH* ONE--HIM WHO IS CALLED THE *HUMAN TORCH?*

DID YOU NOT *OVERHEAR* THEIR SPEECH? IT IS *HIM* THEY *SEEK!*

15

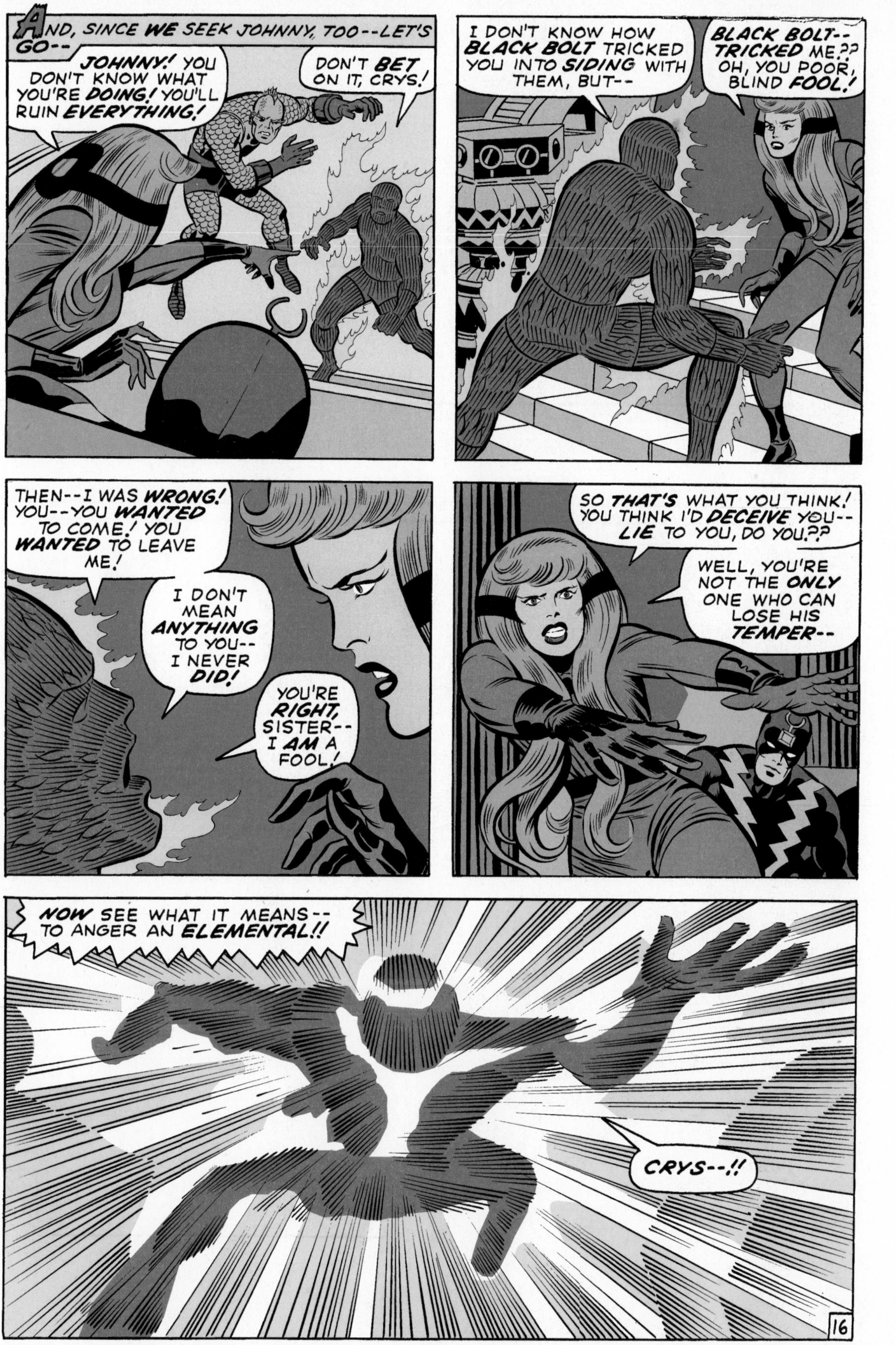
AND, SINCE WE SEEK JOHNNY, TOO--LET'S GO--
JOHNNY! YOU DON'T KNOW WHAT YOU'RE DOING! YOU'LL RUIN EVERYTHING!
DON'T BET ON IT, CRYS!
I DON'T KNOW HOW BLACK BOLT TRICKED YOU INTO SIDING WITH THEM, BUT--
BLACK BOLT--TRICKED ME?? OH, YOU POOR, BLIND FOOL!
THEN--I WAS WRONG! YOU--YOU WANTED TO COME! YOU WANTED TO LEAVE ME!
I DON'T MEAN ANYTHING TO YOU--I NEVER DID!
YOU'RE RIGHT, SISTER--I AM A FOOL!
SO THAT'S WHAT YOU THINK! YOU THINK I'D DECEIVE YOU--LIE TO YOU, DO YOU??
WELL, YOU'RE NOT THE ONLY ONE WHO CAN LOSE HIS TEMPER--
NOW SEE WHAT IT MEANS--TO ANGER AN ELEMENTAL!!
CRYS--!!
16

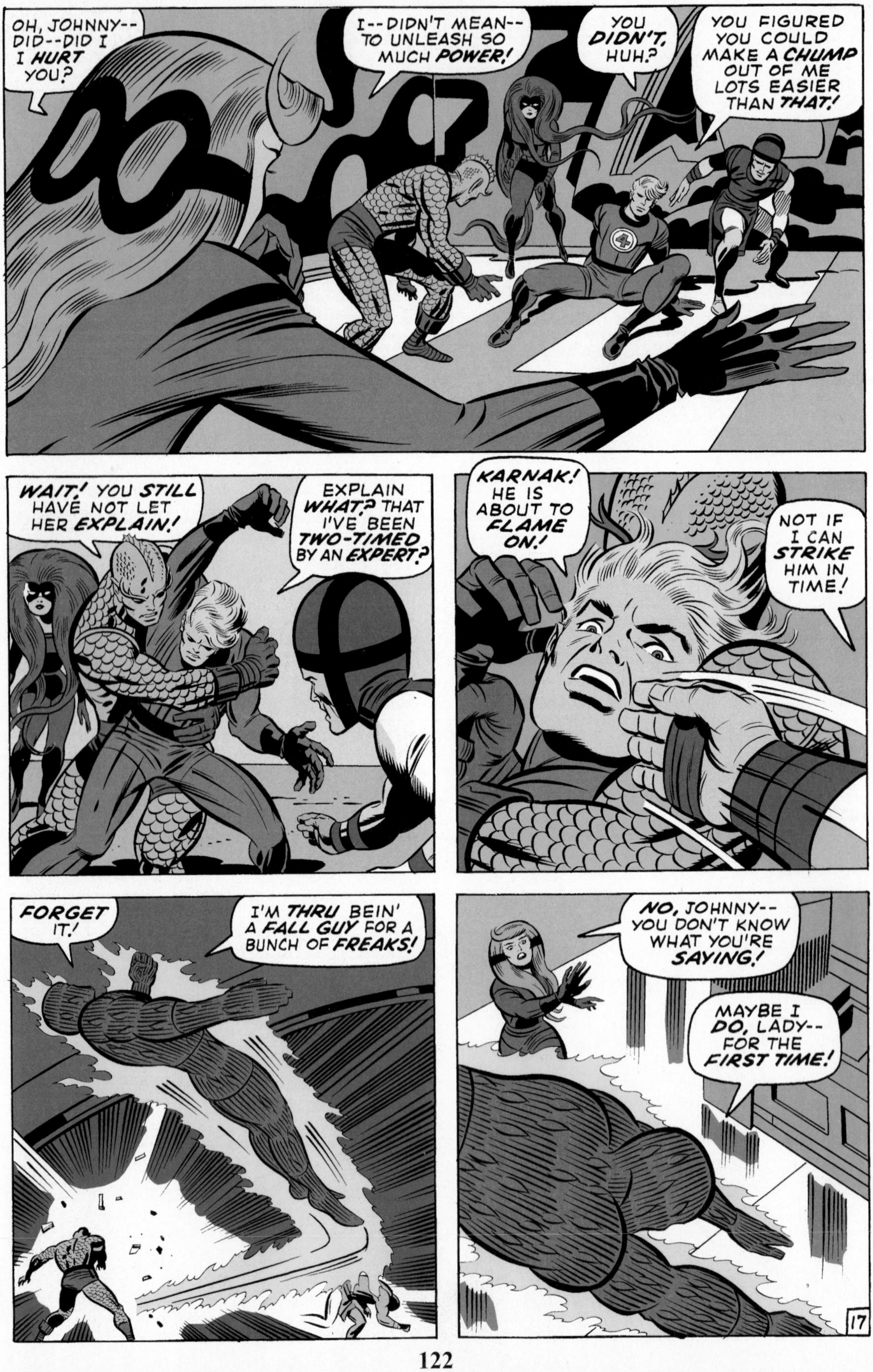
OH, JOHNNY-- DID--DID I HURT YOU?
I--DIDN'T MEAN-- TO UNLEASH SO MUCH POWER!
YOU DIDN'T, HUH?
YOU FIGURED YOU COULD MAKE A CHUMP OUT OF ME LOTS EASIER THAN THAT!
WAIT! YOU STILL HAVE NOT LET HER EXPLAIN!
EXPLAIN WHAT? THAT I'VE BEEN TWO-TIMED BY AN EXPERT?
KARNAK! HE IS ABOUT TO FLAME ON!
NOT IF I CAN STRIKE HIM IN TIME!
FORGET IT!
I'M THRU BEIN' A FALL GUY FOR A BUNCH OF FREAKS!
NO, JOHNNY-- YOU DON'T KNOW WHAT YOU'RE SAYING!
MAYBE I DO, LADY-- FOR THE FIRST TIME!
17

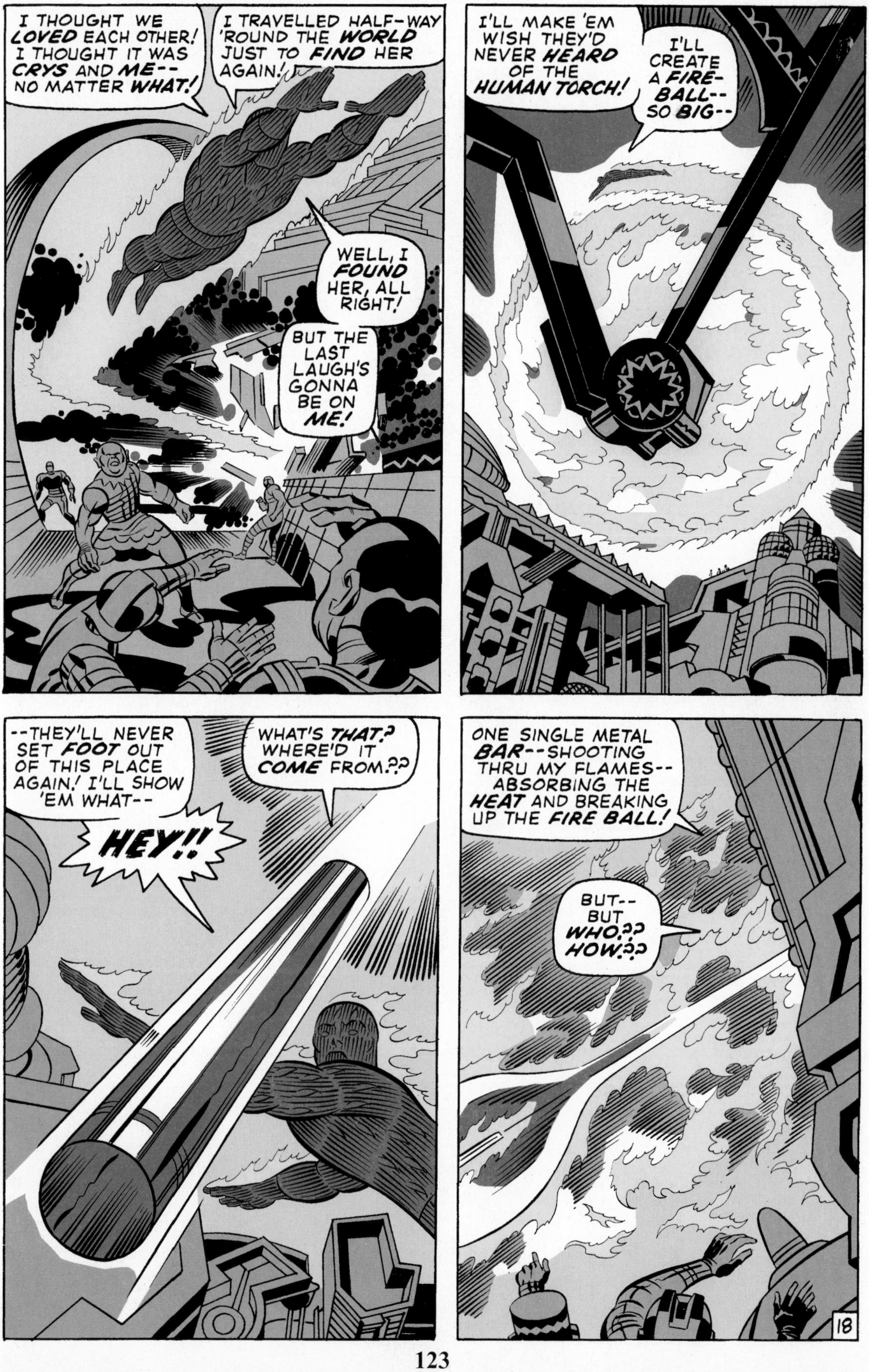
I THOUGHT WE LOVED EACH OTHER! I THOUGHT IT WAS CRYS AND ME-- NO MATTER WHAT!
I TRAVELLED HALF-WAY 'ROUND THE WORLD JUST TO FIND HER AGAIN!
WELL, I FOUND HER, ALL RIGHT!
BUT THE LAST LAUGH'S GONNA BE ON ME!
I'LL MAKE 'EM WISH THEY'D NEVER HEARD OF THE HUMAN TORCH!
I'LL CREATE A FIRE-BALL-- SO BIG--
--THEY'LL NEVER SET FOOT OUT OF THIS PLACE AGAIN! I'LL SHOW 'EM WHAT--
HEY!!
WHAT'S THAT?? WHERE'D IT COME FROM???
ONE SINGLE METAL BAR--SHOOTING THRU MY FLAMES-- ABSORBING THE HEAT AND BREAKING UP THE FIRE BALL!
BUT-- BUT WHO?? HOW???
18

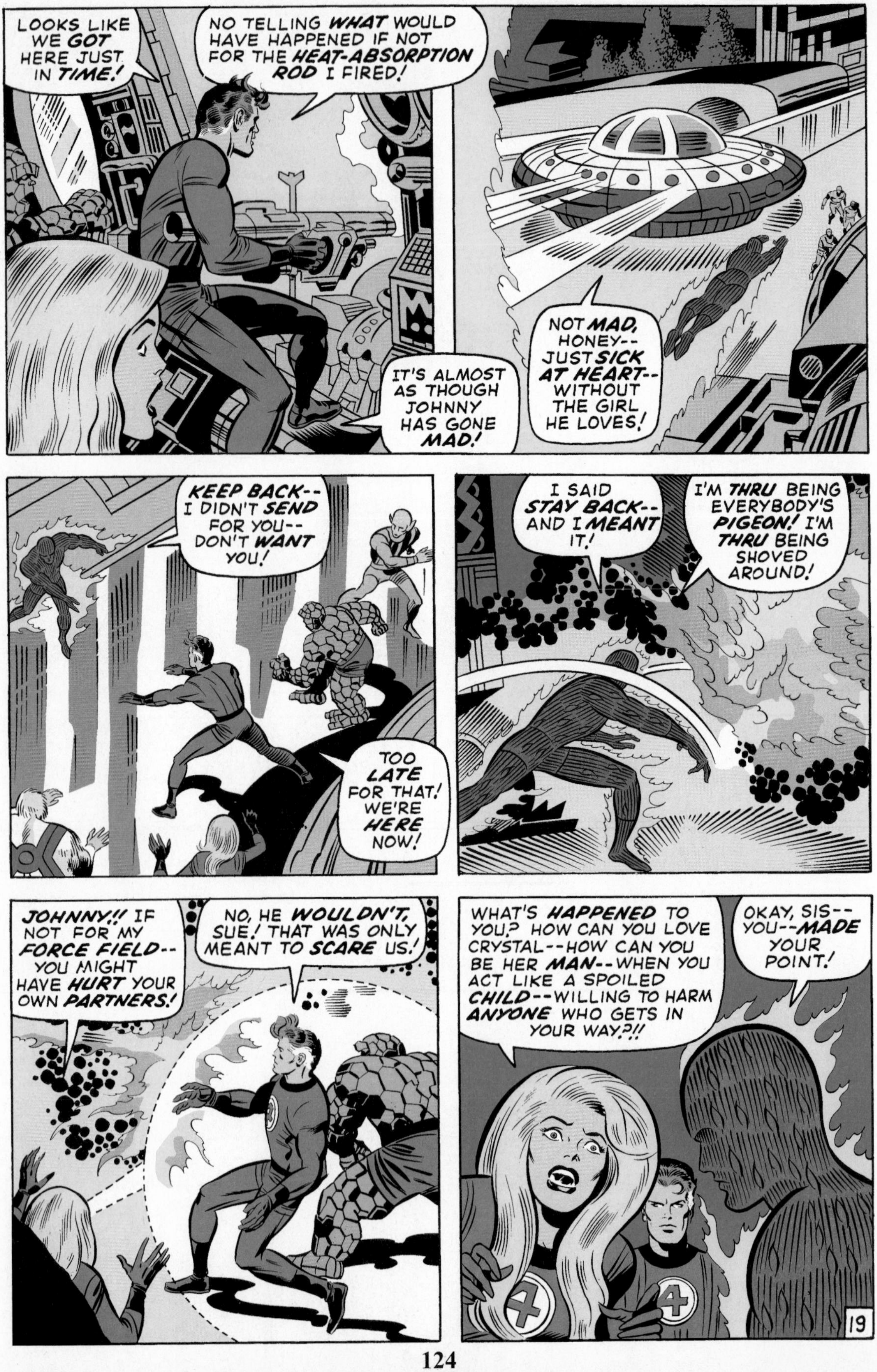
LOOKS LIKE WE GOT HERE JUST IN TIME!
NO TELLING WHAT WOULD HAVE HAPPENED IF NOT FOR THE HEAT-ABSORPTION ROD I FIRED!
IT'S ALMOST AS THOUGH JOHNNY HAS GONE MAD!
NOT MAD, HONEY-- JUST SICK AT HEART-- WITHOUT THE GIRL HE LOVES!
KEEP BACK-- I DIDN'T SEND FOR YOU-- DON'T WANT YOU!
TOO LATE FOR THAT! WE'RE HERE NOW!
I SAID STAY BACK-- AND I MEANT IT!
I'M THRU BEING EVERYBODY'S PIGEON! I'M THRU BEING SHOVED AROUND!
JOHNNY!! IF NOT FOR MY FORCE FIELD-- YOU MIGHT HAVE HURT YOUR OWN PARTNERS!
NO, HE WOULDN'T, SUE! THAT WAS ONLY MEANT TO SCARE US!
WHAT'S HAPPENED TO YOU? HOW CAN YOU LOVE CRYSTAL--HOW CAN YOU BE HER MAN--WHEN YOU ACT LIKE A SPOILED CHILD--WILLING TO HARM ANYONE WHO GETS IN YOUR WAY?!!
OKAY, SIS-- YOU--MADE YOUR POINT!
19

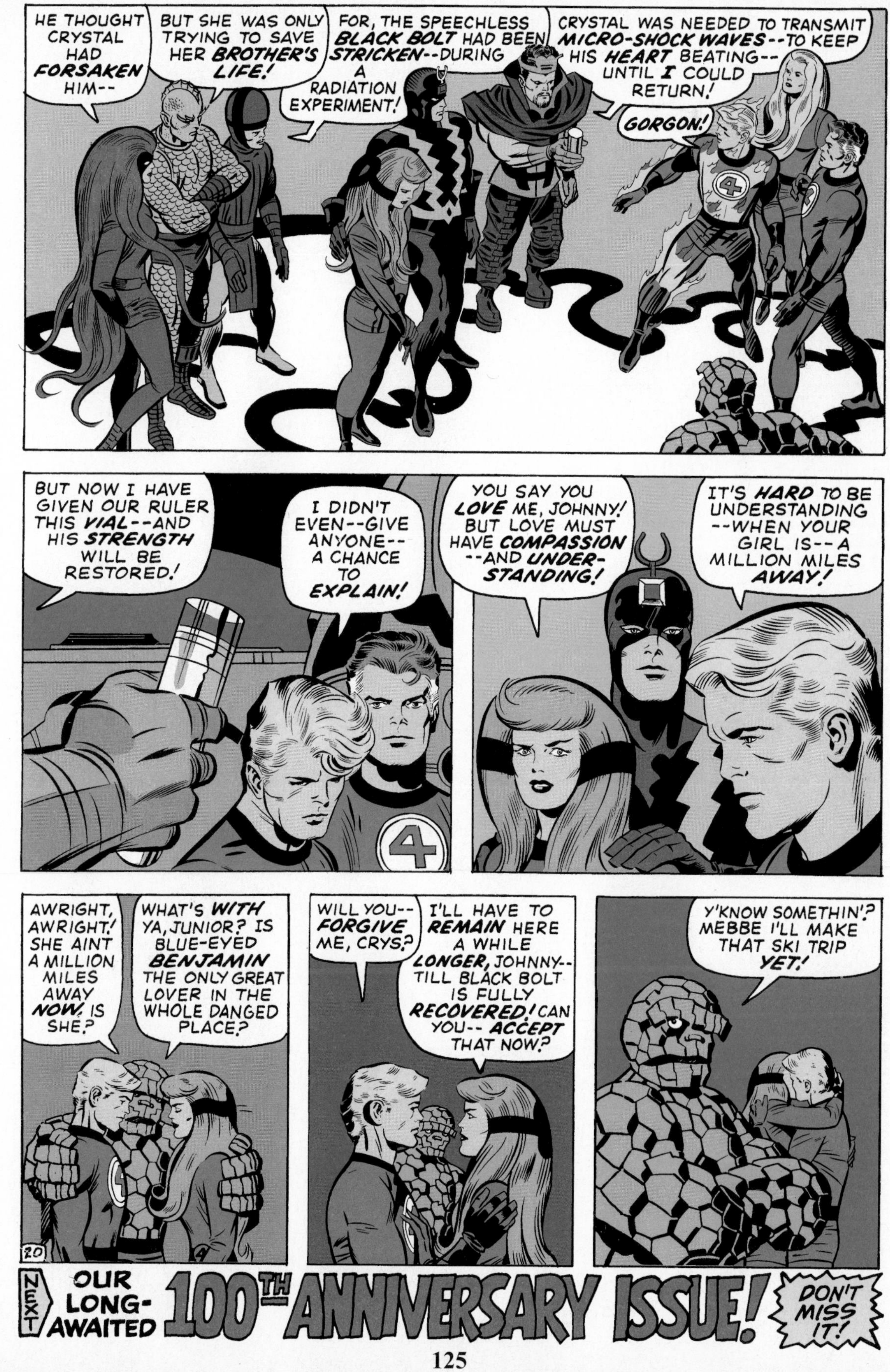

HE THOUGHT CRYSTAL HAD FORSAKEN HIM--
BUT SHE WAS ONLY TRYING TO SAVE HER BROTHER'S LIFE!
FOR, THE SPEECHLESS BLACK BOLT HAD BEEN STRICKEN--DURING A RADIATION EXPERIMENT!
CRYSTAL WAS NEEDED TO TRANSMIT MICRO-SHOCK WAVES--TO KEEP HIS HEART BEATING--UNTIL I COULD RETURN!
GORGON!
BUT NOW I HAVE GIVEN OUR RULER THIS VIAL--AND HIS STRENGTH WILL BE RESTORED!
I DIDN'T EVEN--GIVE ANYONE--A CHANCE TO EXPLAIN!
YOU SAY YOU LOVE ME, JOHNNY! BUT LOVE MUST HAVE COMPASSION--AND UNDER-STANDING!
IT'S HARD TO BE UNDERSTANDING--WHEN YOUR GIRL IS--A MILLION MILES AWAY!
AWRIGHT, AWRIGHT! SHE AINT A MILLION MILES AWAY NOW, IS SHE?
WHAT'S WITH YA, JUNIOR? IS BLUE-EYED BENJAMIN THE ONLY GREAT LOVER IN THE WHOLE DANGED PLACE?
20
WILL YOU--FORGIVE ME, CRYS?
I'LL HAVE TO REMAIN HERE A WHILE LONGER, JOHNNY--TILL BLACK BOLT IS FULLY RECOVERED! CAN YOU--ACCEPT THAT NOW?
Y'KNOW SOMETHIN'? MEBBE I'LL MAKE THAT SKI TRIP YET!
NEXT
OUR LONG-AWAITED 100TH ANNIVERSARY ISSUE!
DON'T MISS IT!

THE WORLD'S GREATEST COMIC MAGAZINE!
FANTASTIC FOUR
15¢
100
JULY
APPROVED BY THE COMICS CODE AUTHORITY
Fantastic Four
THIS IS IT!
THE SPECTACULAR LONG-AWAITED
100TH ANNIVERSARY ISSUE!
FEATURING:
VILLAINS! VILLAINS! VILLAINS!
MARVEL COMICS GROUP
JACK + JOE

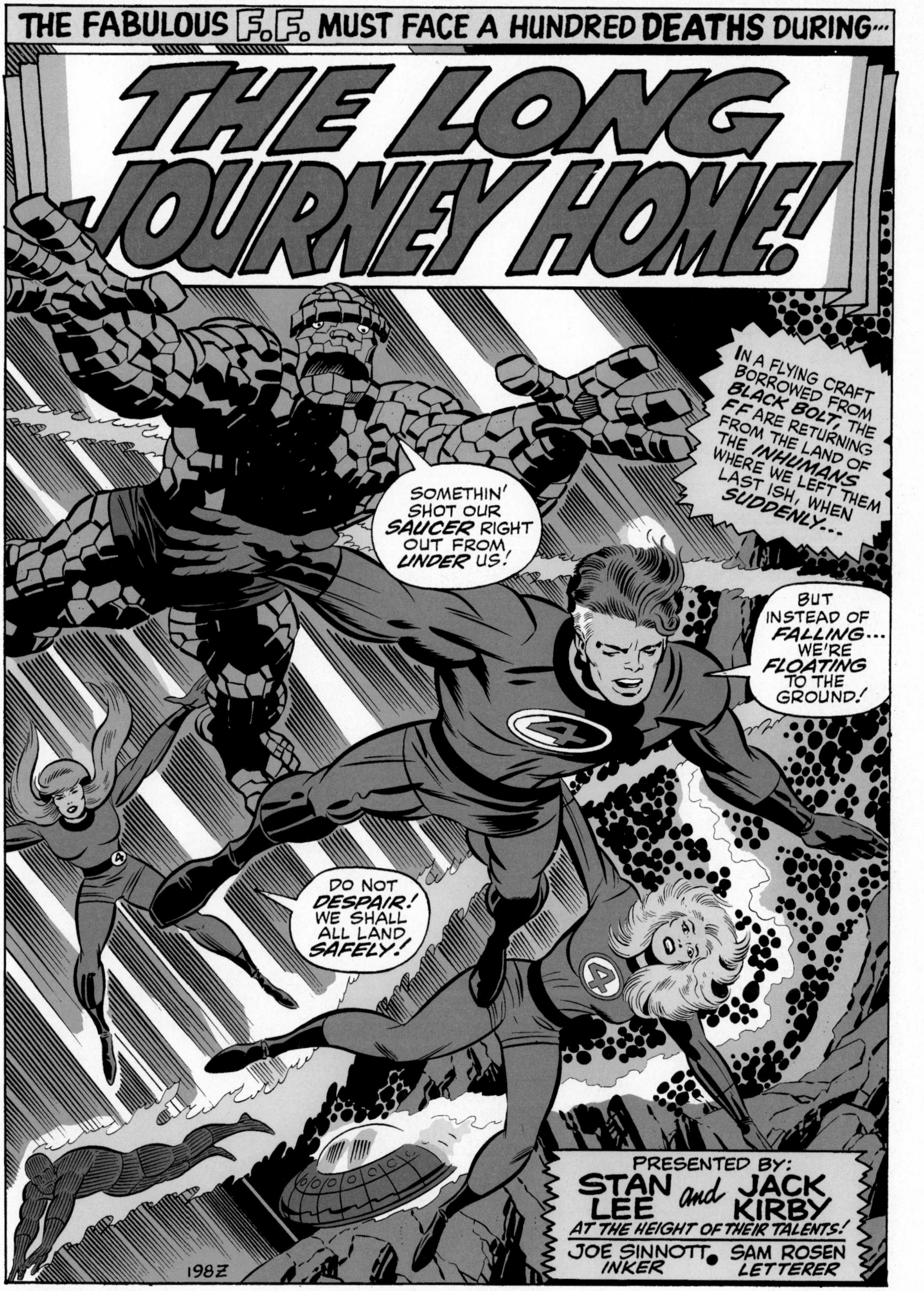
THE FABULOUS F.F. MUST FACE A HUNDRED DEATHS DURING...
THE LONG JOURNEY HOME!
IN A FLYING CRAFT BORROWED FROM BLACK BOLT, THE FF ARE RETURNING FROM THE LAND OF THE INHUMANS WHERE WE LEFT THEM LAST ISH, WHEN SUDDENLY...
SOMETHIN' SHOT OUR SAUCER RIGHT OUT FROM UNDER US!
BUT INSTEAD OF FALLING... WE'RE FLOATING TO THE GROUND!
DO NOT DESPAIR! WE SHALL ALL LAND SAFELY!
PRESENTED BY: STAN LEE and JACK KIRBY
AT THE HEIGHT OF THEIR TALENTS!
JOE SINNOTT • INKER
SAM ROSEN LETTERER
198Z

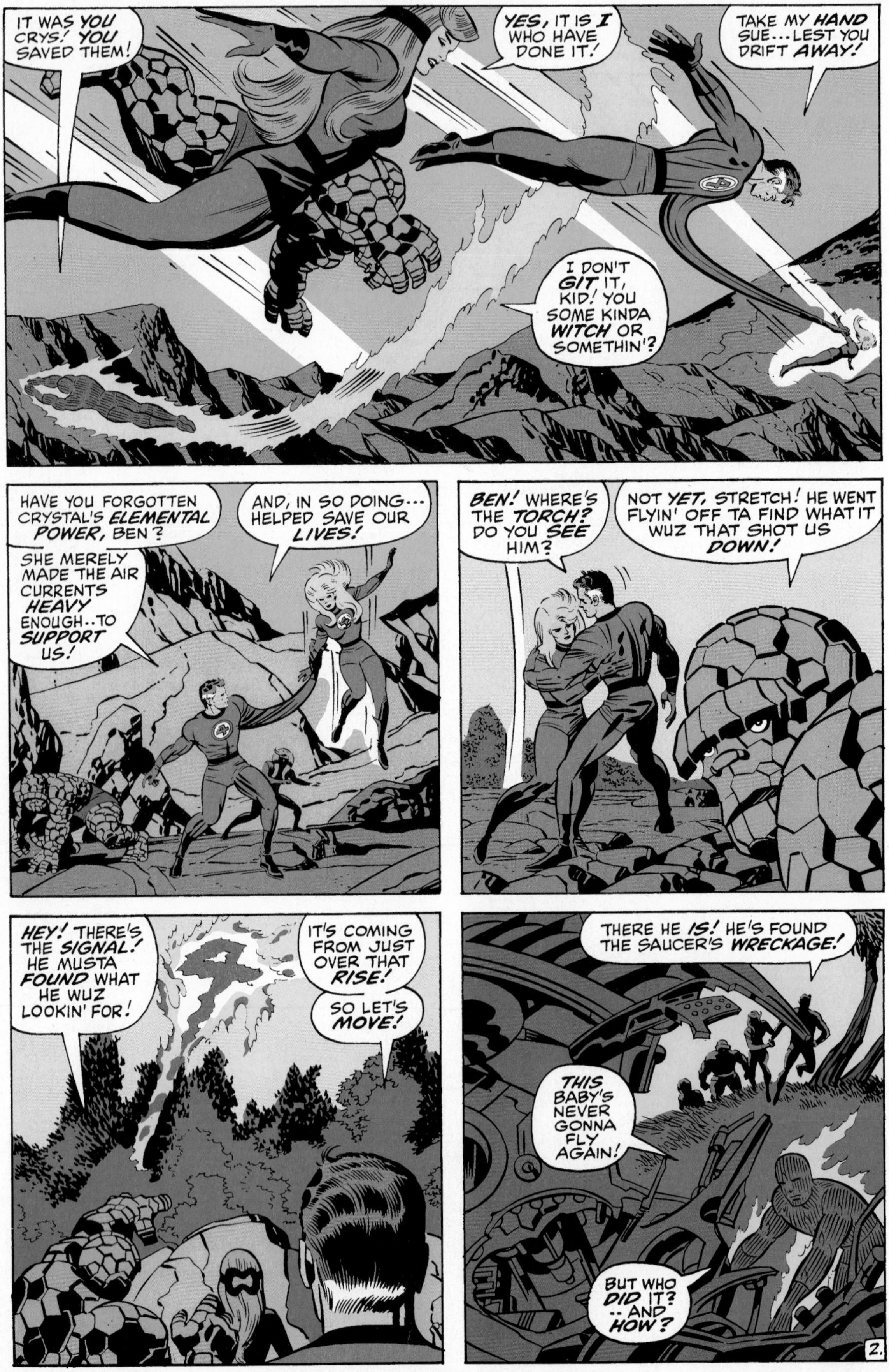
IT WAS YOU CRYS! YOU SAVED THEM!
YES, IT IS I WHO HAVE DONE IT!
TAKE MY HAND SUE... LEST YOU DRIFT AWAY!
I DON'T GIT IT, KID! YOU SOME KINDA WITCH OR SOMETHIN'?
HAVE YOU FORGOTTEN CRYSTAL'S ELEMENTAL POWER, BEN?
SHE MERELY MADE THE AIR CURRENTS HEAVY ENOUGH.. TO SUPPORT US!
AND, IN SO DOING... HELPED SAVE OUR LIVES!
BEN! WHERE'S THE TORCH? DO YOU SEE HIM?
NOT YET, STRETCH! HE WENT FLYIN' OFF TA FIND WHAT IT WUZ THAT SHOT US DOWN!
HEY! THERE'S THE SIGNAL! HE MUSTA FOUND WHAT HE WUZ LOOKIN' FOR!
IT'S COMING FROM JUST OVER THAT RISE!
SO LET'S MOVE!
THERE HE IS! HE'S FOUND THE SAUCER'S WRECKAGE!
THIS BABY'S NEVER GONNA FLY AGAIN!
BUT WHO DID IT? .. AND HOW?
2.

WHATEVER *HIT* US... IT WAS AN UNBELIEVABLY POTENT AND *SOPHISTICATED* WEAPON!

HOW CAN YOU *TELL*, REED?

LOOK AT THE REMAINS OF THE *METAL!* SOMETHING MADE IT SUDDENLY *FALL APART...* NOISE-LESSLY, WITHOUT ANY *WARNING!*

NUTS! EVERY TIME YA TURN AROUND, ANOTHER *MAD SCIENTIST* POPS UP OUTTA THE WOODWORK!

BUT *THIS* TIME, OUR HAPLESS HEROES ARE DESTINED TO FACE FAR *MORE* THAN ONE LONE HOSTILE FOE...

THE *FIRST* BLOW SHALL BE... *MINE!*

CLIK!

TO *KANG THE CONQUEROR* HAS BEEN GIVEN THE HONOR OF *LAUNCHING* THE ATTACK AGAINST THE *FANTASTIC FOUR!*

SHHOOSH!

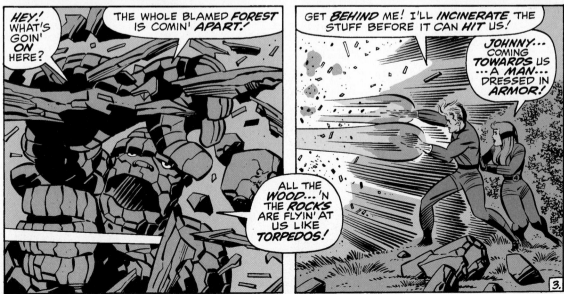

HEY! WHAT'S GOIN' ON HERE?

THE WHOLE BLAMED *FOREST* IS COMIN' *APART!*

ALL THE *WOOD...* 'N THE *ROCKS* ARE FLYIN' AT US LIKE TORPEDOS!

GET *BEHIND* ME! I'LL *INCINERATE* THE STUFF BEFORE IT CAN *HIT* US!

JOHNNY... COMING *TOWARDS* US ...A MAN... DRESSED IN ARMOR!

3.

129

I SEE HIM *TOO!* IT... IT'S *KANG*... THE *CONQUEROR!*

I CAN DROP MY *FORCE FIELD* NOW, DARLING! THE FOREST IS *STILL* AGAIN!

BUT HOW WILL WE STRIKE *BACK* AT KANG?

LEAVE 'IM TA *ME,* SUSIE!

I'VE WAITED FER *YEARS* TA LEAN ON THE BUM!

BEN! *LOOK OUT!*

HEY! HOW DID HE DO THAT?

I DIDN'T TAKE MY *PEEPERS* OFFA HIM FER A *MINNIT!*

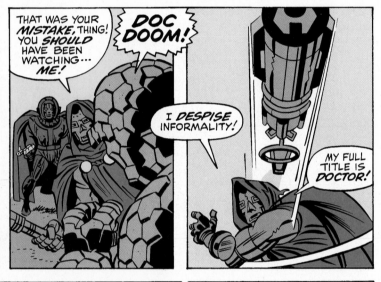

THAT WAS YOUR *MISTAKE,* THING! YOU *SHOULD* HAVE BEEN WATCHING... *ME!*

DOC DOOM!

I *DESPISE* INFORMALITY!

MY FULL TITLE IS *DOCTOR!*

NOW, WHILE YOU PONDER THE PROBLEM OF WHETHER KANG AND *MYSELF* ARE *TWO SEPARATE BEINGS...*

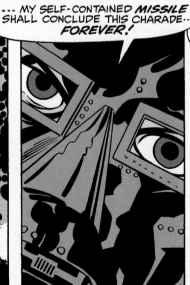

... MY SELF-CONTAINED *MISSILE* SHALL CONCLUDE THIS CHARADE... *FOREVER!*

QUICK THINKING, MRS. RICHARDS!

BUT YOUR *FORCE FIELD* WILL BE *BROKEN* BY MY *NEXT* ATTACK!

4

130

HE'S FOUGHT US *BEFORE*... HE *KNOWS* OUR POWERS!

IF HE SAYS HE CAN *BEAT* US--

BUT HE IS A *STRANGER* TO *MY* POWERS! *WATCH*--!

THE GIRL UPROOTED A *REDWOOD*...WITH ONE SINGLE *GESTURE*!

IT'S *FALLING*... ABOUT TO *CRUSH* US!

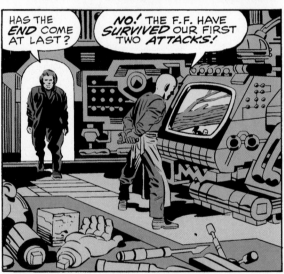

HAS THE *END* COME AT LAST?

NO! THE F.F. HAVE *SURVIVED* OUR FIRST TWO *ATTACKS*!

WHAT DOES IT *MATTER?* WE HAVE PLANNED TOO *LONG*--- TOO *WELL!* *NOTHING* CAN SAVE THEM FROM US!

FOR *YEARS*, THE POWERS OF THE *PUPPET MASTER* WERE NOT GREAT ENOUGH TO *DESTROY* THEM--- BUT *NOW*...

NOW YOU ARE ALLIED WITH THE *THINKER!* AND AFTER TODAY, NEVER *AGAIN* WILL MEN CALL ME *MAD!*

COME! I MUST RETURN TO THE *RADIATION CHAMBER!*

FOR, IF ALL *ELSE* FAILS.... THE FIGURE IN THAT *BLOCK* WILL STILL INSURE OUR *VICTORY!*

5

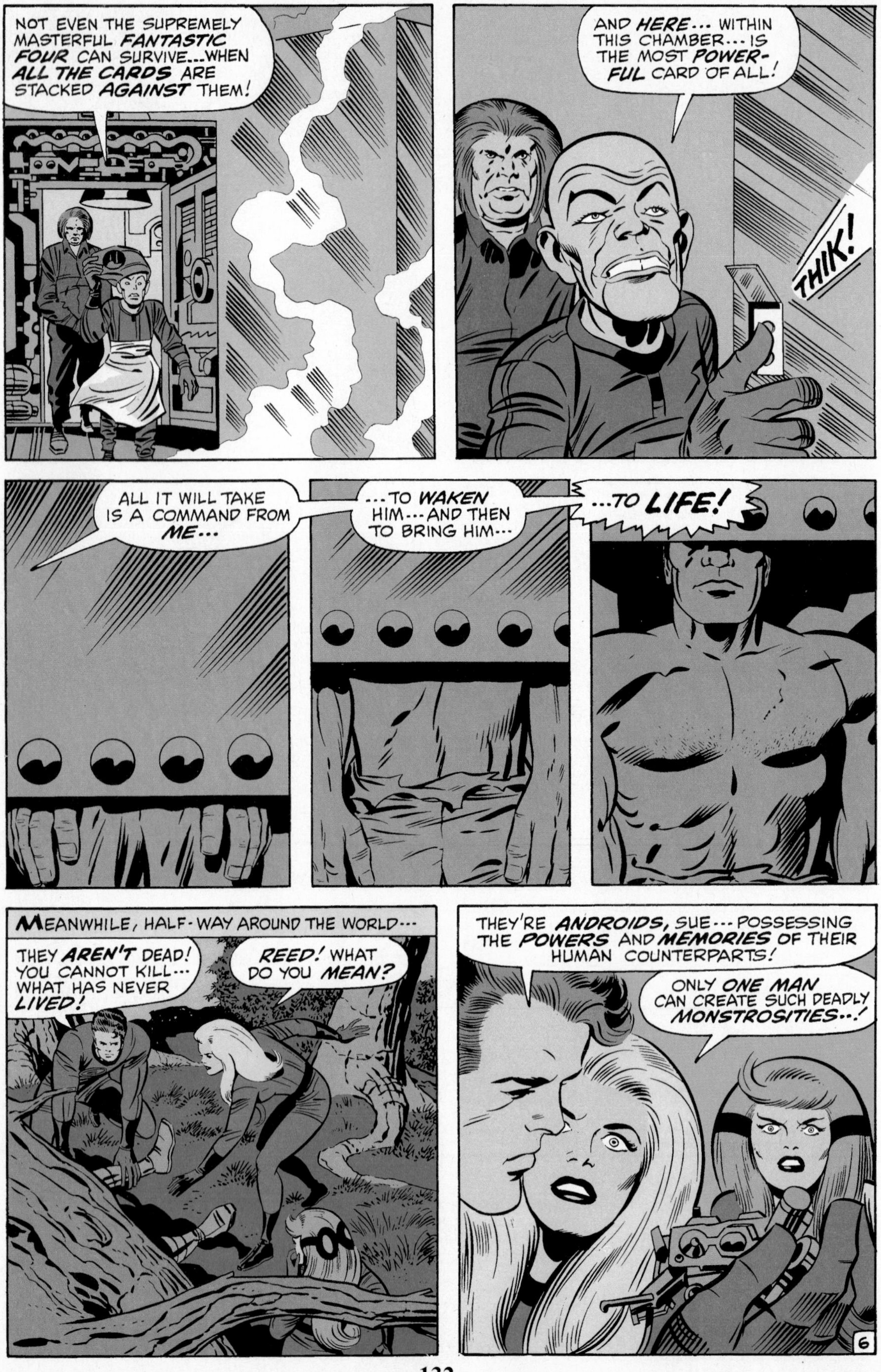
NOT EVEN THE SUPREMELY MASTERFUL FANTASTIC FOUR CAN SURVIVE...WHEN ALL THE CARDS ARE STACKED AGAINST THEM!
AND HERE... WITHIN THIS CHAMBER... IS THE MOST POWER-FUL CARD OF ALL!
THIK!
ALL IT WILL TAKE IS A COMMAND FROM ME...
...TO WAKEN HIM...AND THEN TO BRING HIM...
...TO LIFE!
MEANWHILE, HALF-WAY AROUND THE WORLD...
THEY AREN'T DEAD! YOU CANNOT KILL... WHAT HAS NEVER LIVED!
REED! WHAT DO YOU MEAN?
THEY'RE ANDROIDS, SUE... POSSESSING THE POWERS AND MEMORIES OF THEIR HUMAN COUNTERPARTS!
ONLY ONE MAN CAN CREATE SUCH DEADLY MONSTROSITIES...!
6

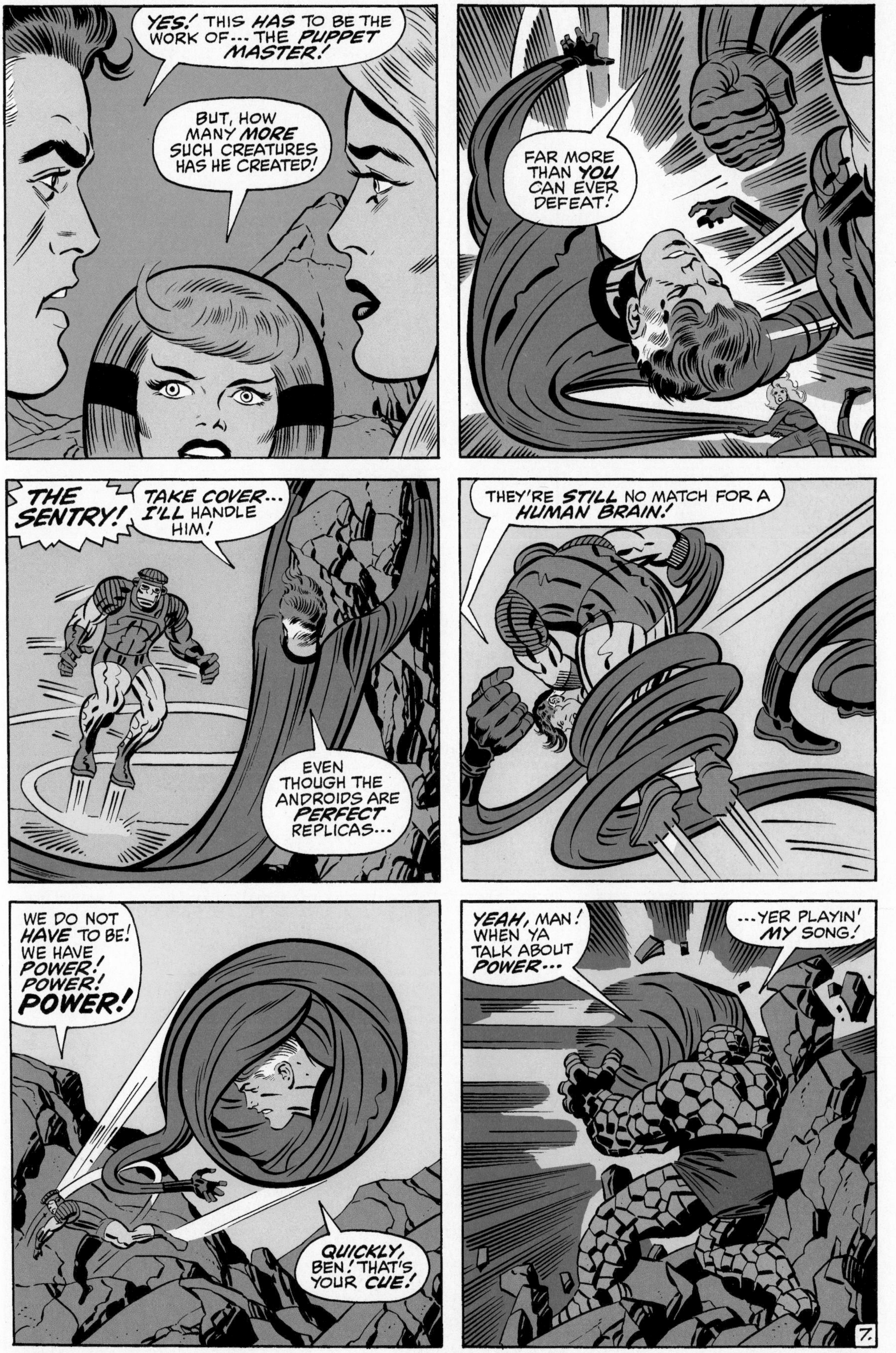
YES! THIS HAS TO BE THE WORK OF... THE PUPPET MASTER!
BUT, HOW MANY MORE SUCH CREATURES HAS HE CREATED!
FAR MORE THAN YOU CAN EVER DEFEAT!
THE SENTRY!
TAKE COVER... I'LL HANDLE HIM!
EVEN THOUGH THE ANDROIDS ARE PERFECT REPLICAS...
THEY'RE STILL NO MATCH FOR A HUMAN BRAIN!
WE DO NOT HAVE TO BE! WE HAVE POWER! POWER! POWER!
QUICKLY, BEN! THAT'S YOUR CUE!
YEAH, MAN! WHEN YA TALK ABOUT POWER...
...YER PLAYIN' MY SONG!
7.

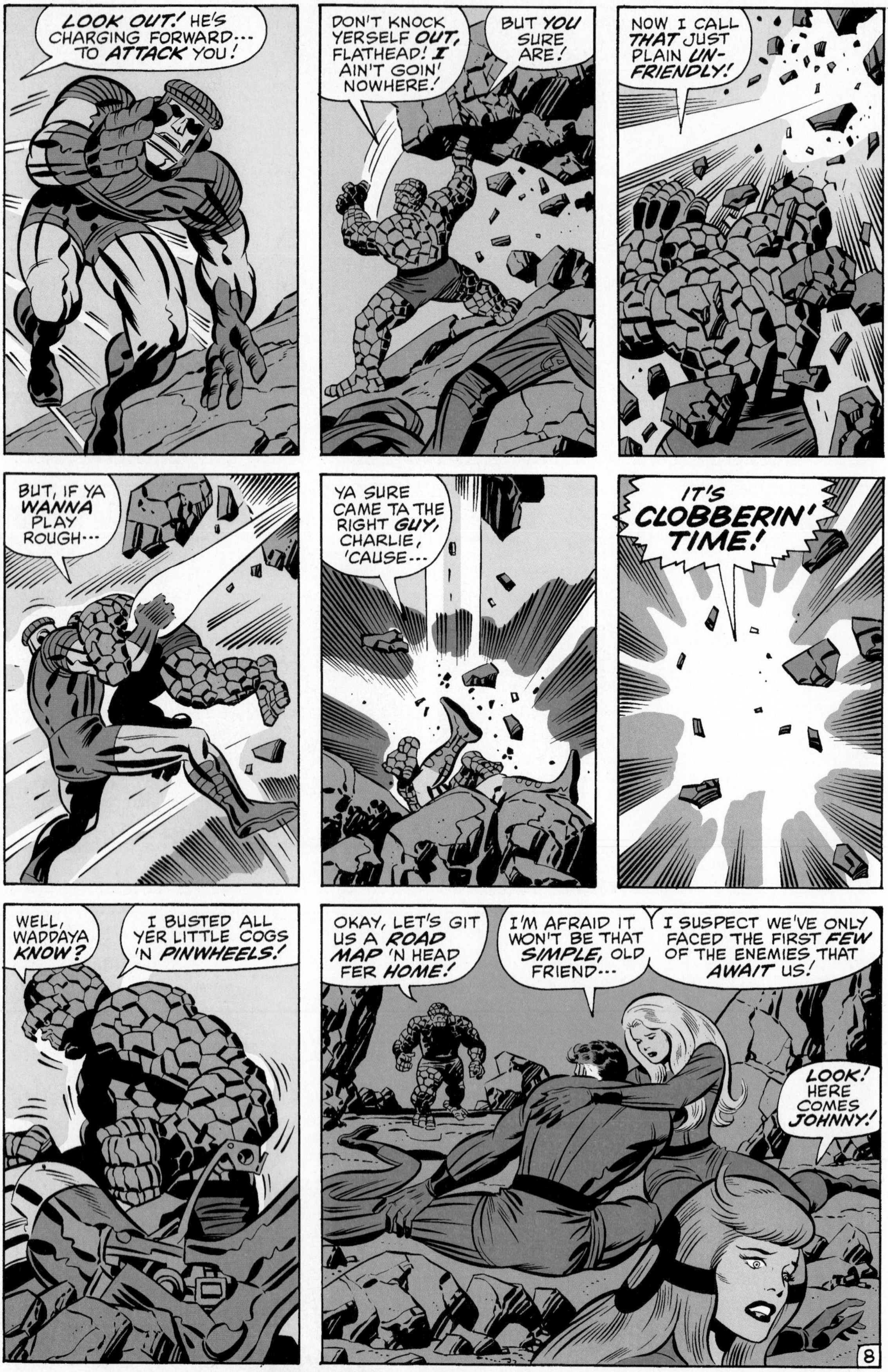
LOOK OUT! HE'S CHARGING FORWARD--- TO ATTACK YOU!
DON'T KNOCK YERSELF OUT, FLATHEAD! I AIN'T GOIN' NOWHERE!
BUT YOU SURE ARE!
NOW I CALL THAT JUST PLAIN UN-FRIENDLY!
BUT, IF YA WANNA PLAY ROUGH---
YA SURE CAME TA THE RIGHT GUY, CHARLIE, 'CAUSE---
IT'S CLOBBERIN' TIME!
WELL, WADDAYA KNOW?
I BUSTED ALL YER LITTLE COGS 'N PINWHEELS!
OKAY, LET'S GIT US A ROAD MAP 'N HEAD FER HOME!
I'M AFRAID IT WON'T BE THAT SIMPLE, OLD FRIEND---
I SUSPECT WE'VE ONLY FACED THE FIRST FEW OF THE ENEMIES THAT AWAIT US!
LOOK! HERE COMES JOHNNY!
8

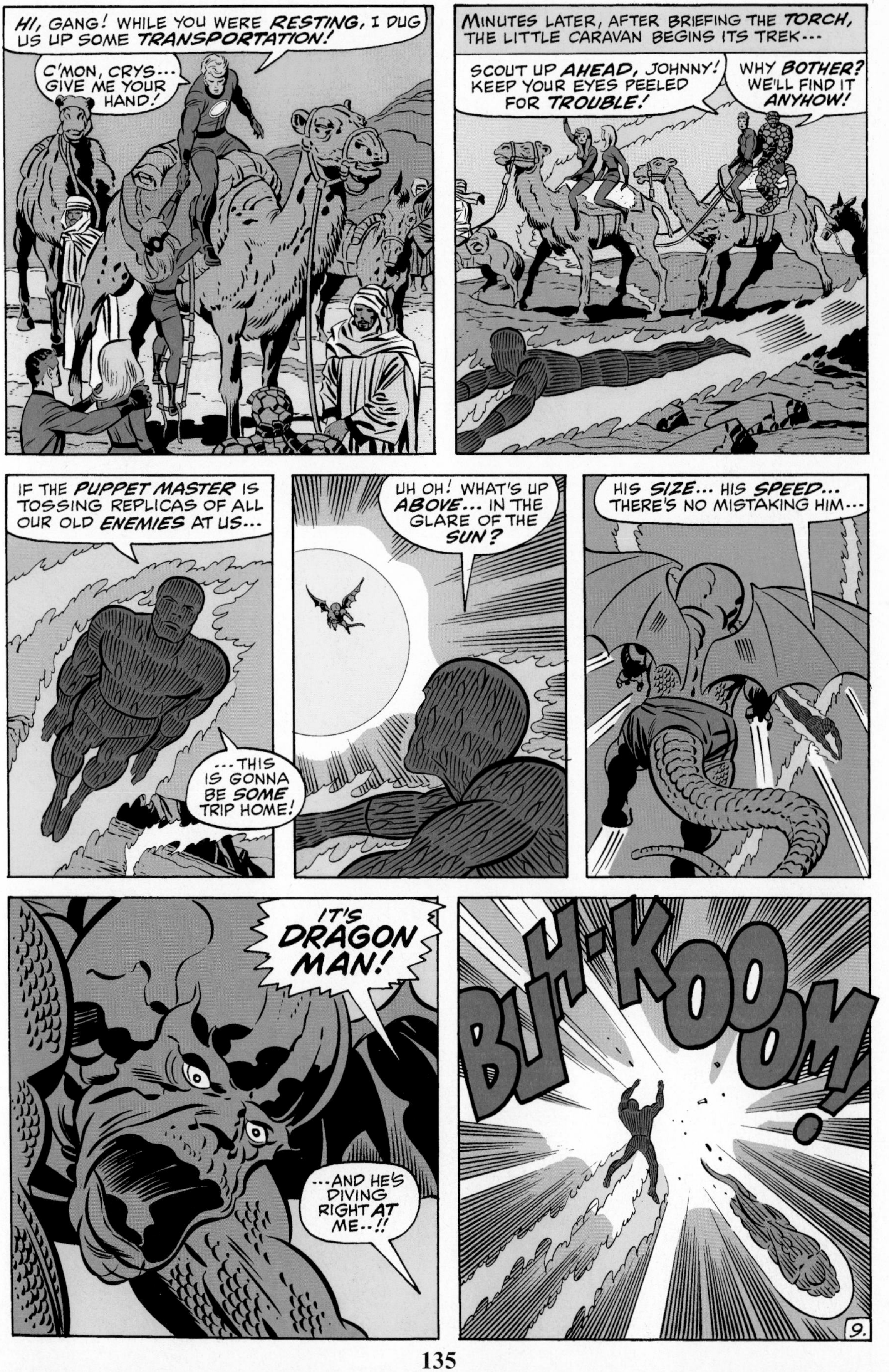
HI, GANG! WHILE YOU WERE RESTING, I DUG US UP SOME TRANSPORTATION!
C'MON, CRYS... GIVE ME YOUR HAND!
MINUTES LATER, AFTER BRIEFING THE TORCH, THE LITTLE CARAVAN BEGINS ITS TREK---
SCOUT UP AHEAD, JOHNNY! KEEP YOUR EYES PEELED FOR TROUBLE!
WHY BOTHER? WE'LL FIND IT ANYHOW!
IF THE PUPPET MASTER IS TOSSING REPLICAS OF ALL OUR OLD ENEMIES AT US...
---THIS IS GONNA BE SOME TRIP HOME!
UH OH! WHAT'S UP ABOVE... IN THE GLARE OF THE SUN?
HIS SIZE... HIS SPEED... THERE'S NO MISTAKING HIM---
IT'S DRAGON MAN!
---AND HE'S DIVING RIGHT AT ME--!!
BUH-KOOOM!
9.

FALL, TORCH... INTO THE SNOW... JUST AS I PLANNED!

IT WILL WEAKEN YOU! IT WILL DIM YOUR FLAME!

THUS MAKING YOU A PERFECT TARGET...

...FOR MY MOST LETHAL ATTACK!

DON'T COUNT ON IT, BIG SHOT!

...NOT WHILE I'VE ENOUGH HEAT LEFT TO FIRE ONE LAST BURST THRU THE MOUNTAIN...

...WHERE IT'LL BUILD UP ENOUGH PRESSURE... TO TRAP YOU...WHEN IT ERUPTS!

MADE IT! THE EXPLOSION CAUGHT HIM FLAT-FOOTED!

BUT I'VE GOT TO REACH THE OTHERS NOW!

WON'T BE MUCH GOOD FOR ANY-THING...TILL I CAN RECHARGE MY FLAME!

THERE THEY ARE NOW!

THEY'RE TRYING TO FORD THAT RIVER---IN A NATIVE FIBER BOAT!

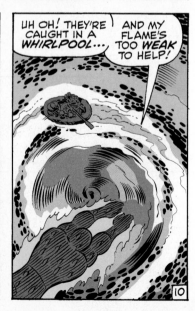

UH OH! THEY'RE CAUGHT IN A WHIRLPOOL....

AND MY FLAME'S TOO WEAK TO HELP!

10

136

IT ISN'T *NATURAL* TO HAVE A WHIRLPOOL HERE! IT--- *BEN!*

WHAT ARE YOU *DOING?*

IF IT AIN'T *NATCHRAL,* THEN SOMETHIN'S *CAUSIN'* IT, RIGHT?

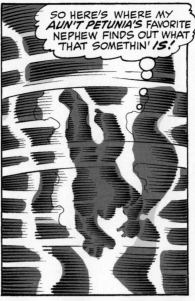

SO HERE'S WHERE MY *AUN'T PETUNIA'S* FAVORITE NEPHEW FINDS OUT WHAT THAT SOMETHIN' *IS!*

OL' *STRETCHO* WUZ *RIGHT,* AS USUAL!

THERE'S SOME KINDA NUTTY *GADGET* DOWN HERE, SPINNIN' THE *WATER* AROUND!

BUT IT AIN'T GONNA DO NO MORE SPINNIN' AFTER *THIS!*

BTAM!

NOW, ALL I GOTTA DO IS *CORK* THINGS UP... 'N GIT BACK UPSTAIRS!

YOU *DID* IT, BEN! THE WHIRLPOOL'S *GONE!*

TOSS ME A HUNK'A *SOAP,* WILLYA?

...SO'S IT WON'T BE A *WASTE!*

FOOL! YOU NEVER SUSPECTED *WHO* PLACED THAT VORTEX MACHINE BELOW!

HUH--??!

IT'S OL' *FISH-FACE...* THE *SUB-MARINER!*

HE'S... *DRAGGIN'* ME DOWN... BUT I GOTTA KICK *REED* 'N THE OTHERS... OUTTA DANGER!

TH-OK!

WE--- WE CAN'T JUST LEAVE THE *THING* BEHIND!

WE HAVEN'T ANY *CHOICE* ...TILL WE COME TO A *STOP!*

11.

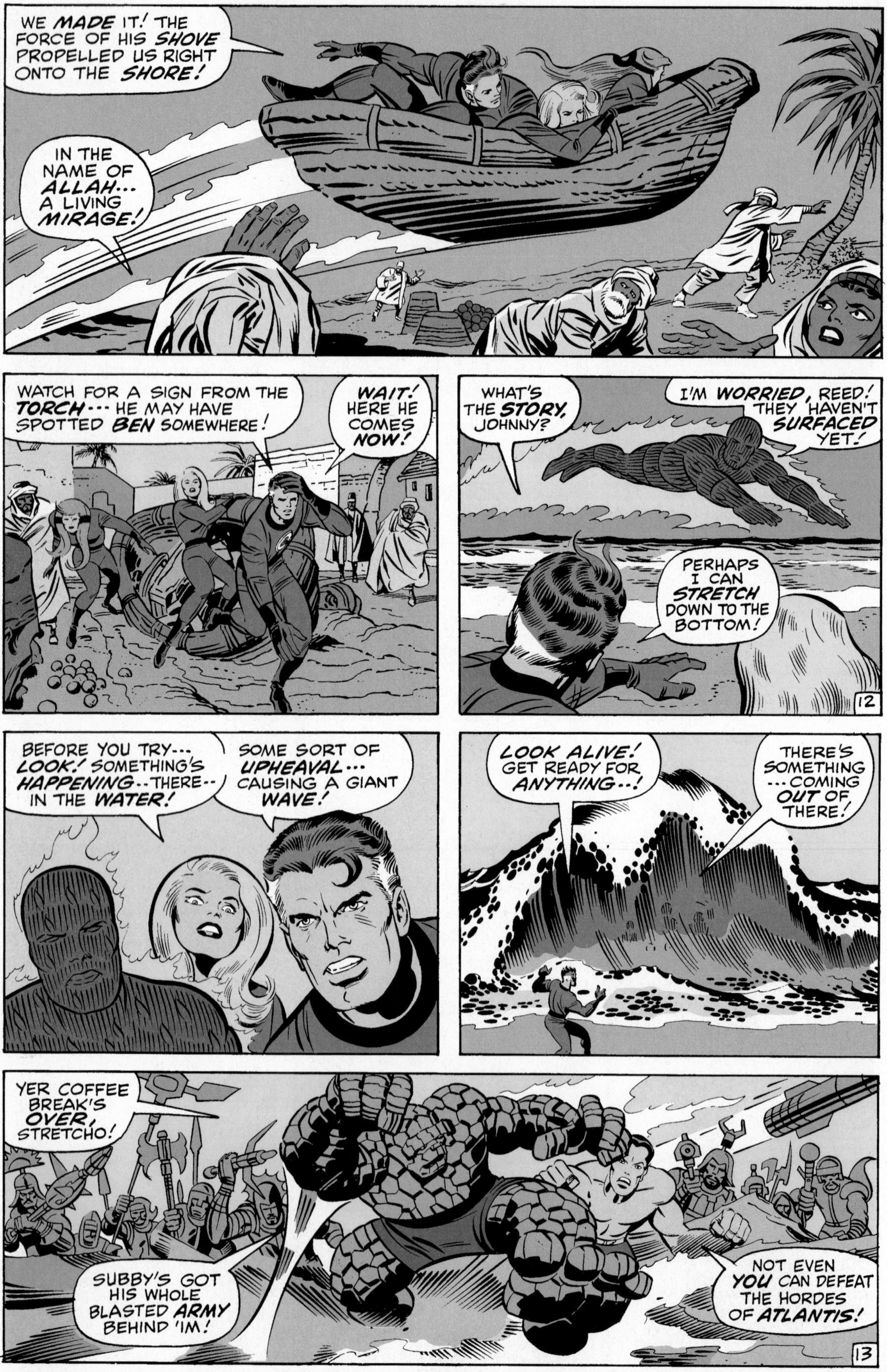

WE MADE IT! THE FORCE OF HIS SHOVE PROPELLED US RIGHT ONTO THE SHORE!
IN THE NAME OF ALLAH... A LIVING MIRAGE!
WATCH FOR A SIGN FROM THE TORCH--- HE MAY HAVE SPOTTED BEN SOMEWHERE!
WAIT! HERE HE COMES NOW!
WHAT'S THE STORY, JOHNNY?
I'M WORRIED, REED! THEY HAVEN'T SURFACED YET!
PERHAPS I CAN STRETCH DOWN TO THE BOTTOM!
12
BEFORE YOU TRY--- LOOK! SOMETHING'S HAPPENING--THERE-- IN THE WATER!
SOME SORT OF UPHEAVAL... CAUSING A GIANT WAVE!
LOOK ALIVE! GET READY FOR ANYTHING--!
THERE'S SOMETHING ...COMING OUT OF THERE!
YER COFFEE BREAK'S OVER, STRETCHO!
SUBBY'S GOT HIS WHOLE BLASTED ARMY BEHIND 'IM!
NOT EVEN YOU CAN DEFEAT THE HORDES OF ATLANTIS!
13

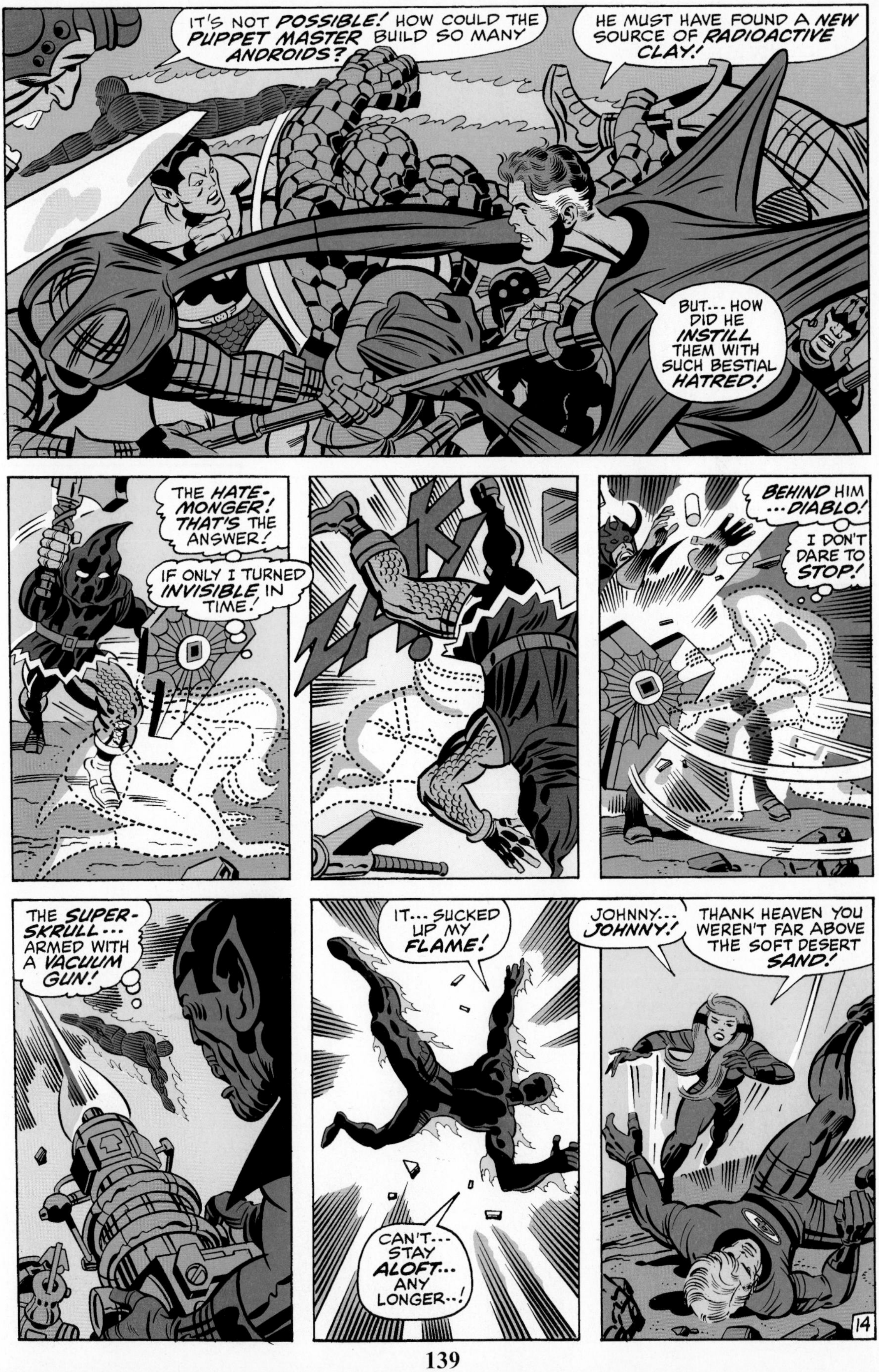
IT'S NOT POSSIBLE! HOW COULD THE PUPPET MASTER BUILD SO MANY ANDROIDS?
HE MUST HAVE FOUND A NEW SOURCE OF RADIOACTIVE CLAY!
BUT--- HOW DID HE INSTILL THEM WITH SUCH BESTIAL HATRED!
THE HATE-MONGER! THAT'S THE ANSWER!
IF ONLY I TURNED INVISIBLE IN TIME!
BEHIND HIM ...DIABLO!
I DON'T DARE TO STOP!
THE SUPER-SKRULL... ARMED WITH A VACUUM GUN!
IT... SUCKED UP MY FLAME!
CAN'T... STAY ALOFT... ANY LONGER..!
JOHNNY... JOHNNY!
THANK HEAVEN YOU WEREN'T FAR ABOVE THE SOFT DESERT SAND!
14

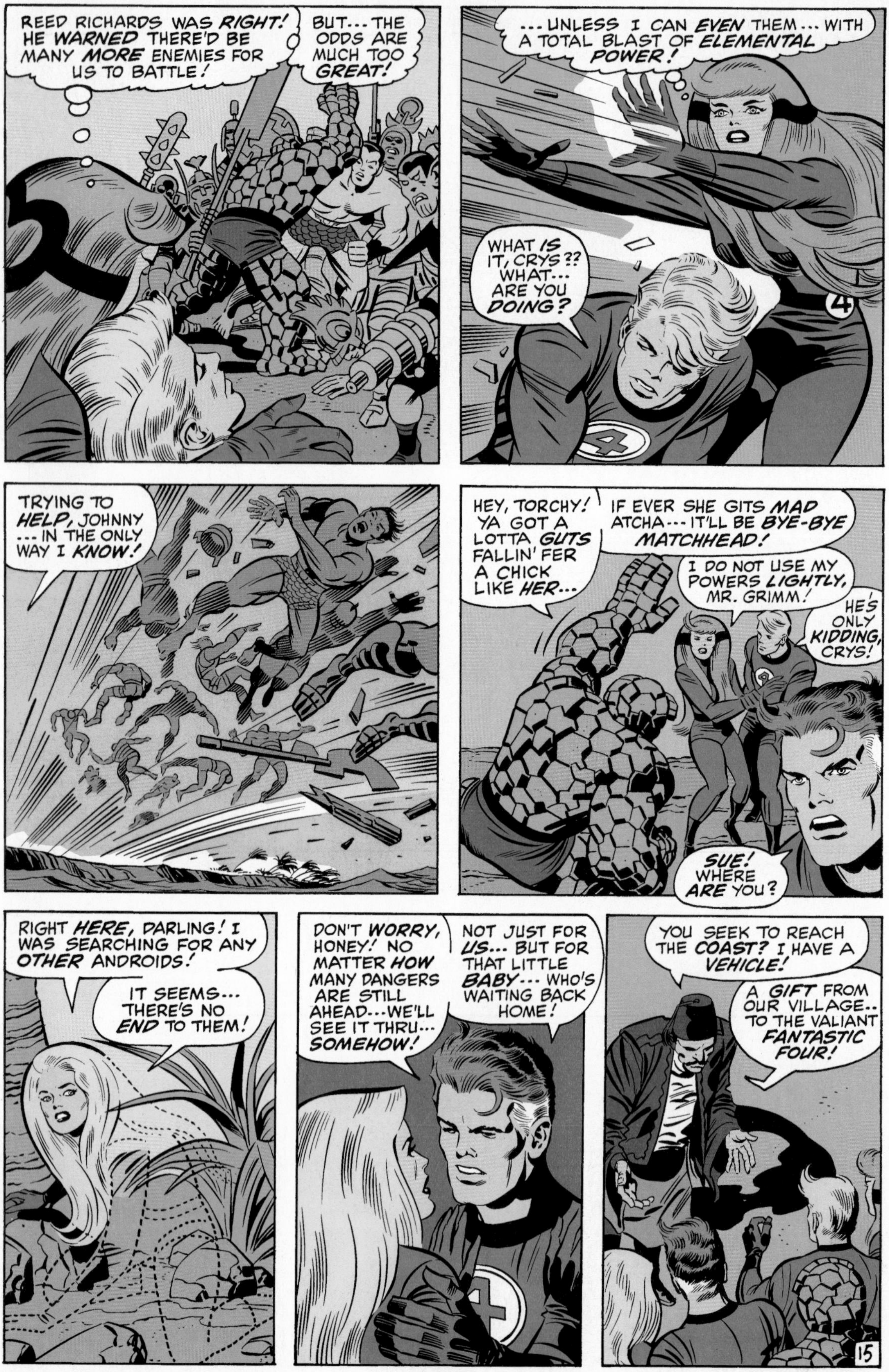
REED RICHARDS WAS RIGHT! HE WARNED THERE'D BE MANY MORE ENEMIES FOR US TO BATTLE!
BUT... THE ODDS ARE MUCH TOO GREAT!
...UNLESS I CAN EVEN THEM... WITH A TOTAL BLAST OF ELEMENTAL POWER!
WHAT IS IT, CRYS?? WHAT... ARE YOU DOING?
TRYING TO HELP, JOHNNY ... IN THE ONLY WAY I KNOW!
HEY, TORCHY! YA GOT A LOTTA GUTS FALLIN' FER A CHICK LIKE HER...
IF EVER SHE GITS MAD ATCHA--- IT'LL BE BYE-BYE MATCHHEAD!
I DO NOT USE MY POWERS LIGHTLY, MR. GRIMM!
HE'S ONLY KIDDING, CRYS!
SUE! WHERE ARE YOU?
RIGHT HERE, DARLING! I WAS SEARCHING FOR ANY OTHER ANDROIDS!
IT SEEMS... THERE'S NO END TO THEM!
DON'T WORRY, HONEY! NO MATTER HOW MANY DANGERS ARE STILL AHEAD...WE'LL SEE IT THRU... SOMEHOW!
NOT JUST FOR US... BUT FOR THAT LITTLE BABY--- WHO'S WAITING BACK HOME!
YOU SEEK TO REACH THE COAST? I HAVE A VEHICLE!
A GIFT FROM OUR VILLAGE.. TO THE VALIANT FANTASTIC FOUR!
15

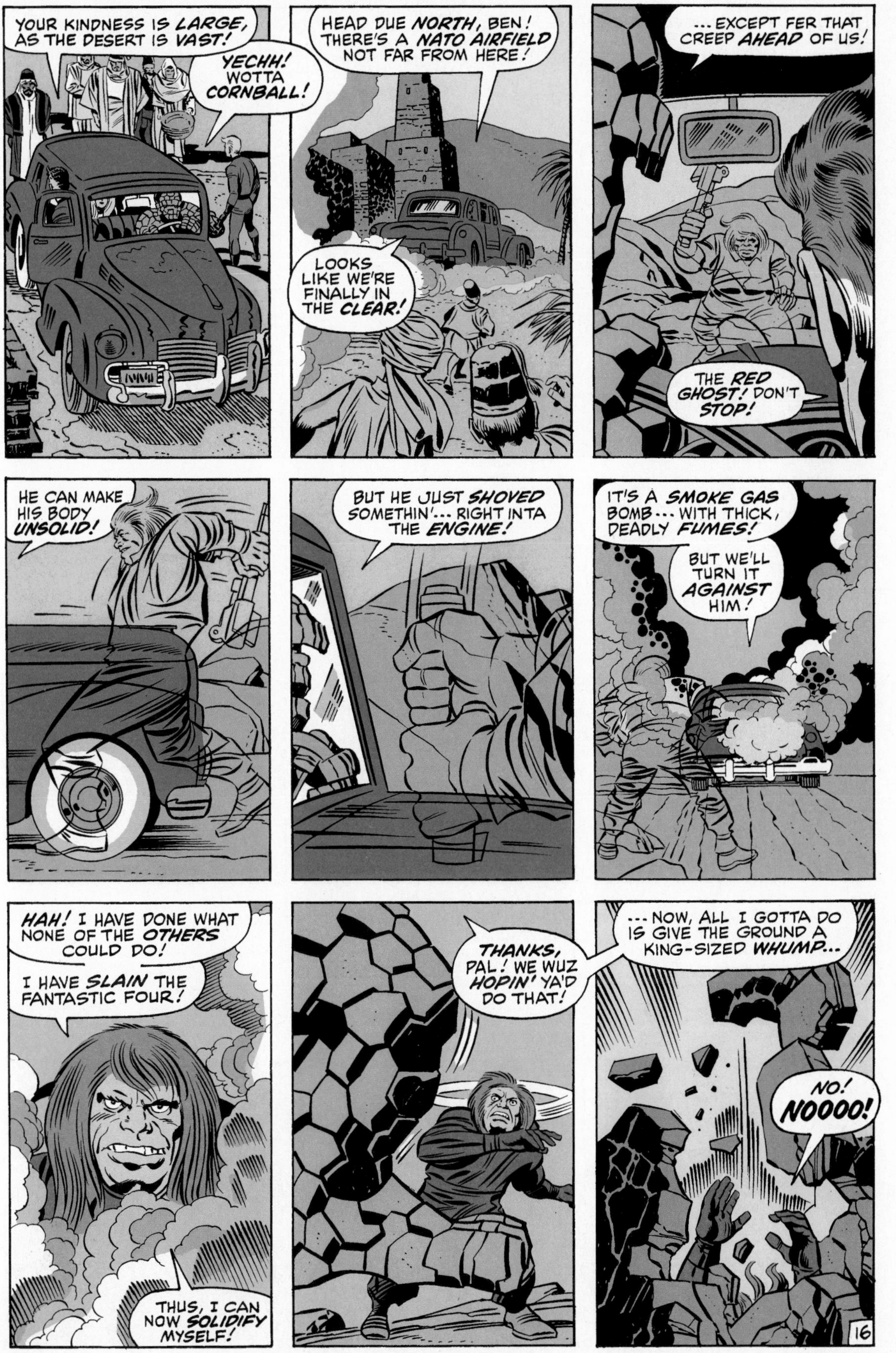
YOUR KINDNESS IS LARGE, AS THE DESERT IS VAST!
YECHH! WOTTA CORNBALL!
HEAD DUE NORTH, BEN! THERE'S A NATO AIRFIELD NOT FAR FROM HERE!
LOOKS LIKE WE'RE FINALLY IN THE CLEAR!
... EXCEPT FER THAT CREEP AHEAD OF US!
THE RED GHOST! DON'T STOP!
HE CAN MAKE HIS BODY UNSOLID!
BUT HE JUST SHOVED SOMETHIN'... RIGHT INTA THE ENGINE!
IT'S A SMOKE GAS BOMB... WITH THICK, DEADLY FUMES!
BUT WE'LL TURN IT AGAINST HIM!
HAH! I HAVE DONE WHAT NONE OF THE OTHERS COULD DO!
I HAVE SLAIN THE FANTASTIC FOUR!
THUS, I CAN NOW SOLIDIFY MYSELF!
THANKS, PAL! WE WUZ HOPIN' YA'D DO THAT!
... NOW, ALL I GOTTA DO IS GIVE THE GROUND A KING-SIZED WHUMP...
NO! NOOOO!
16

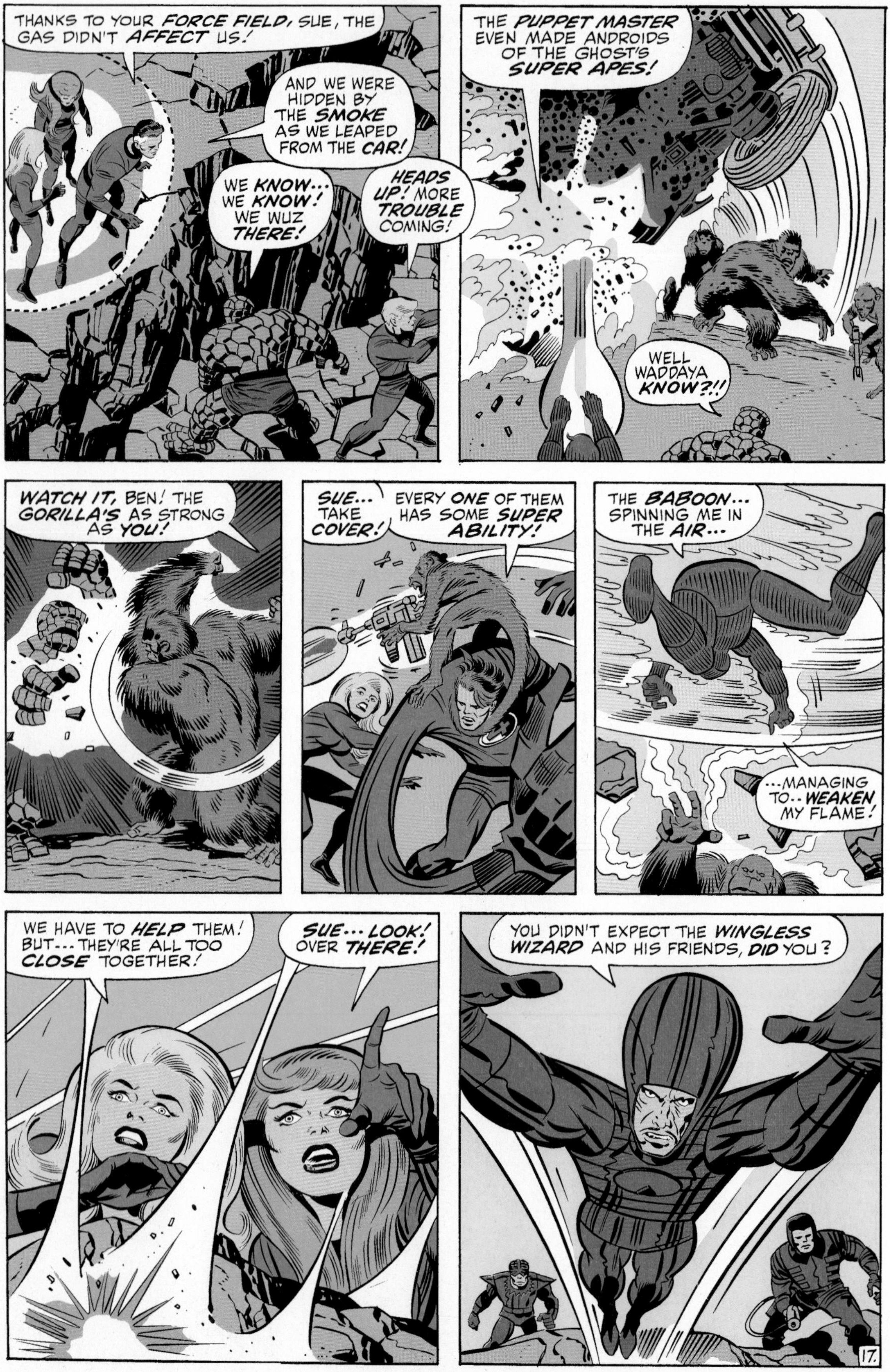
THANKS TO YOUR FORCE FIELD, SUE, THE GAS DIDN'T AFFECT US!
AND WE WERE HIDDEN BY THE SMOKE AS WE LEAPED FROM THE CAR!
WE KNOW... WE KNOW! WE WUZ THERE!
HEADS UP! MORE TROUBLE COMING!
THE PUPPET MASTER EVEN MADE ANDROIDS OF THE GHOST'S SUPER APES!
WELL WADDAYA KNOW?!!
WATCH IT, BEN! THE GORILLA'S AS STRONG AS YOU!
SUE... TAKE COVER!
EVERY ONE OF THEM HAS SOME SUPER ABILITY!
THE BABOON... SPINNING ME IN THE AIR...
...MANAGING TO.. WEAKEN MY FLAME!
WE HAVE TO HELP THEM! BUT--- THEY'RE ALL TOO CLOSE TOGETHER!
SUE... LOOK! OVER THERE!
YOU DIDN'T EXPECT THE WINGLESS WIZARD AND HIS FRIENDS, DID YOU?
17.

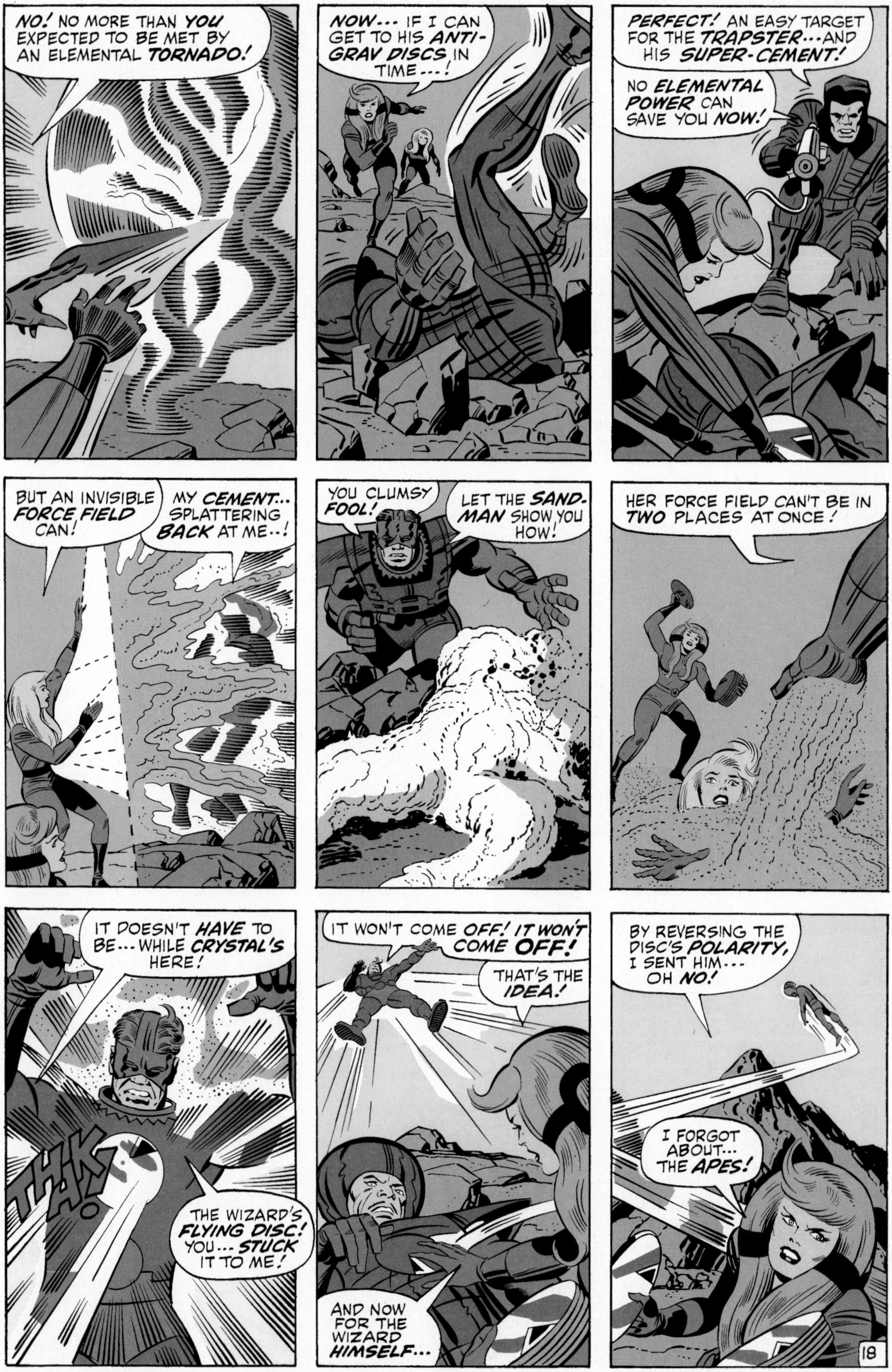
NO! NO MORE THAN YOU EXPECTED TO BE MET BY AN ELEMENTAL TORNADO!
NOW... IF I CAN GET TO HIS ANTI-GRAV DISCS IN TIME...!
PERFECT! AN EASY TARGET FOR THE TRAPSTER...AND HIS SUPER-CEMENT!
NO ELEMENTAL POWER CAN SAVE YOU NOW!
BUT AN INVISIBLE FORCE FIELD CAN!
MY CEMENT... SPLATTERING BACK AT ME..!
YOU CLUMSY FOOL!
LET THE SAND-MAN SHOW YOU HOW!
HER FORCE FIELD CAN'T BE IN TWO PLACES AT ONCE!
IT DOESN'T HAVE TO BE...WHILE CRYSTAL'S HERE!
THAK!
THE WIZARD'S FLYING DISC! YOU... STUCK IT TO ME!
IT WON'T COME OFF! IT WON'T COME OFF!
THAT'S THE IDEA!
AND NOW FOR THE WIZARD HIMSELF...
BY REVERSING THE DISC'S POLARITY, I SENT HIM... OH NO!
I FORGOT ABOUT... THE APES!
18

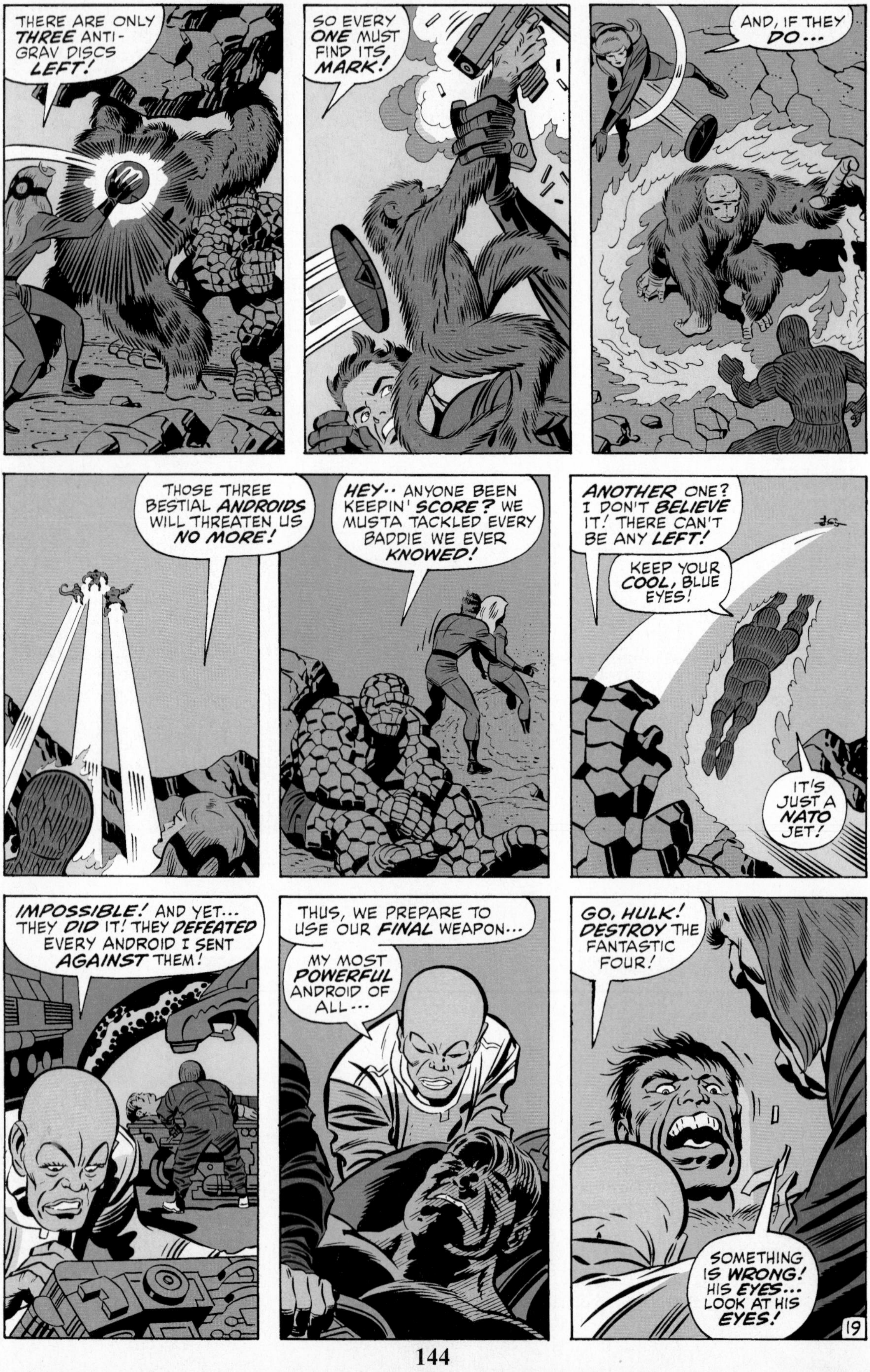
THERE ARE ONLY THREE ANTI-GRAV DISCS LEFT!
SO EVERY ONE MUST FIND ITS MARK!
AND, IF THEY DO...
THOSE THREE BESTIAL ANDROIDS WILL THREATEN US NO MORE!
HEY.. ANYONE BEEN KEEPIN' SCORE? WE MUSTA TACKLED EVERY BADDIE WE EVER KNOWED!
ANOTHER ONE? I DON'T BELIEVE IT! THERE CAN'T BE ANY LEFT!
KEEP YOUR COOL, BLUE EYES!
IT'S JUST A NATO JET!
IMPOSSIBLE! AND YET... THEY DID IT! THEY DEFEATED EVERY ANDROID I SENT AGAINST THEM!
THUS, WE PREPARE TO USE OUR FINAL WEAPON...
MY MOST POWERFUL ANDROID OF ALL...
GO, HULK! DESTROY THE FANTASTIC FOUR!
SOMETHING IS WRONG! HIS EYES... LOOK AT HIS EYES!
19

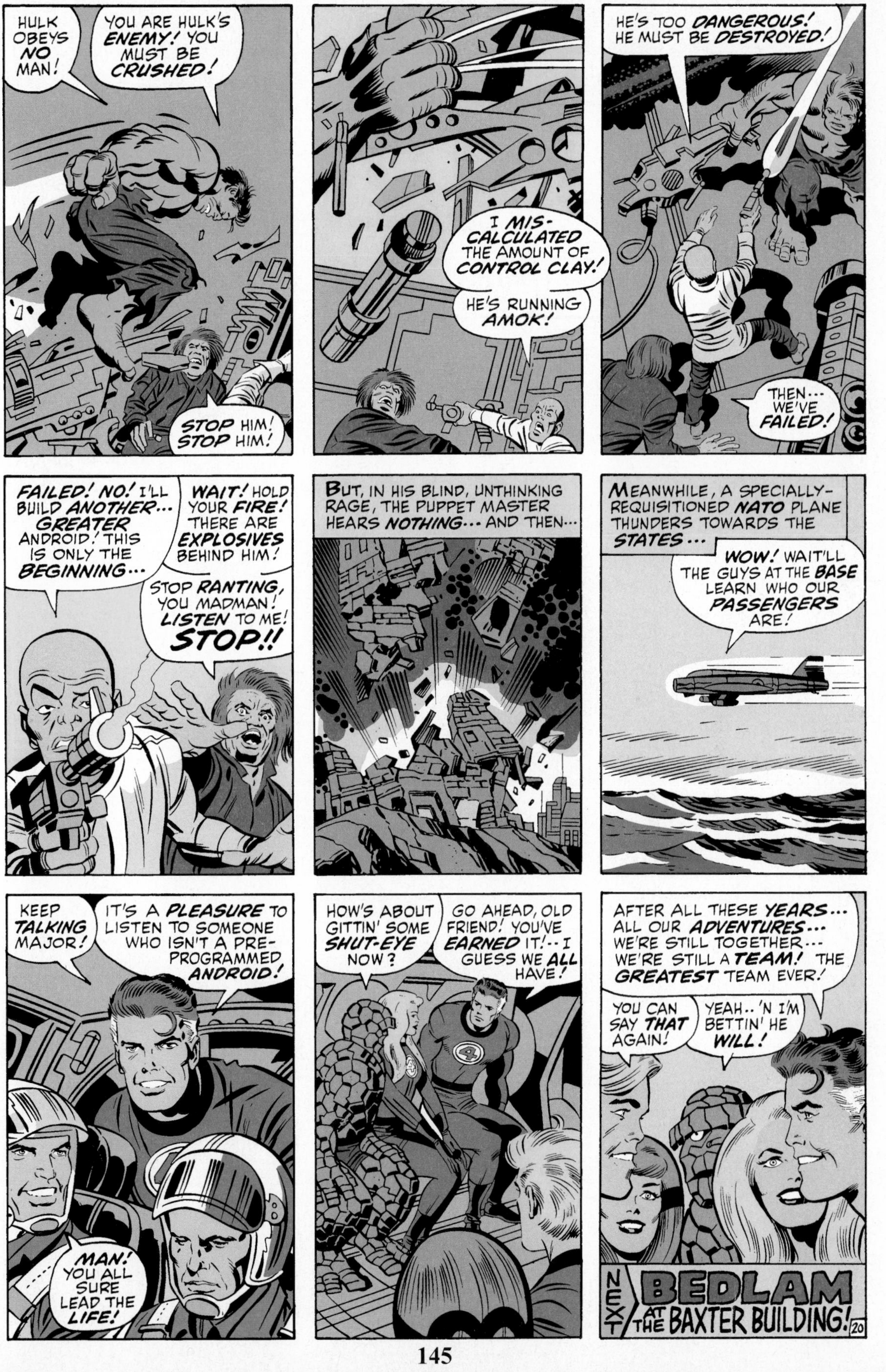
HULK OBEYS NO MAN!
YOU ARE HULK'S ENEMY! YOU MUST BE CRUSHED!
STOP HIM! STOP HIM!
I MIS-CALCULATED THE AMOUNT OF CONTROL CLAY!
HE'S RUNNING AMOK!
HE'S TOO DANGEROUS! HE MUST BE DESTROYED!
THEN... WE'VE FAILED!
FAILED! NO! I'LL BUILD ANOTHER... GREATER ANDROID! THIS IS ONLY THE BEGINNING...
WAIT! HOLD YOUR FIRE! THERE ARE EXPLOSIVES BEHIND HIM!
STOP RANTING, YOU MADMAN! LISTEN TO ME! STOP!!
BUT, IN HIS BLIND, UNTHINKING RAGE, THE PUPPET MASTER HEARS NOTHING... AND THEN...
MEANWHILE, A SPECIALLY-REQUISITIONED NATO PLANE THUNDERS TOWARDS THE STATES...
WOW! WAIT'LL THE GUYS AT THE BASE LEARN WHO OUR PASSENGERS ARE!
KEEP TALKING MAJOR!
IT'S A PLEASURE TO LISTEN TO SOMEONE WHO ISN'T A PRE-PROGRAMMED ANDROID!
MAN! YOU ALL SURE LEAD THE LIFE!
HOW'S ABOUT GITTIN' SOME SHUT-EYE NOW?
GO AHEAD, OLD FRIEND! YOU'VE EARNED IT!-- I GUESS WE ALL HAVE!
AFTER ALL THESE YEARS... ALL OUR ADVENTURES... WE'RE STILL TOGETHER... WE'RE STILL A TEAM! THE GREATEST TEAM EVER!
YOU CAN SAY THAT AGAIN!
YEAH.. 'N I'M BETTIN' HE WILL!
NEXT/ BEDLAM AT THE BAXTER BUILDING!
20

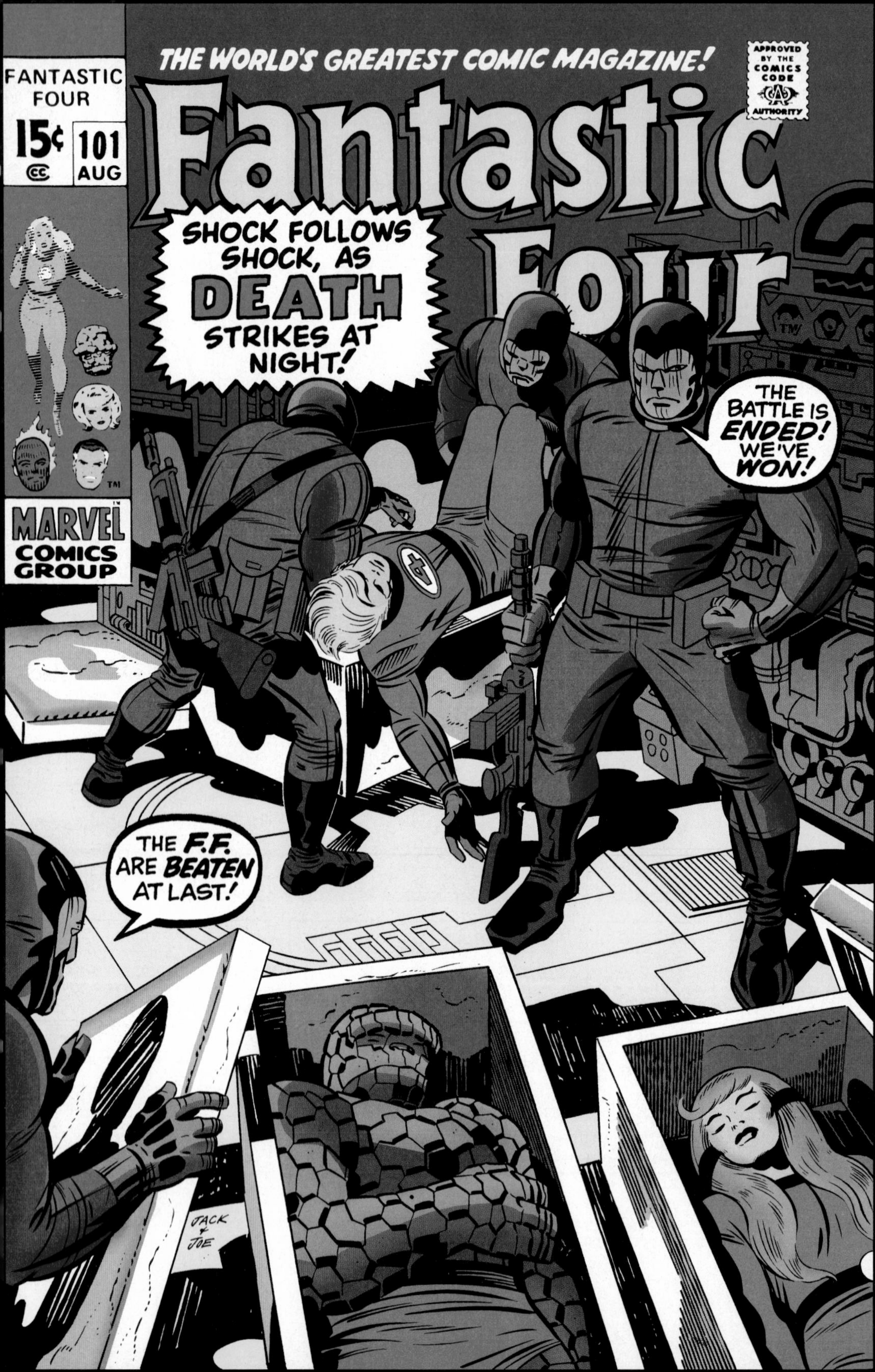
THE WORLD'S GREATEST COMIC MAGAZINE!
FANTASTIC FOUR
15¢
101
AUG
APPROVED BY THE COMICS CODE AUTHORITY
Fantastic Four
SHOCK FOLLOWS SHOCK, AS DEATH STRIKES AT NIGHT!
THE BATTLE IS ENDED! WE'VE WON!
MARVEL COMICS GROUP
THE F.F. ARE BEATEN AT LAST!
JACK + JOE

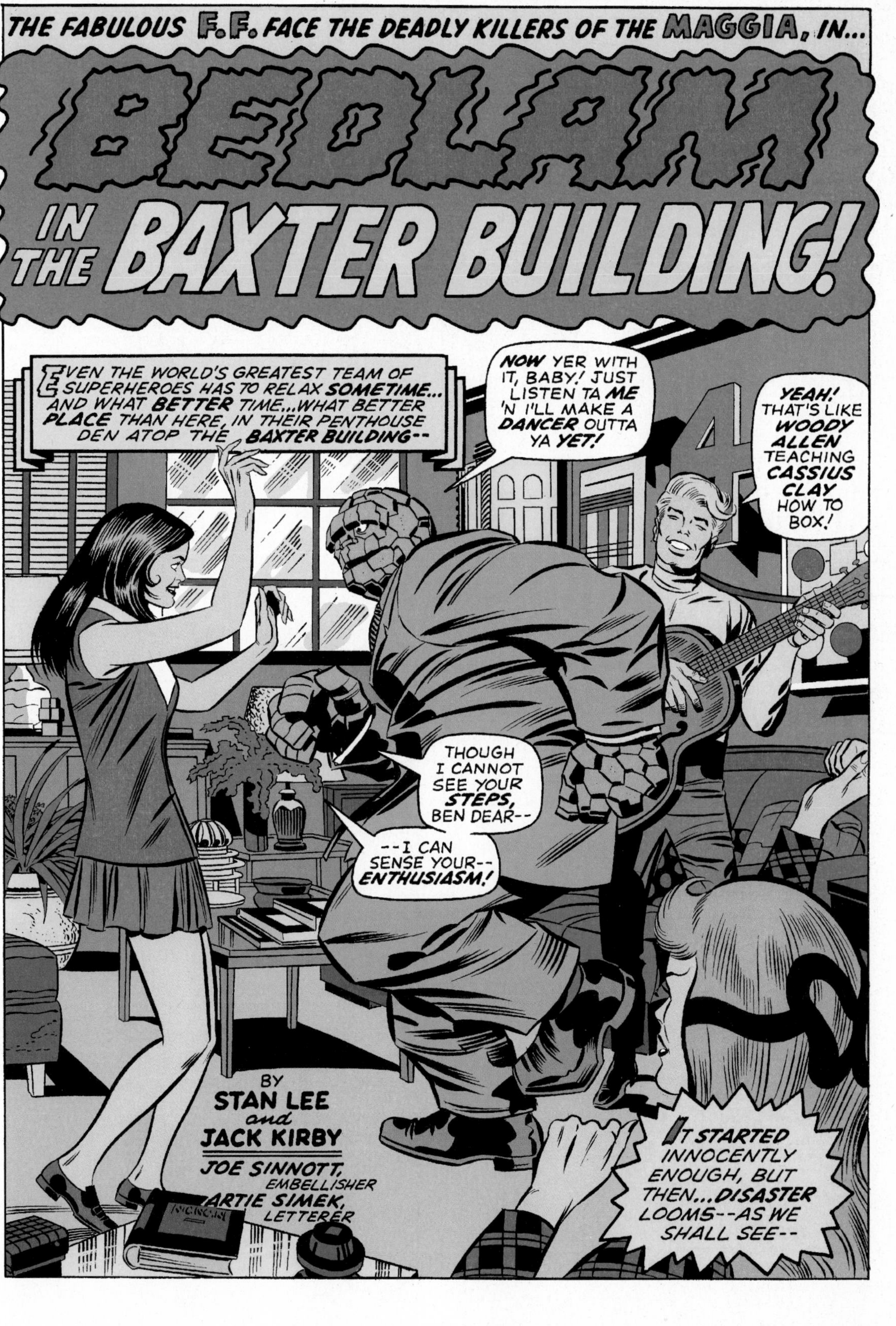

THE FABULOUS F.F. FACE THE DEADLY KILLERS OF THE MAGGIA, IN...
BEDLAM IN THE BAXTER BUILDING!
EVEN THE WORLD'S GREATEST TEAM OF SUPERHEROES HAS TO RELAX SOMETIME... AND WHAT BETTER TIME...WHAT BETTER PLACE THAN HERE, IN THEIR PENTHOUSE DEN ATOP THE BAXTER BUILDING--
NOW YER WITH IT, BABY! JUST LISTEN TA ME 'N I'LL MAKE A DANCER OUTTA YA YET!
YEAH! THAT'S LIKE WOODY ALLEN TEACHING CASSIUS CLAY HOW TO BOX!
THOUGH I CANNOT SEE YOUR STEPS, BEN DEAR--
--I CAN SENSE YOUR-- ENTHUSIASM!
BY STAN LEE and JACK KIRBY
JOE SINNOTT, EMBELLISHER
ARTIE SIMEK, LETTERER
IT STARTED INNOCENTLY ENOUGH, BUT THEN...DISASTER LOOMS--AS WE SHALL SEE--

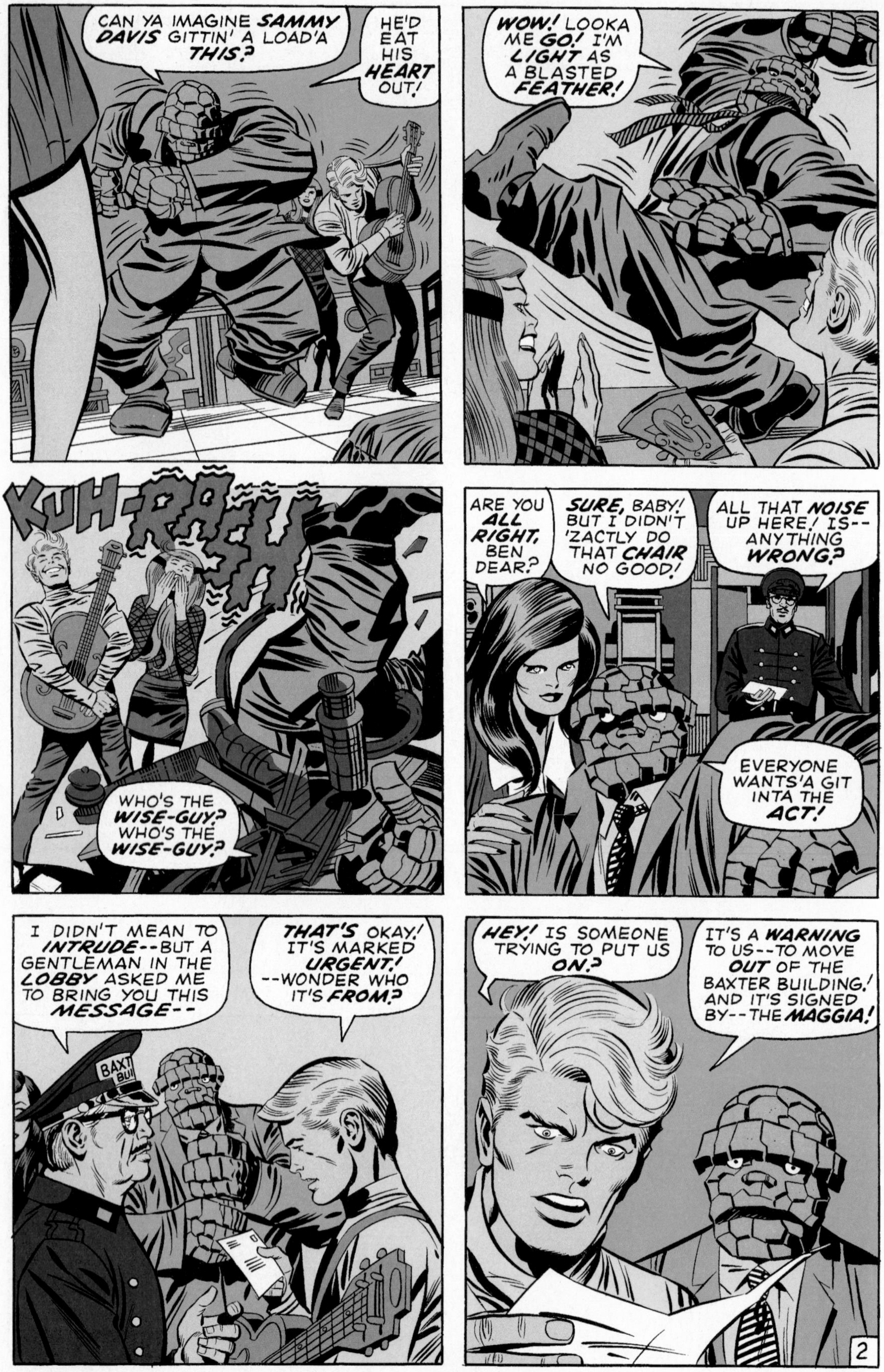

CAN YA IMAGINE SAMMY DAVIS GITTIN' A LOAD'A THIS?
HE'D EAT HIS HEART OUT!
WOW! LOOKA ME GO! I'M LIGHT AS A BLASTED FEATHER!
KUH-RASH
WHO'S THE WISE-GUY? WHO'S THE WISE-GUY?
ARE YOU ALL RIGHT, BEN DEAR?
SURE, BABY! BUT I DIDN'T 'ZACTLY DO THAT CHAIR NO GOOD!
ALL THAT NOISE UP HERE! IS-- ANYTHING WRONG?
EVERYONE WANTS'A GIT INTA THE ACT!
I DIDN'T MEAN TO INTRUDE--BUT A GENTLEMAN IN THE LOBBY ASKED ME TO BRING YOU THIS MESSAGE--
THAT'S OKAY! IT'S MARKED URGENT! --WONDER WHO IT'S FROM?
HEY! IS SOMEONE TRYING TO PUT US ON?
IT'S A WARNING TO US--TO MOVE OUT OF THE BAXTER BUILDING! AND IT'S SIGNED BY--THE MAGGIA!
2

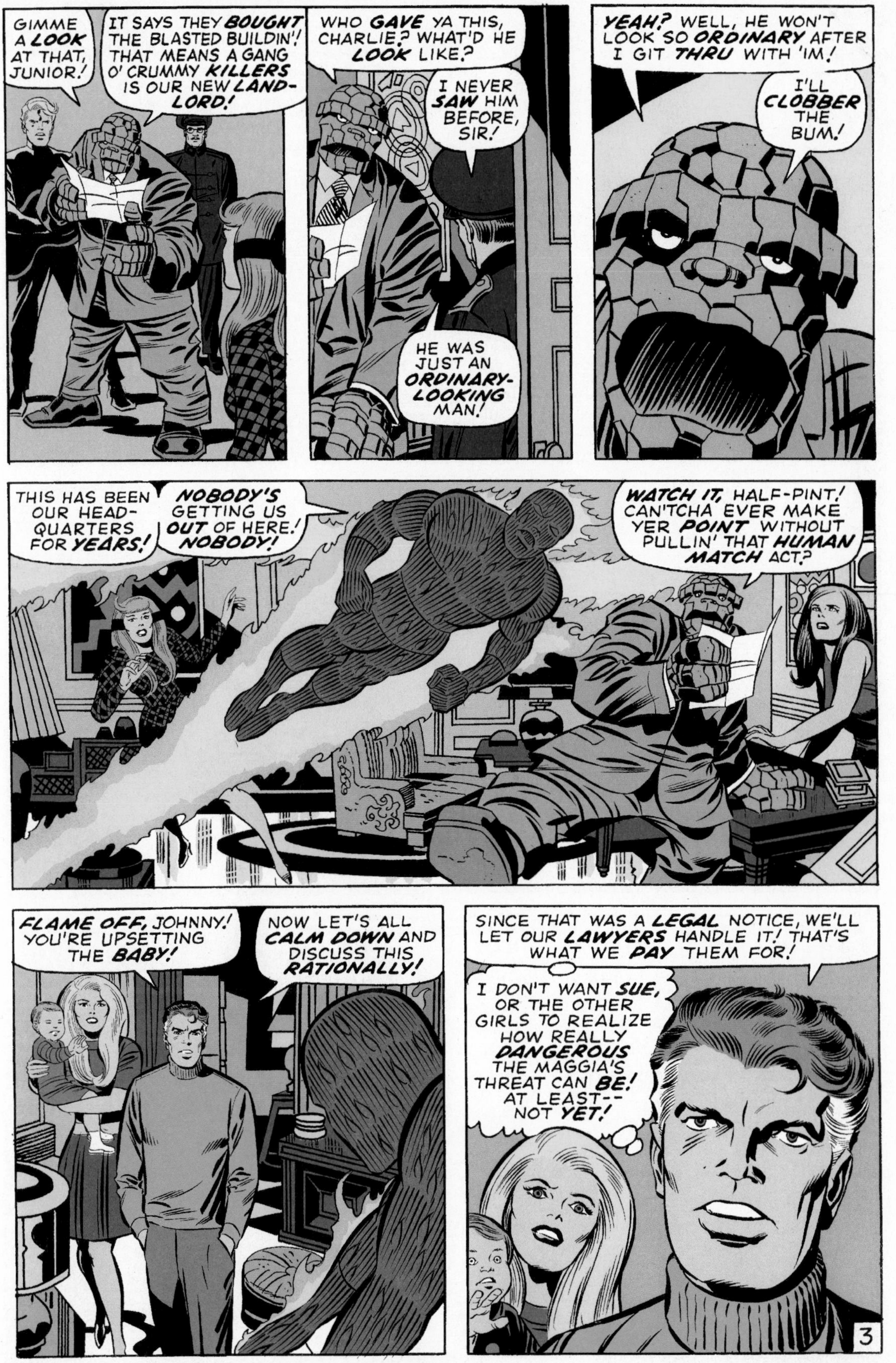
GIMME A LOOK AT THAT, JUNIOR!
IT SAYS THEY BOUGHT THE BLASTED BUILDIN'! THAT MEANS A GANG O' CRUMMY KILLERS IS OUR NEW LAND-LORD!
WHO GAVE YA THIS, CHARLIE? WHAT'D HE LOOK LIKE?
I NEVER SAW HIM BEFORE, SIR!
HE WAS JUST AN ORDINARY-LOOKING MAN!
YEAH? WELL, HE WON'T LOOK SO ORDINARY AFTER I GIT THRU WITH 'IM!
I'LL CLOBBER THE BUM!
THIS HAS BEEN OUR HEAD-QUARTERS FOR YEARS!
NOBODY'S GETTING US OUT OF HERE! NOBODY!
WATCH IT, HALF-PINT! CAN'TCHA EVER MAKE YER POINT WITHOUT PULLIN' THAT HUMAN MATCH ACT?
FLAME OFF, JOHNNY! YOU'RE UPSETTING THE BABY!
NOW LET'S ALL CALM DOWN AND DISCUSS THIS RATIONALLY!
SINCE THAT WAS A LEGAL NOTICE, WE'LL LET OUR LAWYERS HANDLE IT! THAT'S WHAT WE PAY THEM FOR!
I DON'T WANT SUE, OR THE OTHER GIRLS TO REALIZE HOW REALLY DANGEROUS THE MAGGIA'S THREAT CAN BE! AT LEAST-- NOT YET!
3

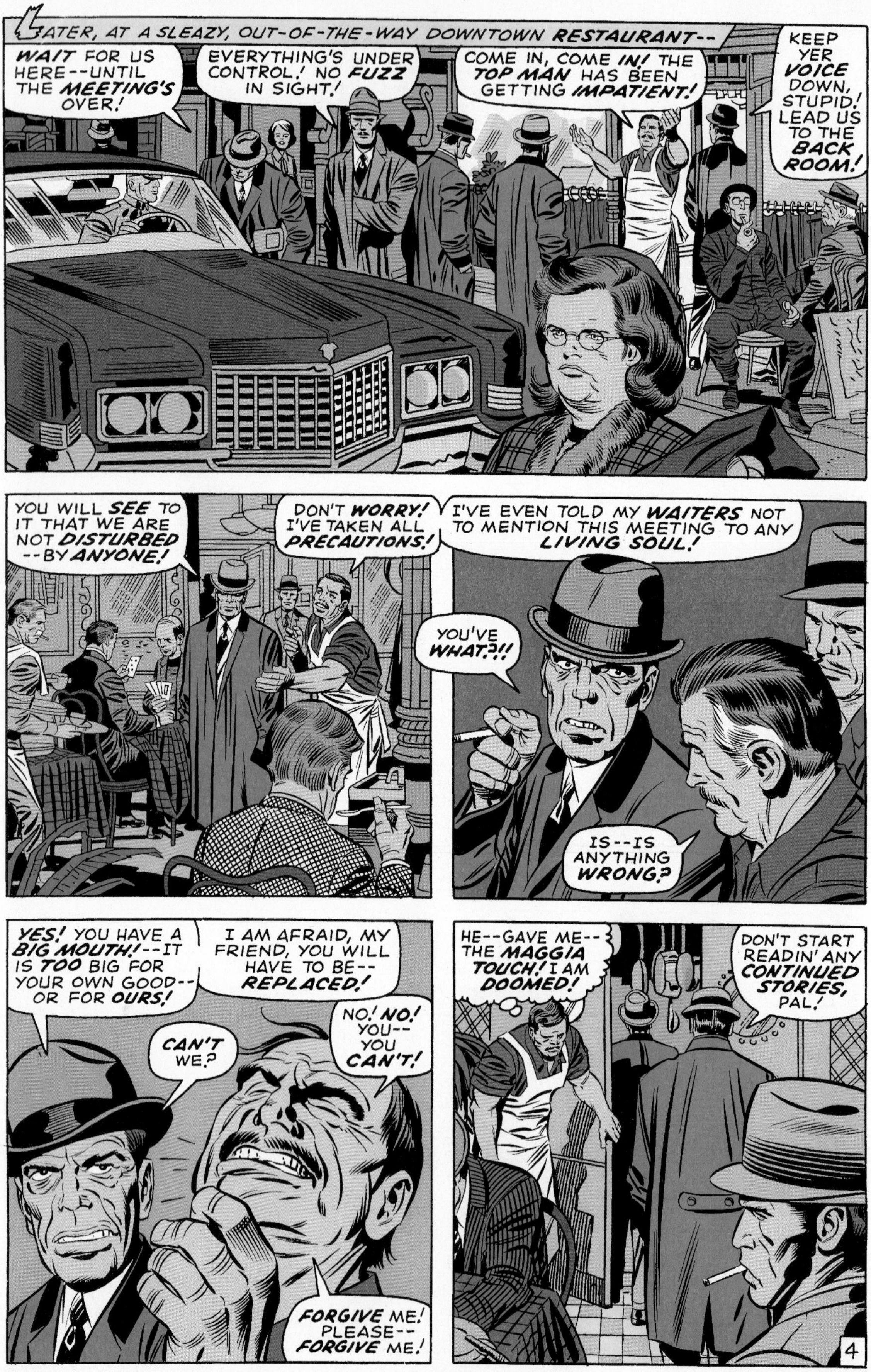
LATER, AT A SLEAZY, OUT-OF-THE-WAY DOWNTOWN RESTAURANT--
WAIT FOR US HERE--UNTIL THE MEETING'S OVER!
EVERYTHING'S UNDER CONTROL! NO FUZZ IN SIGHT!
COME IN, COME IN! THE TOP MAN HAS BEEN GETTING IMPATIENT!
KEEP YER VOICE DOWN, STUPID! LEAD US TO THE BACK ROOM!
YOU WILL SEE TO IT THAT WE ARE NOT DISTURBED --BY ANYONE!
DON'T WORRY! I'VE TAKEN ALL PRECAUTIONS!
I'VE EVEN TOLD MY WAITERS NOT TO MENTION THIS MEETING TO ANY LIVING SOUL!
YOU'VE WHAT?!!
IS--IS ANYTHING WRONG?
YES! YOU HAVE A BIG MOUTH!--IT IS TOO BIG FOR YOUR OWN GOOD--OR FOR OURS!
I AM AFRAID, MY FRIEND, YOU WILL HAVE TO BE--REPLACED!
NO! NO! YOU--YOU CAN'T!
CAN'T WE?
FORGIVE ME! PLEASE--FORGIVE ME!
HE--GAVE ME--THE MAGGIA TOUCH! I AM DOOMED!
DON'T START READIN' ANY CONTINUED STORIES, PAL!
4

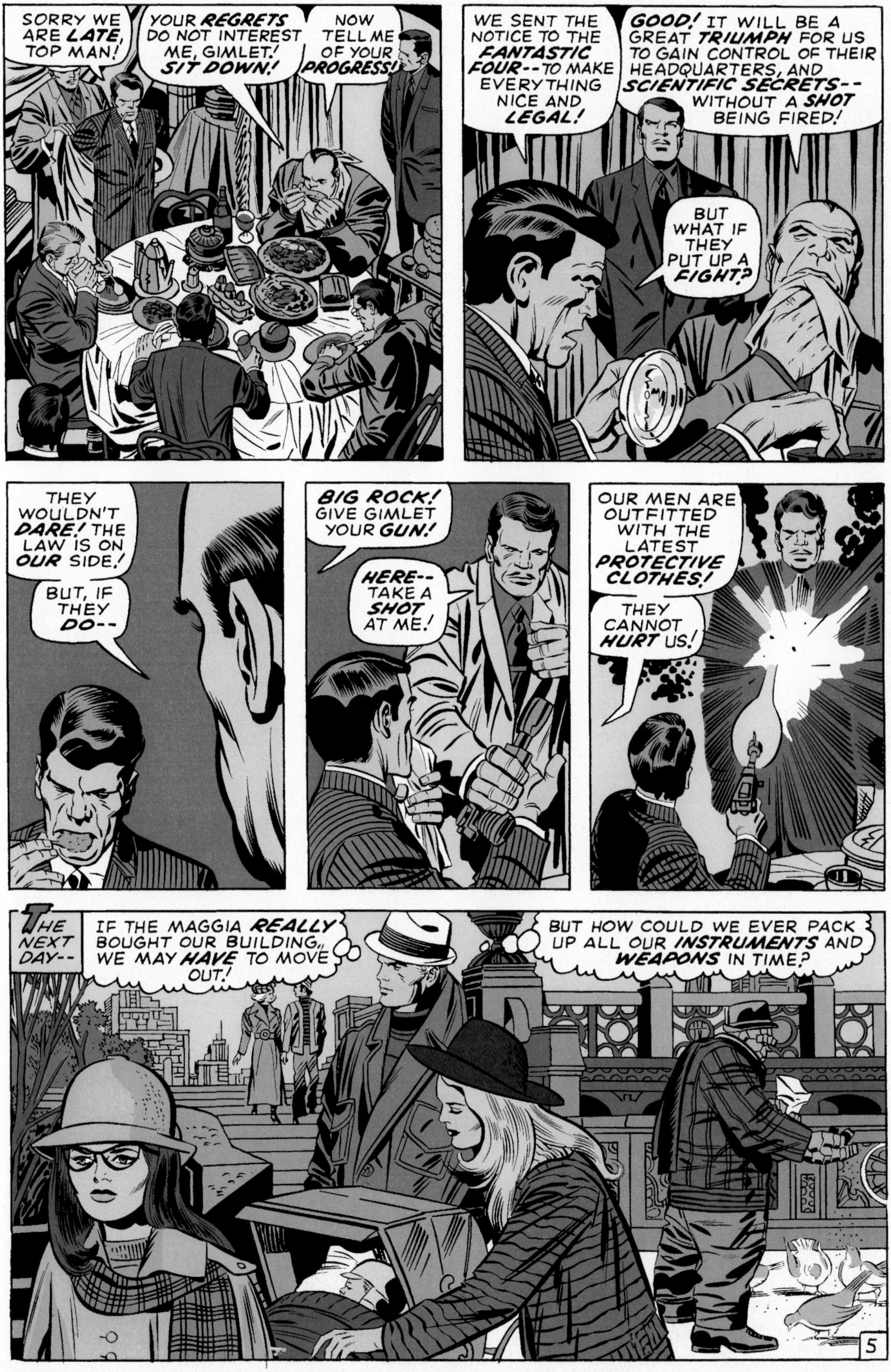
SORRY WE ARE LATE, TOP MAN!
YOUR REGRETS DO NOT INTEREST ME, GIMLET! SIT DOWN!
NOW TELL ME OF YOUR PROGRESS!
WE SENT THE NOTICE TO THE FANTASTIC FOUR--TO MAKE EVERYTHING NICE AND LEGAL!
GOOD! IT WILL BE A GREAT TRIUMPH FOR US TO GAIN CONTROL OF THEIR HEADQUARTERS, AND SCIENTIFIC SECRETS-- WITHOUT A SHOT BEING FIRED!
BUT WHAT IF THEY PUT UP A FIGHT?
THEY WOULDN'T DARE! THE LAW IS ON OUR SIDE!
BUT, IF THEY DO--
BIG ROCK! GIVE GIMLET YOUR GUN!
HERE-- TAKE A SHOT AT ME!
OUR MEN ARE OUTFITTED WITH THE LATEST PROTECTIVE CLOTHES!
THEY CANNOT HURT US!
THE NEXT DAY--
IF THE MAGGIA REALLY BOUGHT OUR BUILDING, WE MAY HAVE TO MOVE OUT!
BUT HOW COULD WE EVER PACK UP ALL OUR INSTRUMENTS AND WEAPONS IN TIME?
5

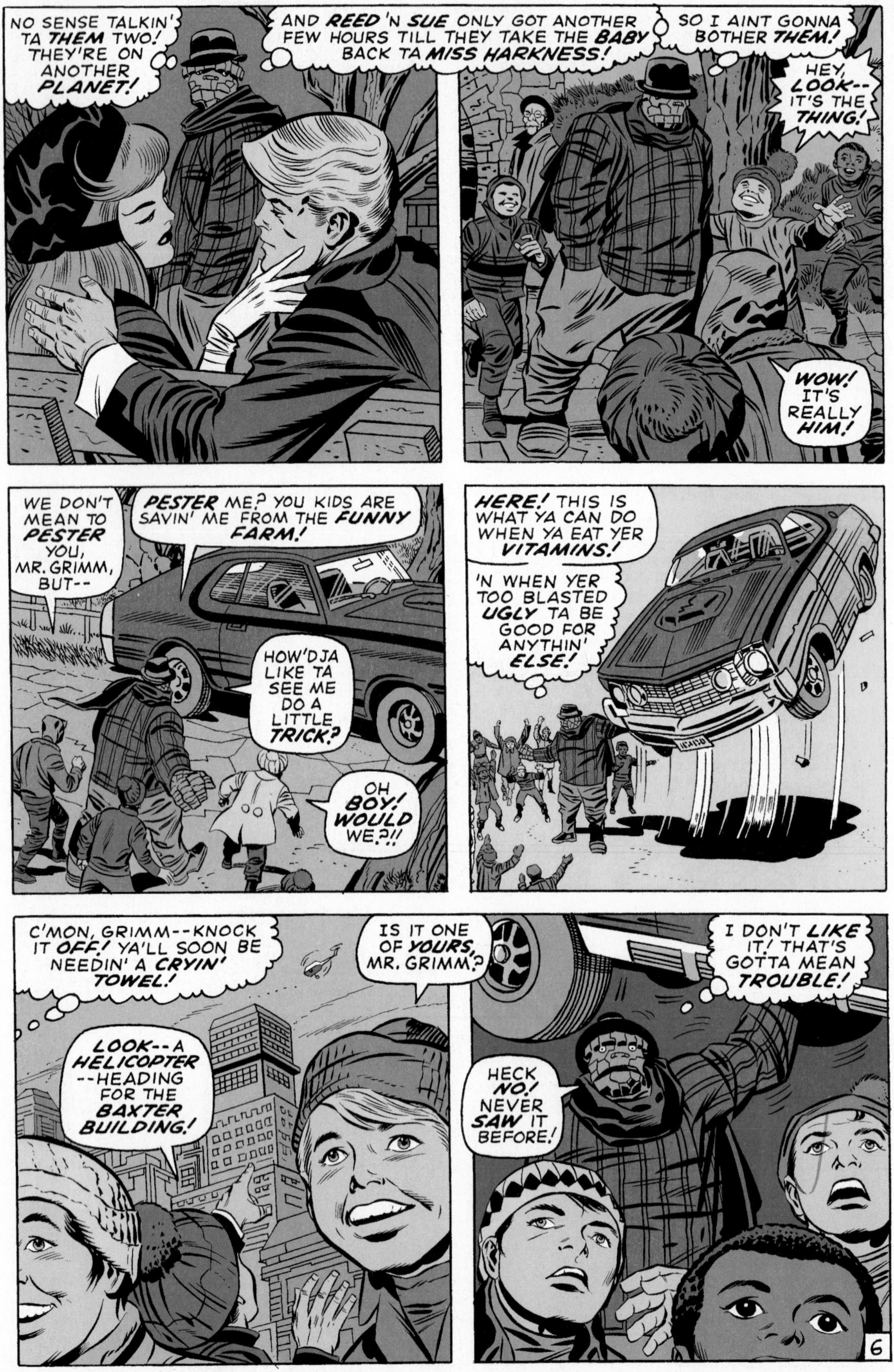

NO SENSE TALKIN' TA THEM TWO! THEY'RE ON ANOTHER PLANET!
AND REED 'N SUE ONLY GOT ANOTHER FEW HOURS TILL THEY TAKE THE BABY BACK TA MISS HARKNESS!
SO I AINT GONNA BOTHER THEM!
HEY, LOOK-- IT'S THE THING!
WOW! IT'S REALLY HIM!
WE DON'T MEAN TO PESTER YOU, MR. GRIMM, BUT--
PESTER ME? YOU KIDS ARE SAVIN' ME FROM THE FUNNY FARM!
HOW'DJA LIKE TA SEE ME DO A LITTLE TRICK?
OH BOY! WOULD WE?!!
HERE! THIS IS WHAT YA CAN DO WHEN YA EAT YER VITAMINS!
'N WHEN YER TOO BLASTED UGLY TA BE GOOD FOR ANYTHIN' ELSE!
C'MON, GRIMM--KNOCK IT OFF! YA'LL SOON BE NEEDIN' A CRYIN' TOWEL!
LOOK--A HELICOPTER --HEADING FOR THE BAXTER BUILDING!
IS IT ONE OF YOURS, MR. GRIMM?
I DON'T LIKE IT! THAT'S GOTTA MEAN TROUBLE!
HECK NO! NEVER SAW IT BEFORE!
6

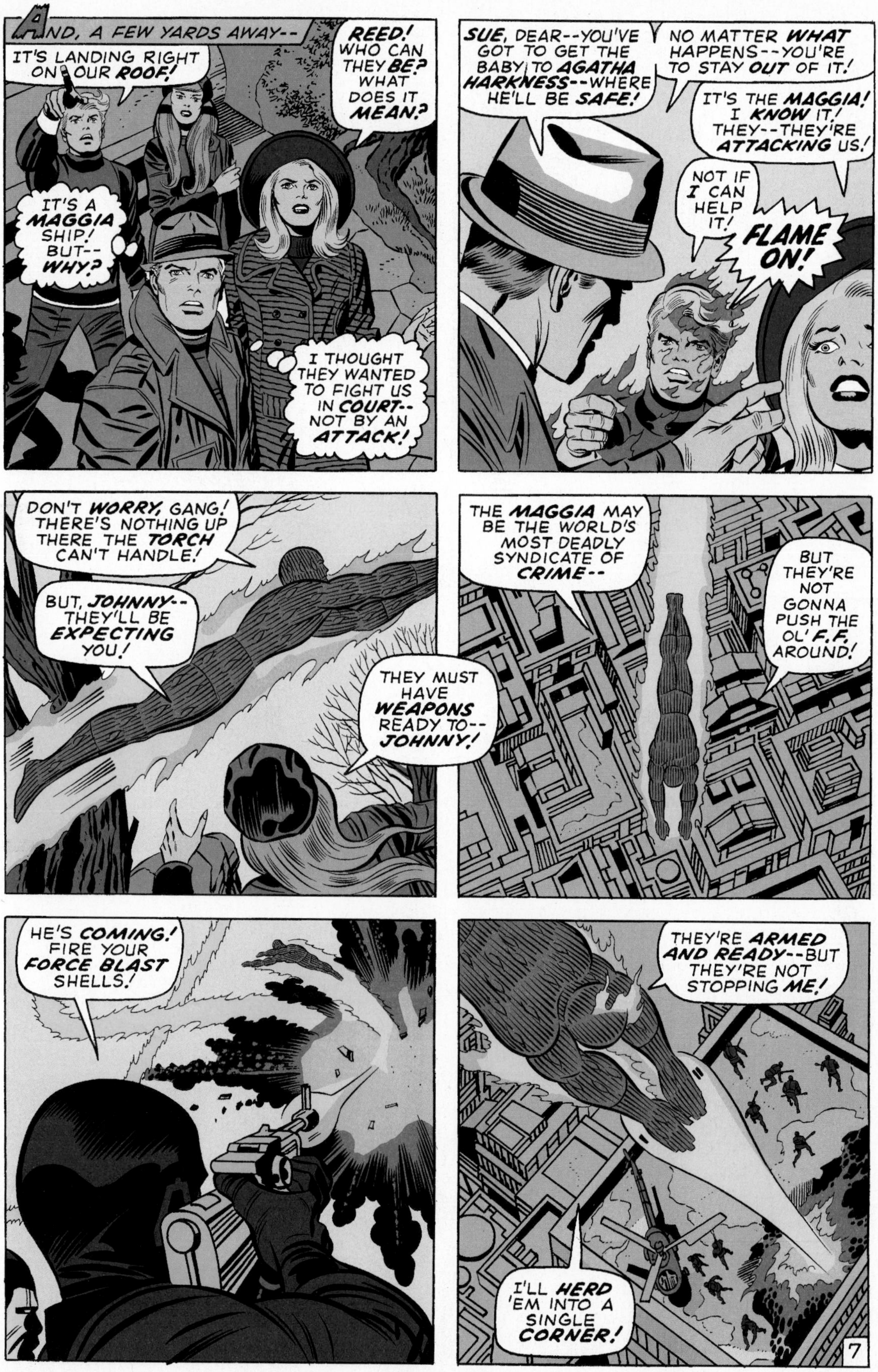
AND, A FEW YARDS AWAY--
IT'S LANDING RIGHT ON OUR ROOF!
REED! WHO CAN THEY BE? WHAT DOES IT MEAN?
IT'S A MAGGIA SHIP! BUT-- WHY?
I THOUGHT THEY WANTED TO FIGHT US IN COURT-- NOT BY AN ATTACK!
SUE, DEAR--YOU'VE GOT TO GET THE BABY TO AGATHA HARKNESS--WHERE HE'LL BE SAFE!
NO MATTER WHAT HAPPENS--YOU'RE TO STAY OUT OF IT!
IT'S THE MAGGIA! I KNOW IT! THEY--THEY'RE ATTACKING US!
NOT IF I CAN HELP IT!
FLAME ON!
DON'T WORRY, GANG! THERE'S NOTHING UP THERE THE TORCH CAN'T HANDLE!
BUT, JOHNNY-- THEY'LL BE EXPECTING YOU!
THEY MUST HAVE WEAPONS READY TO-- JOHNNY!
THE MAGGIA MAY BE THE WORLD'S MOST DEADLY SYNDICATE OF CRIME--
BUT THEY'RE NOT GONNA PUSH THE OL' F.F. AROUND!
HE'S COMING! FIRE YOUR FORCE BLAST SHELLS!
THEY'RE ARMED AND READY--BUT THEY'RE NOT STOPPING ME!
I'LL HERD 'EM INTO A SINGLE CORNER!
7

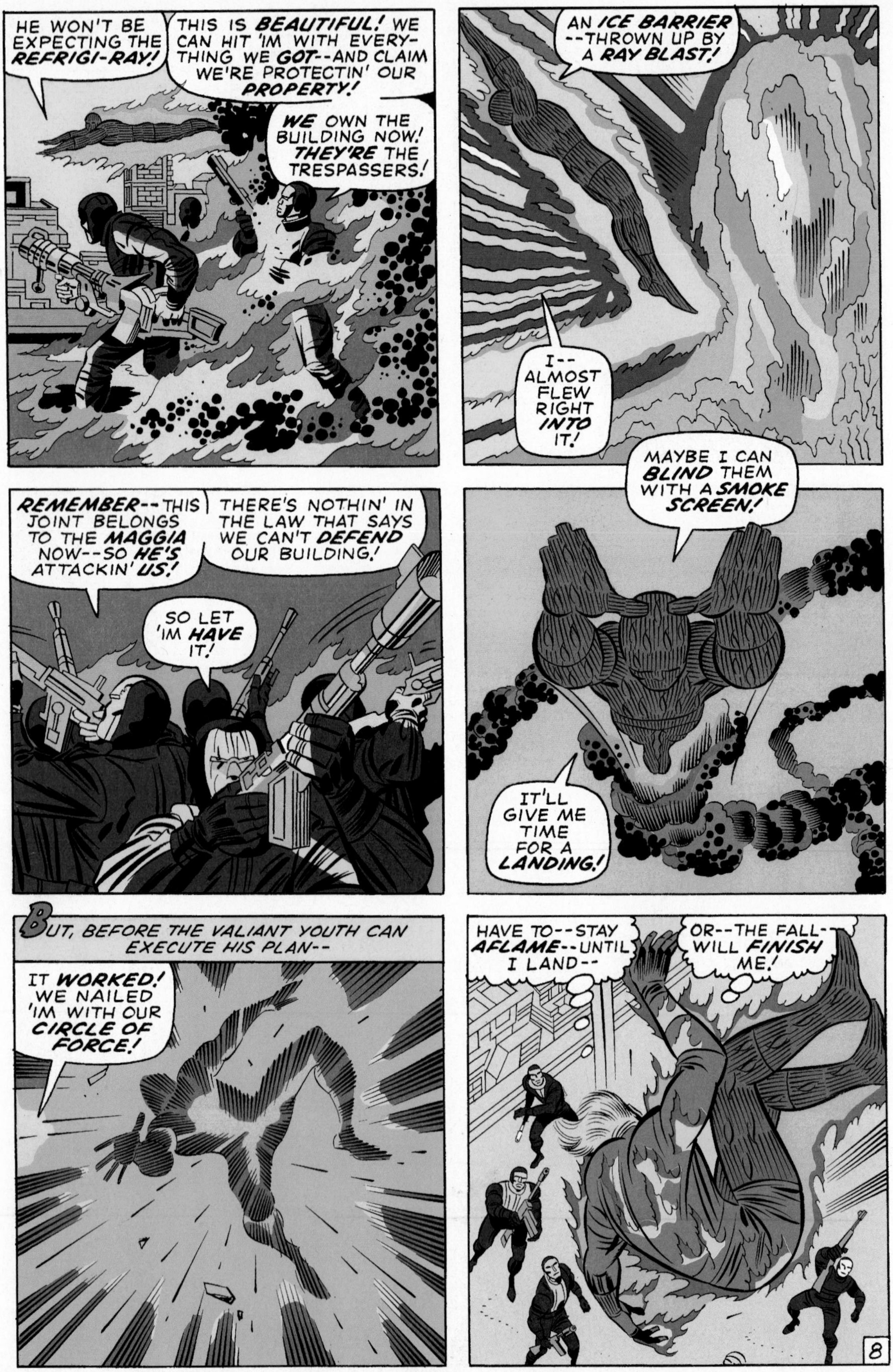
HE WON'T BE EXPECTING THE REFRIGI-RAY!
THIS IS BEAUTIFUL! WE CAN HIT 'IM WITH EVERY-THING WE GOT--AND CLAIM WE'RE PROTECTIN' OUR PROPERTY!
WE OWN THE BUILDING NOW! THEY'RE THE TRESPASSERS!
AN ICE BARRIER --THROWN UP BY A RAY BLAST!
I-- ALMOST FLEW RIGHT INTO IT!
REMEMBER--THIS JOINT BELONGS TO THE MAGGIA NOW--SO HE'S ATTACKIN' US!
THERE'S NOTHIN' IN THE LAW THAT SAYS WE CAN'T DEFEND OUR BUILDING!
SO LET 'IM HAVE IT!
MAYBE I CAN BLIND THEM WITH A SMOKE SCREEN!
IT'LL GIVE ME TIME FOR A LANDING!
BUT, BEFORE THE VALIANT YOUTH CAN EXECUTE HIS PLAN--
IT WORKED! WE NAILED 'IM WITH OUR CIRCLE OF FORCE!
HAVE TO--STAY AFLAME--UNTIL I LAND--
OR--THE FALL-WILL FINISH ME!
8

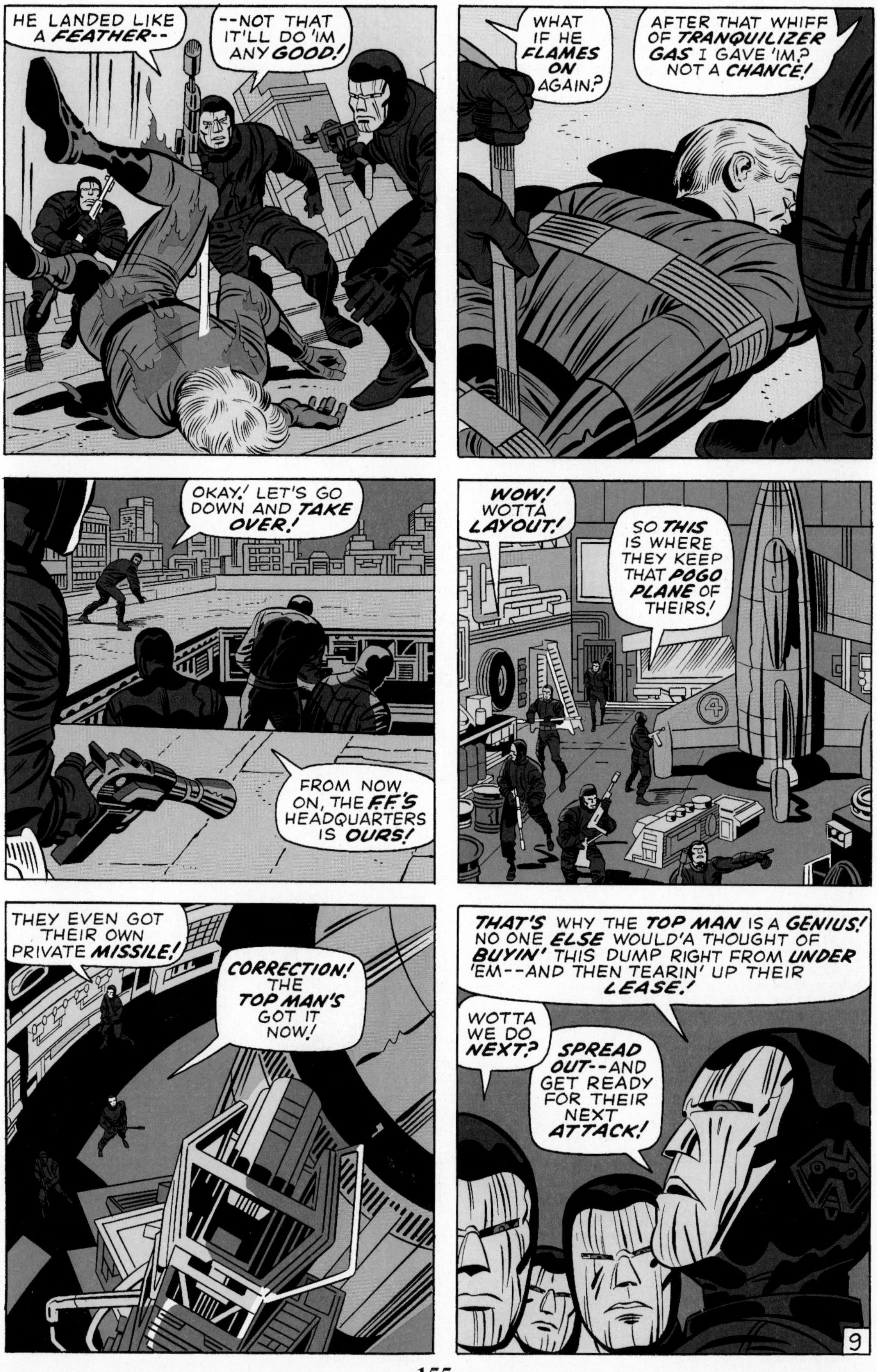
HE LANDED LIKE A FEATHER--
--NOT THAT IT'LL DO 'IM ANY GOOD!
WHAT IF HE FLAMES ON AGAIN?
AFTER THAT WHIFF OF TRANQUILIZER GAS I GAVE 'IM? NOT A CHANCE!
OKAY! LET'S GO DOWN AND TAKE OVER!
FROM NOW ON, THE F.F.'S HEADQUARTERS IS OURS!
WOW! WOTTA LAYOUT!
SO THIS IS WHERE THEY KEEP THAT POGO PLANE OF THEIRS!
THEY EVEN GOT THEIR OWN PRIVATE MISSILE!
CORRECTION! THE TOP MAN'S GOT IT NOW!
THAT'S WHY THE TOP MAN IS A GENIUS! NO ONE ELSE WOULD'A THOUGHT OF BUYIN' THIS DUMP RIGHT FROM UNDER 'EM--AND THEN TEARIN' UP THEIR LEASE!
WOTTA WE DO NEXT?
SPREAD OUT--AND GET READY FOR THEIR NEXT ATTACK!
9

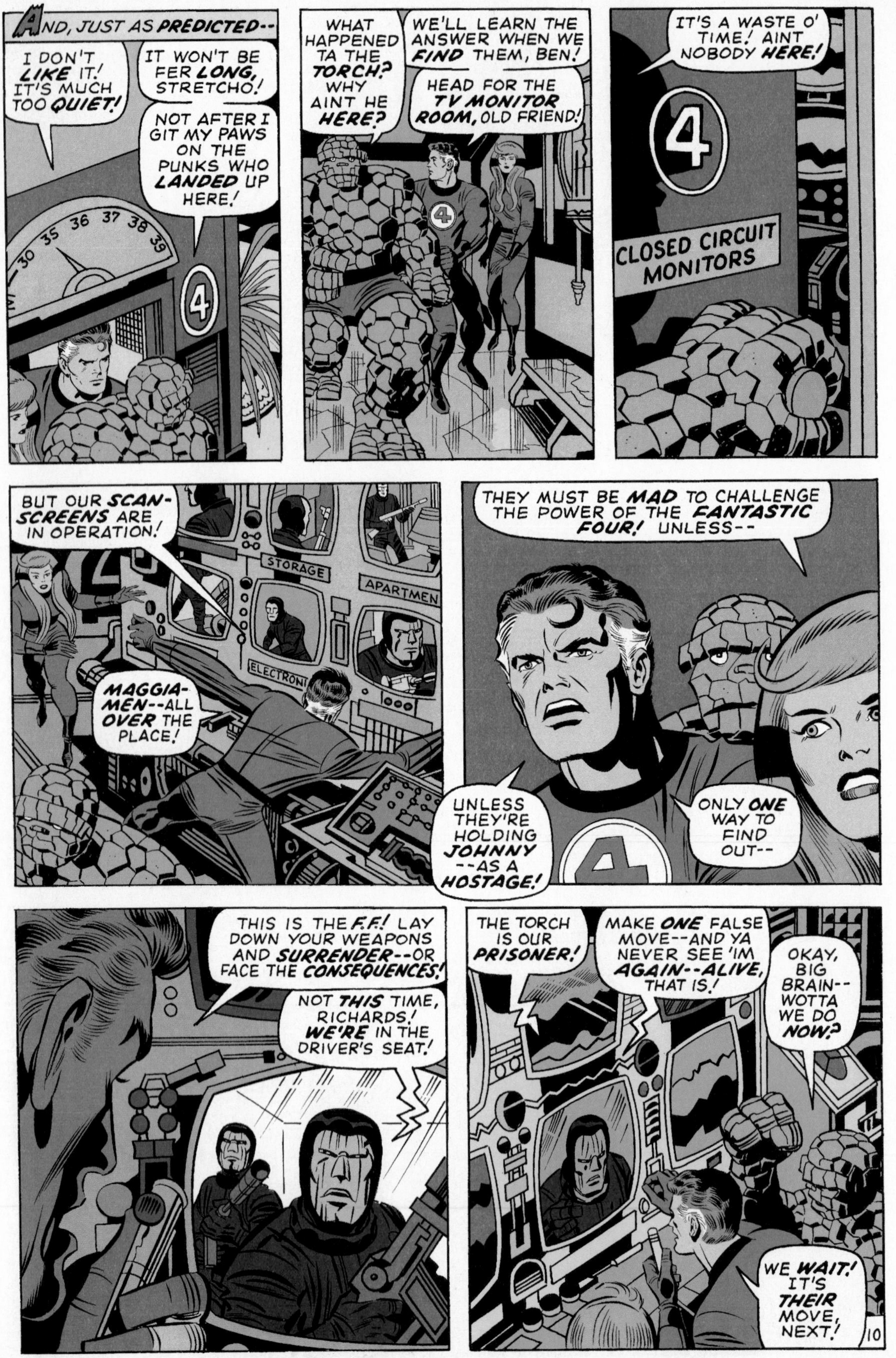
AND, JUST AS PREDICTED--
I DON'T LIKE IT! IT'S MUCH TOO QUIET!
IT WON'T BE FER LONG, STRETCHO!
NOT AFTER I GIT MY PAWS ON THE PUNKS WHO LANDED UP HERE!
30 35 36 37 38 39
4
WHAT HAPPENED TA THE TORCH? WHY AINT HE HERE?
WE'LL LEARN THE ANSWER WHEN WE FIND THEM, BEN!
HEAD FOR THE TV MONITOR ROOM, OLD FRIEND!
4
IT'S A WASTE O' TIME! AINT NOBODY HERE!
4
CLOSED CIRCUIT MONITORS
BUT OUR SCAN-SCREENS ARE IN OPERATION!
STORAGE
APARTMEN
ELECTRONI
MAGGIA-MEN--ALL OVER THE PLACE!
THEY MUST BE MAD TO CHALLENGE THE POWER OF THE FANTASTIC FOUR! UNLESS--
UNLESS THEY'RE HOLDING JOHNNY --AS A HOSTAGE!
ONLY ONE WAY TO FIND OUT--
THIS IS THE F.F.! LAY DOWN YOUR WEAPONS AND SURRENDER--OR FACE THE CONSEQUENCES!
NOT THIS TIME, RICHARDS! WE'RE IN THE DRIVER'S SEAT!
THE TORCH IS OUR PRISONER!
MAKE ONE FALSE MOVE--AND YA NEVER SEE 'IM AGAIN--ALIVE, THAT IS!
OKAY, BIG BRAIN-- WOTTA WE DO NOW?
WE WAIT! IT'S THEIR MOVE, NEXT!
10

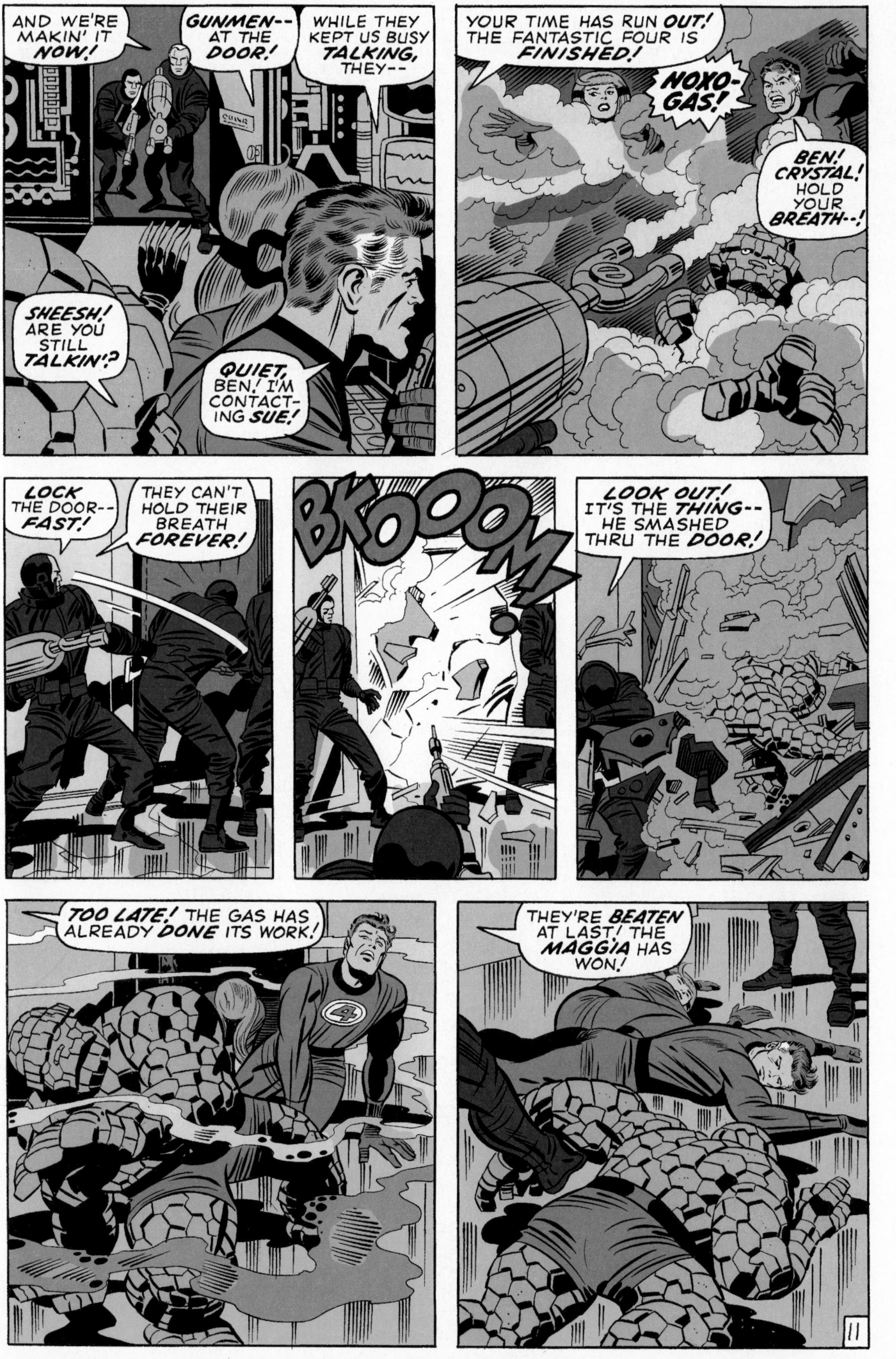
AND WE'RE MAKIN' IT NOW!
GUNMEN-- AT THE DOOR!
WHILE THEY KEPT US BUSY TALKING, THEY--
SHEESH! ARE YOU STILL TALKIN'?
QUIET, BEN! I'M CONTACTING SUE!
YOUR TIME HAS RUN OUT! THE FANTASTIC FOUR IS FINISHED!
NOXO-GAS!
BEN! CRYSTAL! HOLD YOUR BREATH--!
LOCK THE DOOR-- FAST!
THEY CAN'T HOLD THEIR BREATH FOREVER!
BKOOOM!
LOOK OUT! IT'S THE THING-- HE SMASHED THRU THE DOOR!
TOO LATE! THE GAS HAS ALREADY DONE ITS WORK!
THEY'RE BEATEN AT LAST! THE MAGGIA HAS WON!
11

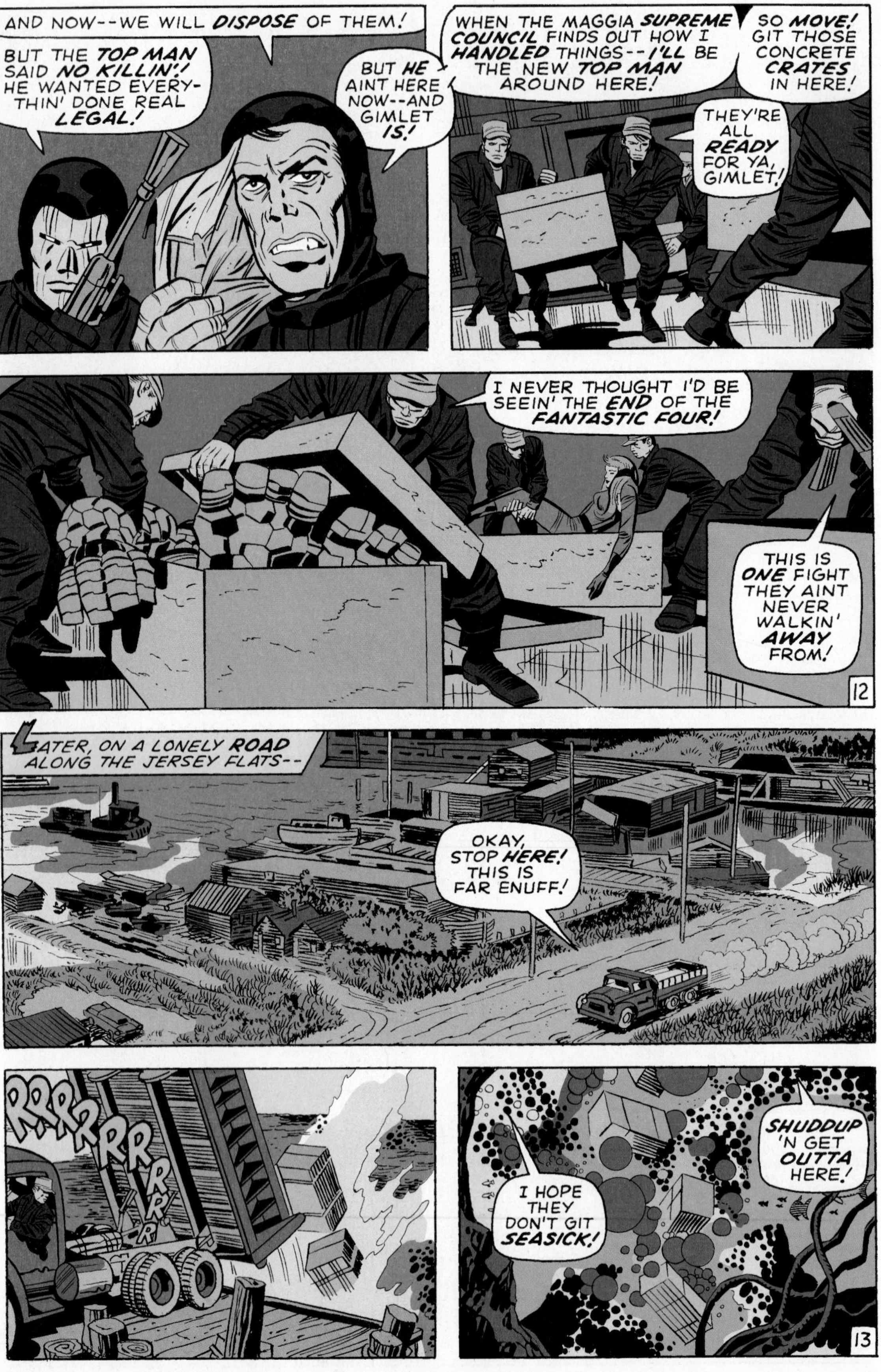
AND NOW--WE WILL DISPOSE OF THEM!
BUT THE TOP MAN SAID NO KILLIN'! HE WANTED EVERY-THIN' DONE REAL LEGAL!
BUT HE AINT HERE NOW--AND GIMLET IS!
WHEN THE MAGGIA SUPREME COUNCIL FINDS OUT HOW I HANDLED THINGS--I'LL BE THE NEW TOP MAN AROUND HERE!
SO MOVE! GIT THOSE CONCRETE CRATES IN HERE!
THEY'RE ALL READY FOR YA, GIMLET!
I NEVER THOUGHT I'D BE SEEIN' THE END OF THE FANTASTIC FOUR!
THIS IS ONE FIGHT THEY AINT NEVER WALKIN' AWAY FROM!
12
LATER, ON A LONELY ROAD ALONG THE JERSEY FLATS--
OKAY, STOP HERE! THIS IS FAR ENUFF!
RRRRRRRRRR
I HOPE THEY DON'T GIT SEASICK!
SHUDDUP 'N GET OUTTA HERE!
13

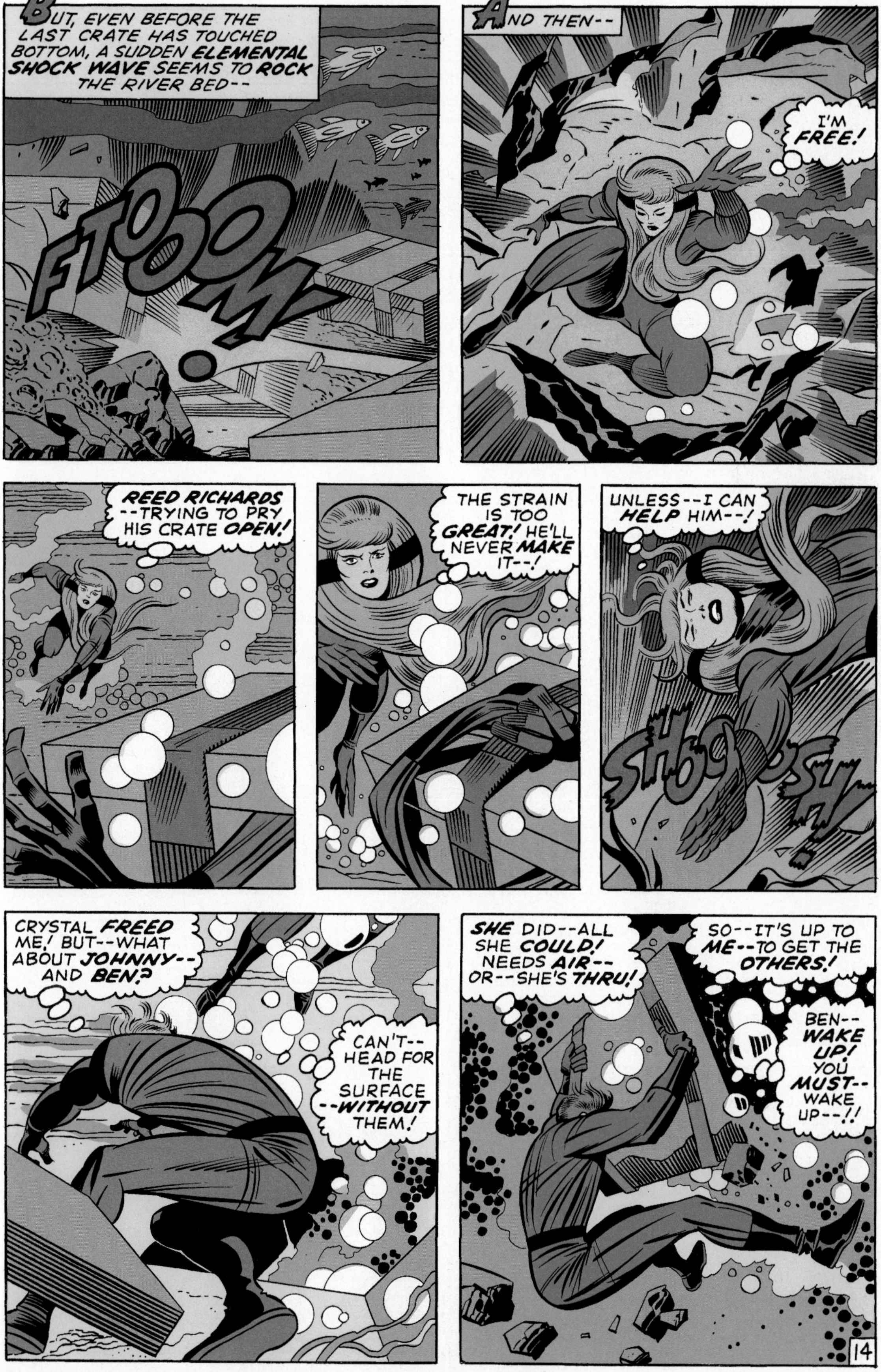
BUT, EVEN BEFORE THE LAST CRATE HAS TOUCHED BOTTOM, A SUDDEN ELEMENTAL SHOCK WAVE SEEMS TO ROCK THE RIVER BED--
FTOOOM!
AND THEN--
I'M FREE!
REED RICHARDS --TRYING TO PRY HIS CRATE OPEN!
THE STRAIN IS TOO GREAT! HE'LL NEVER MAKE IT--!
UNLESS--I CAN HELP HIM--!
SHOOOSH!
CRYSTAL FREED ME! BUT--WHAT ABOUT JOHNNY-- AND BEN?
CAN'T-- HEAD FOR THE SURFACE --WITHOUT THEM!
SHE DID--ALL SHE COULD! NEEDS AIR-- OR--SHE'S THRU!
SO--IT'S UP TO ME--TO GET THE OTHERS!
BEN-- WAKE UP! YOU MUST-- WAKE UP--!!
14

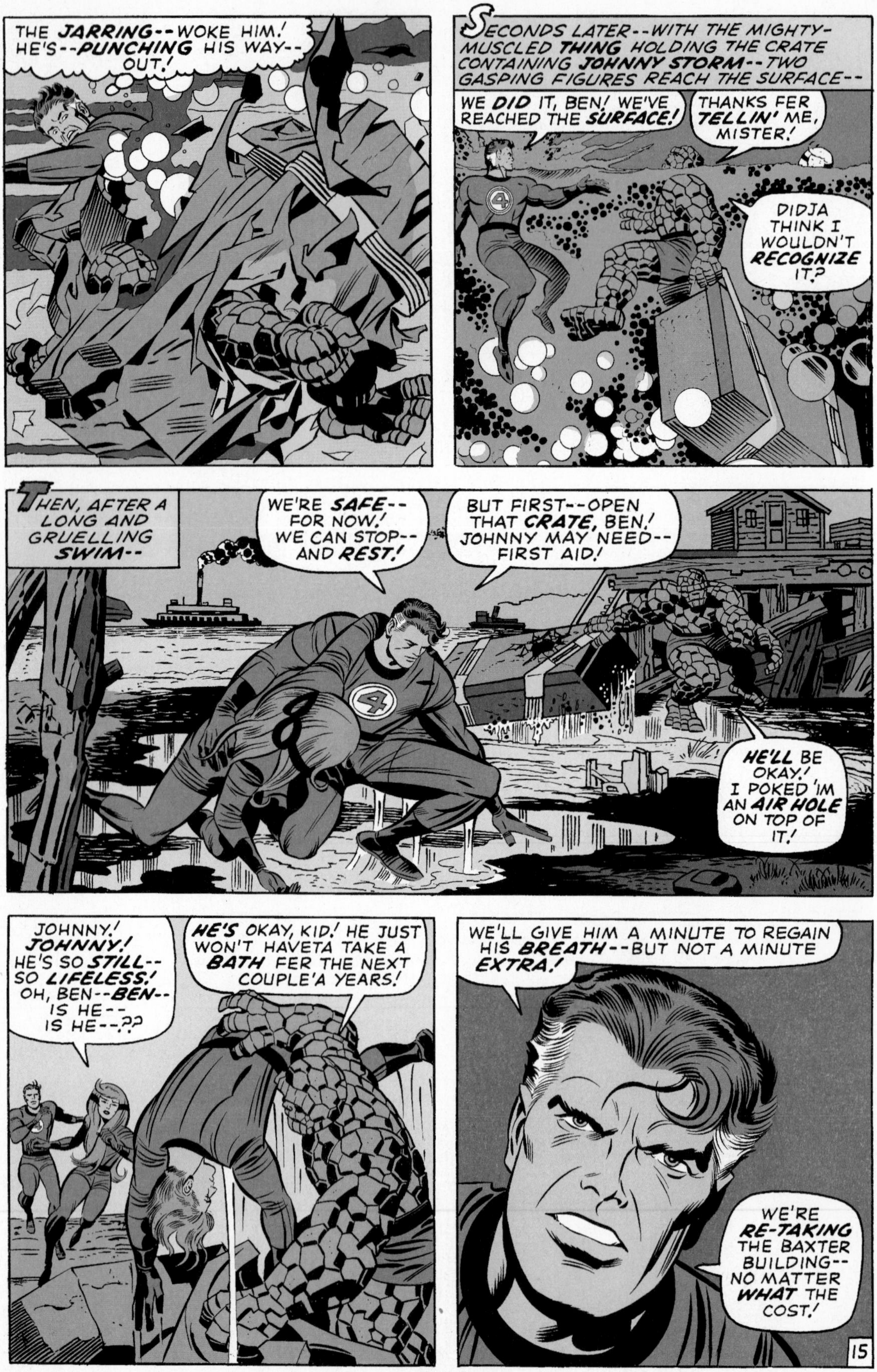

THE JARRING--WOKE HIM! HE'S--PUNCHING HIS WAY--OUT!
SECONDS LATER--WITH THE MIGHTY-MUSCLED THING HOLDING THE CRATE CONTAINING JOHNNY STORM--TWO GASPING FIGURES REACH THE SURFACE--
WE DID IT, BEN! WE'VE REACHED THE SURFACE!
THANKS FER TELLIN' ME, MISTER!
DIDJA THINK I WOULDN'T RECOGNIZE IT?
THEN, AFTER A LONG AND GRUELLING SWIM--
WE'RE SAFE--FOR NOW! WE CAN STOP--AND REST!
BUT FIRST--OPEN THAT CRATE, BEN! JOHNNY MAY NEED--FIRST AID!
HE'LL BE OKAY! I POKED 'IM AN AIR HOLE ON TOP OF IT!
JOHNNY! JOHNNY! HE'S SO STILL--SO LIFELESS! OH, BEN--BEN--IS HE--IS HE--??
HE'S OKAY, KID! HE JUST WON'T HAVETA TAKE A BATH FER THE NEXT COUPLE'A YEARS!
WE'LL GIVE HIM A MINUTE TO REGAIN HIS BREATH--BUT NOT A MINUTE EXTRA!
WE'RE RE-TAKING THE BAXTER BUILDING--NO MATTER WHAT THE COST!
15

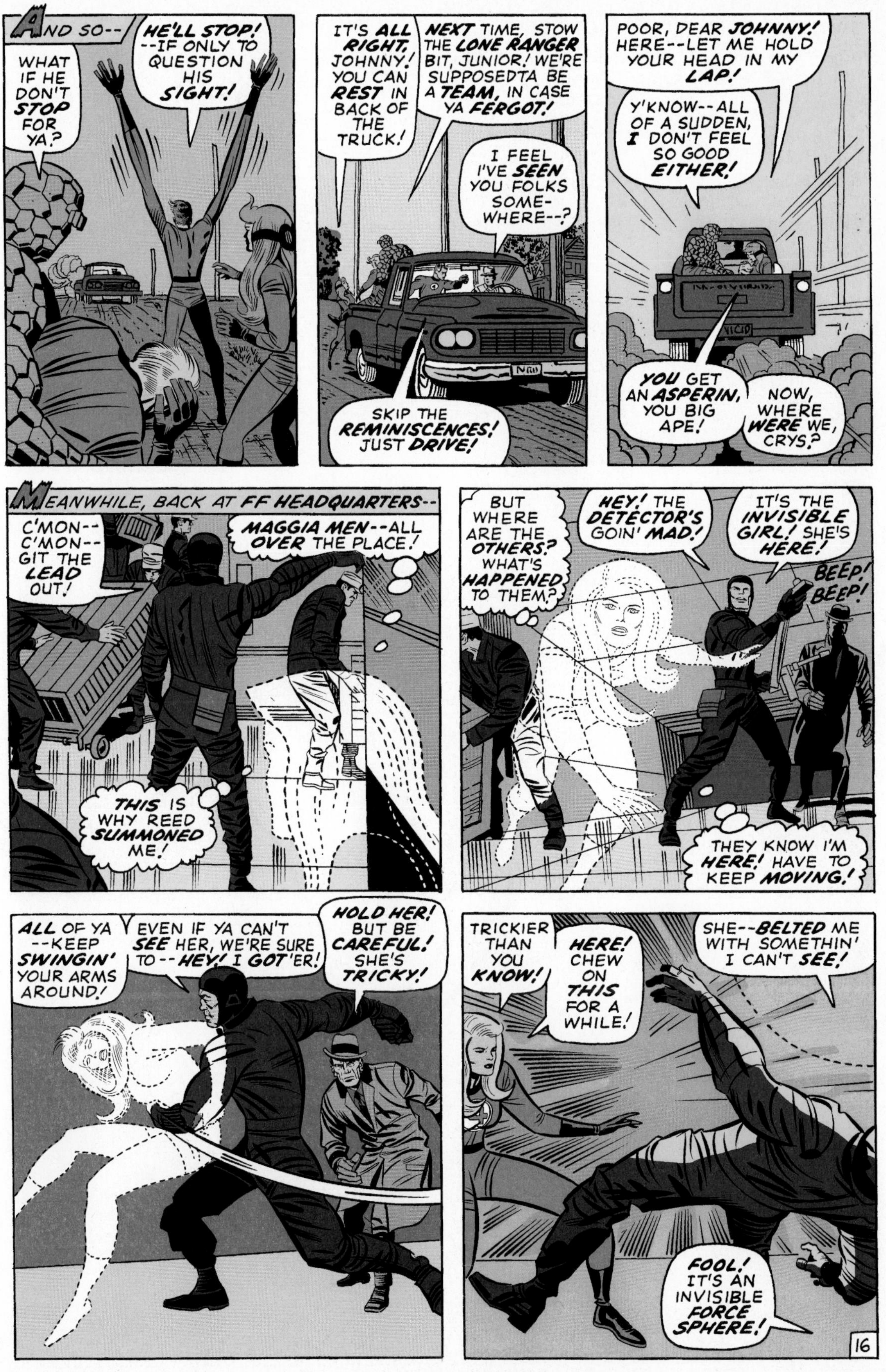
AND SO--
WHAT IF HE DON'T STOP FOR YA?
HE'LL STOP! --IF ONLY TO QUESTION HIS SIGHT!
IT'S ALL RIGHT, JOHNNY! YOU CAN REST IN BACK OF THE TRUCK!
NEXT TIME, STOW THE LONE RANGER BIT, JUNIOR! WE'RE SUPPOSEDTA BE A TEAM, IN CASE YA FERGOT!
I FEEL I'VE SEEN YOU FOLKS SOME-WHERE--?
SKIP THE REMINISCENCES! JUST DRIVE!
POOR, DEAR JOHNNY! HERE--LET ME HOLD YOUR HEAD IN MY LAP!
Y'KNOW--ALL OF A SUDDEN, I DON'T FEEL SO GOOD EITHER!
YOU GET AN ASPERIN, YOU BIG APE!
NOW, WHERE WERE WE, CRYS?
MEANWHILE, BACK AT FF HEADQUARTERS--
C'MON-- C'MON-- GIT THE LEAD OUT!
MAGGIA MEN--ALL OVER THE PLACE!
THIS IS WHY REED SUMMONED ME!
BUT WHERE ARE THE OTHERS? WHAT'S HAPPENED TO THEM?
HEY! THE DETECTOR'S GOIN' MAD!
IT'S THE INVISIBLE GIRL! SHE'S HERE!
BEEP! BEEP!
THEY KNOW I'M HERE! HAVE TO KEEP MOVING!
ALL OF YA --KEEP SWINGIN' YOUR ARMS AROUND!
EVEN IF YA CAN'T SEE HER, WE'RE SURE TO--HEY! I GOT 'ER!
HOLD HER! BUT BE CAREFUL! SHE'S TRICKY!
TRICKIER THAN YOU KNOW!
HERE! CHEW ON THIS FOR A WHILE!
SHE--BELTED ME WITH SOMETHIN' I CAN'T SEE!
FOOL! IT'S AN INVISIBLE FORCE SPHERE!
16

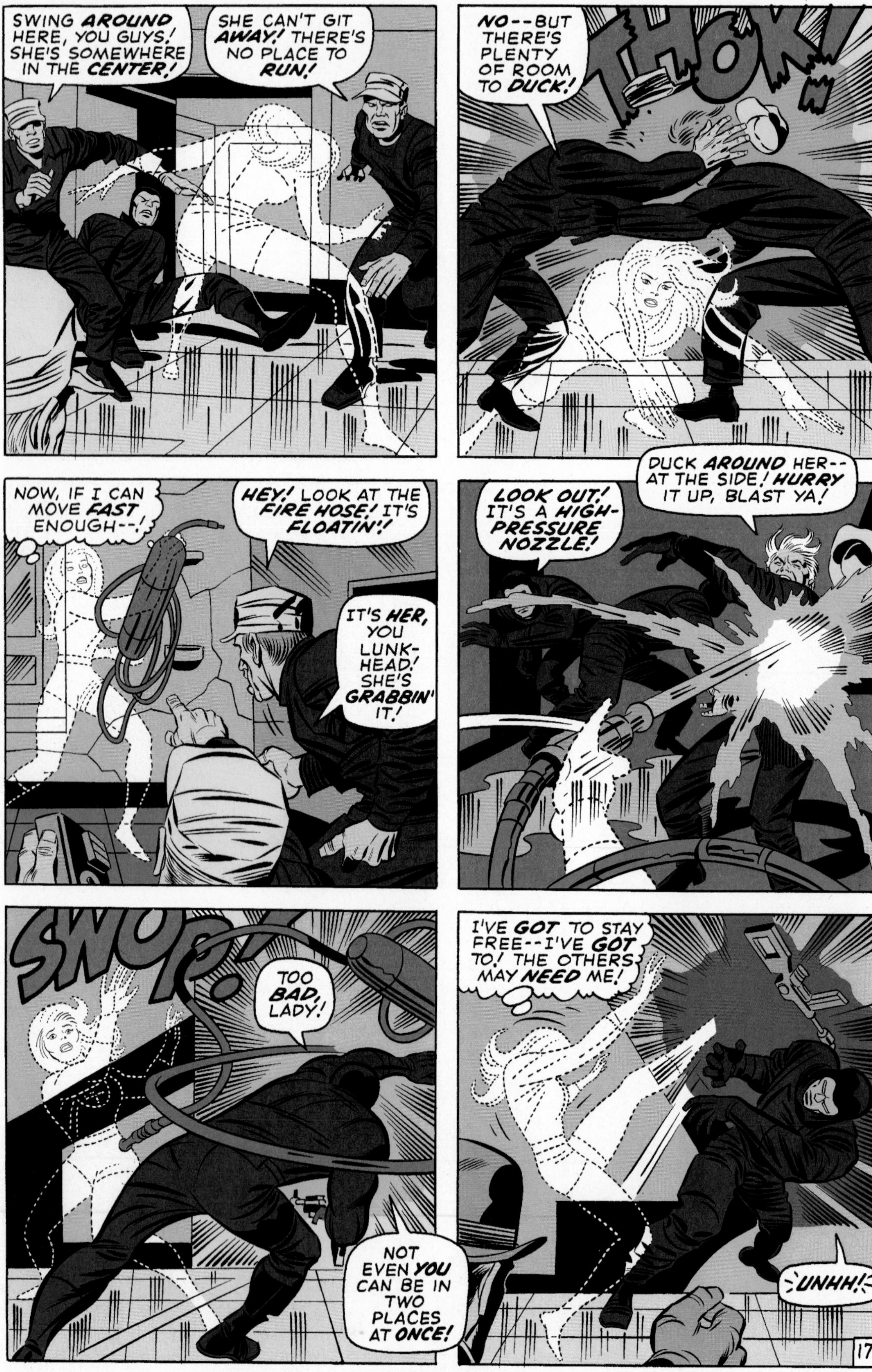
SWING AROUND HERE, YOU GUYS! SHE'S SOMEWHERE IN THE CENTER!
SHE CAN'T GIT AWAY! THERE'S NO PLACE TO RUN!
NO--BUT THERE'S PLENTY OF ROOM TO DUCK!
THOK!
NOW, IF I CAN MOVE FAST ENOUGH--!
HEY! LOOK AT THE FIRE HOSE! IT'S FLOATIN'!
IT'S HER, YOU LUNK-HEAD! SHE'S GRABBIN' IT!
DUCK AROUND HER--AT THE SIDE! HURRY IT UP, BLAST YA!
LOOK OUT! IT'S A HIGH-PRESSURE NOZZLE!
SWOP!
TOO BAD, LADY!
NOT EVEN YOU CAN BE IN TWO PLACES AT ONCE!
I'VE GOT TO STAY FREE--I'VE GOT TO! THE OTHERS MAY NEED ME!
UNHH!
17

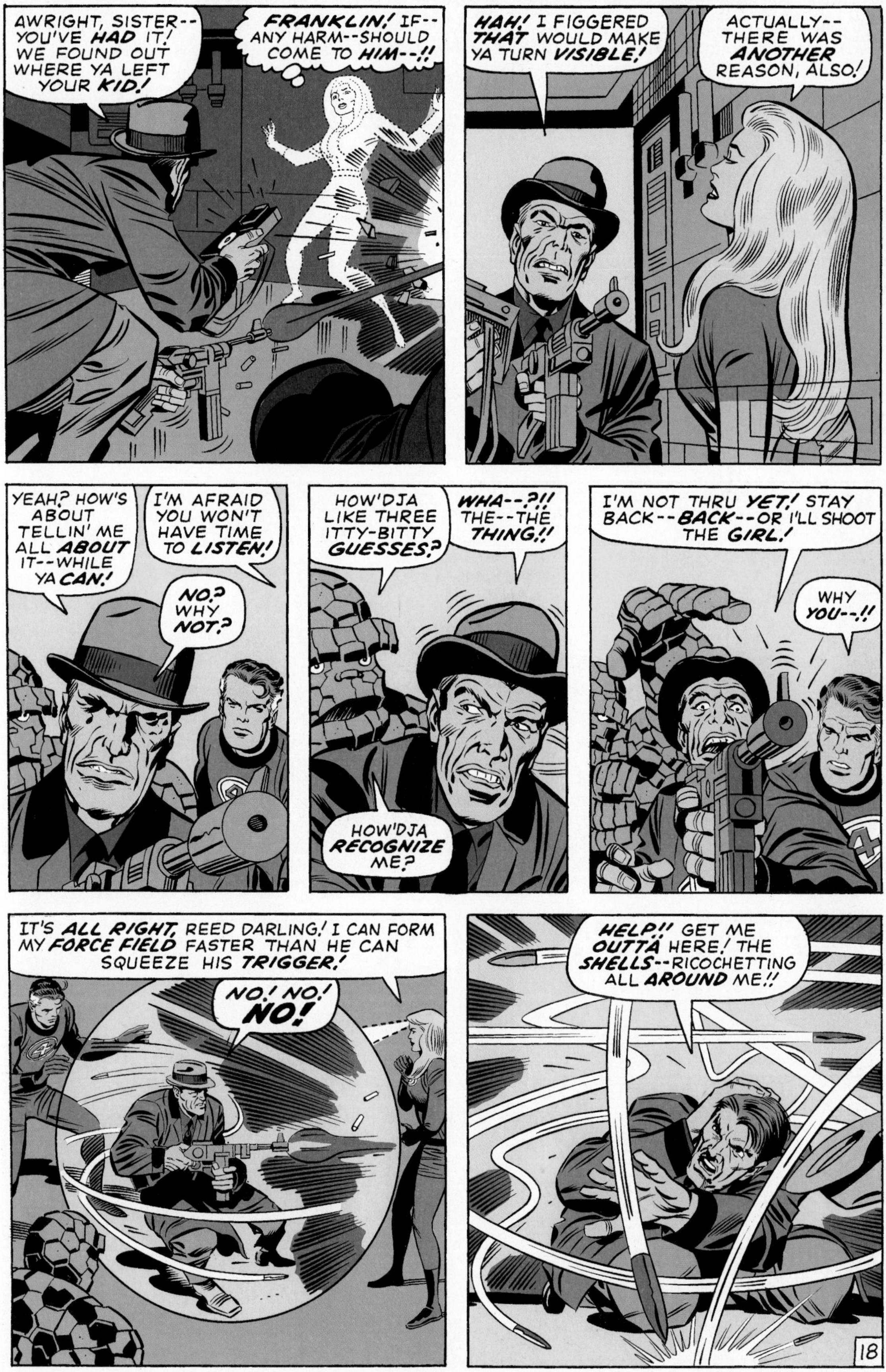

AWRIGHT, SISTER-- YOU'VE HAD IT! WE FOUND OUT WHERE YA LEFT YOUR KID!
FRANKLIN! IF-- ANY HARM--SHOULD COME TO HIM--!!
HAH! I FIGGERED THAT WOULD MAKE YA TURN VISIBLE!
ACTUALLY-- THERE WAS ANOTHER REASON, ALSO!
YEAH? HOW'S ABOUT TELLIN' ME ALL ABOUT IT--WHILE YA CAN!
I'M AFRAID YOU WON'T HAVE TIME TO LISTEN!
NO? WHY NOT?
HOW'DJA LIKE THREE ITTY-BITTY GUESSES?
WHA--?!! THE--THE THING!!
HOW'DJA RECOGNIZE ME?
I'M NOT THRU YET! STAY BACK--BACK--OR I'LL SHOOT THE GIRL!
WHY YOU--!!
IT'S ALL RIGHT, REED DARLING! I CAN FORM MY FORCE FIELD FASTER THAN HE CAN SQUEEZE HIS TRIGGER!
NO! NO! NO!
HELP!! GET ME OUTTA HERE! THE SHELLS--RICOCHETTING ALL AROUND ME!!
18

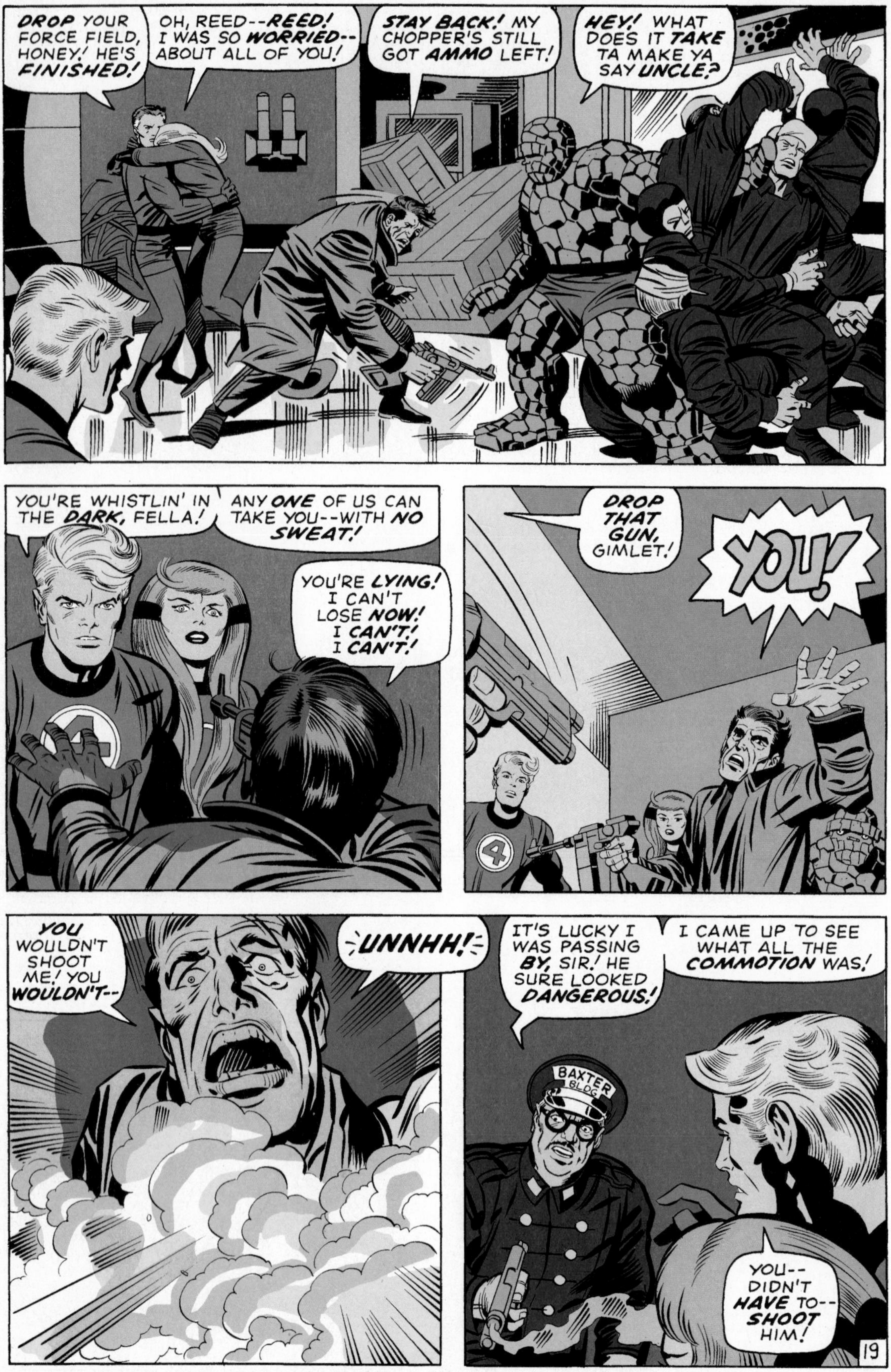
DROP YOUR FORCE FIELD, HONEY! HE'S FINISHED!
OH, REED--REED! I WAS SO WORRIED--ABOUT ALL OF YOU!
STAY BACK! MY CHOPPER'S STILL GOT AMMO LEFT!
HEY! WHAT DOES IT TAKE TA MAKE YA SAY UNCLE?
YOU'RE WHISTLIN' IN THE DARK, FELLA!
ANY ONE OF US CAN TAKE YOU--WITH NO SWEAT!
YOU'RE LYING! I CAN'T LOSE NOW! I CAN'T! I CAN'T!
DROP THAT GUN, GIMLET!
YOU!
YOU WOULDN'T SHOOT ME! YOU WOULDN'T--
UNNHH!
IT'S LUCKY I WAS PASSING BY, SIR! HE SURE LOOKED DANGEROUS!
I CAME UP TO SEE WHAT ALL THE COMMOTION WAS!
BAXTER BLDG
YOU--DIDN'T HAVE TO--SHOOT HIM!
19

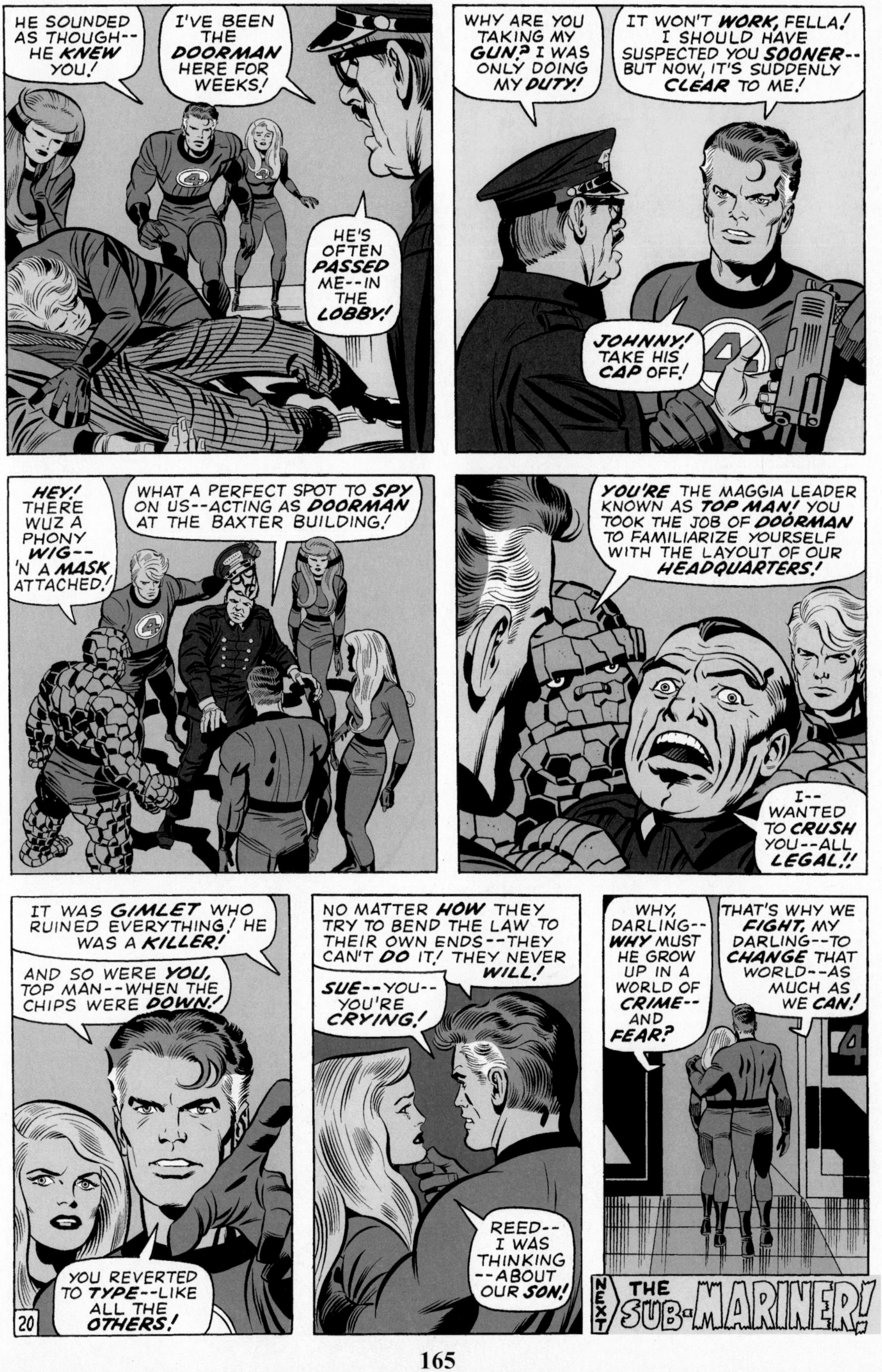
HE SOUNDED AS THOUGH-- HE KNEW YOU!
I'VE BEEN THE DOORMAN HERE FOR WEEKS!
HE'S OFTEN PASSED ME--IN THE LOBBY!
WHY ARE YOU TAKING MY GUN? I WAS ONLY DOING MY DUTY!
IT WON'T WORK, FELLA! I SHOULD HAVE SUSPECTED YOU SOONER-- BUT NOW, IT'S SUDDENLY CLEAR TO ME!
JOHNNY! TAKE HIS CAP OFF!
HEY! THERE WUZ A PHONY WIG-- 'N A MASK ATTACHED!
WHAT A PERFECT SPOT TO SPY ON US--ACTING AS DOORMAN AT THE BAXTER BUILDING!
YOU'RE THE MAGGIA LEADER KNOWN AS TOP MAN! YOU TOOK THE JOB OF DOORMAN TO FAMILIARIZE YOURSELF WITH THE LAYOUT OF OUR HEADQUARTERS!
I--WANTED TO CRUSH YOU--ALL LEGAL!!
IT WAS GIMLET WHO RUINED EVERYTHING! HE WAS A KILLER!
AND SO WERE YOU, TOP MAN--WHEN THE CHIPS WERE DOWN!
YOU REVERTED TO TYPE--LIKE ALL THE OTHERS!
20
NO MATTER HOW THEY TRY TO BEND THE LAW TO THEIR OWN ENDS--THEY CAN'T DO IT! THEY NEVER WILL!
SUE--YOU--YOU'RE CRYING!
REED--I WAS THINKING--ABOUT OUR SON!
WHY, DARLING--WHY MUST HE GROW UP IN A WORLD OF CRIME--AND FEAR?
THAT'S WHY WE FIGHT, MY DARLING--TO CHANGE THAT WORLD--AS MUCH AS WE CAN!
NEXT THE SUB-MARINER!

THE WORLD'S GREATEST COMIC MAGAZINE!
FANTASTIC FOUR
15¢ 102 SEPT
APPROVED BY THE COMICS CODE AUTHORITY
Fantastic Four
MARVEL COMICS GROUP
FEATURING: THE SUPER-STRENGTH OF THE SUB-MARINER!
CRUSH THE FANTASTIC FOUR!
ALSO CO-STARRING: THE MURDEROUS MIGHT OF MAGNETO!
NAMOR HAS GONE MAD! HE'S ATTACKING US!
THIS IS THE ONE YOU'VE BEEN WAITING FOR!
J.R. + J.V.

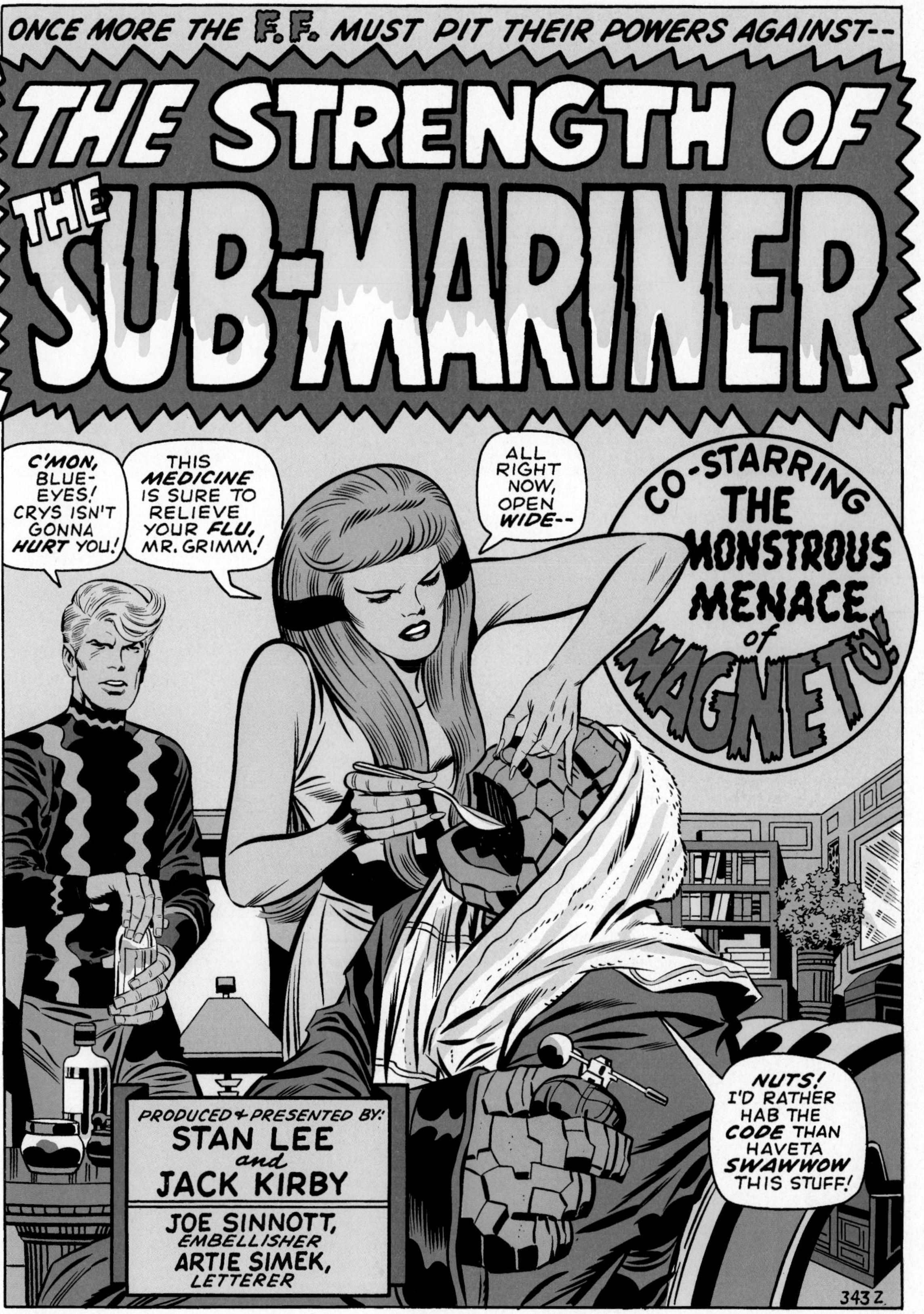
ONCE MORE THE F.F. MUST PIT THEIR POWERS AGAINST--
THE STRENGTH OF THE SUB-MARINER
C'MON, BLUE-EYES! CRYS ISN'T GONNA HURT YOU!
THIS MEDICINE IS SURE TO RELIEVE YOUR FLU, MR. GRIMM.!
ALL RIGHT NOW, OPEN WIDE--
CO-STARRING THE MONSTROUS MENACE of MAGNETO!
PRODUCED & PRESENTED BY: STAN LEE and JACK KIRBY
JOE SINNOTT, EMBELLISHER
ARTIE SIMEK, LETTERER
NUTS! I'D RATHER HAB THE CODE THAN HAVETA SWAWWOW THIS STUFF!
343Z.

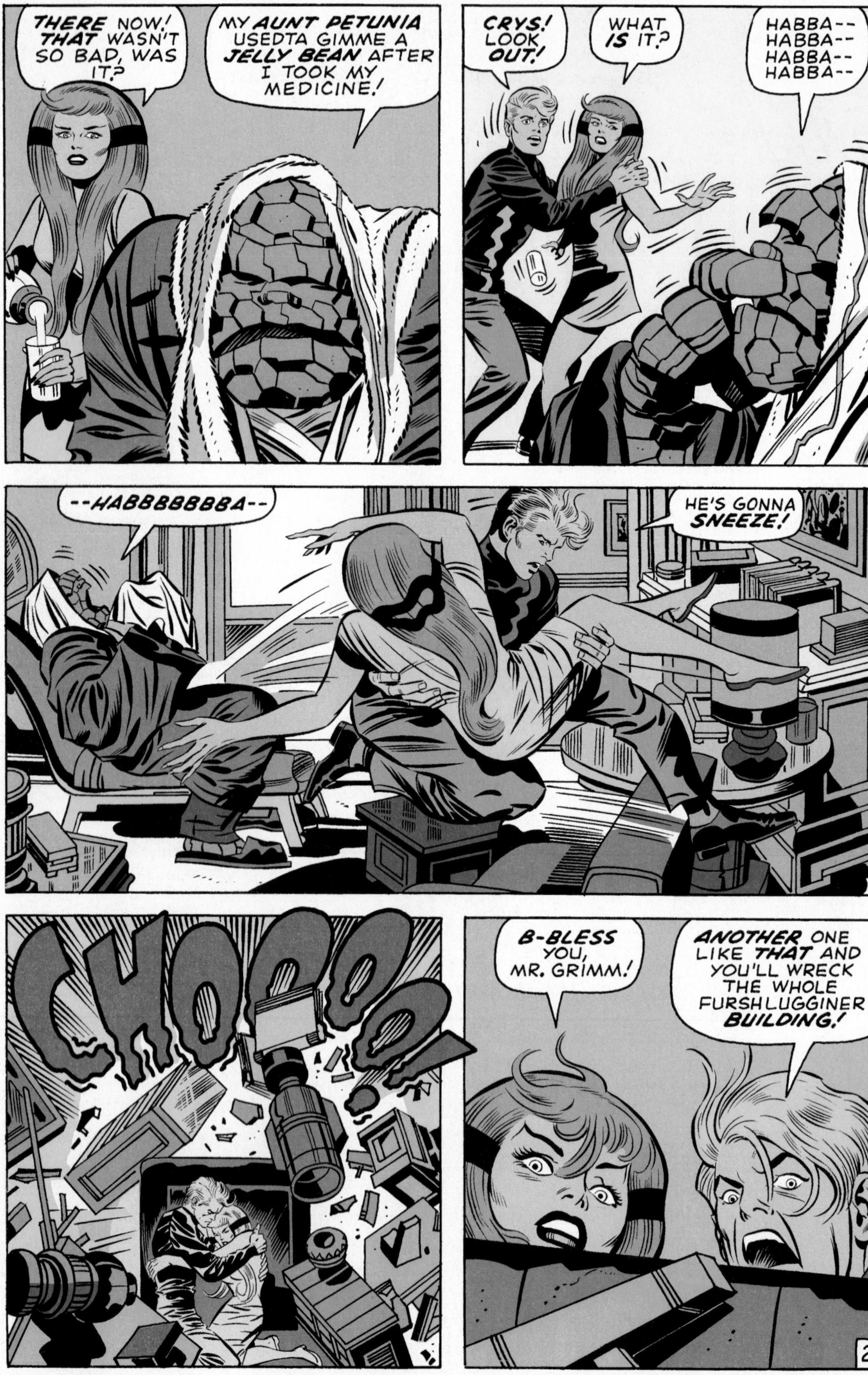
THERE NOW! THAT WASN'T SO BAD, WAS IT?
MY AUNT PETUNIA USEDTA GIMME A JELLY BEAN AFTER I TOOK MY MEDICINE!
CRYS! LOOK OUT!
WHAT IS IT?
HABBA-- HABBA-- HABBA-- HABBA--
--HABBBBBBBA--
HE'S GONNA SNEEZE!
CHOOOO!
B-BLESS YOU, MR. GRIMM!
ANOTHER ONE LIKE THAT AND YOU'LL WRECK THE WHOLE FURSHLUGGINER BUILDING!
2

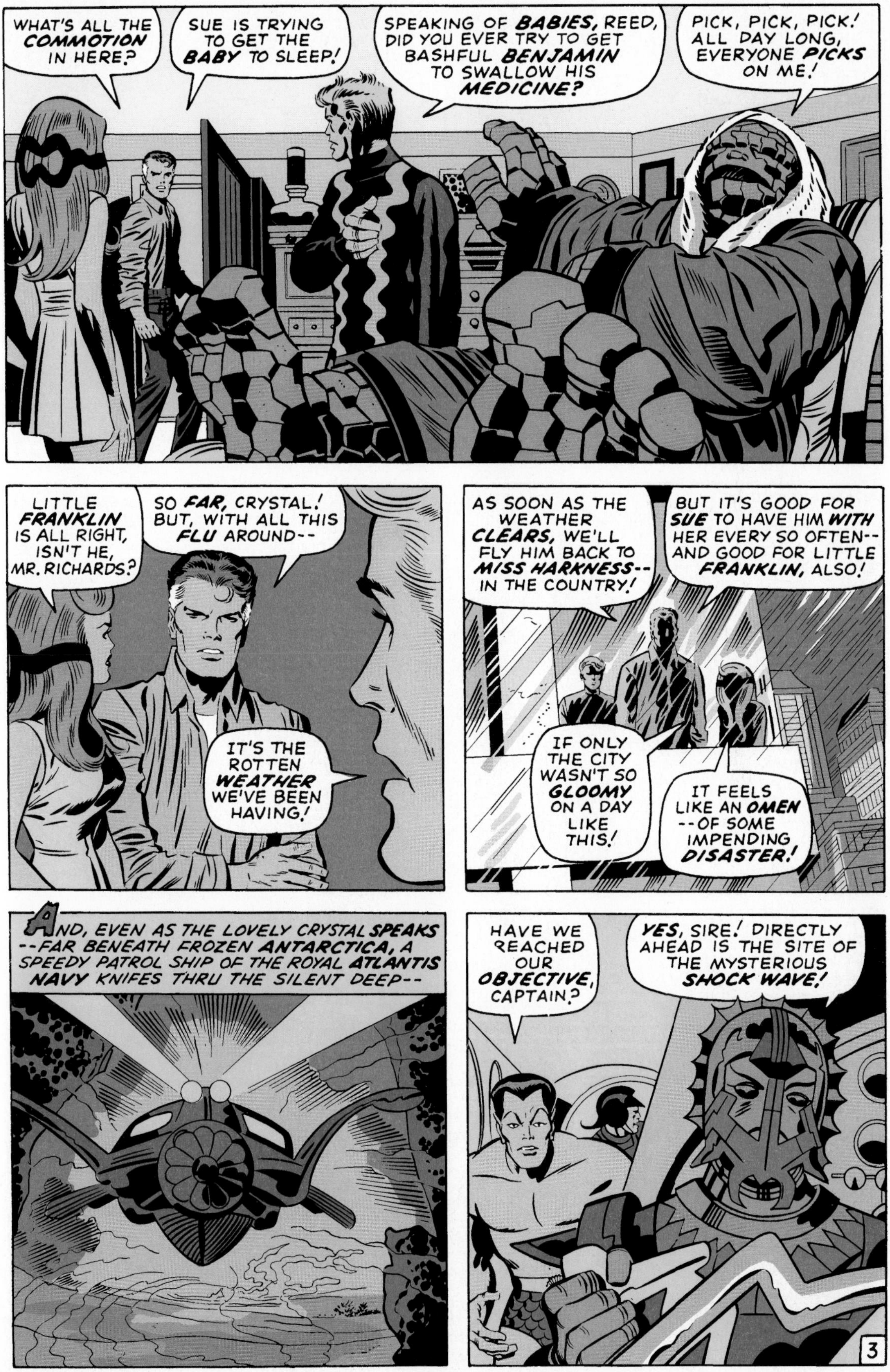

WHAT'S ALL THE COMMOTION IN HERE?
SUE IS TRYING TO GET THE BABY TO SLEEP!
SPEAKING OF BABIES, REED, DID YOU EVER TRY TO GET BASHFUL BENJAMIN TO SWALLOW HIS MEDICINE?
PICK, PICK, PICK! ALL DAY LONG, EVERYONE PICKS ON ME!
LITTLE FRANKLIN IS ALL RIGHT, ISN'T HE, MR. RICHARDS?
SO FAR, CRYSTAL! BUT, WITH ALL THIS FLU AROUND--
IT'S THE ROTTEN WEATHER WE'VE BEEN HAVING!
AS SOON AS THE WEATHER CLEARS, WE'LL FLY HIM BACK TO MISS HARKNESS-- IN THE COUNTRY!
BUT IT'S GOOD FOR SUE TO HAVE HIM WITH HER EVERY SO OFTEN-- AND GOOD FOR LITTLE FRANKLIN, ALSO!
IF ONLY THE CITY WASN'T SO GLOOMY ON A DAY LIKE THIS!
IT FEELS LIKE AN OMEN --OF SOME IMPENDING DISASTER!
AND, EVEN AS THE LOVELY CRYSTAL SPEAKS --FAR BENEATH FROZEN ANTARCTICA, A SPEEDY PATROL SHIP OF THE ROYAL ATLANTIS NAVY KNIFES THRU THE SILENT DEEP--
HAVE WE REACHED OUR OBJECTIVE, CAPTAIN?
YES, SIRE! DIRECTLY AHEAD IS THE SITE OF THE MYSTERIOUS SHOCK WAVE!
3

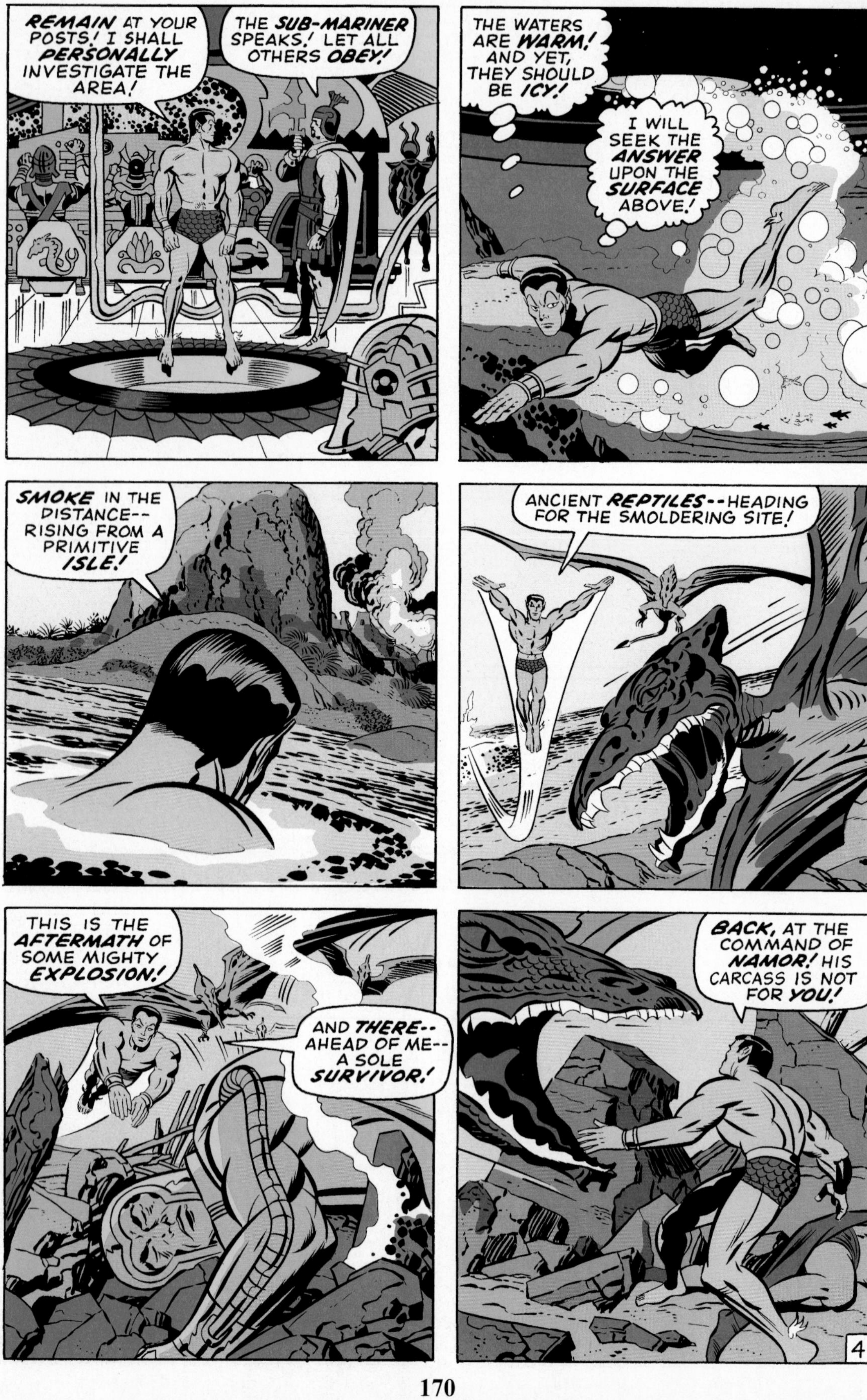
REMAIN AT YOUR POSTS! I SHALL PERSONALLY INVESTIGATE THE AREA!
THE SUB-MARINER SPEAKS! LET ALL OTHERS OBEY!
THE WATERS ARE WARM! AND YET, THEY SHOULD BE ICY!
I WILL SEEK THE ANSWER UPON THE SURFACE ABOVE!
SMOKE IN THE DISTANCE-- RISING FROM A PRIMITIVE ISLE!
ANCIENT REPTILES--HEADING FOR THE SMOLDERING SITE!
THIS IS THE AFTERMATH OF SOME MIGHTY EXPLOSION!
AND THERE-- AHEAD OF ME-- A SOLE SURVIVOR!
BACK, AT THE COMMAND OF NAMOR! HIS CARCASS IS NOT FOR YOU!
4

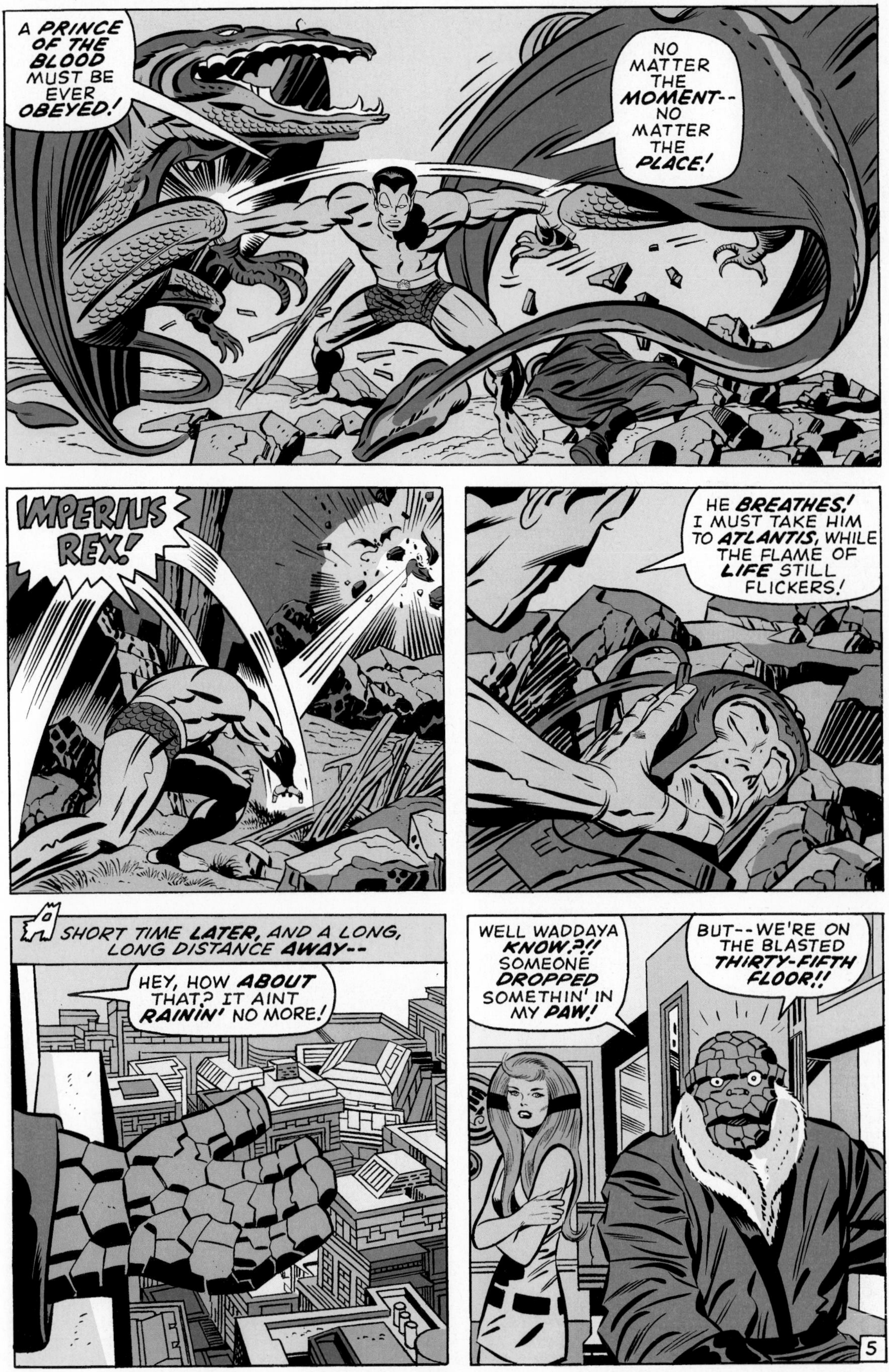
A PRINCE OF THE BLOOD MUST BE EVER OBEYED!
NO MATTER THE MOMENT-- NO MATTER THE PLACE!
IMPERIUS REX!
HE BREATHES! I MUST TAKE HIM TO ATLANTIS, WHILE THE FLAME OF LIFE STILL FLICKERS!
A SHORT TIME LATER, AND A LONG, LONG DISTANCE AWAY--
HEY, HOW ABOUT THAT? IT AINT RAININ' NO MORE!
WELL WADDAYA KNOW.?!! SOMEONE DROPPED SOMETHIN' IN MY PAW!
BUT--WE'RE ON THE BLASTED THIRTY-FIFTH FLOOR!!
5

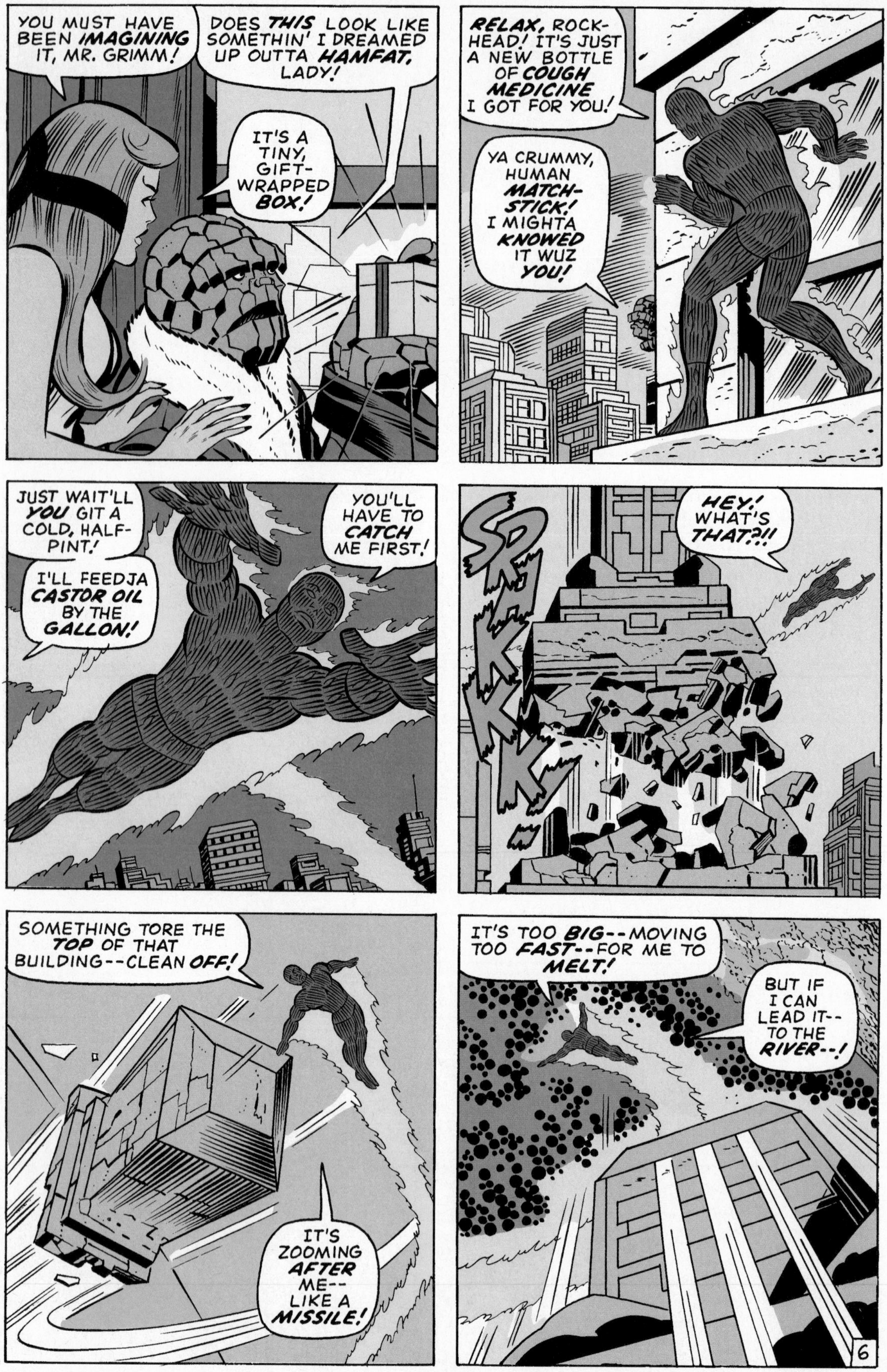
YOU MUST HAVE BEEN IMAGINING IT, MR. GRIMM!
DOES THIS LOOK LIKE SOMETHIN' I DREAMED UP OUTTA HAMFAT, LADY!
IT'S A TINY, GIFT-WRAPPED BOX!
RELAX, ROCK-HEAD! IT'S JUST A NEW BOTTLE OF COUGH MEDICINE I GOT FOR YOU!
YA CRUMMY, HUMAN MATCH-STICK! I MIGHTA KNOWED IT WUZ YOU!
JUST WAIT'LL YOU GIT A COLD, HALF-PINT!
I'LL FEEDJA CASTOR OIL BY THE GALLON!
YOU'LL HAVE TO CATCH ME FIRST!
SPRAKKK
HEY! WHAT'S THAT?!!
SOMETHING TORE THE TOP OF THAT BUILDING--CLEAN OFF!
IT'S ZOOMING AFTER ME--LIKE A MISSILE!
IT'S TOO BIG--MOVING TOO FAST--FOR ME TO MELT!
BUT IF I CAN LEAD IT--TO THE RIVER--!
6

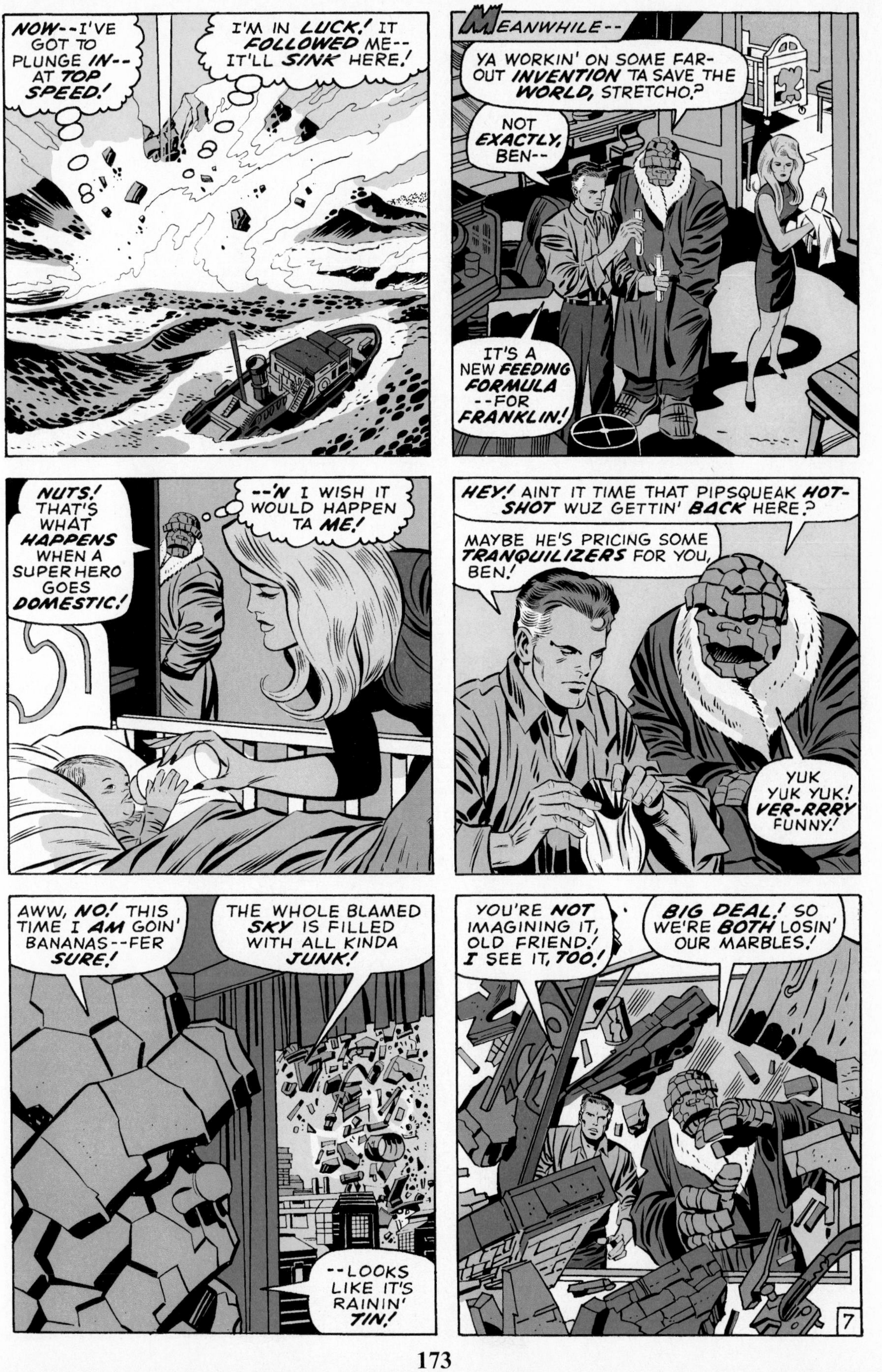
NOW--I'VE GOT TO PLUNGE IN--AT TOP SPEED!
I'M IN LUCK! IT FOLLOWED ME--IT'LL SINK HERE!
MEANWHILE--
YA WORKIN' ON SOME FAR-OUT INVENTION TA SAVE THE WORLD, STRETCHO?
NOT EXACTLY, BEN--
IT'S A NEW FEEDING FORMULA --FOR FRANKLIN!
NUTS! THAT'S WHAT HAPPENS WHEN A SUPER HERO GOES DOMESTIC!
--'N I WISH IT WOULD HAPPEN TA ME!
HEY! AINT IT TIME THAT PIPSQUEAK HOT-SHOT WUZ GETTIN' BACK HERE?
MAYBE HE'S PRICING SOME TRANQUILIZERS FOR YOU, BEN!
YUK YUK YUK! VER-RRRY FUNNY!
AWW, NO! THIS TIME I AM GOIN' BANANAS--FER SURE!
THE WHOLE BLAMED SKY IS FILLED WITH ALL KINDA JUNK!
--LOOKS LIKE IT'S RAININ' TIN!
YOU'RE NOT IMAGINING IT, OLD FRIEND! I SEE IT, TOO!
BIG DEAL! SO WE'RE BOTH LOSIN' OUR MARBLES!
7

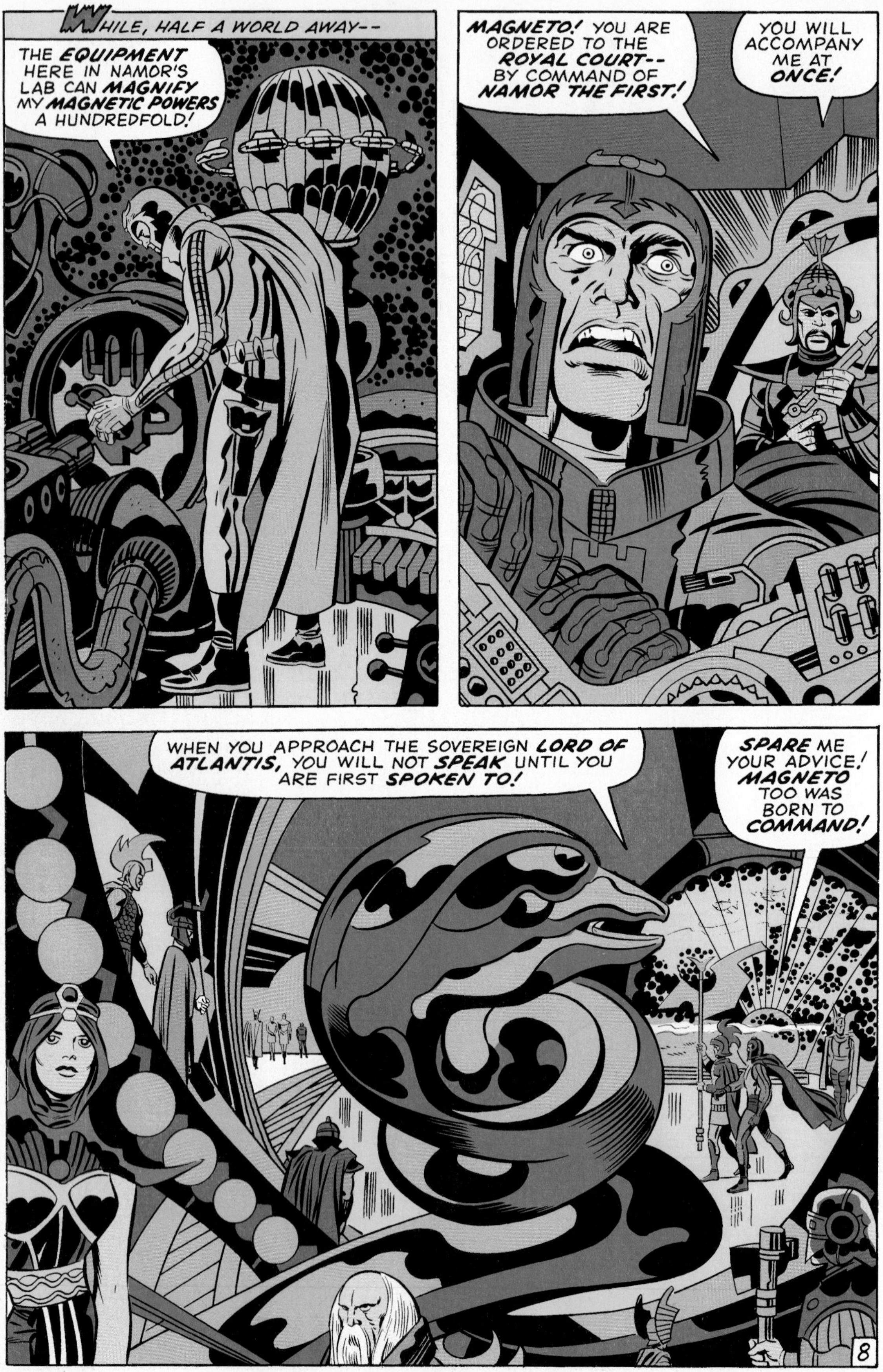
WHILE, HALF A WORLD AWAY--
THE EQUIPMENT HERE IN NAMOR'S LAB CAN MAGNIFY MY MAGNETIC POWERS A HUNDREDFOLD!
MAGNETO! YOU ARE ORDERED TO THE ROYAL COURT-- BY COMMAND OF NAMOR THE FIRST!
YOU WILL ACCOMPANY ME AT ONCE!
WHEN YOU APPROACH THE SOVEREIGN LORD OF ATLANTIS, YOU WILL NOT SPEAK UNTIL YOU ARE FIRST SPOKEN TO!
SPARE ME YOUR ADVICE! MAGNETO TOO WAS BORN TO COMMAND!
8

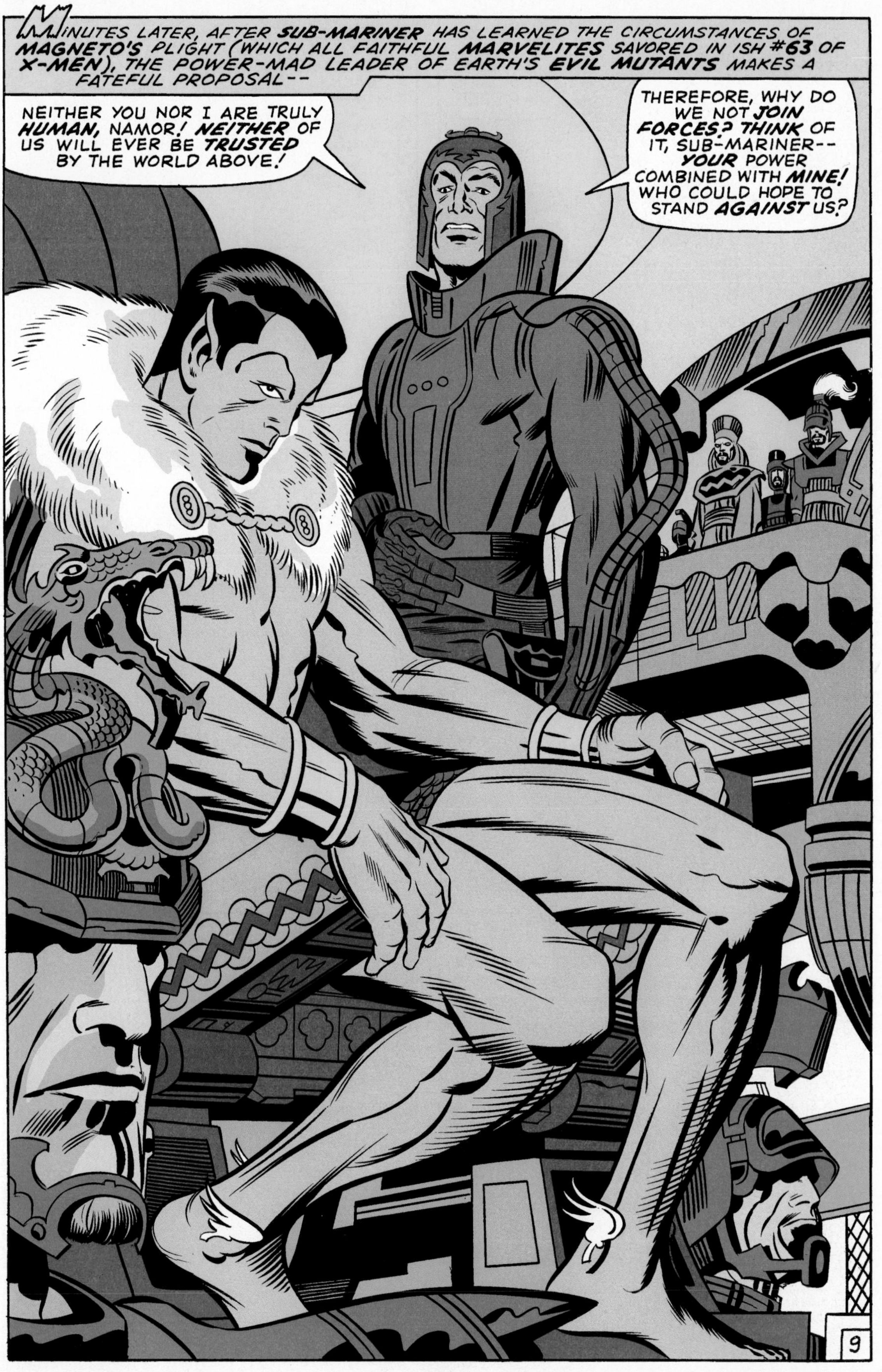
MINUTES LATER, AFTER SUB-MARINER HAS LEARNED THE CIRCUMSTANCES OF MAGNETO'S PLIGHT (WHICH ALL FAITHFUL MARVELITES SAVORED IN ISH #63 OF X-MEN), THE POWER-MAD LEADER OF EARTH'S EVIL MUTANTS MAKES A FATEFUL PROPOSAL--
NEITHER YOU NOR I ARE TRULY HUMAN, NAMOR! NEITHER OF US WILL EVER BE TRUSTED BY THE WORLD ABOVE!
THEREFORE, WHY DO WE NOT JOIN FORCES? THINK OF IT, SUB-MARINER-- YOUR POWER COMBINED WITH MINE! WHO COULD HOPE TO STAND AGAINST US?
9

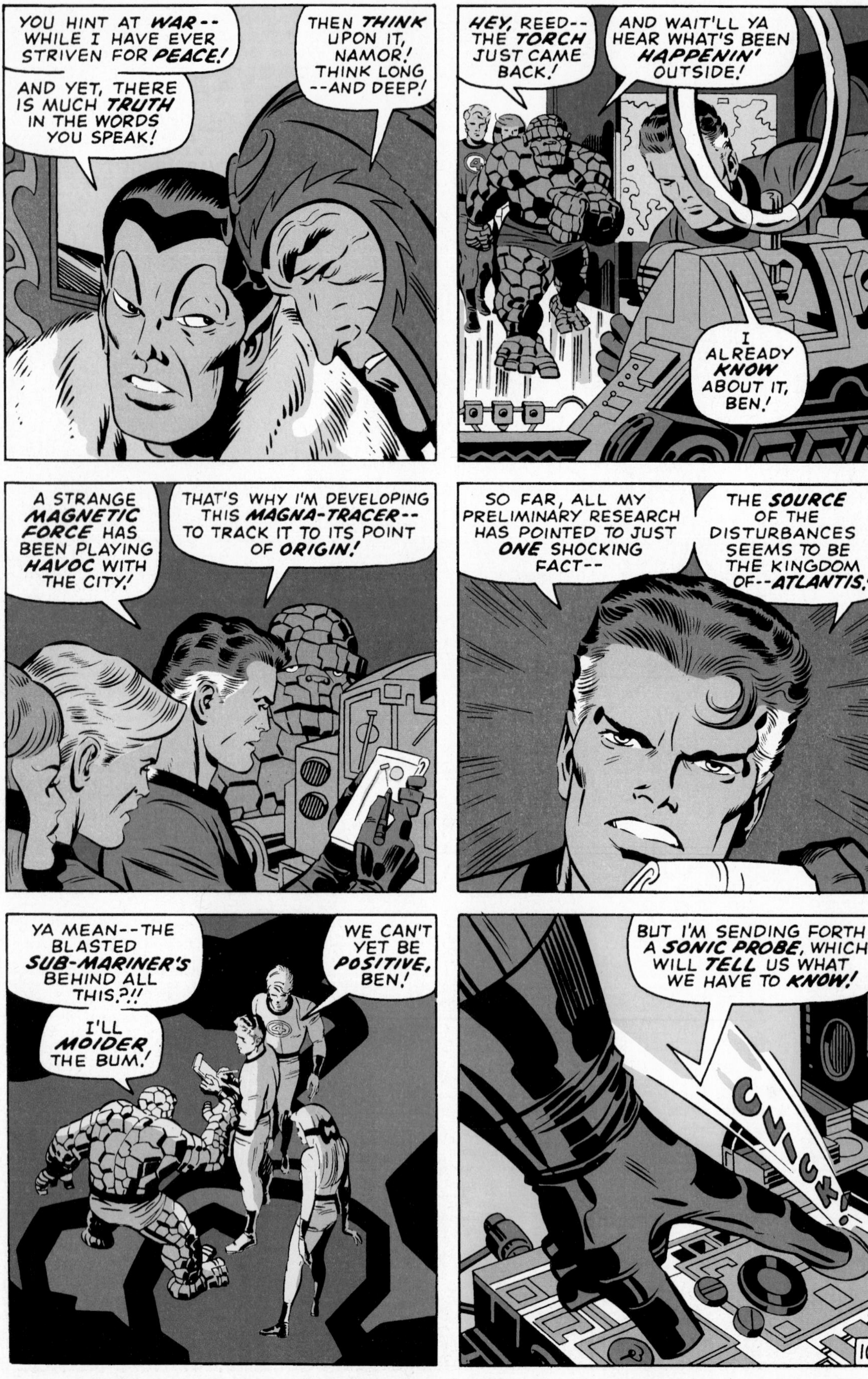

YOU HINT AT WAR-- WHILE I HAVE EVER STRIVEN FOR PEACE!
AND YET, THERE IS MUCH TRUTH IN THE WORDS YOU SPEAK!
THEN THINK UPON IT, NAMOR! THINK LONG --AND DEEP!
HEY, REED-- THE TORCH JUST CAME BACK!
AND WAIT'LL YA HEAR WHAT'S BEEN HAPPENIN' OUTSIDE!
I ALREADY KNOW ABOUT IT, BEN!
A STRANGE MAGNETIC FORCE HAS BEEN PLAYING HAVOC WITH THE CITY!
THAT'S WHY I'M DEVELOPING THIS MAGNA-TRACER-- TO TRACK IT TO ITS POINT OF ORIGIN!
SO FAR, ALL MY PRELIMINARY RESEARCH HAS POINTED TO JUST ONE SHOCKING FACT--
THE SOURCE OF THE DISTURBANCES SEEMS TO BE THE KINGDOM OF--ATLANTIS!
YA MEAN--THE BLASTED SUB-MARINER'S BEHIND ALL THIS?!!
I'LL MOIDER THE BUM!
WE CAN'T YET BE POSITIVE, BEN!
BUT I'M SENDING FORTH A SONIC PROBE, WHICH WILL TELL US WHAT WE HAVE TO KNOW!
CLICK!
10

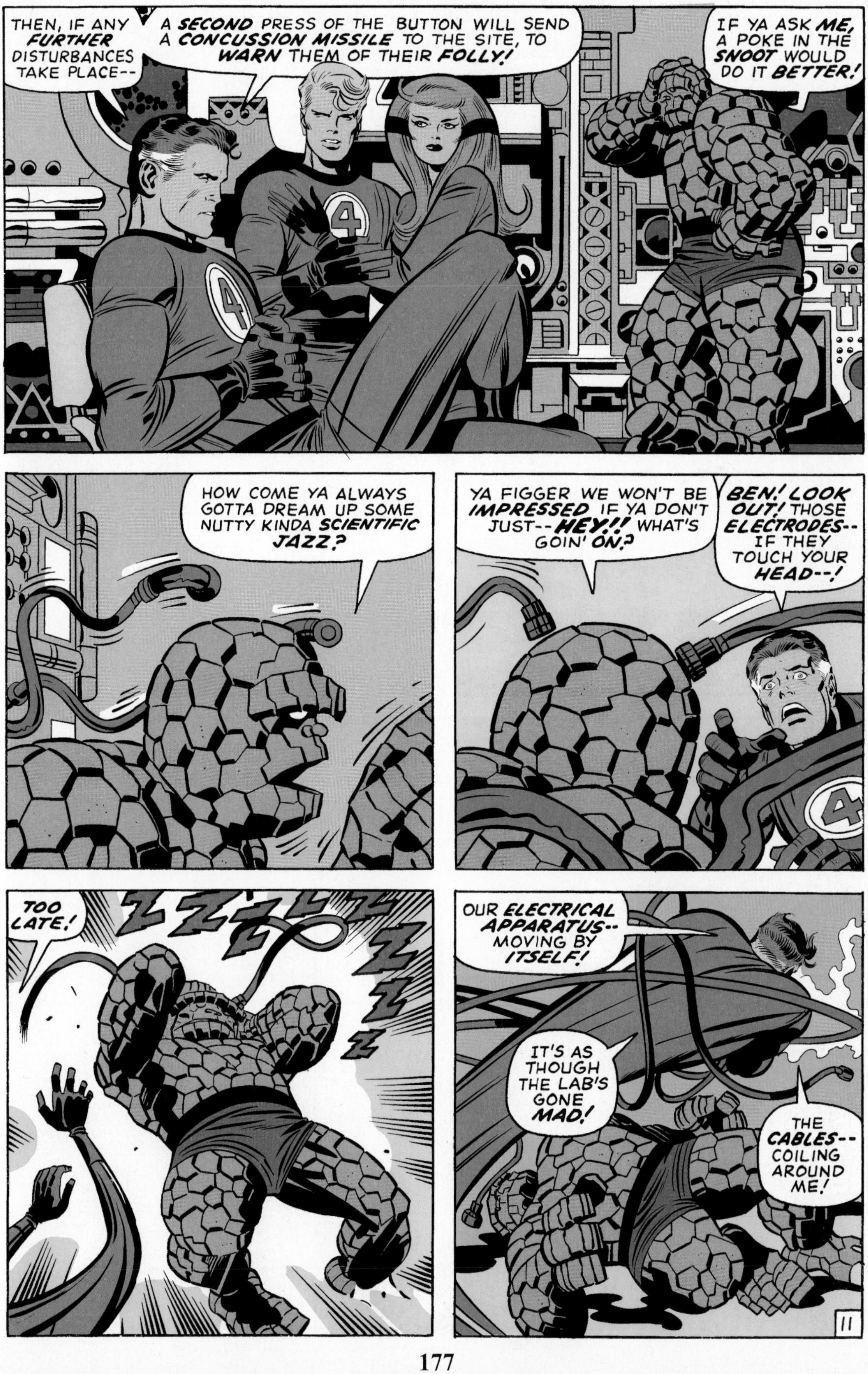
THEN, IF ANY FURTHER DISTURBANCES TAKE PLACE--
A SECOND PRESS OF THE BUTTON WILL SEND A CONCUSSION MISSILE TO THE SITE, TO WARN THEM OF THEIR FOLLY!
IF YA ASK ME, A POKE IN THE SNOOT WOULD DO IT BETTER!
HOW COME YA ALWAYS GOTTA DREAM UP SOME NUTTY KINDA SCIENTIFIC JAZZ?
YA FIGGER WE WON'T BE IMPRESSED IF YA DON'T JUST--HEY!! WHAT'S GOIN' ON?
BEN! LOOK OUT! THOSE ELECTRODES--IF THEY TOUCH YOUR HEAD--!
TOO LATE!
OUR ELECTRICAL APPARATUS--MOVING BY ITSELF!
IT'S AS THOUGH THE LAB'S GONE MAD!
THE CABLES--COILING AROUND ME!
11

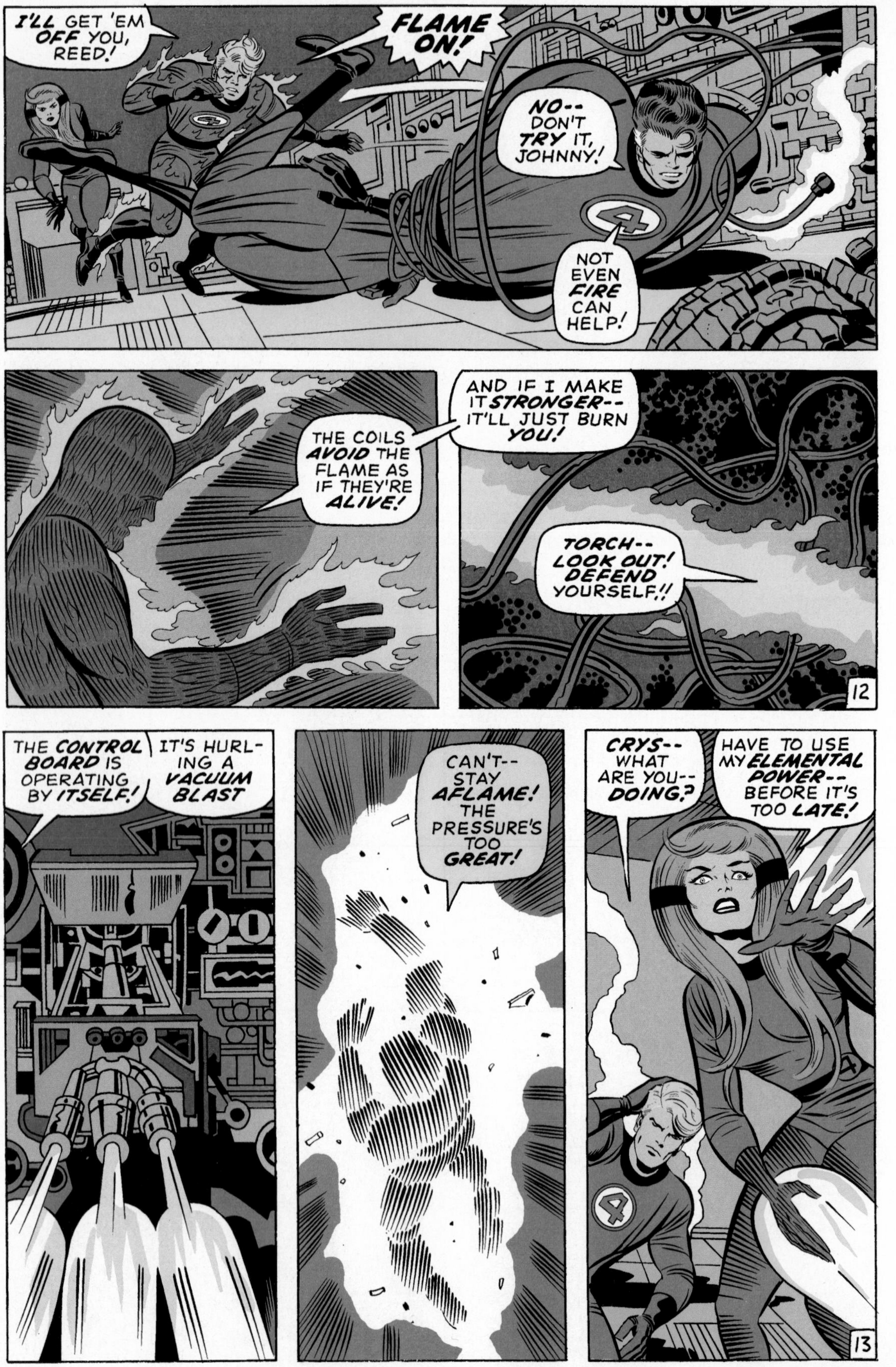
I'LL GET 'EM OFF YOU, REED!
FLAME ON!
NO-- DON'T TRY IT, JOHNNY!
NOT EVEN FIRE CAN HELP!
THE COILS AVOID THE FLAME AS IF THEY'RE ALIVE!
AND IF I MAKE IT STRONGER-- IT'LL JUST BURN YOU!
TORCH-- LOOK OUT! DEFEND YOURSELF!!
12
THE CONTROL BOARD IS OPERATING BY ITSELF!
IT'S HURL-ING A VACUUM BLAST
CAN'T-- STAY AFLAME! THE PRESSURE'S TOO GREAT!
CRYS-- WHAT ARE YOU-- DOING?
HAVE TO USE MY ELEMENTAL POWER-- BEFORE IT'S TOO LATE!
13

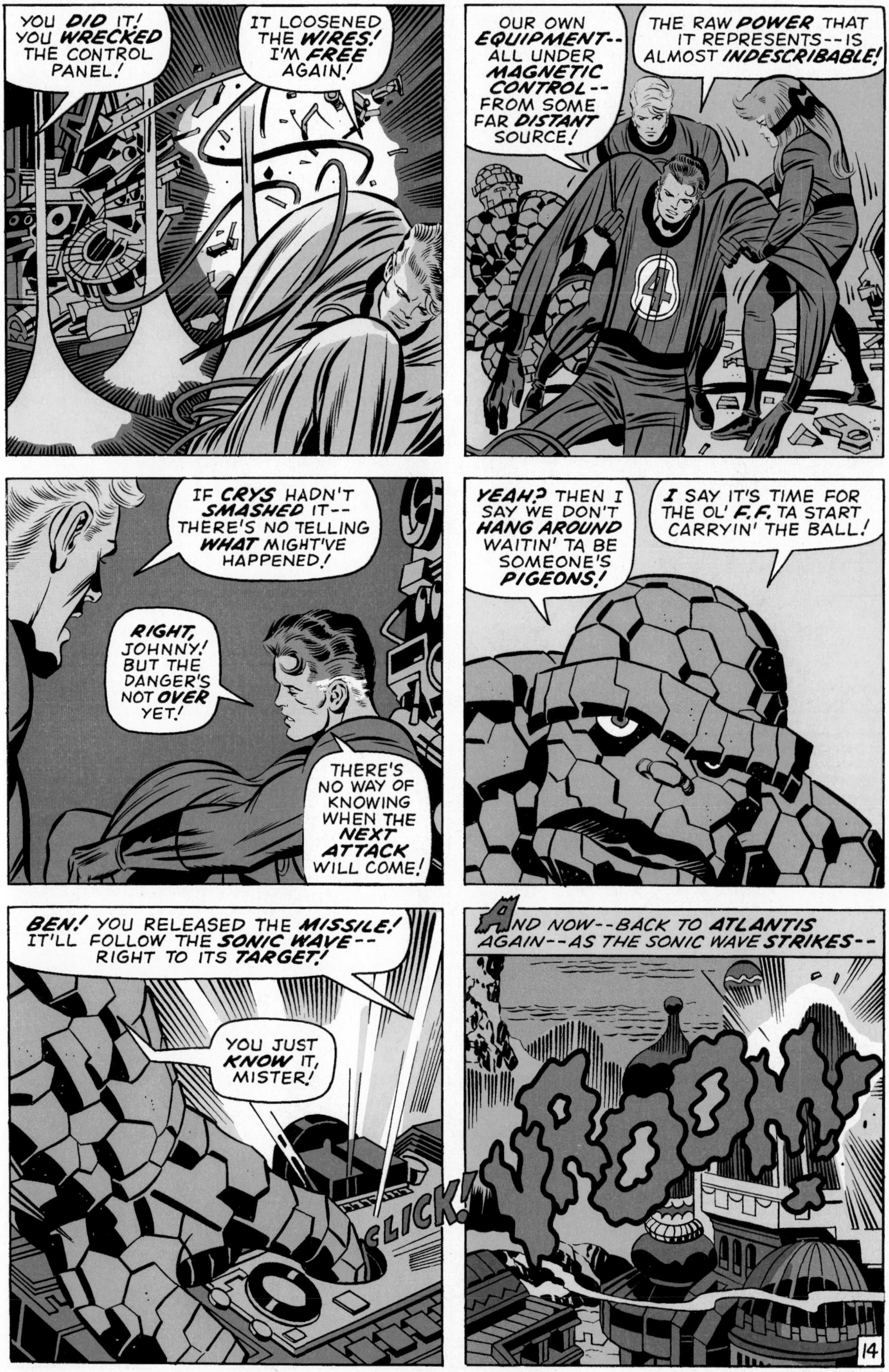
YOU DID IT! YOU WRECKED THE CONTROL PANEL!
IT LOOSENED THE WIRES! I'M FREE AGAIN!
OUR OWN EQUIPMENT-- ALL UNDER MAGNETIC CONTROL-- FROM SOME FAR DISTANT SOURCE!
THE RAW POWER THAT IT REPRESENTS--IS ALMOST INDESCRIBABLE!
IF CRYS HADN'T SMASHED IT-- THERE'S NO TELLING WHAT MIGHT'VE HAPPENED!
RIGHT, JOHNNY! BUT THE DANGER'S NOT OVER YET!
THERE'S NO WAY OF KNOWING WHEN THE NEXT ATTACK WILL COME!
YEAH? THEN I SAY WE DON'T HANG AROUND WAITIN' TA BE SOMEONE'S PIGEONS!
I SAY IT'S TIME FOR THE OL' F.F. TA START CARRYIN' THE BALL!
BEN! YOU RELEASED THE MISSILE! IT'LL FOLLOW THE SONIC WAVE-- RIGHT TO ITS TARGET!
YOU JUST KNOW IT, MISTER!
CLICK!
AND NOW--BACK TO ATLANTIS AGAIN--AS THE SONIC WAVE STRIKES--
BROOM
14

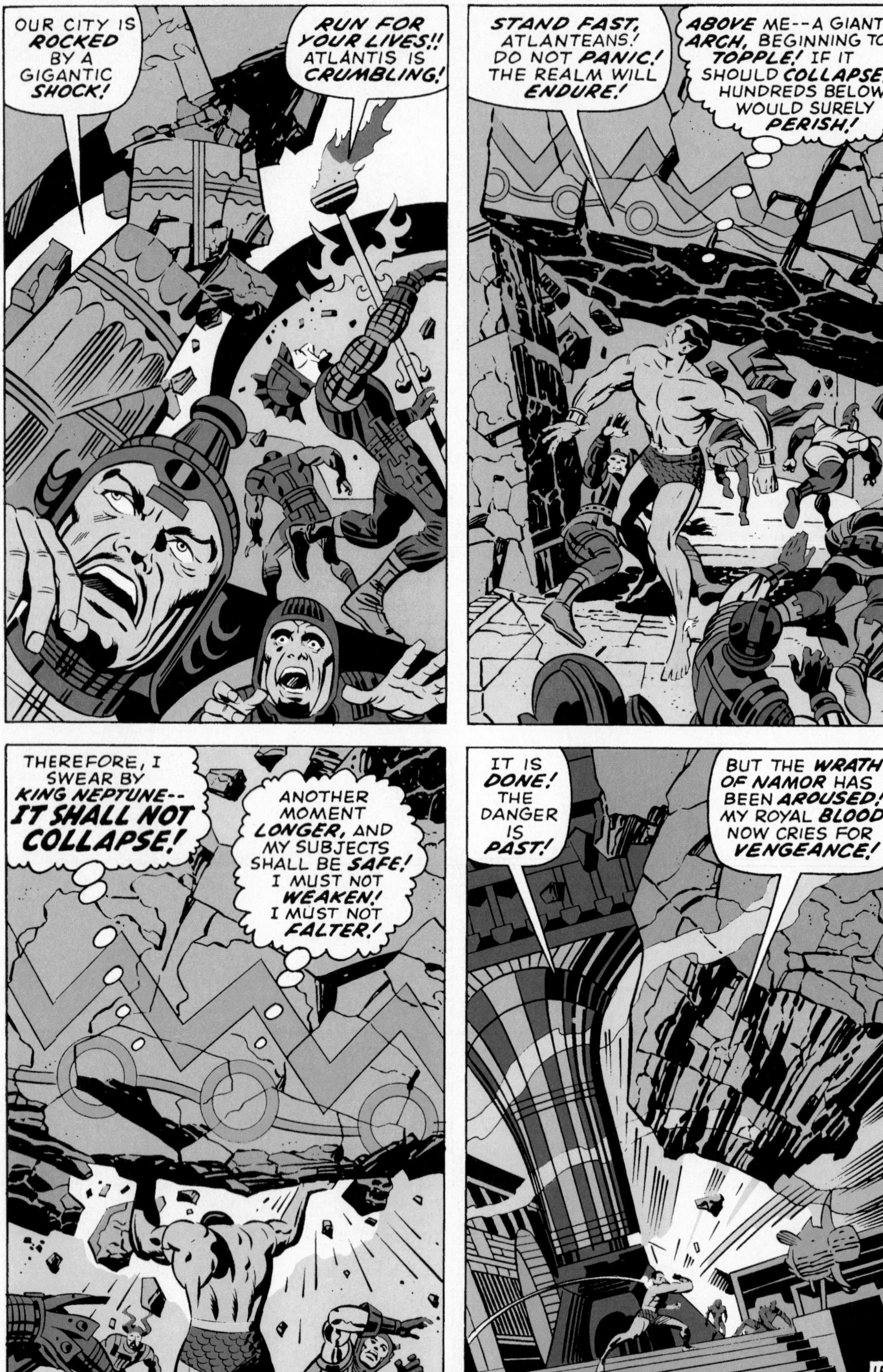
OUR CITY IS ROCKED BY A GIGANTIC SHOCK!
RUN FOR YOUR LIVES!! ATLANTIS IS CRUMBLING!
STAND FAST, ATLANTEANS! DO NOT PANIC! THE REALM WILL ENDURE!
ABOVE ME--A GIANT ARCH, BEGINNING TO TOPPLE! IF IT SHOULD COLLAPSE, HUNDREDS BELOW WOULD SURELY PERISH!
THEREFORE, I SWEAR BY KING NEPTUNE-- IT SHALL NOT COLLAPSE!
ANOTHER MOMENT LONGER, AND MY SUBJECTS SHALL BE SAFE! I MUST NOT WEAKEN! I MUST NOT FALTER!
IT IS DONE! THE DANGER IS PAST!
BUT THE WRATH OF NAMOR HAS BEEN AROUSED! MY ROYAL BLOOD NOW CRIES FOR VENGEANCE!
15

BUT *FIRST*-- THERE MUST BE AN *INQUIRY!*

MAGNETO! HAVE HIM *BROUGHT* TO ME AT *ONCE!*

SIRE! IT SHALL BE *DONE!*

SPEAK! WHAT DO *YOU* KNOW OF THE DEADLY *SHOCK WAVE?*

I KNOW *MORE* THAN YOU *THINK,* SUB-MARINER!

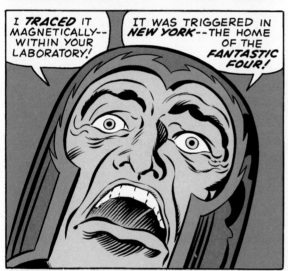

I *TRACED* IT MAGNETICALLY-- WITHIN YOUR LABORATORY!

IT WAS TRIGGERED IN *NEW YORK*-- THE HOME OF THE *FANTASTIC FOUR!*

SO! THEY ATTACK ME *AGAIN!*

I SHOULD HAVE *KNOWN!*

BUT *THIS* TIME YOU NEED NOT FACE THEM *ALONE!*

NOW YOU SHALL HAVE THE AID OF--*MAGNETO!*

I AM *NAMOR* THE FIRST, LORD OF THE *SEA!* I NEED *NO* AID!

DON'T BE A *FOOL!* *TOGETHER*--WE CAN ACCOMPLISH *ANY-THING!*

16

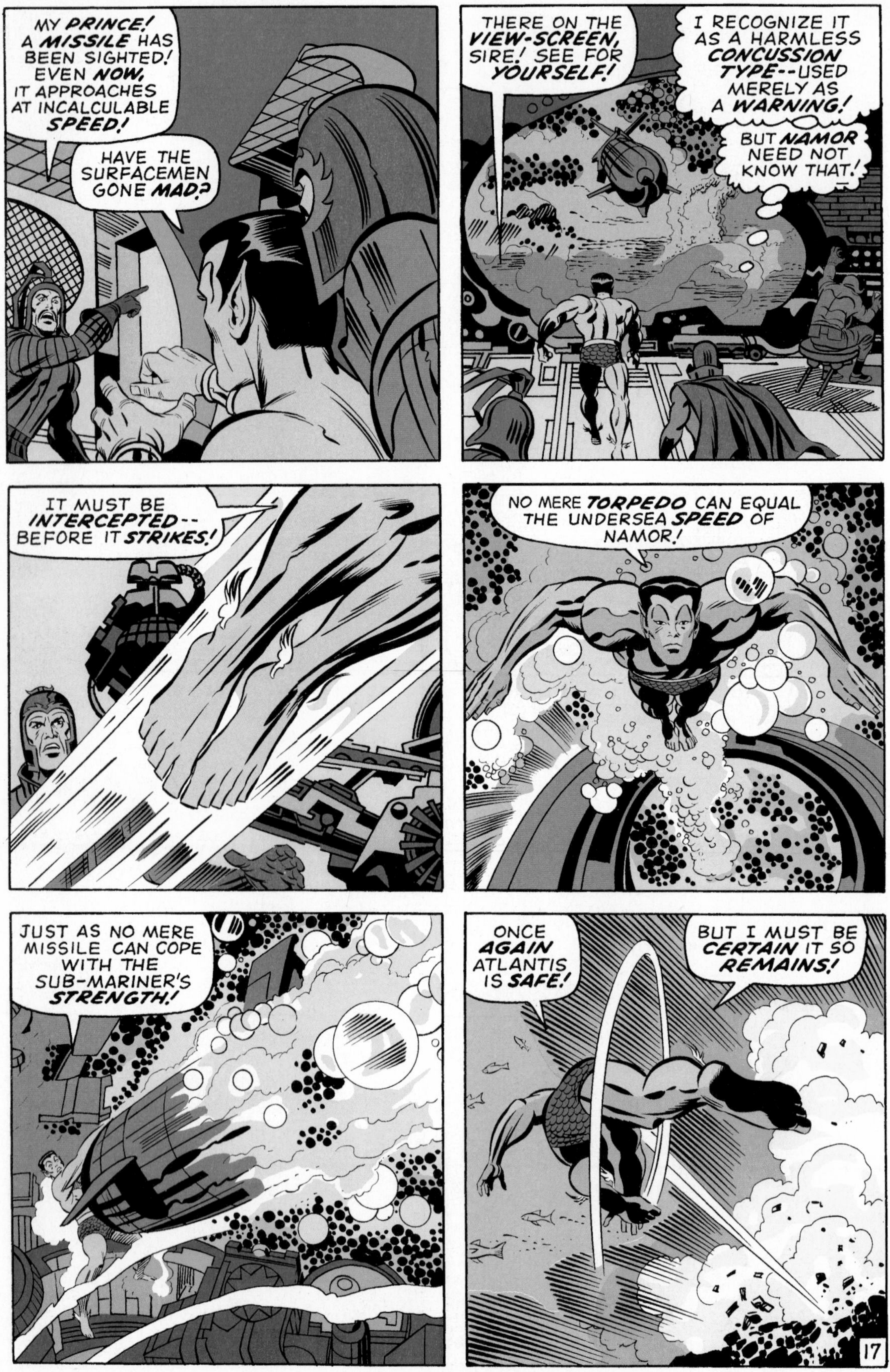
MY PRINCE! A MISSILE HAS BEEN SIGHTED! EVEN NOW, IT APPROACHES AT INCALCULABLE SPEED!
HAVE THE SURFACEMEN GONE MAD?
THERE ON THE VIEW-SCREEN, SIRE! SEE FOR YOURSELF!
I RECOGNIZE IT AS A HARMLESS CONCUSSION TYPE--USED MERELY AS A WARNING!
BUT NAMOR NEED NOT KNOW THAT!
IT MUST BE INTERCEPTED-- BEFORE IT STRIKES!
NO MERE TORPEDO CAN EQUAL THE UNDERSEA SPEED OF NAMOR!
JUST AS NO MERE MISSILE CAN COPE WITH THE SUB-MARINER'S STRENGTH!
ONCE AGAIN ATLANTIS IS SAFE!
BUT I MUST BE CERTAIN IT SO REMAINS!
17

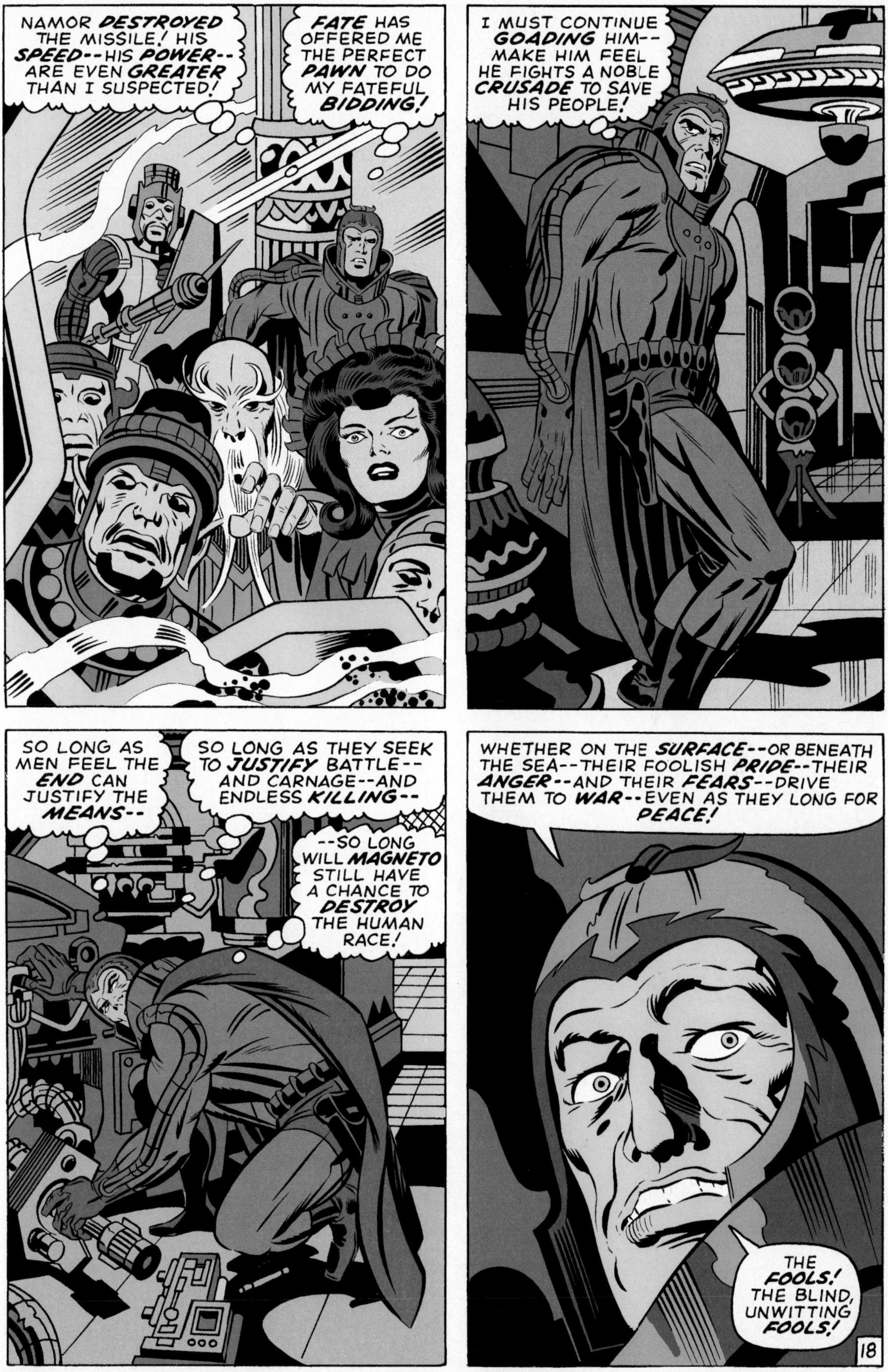

NAMOR DESTROYED THE MISSILE! HIS SPEED--HIS POWER--ARE EVEN GREATER THAN I SUSPECTED!
FATE HAS OFFERED ME THE PERFECT PAWN TO DO MY FATEFUL BIDDING!
I MUST CONTINUE GOADING HIM--MAKE HIM FEEL HE FIGHTS A NOBLE CRUSADE TO SAVE HIS PEOPLE!
SO LONG AS MEN FEEL THE END CAN JUSTIFY THE MEANS--
SO LONG AS THEY SEEK TO JUSTIFY BATTLE--AND CARNAGE--AND ENDLESS KILLING--
--SO LONG WILL MAGNETO STILL HAVE A CHANCE TO DESTROY THE HUMAN RACE!
WHETHER ON THE SURFACE--OR BENEATH THE SEA--THEIR FOOLISH PRIDE--THEIR ANGER--AND THEIR FEARS--DRIVE THEM TO WAR--EVEN AS THEY LONG FOR PEACE!
THE FOOLS! THE BLIND, UNWITTING FOOLS!
18

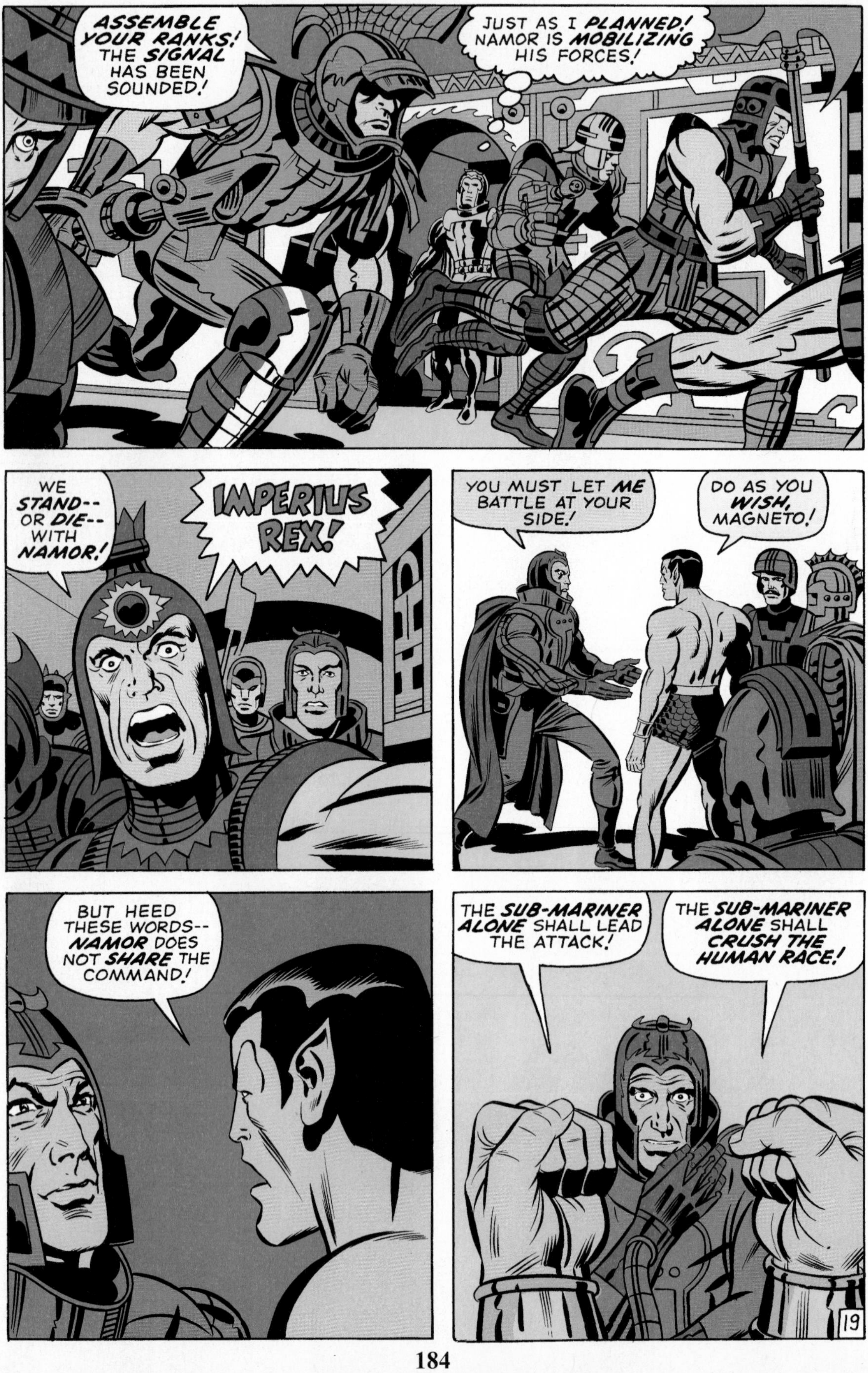
ASSEMBLE YOUR RANKS! THE SIGNAL HAS BEEN SOUNDED!
JUST AS I PLANNED! NAMOR IS MOBILIZING HIS FORCES!
WE STAND-- OR DIE-- WITH NAMOR!
IMPERIUS REX!
YOU MUST LET ME BATTLE AT YOUR SIDE!
DO AS YOU WISH, MAGNETO!
BUT HEED THESE WORDS-- NAMOR DOES NOT SHARE THE COMMAND!
THE SUB-MARINER ALONE SHALL LEAD THE ATTACK!
THE SUB-MARINER ALONE SHALL CRUSH THE HUMAN RACE!
19

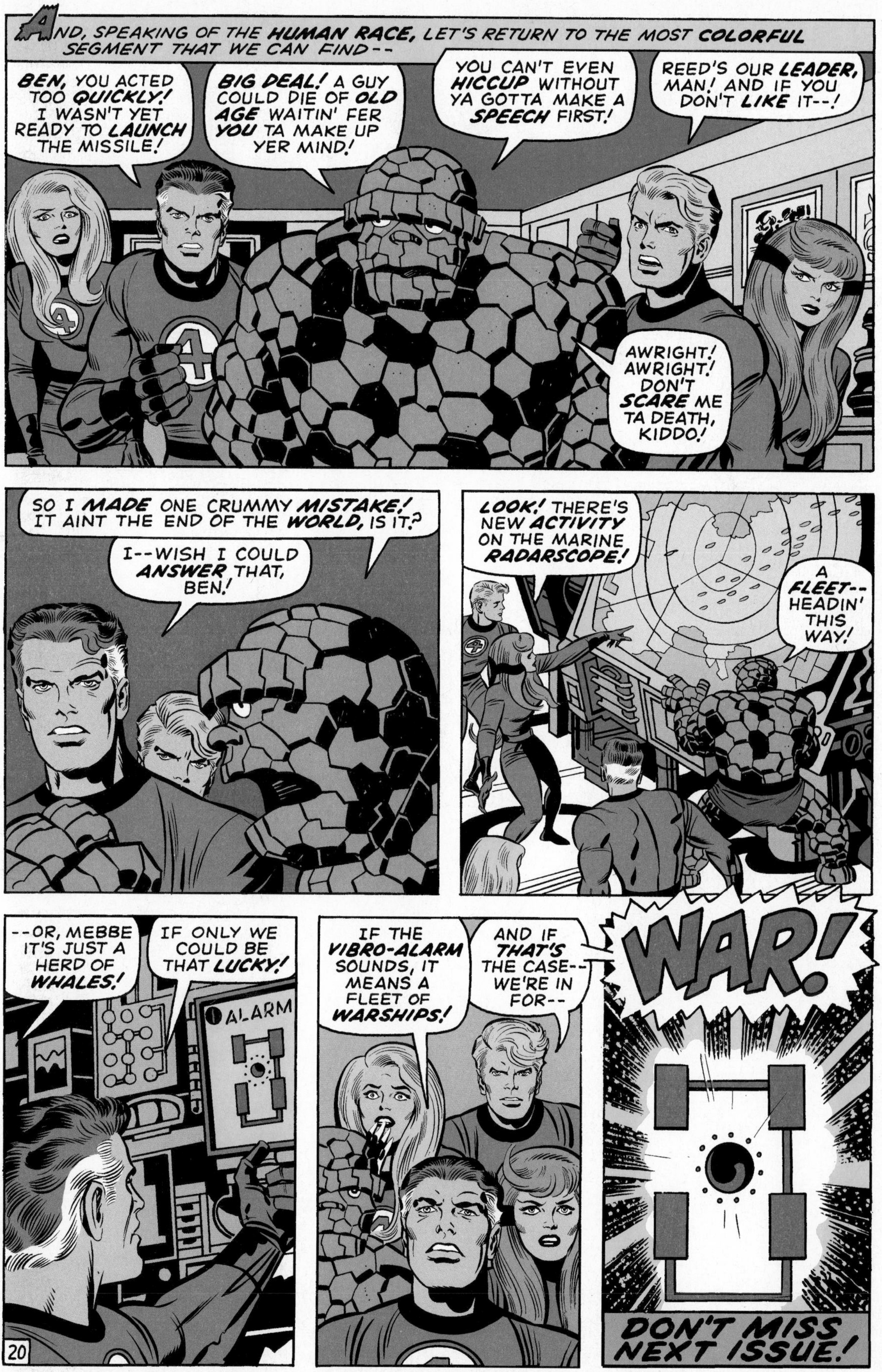
AND, SPEAKING OF THE HUMAN RACE, LET'S RETURN TO THE MOST COLORFUL SEGMENT THAT WE CAN FIND--
BEN, YOU ACTED TOO QUICKLY! I WASN'T YET READY TO LAUNCH THE MISSILE!
BIG DEAL! A GUY COULD DIE OF OLD AGE WAITIN' FER YOU TA MAKE UP YER MIND!
YOU CAN'T EVEN HICCUP WITHOUT YA GOTTA MAKE A SPEECH FIRST!
REED'S OUR LEADER, MAN! AND IF YOU DON'T LIKE IT--!
AWRIGHT! AWRIGHT! DON'T SCARE ME TA DEATH, KIDDO!
SO I MADE ONE CRUMMY MISTAKE! IT AINT THE END OF THE WORLD, IS IT?
I--WISH I COULD ANSWER THAT, BEN!
LOOK! THERE'S NEW ACTIVITY ON THE MARINE RADARSCOPE!
A FLEET--HEADIN' THIS WAY!
--OR, MEBBE IT'S JUST A HERD OF WHALES!
IF ONLY WE COULD BE THAT LUCKY!
ALARM
IF THE VIBRO-ALARM SOUNDS, IT MEANS A FLEET OF WARSHIPS!
AND IF THAT'S THE CASE--WE'RE IN FOR--
WAR!
DON'T MISS NEXT ISSUE!
20

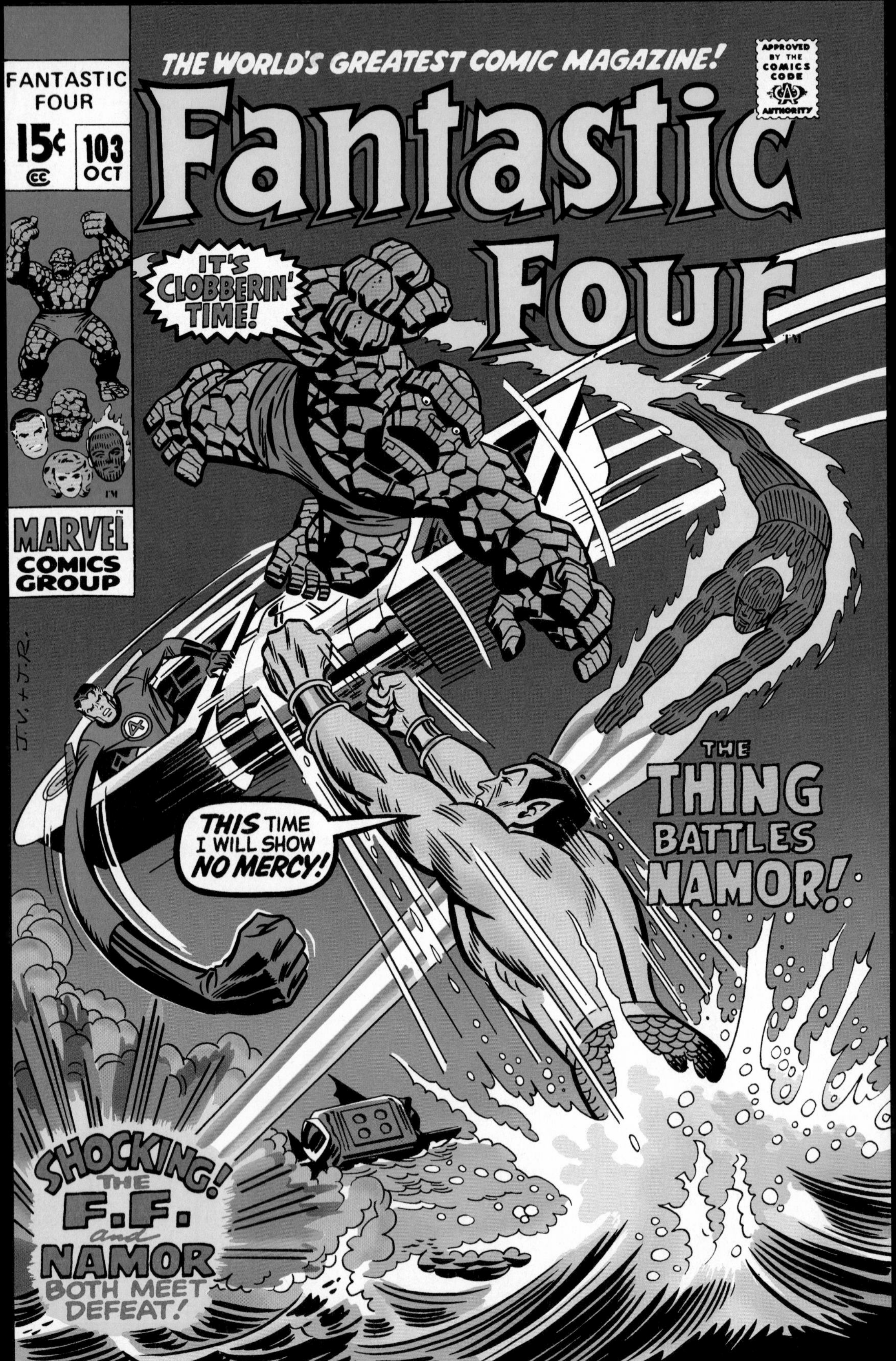
THE WORLD'S GREATEST COMIC MAGAZINE!
APPROVED BY THE COMICS CODE CA AUTHORITY
FANTASTIC FOUR
15¢
103 OCT
Fantastic Four
IT'S CLOBBERIN' TIME!
MARVEL COMICS GROUP
J.V.+J.R.
THIS TIME I WILL SHOW NO MERCY!
THE THING BATTLES NAMOR!
SHOCKING! THE F.F. and NAMOR BOTH MEET DEFEAT!

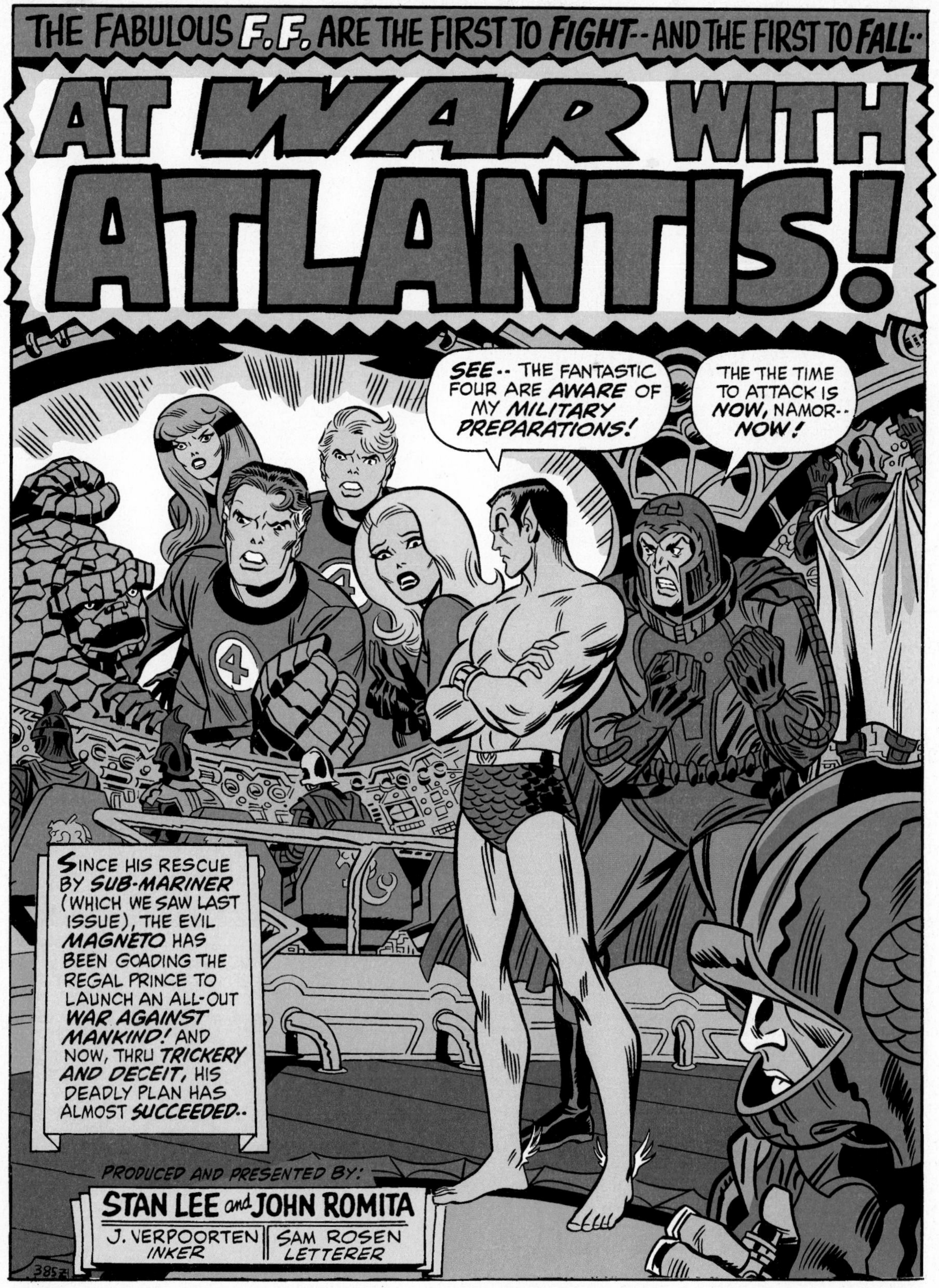
THE FABULOUS F.F. ARE THE FIRST TO FIGHT-- AND THE FIRST TO FALL--
AT WAR WITH ATLANTIS!
SEE-- THE FANTASTIC FOUR ARE AWARE OF MY MILITARY PREPARATIONS!
THE THE TIME TO ATTACK IS NOW, NAMOR-- NOW!
SINCE HIS RESCUE BY SUB-MARINER (WHICH WE SAW LAST ISSUE), THE EVIL MAGNETO HAS BEEN GOADING THE REGAL PRINCE TO LAUNCH AN ALL-OUT WAR AGAINST MANKIND! AND NOW, THRU TRICKERY AND DECEIT, HIS DEADLY PLAN HAS ALMOST SUCCEEDED..
PRODUCED AND PRESENTED BY:
STAN LEE and JOHN ROMITA
J. VERPOORTEN INKER
SAM ROSEN LETTERER

EVEN AS THE TWO, SUPER-POWERED ALLIES *SPEAK*, NAMOR'S MIGHTY *INVASION FLEET* TAKES TO THE SURFACE-- WAITING FOR ITS LEADER'S IMPERIAL *COMMAND*---

ALL IS IN TOTAL *READINESS!*

WE HAVE ATTAINED FULL *COMBAT STRENGTH!*

SEA SCOUTS-- TAKE TO THE *SKIES!*

--FOLLOW PLAN 4 *OBSERVE AND PROTECT!*

MAGNETO-- *STAND BACK!*

NONE TELL *PRINCE NAMOR* WHEN TO GIVE A *COMMAND!*

I DO NOT *LIGHTLY* REGARD THE *LIVES* OF MY FELLOW *ATLANTEANS!*

NOR EVEN THOSE OF THE *SURFACE DWELLERS!*

I CAN'T LET HIM CHANGE HIS MIND *NOW*-- AND I *WON'T!*

MEANWHILE, ATOP THE WORLD-FAMED *BAXTER BUILDING*, THE MOOD IS EQUALLY *GRIM*-- EQUALLY *NERVE-WRACKING*---

I *HAD* TO DO IT! IT WAS MY *DUTY* TO ALERT THE *PENTAGON!*

REED! DOES THAT MEAN-- WAR IS *IN-EVITABLE?*

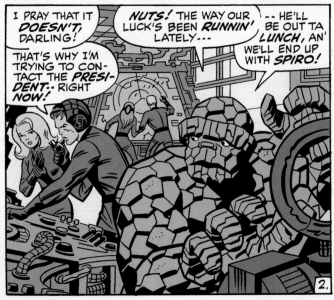

I PRAY THAT IT *DOESN'T,* DARLING!

THAT'S WHY I'M TRYING TO CON-TACT THE *PRESI-DENT*-- RIGHT *NOW!*

NUTS! THE WAY OUR LUCK'S BEEN *RUNNIN'* LATELY---

-- HE'LL BE OUT TA *LUNCH,* AN' WE'LL END UP WITH *SPIRO!*

2.

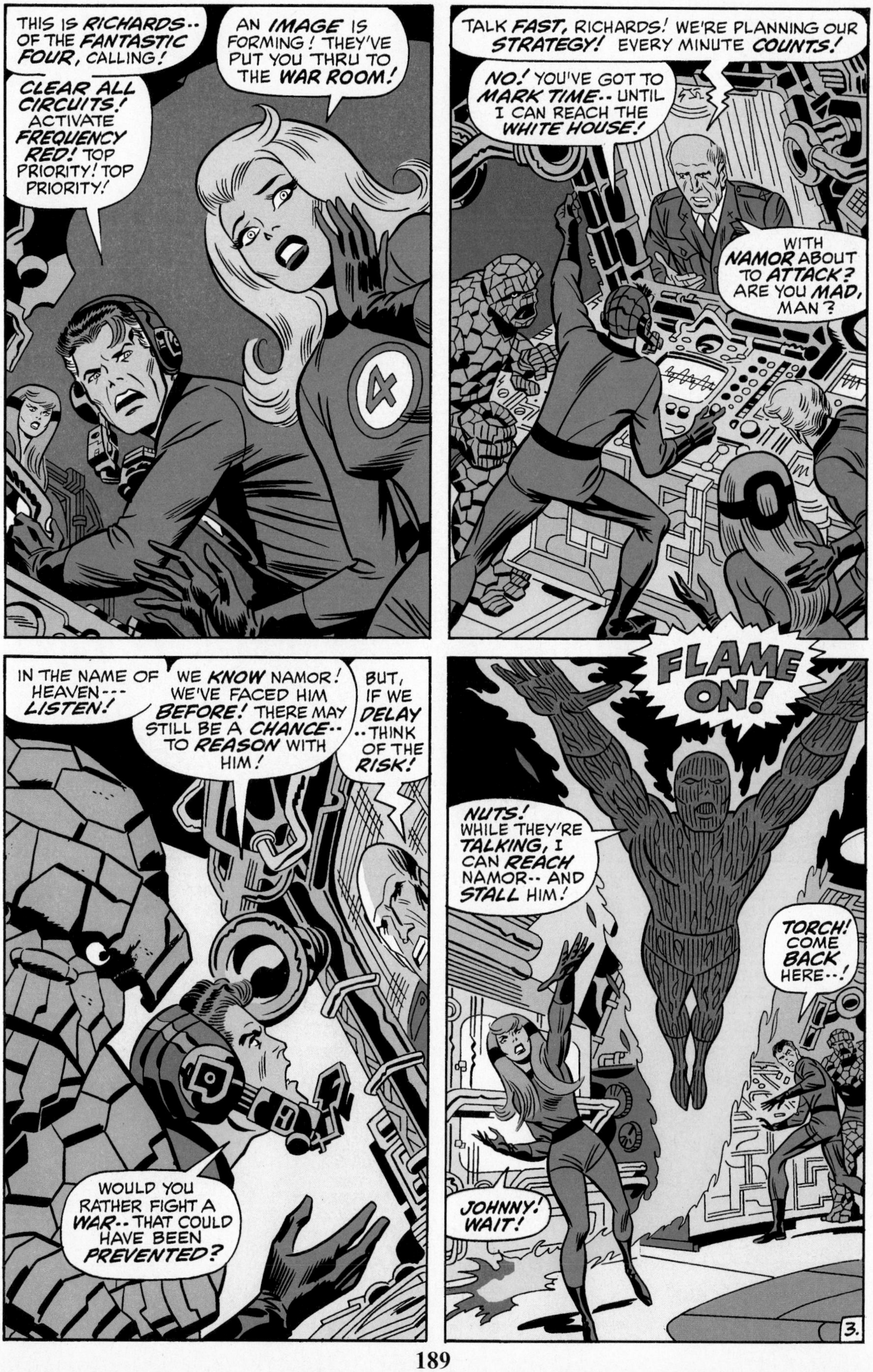
THIS IS RICHARDS.. OF THE FANTASTIC FOUR, CALLING!
CLEAR ALL CIRCUITS! ACTIVATE FREQUENCY RED! TOP PRIORITY! TOP PRIORITY!
AN IMAGE IS FORMING! THEY'VE PUT YOU THRU TO THE WAR ROOM!
TALK FAST, RICHARDS! WE'RE PLANNING OUR STRATEGY! EVERY MINUTE COUNTS!
NO! YOU'VE GOT TO MARK TIME.. UNTIL I CAN REACH THE WHITE HOUSE!
WITH NAMOR ABOUT TO ATTACK? ARE YOU MAD, MAN?
IN THE NAME OF HEAVEN--- LISTEN!
WE KNOW NAMOR! WE'VE FACED HIM BEFORE! THERE MAY STILL BE A CHANCE.. TO REASON WITH HIM!
BUT, IF WE DELAY ..THINK OF THE RISK!
WOULD YOU RATHER FIGHT A WAR.. THAT COULD HAVE BEEN PREVENTED?
FLAME ON!
NUTS! WHILE THEY'RE TALKING, I CAN REACH NAMOR.. AND STALL HIM!
TORCH! COME BACK HERE..!
JOHNNY! WAIT!
3.

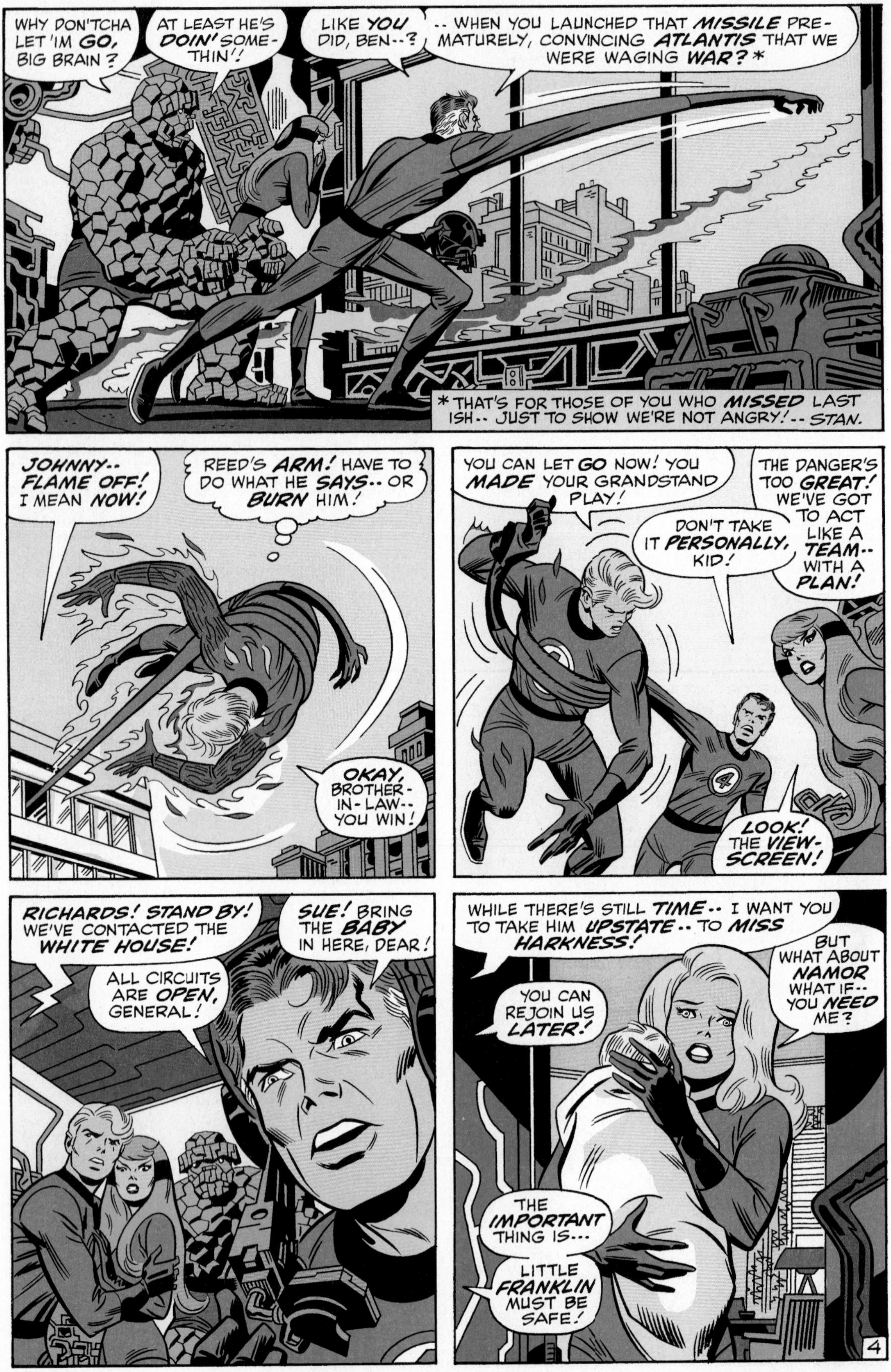
WHY DON'TCHA LET 'IM GO, BIG BRAIN?
AT LEAST HE'S DOIN' SOME-THIN'!
LIKE YOU DID, BEN--?
-- WHEN YOU LAUNCHED THAT MISSILE PRE-MATURELY, CONVINCING ATLANTIS THAT WE WERE WAGING WAR? *
* THAT'S FOR THOSE OF YOU WHO MISSED LAST ISH -- JUST TO SHOW WE'RE NOT ANGRY! -- STAN.
JOHNNY -- FLAME OFF! I MEAN NOW!
REED'S ARM! HAVE TO DO WHAT HE SAYS -- OR BURN HIM!
OKAY, BROTHER-IN-LAW -- YOU WIN!
YOU CAN LET GO NOW! YOU MADE YOUR GRANDSTAND PLAY!
THE DANGER'S TOO GREAT! WE'VE GOT TO ACT LIKE A TEAM -- WITH A PLAN!
DON'T TAKE IT PERSONALLY, KID!
LOOK! THE VIEW-SCREEN!
RICHARDS! STAND BY! WE'VE CONTACTED THE WHITE HOUSE!
ALL CIRCUITS ARE OPEN, GENERAL!
SUE! BRING THE BABY IN HERE, DEAR!
WHILE THERE'S STILL TIME -- I WANT YOU TO TAKE HIM UPSTATE -- TO MISS HARKNESS!
BUT WHAT ABOUT NAMOR WHAT IF -- YOU NEED ME?
YOU CAN REJOIN US LATER!
THE IMPORTANT THING IS...
LITTLE FRANKLIN MUST BE SAFE!
4

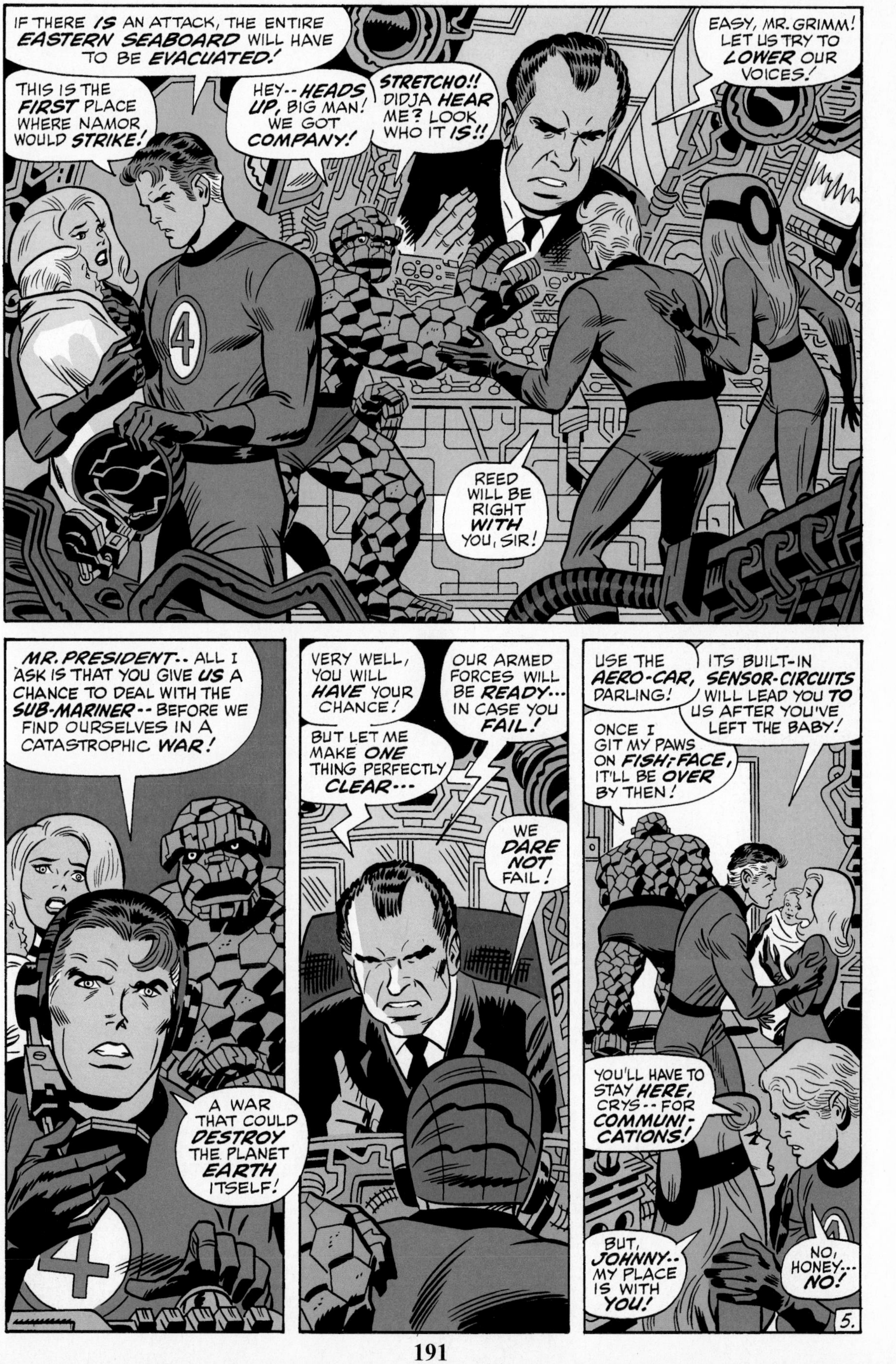
IF THERE IS AN ATTACK, THE ENTIRE EASTERN SEABOARD WILL HAVE TO BE EVACUATED!
THIS IS THE FIRST PLACE WHERE NAMOR WOULD STRIKE!
HEY-- HEADS UP, BIG MAN! WE GOT COMPANY!
STRETCHO!! DIDJA HEAR ME? LOOK WHO IT IS!!
EASY, MR. GRIMM! LET US TRY TO LOWER OUR VOICES!
REED WILL BE RIGHT WITH YOU, SIR!
MR. PRESIDENT-- ALL I ASK IS THAT YOU GIVE US A CHANCE TO DEAL WITH THE SUB-MARINER-- BEFORE WE FIND OURSELVES IN A CATASTROPHIC WAR!
A WAR THAT COULD DESTROY THE PLANET EARTH ITSELF!
VERY WELL, YOU WILL HAVE YOUR CHANCE!
BUT LET ME MAKE ONE THING PERFECTLY CLEAR---
OUR ARMED FORCES WILL BE READY... IN CASE YOU FAIL!
WE DARE NOT FAIL!
USE THE AERO-CAR, DARLING!
ITS BUILT-IN SENSOR-CIRCUITS WILL LEAD YOU TO US AFTER YOU'VE LEFT THE BABY!
ONCE I GIT MY PAWS ON FISH-FACE, IT'LL BE OVER BY THEN!
YOU'LL HAVE TO STAY HERE, CRYS-- FOR COMMUNI-CATIONS!
BUT, JOHNNY-- MY PLACE IS WITH YOU!
NO, HONEY... NO!
5.

LIKE REED *SAID*-- WE'RE A *TEAM*-- WE HAVE TO *ACT* LIKE A TEAM...

AND *HE'S* THE ONE WHO CALLS THE *SIGNALS*!

YOU'RE *NEEDED* HERE, CRYS! DON'T LET US *DOWN*!

THIS IS THE *LAST* TIME-- I WILL STAY *BEHIND*!

*M*INUTES LATER, ATOP THE LANDING-STRIP *ROOF*...

TRY NOT TO *WORRY*, DEAR! PERHAPS IT'S JUST A *FALSE* ALARM!

DO *YOU* BELIEVE THAT, REED?

THERE'S -- NO MORE TIME-- TO *TALK*! HERE COMES THE *FANTASTI-CAR*!

SEE HOW HE'S *LOOKING* AT YOU -- WITH SUCH LOVING *TRUST*!

WE WON'T *FAIL* YOU, LITTLE FELLA! YOU DESERVE SOMETHING *BETTER* THAN-- *WAR*!

REED, *DARLING*-- WHEN WILL WE EVER BE ABLE TO HAVE A *PEACEFUL* LIFE?

MAYBE *NEVER*, MY LOVE! BUT AT LEAST WE HAVE-- EACH *OTHER*!

IF YER THRU FANNIN' THE *BREEZE* NOW, STRETCHO...

LET'S GIT *GOIN'*!

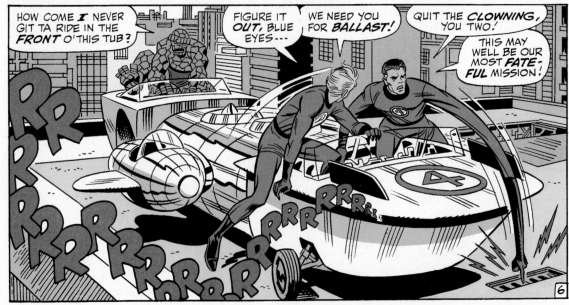

HOW COME *I* NEVER GIT TA RIDE IN THE *FRONT* O'THIS TUB?

FIGURE IT *OUT*, BLUE EYES...

WE NEED YOU FOR *BALLAST*!

QUIT THE *CLOWNING*, YOU TWO!

THIS MAY WELL BE OUR MOST *FATE-FUL* MISSION!

6

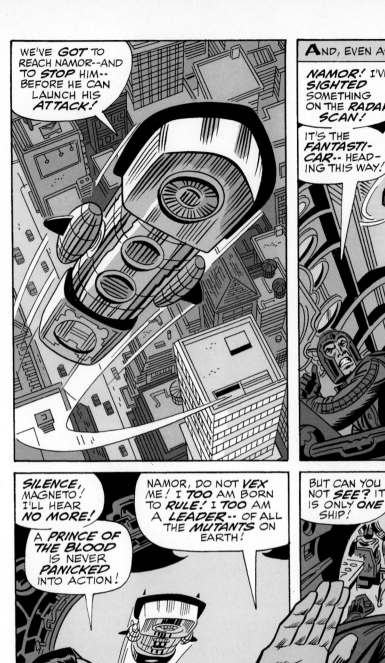

WE'VE **GOT** TO REACH NAMOR--AND TO **STOP** HIM--BEFORE HE CAN LAUNCH HIS **ATTACK!**

AND, EVEN AS REED RICHARDS **SPEAKS**---

NAMOR! I'VE **SIGHTED** SOMETHING ON THE **RADAR-SCAN!**

IT'S THE **FANTASTI-CAR!**--HEADING THIS WAY!

NOW ARE YOU CONVINCED? **NOW** WILL YOU GIVE THE ORDER TO **ATTACK?**

THE **FANTASTIC FOUR**--APPROACHING **MY** DOMAIN?

IF YOU WAIT ANY **LONGER**--IT COULD BE **TOO LATE!**

SILENCE, MAGNETO! I'LL HEAR **NO MORE!**

A **PRINCE OF THE BLOOD** IS NEVER **PANICKED** INTO ACTION!

NAMOR, DO NOT **VEX** ME! I **TOO** AM BORN TO **RULE!** I **TOO** AM A **LEADER**-- OF ALL THE **MUTANTS** ON EARTH!

AND **I** SAY-- **ATTACK!**

BUT CAN YOU NOT **SEE?** IT IS ONLY **ONE** SHIP!

KLACK!

NOW IS MY CHANCE-- WHILE HIS GAZE IS **AVERTED!**

I'LL USE MY OWN **MAGNETIC POWER** TO DO WHAT **HE** WILL NOT!

7.

193

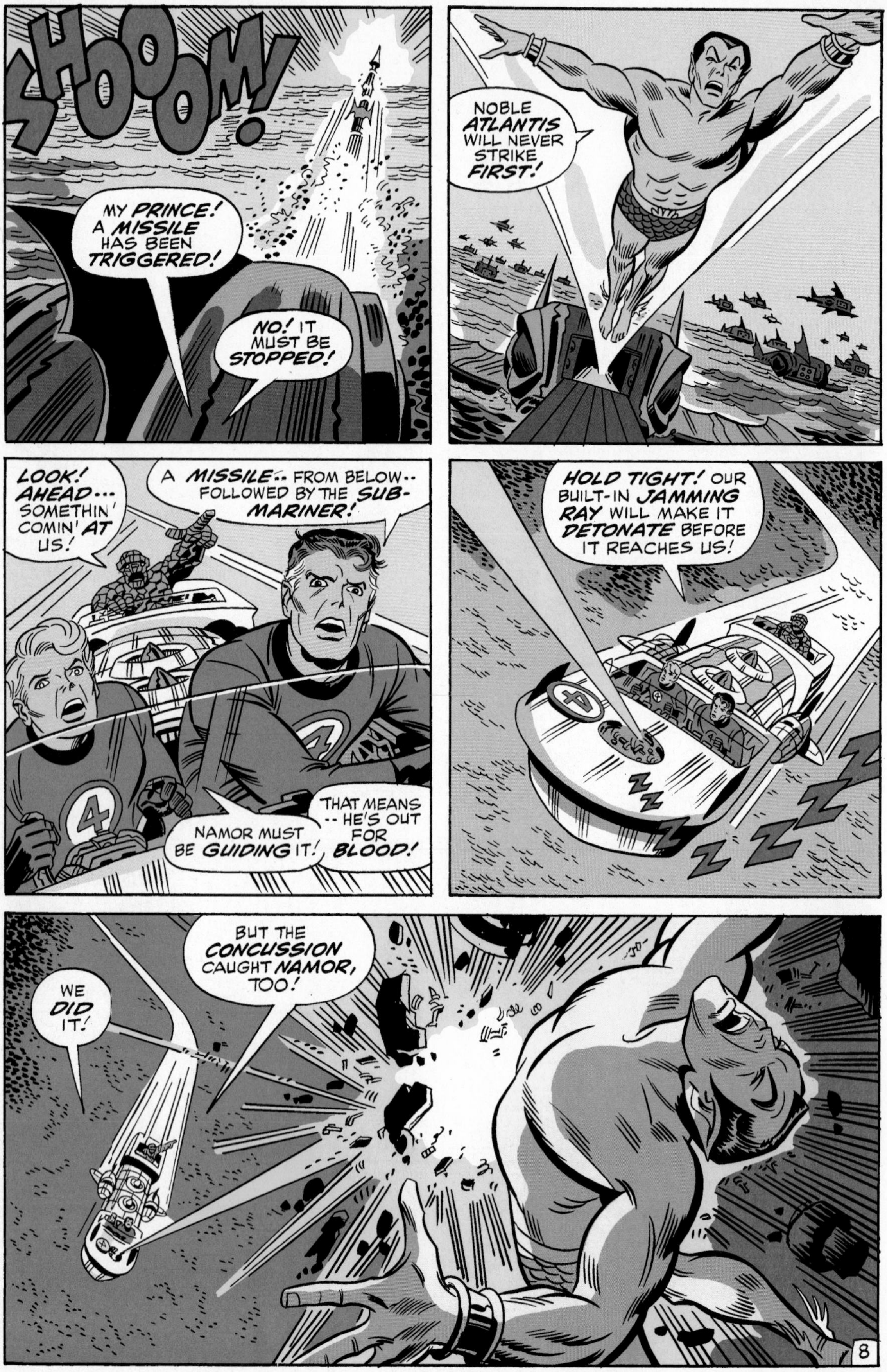
SHOOOOM!
MY PRINCE! A MISSILE HAS BEEN TRIGGERED!
NO! IT MUST BE STOPPED!
NOBLE ATLANTIS WILL NEVER STRIKE FIRST!
LOOK! AHEAD... SOMETHIN' COMIN' AT US!
A MISSILE -- FROM BELOW -- FOLLOWED BY THE SUB-MARINER!
NAMOR MUST BE GUIDING IT!
THAT MEANS -- HE'S OUT FOR BLOOD!
HOLD TIGHT! OUR BUILT-IN JAMMING RAY WILL MAKE IT DETONATE BEFORE IT REACHES US!
WE DID IT!
BUT THE CONCUSSION CAUGHT NAMOR, TOO!
8

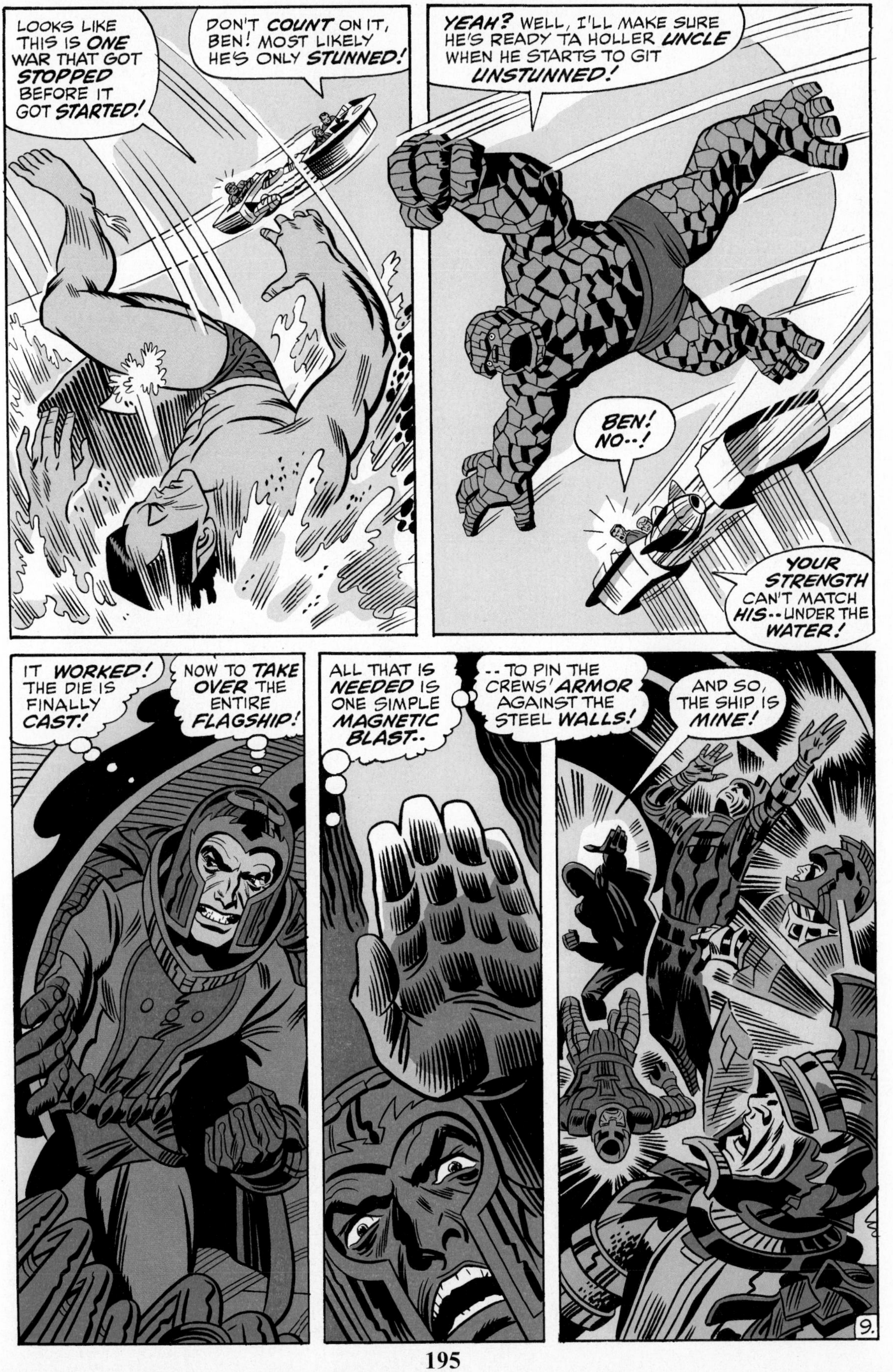
LOOKS LIKE THIS IS ONE WAR THAT GOT STOPPED BEFORE IT GOT STARTED!
DON'T COUNT ON IT, BEN! MOST LIKELY HE'S ONLY STUNNED!
YEAH? WELL, I'LL MAKE SURE HE'S READY TA HOLLER UNCLE WHEN HE STARTS TO GIT UNSTUNNED!
BEN! NO--!
YOUR STRENGTH CAN'T MATCH HIS--UNDER THE WATER!
IT WORKED! THE DIE IS FINALLY CAST!
NOW TO TAKE OVER THE ENTIRE FLAGSHIP!
ALL THAT IS NEEDED IS ONE SIMPLE MAGNETIC BLAST--
--TO PIN THE CREWS' ARMOR AGAINST THE STEEL WALLS!
AND SO, THE SHIP IS MINE!
9.

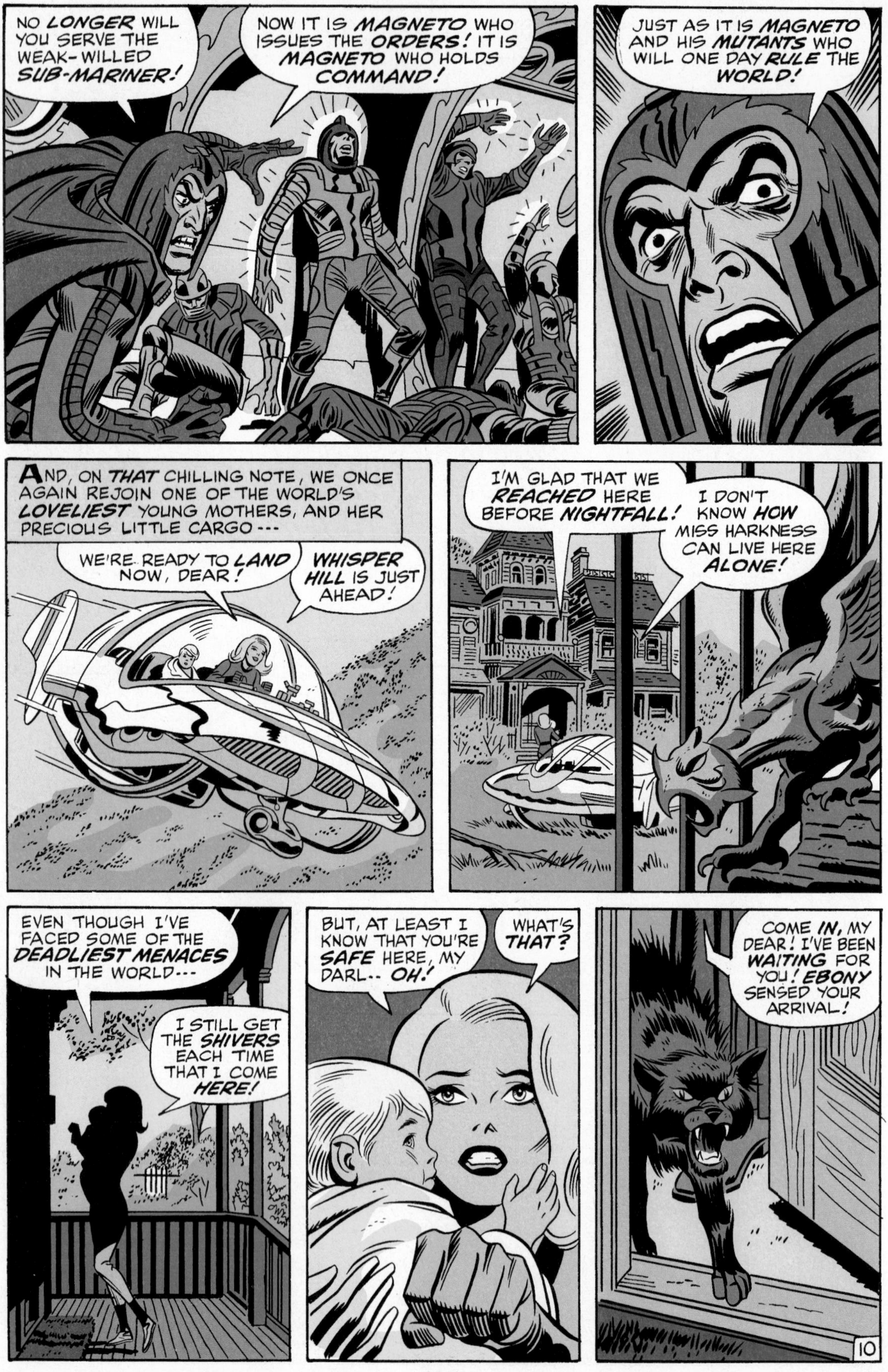

NO LONGER WILL YOU SERVE THE WEAK-WILLED SUB-MARINER!
NOW IT IS MAGNETO WHO ISSUES THE ORDERS! IT IS MAGNETO WHO HOLDS COMMAND!
JUST AS IT IS MAGNETO AND HIS MUTANTS WHO WILL ONE DAY RULE THE WORLD!
AND, ON THAT CHILLING NOTE, WE ONCE AGAIN REJOIN ONE OF THE WORLD'S LOVELIEST YOUNG MOTHERS, AND HER PRECIOUS LITTLE CARGO---
WE'RE READY TO LAND NOW, DEAR!
WHISPER HILL IS JUST AHEAD!
I'M GLAD THAT WE REACHED HERE BEFORE NIGHTFALL!
I DON'T KNOW HOW MISS HARKNESS CAN LIVE HERE ALONE!
EVEN THOUGH I'VE FACED SOME OF THE DEADLIEST MENACES IN THE WORLD---
I STILL GET THE SHIVERS EACH TIME THAT I COME HERE!
BUT, AT LEAST I KNOW THAT YOU'RE SAFE HERE, MY DARL-- OH!
WHAT'S THAT?
COME IN, MY DEAR! I'VE BEEN WAITING FOR YOU! EBONY SENSED YOUR ARRIVAL!
10

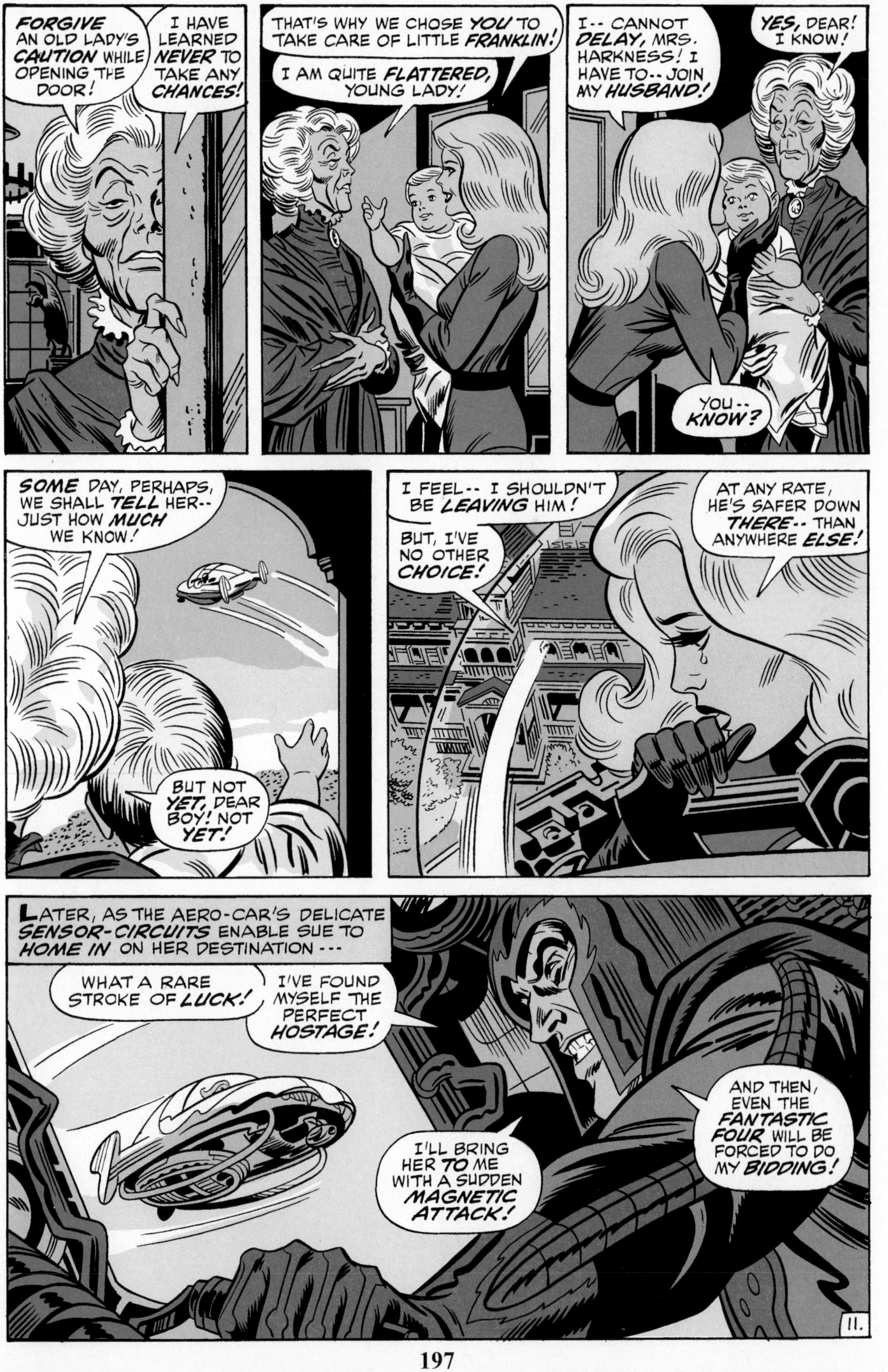
FORGIVE AN OLD LADY'S CAUTION WHILE OPENING THE DOOR!
I HAVE LEARNED NEVER TO TAKE ANY CHANCES!
THAT'S WHY WE CHOSE YOU TO TAKE CARE OF LITTLE FRANKLIN!
I AM QUITE FLATTERED, YOUNG LADY!
I-- CANNOT DELAY, MRS. HARKNESS! I HAVE TO-- JOIN MY HUSBAND!
YES, DEAR! I KNOW!
YOU-- KNOW?
SOME DAY, PERHAPS, WE SHALL TELL HER-- JUST HOW MUCH WE KNOW!
BUT NOT YET, DEAR BOY! NOT YET!
I FEEL-- I SHOULDN'T BE LEAVING HIM!
BUT, I'VE NO OTHER CHOICE!
AT ANY RATE, HE'S SAFER DOWN THERE-- THAN ANYWHERE ELSE!
LATER, AS THE AERO-CAR'S DELICATE SENSOR-CIRCUITS ENABLE SUE TO HOME IN ON HER DESTINATION ---
WHAT A RARE STROKE OF LUCK!
I'VE FOUND MYSELF THE PERFECT HOSTAGE!
I'LL BRING HER TO ME WITH A SUDDEN MAGNETIC ATTACK!
AND THEN, EVEN THE FANTASTIC FOUR WILL BE FORCED TO DO MY BIDDING!
11.

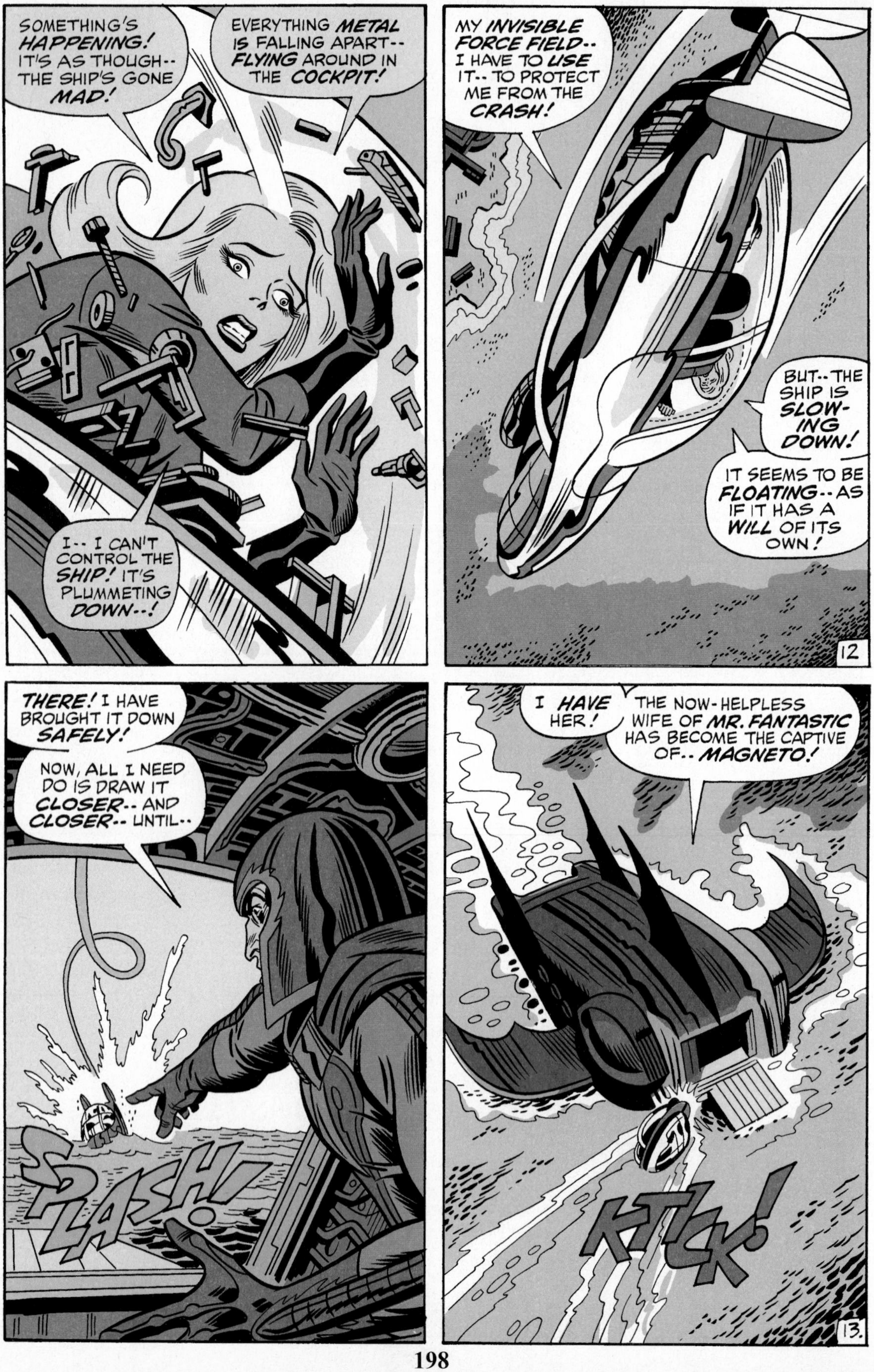
SOMETHING'S HAPPENING! IT'S AS THOUGH-- THE SHIP'S GONE MAD!
EVERYTHING METAL IS FALLING APART-- FLYING AROUND IN THE COCKPIT!
I-- I CAN'T CONTROL THE SHIP! IT'S PLUMMETING DOWN--!
MY INVISIBLE FORCE FIELD-- I HAVE TO USE IT-- TO PROTECT ME FROM THE CRASH!
BUT-- THE SHIP IS SLOWING DOWN!
IT SEEMS TO BE FLOATING-- AS IF IT HAS A WILL OF ITS OWN!
12
THERE! I HAVE BROUGHT IT DOWN SAFELY!
NOW, ALL I NEED DO IS DRAW IT CLOSER-- AND CLOSER-- UNTIL--
SPLASH!
I HAVE HER!
THE NOW-HELPLESS WIFE OF MR. FANTASTIC HAS BECOME THE CAPTIVE OF-- MAGNETO!
KTICK!
13.

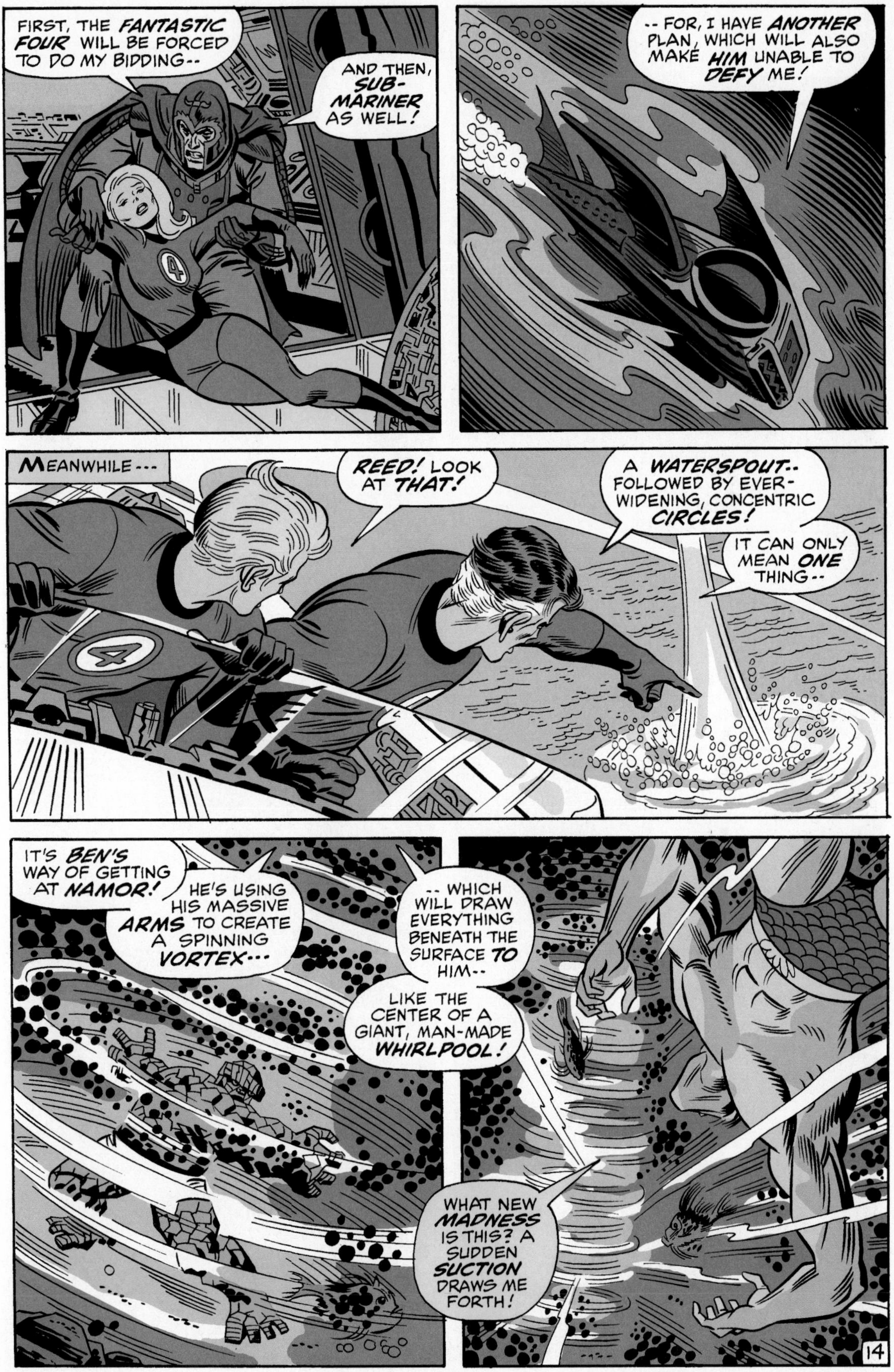
FIRST, THE FANTASTIC FOUR WILL BE FORCED TO DO MY BIDDING--
AND THEN, SUB-MARINER AS WELL!
-- FOR, I HAVE ANOTHER PLAN, WHICH WILL ALSO MAKE HIM UNABLE TO DEFY ME!
MEANWHILE ---
REED! LOOK AT THAT!
A WATERSPOUT-- FOLLOWED BY EVER-WIDENING, CONCENTRIC CIRCLES!
IT CAN ONLY MEAN ONE THING--
IT'S BEN'S WAY OF GETTING AT NAMOR!
HE'S USING HIS MASSIVE ARMS TO CREATE A SPINNING VORTEX---
-- WHICH WILL DRAW EVERYTHING BENEATH THE SURFACE TO HIM--
LIKE THE CENTER OF A GIANT, MAN-MADE WHIRLPOOL!
WHAT NEW MADNESS IS THIS? A SUDDEN SUCTION DRAWS ME FORTH!
14

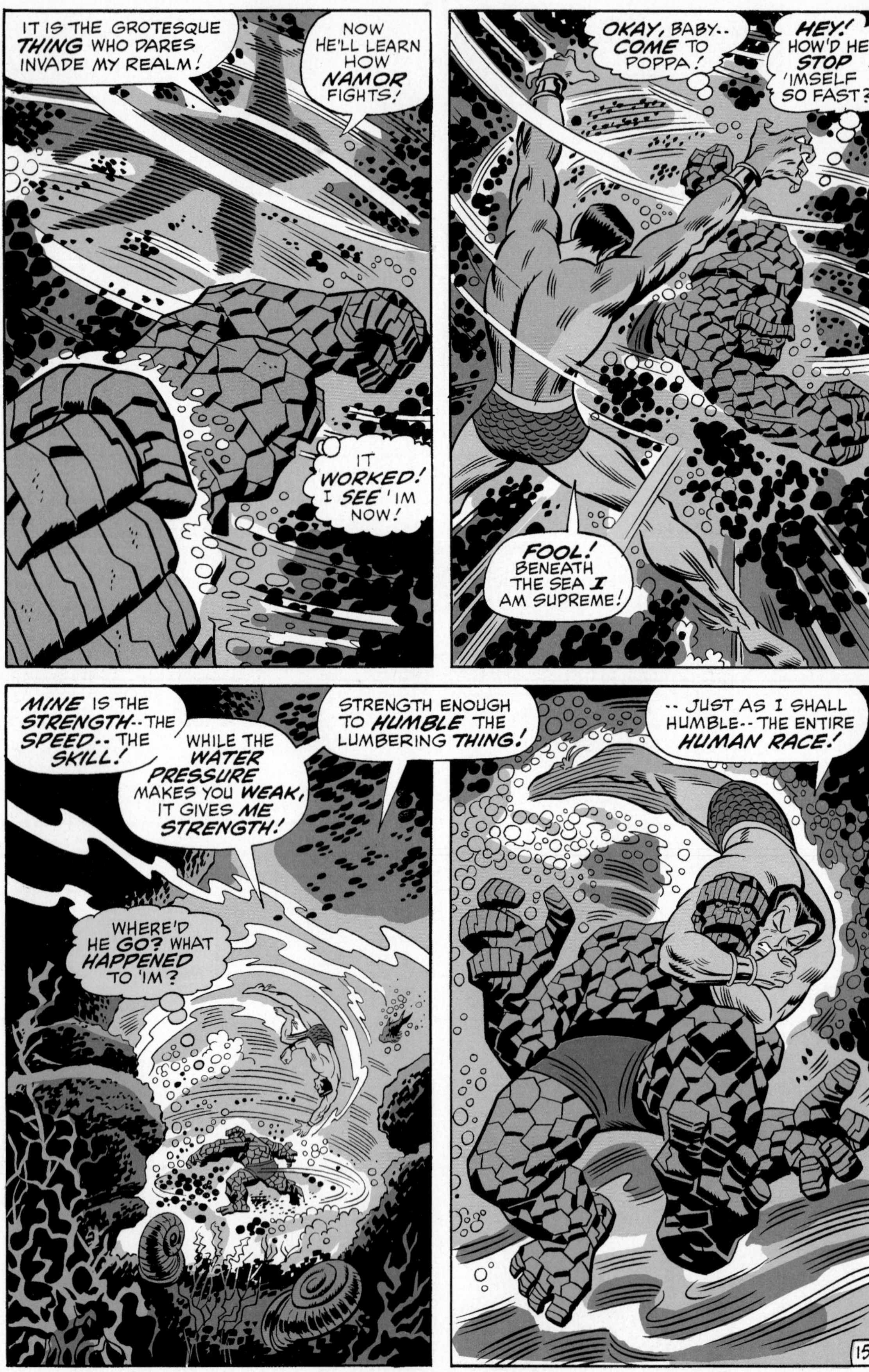
IT IS THE GROTESQUE THING WHO DARES INVADE MY REALM!
NOW HE'LL LEARN HOW NAMOR FIGHTS!
IT WORKED! I SEE 'IM NOW!
OKAY, BABY.. COME TO POPPA!
HEY! HOW'D HE STOP 'IMSELF SO FAST?
FOOL! BENEATH THE SEA I AM SUPREME!
MINE IS THE STRENGTH--THE SPEED.. THE SKILL!
WHILE THE WATER PRESSURE MAKES YOU WEAK, IT GIVES ME STRENGTH!
STRENGTH ENOUGH TO HUMBLE THE LUMBERING THING!
WHERE'D HE GO? WHAT HAPPENED TO 'IM?
-- JUST AS I SHALL HUMBLE-- THE ENTIRE HUMAN RACE!
15

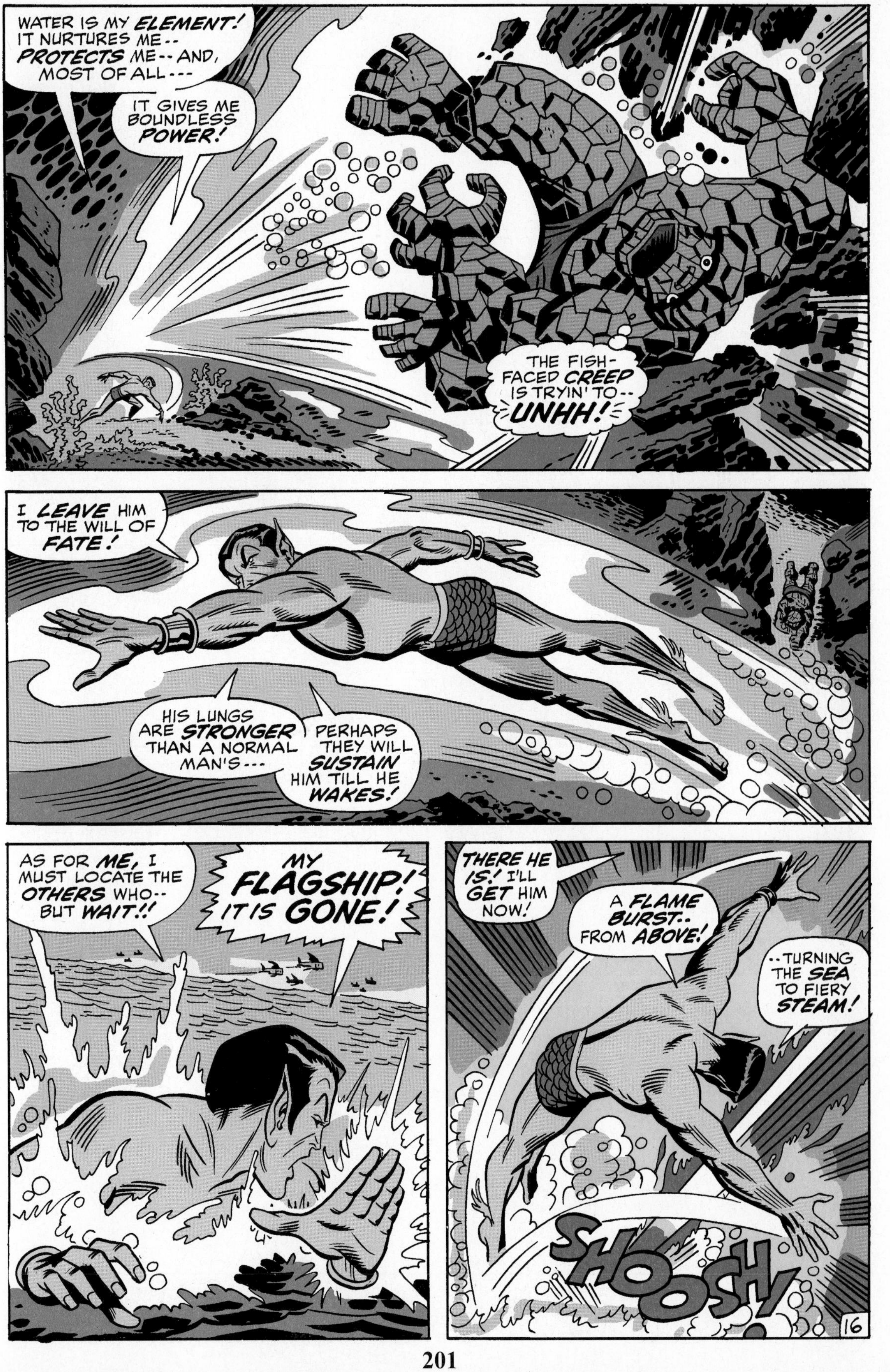

WATER IS MY ELEMENT! IT NURTURES ME-- PROTECTS ME-- AND, MOST OF ALL---
IT GIVES ME BOUNDLESS POWER!
THE FISH-FACED CREEP IS TRYIN' TO-- UNHH!
I LEAVE HIM TO THE WILL OF FATE!
HIS LUNGS ARE STRONGER THAN A NORMAL MAN'S---
PERHAPS THEY WILL SUSTAIN HIM TILL HE WAKES!
AS FOR ME, I MUST LOCATE THE OTHERS WHO-- BUT WAIT!!
MY FLAGSHIP! IT IS GONE!
THERE HE IS! I'LL GET HIM NOW!
A FLAME BURST.. FROM ABOVE!
..TURNING THE SEA TO FIERY STEAM!
SHOOSH!
16

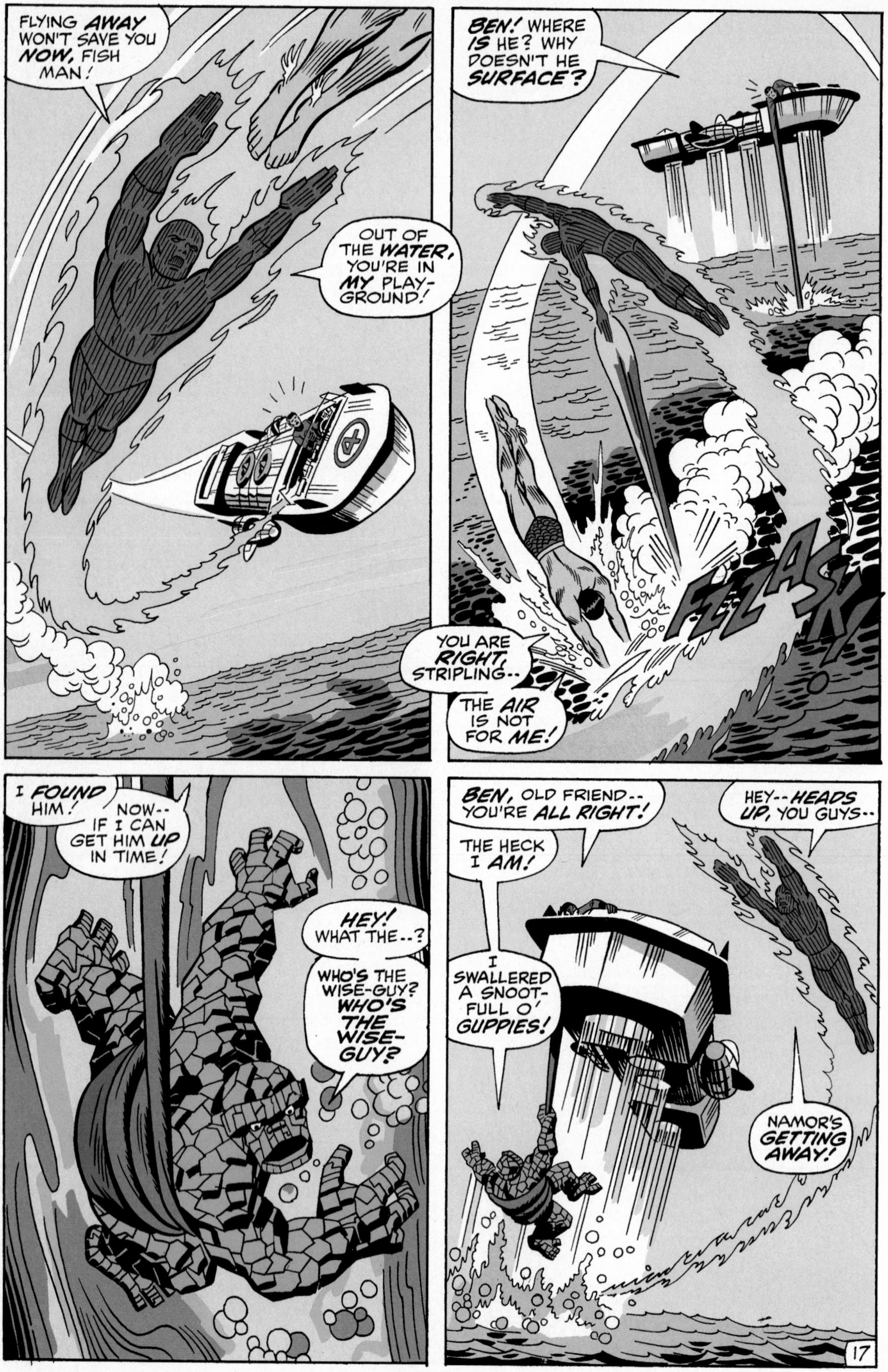
FLYING AWAY WON'T SAVE YOU NOW, FISH MAN!
OUT OF THE WATER, YOU'RE IN MY PLAY-GROUND!
BEN! WHERE IS HE? WHY DOESN'T HE SURFACE?
FZZASK!
YOU ARE RIGHT, STRIPLING..
THE AIR IS NOT FOR ME!
I FOUND HIM!
NOW-- IF I CAN GET HIM UP IN TIME!
HEY! WHAT THE..?
WHO'S THE WISE-GUY? WHO'S THE WISE-GUY?
BEN, OLD FRIEND-- YOU'RE ALL RIGHT!
THE HECK I AM!
I SWALLERED A SNOOT-FULL O' GUPPIES!
HEY--HEADS UP, YOU GUYS..
NAMOR'S GETTING AWAY!
17

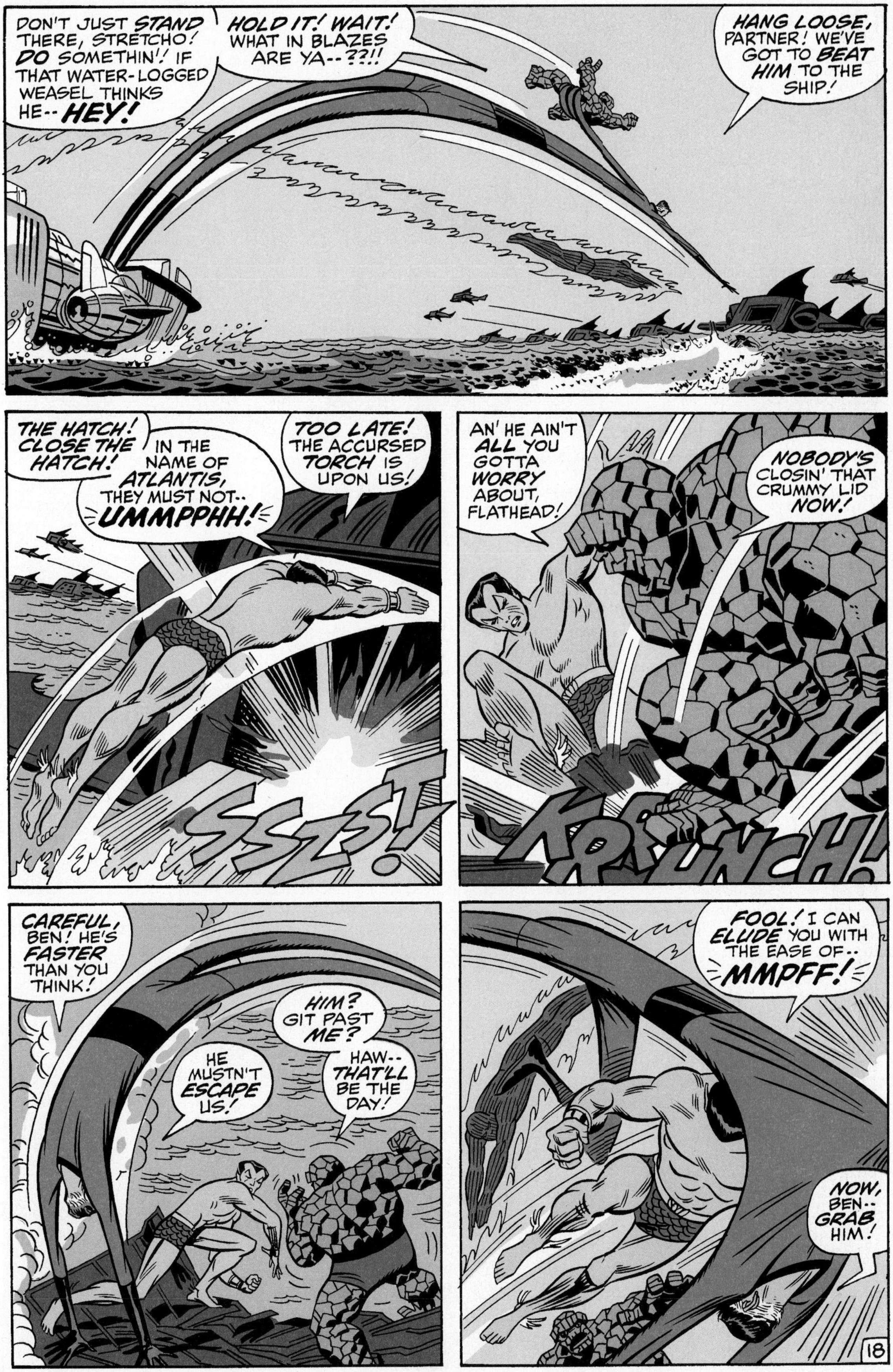
DON'T JUST STAND THERE, STRETCHO! DO SOMETHIN'! IF THAT WATER-LOGGED WEASEL THINKS HE-- HEY!
HOLD IT! WAIT! WHAT IN BLAZES ARE YA--??!!
HANG LOOSE, PARTNER! WE'VE GOT TO BEAT HIM TO THE SHIP!
THE HATCH! CLOSE THE HATCH!
IN THE NAME OF ATLANTIS, THEY MUST NOT.. UMMPPHH!
TOO LATE! THE ACCURSED TORCH IS UPON US!
SSZZST!
AN' HE AIN'T ALL YOU GOTTA WORRY ABOUT, FLATHEAD!
NOBODY'S CLOSIN' THAT CRUMMY LID NOW!
KRRUNCH!
CAREFUL, BEN! HE'S FASTER THAN YOU THINK!
HIM? GIT PAST ME?
HE MUSTN'T ESCAPE US!
HAW-- THAT'LL BE THE DAY!
FOOL! I CAN ELUDE YOU WITH THE EASE OF.. MMPFF!
NOW, BEN.. GRAB HIM!
18

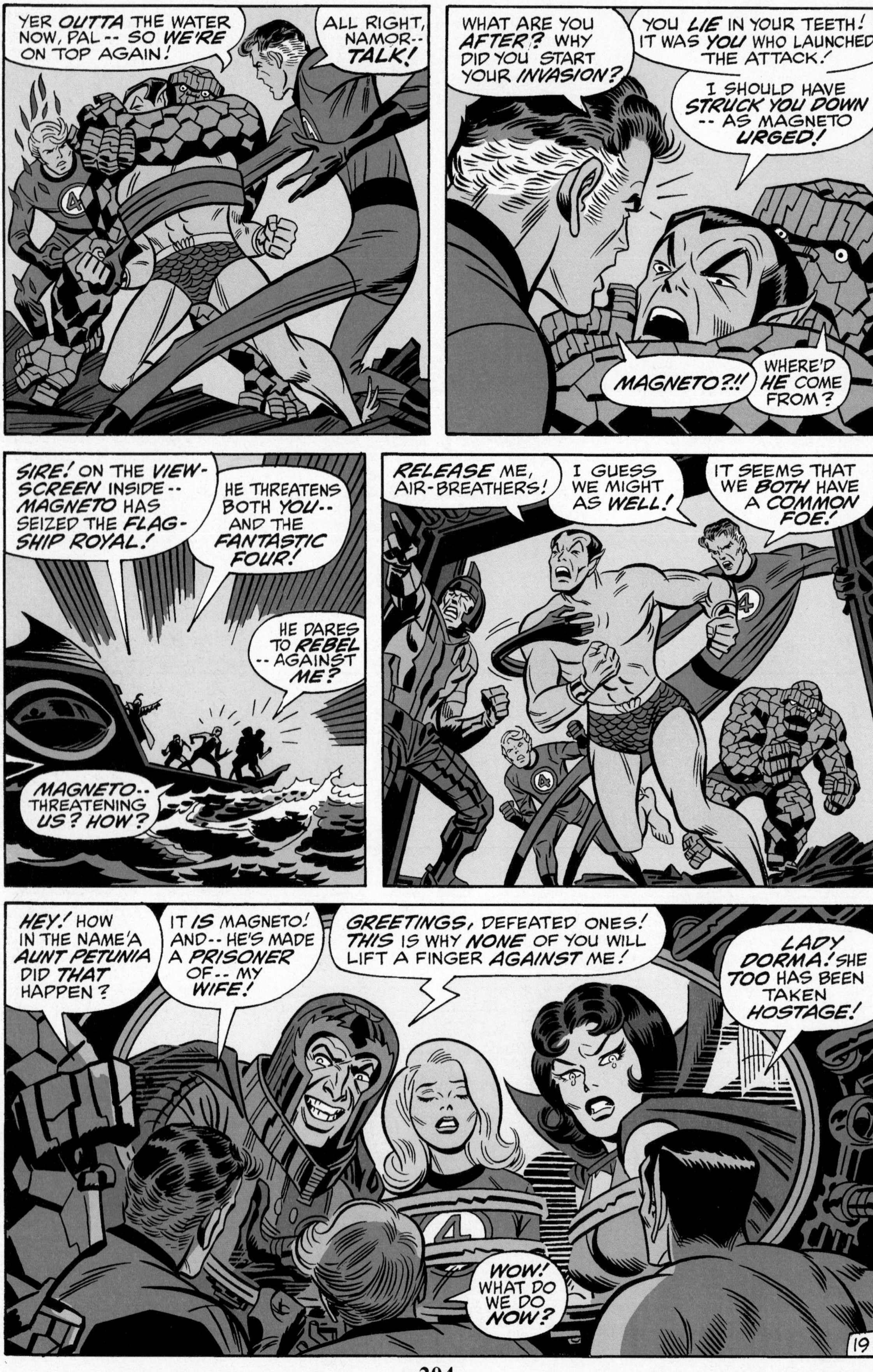

YER OUTTA THE WATER NOW, PAL -- SO WE'RE ON TOP AGAIN!
ALL RIGHT, NAMOR -- TALK!
WHAT ARE YOU AFTER? WHY DID YOU START YOUR INVASION?
YOU LIE IN YOUR TEETH! IT WAS YOU WHO LAUNCHED THE ATTACK!
I SHOULD HAVE STRUCK YOU DOWN -- AS MAGNETO URGED!
MAGNETO?!!
WHERE'D HE COME FROM?
SIRE! ON THE VIEW-SCREEN INSIDE -- MAGNETO HAS SEIZED THE FLAG-SHIP ROYAL!
HE THREATENS BOTH YOU -- AND THE FANTASTIC FOUR!
HE DARES TO REBEL -- AGAINST ME?
MAGNETO -- THREATENING US? HOW?
RELEASE ME, AIR-BREATHERS!
I GUESS WE MIGHT AS WELL!
IT SEEMS THAT WE BOTH HAVE A COMMON FOE!
HEY! HOW IN THE NAME'A AUNT PETUNIA DID THAT HAPPEN?
IT IS MAGNETO! AND -- HE'S MADE A PRISONER OF -- MY WIFE!
GREETINGS, DEFEATED ONES! THIS IS WHY NONE OF YOU WILL LIFT A FINGER AGAINST ME!
LADY DORMA! SHE TOO HAS BEEN TAKEN HOSTAGE!
WOW! WHAT DO WE DO NOW?
19

IF ONE SINGLE *HAIR* OF MY LADY'S HEAD SHOULD BE *HARMED*--

HOLD IT, NAMOR! *THREATS* WON'T HELP US *NOW!*

DORMA IS TRYING TO *TELL* US SOMETHING--!

FORGIVE ME, MY LORD! I WAS *LURED* INTO YOUR FLAGSHIP-- THINKING *YOU* WERE THERE!

BUT, I *BEG* YOU-- FEAR *NOT* FOR MY SAFETY--

YOU MUST DO-- WHAT MUST BE *DONE!*

I *WARN* YOU, MAGNETO-- IF YOU THINK TO *DEFY* THE POWER OF *ATLANTIS*--

YEAH! 'N HOW ABOUT THE COCKAMAMIE *FANTASTIC FOUR?!!*

HE'S *RIGHT!* HE'S GOT ALL THE *ACES!*

YOU DO NOT *IMPRESS* ME! THE TRUMP CARDS ARE *MINE!*

YOU *KNOW* THAT YOU MUST *SERVE* ME, WHILE I HOLD THE ONES YOU *LOVE!*

NUTS! LET 'EM KEEP *YAKKIN'*-- MEANTIME I'LL TAKE ATLANTIS *APART* TILL I *FIND* ME THAT PUNK!

YOU *CAN'T,* BIG BUDDY! THERE'S TOO MUCH AT *STAKE!*

HUMAN LIFE MEANS *NOTHING* TO MAGNETO!

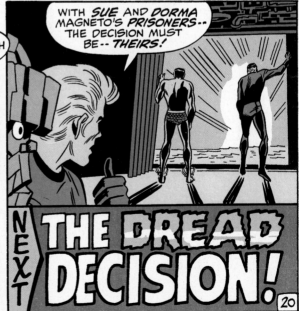

WITH *SUE* AND DORMA MAGNETO'S *PRISONERS*-- THE DECISION MUST BE-- *THEIRS!*

NEXT **THE DREAD DECISION!**

20

THE WORLD'S GREATEST COMIC MAGAZINE!
FANTASTIC FOUR
15¢ 104 NOV
APPROVED BY THE COMICS CODE AUTHORITY
Fantastic Four
MARVEL COMICS GROUP
ATTACK ME AND THOSE YOU LOVE MOST WILL DIE!
NOTHING MUST STOP US!
WE HAVE NO CHOICE--
THE HUMAN RACE IS AT STAKE!
THE CONQUEROR SAYS DIE!

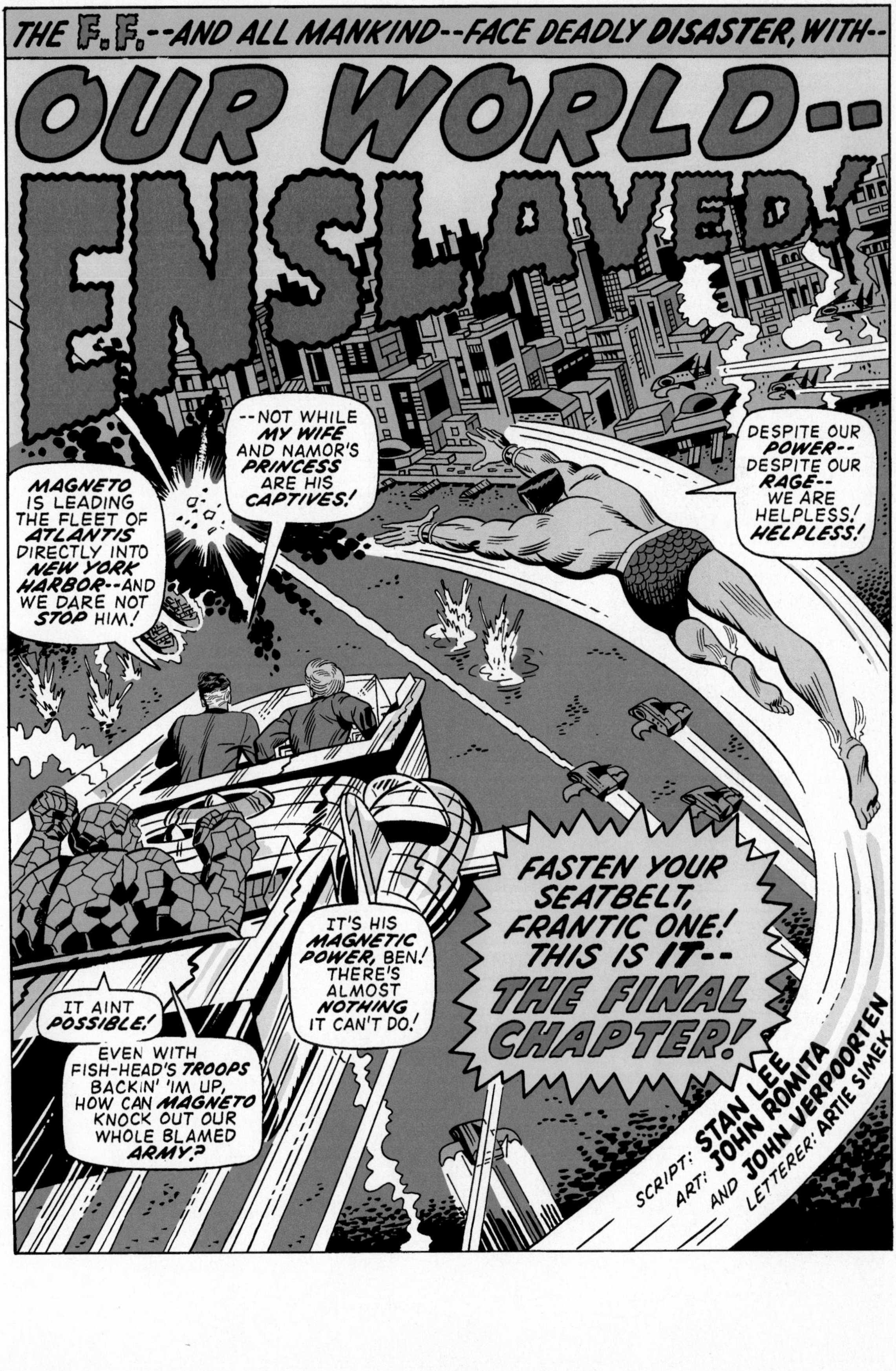

THE F.F.--AND ALL MANKIND--FACE DEADLY DISASTER, WITH--
OUR WORLD--ENSLAVED!
MAGNETO IS LEADING THE FLEET OF ATLANTIS DIRECTLY INTO NEW YORK HARBOR--AND WE DARE NOT STOP HIM!
--NOT WHILE MY WIFE AND NAMOR'S PRINCESS ARE HIS CAPTIVES!
DESPITE OUR POWER--DESPITE OUR RAGE--WE ARE HELPLESS! HELPLESS!
FASTEN YOUR SEATBELT, FRANTIC ONE! THIS IS IT--THE FINAL CHAPTER!
IT'S HIS MAGNETIC POWER, BEN! THERE'S ALMOST NOTHING IT CAN'T DO!
IT AINT POSSIBLE!
EVEN WITH FISH-HEAD'S TROOPS BACKIN' 'IM UP, HOW CAN MAGNETO KNOCK OUT OUR WHOLE BLAMED ARMY?
SCRIPT: STAN LEE
ART: JOHN ROMITA AND JOHN VERPOORTEN
LETTERER: ARTIE SIMEK

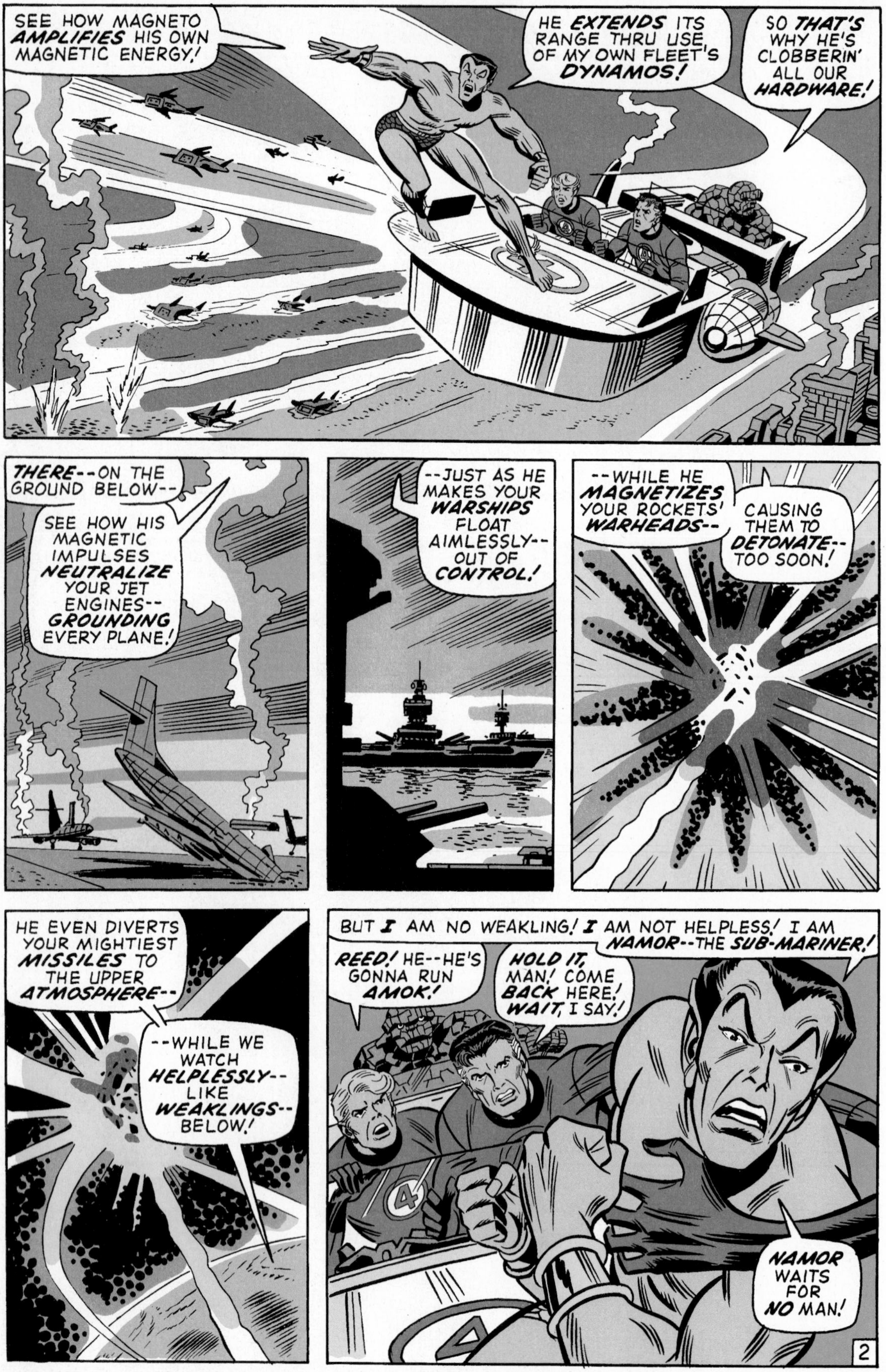
SEE HOW MAGNETO AMPLIFIES HIS OWN MAGNETIC ENERGY!
HE EXTENDS ITS RANGE THRU USE OF MY OWN FLEET'S DYNAMOS!
SO THAT'S WHY HE'S CLOBBERIN' ALL OUR HARDWARE!
THERE--ON THE GROUND BELOW--
SEE HOW HIS MAGNETIC IMPULSES NEUTRALIZE YOUR JET ENGINES--GROUNDING EVERY PLANE!
--JUST AS HE MAKES YOUR WARSHIPS FLOAT AIMLESSLY--OUT OF CONTROL!
--WHILE HE MAGNETIZES YOUR ROCKETS' WARHEADS--
CAUSING THEM TO DETONATE--TOO SOON!
HE EVEN DIVERTS YOUR MIGHTIEST MISSILES TO THE UPPER ATMOSPHERE--
--WHILE WE WATCH HELPLESSLY--LIKE WEAKLINGS--BELOW!
BUT I AM NO WEAKLING! I AM NOT HELPLESS! I AM NAMOR--THE SUB-MARINER!
REED! HE--HE'S GONNA RUN AMOK!
HOLD IT, MAN! COME BACK HERE! WAIT, I SAY!
NAMOR WAITS FOR NO MAN!
2

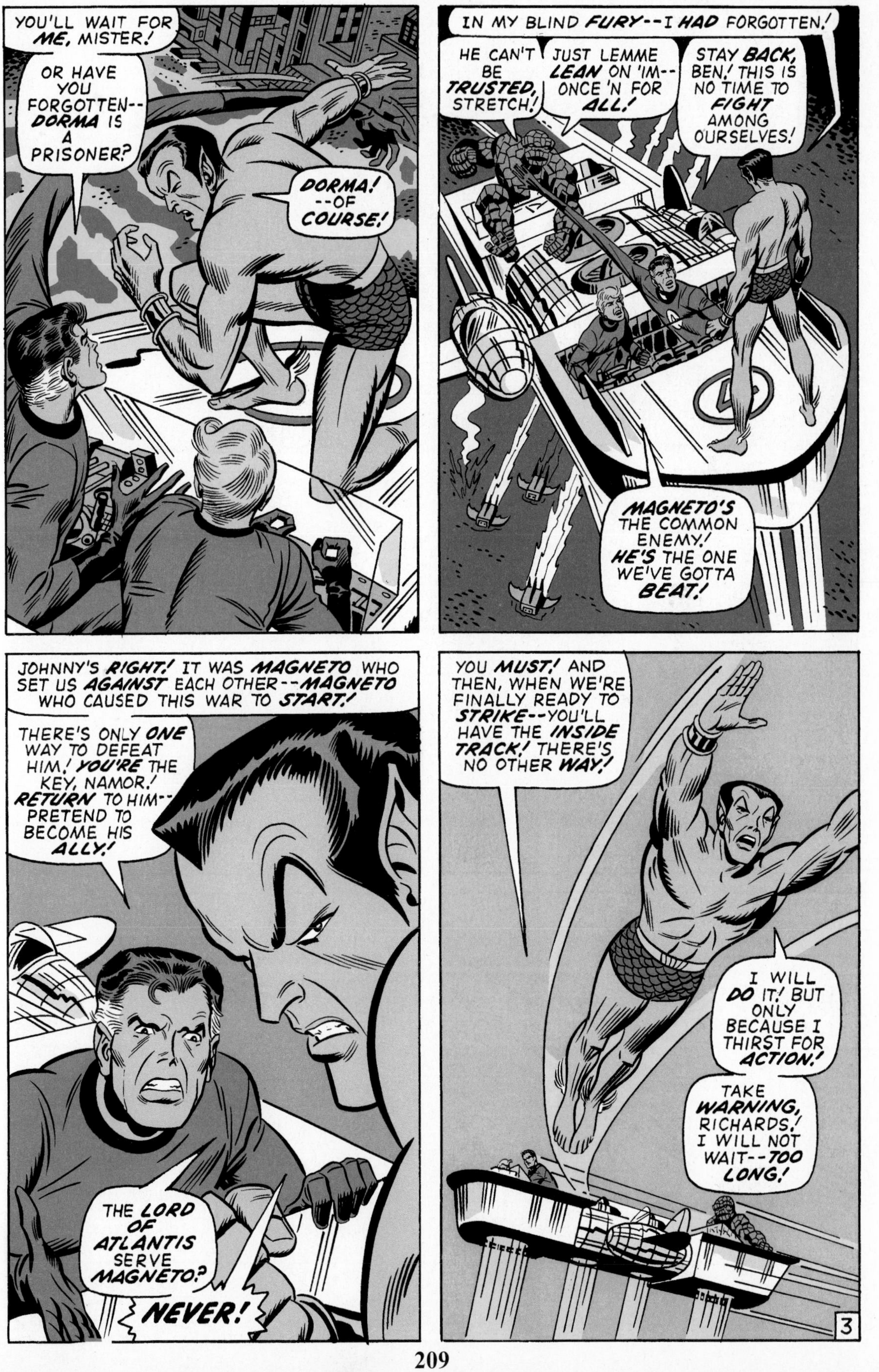

YOU'LL WAIT FOR ME, MISTER!
OR HAVE YOU FORGOTTEN--DORMA IS A PRISONER?
DORMA! --OF COURSE!
IN MY BLIND FURY--I HAD FORGOTTEN!
HE CAN'T BE TRUSTED, STRETCH!
JUST LEMME LEAN ON 'IM--ONCE 'N FOR ALL!
STAY BACK, BEN! THIS IS NO TIME TO FIGHT AMONG OURSELVES!
MAGNETO'S THE COMMON ENEMY! HE'S THE ONE WE'VE GOTTA BEAT!
JOHNNY'S RIGHT! IT WAS MAGNETO WHO SET US AGAINST EACH OTHER--MAGNETO WHO CAUSED THIS WAR TO START!
THERE'S ONLY ONE WAY TO DEFEAT HIM! YOU'RE THE KEY, NAMOR! RETURN TO HIM--PRETEND TO BECOME HIS ALLY!
THE LORD OF ATLANTIS SERVE MAGNETO?
NEVER!
YOU MUST! AND THEN, WHEN WE'RE FINALLY READY TO STRIKE--YOU'LL HAVE THE INSIDE TRACK! THERE'S NO OTHER WAY!
I WILL DO IT! BUT ONLY BECAUSE I THIRST FOR ACTION!
TAKE WARNING, RICHARDS! I WILL NOT WAIT--TOO LONG!
3

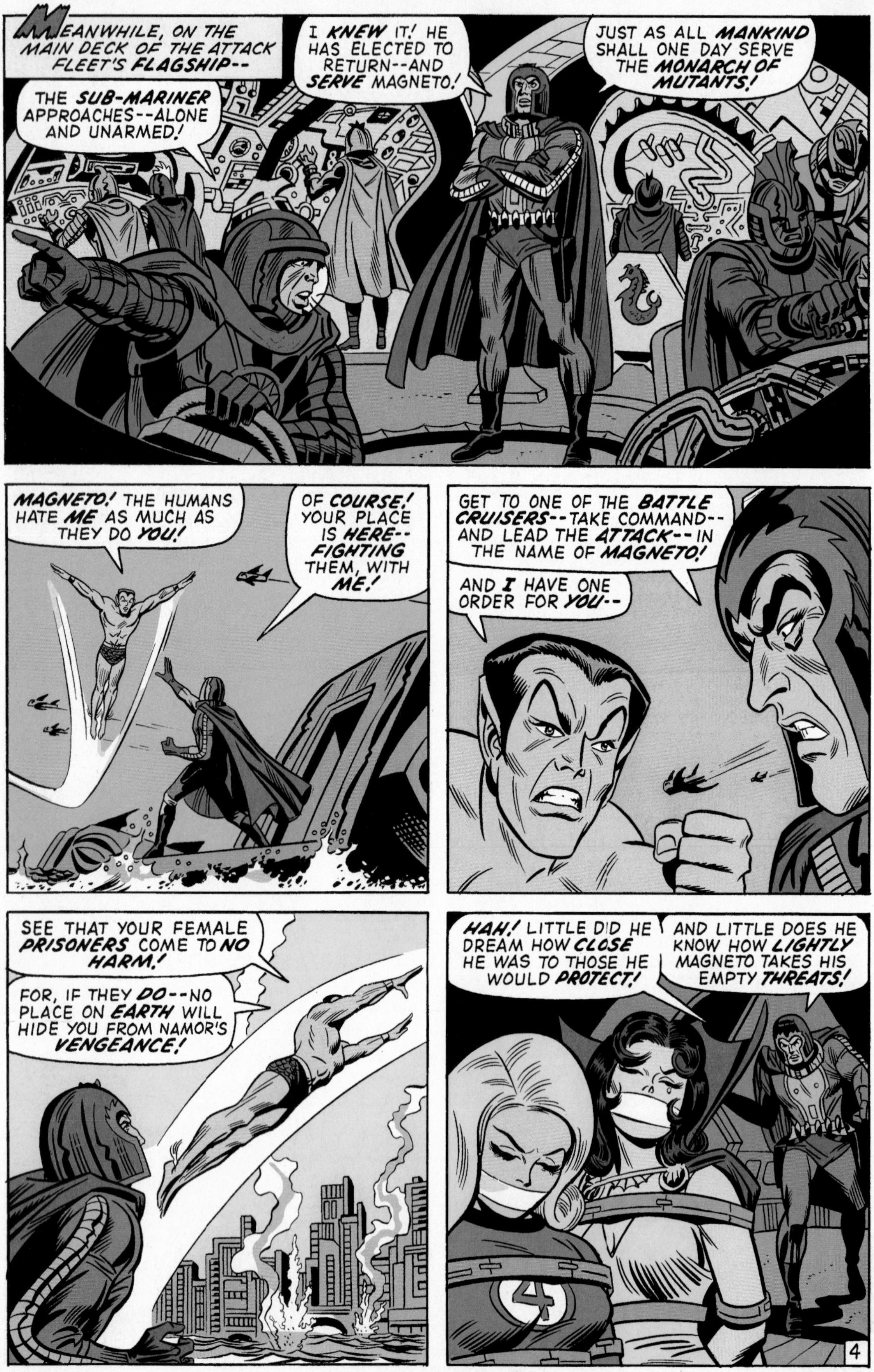
MEANWHILE, ON THE MAIN DECK OF THE ATTACK FLEET'S FLAGSHIP--
THE SUB-MARINER APPROACHES--ALONE AND UNARMED!
I KNEW IT! HE HAS ELECTED TO RETURN--AND SERVE MAGNETO!
JUST AS ALL MANKIND SHALL ONE DAY SERVE THE MONARCH OF MUTANTS!
MAGNETO! THE HUMANS HATE ME AS MUCH AS THEY DO YOU!
OF COURSE! YOUR PLACE IS HERE--FIGHTING THEM, WITH ME!
GET TO ONE OF THE BATTLE CRUISERS--TAKE COMMAND--AND LEAD THE ATTACK--IN THE NAME OF MAGNETO!
AND I HAVE ONE ORDER FOR YOU--
SEE THAT YOUR FEMALE PRISONERS COME TO NO HARM!
FOR, IF THEY DO--NO PLACE ON EARTH WILL HIDE YOU FROM NAMOR'S VENGEANCE!
HAH! LITTLE DID HE DREAM HOW CLOSE HE WAS TO THOSE HE WOULD PROTECT!
AND LITTLE DOES HE KNOW HOW LIGHTLY MAGNETO TAKES HIS EMPTY THREATS!
4

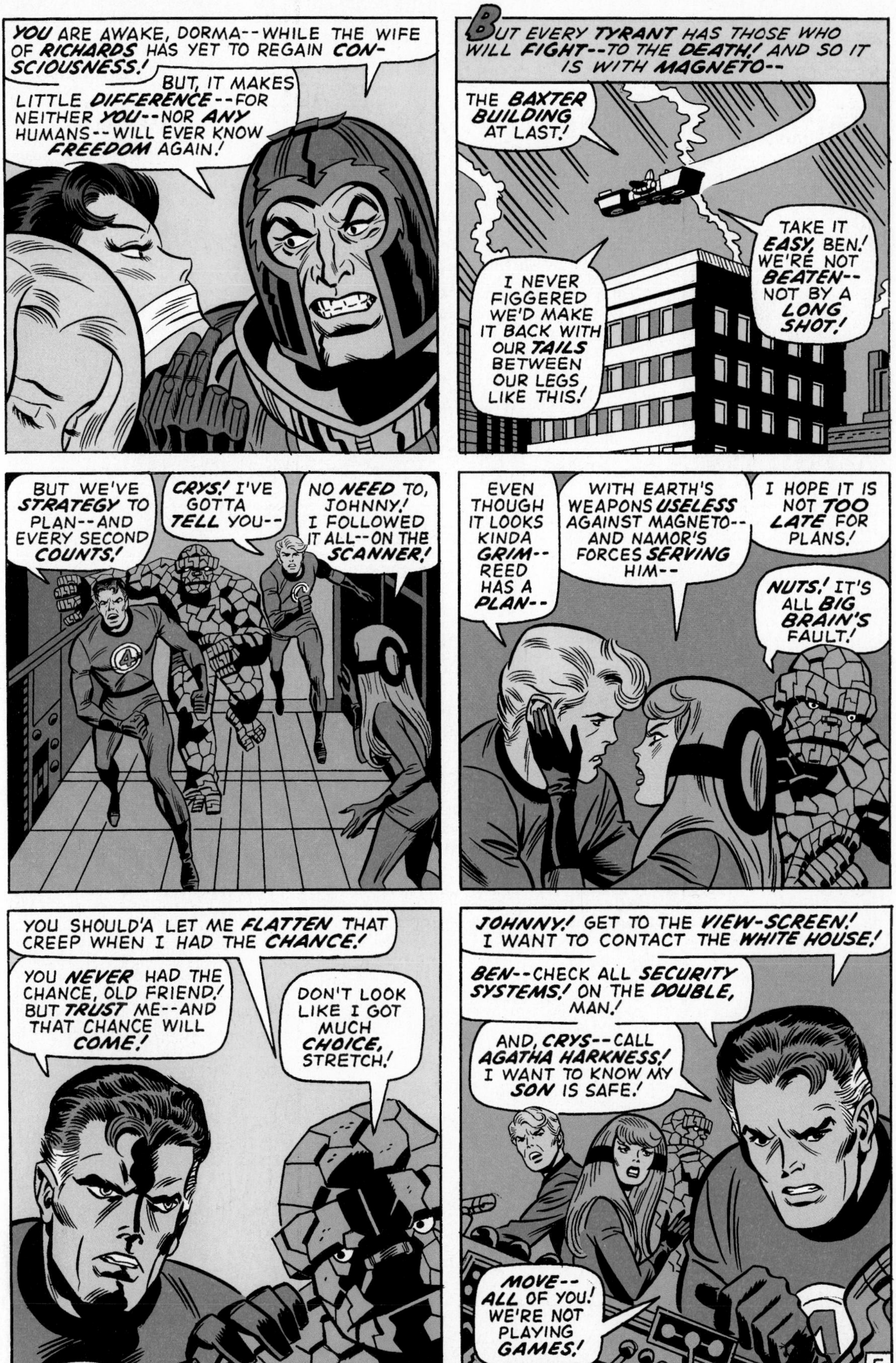
YOU ARE AWAKE, DORMA--WHILE THE WIFE OF RICHARDS HAS YET TO REGAIN CONSCIOUSNESS.!
BUT, IT MAKES LITTLE DIFFERENCE--FOR NEITHER YOU--NOR ANY HUMANS--WILL EVER KNOW FREEDOM AGAIN.!
BUT EVERY TYRANT HAS THOSE WHO WILL FIGHT--TO THE DEATH! AND SO IT IS WITH MAGNETO--
THE BAXTER BUILDING AT LAST!
I NEVER FIGGERED WE'D MAKE IT BACK WITH OUR TAILS BETWEEN OUR LEGS LIKE THIS!
TAKE IT EASY, BEN! WE'RE NOT BEATEN--NOT BY A LONG SHOT!
BUT WE'VE STRATEGY TO PLAN--AND EVERY SECOND COUNTS!
CRYS! I'VE GOTTA TELL YOU--
NO NEED TO, JOHNNY! I FOLLOWED IT ALL--ON THE SCANNER!
EVEN THOUGH IT LOOKS KINDA GRIM--REED HAS A PLAN--
WITH EARTH'S WEAPONS USELESS AGAINST MAGNETO--AND NAMOR'S FORCES SERVING HIM--
I HOPE IT IS NOT TOO LATE FOR PLANS!
NUTS! IT'S ALL BIG BRAIN'S FAULT!
YOU SHOULD'A LET ME FLATTEN THAT CREEP WHEN I HAD THE CHANCE!
YOU NEVER HAD THE CHANCE, OLD FRIEND! BUT TRUST ME--AND THAT CHANCE WILL COME!
DON'T LOOK LIKE I GOT MUCH CHOICE, STRETCH!
JOHNNY! GET TO THE VIEW-SCREEN! I WANT TO CONTACT THE WHITE HOUSE!
BEN--CHECK ALL SECURITY SYSTEMS! ON THE DOUBLE, MAN!
AND, CRYS--CALL AGATHA HARKNESS! I WANT TO KNOW MY SON IS SAFE!
MOVE--ALL OF YOU! WE'RE NOT PLAYING GAMES!
5

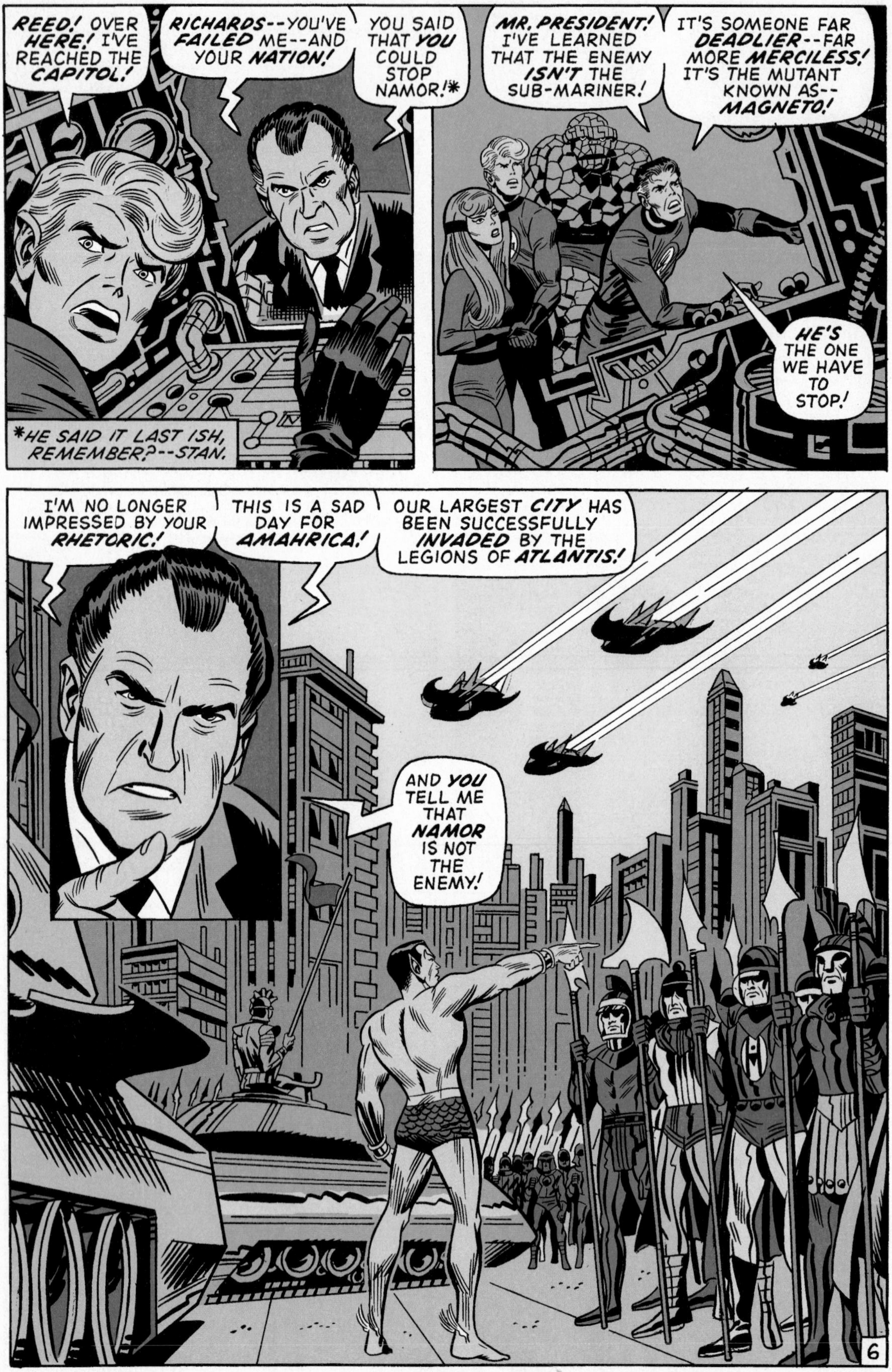
REED! OVER HERE! I'VE REACHED THE CAPITOL!
RICHARDS--YOU'VE FAILED ME--AND YOUR NATION!
YOU SAID THAT YOU COULD STOP NAMOR!*
*HE SAID IT LAST ISH, REMEMBER?--STAN.
MR. PRESIDENT! I'VE LEARNED THAT THE ENEMY ISN'T THE SUB-MARINER!
IT'S SOMEONE FAR DEADLIER--FAR MORE MERCILESS! IT'S THE MUTANT KNOWN AS--MAGNETO!
HE'S THE ONE WE HAVE TO STOP!
I'M NO LONGER IMPRESSED BY YOUR RHETORIC!
THIS IS A SAD DAY FOR AMAHRICA!
OUR LARGEST CITY HAS BEEN SUCCESSFULLY INVADED BY THE LEGIONS OF ATLANTIS!
AND YOU TELL ME THAT NAMOR IS NOT THE ENEMY!
6

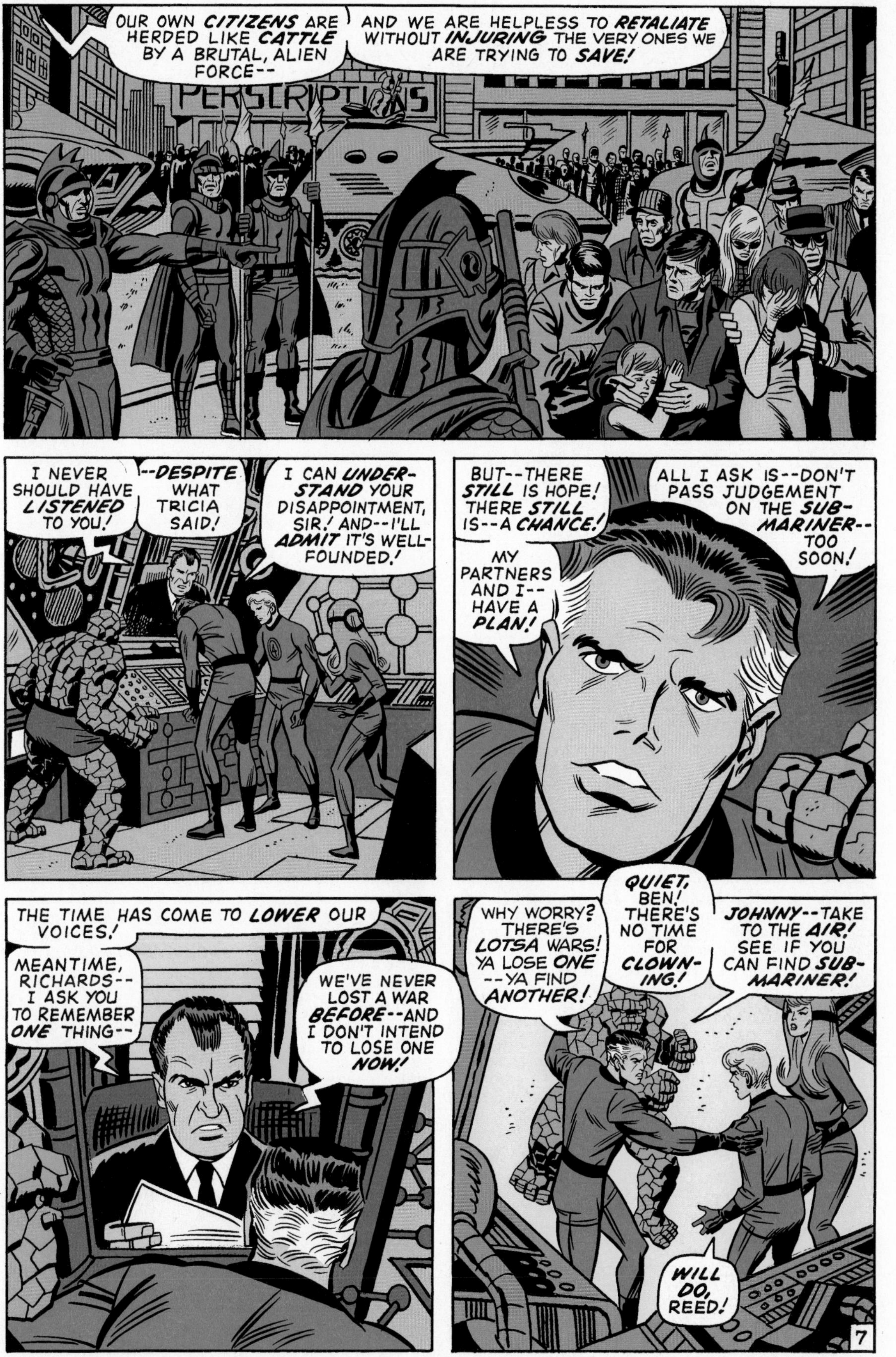
OUR OWN CITIZENS ARE HERDED LIKE CATTLE BY A BRUTAL, ALIEN FORCE--
AND WE ARE HELPLESS TO RETALIATE WITHOUT INJURING THE VERY ONES WE ARE TRYING TO SAVE!
PERSCRIPTIONS
I NEVER SHOULD HAVE LISTENED TO YOU!
--DESPITE WHAT TRICIA SAID!
I CAN UNDERSTAND YOUR DISAPPOINTMENT, SIR! AND--I'LL ADMIT IT'S WELL-FOUNDED!
BUT--THERE STILL IS HOPE! THERE STILL IS--A CHANCE!
MY PARTNERS AND I--HAVE A PLAN!
ALL I ASK IS--DON'T PASS JUDGEMENT ON THE SUB-MARINER--TOO SOON!
THE TIME HAS COME TO LOWER OUR VOICES!
MEANTIME, RICHARDS--I ASK YOU TO REMEMBER ONE THING--
WE'VE NEVER LOST A WAR BEFORE--AND I DON'T INTEND TO LOSE ONE NOW!
WHY WORRY? THERE'S LOTSA WARS! YA LOSE ONE--YA FIND ANOTHER!
QUIET, BEN! THERE'S NO TIME FOR CLOWNING!
JOHNNY--TAKE TO THE AIR! SEE IF YOU CAN FIND SUB-MARINER!
WILL DO, REED!
7

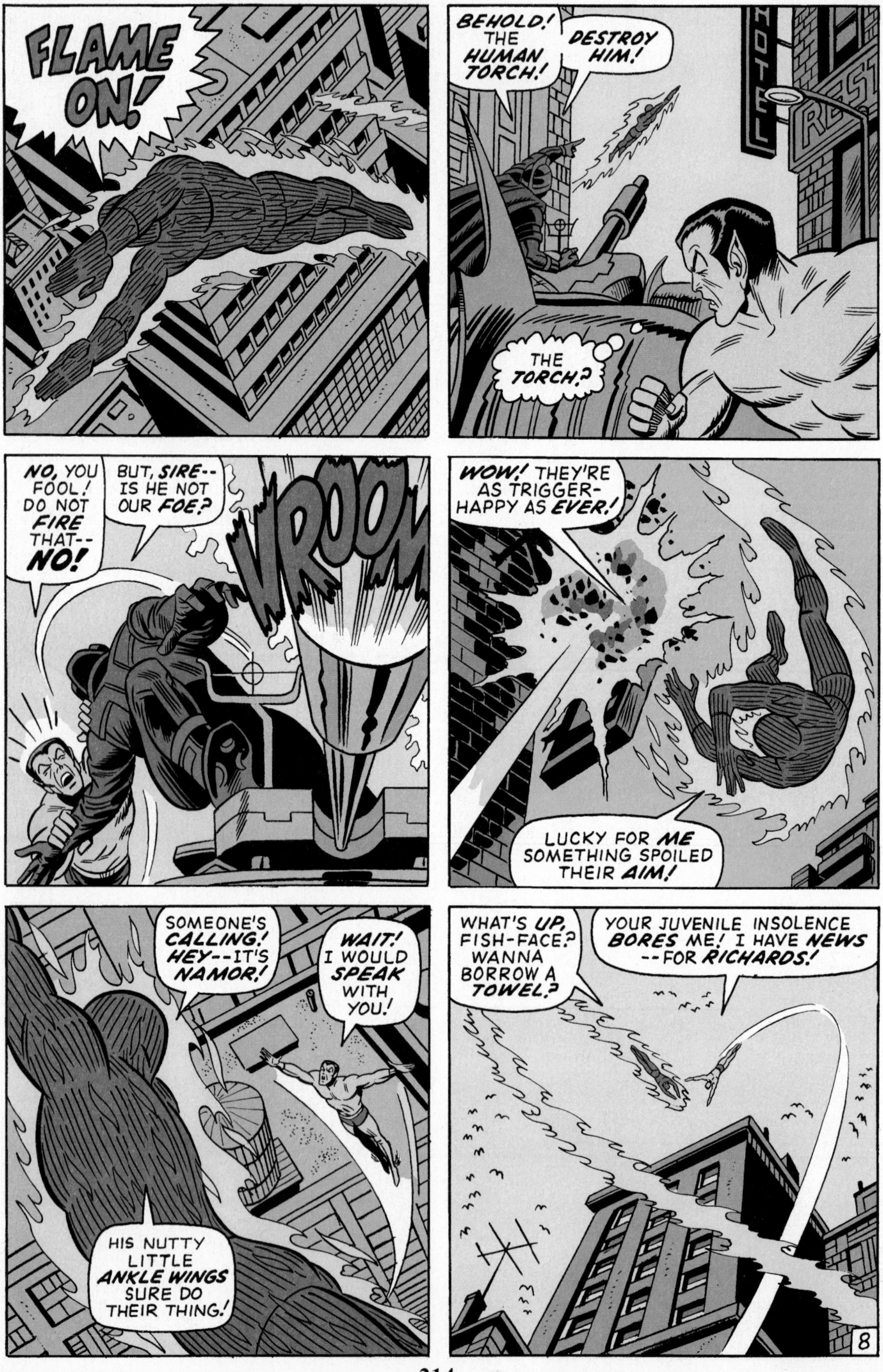
FLAME ON!
BEHOLD! THE HUMAN TORCH!
DESTROY HIM!
HOTEL
REST
THE TORCH?
NO, YOU FOOL! DO NOT FIRE THAT-- NO!
BUT, SIRE-- IS HE NOT OUR FOE?
VROOM
WOW! THEY'RE AS TRIGGER-HAPPY AS EVER!
LUCKY FOR ME SOMETHING SPOILED THEIR AIM!
SOMEONE'S CALLING! HEY--IT'S NAMOR!
WAIT! I WOULD SPEAK WITH YOU!
HIS NUTTY LITTLE ANKLE WINGS SURE DO THEIR THING!
WHAT'S UP, FISH-FACE? WANNA BORROW A TOWEL?
YOUR JUVENILE INSOLENCE BORES ME! I HAVE NEWS --FOR RICHARDS!
8

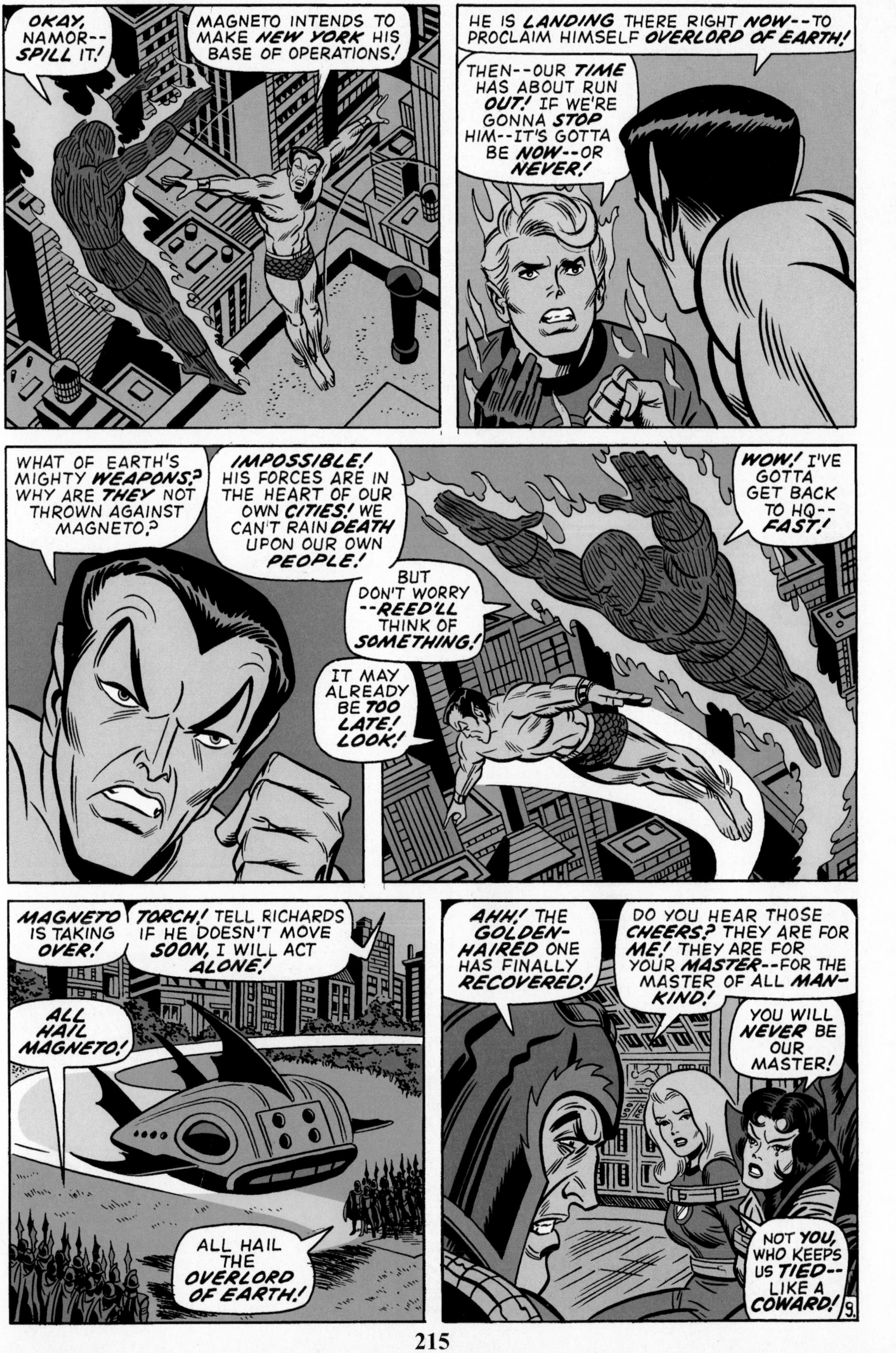
OKAY, NAMOR-- SPILL IT!
MAGNETO INTENDS TO MAKE NEW YORK HIS BASE OF OPERATIONS!
HE IS LANDING THERE RIGHT NOW--TO PROCLAIM HIMSELF OVERLORD OF EARTH!
THEN--OUR TIME HAS ABOUT RUN OUT! IF WE'RE GONNA STOP HIM--IT'S GOTTA BE NOW--OR NEVER!
WHAT OF EARTH'S MIGHTY WEAPONS? WHY ARE THEY NOT THROWN AGAINST MAGNETO?
IMPOSSIBLE! HIS FORCES ARE IN THE HEART OF OUR OWN CITIES! WE CAN'T RAIN DEATH UPON OUR OWN PEOPLE!
BUT DON'T WORRY --REED'LL THINK OF SOMETHING!
WOW! I'VE GOTTA GET BACK TO HQ-- FAST!
IT MAY ALREADY BE TOO LATE! LOOK!
MAGNETO IS TAKING OVER!
TORCH! TELL RICHARDS IF HE DOESN'T MOVE SOON, I WILL ACT ALONE!
ALL HAIL MAGNETO!
ALL HAIL THE OVERLORD OF EARTH!
AHH! THE GOLDEN-HAIRED ONE HAS FINALLY RECOVERED!
DO YOU HEAR THOSE CHEERS? THEY ARE FOR ME! THEY ARE FOR YOUR MASTER--FOR THE MASTER OF ALL MAN-KIND!
YOU WILL NEVER BE OUR MASTER!
NOT YOU, WHO KEEPS US TIED--LIKE A COWARD!
9.

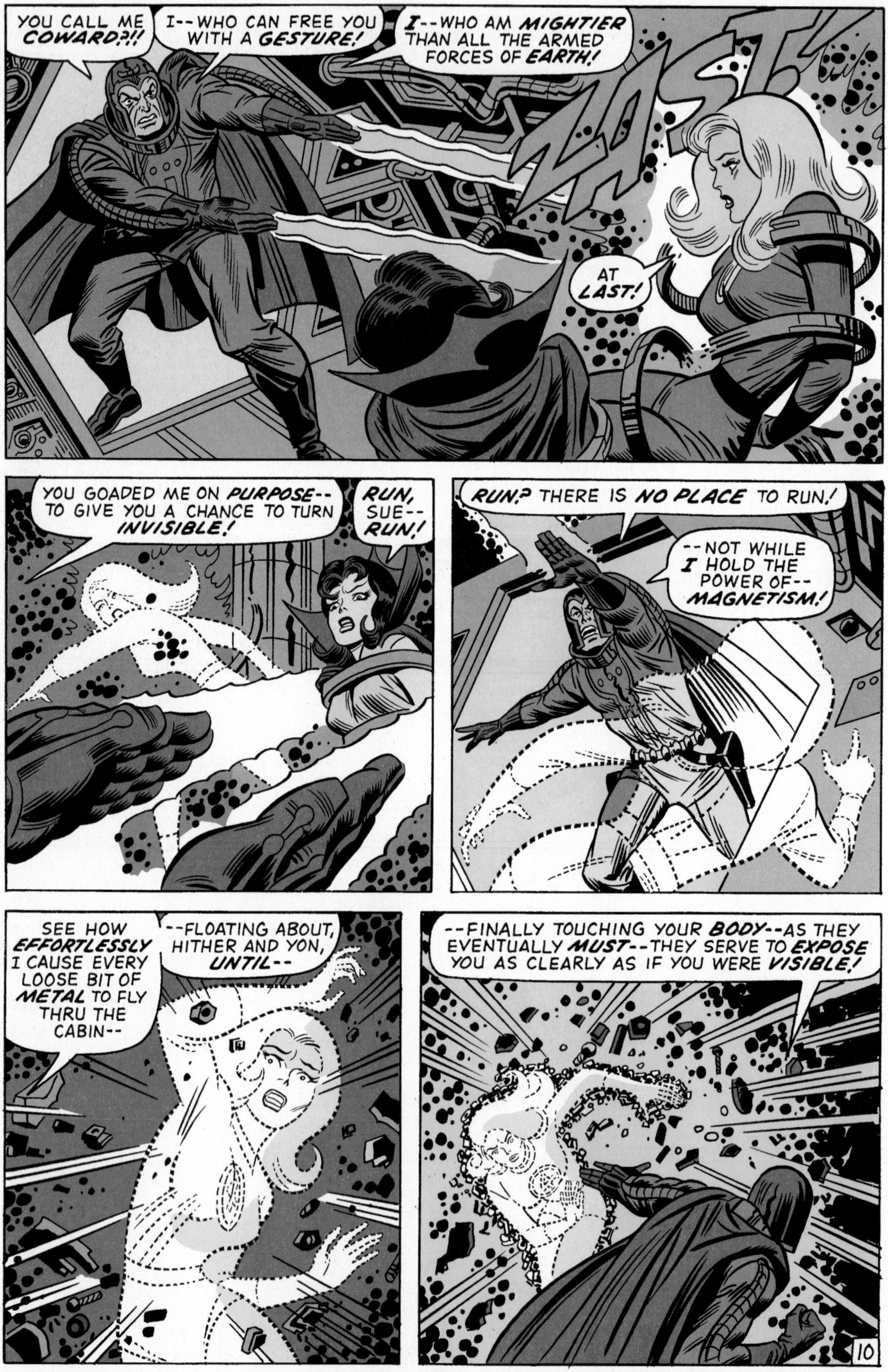
YOU CALL ME COWARD?!!
I--WHO CAN FREE YOU WITH A GESTURE!
I--WHO AM MIGHTIER THAN ALL THE ARMED FORCES OF EARTH!
ZLAST!
AT LAST!
YOU GOADED ME ON PURPOSE-- TO GIVE YOU A CHANCE TO TURN INVISIBLE!
RUN, SUE-- RUN!
RUN? THERE IS NO PLACE TO RUN!
--NOT WHILE I HOLD THE POWER OF-- MAGNETISM!
SEE HOW EFFORTLESSLY I CAUSE EVERY LOOSE BIT OF METAL TO FLY THRU THE CABIN--
--FLOATING ABOUT, HITHER AND YON, UNTIL--
--FINALLY TOUCHING YOUR BODY--AS THEY EVENTUALLY MUST--THEY SERVE TO EXPOSE YOU AS CLEARLY AS IF YOU WERE VISIBLE!
10

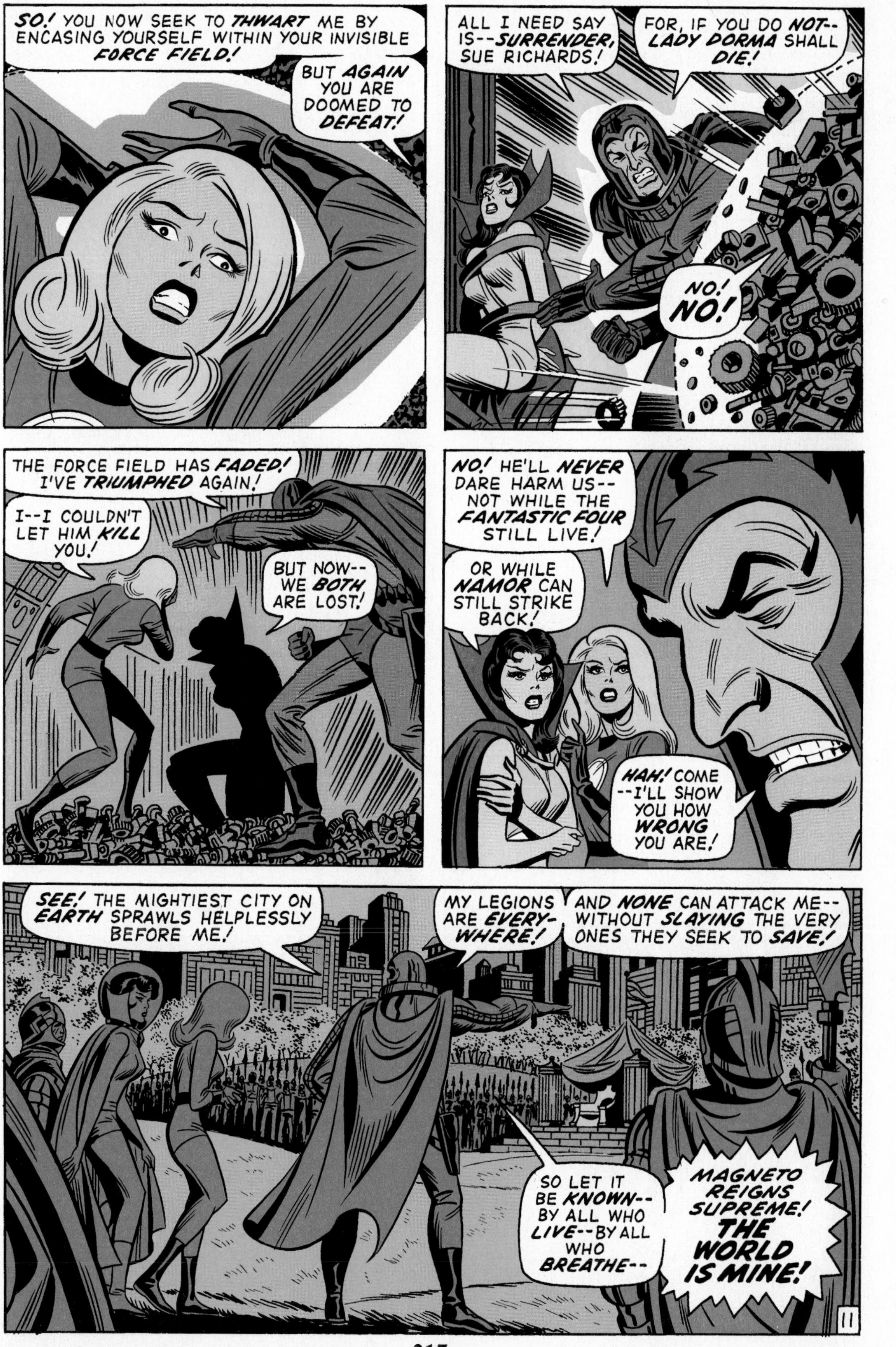
SO! YOU NOW SEEK TO THWART ME BY ENCASING YOURSELF WITHIN YOUR INVISIBLE FORCE FIELD!
BUT AGAIN YOU ARE DOOMED TO DEFEAT!
ALL I NEED SAY IS--SURRENDER, SUE RICHARDS!
FOR, IF YOU DO NOT--LADY DORMA SHALL DIE!
NO! NO!
THE FORCE FIELD HAS FADED! I'VE TRIUMPHED AGAIN!
I--I COULDN'T LET HIM KILL YOU!
BUT NOW--WE BOTH ARE LOST!
NO! HE'LL NEVER DARE HARM US--NOT WHILE THE FANTASTIC FOUR STILL LIVE!
OR WHILE NAMOR CAN STILL STRIKE BACK!
HAH! COME--I'LL SHOW YOU HOW WRONG YOU ARE!
SEE! THE MIGHTIEST CITY ON EARTH SPRAWLS HELPLESSLY BEFORE ME!
MY LEGIONS ARE EVERY-WHERE!
AND NONE CAN ATTACK ME--WITHOUT SLAYING THE VERY ONES THEY SEEK TO SAVE!
SO LET IT BE KNOWN--BY ALL WHO LIVE--BY ALL WHO BREATHE--
MAGNETO REIGNS SUPREME! THE WORLD IS MINE!
11

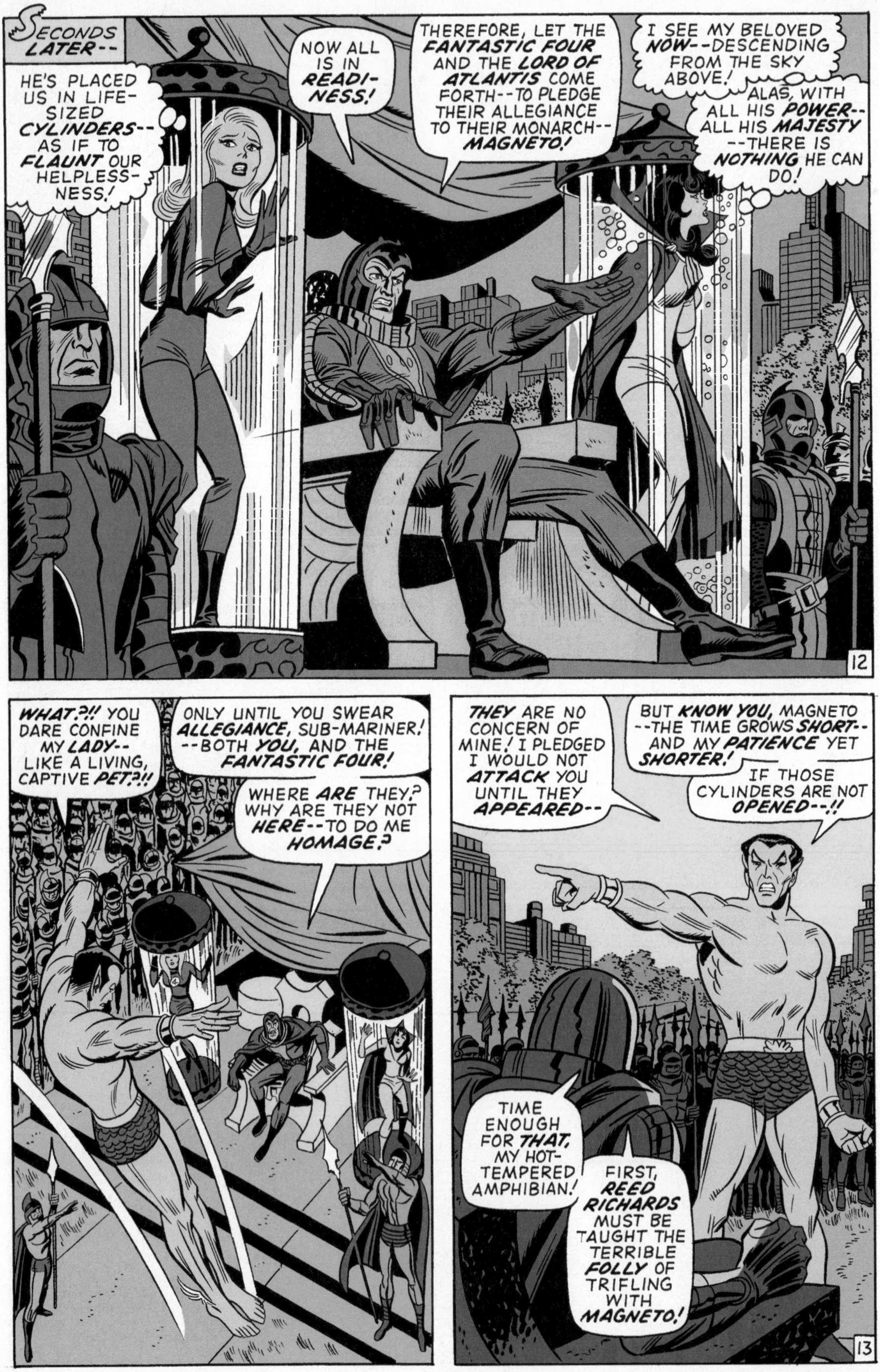
SECONDS LATER--
HE'S PLACED US IN LIFE-SIZED CYLINDERS--AS IF TO FLAUNT OUR HELPLESSNESS!
NOW ALL IS IN READINESS!
THEREFORE, LET THE FANTASTIC FOUR AND THE LORD OF ATLANTIS COME FORTH--TO PLEDGE THEIR ALLEGIANCE TO THEIR MONARCH--MAGNETO!
I SEE MY BELOVED NOW--DESCENDING FROM THE SKY ABOVE!
ALAS, WITH ALL HIS POWER--ALL HIS MAJESTY--THERE IS NOTHING HE CAN DO!
12
WHAT?!! YOU DARE CONFINE MY LADY--LIKE A LIVING, CAPTIVE PET?!!
ONLY UNTIL YOU SWEAR ALLEGIANCE, SUB-MARINER! --BOTH YOU, AND THE FANTASTIC FOUR!
WHERE ARE THEY? WHY ARE THEY NOT HERE--TO DO ME HOMAGE?
THEY ARE NO CONCERN OF MINE! I PLEDGED I WOULD NOT ATTACK YOU UNTIL THEY APPEARED--
BUT KNOW YOU, MAGNETO--THE TIME GROWS SHORT--AND MY PATIENCE YET SHORTER!
IF THOSE CYLINDERS ARE NOT OPENED--!!
TIME ENOUGH FOR THAT, MY HOT-TEMPERED AMPHIBIAN!
FIRST, REED RICHARDS MUST BE TAUGHT THE TERRIBLE FOLLY OF TRIFLING WITH MAGNETO!
13

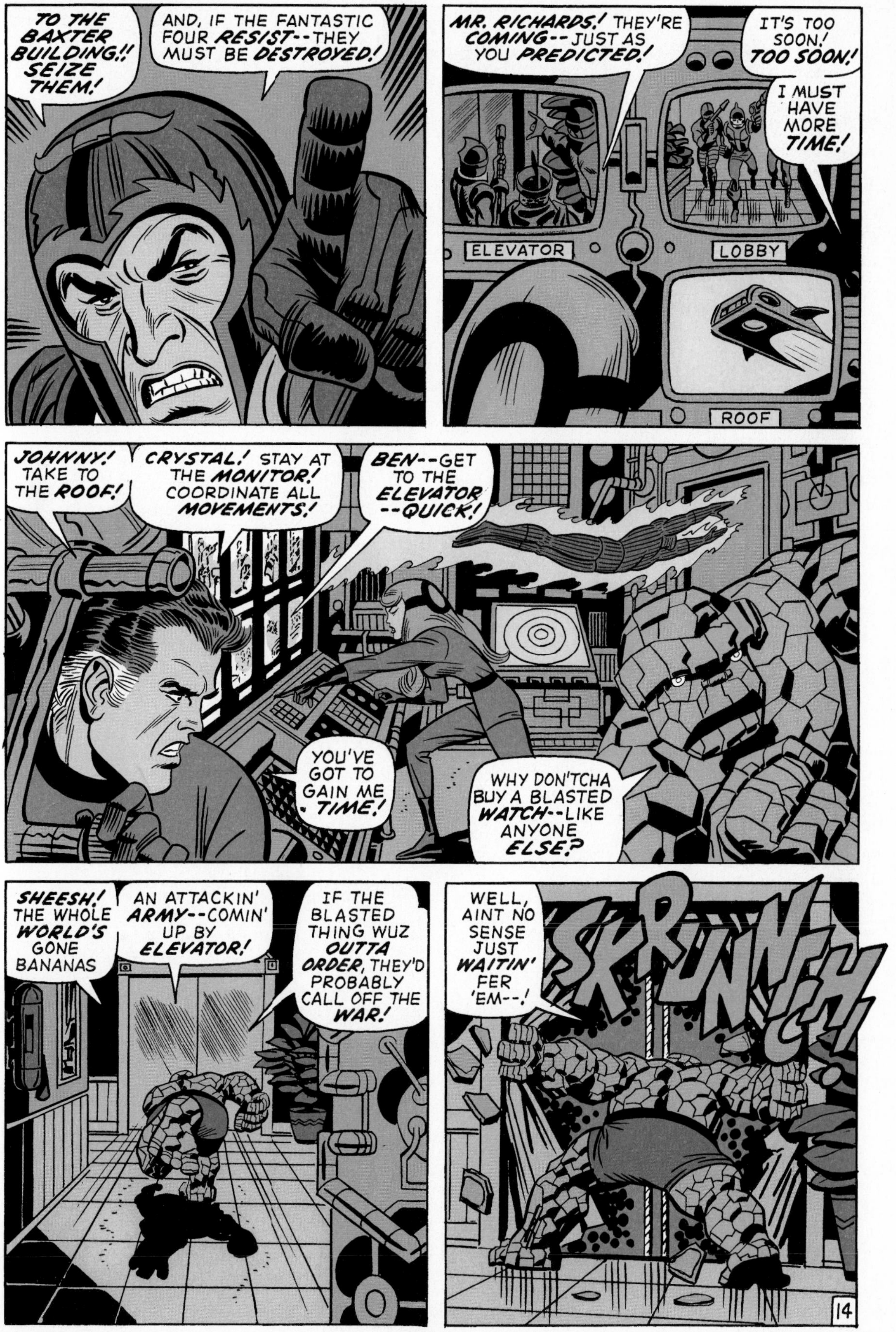
TO THE BAXTER BUILDING!! SEIZE THEM!
AND, IF THE FANTASTIC FOUR RESIST--THEY MUST BE DESTROYED!
MR. RICHARDS! THEY'RE COMING--JUST AS YOU PREDICTED!
IT'S TOO SOON! TOO SOON!
I MUST HAVE MORE TIME!
ELEVATOR
LOBBY
ROOF
JOHNNY! TAKE TO THE ROOF!
CRYSTAL! STAY AT THE MONITOR! COORDINATE ALL MOVEMENTS!
BEN--GET TO THE ELEVATOR --QUICK!
YOU'VE GOT TO GAIN ME TIME!
WHY DON'TCHA BUY A BLASTED WATCH--LIKE ANYONE ELSE?
SHEESH! THE WHOLE WORLD'S GONE BANANAS
AN ATTACKIN' ARMY--COMIN' UP BY ELEVATOR!
IF THE BLASTED THING WUZ OUTTA ORDER, THEY'D PROBABLY CALL OFF THE WAR!
WELL, AINT NO SENSE JUST WAITIN' FER 'EM--!
SKRUNNCH!
14

I CAN GIT 'EM *UP* HERE A HECKUVA LOT *FASTER* THAN THESE CRUMMY *CABLES* CAN!

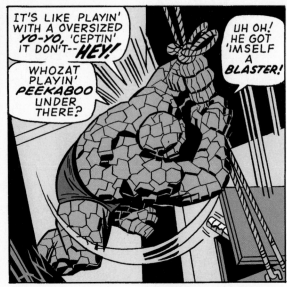

IT'S LIKE PLAYIN' WITH A OVERSIZED *YO-YO,* 'CEPTIN' IT DON'T-- *HEY!*

WHOZAT PLAYIN' *PEEKABOO* UNDER THERE?

UH OH! HE GOT 'IMSELF A *BLASTER!*

IT DON'T LOOK LIKE NO ORDINARY *POP-GUN!* I BETTER-- *UNHH!--*

FIRE! BEFORE HE GETS *AWAY!* GOOD! *GOOD!*

NOT EVEN THE *THING'S* BESTIAL STRENGTH CAN STAND UP TO THE MOST POTENT *STUN GUN* IN ALL ATLANTIS!

AND NOW FOR THE *OTHERS!*

MR. RICHARDS! THE HALLWAY MONITOR SHOWS BEN GRIMM HAS *FALLEN!*

THE INVADERS ARE IN THE *CORRIDOR!*

STAND BACK, GIRL! I'VE GOT TO *STOP* THEM FROM COMING *CLOSER!*

SWOK!

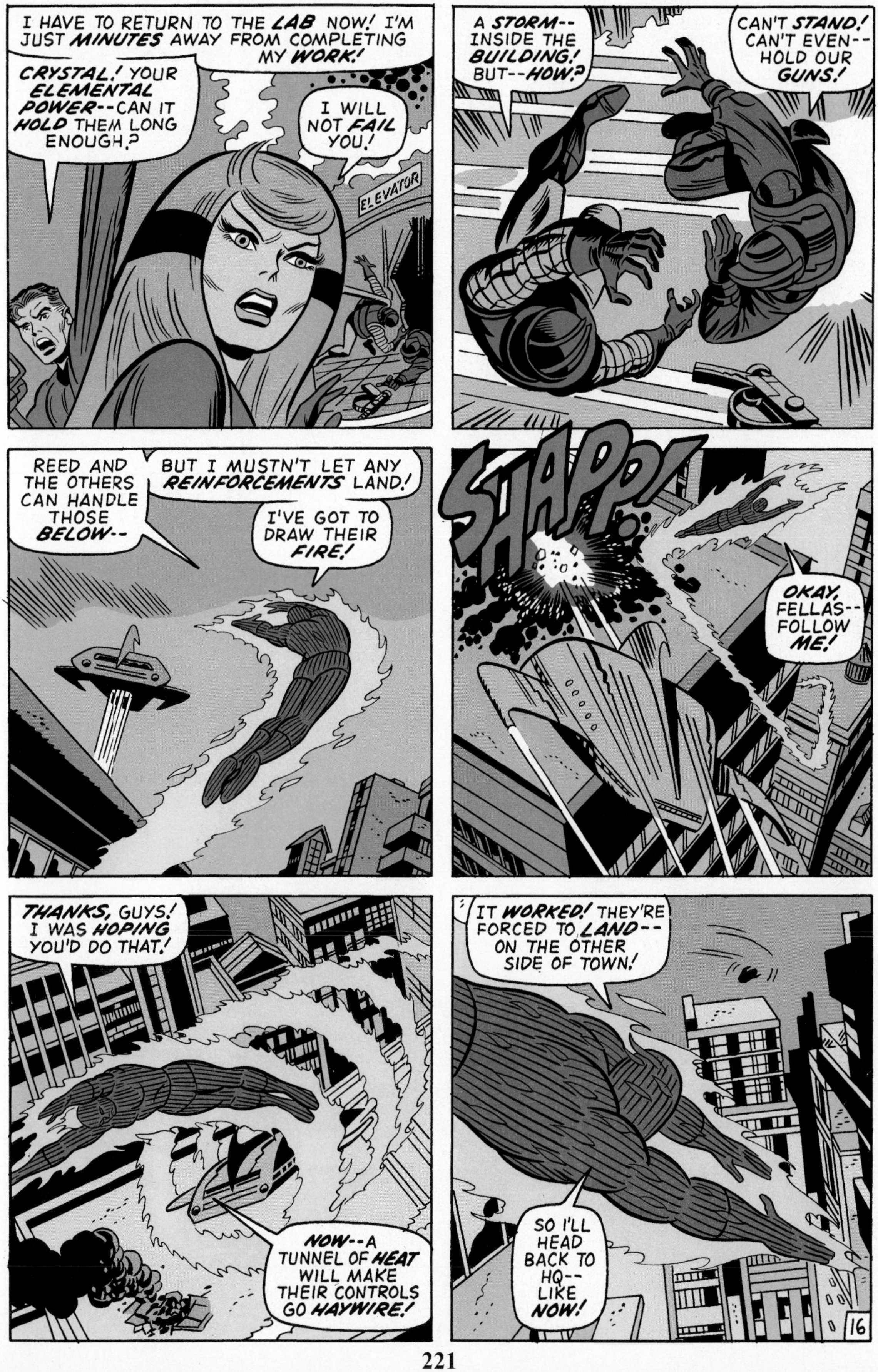
I HAVE TO RETURN TO THE LAB NOW! I'M JUST MINUTES AWAY FROM COMPLETING MY WORK!
CRYSTAL! YOUR ELEMENTAL POWER--CAN IT HOLD THEM LONG ENOUGH?
I WILL NOT FAIL YOU!
ELEVATOR
A STORM--INSIDE THE BUILDING! BUT--HOW?
CAN'T STAND! CAN'T EVEN--HOLD OUR GUNS!
REED AND THE OTHERS CAN HANDLE THOSE BELOW--
BUT I MUSTN'T LET ANY REINFORCEMENTS LAND!
I'VE GOT TO DRAW THEIR FIRE!
SHAPP!
OKAY, FELLAS--FOLLOW ME!
THANKS, GUYS! I WAS HOPING YOU'D DO THAT!
NOW--A TUNNEL OF HEAT WILL MAKE THEIR CONTROLS GO HAYWIRE!
IT WORKED! THEY'RE FORCED TO LAND--ON THE OTHER SIDE OF TOWN!
SO I'LL HEAD BACK TO HQ--LIKE NOW!
16

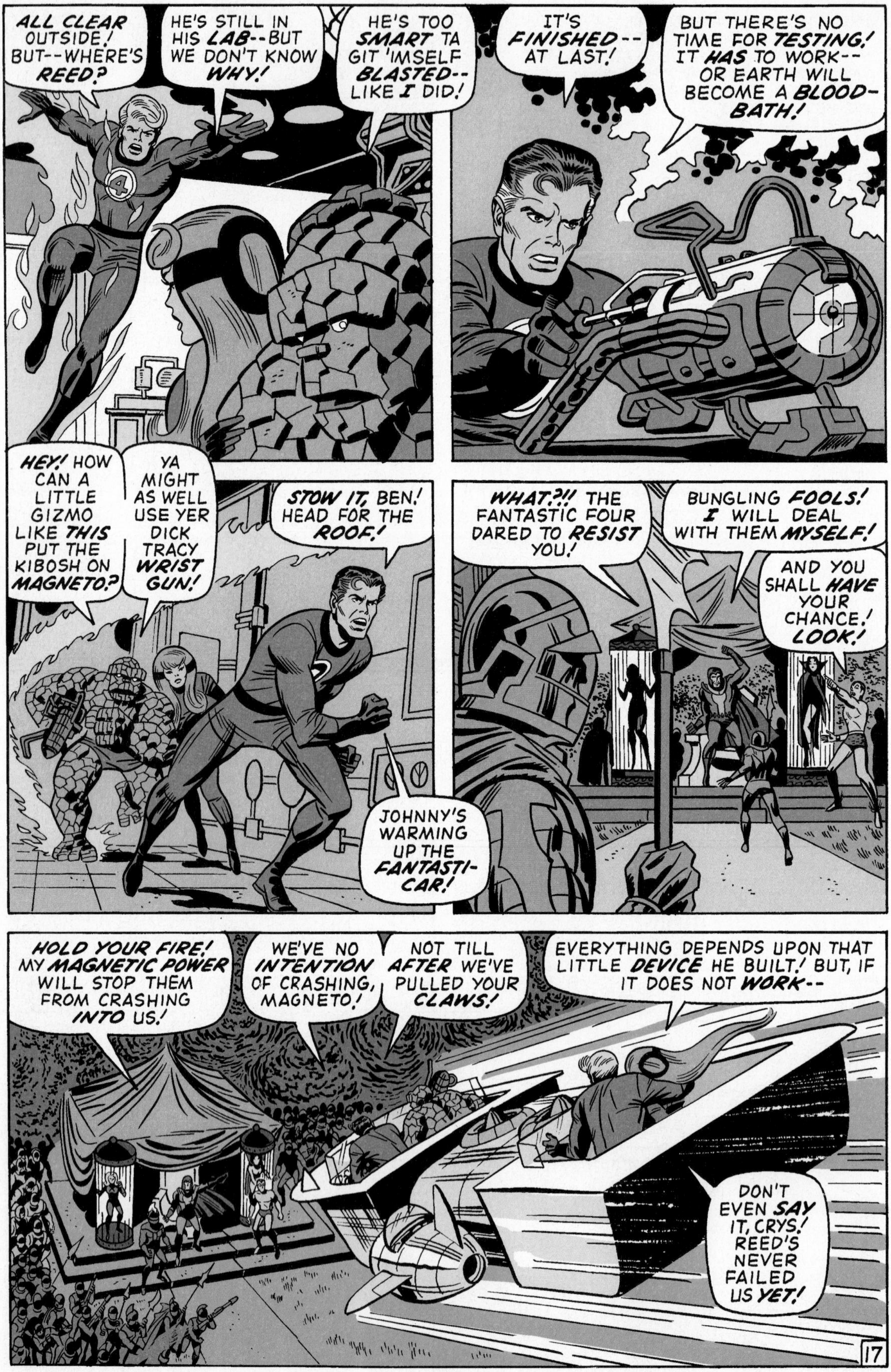
ALL CLEAR OUTSIDE! BUT--WHERE'S REED?
HE'S STILL IN HIS LAB--BUT WE DON'T KNOW WHY!
HE'S TOO SMART TA GIT 'IMSELF BLASTED--LIKE I DID!
IT'S FINISHED--AT LAST!
BUT THERE'S NO TIME FOR TESTING! IT HAS TO WORK--OR EARTH WILL BECOME A BLOOD-BATH!
HEY! HOW CAN A LITTLE GIZMO LIKE THIS PUT THE KIBOSH ON MAGNETO?
YA MIGHT AS WELL USE YER DICK TRACY WRIST GUN!
STOW IT, BEN! HEAD FOR THE ROOF!
JOHNNY'S WARMING UP THE FANTASTI-CAR!
WHAT?!! THE FANTASTIC FOUR DARED TO RESIST YOU!
BUNGLING FOOLS! I WILL DEAL WITH THEM MYSELF!
AND YOU SHALL HAVE YOUR CHANCE! LOOK!
HOLD YOUR FIRE! MY MAGNETIC POWER WILL STOP THEM FROM CRASHING INTO US!
WE'VE NO INTENTION OF CRASHING, MAGNETO!
NOT TILL AFTER WE'VE PULLED YOUR CLAWS!
EVERYTHING DEPENDS UPON THAT LITTLE DEVICE HE BUILT! BUT, IF IT DOES NOT WORK--
DON'T EVEN SAY IT, CRYS! REED'S NEVER FAILED US YET!
17

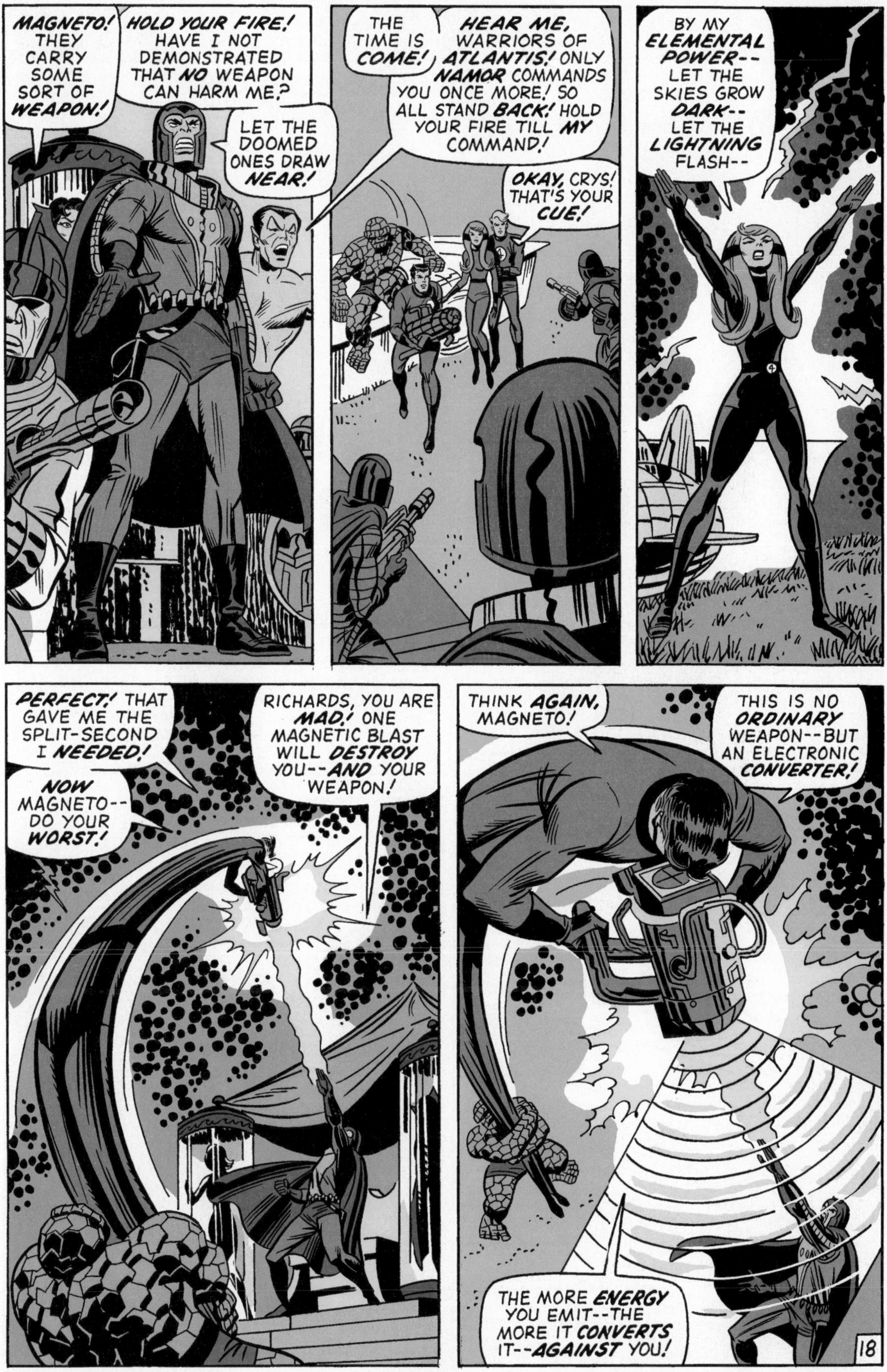
MAGNETO! THEY CARRY SOME SORT OF WEAPON!
HOLD YOUR FIRE! HAVE I NOT DEMONSTRATED THAT NO WEAPON CAN HARM ME?
LET THE DOOMED ONES DRAW NEAR!
THE TIME IS COME!
HEAR ME, WARRIORS OF ATLANTIS! ONLY NAMOR COMMANDS YOU ONCE MORE! SO ALL STAND BACK! HOLD YOUR FIRE TILL MY COMMAND!
OKAY, CRYS! THAT'S YOUR CUE!
BY MY ELEMENTAL POWER-- LET THE SKIES GROW DARK-- LET THE LIGHTNING FLASH--
PERFECT! THAT GAVE ME THE SPLIT-SECOND I NEEDED!
NOW MAGNETO-- DO YOUR WORST!
RICHARDS, YOU ARE MAD! ONE MAGNETIC BLAST WILL DESTROY YOU--AND YOUR WEAPON!
THINK AGAIN, MAGNETO!
THIS IS NO ORDINARY WEAPON--BUT AN ELECTRONIC CONVERTER!
THE MORE ENERGY YOU EMIT--THE MORE IT CONVERTS IT--AGAINST YOU!
18

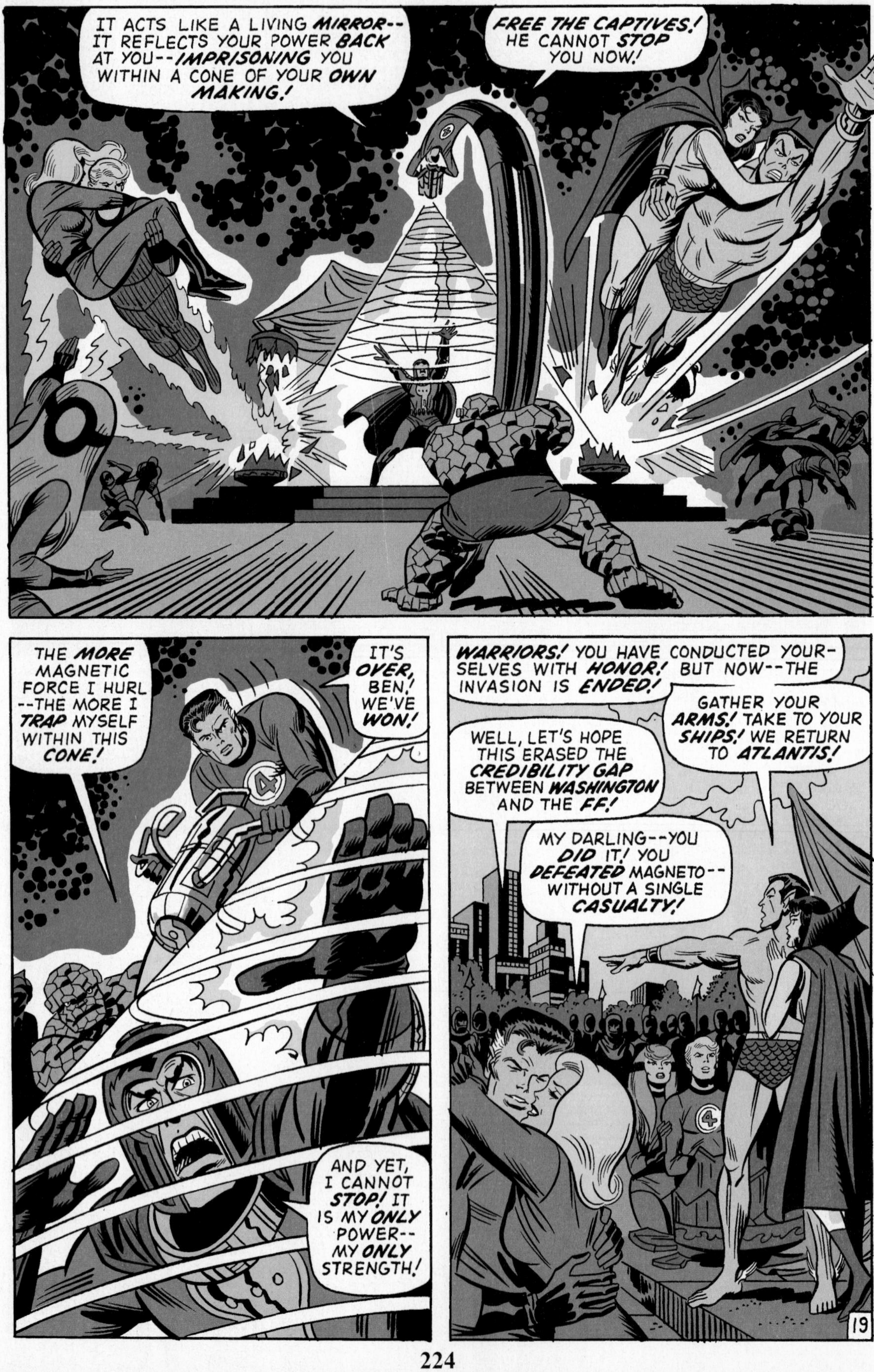
IT ACTS LIKE A LIVING MIRROR-- IT REFLECTS YOUR POWER BACK AT YOU--IMPRISONING YOU WITHIN A CONE OF YOUR OWN MAKING!
FREE THE CAPTIVES! HE CANNOT STOP YOU NOW!
THE MORE MAGNETIC FORCE I HURL --THE MORE I TRAP MYSELF WITHIN THIS CONE!
IT'S OVER, BEN! WE'VE WON!
AND YET, I CANNOT STOP! IT IS MY ONLY POWER-- MY ONLY STRENGTH!
WARRIORS! YOU HAVE CONDUCTED YOURSELVES WITH HONOR! BUT NOW--THE INVASION IS ENDED!
GATHER YOUR ARMS! TAKE TO YOUR SHIPS! WE RETURN TO ATLANTIS!
WELL, LET'S HOPE THIS ERASED THE CREDIBILITY GAP BETWEEN WASHINGTON AND THE FF!
MY DARLING--YOU DID IT! YOU DEFEATED MAGNETO-- WITHOUT A SINGLE CASUALTY!
19

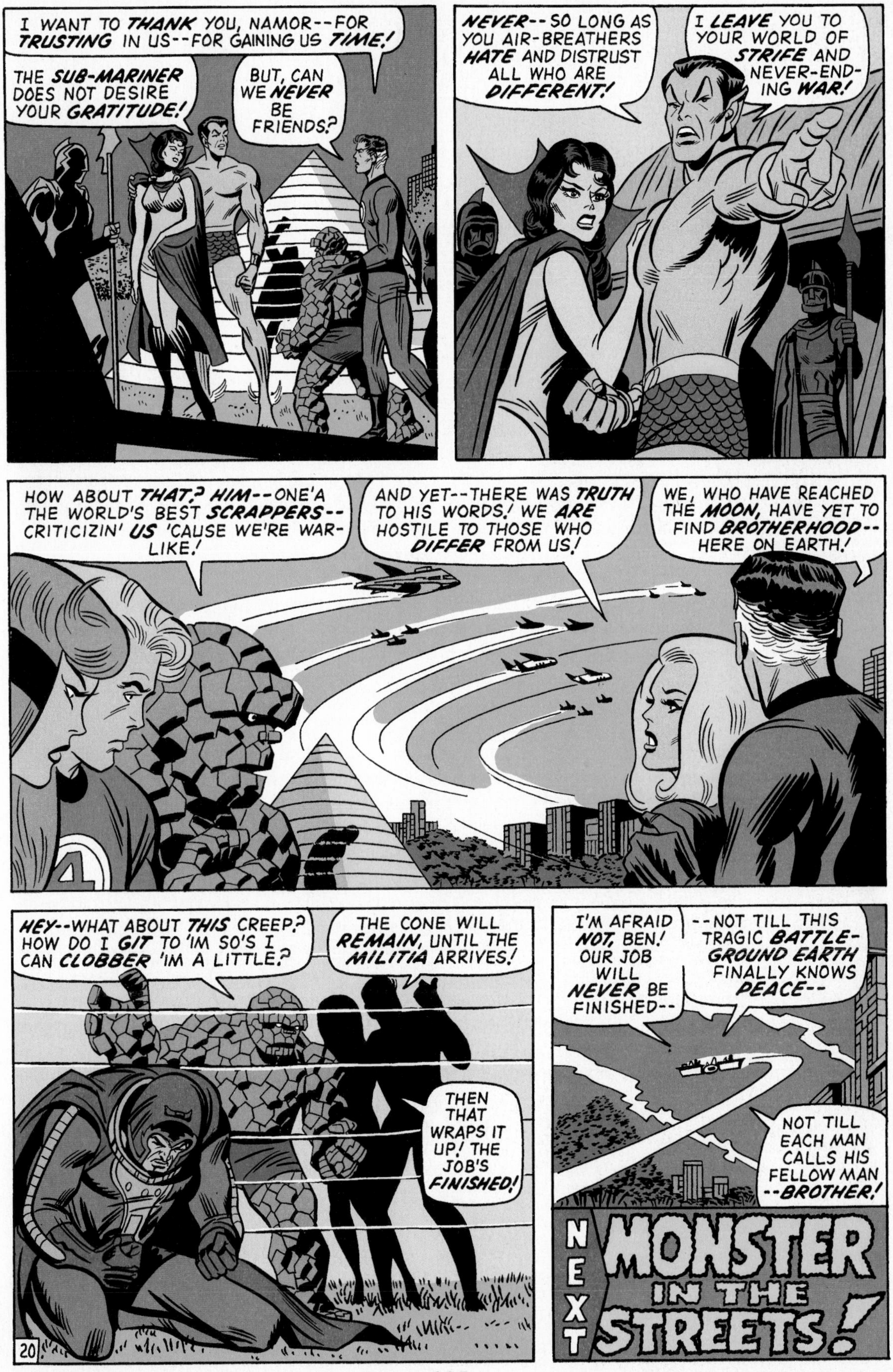
I WANT TO THANK YOU, NAMOR--FOR TRUSTING IN US--FOR GAINING US TIME!
THE SUB-MARINER DOES NOT DESIRE YOUR GRATITUDE!
BUT, CAN WE NEVER BE FRIENDS?
NEVER--SO LONG AS YOU AIR-BREATHERS HATE AND DISTRUST ALL WHO ARE DIFFERENT!
I LEAVE YOU TO YOUR WORLD OF STRIFE AND NEVER-ENDING WAR!
HOW ABOUT THAT? HIM--ONE'A THE WORLD'S BEST SCRAPPERS--CRITICIZIN' US 'CAUSE WE'RE WAR-LIKE!
AND YET--THERE WAS TRUTH TO HIS WORDS! WE ARE HOSTILE TO THOSE WHO DIFFER FROM US!
WE, WHO HAVE REACHED THE MOON, HAVE YET TO FIND BROTHERHOOD--HERE ON EARTH!
HEY--WHAT ABOUT THIS CREEP? HOW DO I GIT TO 'IM SO'S I CAN CLOBBER 'IM A LITTLE?
THE CONE WILL REMAIN, UNTIL THE MILITIA ARRIVES!
THEN THAT WRAPS IT UP! THE JOB'S FINISHED!
20
I'M AFRAID NOT, BEN! OUR JOB WILL NEVER BE FINISHED--
--NOT TILL THIS TRAGIC BATTLEGROUND EARTH FINALLY KNOWS PEACE--
NOT TILL EACH MAN CALLS HIS FELLOW MAN--BROTHER!
NEXT
MONSTER IN THE STREETS!

FANTASTIC FOUR #108: KIRBY'S WAY
BY JOHN MORROW

Fantastic Four #108 has quite a history behind it. It was originally meant to be #102, but Stan Lee apparently felt that Jack Kirby's story, as submitted, wasn't dialogueable. So Stan ran the story intended for *FF* #103 (which Kirby turned in along with his resignation from Marvel in 1969) in #102, and put the rejected art on the shelf for a few months. The Bullpen eventually chopped Kirby's originals up, rearranged panels, had John Buscema add some filler art, changed the ending, sent the whole thing to Joe Sinnott to ink, and published it (not so coincidentally) the same month Kirby's *New Gods* #1 came out at DC Comics. The end result was a real mess that, quite frankly, didn't make much sense.

But just how bad was Kirby's original story? Judge for yourself. Presented here is my attempt to put the story back into its original form, using the Kirby art that didn't make the cut. Comic art dealer Mitch Itkowitz came across many of the discarded pencils in the Marvel files a few years ago, and had them returned to Jack. A few panels are still missing, and you'll see those indicated by question marks. Since Kirby's original story and the published version had major differences, I deleted the published dialogue and page numbers to avoid confusion. In quotes (" ") accompanying the pencil panels are Jack's original margin notes for Stan Lee to dialogue by (these are numbered to coincide with the panel numbers). With just the few margin notes here to accompany Kirby's powerful art, it's easy enough to get an idea of the story he set out to tell originally.

Some of the later pages were renumbered more than once during the alterations, making reassembly a difficult task (apparently, the hatchet job went through several revisions). One thing that helped immensely in reassembling this story was the fact that Kirby worked on a grid. By simply following his standard *FF* grid from this period, you can usually tell if panels were falling in the right place on a given page.

There were some major differences in the two versions. Just what is going on in the introduction on page 2 is unclear, and maybe this confusion at the opening of the story is the reason Stan decided it was unusable. Unlike the published version of this story, Kirby's version dealt with a force called Mega-Power, not Nega-Power, and had nothing to do with the Negative Zone. And the villain Janus didn't die in the end (a plot twist that I always thought seemed very un-Kirbylike).

This story didn't break any new ground, but there are some really nice bits that got left on the Bullpen floor; those simple, down-to-earth touches like Reed and Sue's casual clothes on page 2 and the Thing's sweater on page 8, and Sue taking baby Franklin from Crystal on page 2. These seemingly minor details make the FF seem like real people, and were a big part of the sense of family fans felt reading the comics of the Lee/Kirby era. The very lack of this type of storytelling detail is one of the reasons the FF has never reached the heights it attained while Kirby was on it.

But rather than dwell on the negative, let's celebrate the end of the classic Lee/Kirby run on *Fantastic Four* by enjoying this look at one of Jack's final efforts on the FF, as he originally intended it to be seen.

John Morrow is editor and publisher of The Jack Kirby Collector, *a quarterly magazine about Kirby's life and career that is currently in its 12th year of publication. His company, TwoMorrows Publishing, launched in 1994 and is the industry's leading publisher of books and magazines about comics artists and comics history. Find out more at www.twomorrows.com*

PAGE 1

1. *"Famous archaeologist has dug up statue of the twin gods Janus--wants to verify it's date with Reed Richard's equipment--"* **2. Stan Lee border note:** *"Art Dealer- Why did Alicia do that strange statue?"* **3. Stan Lee border note:** *"Reed- It represents one of our greatest cases."* **4.** *"One face of the statue is calm--wholesome. Other face is evil--savage."* **5.** *"Why should statue have been unearthed at this particular time?"* Editorial notes pointing to Crystal and Sue request for their positions to be swapped.

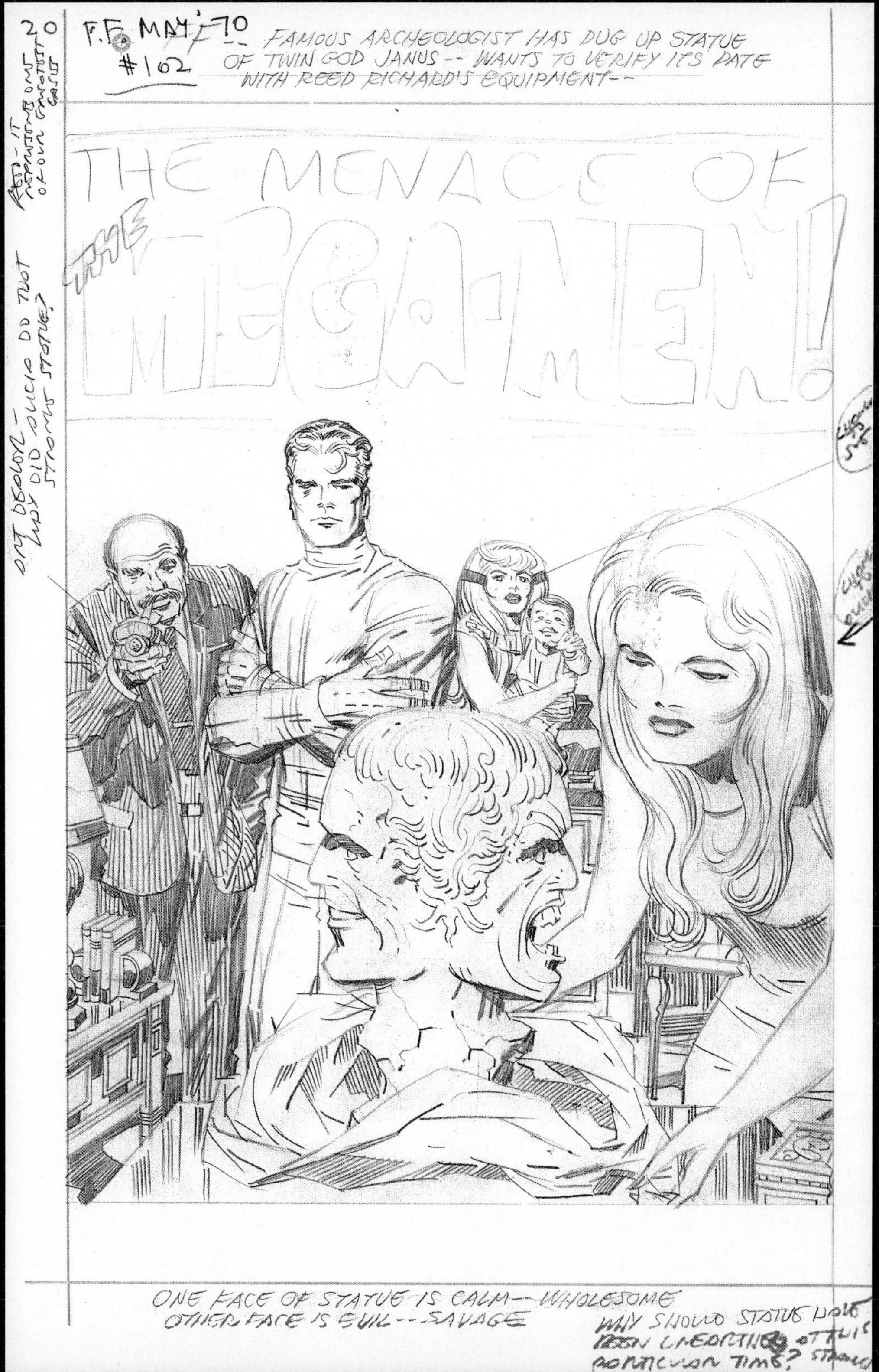

20
F.F. MAY '70
#102
FAMOUS ARCHEOLOGIST HAS DUG UP STATUE OF TWIN GOD JANUS -- WANTS TO VERIFY IT'S DATE WITH REED RICHARD'S EQUIPMENT--
THE MENACE OF THE MEGA-MEN!
ONE FACE OF STATUE IS CALM-- WHOLESOME
OTHER FACE IS EVIL--SAVAGE

Page 2

Panel 1. *"Even ancients pondered problem that still plagues man today."* **2.** *"This radiation test will prove date conclusively."* **3.** *"The rays react."* **4.** *"This intensity meter places statue at 4000 B.C."* **5.** *"That fierce face--thank goodness we've progressed today."* **6.** (From *Fantastic Four* #108, Page 1. The panel was cropped when published.)

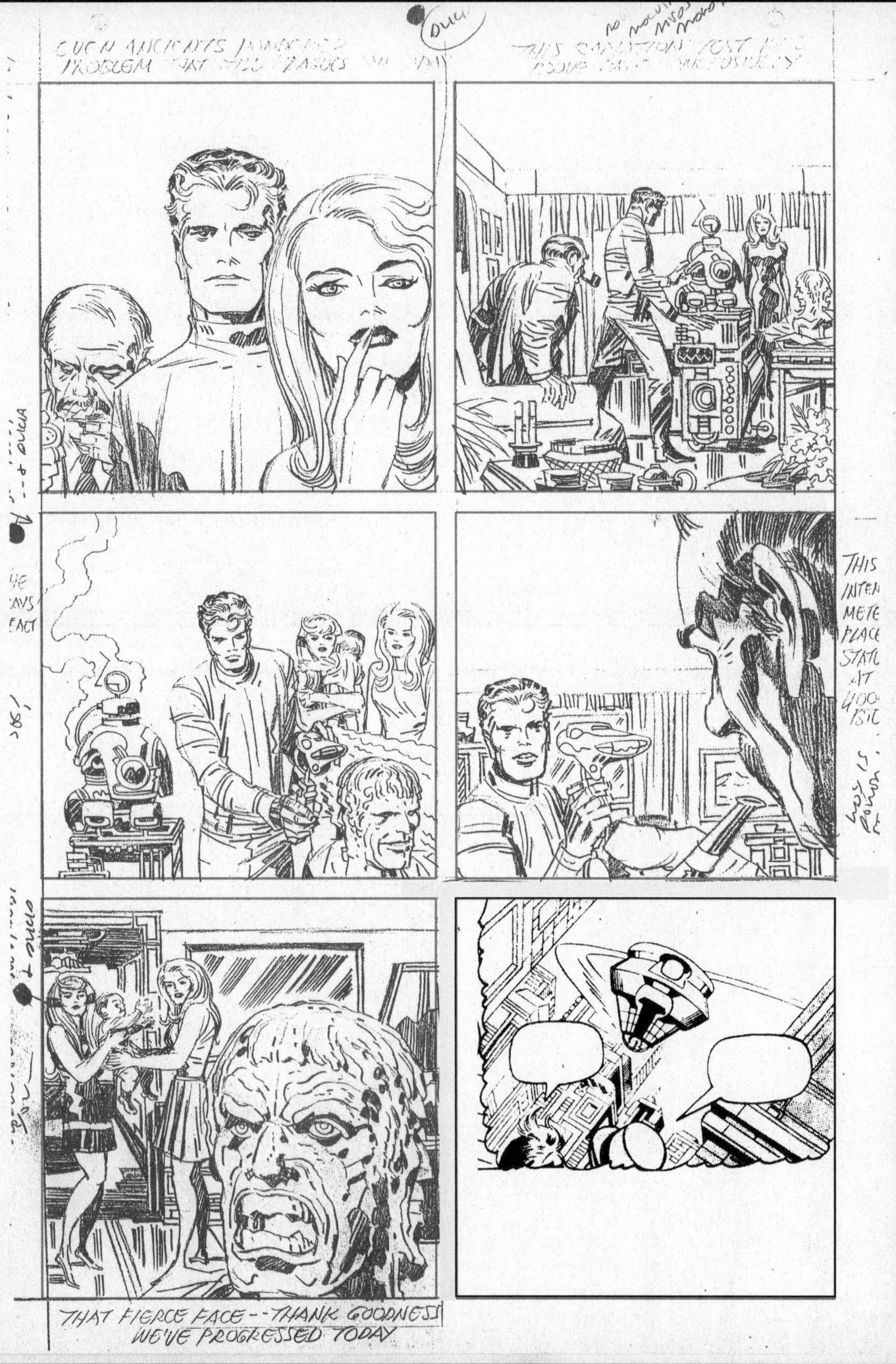
THIS
INTEN
METE
PLACE
STATU
AT
400
BC
THAT FIERCE FACE--THANK GOODNESS
WE'VE PROGRESSED TODAY

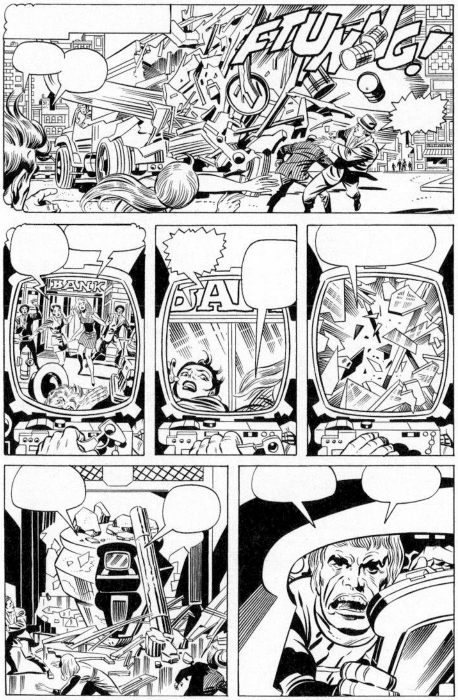
FTUNNG!
BANK

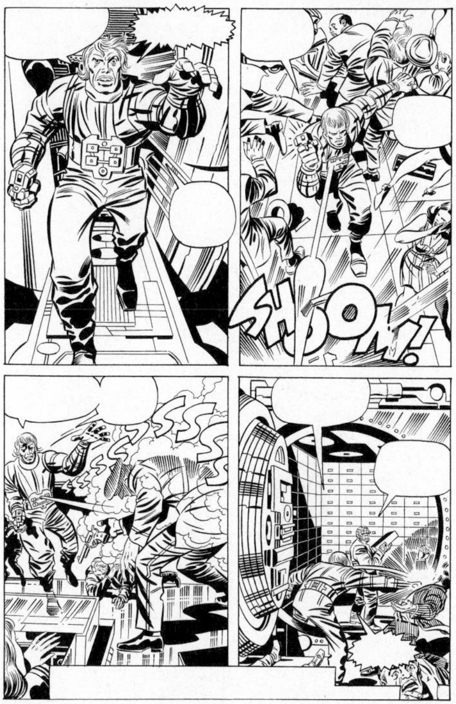
SHOOM!

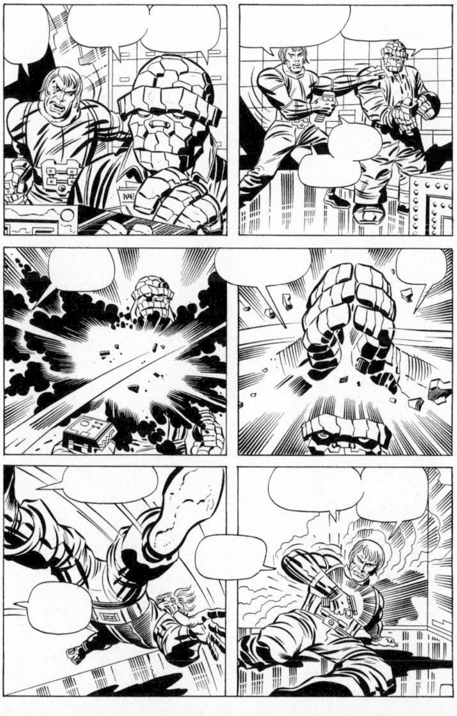

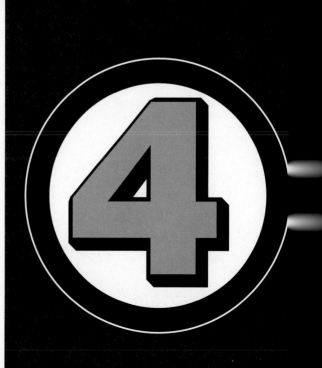

THIS GIVES INTRUDER TEMPORARY STRENGTH -- HE BOPS BEN HARD

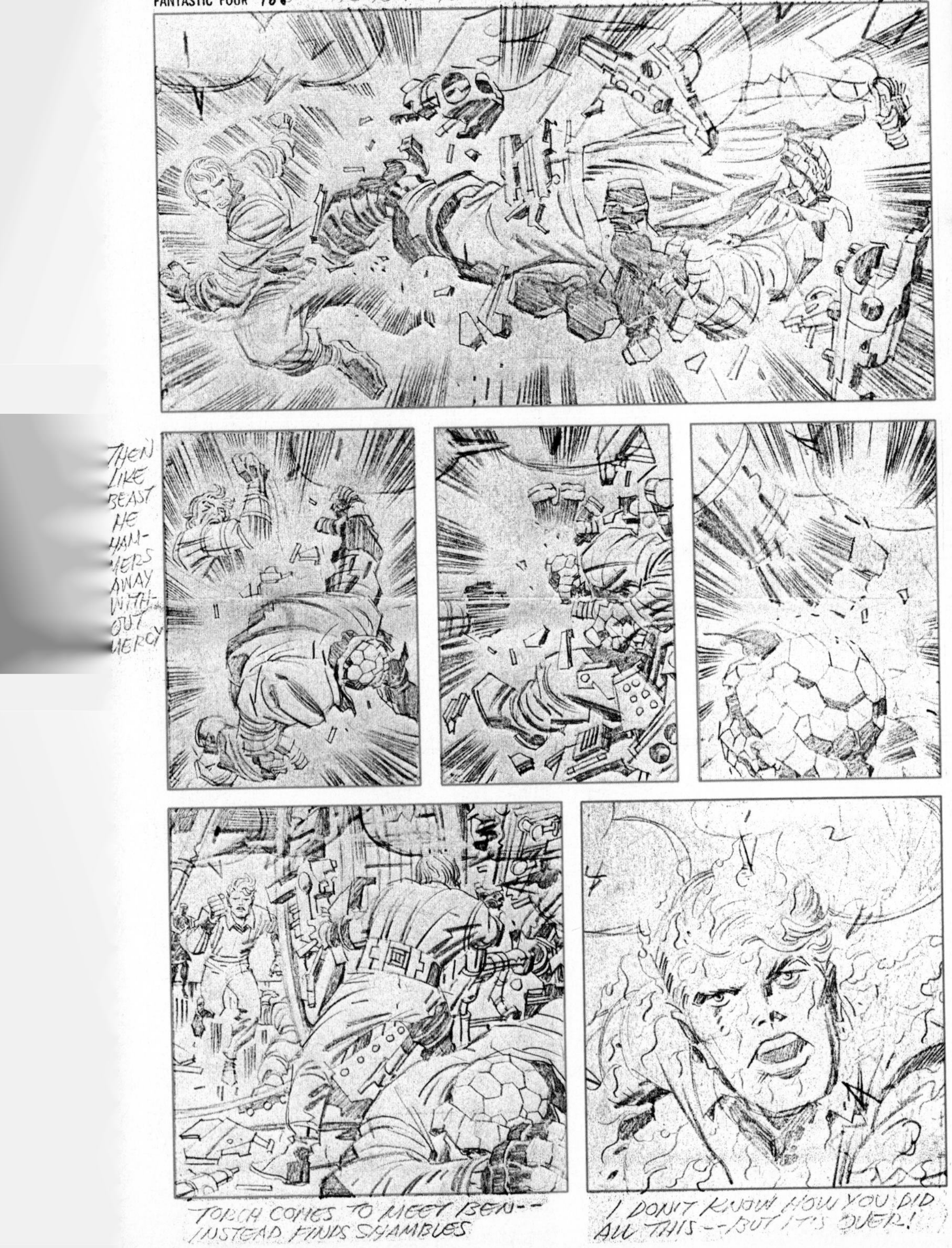

THEN LIKE BEAST HE HAMMERS AWAY WITHOUT MERCY

TORCH COMES TO MEET BEN-- INSTEAD FINDS SHAMBLES

I DON'T KNOW HOW YOU DID ALL THIS--BUT IT'S OVER!

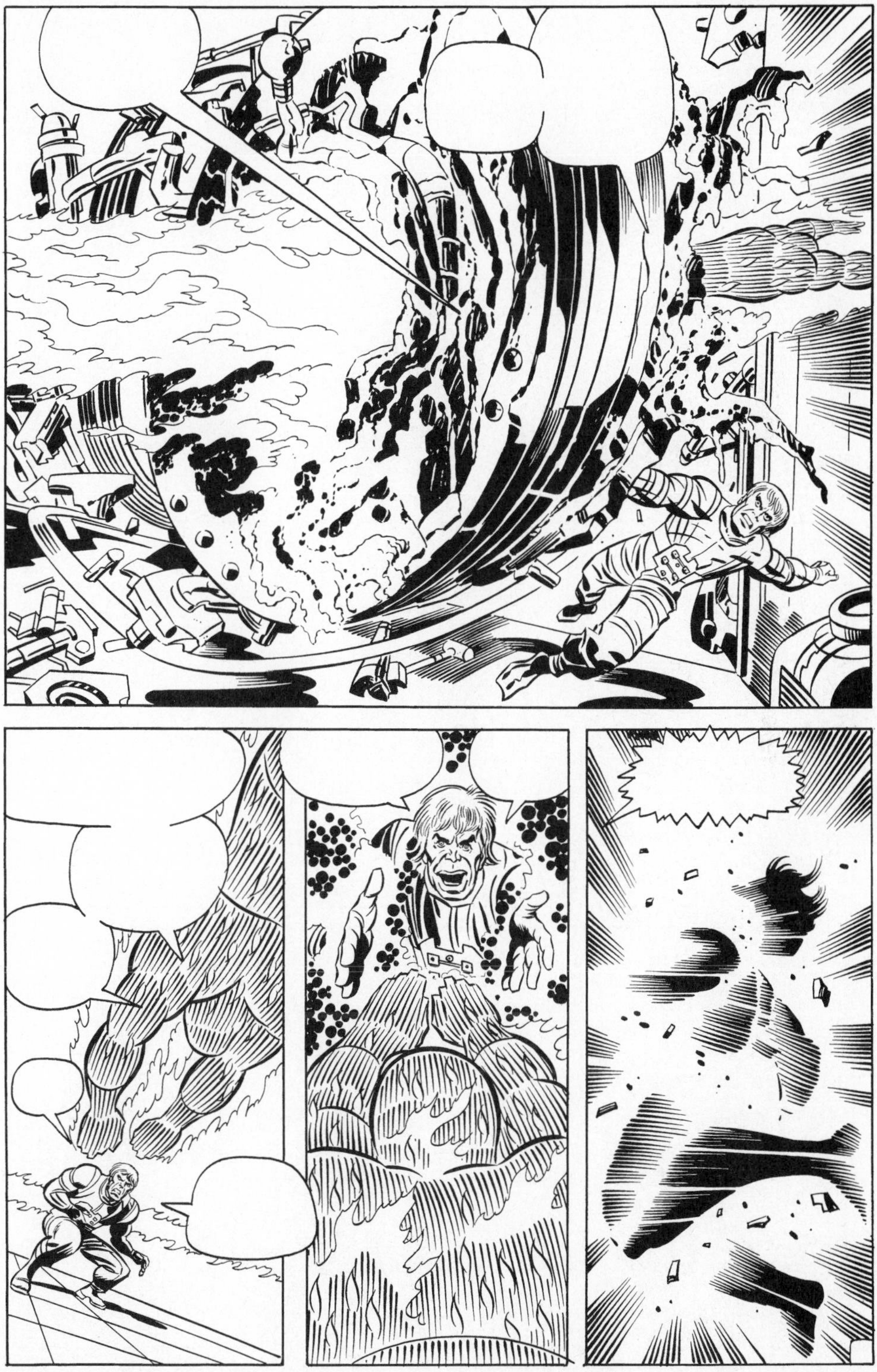

anel 1. "Torch whirls in ______ nightmare." (From Fantastic Four #108, page 7, Panels 1-3) 2. "______ like bad dream." 3. "Torch wakes up in ______" 4. "Ben says we blew it--the guy got away with a million bucks." 5. (missing panel) 6. "Yeah--he's now number one--on the ten most wanted felons!" 7. "We can't stay here! Let's get him--" "Reed says cool it--he's following a lead."

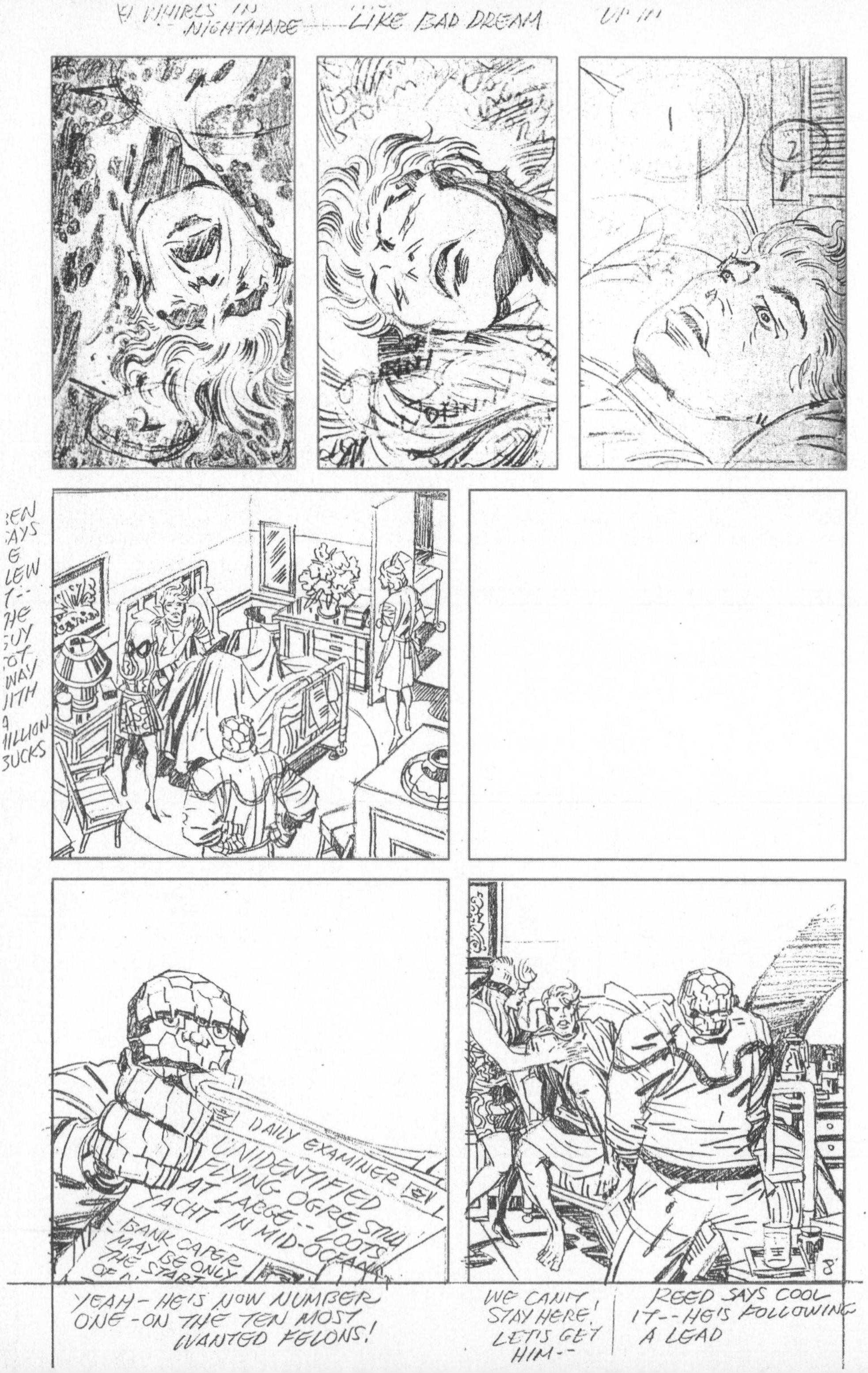

WHIRLS IN NIGHTMARE
LIKE BAD DREAM
UP IN
BEN SAYS WE BLEW IT-- THE GUY GOT AWAY WITH A MILLION BUCKS
DAILY EXAMINER
UNIDENTIFIED FLYING OGRE STILL AT LARGE-- LOOTS YACHT IN MID-OCEAN
BANK CAPER MAY BE ONLY THE START
YEAH-- HE'S NOW NUMBER ONE - ON THE TEN MOST WANTED FELONS!
WE CAN'T STAY HERE! LET'S GET HIM--
REED SAYS COOL IT-- HE'S FOLLOWING A LEAD

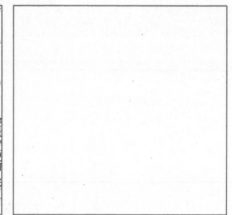

Panel 1. (From *Fantastic Four* #108, Page 15, Panel 4.) **2-5.** (Missing panels, possibly showing Sue planting mini-camera in Janus' house.)

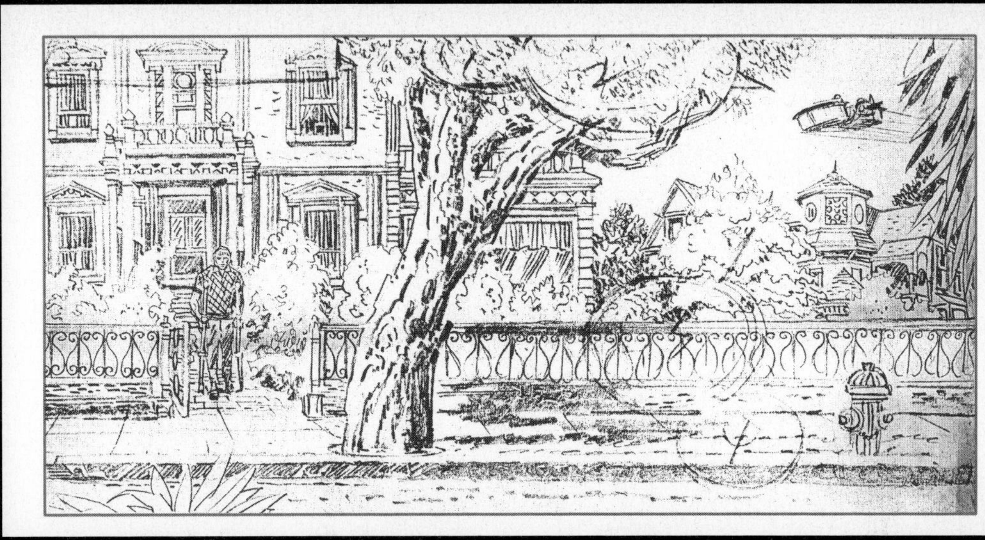

PAGE 10

Panels 1-2. (Missing panels, possibly showing Sue planting a mini-camera in Janus' house.) **3.** *"Reed is amazed at mildness of Prof, who is complete opposite of Ben's description."* **5.** *"Meanwhile, the Prof's evil brother has been watching--he says Richards must be flabbergasted."* **6.** *"Prof says--why did you have to come after all these years?" "Because you're a perfect cover, brother--"*

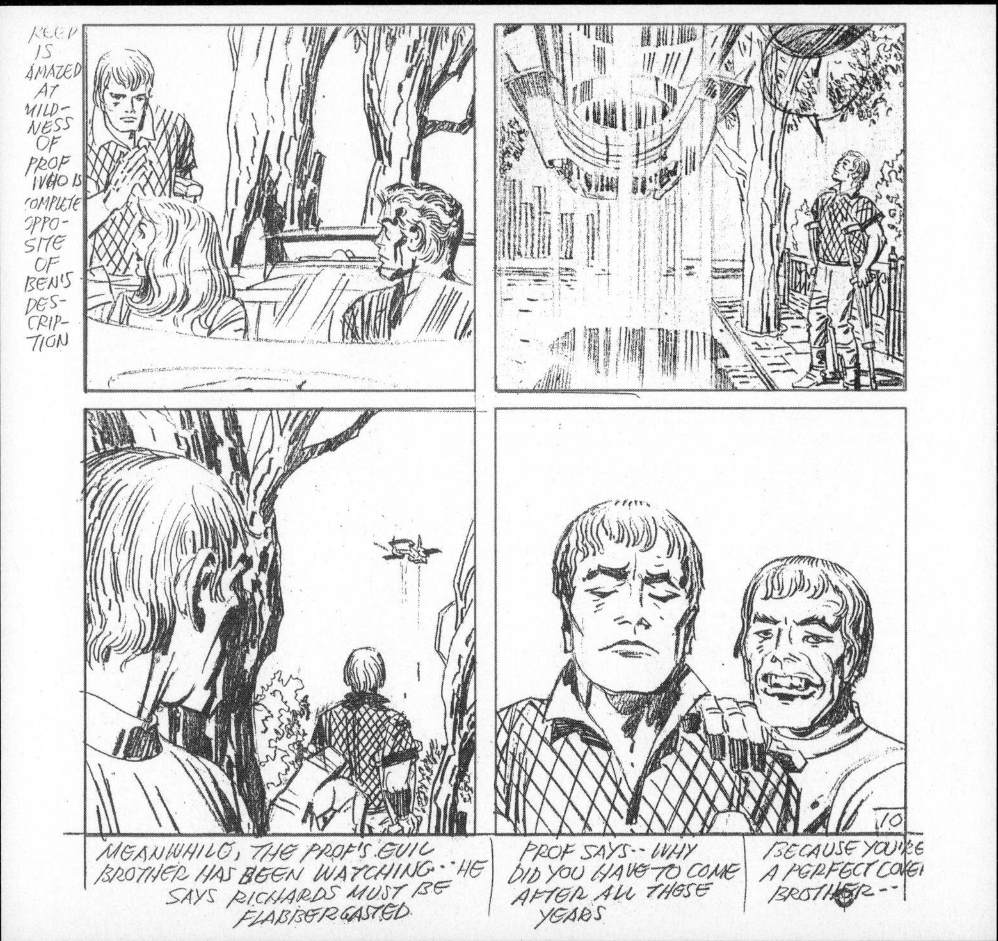
IS AMAZED AT MILD-NESS OF PROF WHO IS COMPLETE OPPO-SITE OF BEN'S DES-CRIP-TION
MEANWHILE, THE PROF'S EVIL BROTHER HAS BEEN WATCHING--HE SAYS RICHARDS MUST BE FLABBERGASTED
PROF SAYS--WHY DID YOU HAVE TO COME AFTER ALL THESE YEARS
BECAUSE YOU'RE A PERFECT COVER BROTHER--
10

Panel 1. *"I've been away perfecting Mega-Power. Now--I'll gain money-power."* **2.** *"You won't talk. The town won't talk--or it's curtains!"* **3.** *"Stick with me. With Mega-Power--I may even help you walk again."* **4.** *"Right now I'm going to be busy in lab. Richards didn't go away without bugging the house."* **5.** *"I've got instruments to trace his bugs and destroy them. Now leave me."* **6.** *"Yes--my plans don't stop here--I'll empty that whole city of its money."* **7.** (From *Fantastic Four* #108, Page 7, Panel 6.)

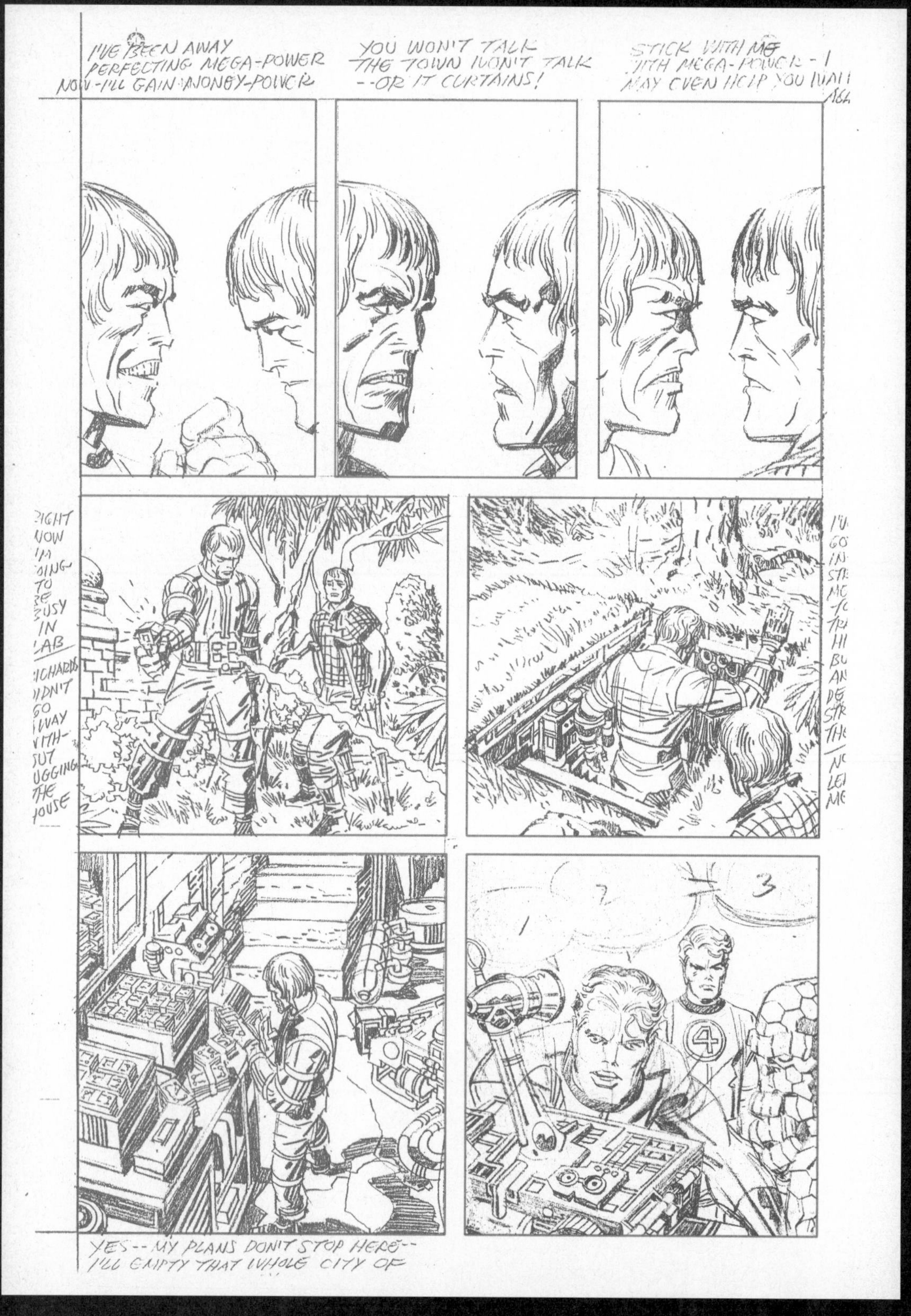
I'VE BEEN AWAY PERFECTING MEGA-POWER NOW-I'LL GAIN MONEY-POWER
YOU WON'T TALK THE TOWN WON'T TALK --OR IT CURTAINS!
STICK WITH ME WITH MEGA-POWER - I MAY EVEN HELP YOU
RIGHT NOW I'M GOING TO BE BUSY IN LAB RICHARDS DIDN'T GO AWAY WITH-OUT BUGGING THE HOUSE
YES--MY PLANS DON'T STOP HERE-- I'LL EMPTY THAT WHOLE CITY OF

Pages 12-13

This page would have been split into two half pages, with ads running under them--a practice that got a 20-page story out of only 19 pages of art. **Panels 1-2.** (From *Fantastic Four* #108, Page 8, Panels 2-3.) **3.** (From *Fantastic Four* #108, Page 8, Panel 6.) **4.** *“______ with mini-camera”* (From *Fantastic Four* #108, Page 9, Panel 1.) **5.** *“What happened?” “Ben says--Reed’s mini-camera blew up in our faces--that’s what!”* **6.** *“That was no malfunction--that was Mega-Power. Listen Sue--I have a nutty idea--”*

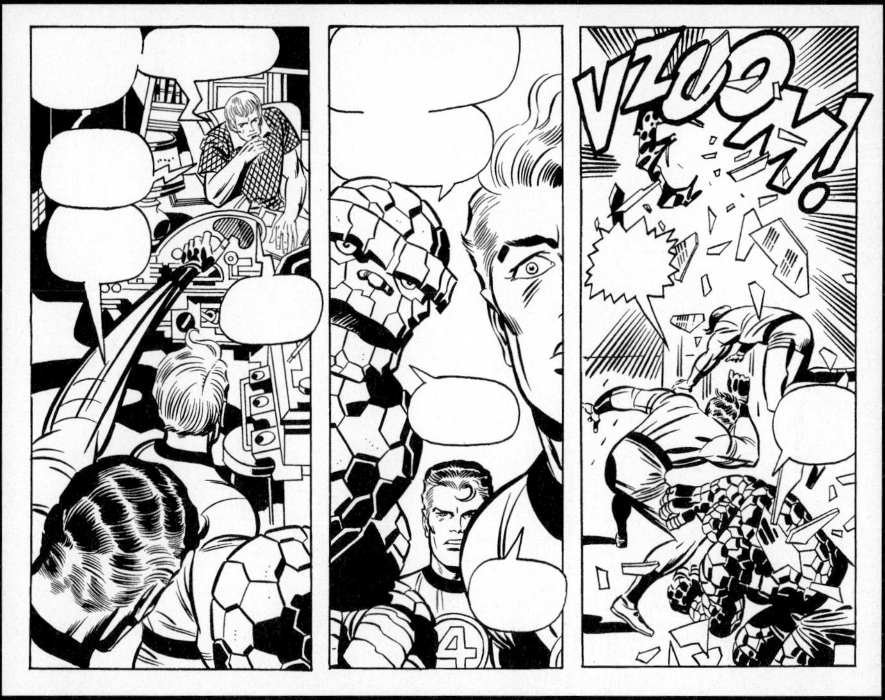
VZOOM!

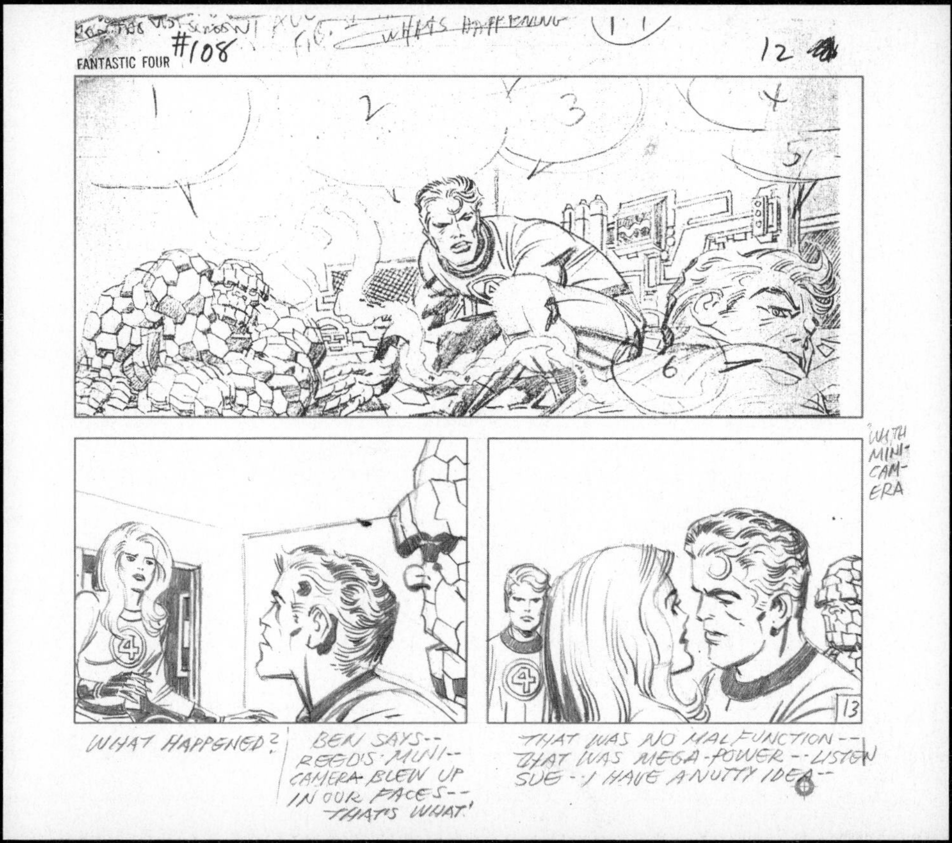
FANTASTIC FOUR #108
12
WITH MINI-CAMERA
13
WHAT HAPPENED?
BEN SAYS--REED'S MINI-CAMERA BLEW UP IN OUR FACES--THAT'S WHAT!
THAT WAS NO MALFUNCTION--THAT WAS MEGA-POWER--LISTEN SUE--I HAVE A NUTTY IDEA--

PAGE 14

Panel 1. *"Let him give her crazy ideas--I'll take action--the real culprit must be in city ______ right now!"* **2.** *"We'll take the Pogo Plane on upper floor. We'll scout around until we nail this bird."* **3.** "Ray shoots out from Johnny's belt. It strikes 'up' button." **6.** *"Ben says--you can't have girls tagging along all the time--Alicia's visiting ______"* **7.** *"Boy--these controls feel great--did you know I was a World War 2 ace?"*

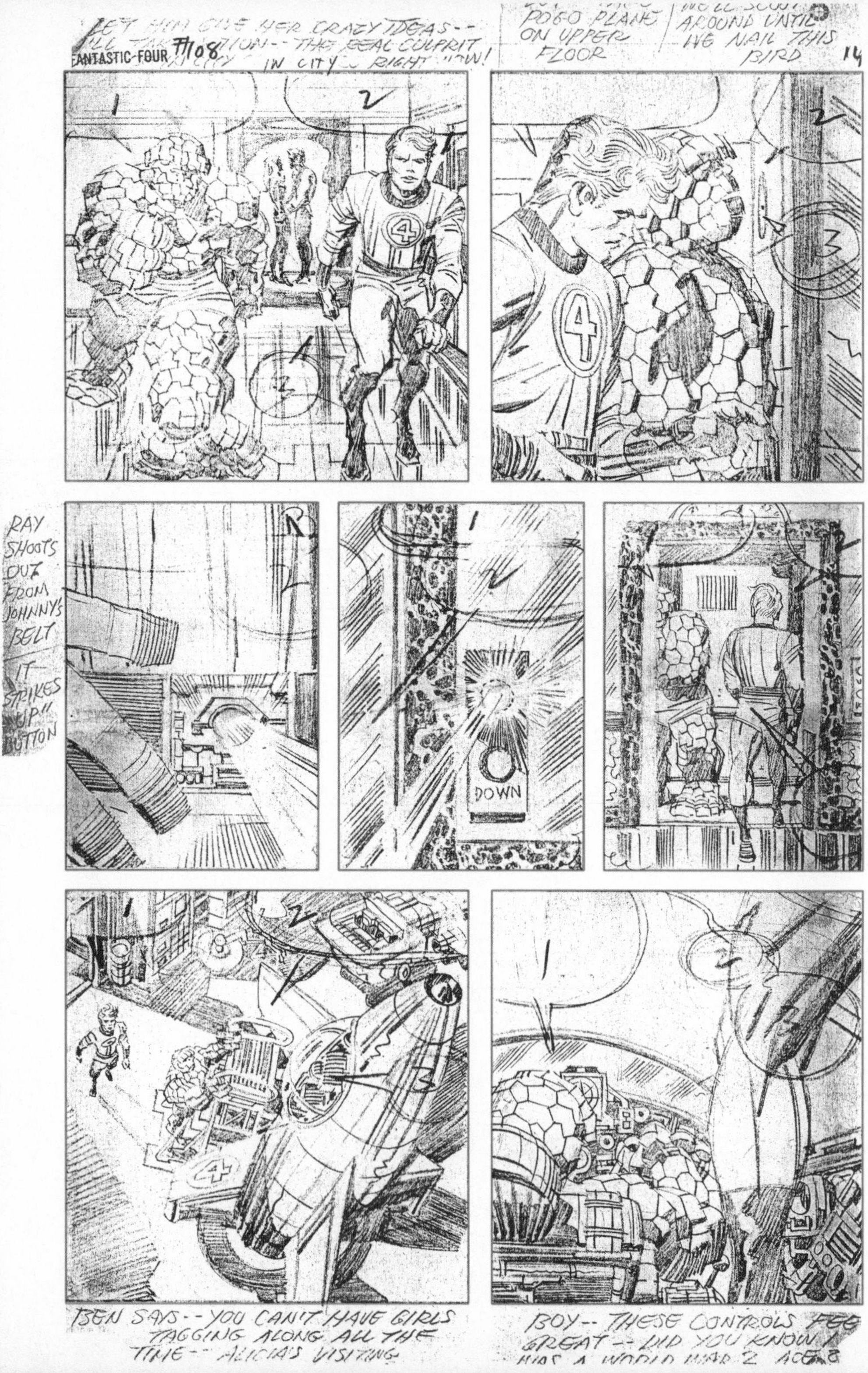

FANTASTIC FOUR
POGO PLANE ON UPPER FLOOR
AROUND UNTIL WE NAIL THIS BIRD
14
RAY SHOOTS OUT FROM JOHNNY'S BELT
IT STRIKES "UP" BUTTON
DOWN
BEN SAYS--YOU CAN'T HAVE GIRLS TAGGING ALONG ALL THE TIME--ALICIA'S VISITING
BOY--THESE CONTROLS FEEL GREAT--DID YOU KNOW I WAS A WORLD WAR 2 ACE

Page 15

Panel 1. *"How's this for a takeoff--she handles great!"* **2.** *"_______ friend's crummy craft! I'll take him like the Red Baron."* **3.** *"You see what I see?"* **4.** *"Flying debris from street below. Ripped out by Mega-Power! Let's go!"* **6.** *"He sees plane! I can't leave without a parting shot--"*

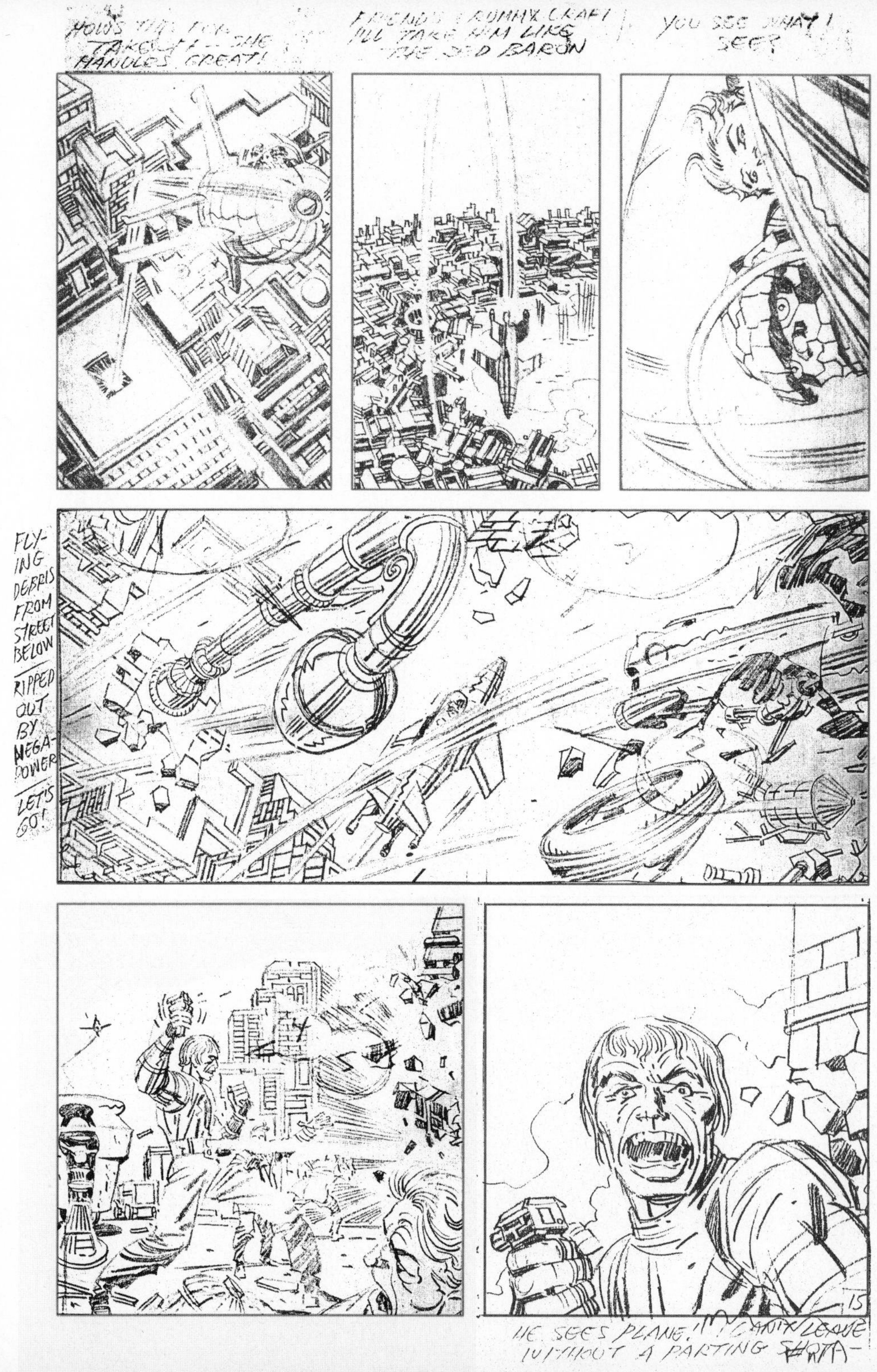
FRIEND'S CRUMMY CRAFT I'LL TAKE HIM LIKE THE RED BARON
YOU SEE WHAT I SEE
FLY-ING DEBRIS FROM STREET BELOW
RIPPED OUT BY MEGA-POWER
LET'S GO!
15
HE SEES PLANE! I CAN'T LEAVE WITHOUT A PARTING SHOT--

PAGE 16

Panels 1-2. (From *Fantastic Four* #108, Page 13, Panels 1-2. Originals were cropped.) **3.** *"Ben! The cockpit's frozen tight! Ben says Flame On, kid. Get out! I can't control it."* **3-7.** (From *Fantastic Four* #108, Page 14, Panels 1-5.)

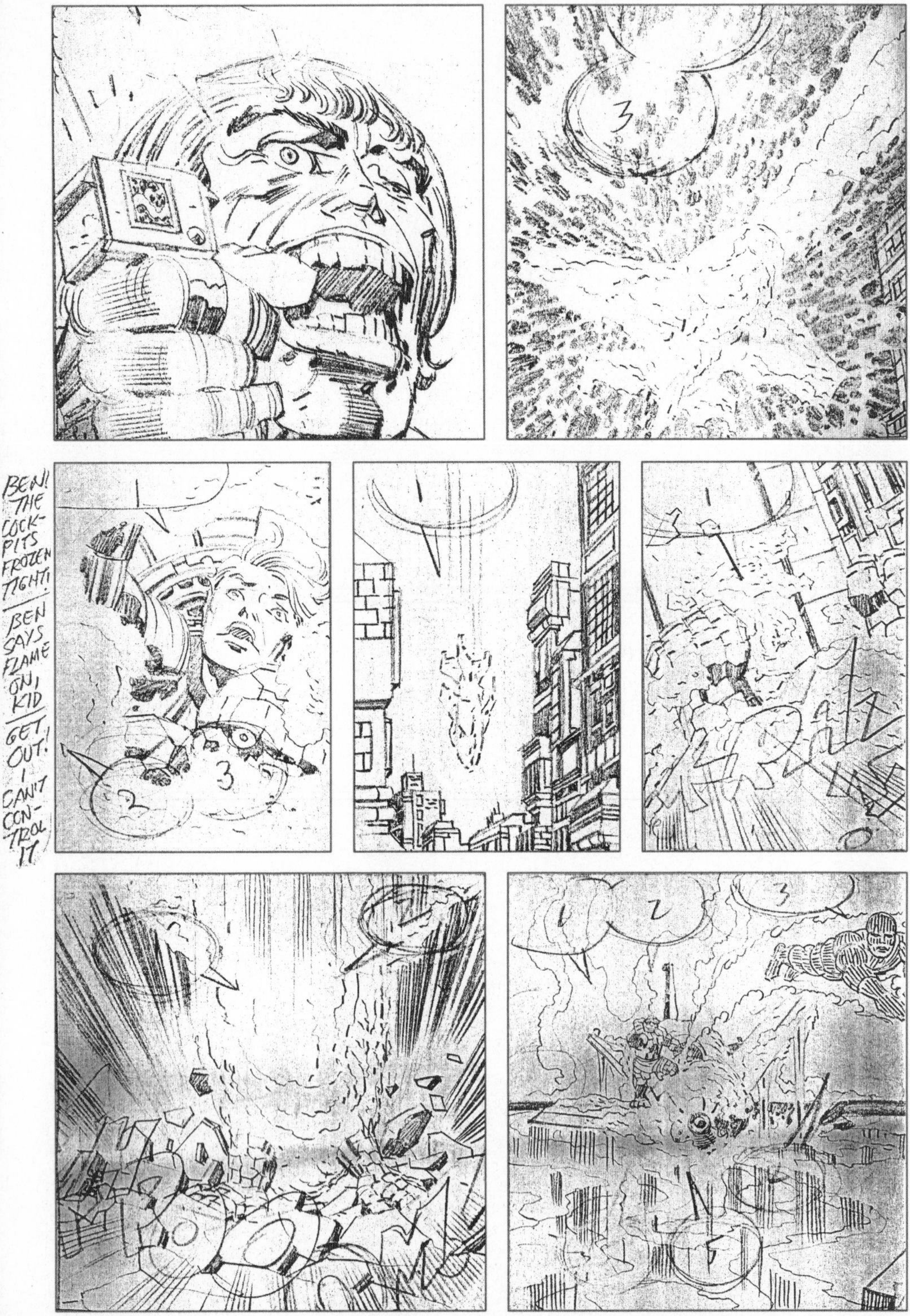

BEN! THE COCK-PITS FROZEN TIGHT!
BEN SAYS FLAME ON, KID
GET OUT! I CAN'T CON-TROL IT

Panels 1-2. (From *Fantastic Four* #108, Page 14, Panels 6-7.) 3. *"Bruised people say 'are we in his power? Can you stop him?"* 3-5. (From *Fantastic Four* #108, Page 15, Panels 1-3.) 6-7. (From *Fantastic Four* #108, Page 16, Panels 3-4.)

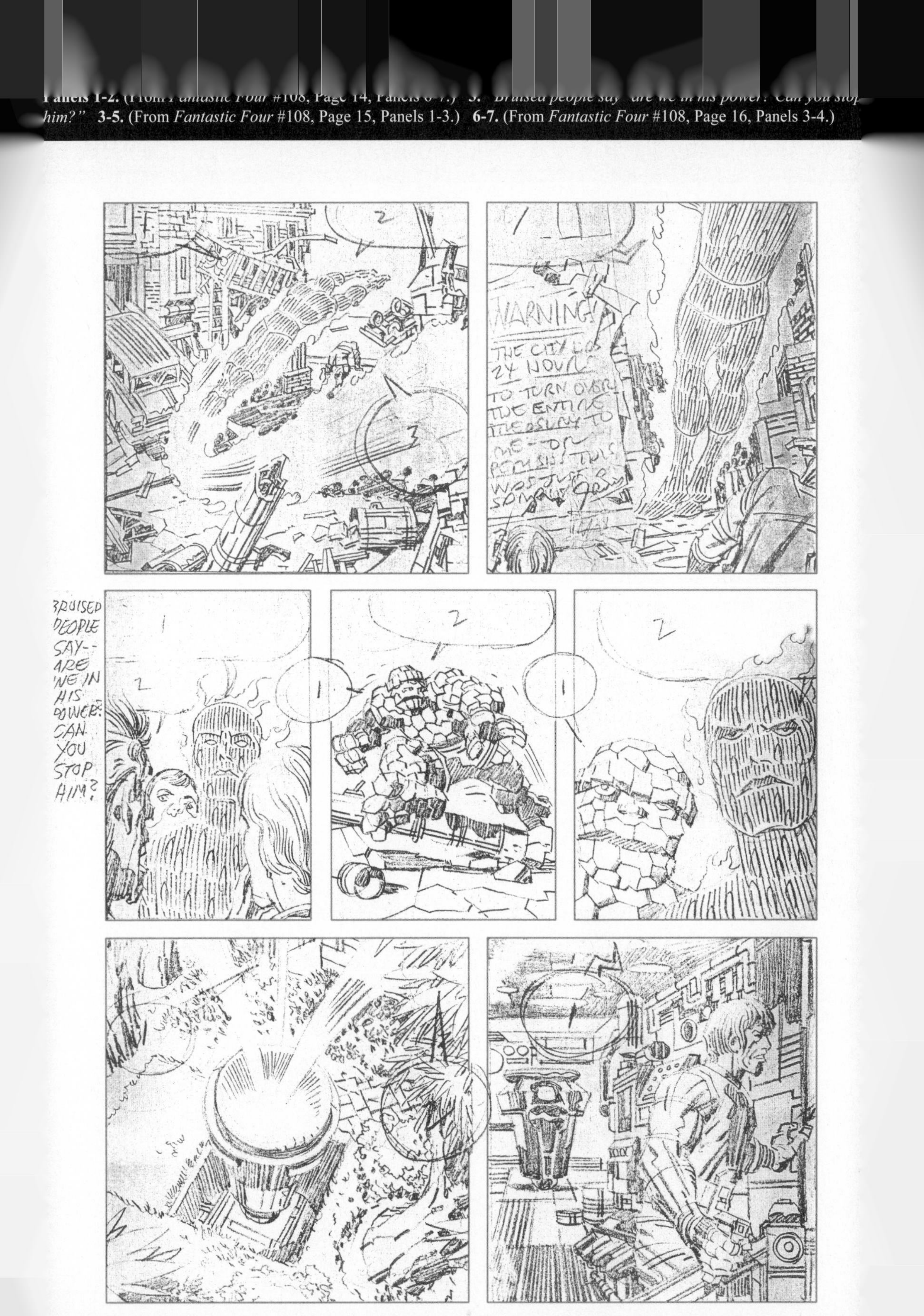
WARNING!
BRUISED PEOPLE SAY-- ARE WE IN HIS POWER? CAN YOU STOP HIM?

Page 18

Panels 1-2. (From *Fantastic Four* #108, Page 16, Panels 5-6.) **3-7.** (From *Fantastic Four* #108, Page 17, Panels 1-5.)

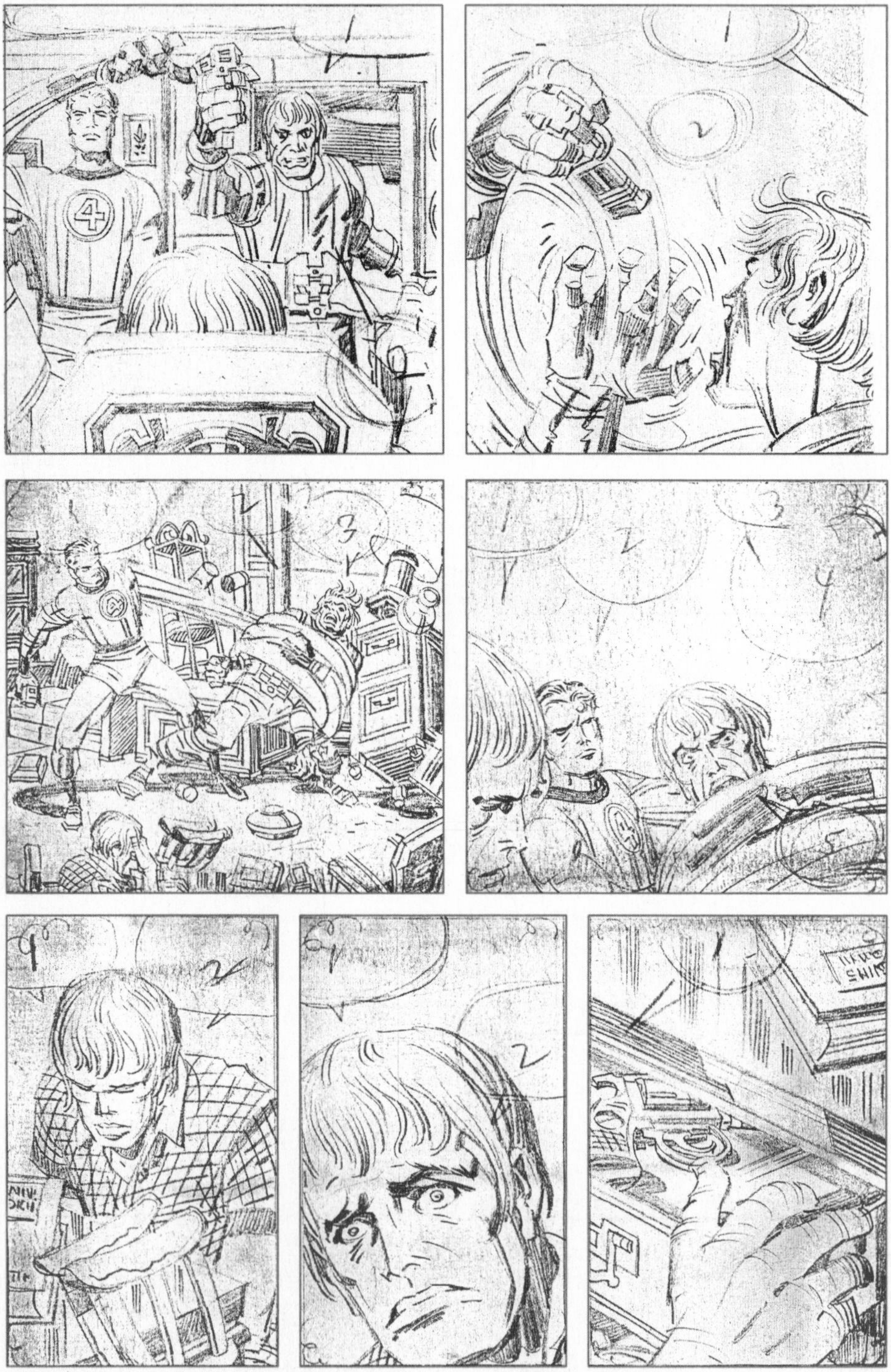

PAGE 19

Panel 1. (From *Fantastic Four* #108, Page 17, Panel 6.) **2-3.** (No Margin Notes Visible.) **4.** *"She grabs gun before twin can reach for it." "Reed says--use gun to cover bad twin, Sue!"* **5.** *"Reed says to good twin--you're a fool you know. The criminal's path is no solution."* **6.** (Margin notes are erased.) **7.** *"Reed touches good twin's feet with trigger."* (The page number "19" has been erased, but is visible.)

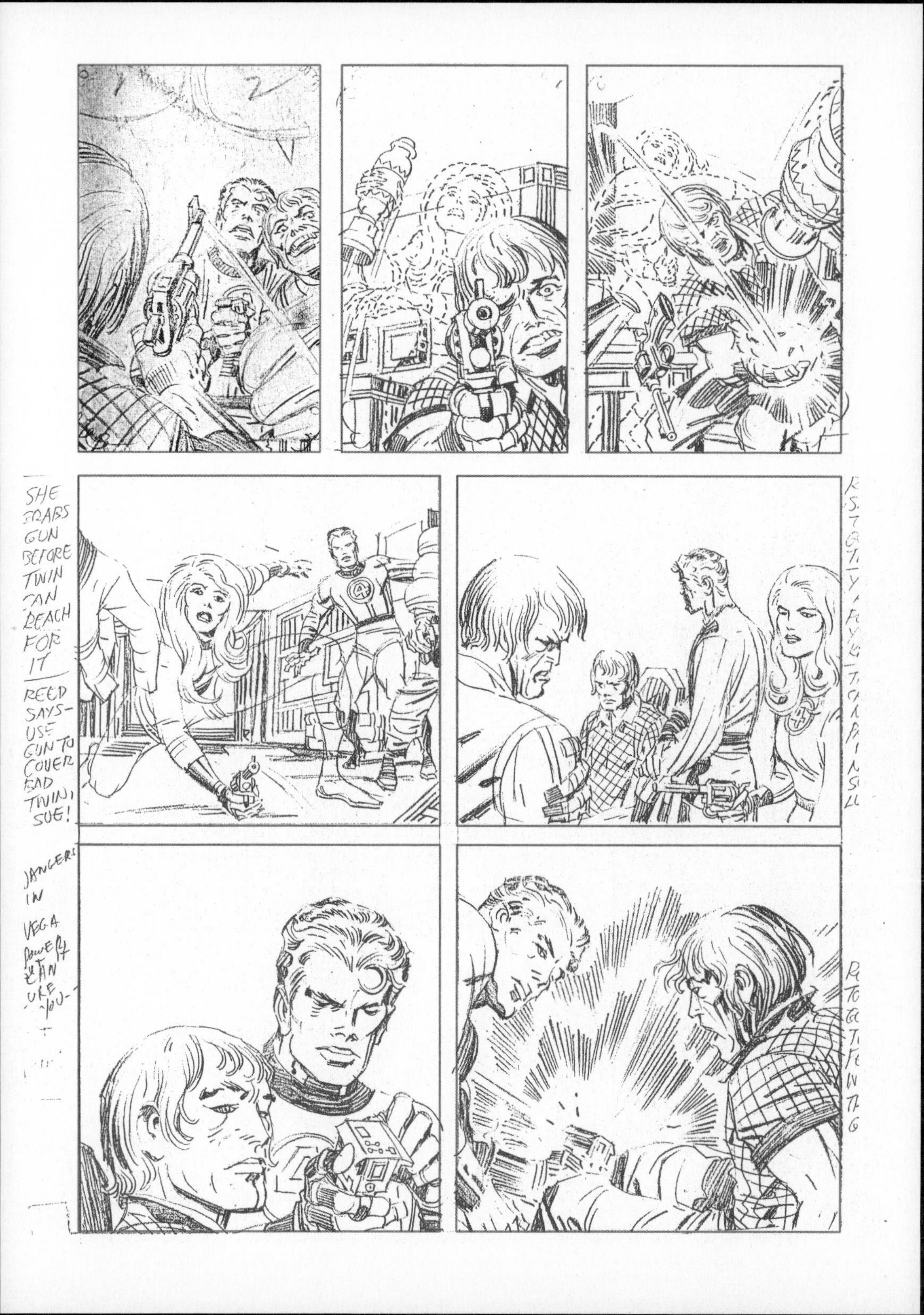

SHE GRABS GUN BEFORE TWIN CAN REACH FOR IT
REED SAYS- USE GUN TO COVER BAD TWIN, SUE!

Panel 1. (Margin Notes have been erased.) **2.** *"Who can tell what Mega-power can do!"* **3.** *"Don't trust him! Get him while you can! I'll handle the girl!"* (Note the scalloped corners, indicating this was considered for a flashback scene in *Fantastic Four* #108.) **4.** (Margin Notes have been erased.) **5-7.** (Missing Panels.)

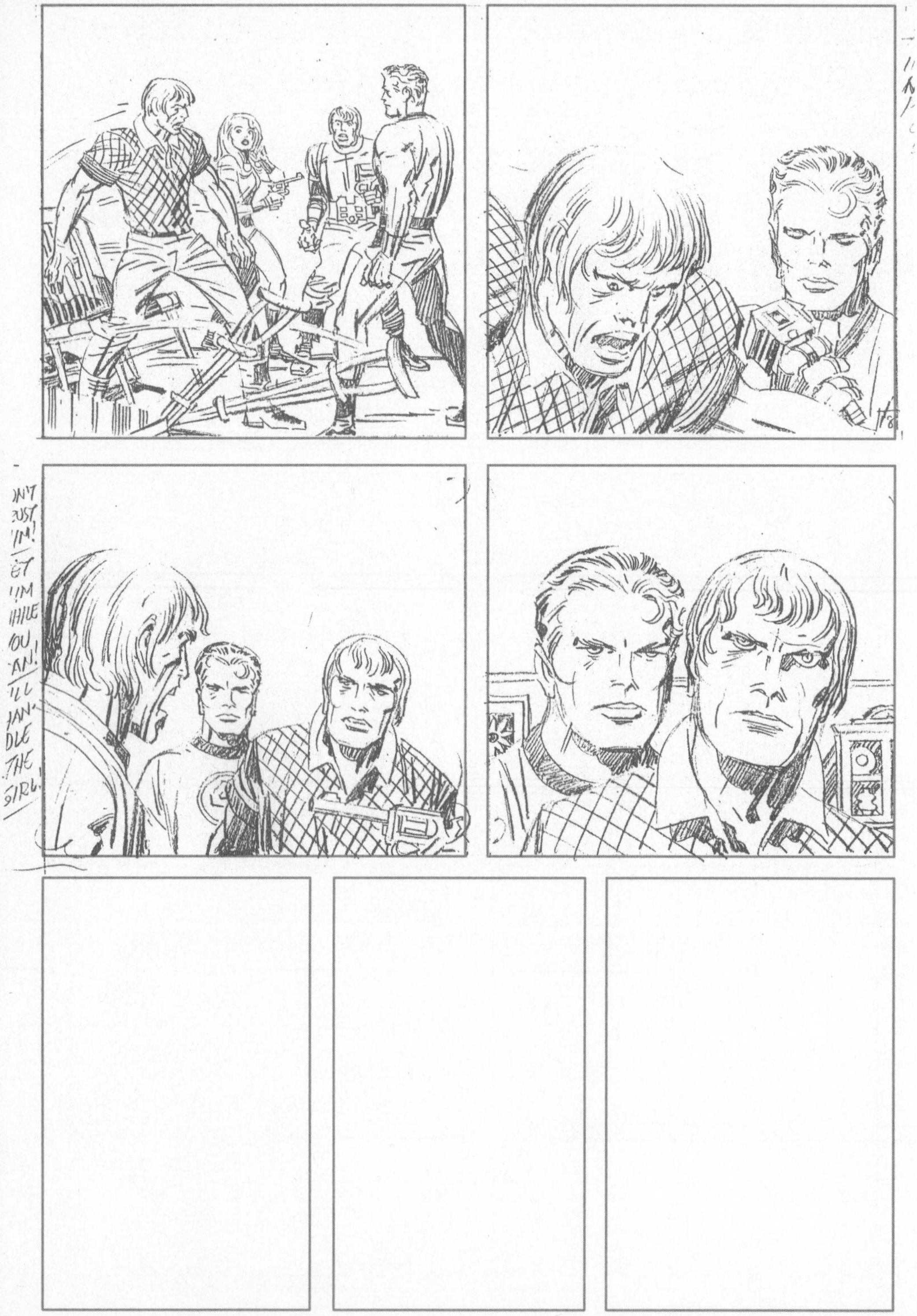

WITH REED RICHARD'S EQUIPMENT--

FANTASTIC FOUR: THE LOST ADVENTURE

Between 1961 and 1970, Stan Lee and Jack Kirby produced 102 consecutive issues of *Fantastic Four*, as well as six Annuals. However, there was a 103rd issue that they'd begun working on, but never completed.

While portions of that story saw print some months later as an extended flashback sequence in *Fantastic Four* #108, the original incarnation of that tale has never been finished—until now!

Working from Jack Kirby's penciled pages and their extensive border notes, Stan Lee and Joe Sinnott have reunited to complete what they'd begun 38 years earlier, aided in part by Ron Frenz and Chris Sotomayor.

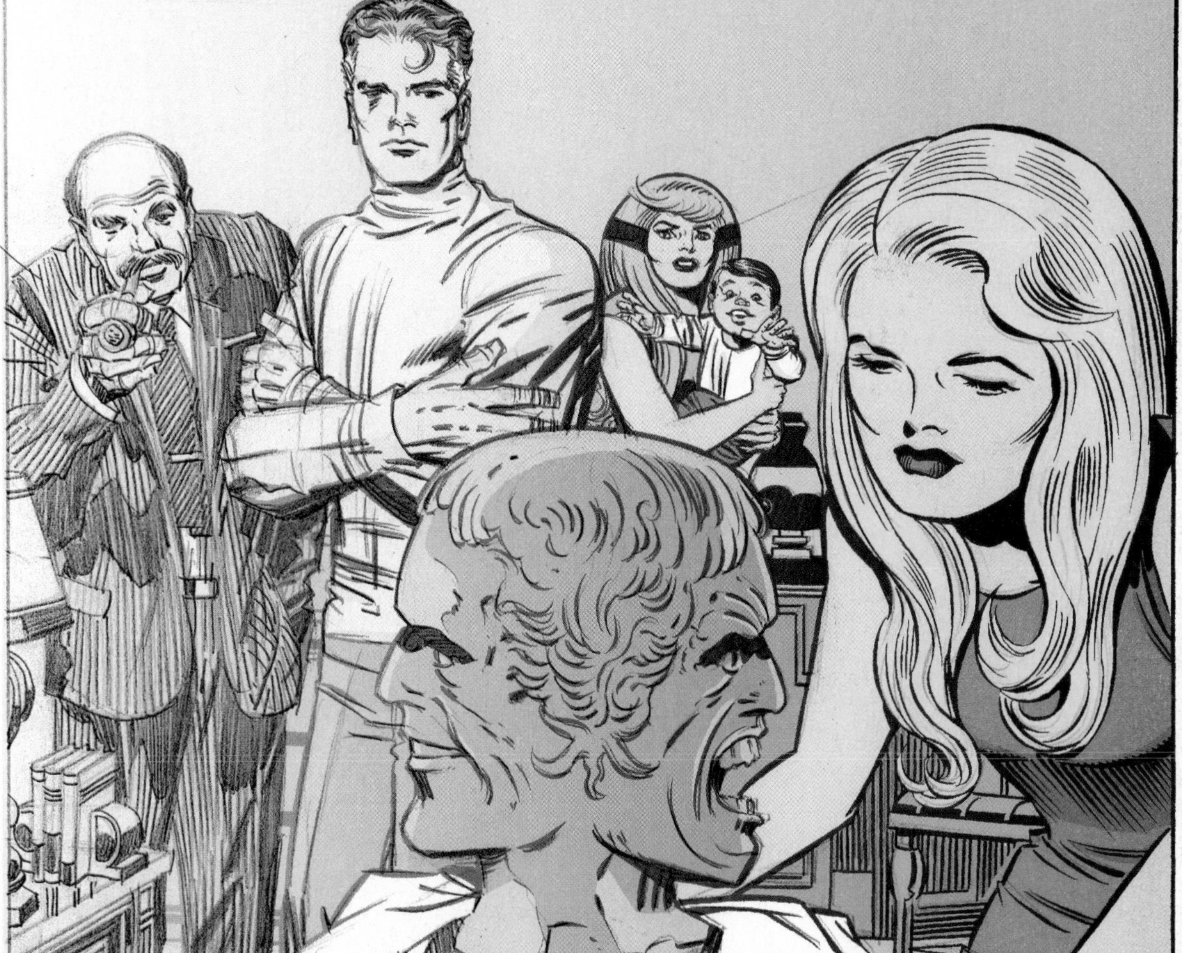

ONE FACE OF STATUE IS CALM--WHOLESOME

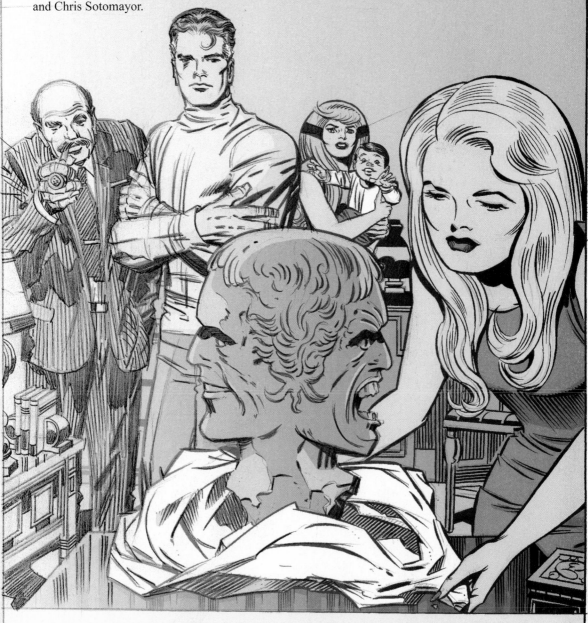

MARVEL

Fantastic Four®

THE LOST ADVENTURE

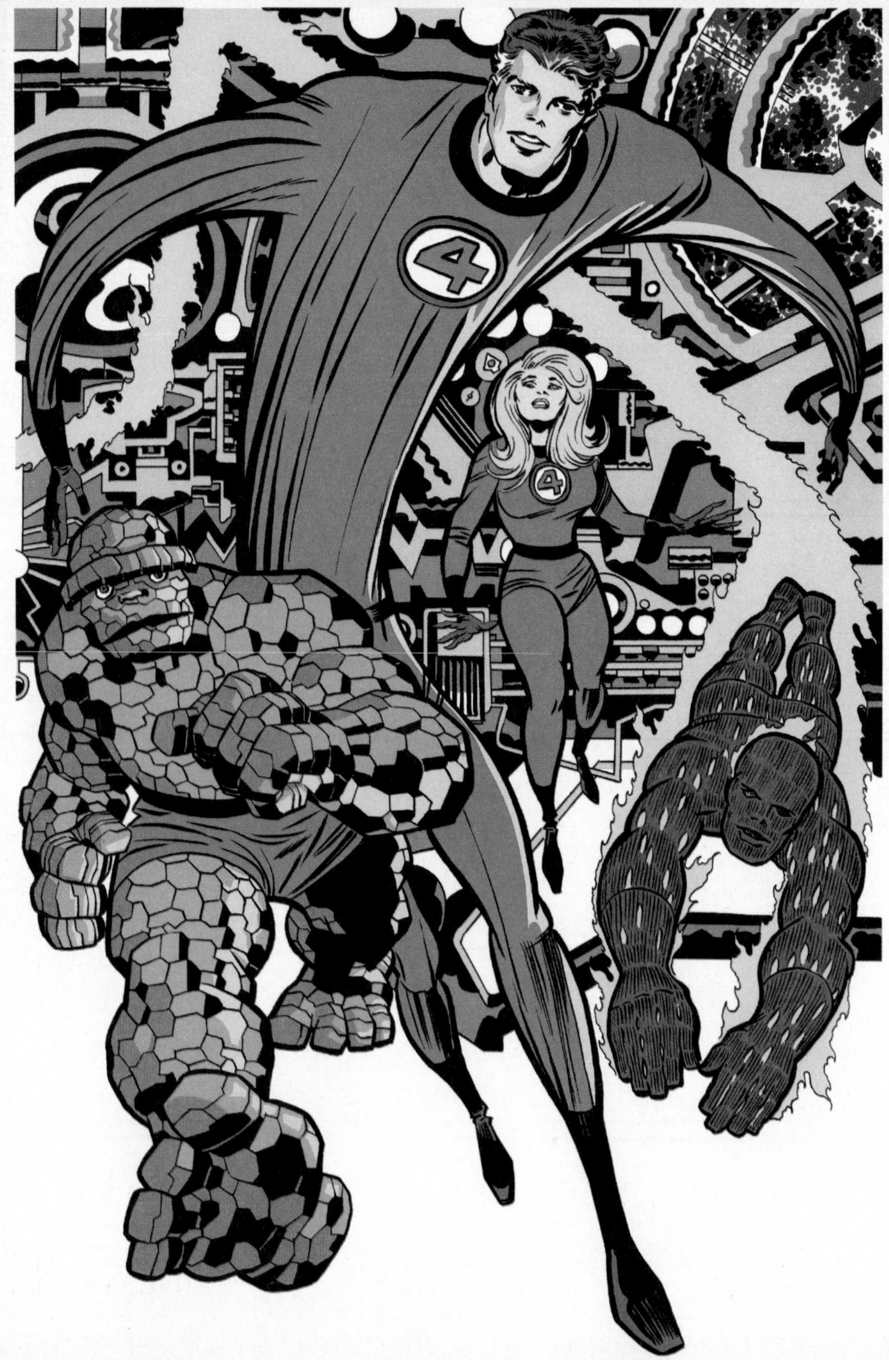

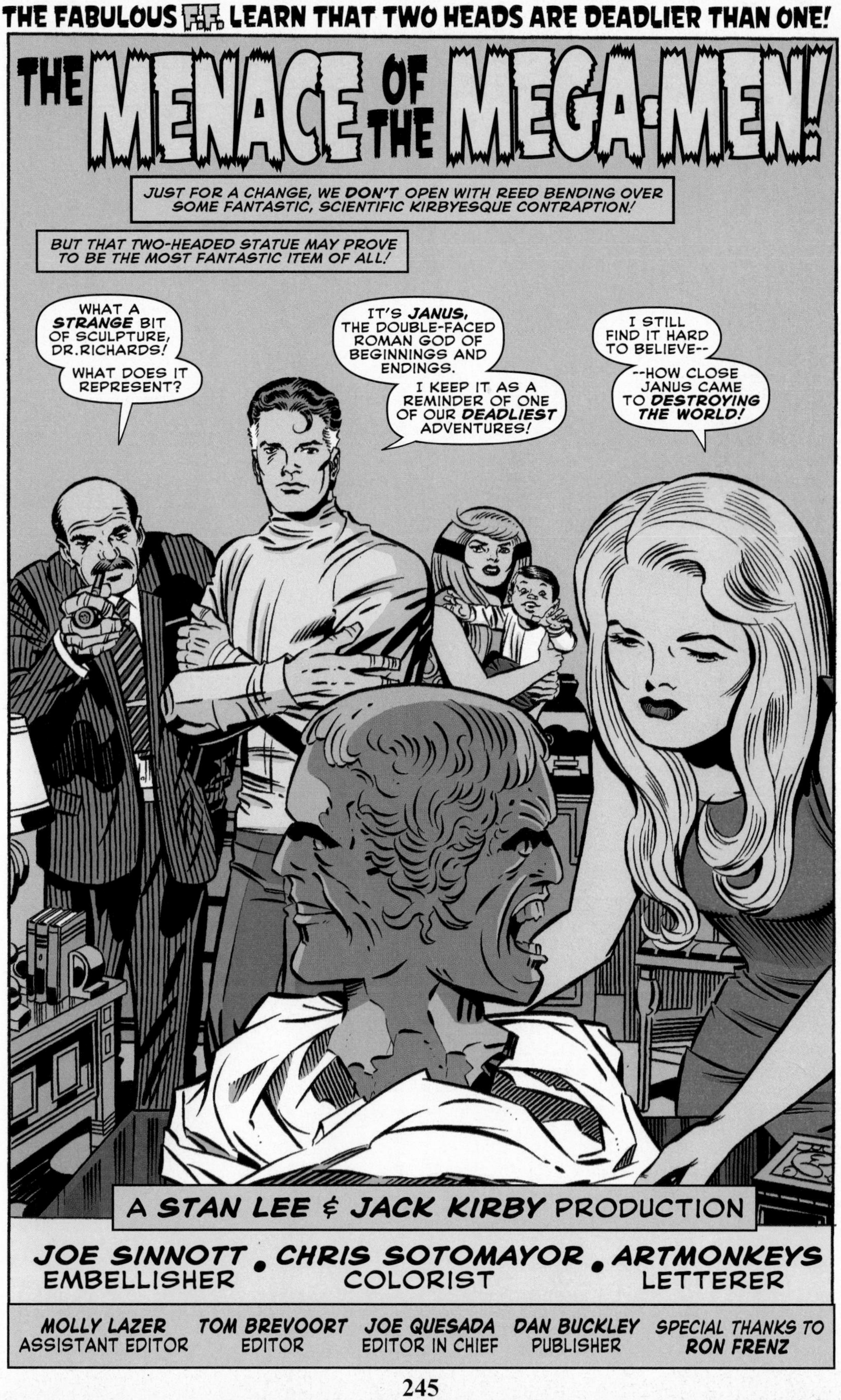
THE FABULOUS F.F. LEARN THAT TWO HEADS ARE DEADLIER THAN ONE!
THE MENACE OF THE MEGA-MEN!
JUST FOR A CHANGE, WE DON'T OPEN WITH REED BENDING OVER SOME FANTASTIC, SCIENTIFIC KIRBYESQUE CONTRAPTION!
BUT THAT TWO-HEADED STATUE MAY PROVE TO BE THE MOST FANTASTIC ITEM OF ALL!
WHAT A STRANGE BIT OF SCULPTURE, DR. RICHARDS!
WHAT DOES IT REPRESENT?
IT'S JANUS, THE DOUBLE-FACED ROMAN GOD OF BEGINNINGS AND ENDINGS.
I KEEP IT AS A REMINDER OF ONE OF OUR DEADLIEST ADVENTURES!
I STILL FIND IT HARD TO BELIEVE--
--HOW CLOSE JANUS CAME TO DESTROYING THE WORLD!
A STAN LEE & JACK KIRBY PRODUCTION
JOE SINNOTT EMBELLISHER • CHRIS SOTOMAYOR COLORIST • ARTMONKEYS LETTERER
MOLLY LAZER ASSISTANT EDITOR
TOM BREVOORT EDITOR
JOE QUESADA EDITOR IN CHIEF
DAN BUCKLEY PUBLISHER
SPECIAL THANKS TO RON FRENZ

DESTROYING THE WORLD, *INDEED!*

I'M A *SCIENTIST,* MY DEAR SUSAN.

I DON'T DEAL IN COMICBOOK PHRASEOLOGY.

THERE WAS NO OTHER WAY TO PUT IT, MY FRIEND.

IT'S STILL HARD TO BELIEVE IT EVER HAPPENED!

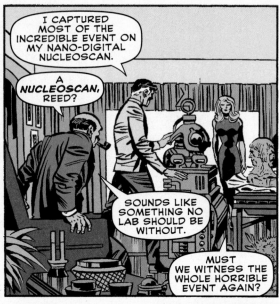

I CAPTURED MOST OF THE INCREDIBLE EVENT ON MY NANO-DIGITAL NUCLEOSCAN.

A *NUCLEOSCAN,* REED?

SOUNDS LIKE SOMETHING NO LAB SHOULD BE WITHOUT.

MUST WE WITNESS THE WHOLE HORRIBLE EVENT AGAIN?

DR. CLAYMORE FEELS YOU WERE INDULGING IN HYPERBOLE, SUE.

AFTER HE SEES WHAT I'M ABOUT TO SHOW HIM--

--PERHAPS HE'LL HAVE MORE RESPECT FOR "COMICBOOK PHRASEOLOGY"!

REED, WE'VE BEEN FRIENDS FOR YEARS.

I'M WELL AWARE OF YOUR AMAZING EXPLOITS.

BUT I'VE NEVER HEARD OF ANY SO-CALLED *JANUS* CAPER!

THAT'S RIGHT, CLAY. I'VE NEVER SPOKEN OF IT.

BUT I WANT TO PROVE TO YOU THAT MY LOVELY WIFE DIDN'T EXAGGERATE--

--WHEN SHE SAID JANUS ALMOST DESTROYED THE WORLD!

"YOU WERE AT AN ARCHEOLOGICAL DIG IN TIBET, CLAY, WHEN A STRANGE, GYROSCOPIC AIRCRAFT ATTACKED THE CENTER OF NEW YORK!"

WOW! WILLYA LOOK AT *THAT?*

WHAT'S IT ADVERTISING?

246

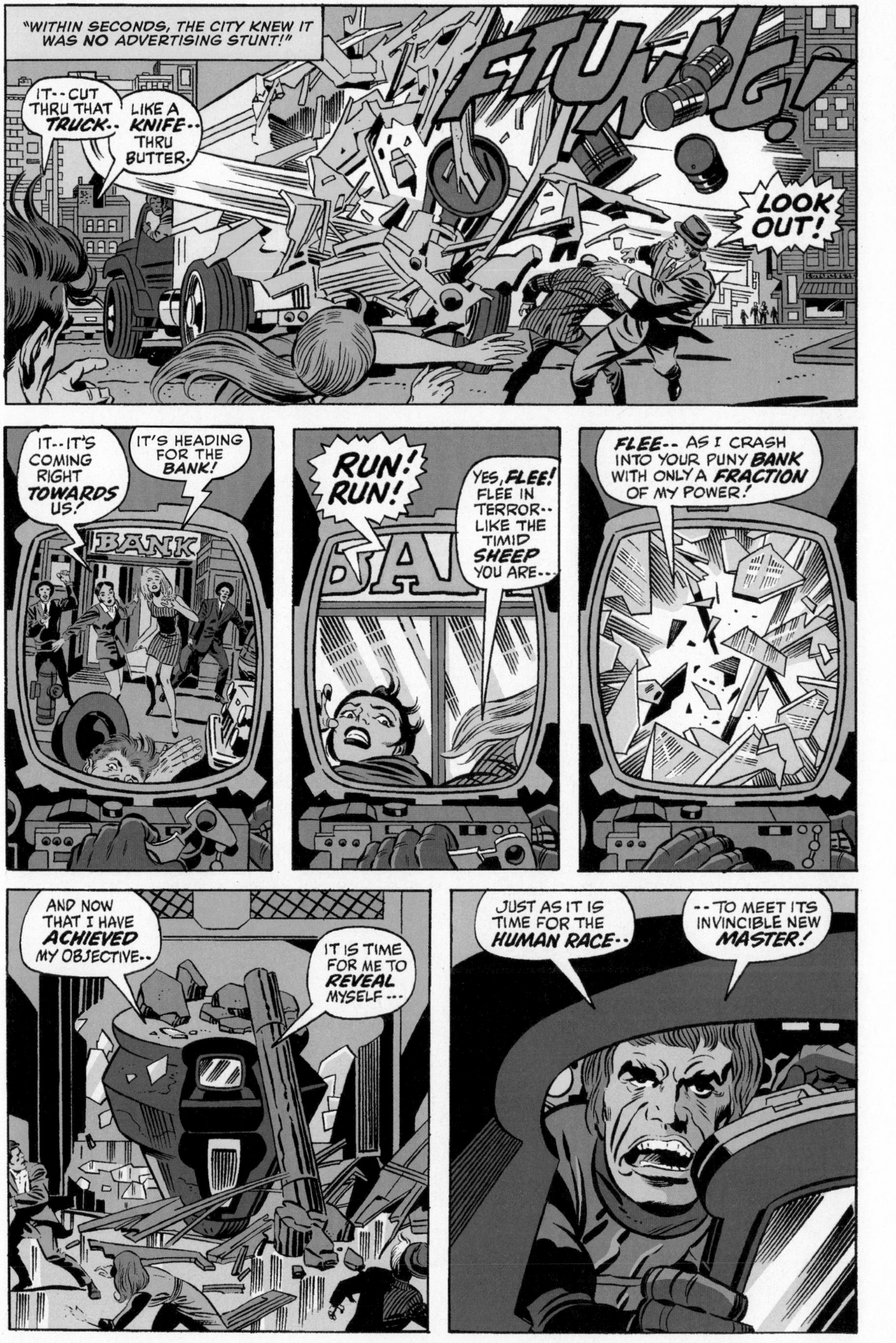
"WITHIN SECONDS, THE CITY KNEW IT WAS NO ADVERTISING STUNT!"
FTUNNG!
IT--CUT THRU THAT TRUCK--
LIKE A KNIFE-- THRU BUTTER.
LOOK OUT!
IT--IT'S COMING RIGHT TOWARDS US!
IT'S HEADING FOR THE BANK!
BANK
RUN! RUN!
YES, FLEE! FLEE IN TERROR-- LIKE THE TIMID SHEEP YOU ARE--
FLEE-- AS I CRASH INTO YOUR PUNY BANK WITH ONLY A FRACTION OF MY POWER!
AND NOW THAT I HAVE ACHIEVED MY OBJECTIVE--
IT IS TIME FOR ME TO REVEAL MYSELF---
JUST AS IT IS TIME FOR THE HUMAN RACE--
--TO MEET ITS INVINCIBLE NEW MASTER!

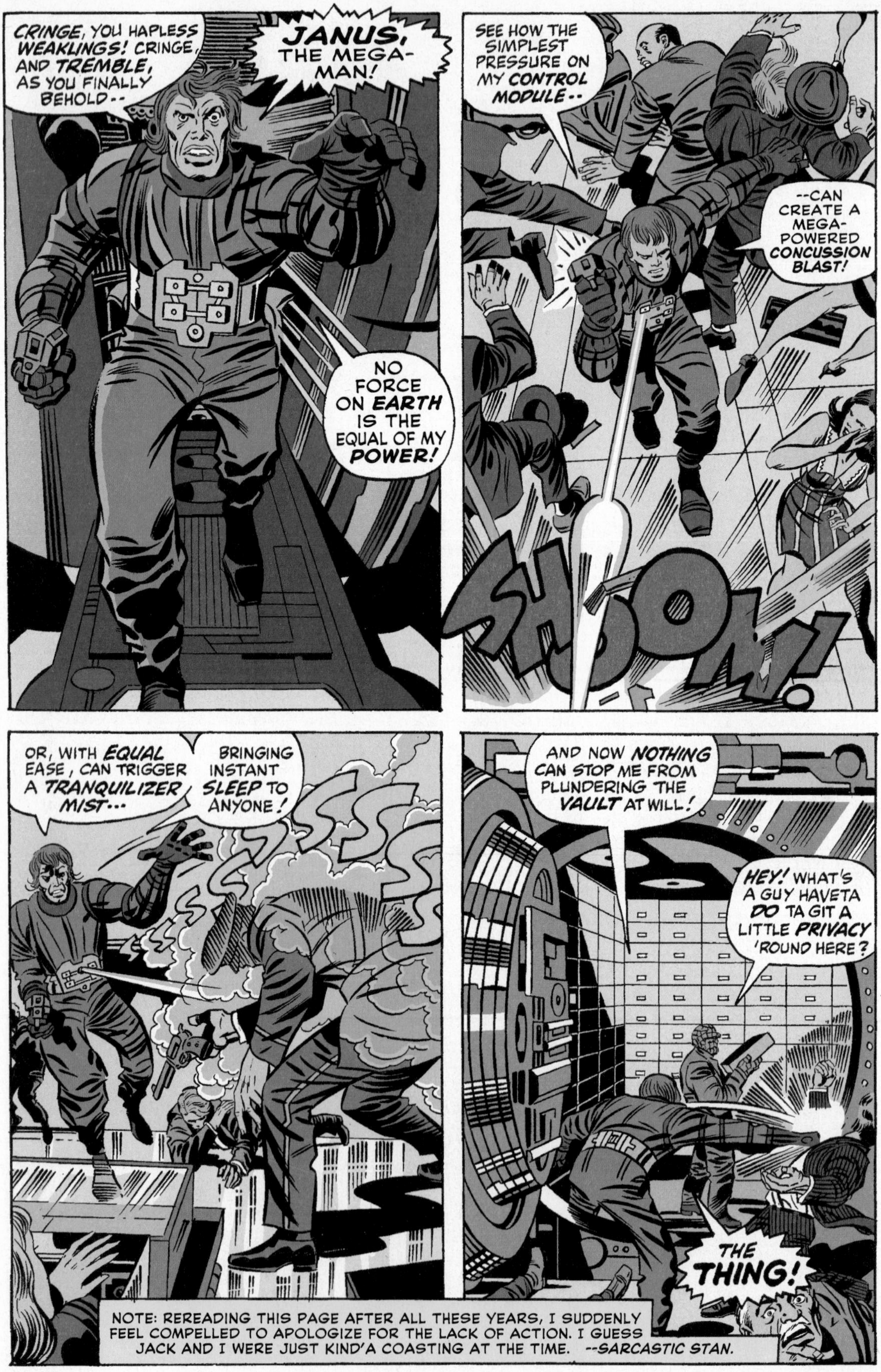
CRINGE, YOU HAPLESS WEAKLINGS! CRINGE, AND TREMBLE, AS YOU FINALLY BEHOLD--
JANUS, THE MEGA-MAN!
NO FORCE ON EARTH IS THE EQUAL OF MY POWER!
SEE HOW THE SIMPLEST PRESSURE ON MY CONTROL MODULE--
--CAN CREATE A MEGA-POWERED CONCUSSION BLAST!
SHOOM!
OR, WITH EQUAL EASE, CAN TRIGGER A TRANQUILIZER MIST...
BRINGING INSTANT SLEEP TO ANYONE!
AND NOW NOTHING CAN STOP ME FROM PLUNDERING THE VAULT AT WILL!
HEY! WHAT'S A GUY HAVETA DO TA GIT A LITTLE PRIVACY 'ROUND HERE?
THE THING!
NOTE: REREADING THIS PAGE AFTER ALL THESE YEARS, I SUDDENLY FEEL COMPELLED TO APOLOGIZE FOR THE LACK OF ACTION. I GUESS JACK AND I WERE JUST KIND'A COASTING AT THE TIME. --SARCASTIC STAN.

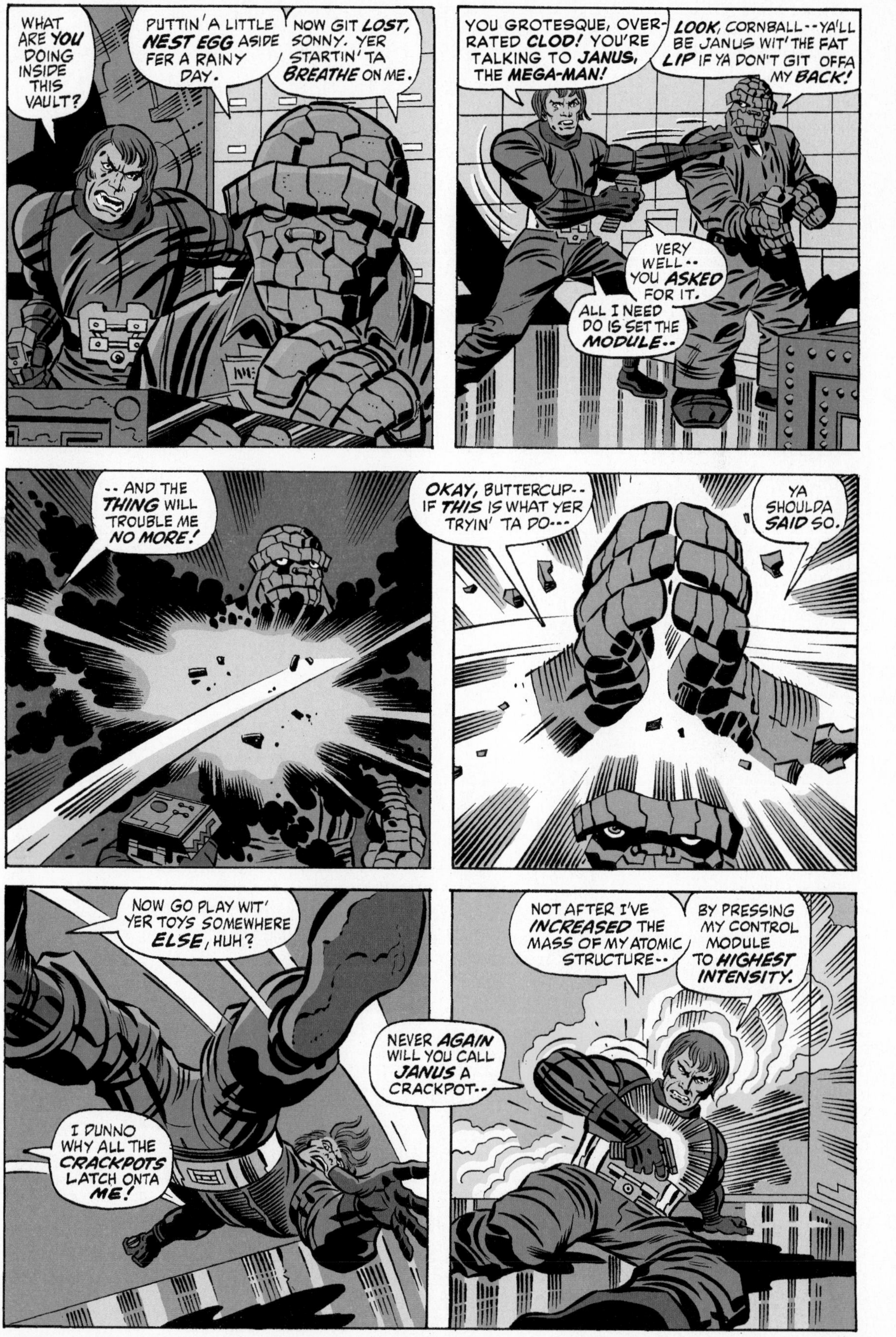
WHAT ARE YOU DOING INSIDE THIS VAULT?
PUTTIN' A LITTLE NEST EGG ASIDE FER A RAINY DAY.
NOW GIT LOST, SONNY. YER STARTIN' TA BREATHE ON ME.
YOU GROTESQUE, OVER-RATED CLOD! YOU'RE TALKING TO JANUS, THE MEGA-MAN!
LOOK, CORNBALL--YA'LL BE JANUS WIT' THE FAT LIP IF YA DON'T GIT OFFA MY BACK!
VERY WELL-- YOU ASKED FOR IT.
ALL I NEED DO IS SET THE MODULE--
-- AND THE THING WILL TROUBLE ME NO MORE!
OKAY, BUTTERCUP-- IF THIS IS WHAT YER TRYIN' TA DO---
YA SHOULDA SAID SO.
NOW GO PLAY WIT' YER TOYS SOMEWHERE ELSE, HUH?
I DUNNO WHY ALL THE CRACKPOTS LATCH ONTA ME!
NOT AFTER I'VE INCREASED THE MASS OF MY ATOMIC STRUCTURE--
BY PRESSING MY CONTROL MODULE TO HIGHEST INTENSITY.
NEVER AGAIN WILL YOU CALL JANUS A CRACKPOT--

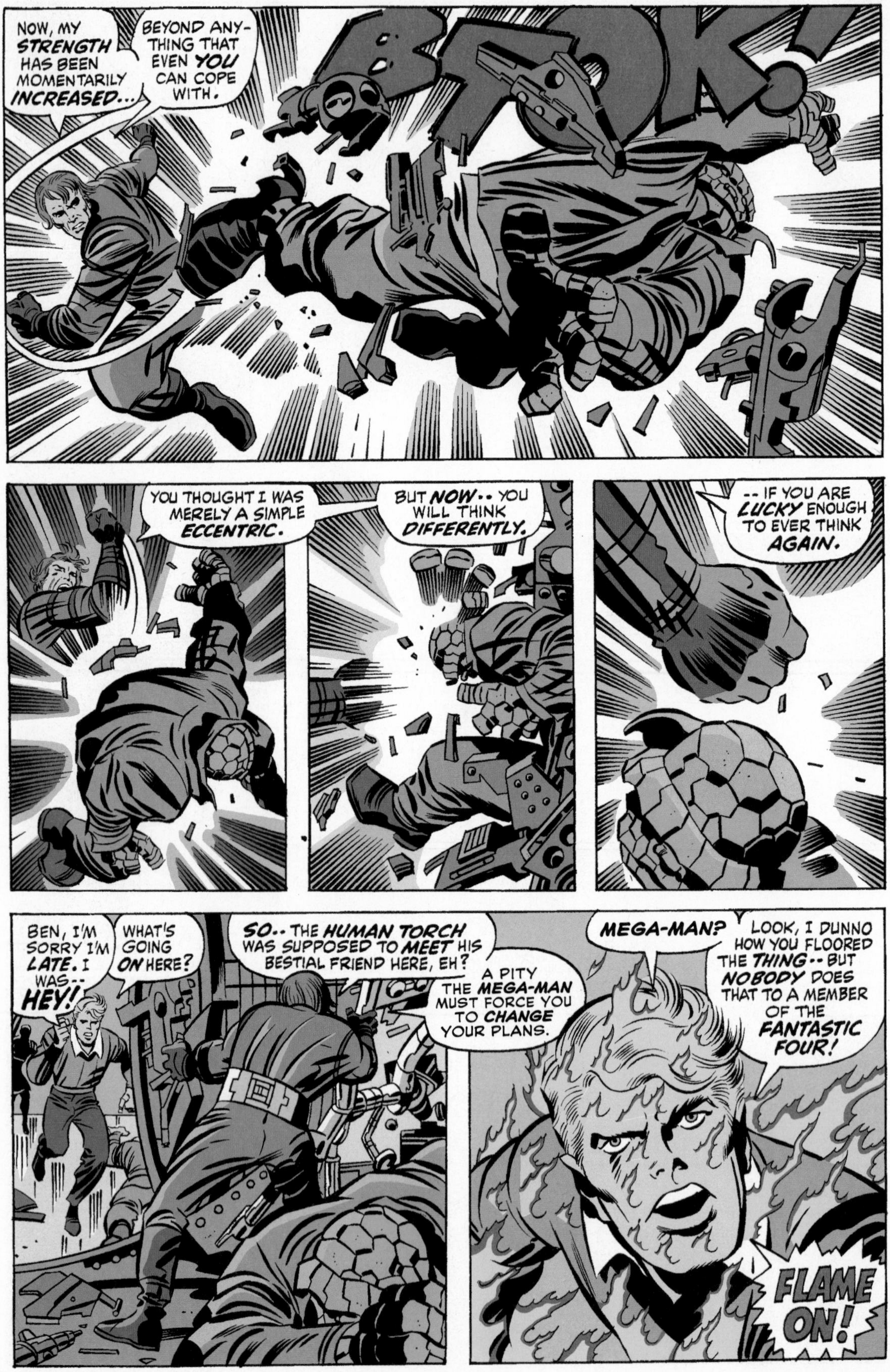
BRAK!
NOW, MY STRENGTH HAS BEEN MOMENTARILY INCREASED...
BEYOND ANYTHING THAT EVEN YOU CAN COPE WITH.
YOU THOUGHT I WAS MERELY A SIMPLE ECCENTRIC.
BUT NOW.. YOU WILL THINK DIFFERENTLY.
-- IF YOU ARE LUCKY ENOUGH TO EVER THINK AGAIN.
BEN, I'M SORRY I'M LATE. I WAS-- HEY!
WHAT'S GOING ON HERE?
SO.. THE HUMAN TORCH WAS SUPPOSED TO MEET HIS BESTIAL FRIEND HERE, EH?
A PITY THE MEGA-MAN MUST FORCE YOU TO CHANGE YOUR PLANS.
MEGA-MAN?
LOOK, I DUNNO HOW YOU FLOORED THE THING -- BUT NOBODY DOES THAT TO A MEMBER OF THE FANTASTIC FOUR!
FLAME ON!

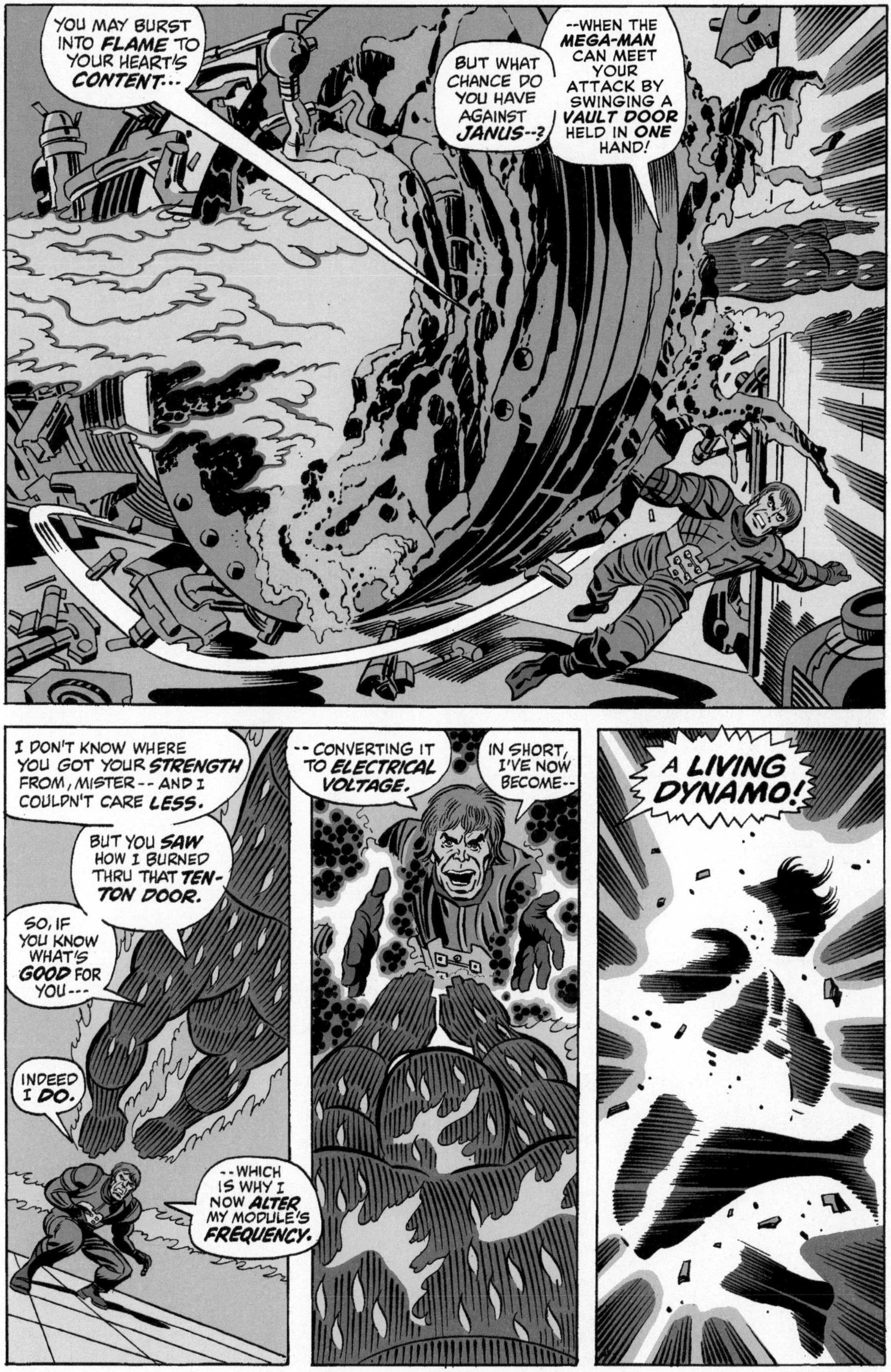
YOU MAY BURST INTO FLAME TO YOUR HEART'S CONTENT...
BUT WHAT CHANCE DO YOU HAVE AGAINST JANUS--?
--WHEN THE MEGA-MAN CAN MEET YOUR ATTACK BY SWINGING A VAULT DOOR HELD IN ONE HAND!
I DON'T KNOW WHERE YOU GOT YOUR STRENGTH FROM, MISTER -- AND I COULDN'T CARE LESS.
BUT YOU SAW HOW I BURNED THRU THAT TEN-TON DOOR.
SO, IF YOU KNOW WHAT'S GOOD FOR YOU---
INDEED I DO.
--WHICH IS WHY I NOW ALTER MY MODULE'S FREQUENCY.
--CONVERTING IT TO ELECTRICAL VOLTAGE.
IN SHORT, I'VE NOW BECOME--
A LIVING DYNAMO!

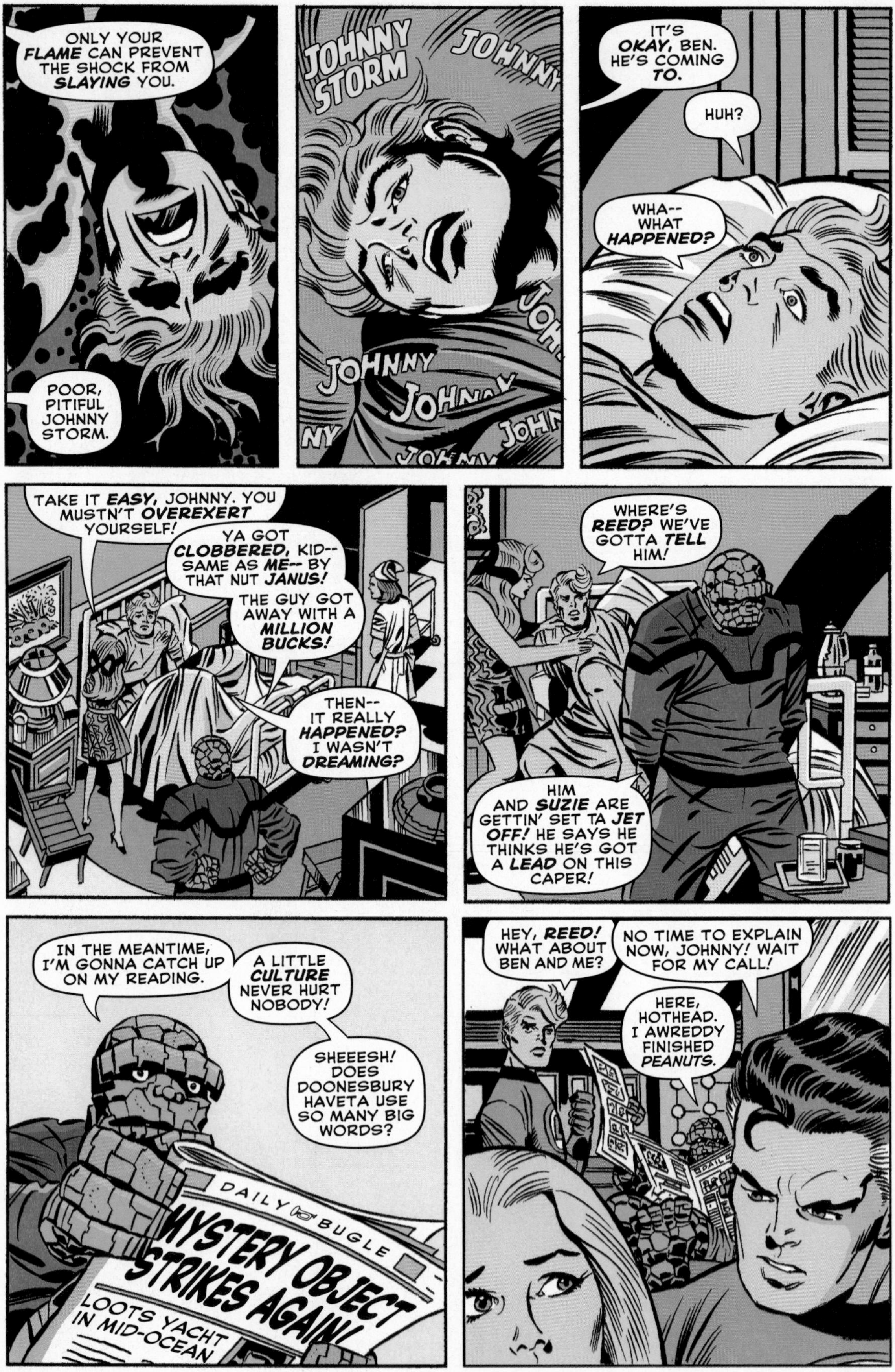
ONLY YOUR FLAME CAN PREVENT THE SHOCK FROM SLAYING YOU.
POOR, PITIFUL JOHNNY STORM.
JOHNNY STORM
JOHNNY
JOHNNY
IT'S OKAY, BEN. HE'S COMING TO.
HUH?
WHA-- WHAT HAPPENED?
TAKE IT EASY, JOHNNY. YOU MUSTN'T OVEREXERT YOURSELF!
YA GOT CLOBBERED, KID-- SAME AS ME-- BY THAT NUT JANUS!
THE GUY GOT AWAY WITH A MILLION BUCKS!
THEN-- IT REALLY HAPPENED? I WASN'T DREAMING?
WHERE'S REED? WE'VE GOTTA TELL HIM!
HIM AND SUZIE ARE GETTIN' SET TA JET OFF! HE SAYS HE THINKS HE'S GOT A LEAD ON THIS CAPER!
IN THE MEANTIME, I'M GONNA CATCH UP ON MY READING.
A LITTLE CULTURE NEVER HURT NOBODY!
SHEEESH! DOES DOONESBURY HAVETA USE SO MANY BIG WORDS?
DAILY BUGLE
MYSTERY OBJECT STRIKES AGAIN!
LOOTS YACHT IN MID-OCEAN
HEY, REED! WHAT ABOUT BEN AND ME?
NO TIME TO EXPLAIN NOW, JOHNNY! WAIT FOR MY CALL!
HERE, HOTHEAD. I AWREDDY FINISHED PEANUTS.

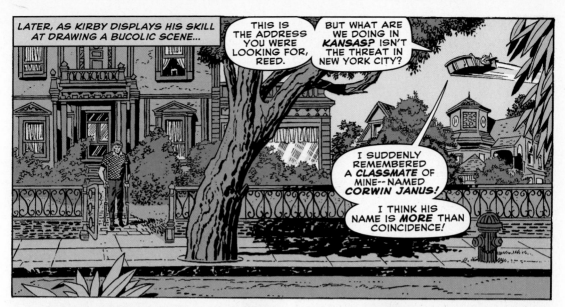

LATER, AS KIRBY DISPLAYS HIS SKILL AT DRAWING A BUCOLIC SCENE...

THIS IS THE ADDRESS YOU WERE LOOKING FOR, REED.

BUT WHAT ARE WE DOING IN *KANSAS?* ISN'T THE THREAT IN NEW YORK CITY?

I SUDDENLY REMEMBERED A *CLASSMATE* OF MINE-- NAMED *CORWIN JANUS!*

I THINK HIS NAME IS *MORE* THAN COINCIDENCE!

THAT'S *HIM!* HE BECAME A RECLUSE AFTER AN ACCIDENT CRIPPLED HIM.

BUT WHAT HAS HE TO DO WITH--?

THAT'S WHAT WE'RE HERE TO FIND OUT!

TURN *INVISIBLE,* DEAR! WHILE I KEEP JANUS OCCUPIED, YOU ENTER HIS HOUSE AND PLANT THIS *MINI-CAMERA!*

THE *FANTASTI-CAR!* I'D RECOGNIZE IT ANYWHERE!

BUT *WHY*--?

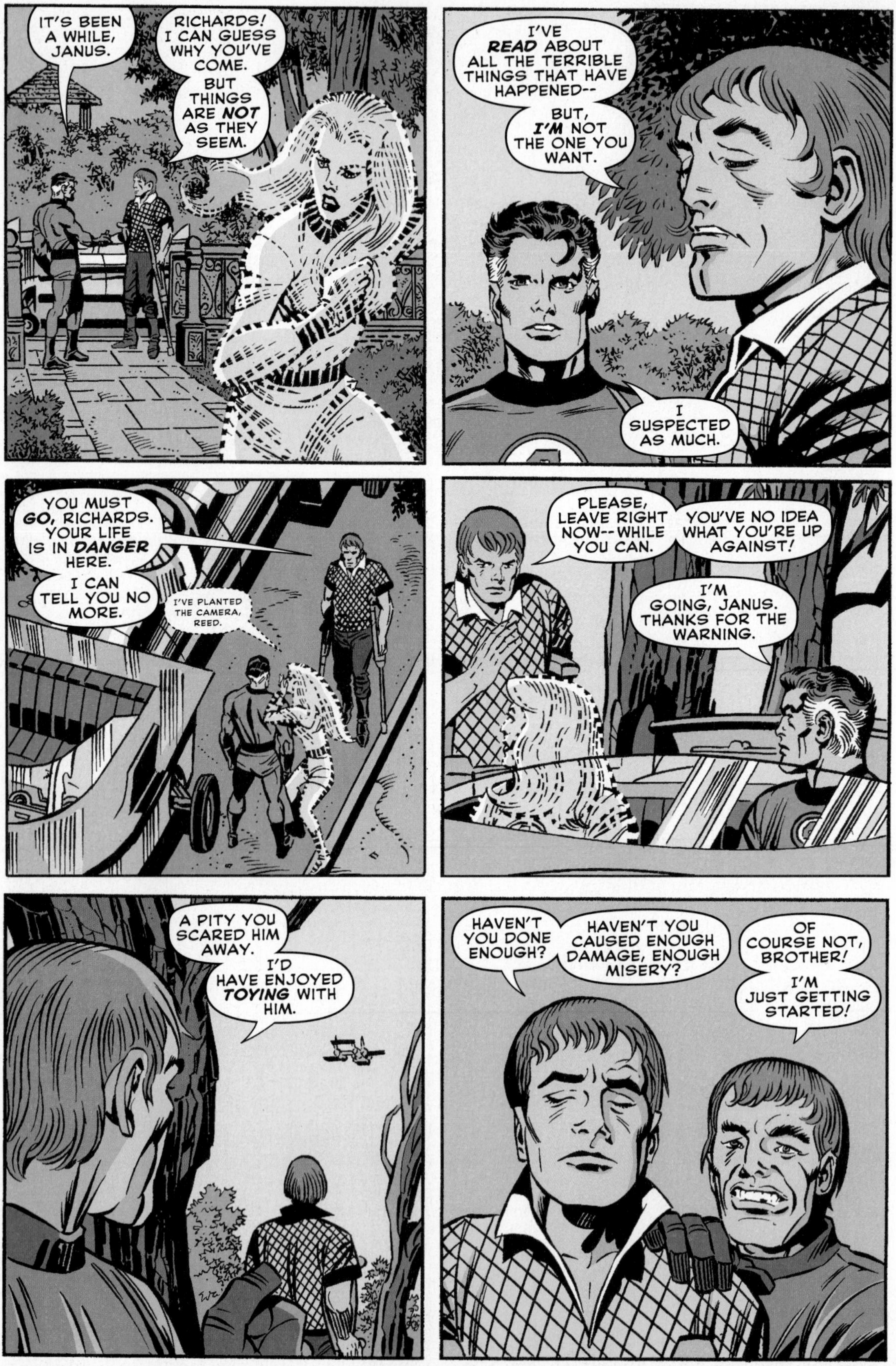
IT'S BEEN A WHILE, JANUS.
RICHARDS! I CAN GUESS WHY YOU'VE COME.
BUT THINGS ARE NOT AS THEY SEEM.
I'VE READ ABOUT ALL THE TERRIBLE THINGS THAT HAVE HAPPENED--
BUT, I'M NOT THE ONE YOU WANT.
I SUSPECTED AS MUCH.
YOU MUST GO, RICHARDS. YOUR LIFE IS IN DANGER HERE.
I CAN TELL YOU NO MORE.
I'VE PLANTED THE CAMERA, REED.
PLEASE, LEAVE RIGHT NOW--WHILE YOU CAN.
YOU'VE NO IDEA WHAT YOU'RE UP AGAINST!
I'M GOING, JANUS. THANKS FOR THE WARNING.
A PITY YOU SCARED HIM AWAY.
I'D HAVE ENJOYED TOYING WITH HIM.
HAVEN'T YOU DONE ENOUGH?
HAVEN'T YOU CAUSED ENOUGH DAMAGE, ENOUGH MISERY?
OF COURSE NOT, BROTHER!
I'M JUST GETTING STARTED!

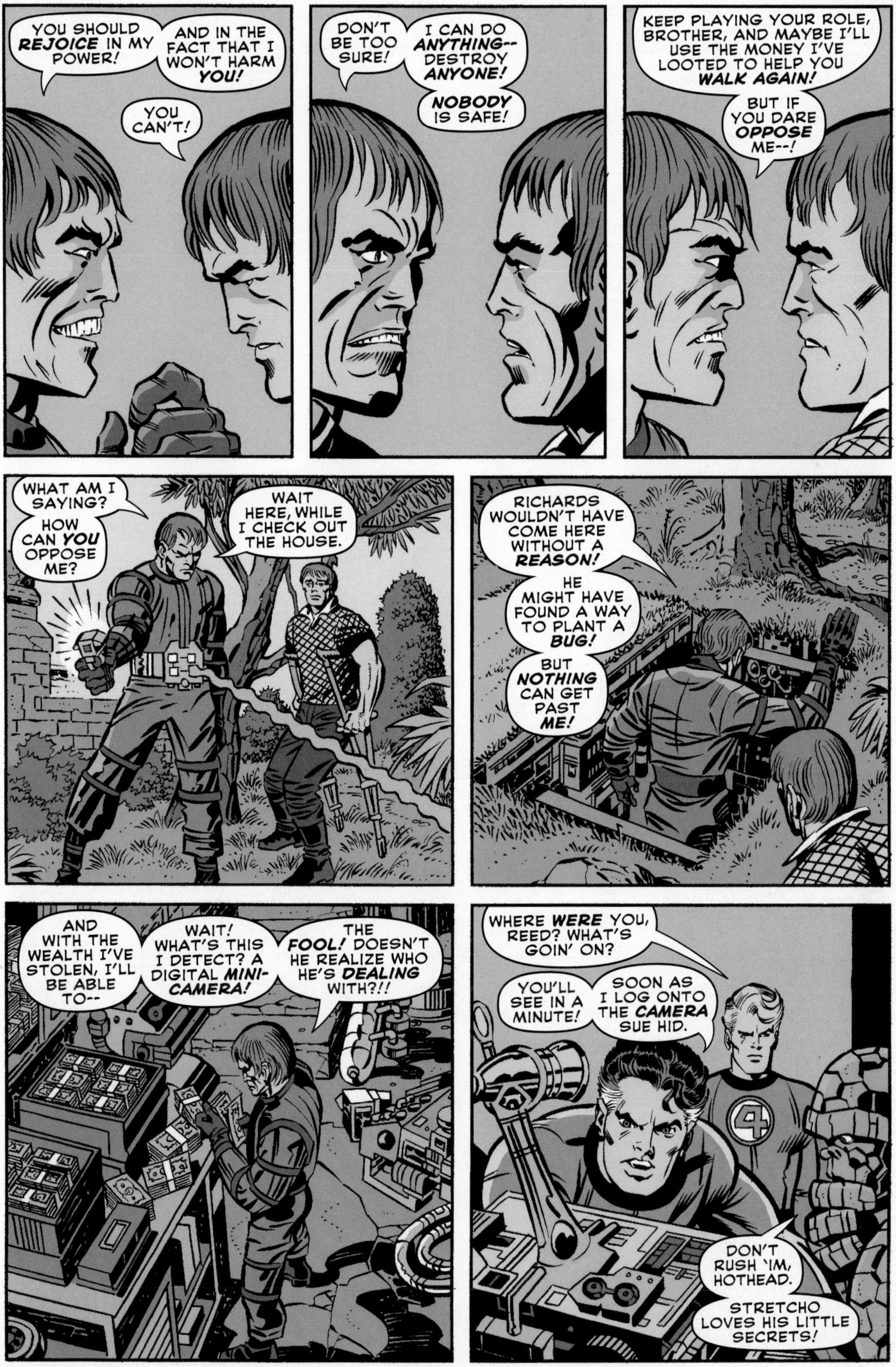
YOU SHOULD REJOICE IN MY POWER!
AND IN THE FACT THAT I WON'T HARM YOU!
YOU CAN'T!
DON'T BE TOO SURE!
I CAN DO ANYTHING-- DESTROY ANYONE!
NOBODY IS SAFE!
KEEP PLAYING YOUR ROLE, BROTHER, AND MAYBE I'LL USE THE MONEY I'VE LOOTED TO HELP YOU WALK AGAIN!
BUT IF YOU DARE OPPOSE ME--!
WHAT AM I SAYING?
HOW CAN YOU OPPOSE ME?
WAIT HERE, WHILE I CHECK OUT THE HOUSE.
RICHARDS WOULDN'T HAVE COME HERE WITHOUT A REASON!
HE MIGHT HAVE FOUND A WAY TO PLANT A BUG!
BUT NOTHING CAN GET PAST ME!
AND WITH THE WEALTH I'VE STOLEN, I'LL BE ABLE TO--
WAIT! WHAT'S THIS I DETECT? A DIGITAL MINI-CAMERA!
THE FOOL! DOESN'T HE REALIZE WHO HE'S DEALING WITH?!!
WHERE WERE YOU, REED? WHAT'S GOIN' ON?
YOU'LL SEE IN A MINUTE!
SOON AS I LOG ONTO THE CAMERA SUE HID.
DON'T RUSH 'IM, HOTHEAD.
STRETCHO LOVES HIS LITTLE SECRETS!

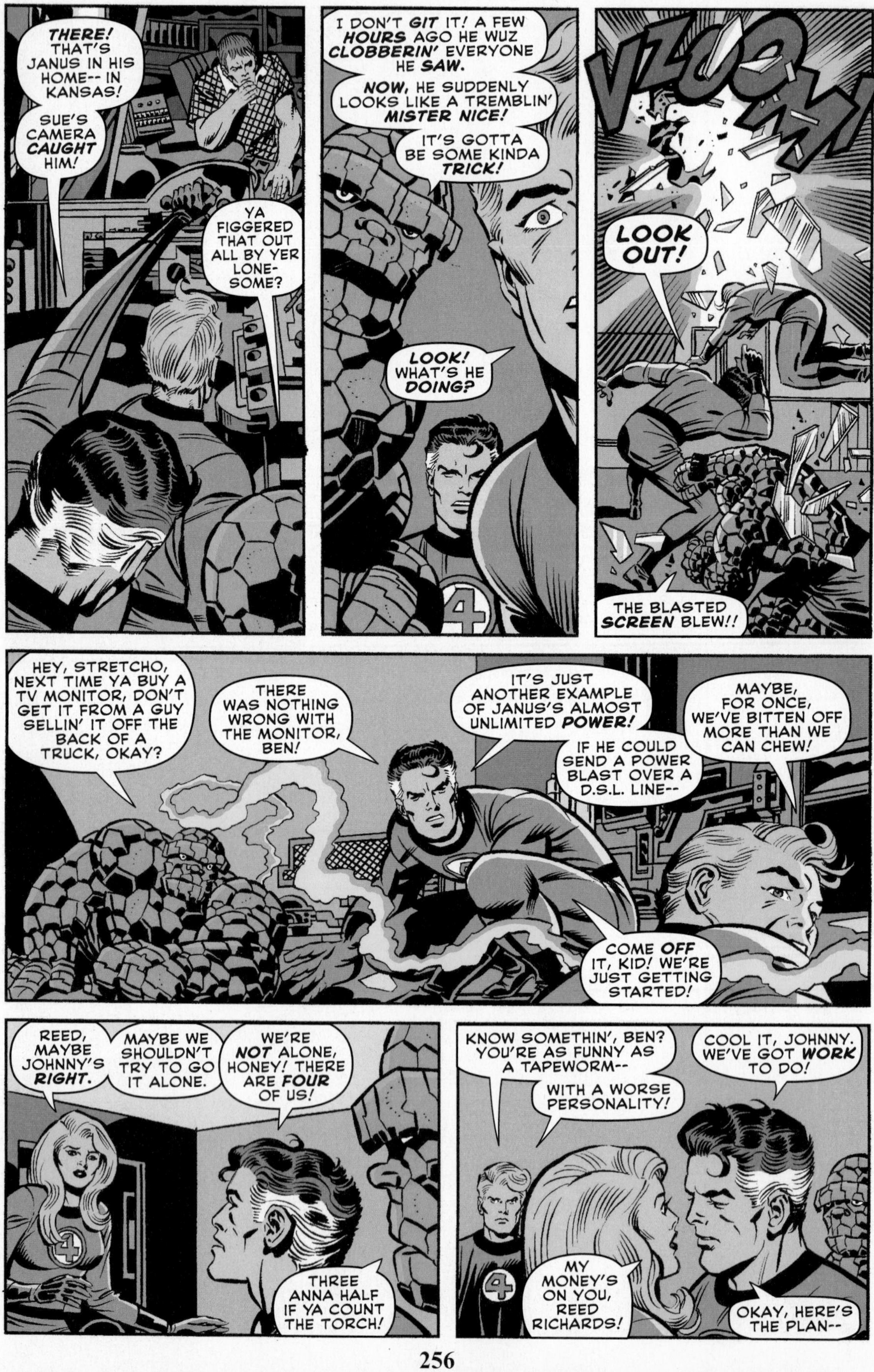
THERE! THAT'S JANUS IN HIS HOME-- IN KANSAS!
SUE'S CAMERA CAUGHT HIM!
YA FIGGERED THAT OUT ALL BY YER LONESOME?
I DON'T GIT IT! A FEW HOURS AGO HE WUZ CLOBBERIN' EVERYONE HE SAW.
NOW, HE SUDDENLY LOOKS LIKE A TREMBLIN' MISTER NICE!
IT'S GOTTA BE SOME KINDA TRICK!
LOOK! WHAT'S HE DOING?
VZOOM
LOOK OUT!
THE BLASTED SCREEN BLEW!!
HEY, STRETCHO, NEXT TIME YA BUY A TV MONITOR, DON'T GET IT FROM A GUY SELLIN' IT OFF THE BACK OF A TRUCK, OKAY?
THERE WAS NOTHING WRONG WITH THE MONITOR, BEN!
IT'S JUST ANOTHER EXAMPLE OF JANUS'S ALMOST UNLIMITED POWER!
IF HE COULD SEND A POWER BLAST OVER A D.S.L. LINE--
MAYBE, FOR ONCE, WE'VE BITTEN OFF MORE THAN WE CAN CHEW!
COME OFF IT, KID! WE'RE JUST GETTING STARTED!
REED, MAYBE JOHNNY'S RIGHT.
MAYBE WE SHOULDN'T TRY TO GO IT ALONE.
WE'RE NOT ALONE, HONEY! THERE ARE FOUR OF US!
THREE ANNA HALF IF YA COUNT THE TORCH!
KNOW SOMETHIN', BEN? YOU'RE AS FUNNY AS A TAPEWORM--
WITH A WORSE PERSONALITY!
COOL IT, JOHNNY. WE'VE GOT WORK TO DO!
MY MONEY'S ON YOU, REED RICHARDS!
OKAY, HERE'S THE PLAN--

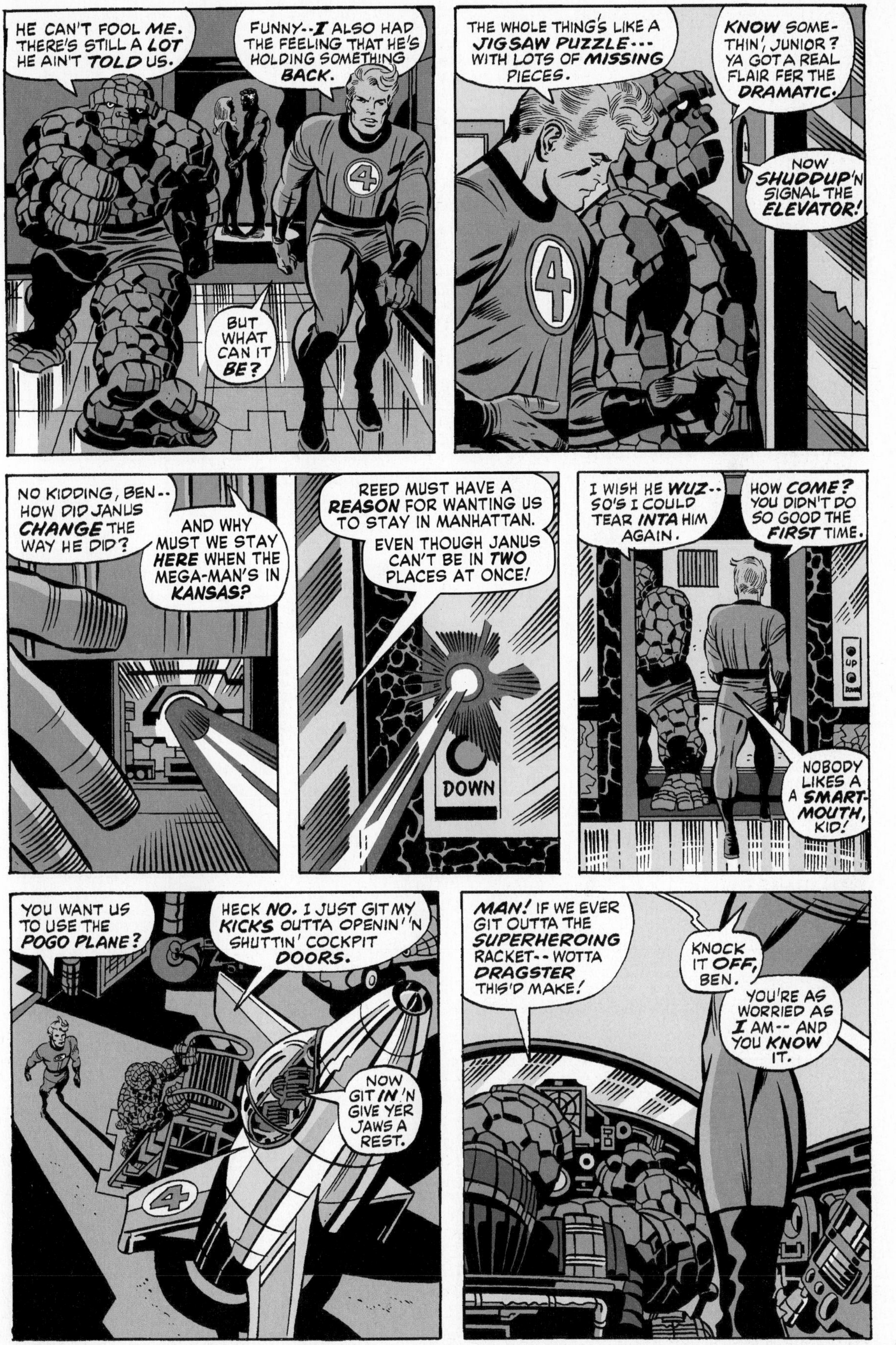
HE CAN'T FOOL ME. THERE'S STILL A LOT HE AIN'T TOLD US.
FUNNY--I ALSO HAD THE FEELING THAT HE'S HOLDING SOMETHING BACK.
BUT WHAT CAN IT BE?
THE WHOLE THING'S LIKE A JIGSAW PUZZLE--- WITH LOTS OF MISSING PIECES.
KNOW SOME-THIN', JUNIOR? YA GOT A REAL FLAIR FER THE DRAMATIC.
NOW SHUDDUP'N SIGNAL THE ELEVATOR!
NO KIDDING, BEN-- HOW DID JANUS CHANGE THE WAY HE DID?
AND WHY MUST WE STAY HERE WHEN THE MEGA-MAN'S IN KANSAS?
REED MUST HAVE A REASON FOR WANTING US TO STAY IN MANHATTAN.
EVEN THOUGH JANUS CAN'T BE IN TWO PLACES AT ONCE!
DOWN
I WISH HE WUZ-- SO'S I COULD TEAR INTA HIM AGAIN.
HOW COME? YOU DIDN'T DO SO GOOD THE FIRST TIME.
UP
DOWN
NOBODY LIKES A SMART-MOUTH, KID!
YOU WANT US TO USE THE POGO PLANE?
HECK NO. I JUST GIT MY KICKS OUTTA OPENIN' 'N SHUTTIN' COCKPIT DOORS.
NOW GIT IN 'N GIVE YER JAWS A REST.
MAN! IF WE EVER GIT OUTTA THE SUPERHEROING RACKET-- WOTTA DRAGSTER THIS'D MAKE!
KNOCK IT OFF, BEN.
YOU'RE AS WORRIED AS I AM-- AND YOU KNOW IT.

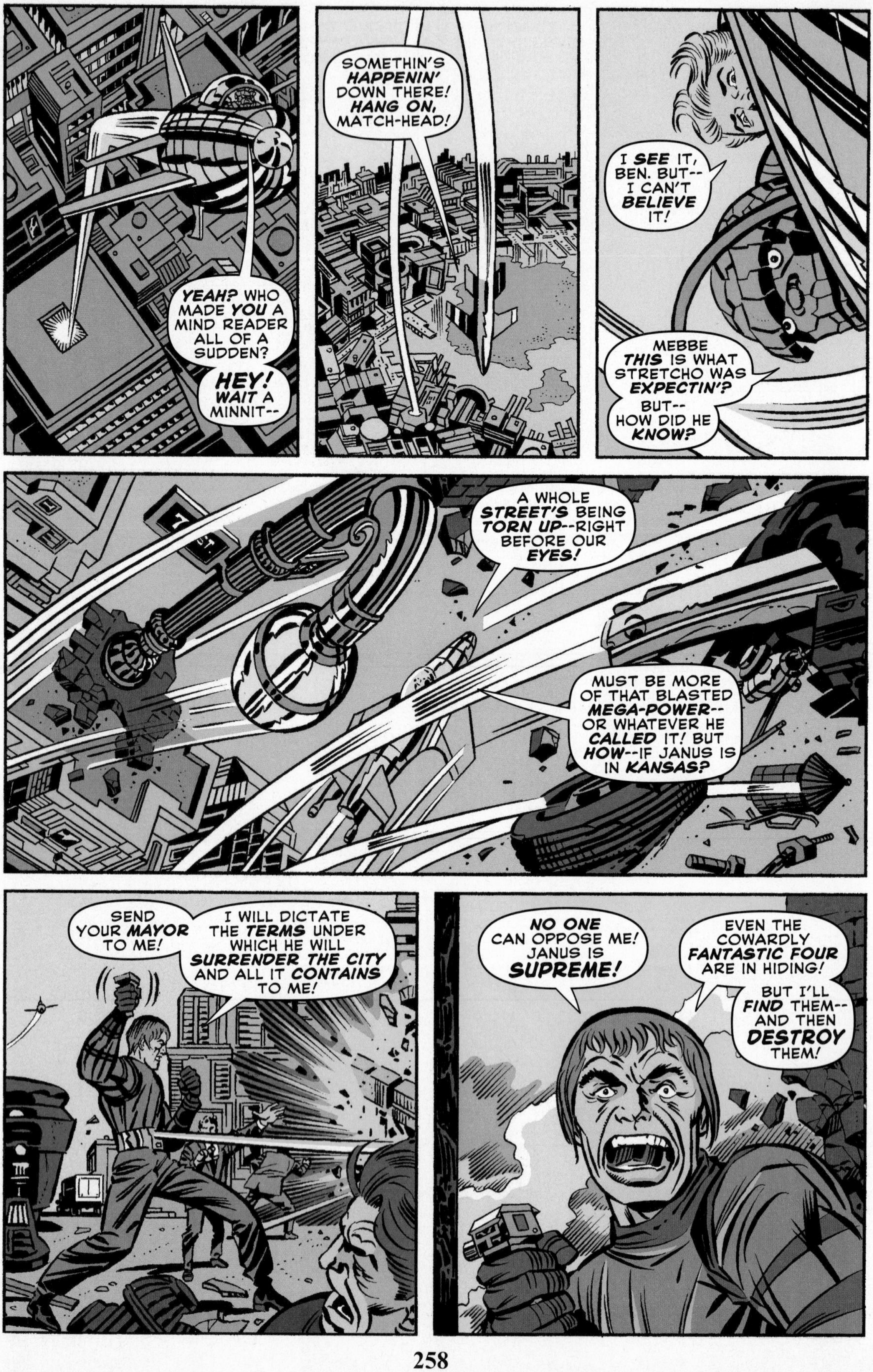
YEAH? WHO MADE YOU A MIND READER ALL OF A SUDDEN?
HEY! WAIT A MINNIT--
SOMETHIN'S HAPPENIN' DOWN THERE! HANG ON, MATCH-HEAD!
I SEE IT, BEN. BUT-- I CAN'T BELIEVE IT!
MEBBE THIS IS WHAT STRETCHO WAS EXPECTIN'? BUT-- HOW DID HE KNOW?
A WHOLE STREET'S BEING TORN UP--RIGHT BEFORE OUR EYES!
MUST BE MORE OF THAT BLASTED MEGA-POWER-- OR WHATEVER HE CALLED IT! BUT HOW--IF JANUS IS IN KANSAS?
SEND YOUR MAYOR TO ME!
I WILL DICTATE THE TERMS UNDER WHICH HE WILL SURRENDER THE CITY AND ALL IT CONTAINS TO ME!
NO ONE CAN OPPOSE ME! JANUS IS SUPREME!
EVEN THE COWARDLY FANTASTIC FOUR ARE IN HIDING!
BUT I'LL FIND THEM-- AND THEN DESTROY THEM!

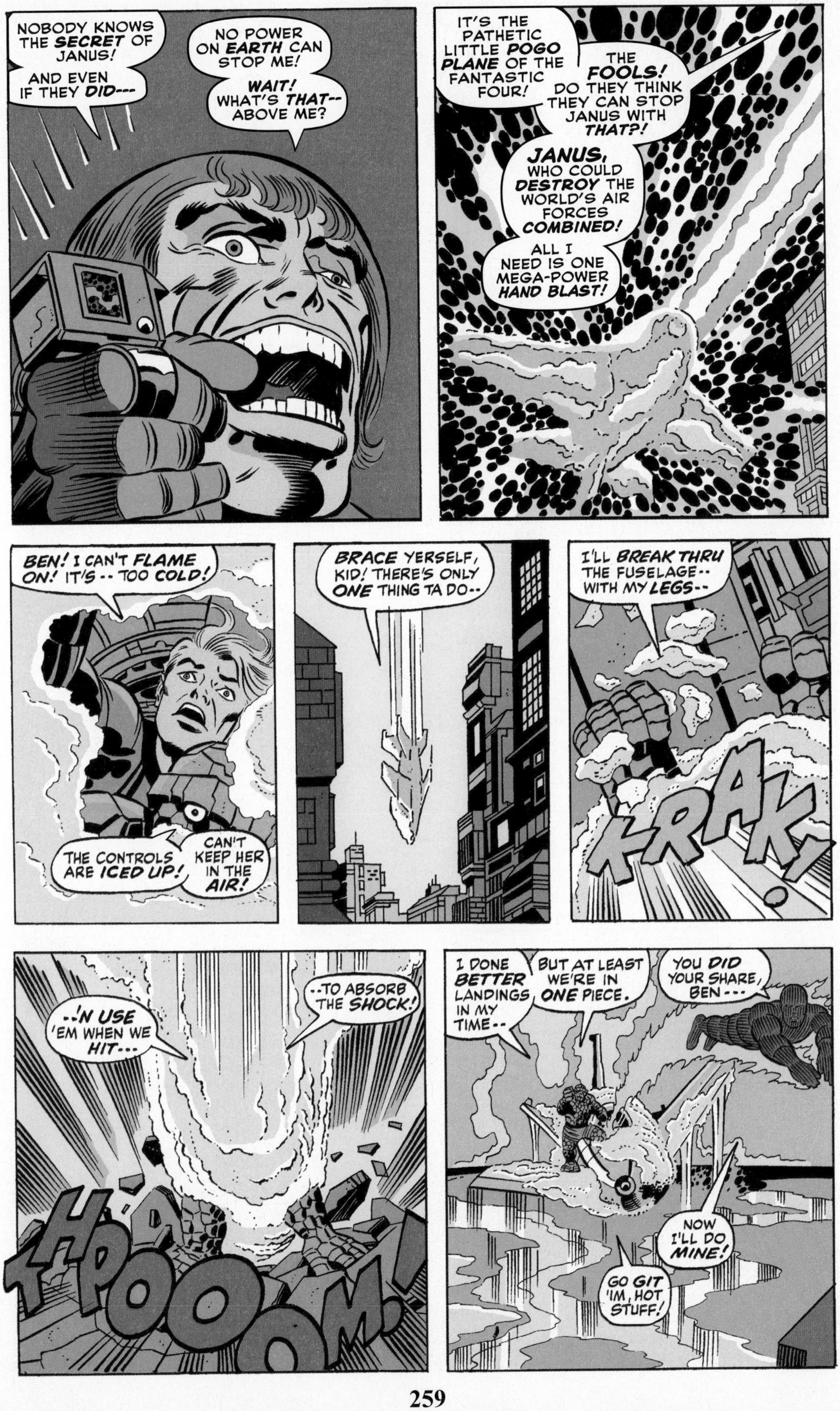
NOBODY KNOWS THE SECRET OF JANUS!
AND EVEN IF THEY DID---
NO POWER ON EARTH CAN STOP ME!
WAIT! WHAT'S THAT-- ABOVE ME?
IT'S THE PATHETIC LITTLE POGO PLANE OF THE FANTASTIC FOUR!
THE FOOLS! DO THEY THINK THEY CAN STOP JANUS WITH THAT?!
JANUS, WHO COULD DESTROY THE WORLD'S AIR FORCES COMBINED!
ALL I NEED IS ONE MEGA-POWER HAND BLAST!
BEN! I CAN'T FLAME ON! IT'S -- TOO COLD!
THE CONTROLS ARE ICED UP!
CAN'T KEEP HER IN THE AIR!
BRACE YERSELF, KID! THERE'S ONLY ONE THING TA DO--
I'LL BREAK THRU THE FUSELAGE-- WITH MY LEGS--
KRAK!
--'N USE 'EM WHEN WE HIT---
--TO ABSORB THE SHOCK!
THPOOOM!
I DONE BETTER LANDINGS IN MY TIME--
BUT AT LEAST WE'RE IN ONE PIECE.
YOU DID YOUR SHARE, BEN---
NOW I'LL DO MINE!
GO GIT 'IM, HOT STUFF!

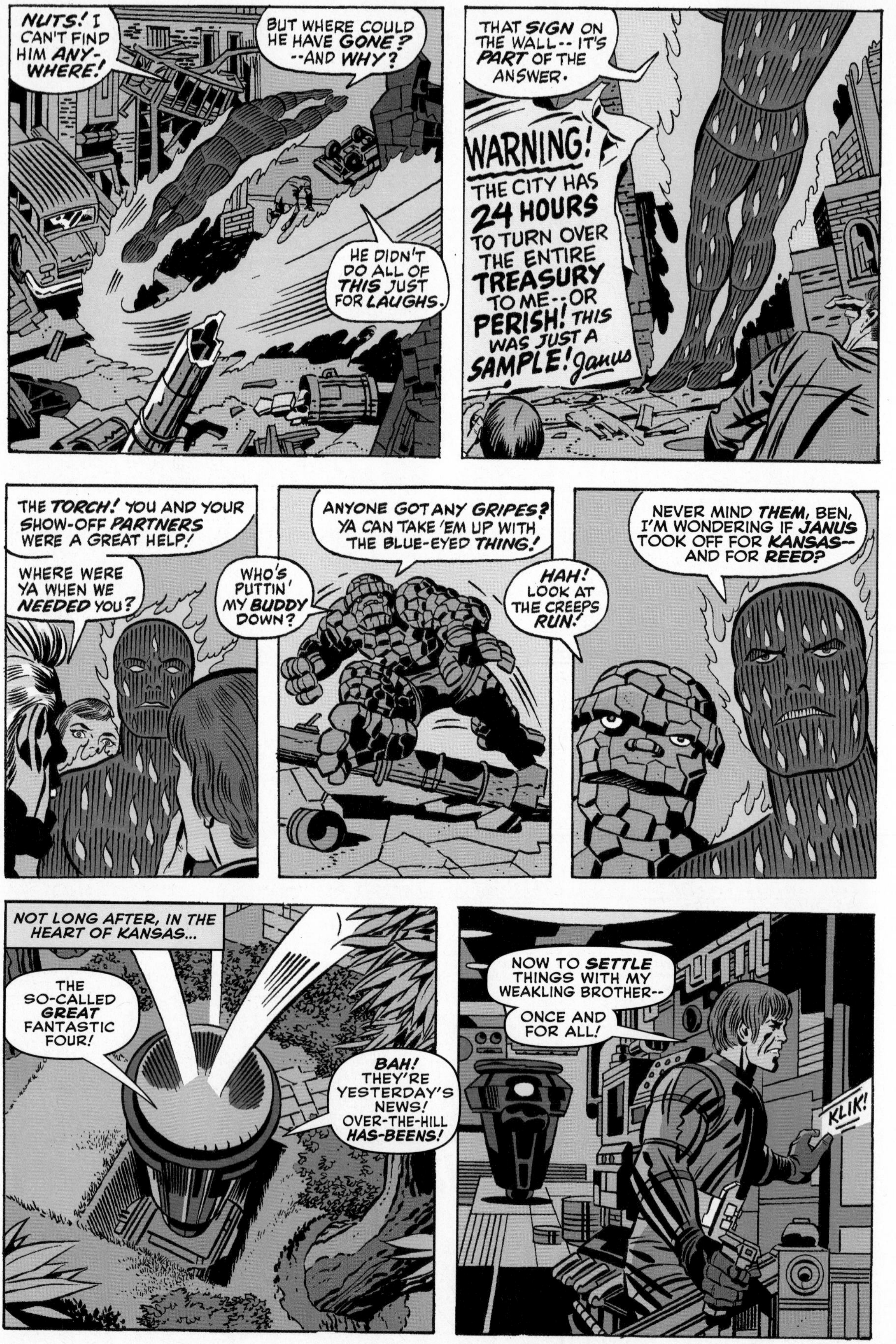
NUTS! I CAN'T FIND HIM ANY-WHERE!
BUT WHERE COULD HE HAVE GONE? --AND WHY?
HE DIDN'T DO ALL OF THIS JUST FOR LAUGHS.
THAT SIGN ON THE WALL-- IT'S PART OF THE ANSWER.
WARNING! THE CITY HAS 24 HOURS TO TURN OVER THE ENTIRE TREASURY TO ME--OR PERISH! THIS WAS JUST A SAMPLE! Janus
THE TORCH! YOU AND YOUR SHOW-OFF PARTNERS WERE A GREAT HELP!
WHERE WERE YA WHEN WE NEEDED YOU?
ANYONE GOT ANY GRIPES? YA CAN TAKE 'EM UP WITH THE BLUE-EYED THING!
WHO'S PUTTIN' MY BUDDY DOWN?
HAH! LOOK AT THE CREEPS RUN!
NEVER MIND THEM, BEN, I'M WONDERING IF JANUS TOOK OFF FOR KANSAS-- AND FOR REED?
NOT LONG AFTER, IN THE HEART OF KANSAS...
THE SO-CALLED GREAT FANTASTIC FOUR!
BAH! THEY'RE YESTERDAY'S NEWS! OVER-THE-HILL HAS-BEENS!
NOW TO SETTLE THINGS WITH MY WEAKLING BROTHER--
ONCE AND FOR ALL!
KLIK!

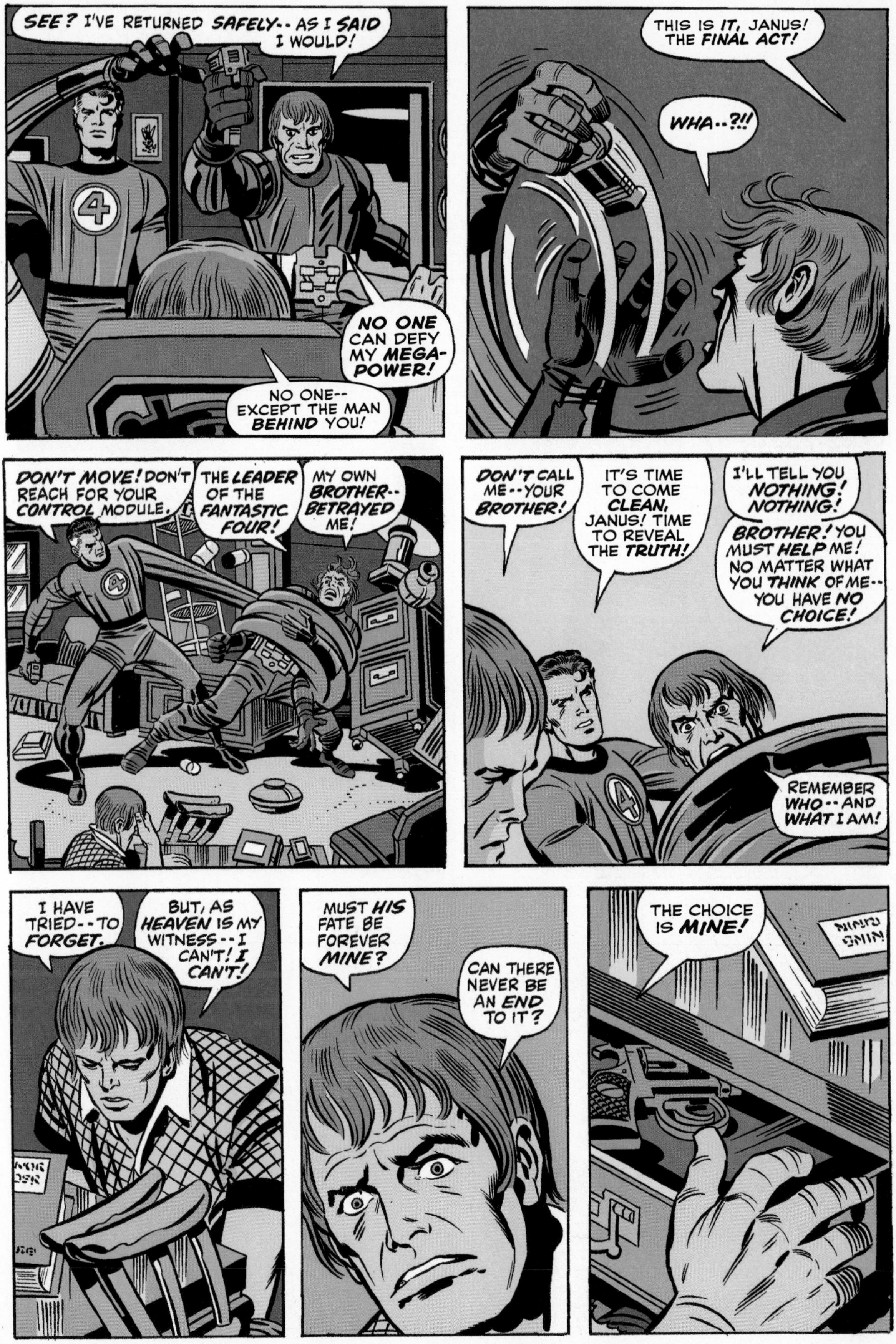
SEE? I'VE RETURNED SAFELY-- AS I SAID I WOULD!
NO ONE CAN DEFY MY MEGA-POWER!
NO ONE-- EXCEPT THE MAN BEHIND YOU!
THIS IS IT, JANUS! THE FINAL ACT!
WHA--?!!
DON'T MOVE! DON'T REACH FOR YOUR CONTROL MODULE.
THE LEADER OF THE FANTASTIC FOUR!
MY OWN BROTHER-- BETRAYED ME!
DON'T CALL ME--YOUR BROTHER!
IT'S TIME TO COME CLEAN, JANUS! TIME TO REVEAL THE TRUTH!
I'LL TELL YOU NOTHING! NOTHING!
BROTHER! YOU MUST HELP ME! NO MATTER WHAT YOU THINK OF ME-- YOU HAVE NO CHOICE!
REMEMBER WHO-- AND WHAT I AM!
I HAVE TRIED--TO FORGET.
BUT, AS HEAVEN IS MY WITNESS--I CAN'T! I CAN'T!
MUST HIS FATE BE FOREVER MINE?
CAN THERE NEVER BE AN END TO IT?
THE CHOICE IS MINE!

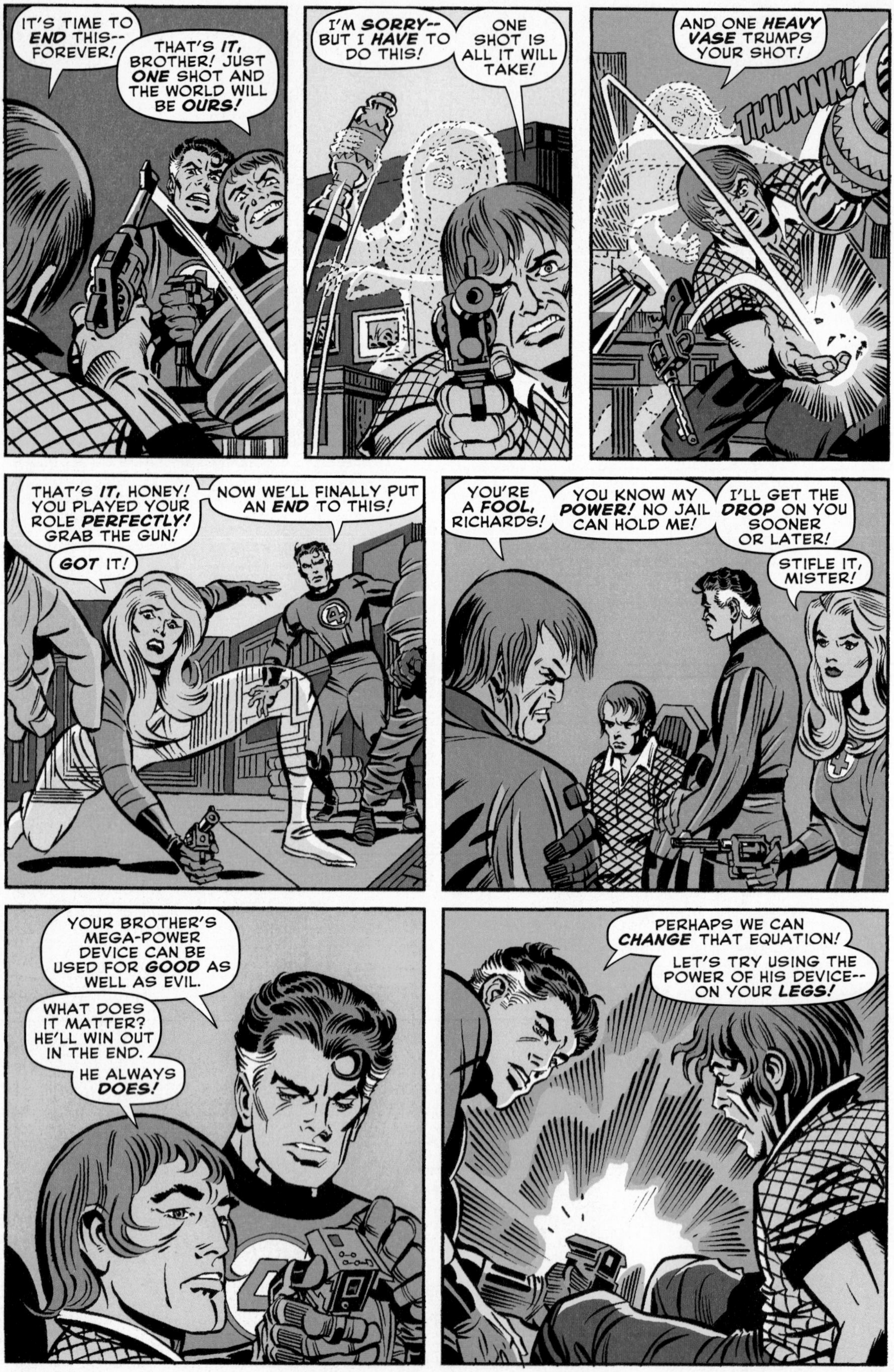
IT'S TIME TO END THIS-- FOREVER!
THAT'S IT, BROTHER! JUST ONE SHOT AND THE WORLD WILL BE OURS!
I'M SORRY-- BUT I HAVE TO DO THIS!
ONE SHOT IS ALL IT WILL TAKE!
AND ONE HEAVY VASE TRUMPS YOUR SHOT!
THUNNK!
THAT'S IT, HONEY! YOU PLAYED YOUR ROLE PERFECTLY! GRAB THE GUN!
NOW WE'LL FINALLY PUT AN END TO THIS!
GOT IT!
YOU'RE A FOOL, RICHARDS!
YOU KNOW MY POWER! NO JAIL CAN HOLD ME!
I'LL GET THE DROP ON YOU SOONER OR LATER!
STIFLE IT, MISTER!
YOUR BROTHER'S MEGA-POWER DEVICE CAN BE USED FOR GOOD AS WELL AS EVIL.
WHAT DOES IT MATTER? HE'LL WIN OUT IN THE END.
HE ALWAYS DOES!
PERHAPS WE CAN CHANGE THAT EQUATION!
LET'S TRY USING THE POWER OF HIS DEVICE-- ON YOUR LEGS!

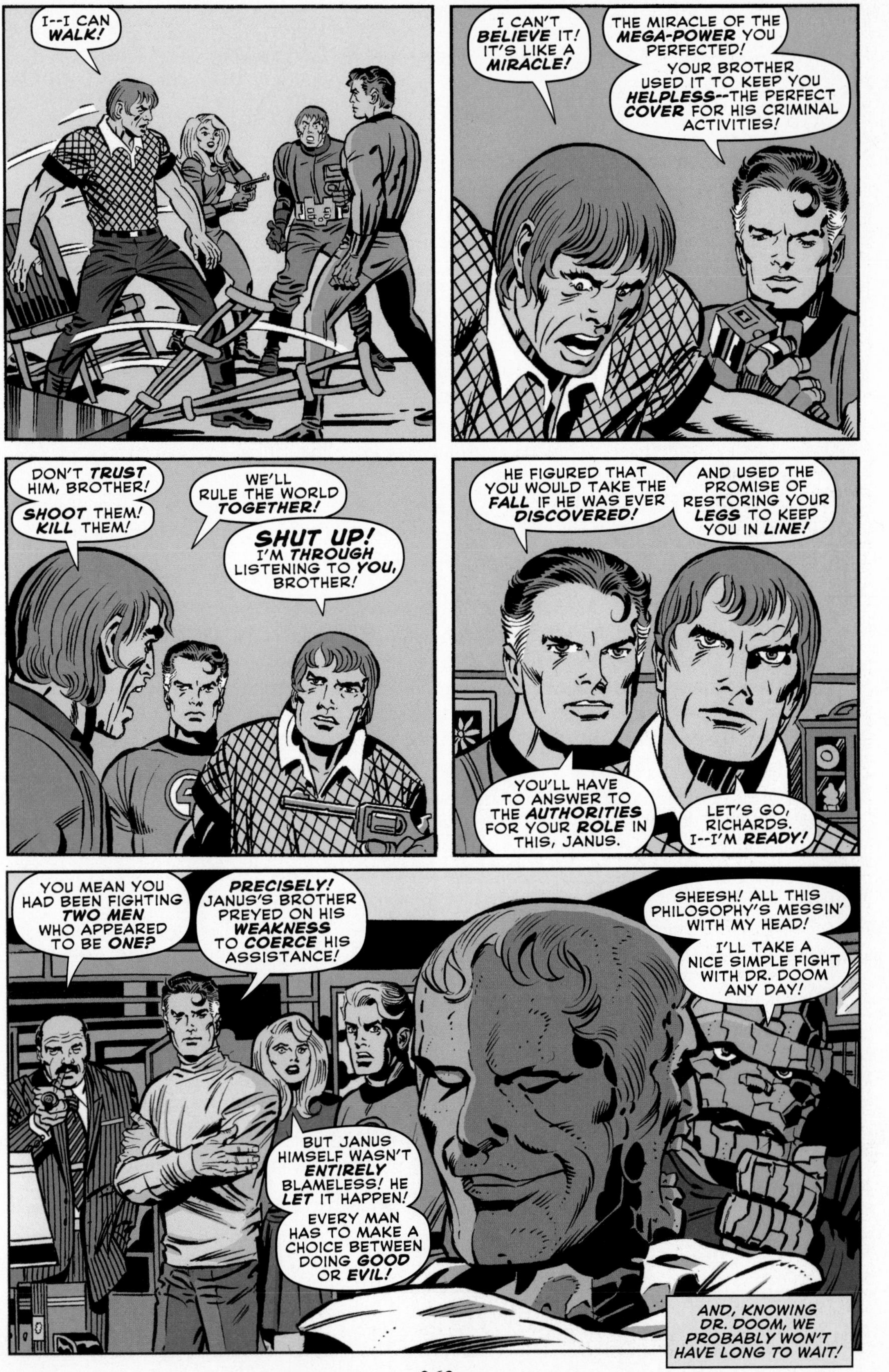
I--I CAN WALK!
I CAN'T BELIEVE IT! IT'S LIKE A MIRACLE!
THE MIRACLE OF THE MEGA-POWER YOU PERFECTED!
YOUR BROTHER USED IT TO KEEP YOU HELPLESS--THE PERFECT COVER FOR HIS CRIMINAL ACTIVITIES!
DON'T TRUST HIM, BROTHER!
SHOOT THEM! KILL THEM!
WE'LL RULE THE WORLD TOGETHER!
SHUT UP! I'M THROUGH LISTENING TO YOU, BROTHER!
HE FIGURED THAT YOU WOULD TAKE THE FALL IF HE WAS EVER DISCOVERED!
AND USED THE PROMISE OF RESTORING YOUR LEGS TO KEEP YOU IN LINE!
YOU'LL HAVE TO ANSWER TO THE AUTHORITIES FOR YOUR ROLE IN THIS, JANUS.
LET'S GO, RICHARDS. I--I'M READY!
YOU MEAN YOU HAD BEEN FIGHTING TWO MEN WHO APPEARED TO BE ONE?
PRECISELY! JANUS'S BROTHER PREYED ON HIS WEAKNESS TO COERCE HIS ASSISTANCE!
BUT JANUS HIMSELF WASN'T ENTIRELY BLAMELESS! HE LET IT HAPPEN!
EVERY MAN HAS TO MAKE A CHOICE BETWEEN DOING GOOD OR EVIL!
SHEESH! ALL THIS PHILOSOPHY'S MESSIN' WITH MY HEAD!
I'LL TAKE A NICE SIMPLE FIGHT WITH DR. DOOM ANY DAY!
AND, KNOWING DR. DOOM, WE PROBABLY WON'T HAVE LONG TO WAIT!

INSPIRATION
BY DICK AYERS

Working with Stan and Jack was an inspiration.

It started with a telephone call from Stan in which he said he realized I always preferred to do my own penciling, inking and lettering ever since I started working for him in October 1951 and it was then August 1959. Stan asked me to ink a cover for *Wyatt Earp* that Jack Kirby had penciled. I inked it, but I wasn't happy with it because I had just inked as it was penciled. Stan must've seen something he liked for he sent me a six-page monster story, "Monstro, The Menace From The Murky Depths." That story inspired me so much I had fun drawing over the pencils, and Stan liked the inking I did enough that he wrote me a letter in praise of the job that I have framed and hanging on the wall in my studio.

Jack Kirby evidently liked my inking of his monster penciling. He asked me to take the place of Wally Wood and ink his Sunday and Daily *Sky Masters* newspaper strip. That I did from September 1959 until December 1960—123 weeks total. At the same time I was inking the Atlas monster stories and a lot of super-hero stories that were showing increased signs of popularity.

And then, in March 1962, Stan assigned me the sixth issue of *Fantastic Four* to ink. Jack Kirby, of course, penciled. It wasn't our first time working together but, I might say, it was our first time on a tight deadline schedule. I think the three of us thrived on tight schedules. Stan would always put the "date due" at the top of his script's first page and I would always try to be a day or two ahead of that. With Jack there was two deadlines. His *Sky Masters* would always arrive Special Delivery at 7:30 a.m. He was never late either. Stan had a system where, if I hand-delivered a story, he'd hand me a script and, if I was mailing the story and telephoned him the day before, he'd special delivery mail it so I'd have the story the next day and not lose a day's production. We became a trio that must've been a publisher's dream.

I don't think Jack had the advantage I had inking his pencils. Artie Simek lettered the penciled pages before I got them to ink and that meant I got to read Stan's captions and dialog as I inked! I'd get to sense the dramatics Stan wanted and inked accordingly. Jack had the blank page and possibly a synopsis to guide him. To this day when I write a story or a graphic novel, as I am doing this week as I write, I write and letter my story first and then draw to fit my writing with the drawing. That is the benefit of illustrating Stan's scripts. We worked that way for a long time. A telephoned synopsis would more than suffice.

Of all the villains in *Fantastic Four* that I inked, I have one favorite... he's from *FF #7*... his name is Kurrgo, Master of Planet X. It happened that I parted with that page for what amounted to $75.00! And a short time ago I saw it advertised for $2,000.00! I was awakened to an important philosophy. Think about something more than drawing or illustrating—think business.

Dick Ayers

2006

Stan Lee's letter praising Dick Ayers' inking work over Jack Kirby on *Tales of Suspense* #8's "Monstro." On the basis of his exceptional work on this story, Ayers would become Kirby's main inker at Marvel for the next five years.

MAGAZINE MANAGEMENT COMPANY
655 MADISON AVENUE, NEW YORK 21, N.Y. • TEmpleton 8-7900

8/25/59

Dick:

You did a swell job inking Kirby's MONSTRO
story.

So, here's the cover of that mag for you to ink,
also. It's due this Friday 8/28 if possible--
if not, Monday will be okay.

I've enclosed another 6-page strip as well for you
to ink. It It has a long deadline-- I won't need it
till Septemeber 10th. Of course, if you send it
to me sooner, that's fine-- but you needn't rush.

I'll try to send you as much inking as I can--- don't
expect TOO much because we don't HAVE that much--
these twelve pages in a row is an unusual situation...
however, whatever DOES come along I'll give you first
crack at.

All best-

ON, AND ON!
BY JOE SINNOTT

To comment on my association with Stan Lee and Jack Kirby on our incredible run with *The Fantastic Four* is a monumental challenge. As I review the books we worked on, it brings with it the realization of what classics they really were. In my humble opinion, and not because I was part of it, these issues were consistently the best in story and art over an extended period of time that comics ever produced. Of course, the creation of Dr. Doom, who appeared in *Fantastic Four* #5, introduced what was to become Marvel's greatest villain, and he remains so after these many hundreds of stories, but my favorite stretch of the *FF* began with issue #45, "Among Us Hide the Inhumans!" What a wealth of great characters created by Stan and Jack during this period: Black Bolt, Lockjaw, Crystal, Medusa, Gorgon, etc., to be followed up by the mind-boggling combination of Galactus and the Silver Surfer in issue #48.

I can't help but feel that Jack and Stan were at their creative best during the run from #45 into the #50s. "This Man, This Monster" from issue #51 is a favorite of mine, and of many others that I have spoken with down through the years. It was one of Jack's most effective and powerful covers and splashes due to its heartfelt simplicity. The splash to "Among Us Hide the Inhumans" has always been one of my favorites art-wise because I love drawing and inking craggy, broken rocks and falling bricks (more about this later). This brings to mind the cover of *FF* #47—what a great layout by Jack. *And* the broken, craggy, falling rocks—I just love it!

A whole article could be written just on Galactus and the Silver Surfer. What a combination from a pencil-and-ink perspective! Galactus was a time-consuming effort, but well worth it. I must mention what a great cover #49 was, "If This Be Doomsday!" I've been asked to recreate it many times. We all used to look forward to Jack's full-page art. In the "Doomsday" story, page two, see how powerful Galactus is standing before the Watcher!

I always felt that the Silver Surfer was one of Stan and Jack's greatest creations—you could do so much with him. He made the art come alive. "The Startling Saga of the Silver Surfer" was a fun story to work on because of the Surfer, of course, but I also loved it when Johnny and Wyatt Wingfoot were on campus together.

I'd be remiss if I didn't mention another favorite character and storyline that I had the satisfaction of working on—the first appearance of the Black Panther. *Fantastic Four* #52 and #53 were particularly interesting to work on—especially the splash to #53.

Some later books where Jack excelled with his brilliant line art and ideas were "The Thing Enslaved," "Ben Grimm Killer," "Doomsday on the Moon," and "Tomorrow--World War Three!"—all were great joys to be part of. In fact, page eight of "World War Three" (issue #95) is my favorite of all the pages Jack and I collaborated on. I had a ball with it! I could say the same for page six in "Doomsday on the Moon!"—what fun!

In fact, working with Stan and Jack on this long, 102-issue run of *The Fantastic Four* was extremely fun, satisfying and exciting. I've often wished that we could have continued on, and on!

Joe Sinnott

2006

(**Above**) Jack Kirby and Joe Sinnott at a 1975 comic convention. Photo by Mark Sinnott. (**Below**) Joe Sinnott and Stan Lee at a 1995 Sotheby's auction. Photo by Betty Sinnott.

THE FALL OF '61
BY ROY THOMAS

The day in early August of 1961 that I bought *The Fantastic Four* #1 off the stands, it instantly became a comic whose next issue I looked forward to. Even when it had been joined by numerous other Marvel titles before I went to work for Stan Lee in mid-1965, it was still my favorite of them all…mostly because of the ever-lovin', blue-eyed Thing.

I wrote at length about the series' early milestones, and what they meant to me, in the 2005 *The Fantastic Four Omnibus* of the first thirty issues of "The World's Greatest Comic Magazine." So, when asked to write about the *FF* for this landmark tenth *Masterworks* volume, it was tempting to just pick up where I left off and rhapsodize about the "Galactus Trilogy" in #48-50—the Black Panther in #52-53—the Kree in #64-65 (whom I later had go to war with Stan and Jack's Skrulls in *The Avengers*)—"Him" in #67 (whom Gil Kane and I turned into Warlock)—that Dr. Doom riff on TV's *Prisoner* in #84—that planet of the underworld in #92-93—and even about how John Romita took over the penciling chores so masterfully with #103-104 that the sales on *FF* actually went *up* for a time after Jack made his 1970 leap to DC.

But I'll leave it to others to do that, more eloquently than I could. What I thought might be fun to do here would be to reprint the *very first review* the *FF* ever got.

For, as a brand new college grad in August 1961, I sat right down and wrote about *FF* #1 for *Alter-Ego,* the comics fanzine I helped Dr. Jerry Bails put out. Actually, it appeared instead in Jerry's new publication *The Comicollector,* but here's what a few hundred readers encountered when that ad-filled fanzine arrived in their mailboxes, in the fall of '61:

FOUR OF A KIND

It was bound to happen! The Human Torch is back, flaming his way across the heavens, scorching everything in his fiery path.

But wait—something has been added. For this Human Torch is a blond-haired teenager, whose major interest in life, when he's not setting fire to USAF jets, is tinkering with hot-rods! And he's not alone, for with him are three other, new super-heroes: his sister, the Invisible Girl, who fades in and out of sight with alarming irregularity; the group's leader, Mr. Fantastic, who possesses the ability to stretch to an amazing variety of sizes and shapes; and, to top it all off, The Thing, endowed with tremendous physical strength which he (it?) generally uses for good, but looking like a monstrous cross between a walking boulder and a Gil monster!

Yes, these are The Fantastic Four, *heroes of a new comic put out bi-monthly by Canam Publishers Corporation. Produced by Stan Lee [EDITOR'S NOTE: Mr. Lee was formerly an editor of the Timely group of comics, which featured the original Human Torch] and Jack Kirby (of the old-time Simon and Kirby team, which originated Captain America, the Guardian, Stuntman, Challengers of the Unknown, and many others), this comic stands somewhere between the* Challengers of the Unknown *and the new* Justice League of America.

Despite its faults—and this first issue has some glaring ones—The Fantastic Four holds promise of becoming one of the better comics now on the stands, in this reviewer's opinion. Especially gratifying is the re-revival of the Torch, undoubtedly one of the most interesting super-hero concepts of all time. The Four's leader, Mr. Fantastic, is also a welcome character, as appearances by Elongated Man in The Flash have so far been too spotty to be satisfying.

The really outstanding feature of this comic, however—which somehow seems more like a mag of the '40s than of the '60s—is the hero known as The Thing! Not since The Heap ran rampant in the old Airboy Comics a decade or more ago has there been such a frightening champion of justice. Perhaps the reader of this comic era—who do not appear to like some of the old ideas—will not take kindly to such an unlikely hero; but I sincerely hope that they do, for something is needed in a period of all-too-handsome supermen to remind us that goodness of heart and an attractive physical appearance are not necessarily synonymous.

Unfortunately, this first issue also leaves a lot to be desired. Invisible Girl's power, apparently unsupplemented by the ability to walk through walls, etc., is such that her role is a minor one; the three humans wear drab clothing that would never really stand the rigors of a monster-filled adventure such as this one; Mr. Fantastic's stretching power (like that of Elongated Man) is still too limited for him to be considered the true successor of Plastic Man or a great one in his own right; and, worst of all, the drawing of this third version of the Human Torch is almost pathetic in some panels, crying for a return to something like the old Burgos version.

It is too early yet to judge fully the Fantastic Four, but I for one cast my vote in favor of them. With a little added imagination in both stories and artwork—plus perhaps the addition of a fifth character, such as the Sub-Mariner or someone like the old Purple Claw—I think this comic would be worthy of a large circulation. One interesting aspect of this comic—are you listening, Don Thompson?—is that The Thing is a rather rebellious creature who is often at the point of fighting to the death with the leader, Mr. Fantastic, and is, to say the least, extremely contemptuous of his leadership. This feature alone, especially if and when the Torch begins to get in on this running feud, would make it well worth any super-hero fan's dime.

However, Alter-Ego would like to hear from others who have read the first issue, or who purchase the second, which will hit the stands the first week of October. We'd like to hear what other comics fans think of The Fantastic Four, its good and bad points. Who knows—this reviewer may have been the only person who bought a copy!

—Roy Thomas

Fortunately, I was wrong about *that* one.

2006

THE WORLD'S GREATEST COMIC MAGAZINE
BY MARK EVANIER

One of the many amazing things about the Lee-Kirby run on *Fantastic Four* was that it didn't have to end when it did.

102 issues? (More if you count annuals and specials.) That isn't enough? Not for me, it wasn't.

People cite it as an amazing achievement not just of quantity or quality but of quantity *of* quality. I've heard other writers and artists speak of the benchmark as some world record they could never hope to equal…but really, Stan and Jack did it without breaking much of a sweat. They were both very prolific and how many issues they did of a book had everything to do with where they were needed.

Jack Kirby drew seven issues of *The Avengers* before Stan decided he needed Jack on some other book. If Stan had left him there, Jack would have drawn 102 issues of *The Avengers*.

Or more. He only left *Fantastic Four* when he did because he left Marvel, and he only left Marvel because of a business dispute with the folks then in charge of the company. If that hadn't happened, Jack could have done another 102 issues. He could have done a lot more than that, even. The man had a fierce work ethic and prided himself on never "burning out," of always finding a way to keep it fresh and challenging.

And if the contractual quarrel had been resolved and Jack had stayed, I'll bet Stan would have, too. Not long afterward, he moved more into the business division and also into managing Marvel's TV and movie projects. Still, if Jack had been there to do what he did on *Fantastic Four*, I just bet Stan would have made the time to work on it. I'm sorry that didn't happen.

I have two personal stories that oughta be in this book. One was from the day I first met Jack Kirby, which was the second Tuesday in July of 1969. A group of my friends and I motored down to Irvine, California where he and his family were then living.

Just coming off Kirby's battered, well-worn drawing table was *Fantastic Four* #97, "The Monster From the Lost Lagoon," which appears in this volume. It was almost finished—a few figures were still in rough pencil—and it was magnificent. My friends and I had never seen uninked Kirby pencil art before and we were stunned. As good as most of Jack's many inkers were, there was something magical about Kirby art in the raw, unembellished state.

In the fourth panel of page five, there was a figure of Johnny Storm walking towards his sister and waving. It was one of the drawings Jack had not yet completed.

My friends had mentioned to Jack that I was an artist, which was stretching the definition of that word beyond all recognition. I drew a little, certainly not at a professional level. To my amazement, Jack asked me to sit at his drawing board, pick up one of his pencils and finish the drawing of Johnny Storm.

I thought he was kidding. *Me?* I told him my abilities were far below the standard of even the poorest-drawn comic book, let alone one drawn by Jack "King" Kirby. "Don't worry," he said. "Just draw his hand. It'll be fine." And he sat me down, handed me a pencil and wandered over to light his pipe as, fingers trembling, I drew in an outstretched hand on the figure.

I drew very lightly, figuring that as soon as we left, he'd erase what I'd done and do it properly. Which I'm sure is just what he did.

Later—years later—I realized why he'd had me do that, and it wasn't to test me out as a potential assistant. (That kind of assistant, Kirby neither wanted nor needed.) Jack loved to inspire young talent, and he thought it would inspire me to be even a small part of a real comic book. Which I guess it did.

I don't think "The Monster From the Lost Lagoon" was the best story Lee and Kirby ever did. I wouldn't even put it in their top fifty. But there will always be something special about it to me. That one panel, especially.

The other story: A few months later, Jack did hire me as an assistant, mostly for things other than drawing. Almost one year to the day after I met Kirby, I paid my first visit to the Marvel offices in New York and met, among others whose work I'd long admired, John Romita. He was sitting at his drawing table, working on his second issue of *Fantastic Four*, trembling pretty much the way I'd trembled when Jack had made me draw in that hand.

When he heard who I worked for, he sat me down and we chatted for a half-hour or so. John did not feel equal to the assignment before him and hoped, I guess, that just speaking of Jack would give him some insight. Perhaps I'd absorbed a few bolts of Kirby energy and could transmit them to him.

I guess it was an intimidating thing, following Kirby like that. Johnny Romita was one of my favorite artists...the guy who'd replaced Steve Ditko on Spider-Man. I reminded him that a lot of us had thought no one could ever succeed on that strip and he had. "Yeah," he muttered. "But this is The World's Greatest Comic Magazine." He took it so seriously that it did not surprise me that he drew one more issue, then handed off to John Buscema.

Was the *Fantastic Four* The World's Greatest Comic Magazine? I can think of other contenders, including a few by Lee and Kirby. Still, viewed as a body of work, ringing in innovations and laying the foundation for The Marvel Age of Comics, those 102 issues sure looked and felt like The World's Greatest Comic Magazine. All the Marvel books of that era were filled with excitement but there was something about a new *F.F.* When you picked it up, you never knew what new, exciting element would be in there...but you knew there'd be something.

Stan and Jack never let us down. Not for 102 issues, they didn't.

2006

THE CHANGING OF THE GUARD
BY GREG THEAKSTON

As the '60s drew to a close everything was as different as it could be from the decade's start.

When the first issue of *The Fantastic Four* hit the stands Kennedy was President, television was broadcast in black and white, most Americans had never heard of Viet Nam, and the space-race had just begun

Ten years is a long time in the entertainment industry, and in the comics in particular. At Marvel (then known as Atlas), prior to the super-hero revival, artists made their living doing hit-and-run eight page features for the anthology books, and there was a shifting-sands feeling in the air at all times. Marvel had nearly gone out of business four years before, and it seemed like it might happen again at any minute. From high-man Stan down to the letterers, everyone was nervous.

Then, very quietly, a step at a time, Marvel took root and grew. Three years later, the sharecropper creators had now settled at the Goodman Plantation, and work seemed reasonably guaranteed. As a bonus, the stories were far more interesting to both the talent and readers alike. The longer tales allowed for character development and continuity of situation, with previously unseen complexity.

And it wasn't just the books that were changing. Working conditions at Marvel didn't resemble the way the rest of the business was punching out the comics. The artists actually got to hash out the story with the writer/editor, and were given much latitude in the pacing and direction of the tales they were telling. As the books developed, Lee began to knit a universe where everybody knew everybody else, and there were more guest stars than the Batman television show.

The change the public never got to see was the newfound confidence around the office. Now, there was no chance Goodman was going to pull the rug out from under them as Marvel challenged the competition in a way they hadn't for years. Eventually, distribution loosened up and new titles were piled onto the roster. Stan jumped from writer/editor into the publisher seat, Steve Ditko left, fresh talent arrived, and new offices were populated by a large production staff famously known as the Batty Bullpen.

Jack Kirby saw and felt the change as well. After a decade on *Thor* and *The Fantastic Four*, he was ready to institute a whole new wave of heroes, built on the foundations of his previous creations. However, lack of control of those creations vexed him, and it was only a matter of time before he left the company.

This volume completes Stan and Jack's 103-issue collaboration that birthed an entire universe, and is the demarcation point between the battle to create a new, successful comics company and the smooth-sailing home of popular icons. 45 rpm records had given way to stereo albums, black and white movies to color, and brush-cuts to Hippie hair...and man had finally walked on the moon.

A decade later everything had changed, especially Marvel Comics.

2006

The Fantastic Four #94 unused cover art
by Jack Kirby & unknown

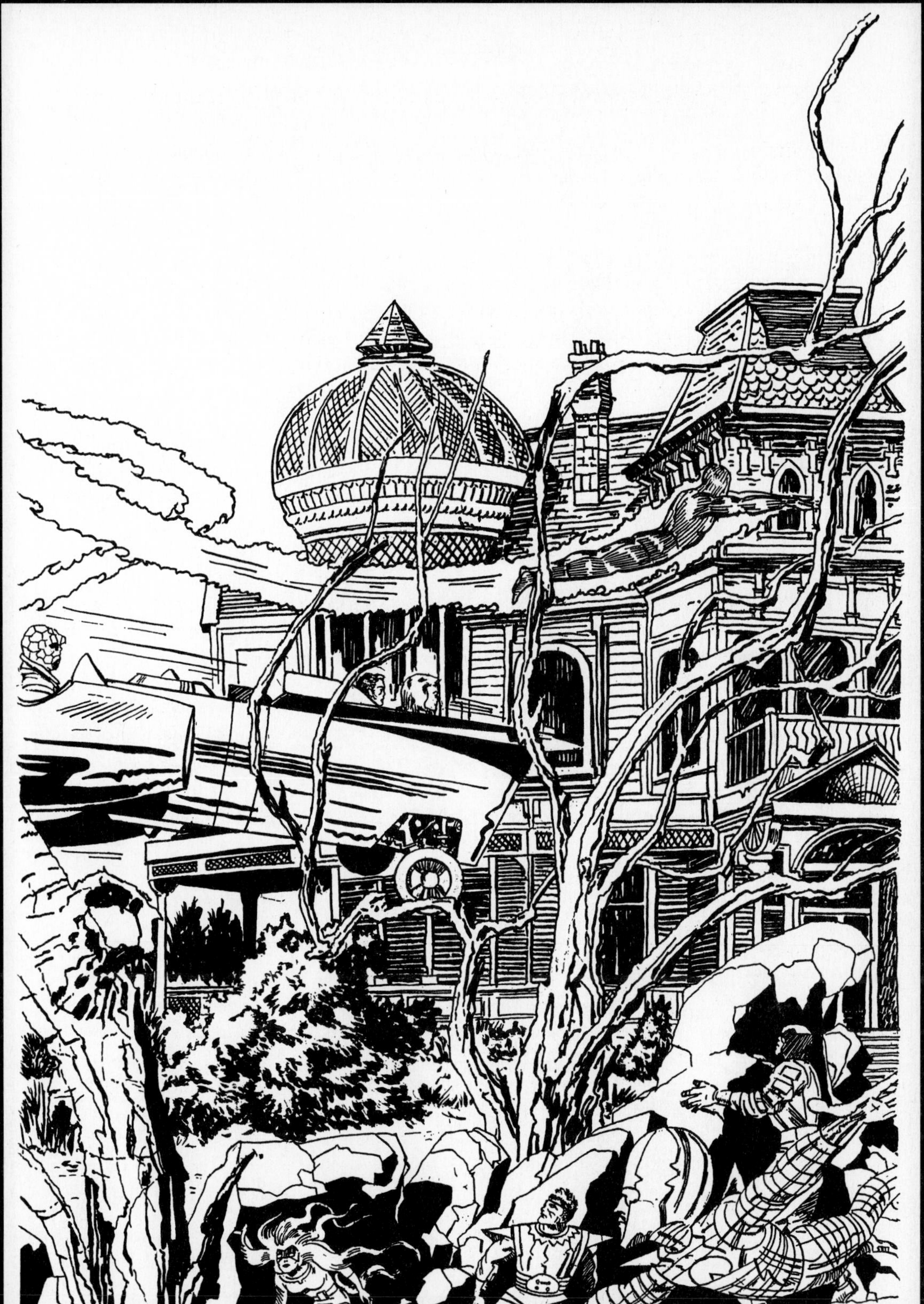

The Fantastic Four #100 cover original art
by Jack Kirby & Joe Sinnott

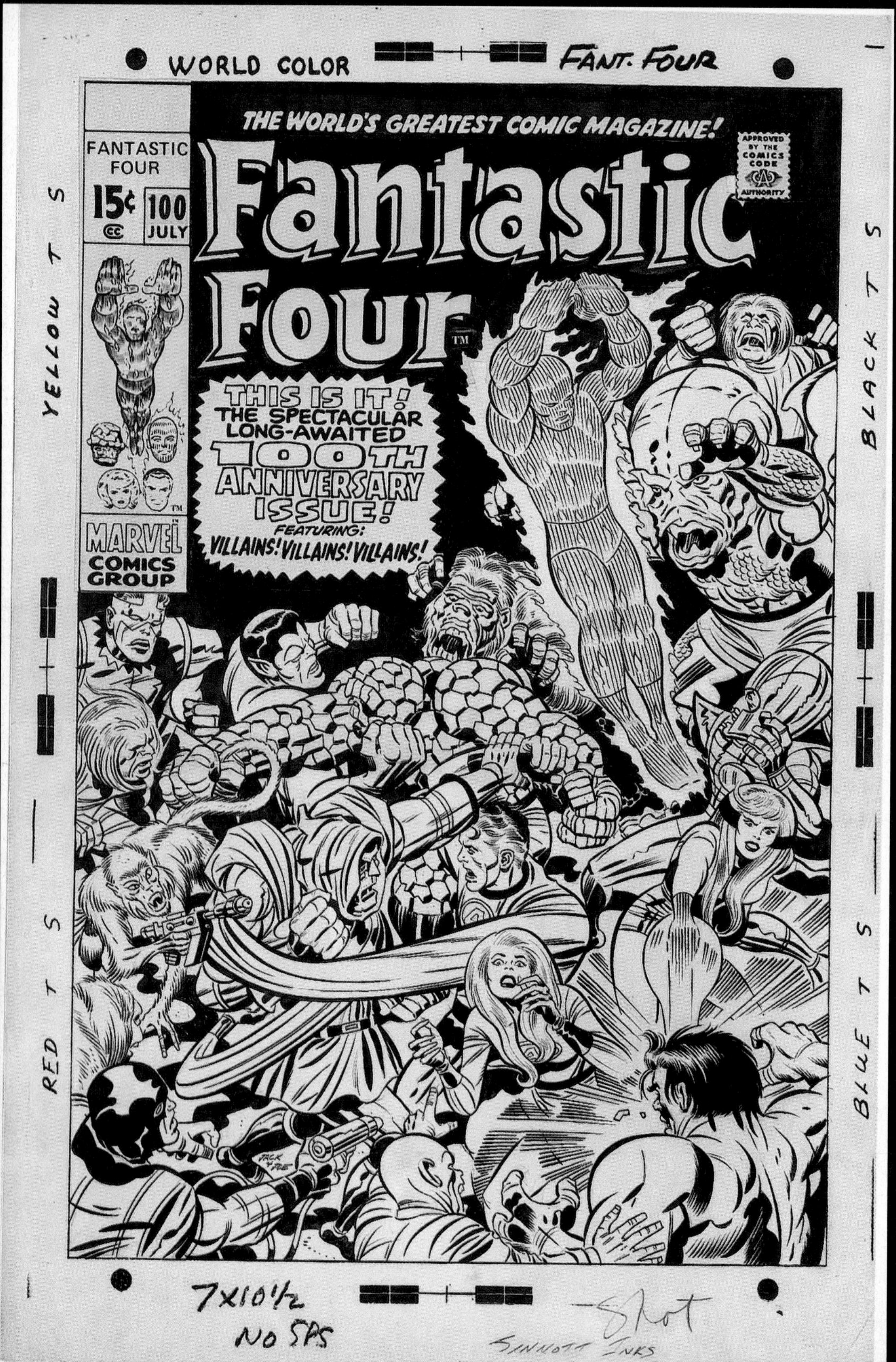
WORLD COLOR
FANT. FOUR
THE WORLD'S GREATEST COMIC MAGAZINE!
APPROVED BY THE COMICS CODE AUTHORITY
FANTASTIC FOUR
15¢
100
JULY
Fantastic Four
THIS IS IT! THE SPECTACULAR LONG-AWAITED 100TH ANNIVERSARY ISSUE!
FEATURING: VILLAINS! VILLAINS! VILLAINS!
MARVEL COMICS GROUP
YELLOW T S
BLACK T S
RED T S
BLUE T S
JACK + JOE
7x10½
NO SPS
SINNOTT INKS

Courtesy Heritage Auctions

The Fantastic Four #104 house ad
from November 1970 titles

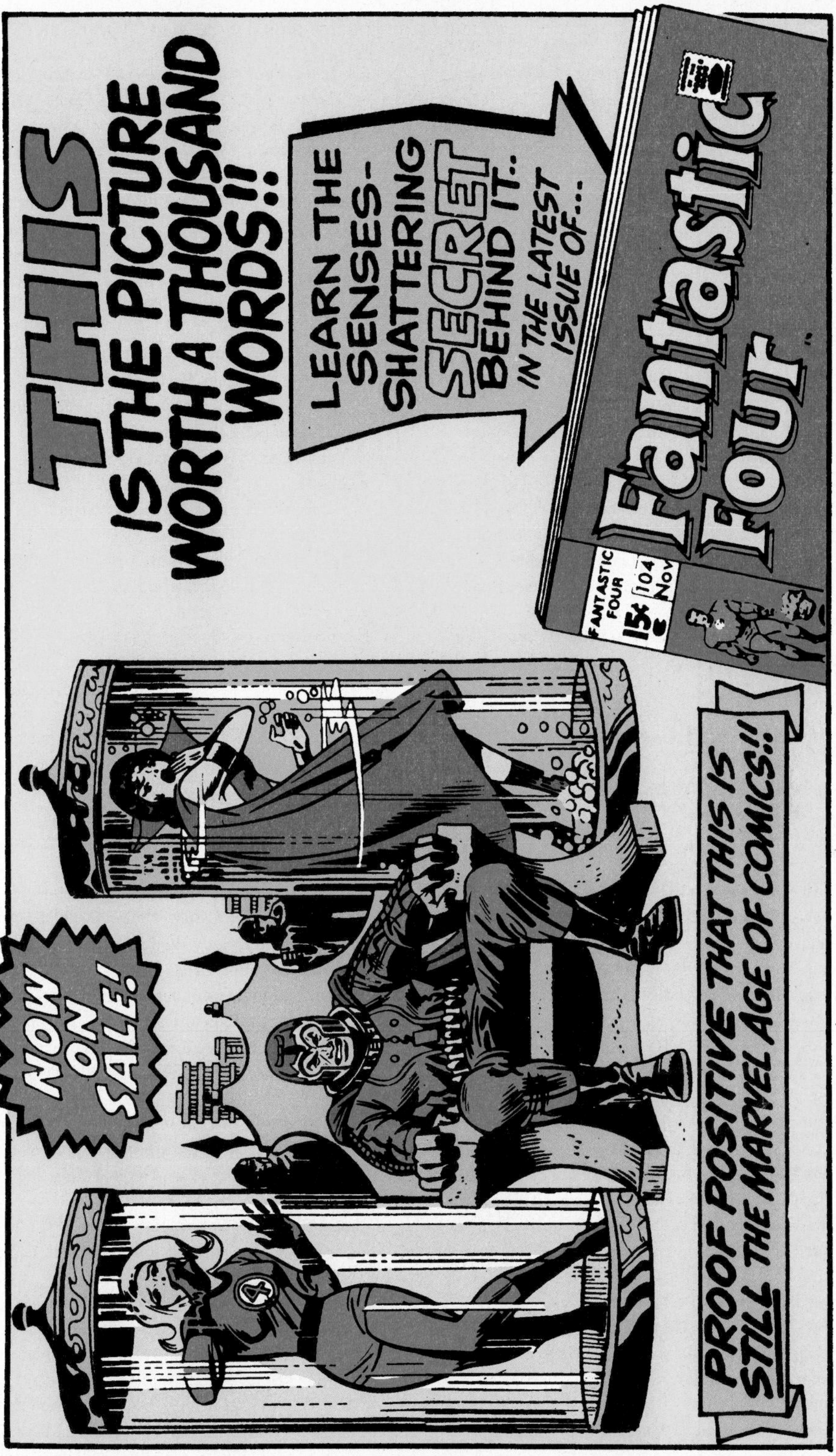
NOW ON SALE!
THIS IS THE PICTURE WORTH A THOUSAND WORDS!!
LEARN THE SENSES-SHATTERING SECRET BEHIND IT.. IN THE LATEST ISSUE OF...
Fantastic Four
FANTASTIC FOUR 15¢
104 NOV
PROOF POSITIVE THAT THIS IS STILL THE MARVEL AGE OF COMICS!!

THE FIRST ONE HUNDRED (AND TWO) DAYS:
A LEE/KIRBY *FANTASTIC FOUR* LEXICON

In 1961 America rocketed into the space race with its eyes set on the moon. Meanwhile, Stan Lee and Jack Kirby launched the Marvel Universe on a trip beyond anyone's wildest imagination. Across 102 consecutive issues of *The Fantastic Four*, the fruits of their creative collaboration remain unparalleled more than 50 years later.

Fantastic Four #1 (Nov. '61) - *Mr. Fantastic, Invisible Girl, Human Torch, Thing, Mole Man, Moloids*

Fantastic Four #2 (Jan. '62) - *Skrulls*

Fantastic Four #3 (Mar. '62) - *Miracle Man, first FF in costume, the Fantasti-car, the Baxter Building*

Fantastic Four #4 (May '62) - Sub-Mariner, *Giganto*

Fantastic Four #5 (Jul. '62) - *Dr. Doom, Doombots*

Fantastic Four #6 (Sep. '62) - Sub-Mariner, Dr. Doom, *The Yancy Street Gang*

Fantastic Four #7 (Oct. '62) - *Kurrgo*

Fantastic Four #8 (Nov. '62) - *Alicia Masters, Puppet Master*

Fantastic Four #9 (Dec. '62) - Sub-Mariner, Bob Hope, Bing Crosby, Alfred Hitchcock, Jim Arness, Dean Martin, Jackie Gleason, Amanda Blake

Fantastic Four #10 (Jan. '63) - Alicia Masters, Dr. Doom, Stan Lee, Jack Kirby

Fantastic Four #11 (Feb. '63) - *Willie Lumpkin, Impossible Man*

Fantastic Four #12 (Mar. '63) - Gen. Thunderbolt Ross, Rick Jones, Hulk, *The Wrecker (Karl Kort),* Captain Nelson

Fantastic Four #13 (Apr. '63) - *Red Ghost, the Super-Apes (Mikhlo, Igor, Peotor), The Watcher (Uatu), Blue Area of the Moon*

Fantastic Four #14 (May '63) - Alicia Masters, Puppet Master, Sub-Mariner

Fantastic Four #15 (Jun. '63) - *Mad Thinker, the Awesome Android*

Fantastic Four #16 (Jul. '63) - Wasp, Ant-Man, Alicia Masters, *Princess Pearla,* Dr. Doom

Fantastic Four #17 (Aug. '63) - Dr. Doom, Alicia Masters, Ant-Man, John F. Kennedy

Fantastic Four #18 (Sep. '63) - *Super-Skrull, Skrull Emperor Dorrek*

Fantastic Four #19 (Oct. '63) - *Rama-Tut,* Alicia Masters,

Fantastic Four #20 (Nov. '63) - *Molecule Man,* Alicia Masters, The Watcher

Fantastic Four Annual #1 (1963) - Sub-Mariner, Lady Dorma, *Warlord Krang,* Princess Fen, Alicia Masters, Leonard McKenzie, Nikita Khrushchev; Spider-Man

Fantastic Four #21 (Dec. '63) - *Hate-Monger (Adolf Hitler),* Nick Fury (as C.I.A. colonel), Alicia Masters

Fantastic Four #22 (Jan. '64) - Mole Man

Fantastic Four #23 (Feb. '64) - *Bull Brogin, Handsome Harry Phillips, Yogi Dakor,* Dr. Doom

Fantastic Four #24 (Mar. '64) - *Infant Terrible,* Alicia Masters

Fantastic Four #25 (Apr. '64) - Hulk, Rick Jones, The Avengers (Iron Man, Wasp, Captain America, Thor, Giant-Man), Alicia Masters

Fantastic Four #26 (May '64) - Hulk, Rick Jones, The Avengers (Iron Man, Wasp, Captain America, Thor, Giant-Man)

Fantastic Four #27 (Jun. '64) - Sub-Mariner, Dr. Strange

Fantastic Four #28 (Jul. '64) - Mad Thinker, the Awesome Android, Puppet Master, Alicia Masters, Professor Xavier, The X-Men (Cyclops, Marvel Girl, Angel, Beast, Iceman)

Fantastic Four #29 (Aug. '64) - Red Ghost, the Super-Apes (Mikhlo, Igor, Peotor), Alicia Masters, The Watcher

Fantastic Four #30 (Sep. '64) - *Diablo*

Fantastic Four Annual #2 (1964) - Dr. Doom (origin), *Boris, Werner Von Doom, Latveria;* Rama-Tut

Fantastic Four #31 (Oct. '64) - *Franklin Storm,* Mole Man, The Avengers (Iron Man, Wasp, Giant-Man, Thor, Captain America)

Fantastic Four #32 (Nov. '64) - Super-Skrull, death of Franklin Storm, Alicia Masters

Fantastic Four #33 (Dec. '64) - Sub-Mariner, *Attuma,* Dorma

Fantastic Four #34 (Jan. '65) - *Gregory Gideon, Thomas Gideon,* Alicia Masters

Fantastic Four #35 (Feb. '65) - *Dragon Man, Gregson Gilbert,* Diablo, Prof. Xavier, Scott Summers, Peter Parker, *Reed and Sue engaged*

Fantastic Four #36 (Mar. '65) - *The Frightful Four (Medusa,* Wizard, Sandman, Paste-Pot Pete), Professor Xavier, The X-Men (Cyclops, Marvel Girl, Angel, Beast, Iceman), The Avengers (Iron Man, Wasp, Captain America, Thor, Giant-Man), Alicia Masters, Rick Jones

Fantastic Four #37 (Apr. '65) - *Skrull Princess Anelle, Morrat,* Skrull Emperor Dorrek, Alicia Masters

Fantastic Four #38 (May '65) - The Frightful Four (Medusa, Wizard, Sandman, Trapster [formerly Paste-Pot Pete])

Fantastic Four #39 (Jun. '65) - Dr. Doom, Daredevil

Fantastic Four #40 (Jul. '65) - Dr. Doom, Daredevil

Fantastic Four #41 (Aug. '65) - The Frightful Four (Medusa, Wizard, Sandman, Trapster), Alicia Masters

Fantastic Four #42 (Sept. '65) - The Frightful Four (Medusa, Wizard, Sandman, Trapster)

Fantastic Four #43 (Oct. '65) - The Frightful Four (Medusa, Wizard, Sandman, Trapster), Dr. Doom

Fantastic Four Annual #3 (1965) - *Wedding of Reed and Sue,* Spider-Man, The X-Men (Cyclops, Marvel Girl, Angel, Beast, Iceman), Professor Xavier, The Avengers (Captain America, Quicksilver, Hawkeye), Dr. Strange, Iron Man, Thor, Daredevil, Foggy Nelson, Karen Page, Alicia Masters, Rick Jones, Nick Fury, Gabe Jones, Dum Dum Dugan, Patsy Walker, Hedy Wolfe, Dr. Doom, Puppet Master, Red Ghost, the Super-Apes (Mikhlo, Igor, Peotor), Mole Man, Grey Gargoyle, Mandarin, Kang, Black Knight II, Enchantress, Executioner, Cobra, Mr. Hyde, Unicorn, Eel, Electro, Human Top, Diablo, Porcupine, Beetle, Living Laser, Super-Skrull, Mad Thinker, the Awesome Android, Attuma, The Watcher, Stan Lee, Jack Kirby

Fantastic Four #44 (Nov. '65) - Medusa, Dragon Man, *Gorgon*

Fantastic Four #45 (Dec. '65) - Dragon Man, Sandman, Trapster, *The Inhumans (Gorgon, Black Bolt, Triton, Karnak, Crystal, Lockjaw)*

Fantastic Four #46 (Jan. '66) - *Seeker,* The Inhumans (Black Bolt, Gorgon, Triton, Karnak, Crystal, Lockjaw, Medusa), Dragon Man

Fantastic Four #47 (Feb. '66) - *Maximus the Mad, Alpha Primitives, Attilan,* Seeker, The Inhumans (Black Bolt, Gorgon, Triton, Karnak, Crystal, Lockjaw, Medusa), Dragon Man, Alicia Masters

Fantastic Four #48 (Mar. '66) - The Inhumans (Black Bolt, Gorgon, Karnak, Crystal, Medusa), Maximus, Seeker, *Silver Surfer, Galactus,* The Watcher, Skrulls

Fantastic Four #49 (Apr. '66) - Galactus, The Watcher, Silver Surfer, *Punisher,* Alicia Masters

Fantastic Four #50 (May '66) - Galactus, Silver Surfer, The Watcher, *the Ultimate Nullifier*, Alicia Masters, *Ricardo Jones, Johnny leaves for college, Coach Thorne, Belle Thorne, Whitey Mullins, Dean Asher, Wyatt Wingfoot*

Fantastic Four #51 (Jun. '66) - Ricardo Jones, Alicia Masters, *The Negative Zone,* Wyatt Wingfoot, Whitey Mullins, Coach Thorne, Belle Thorne

Fantastic Four #52 (Jul. '66) - *Black Panther, Wakanda,* Wyatt Wingfoot, Maximus, The Inhumans (Black Bolt, Gorgon, Karnak, Crystal, Medusa)

Fantastic Four #53 (Aug. '66) - Black Panther, *Klaw, Vibranium,* Wyatt Wingfoot

Fantastic Four #54 (Sep. '66) - The Inhumans (Black Bolt, Gorgon, Karnak, Triton, Medusa, Crystal), Maximus, Black Panther, Wyatt Wingfoot, *Wanderer (Prester John)*

Fantastic Four #55 (Oct. '66) - Silver Surfer, Alicia Masters, Wyatt Wingfoot, Lockjaw

Fantastic Four #56 (Nov. '66) - Klaw, Silver Surfer, Maximus, The Inhumans (Black Bolt, Gorgon, Karnak, Medusa, Crystal, Lockjaw), Wyatt Wingfoot, Black Panther, Dr. Doom

Fantastic Four Annual #4 (1966) - Mad Thinker, *Quasimodo,* original Human Torch, Lockjaw, Wyatt Wingfoot

Fantastic Four #57 (Dec. '66) - Dr. Doom, Silver Surfer, Sandman, Wizard, Wyatt Wingfoot, The Inhumans (Black Bolt, Karnak, Gorgon, Triton, Medusa, Crystal, Lockjaw), Maximus

Fantastic Four #58 (Jan. '67) - Dr. Doom, Silver Surfer, Wyatt Wingfoot, Lockjaw

Fantastic Four #59 (Feb. '67) - Dr. Doom, Silver Surfer, Wyatt Wingfoot, The Inhumans (Black Bolt, Karnak, Gorgon, Triton, Medusa, Crystal), Maximus

Fantastic Four #60 (Mar. '67) - Dr. Doom, Silver Surfer, Wyatt Wingfoot, The Inhumans (Black Bolt, Karnak, Gorgon, Triton, Medusa, Crystal), The Watcher

Fantastic Four #61 (Apr. '67) - Silver Surfer, Sandman, Wyatt Wingfoot, Coach Thorne, Peter Parker, Mary Jane Watson, The Inhumans (Black Bolt, Karnak, Gorgon, Triton, Medusa, Crystal, Lockjaw)

Fantastic Four #62 (May '67) - *Blastaar,* Sandman, The Inhumans (Black Bolt, Karnak, Gorgon, Triton, Medusa, Crystal, Lockjaw)

Fantastic Four #63 (Jun. '67) - Blastaar, Sandman, Triton, Crystal

Fantastic Four #64 (Jul. '67) - *Kree Sentry 459,* Crystal, Triton, Lockjaw

Fantastic Four #65 (Aug. '67) - *Ronan the Accuser, Kree Supreme Intelligence,* Crystal, Alicia Masters, *Jerome Hamilton*

Fantastic Four #66 (Sep. '67) - Crystal, Alicia Masters, *The Enclave* (Jerome Hamilton, *Carlo Zota, Wladyslav Shinski, Maris Morlak*), *The Beehive*

Fantastic Four #67 (Oct. '67) - Crystal, Alicia Masters, The Enclave (Jerome Hamilton, Maris Morlak, Wladyslav Shinski, Carlo Zota), *Him (Adam Warlock)*

Fantastic Four Annual #5 (1967) - *Psycho-Man, Live Wire, Ivan, Shell-Shock,* Black Panther, The Inhumans (Black Bolt, Karnak, Gorgon, Medusa, Crystal, Lockjaw), *Sue announces pregnancy;* Stan Lee, Jack Kirby; Silver Surfer, Quasimodo

Fantastic Four #68 (Nov. '67) - Mad Thinker, *Jose Santini,* Crystal, Alicia Masters

Fantastic Four #69 (Dec. '67) - Mad Thinker, Jose Santini, Crystal, Alicia Masters

Fantastic Four #70 (Jan. '68) - Mad Thinker, Jose Santini, *Mad Thinker's Killer Android,* Crystal

Fantastic Four #71 (Feb. '68) - Mad Thinker's Killer Android, Crystal

Fantastic Four #72 (Mar. '68) - Silver Surfer, The Watcher, Crystal, *Sue takes leave from team*

Fantastic Four #73 (Apr. '68) - Daredevil, Spider-Man, Thor

Fantastic Four #74 (May '68) - Silver Surfer, Galactus, Punisher, Crystal, Alicia Masters

Fantastic Four #75 (Jun. '68) - Galactus, Silver Surfer, *The Microverse,* Crystal

Fantastic Four #76 (Jul. '68) - Galactus, Silver Surfer, Crystal, Psycho-Man

Fantastic Four #77 (Aug. '68) - Galactus, Silver Surfer, Crystal, Psycho-Man

Fantastic Four #78 (Sep. '68) - Wizard, Crystal

Fantastic Four #79 (Oct. '68) - Crystal, *Sergius O'Hoolihan,* Alicia Masters, *Mad Thinker's Powerhouse Android*

Fantastic Four #80 (Nov. '68) - Wyatt Wingfoot, *Silent Fox, Tomazooma*

Fantastic Four Annual #6 (1968) - *Annihilus, birth of Reed and Sue's son*

Fantastic Four #81 (Dec. '68) - Wizard, *Crystal joins team*

Fantastic Four #82 (Jan. '69) - The Inhumans (Black Bolt, Karnak, Gorgon, Triton, Medusa, Lockjaw), Maximus, *Zorr*

Fantastic Four #83 (Feb. '69) - The Inhumans (Black Bolt, Karnak, Gorgon, Triton, Medusa), Maximus, Zorr, Baby Richards

Fantastic Four #84 (Mar. '69) - Dum Dum Dugan, Nick Fury, Dr. Doom

Fantastic Four #85 (Apr. '69) - Dr. Doom, *Hauptmann*

Fantastic Four #86 (May '69) - Dr. Doom, Hauptmann, *Sue returns to team*

Fantastic Four #87 (Jun. '69) - Dr. Doom, Hauptmann

Fantastic Four #88 (Jul. '69) - Mole Man, Baby Richards, Alicia Masters

Fantastic Four #89 (Aug. '69) - Mole Man, *Skrull Slaver*

Fantastic Four #90 (Sep. '69) - Mole Man, Alicia Masters, Baby Richards, Skrull Slaver

Fantastic Four #91 (Oct. '69) - Alicia Masters, Baby Richards, Skrull Slaver, *Boss Barker, Slave-Keeper, Taxtor, Torgo*

Fantastic Four #92 (Nov. '69) - Torgo, Slave-Keeper

Fantastic Four #93 (Dec. '69) - Torgo, Boss Barker, Skrull Slaver

Fantastic Four #94 (Jan. '70) - *Baby Richards named (Franklin Benjamin Richards),* The Frightful Four, (Medusa, Sandman, Wizard, Trapster, *Agatha Harkness, Ebony*

Fantastic Four #95 (Feb. '70) - Medusa, *Monocle*

Fantastic Four #96 (Mar. '70) - Mad Thinker, *Mr. Fantastic Android, Human Torch Android, Invisible Girl Android, Thing Android*

Fantastic Four #97 (Apr. '70) - Franklin Richards, *Quon male, Quon female*

Fantastic Four #98 (May '70) - Alicia Masters, Franklin Richards, Kree Sentry 459, Neil Armstrong

Fantastic Four #99 (Jun. '70) - The Inhumans (Medusa, Black Bolt, Triton, Karnak, Gorgon)

Fantastic Four #100 (Jul. '70) - Puppet Master, Mad Thinker, *androids (Kree Sentry, Dragon Man, Kang, Dr. Doom, Sub-Mariner, Hate-Monger, Wizard, Sandman, Hulk, Red Ghost, the Super-Apes [Mikhlo, Igor, Peotor])*

Fantastic Four #101 (Aug. '70) - *Gimlet, Top Man,* Alicia Masters, Franklin Richards

Fantastic Four #102 (Sep. '70) - Sub-Mariner, Magneto, Franklin Richards

•*Blue type denotes first appearance*

Research by Sean Kleefeld

BIOGRAPHIES

STAN LEE

Stanley Lieber was born in New York City in 1922, the oldest son of Jewish immigrants from Romania. Upon an early graduation from high school, Stan was thrust in to the Depression-era economy. Meanwhile, Martin Goodman's Timely Comics needed staff, and Stan, Goodman's wife's cousin, joined as an assistant editor. His youthful aspiration was to one day write the "Great American Novel," so for his comic book work he adopted a pseudonym: Stan Lee. This way, he could reserve his real name for that novel-to-be.

He quickly graduated from simple text pieces to full-length stories, and before long his proficiency on the job earned him the position of managing editor while still a teenager. His tenure in the '50s saw the company's expansion (under the name Atlas) to include horror, crime, Western, war, satire and romance comics.

All this was a prelude to the Marvel Age of Comics, ushered in under the auspices of Stan Lee and a small stable of artists including the formidably talented Jack Kirby and Steve Ditko. Responding to Martin Goodman's challenge to find a way to find a way to revitalize dwindling sales, Lee figured he would co-opt the super-hero revival at DC Comics and add his own magic to the mix: Instead of being perfect invulnerable champions, Marvel's heroes would be normal, fallible, imperfect people forced to cope with their newfound superhuman traits just as the average person might.

Lee's innovation sent shock waves throughout comics, and within a few years, Marvelmania was taking hold. Under his direction, the Fantastic Four, Spider-Man, Iron Man, Thor, Doctor Strange and the Incredible Hulk flourished in the shared universe they inhabited. Lee developed the idea that these larger-than-life heroes would meet each other in crossovers from title to title, thus broadening the story possibilities for eager fans.

In addition to bringing a new twist to the life of the super hero, Lee also brought the reader inside Marvel's "Batty Bullpen," creating a sense of camaraderie and special membership. His friendly and enthusiastic banter in letters pages, house ads and Bullpen Bulletins brought Marvel Comics to a level of familiarity with their fans that had kids and college students proudly professing themselves to be "True Believers."

At one time, Lee wrote virtually every comic that Marvel published during the '60s. But when he was promoted to publisher in 1971, his writing had to take a backseat, and by the mid-'70s, he semi-retired from scripting duties. Over the years, Lee has returned to write scripts for the occasional single issue or series, focusing on Marvel's ventures into television and movie development. His standing in the field was recognized with his induction into the Eisner Hall of Fame in 1994, and to this day, he remains Marvel Comics' single greatest ambassador to the world.

JACK KIRBY

Jacob Kurtzberg was born in 1917 and grew up in New York's gritty Lower East Side. It would be many years before he would adopt the name Jack Kirby, but his experiences in the neighborhood would help inform the work that later made him a legend. Unlike many of his rough-and-tumble peers, his imagination inspired him to look beyond the commonality of everyday life. He was inclined at an early age to pursue drawing, and he was also a guy who wanted to "get things done." This hard work ethic and ambition took him places most men of humble stations would never dream of going.

After early strip work helped get his name out to employers, a fateful meeting with artist Joe Simon connected the two at the hip and vaulted both of them into comics prominence. Together, they developed Captain America for Timely Comics, and Kirby immediately helped redefine what comics could be with his innovative page designs and proportion-exploding panels.

Soon, Simon and Kirby were working at National/DC, turning out hit kid-gang comics like *Newsboy Legion* and *Boy Commandos*, as well as super-hero fare like Sandman and Manhunter. He served honorably in World War II, with combat duties that took him through the European theater.

After the war, Simon and Kirby established the romance genre with *Young Romance*, produced titles including *Boy's Ranch*, *Black Magic* and *Fighting American*, and started their own imprint, Mainline. Kirby followed with *Challengers of the Unknown*, Green Arrow and the strip *Sky Masters of the Space Force*. By 1958, he began a prolific output at Atlas/Marvel that covered Western, war and monster genres. When it came time to launch the Marvel Age of Comics, Kirby brought his dynamic layouts, unparalleled action and unbridled creativity to the fore in books like *Fantastic Four*, *Avengers*, *X-Men*, *Incredible Hulk* and *Thor*, leaving his unmistakable stamp on the characters.

Through it all, he earned the nickname "The King," and his way of doing things became so popular that it set the tone throughout the '60s; before they were entrusted with taking over completely, new artists were often assimilated on to books by working over Kirby's layouts. Kirby left Marvel for DC in 1970, this time handling scripting chores as well as art duties. His "Fourth World" books, along with *Kamandi*, *OMAC* and *The Demon*, were just a few of the highlights of his tenure at DC before returning to Marvel in the late '70s to lend his imagination to *The Eternals*, *Devil Dinosaur* and *Machine Man*. He also returned to the pages of *Captain America*, the character he had first made famous 35 years previously.

Kirby was inducted into the Eisner Hall of Fame's 1987 inaugural class and continued creating comics throughout the '90s until passing away in 1994, a creative giant for whom the word "legend" may be too small a title.

JOHN ROMITA

Without question one of the most loved and influential artists to grace the pages of Marvel Comics, John Romita was born in 1930 and, fresh out of a fine arts high school, quickly joined the ranks of comic-book artists. Romita broke into the field at Atlas, the 1950s incarnation of Marvel Comics, contributing to their many war, Western, horror, and jungle adventure series, as well as the 1953-54 revival of Captain America.

After the 1957 Atlas implosion, he moved to DC, working on romance titles including *Secret Hearts*, *Girls' Love Stories* and *Young Love*. It wasn't until 1966 that he returned to Marvel and the super-hero genre in the pages of *Daredevil* #12-19, including a guest appearance by a certain friendly neighborhood Spider-Man. Having done such a confident rendering of Spider-Man in the pages of *Daredevil*, it was an easy choice to tap Romita as the new artist on what was fast becoming Marvel's most important title—*The Amazing Spider-Man*.

After a few issues struggling in the mold of Steve Ditko, Romita came into his own with a bold style regarded as one of the most iconic in comic-book art. John developed a look for Peter Parker and his world that would define the character for years to come. His more muscular and firm figure drawings added a bolder flair to the book, and his years of drawing beautiful women in DC's romance books paid off big-time with definitive renderings of Gwen Stacy and the introduction of Mary Jane Watson.

For the better part of the next seven years, Romita drew *The Amazing Spider-Man* (spelled at times by Gil Kane). He also did a brief stint on *The Fantastic Four*, being the first to draw the book after Jack Kirby's 103-issue tenure, and returned to Captain America for another acclaimed run.

It was about this time when Romita was anointed art director for Marvel. Though his responsibilities kept him from drawing a monthly series, John had perhaps an even greater influence over the look and feel of the line. In addition to drawing countless covers, he also designed characters from the Punisher to Wolverine as well as the Spider-Man balloon for the Macy's Thanksgiving Day Parade. He also trained the next generation of artists in Marvel's Art Department, known as Romita's Raiders.

Romita's stature in the field was recognized by his induction into the Eisner Hall of Fame in 2002. To this day, though semi-retired, Romita steps up to the drawing board to lend his mastery of the medium to the occasional cover or story. Beyond that, though, the Romita legacy is in safekeeping with John Romita Jr., who is now—much like his father was at the height of his career—setting the tempo for the look of Marvel Comics.

RON FRENZ

Few can match Ron Frenz when it comes to consistency and longevity as an artist. He notched accomplished runs on the field's two most revered and influential characters, Spider-Man and Superman, and carried each through controversial new costume designs. When the 22-year-old broke into the industry, he began as co-penciler of *Ka-Zar the Savage*, and then *Star Wars*. Proving himself on those books, Frenz succeeded John Romita Jr. on *Amazing Spider-Man*, his artwork channeling Steve Ditko's original web-slinger. Next, he joined Tom DeFalco on a six-year-long run on *Thor* with a new look and identity for Marvel's Thunder God. Their efforts led to *Thunderstrike*, a spin-off title featuring Eric Masterson, and the creation of the New Warriors. After an influential run on DC's *Superman*, Frenz returned to Marvel to team with DeFalco on the launch of the MC2 Universe, home of Spider-Girl, the fan-favorite Marvel heroine, for which he drew dozens of issues right up to her final miniseries, *Spectacular Spider-Girl*. In 2001, Frenz joined Kurt Busiek and Erik Larsen on their revival of *The Defenders*, and was part of the jam unit that drew the Lee/Kirby homage *Fantastic Four: The World's Greatest Comics Magazine*. His most recent project is the 2013 IDW revival of *G.I. Joe: A Real American Hero* with series originator Larry Hama.

Biographies researched and written by John Rhett Thomas

THE MARVEL MASTERWORKS

ALSO AVAILABLE IN HARDCOVER

THE MARVEL AGE

It was August 1961 and change was hitting the newsstands. *Fantastic Four* #1 did not feature the squeaky-clean heroes of yesteryear. These were real characters placed in extraordinary circumstances. They lived together, they fought among themselves—and sometimes, they even lost to the bad guys. This was more than a change in attitude: It was the beginning of something entirely different—the Marvel Age of Comics!

Thanks to the fertile imaginations of Stan Lee, Jack Kirby, Steve Ditko and others, an unending list of heroes followed the FF with ever-increasing acclaim and popularity: the Amazing Spider-Man, the Mighty Thor, the Incredible Hulk, Daredevil, Iron Man and the X-Men, to name but a few. These were the Marvel heroes, born of conflict and a continuous struggle to balance human lives with superhuman responsibilities.

The *Marvel Masterworks* series was created to give comic-book readers everywhere the chance to experience the greatest comics the world has known as they were originally presented.

THE AMAZING SPIDER-MAN VOLS. 1-15
ANT-MAN/GIANT-MAN VOLS. 1-2
THE AVENGERS VOLS. 1-13
THE BLACK PANTHER VOL. 1
CAPTAIN AMERICA VOLS. 1-6
CAPTAIN MARVEL VOLS. 1-4
DAREDEVIL VOLS. 1-7
DEATHLOK VOL. 1
THE DEFENDERS VOLS. 1-4
DOCTOR STRANGE VOLS. 1-6
THE FANTASTIC FOUR VOLS. 1-15
THE HUMAN TORCH VOLS. 1-2
THE INCREDIBLE HULK VOLS. 1-7
THE INHUMANS VOLS. 1-2
THE INVINCIBLE IRON MAN VOLS. 1-8
IRON FIST VOLS. 1-2
KA-ZAR VOL. 1
MARVEL TEAM-UP VOLS. 1-2
MARVEL TWO-IN-ONE VOL. 1
NICK FURY, AGENT OF S.H.I.E.L.D. VOLS. 1-3
RAWHIDE KID VOLS. 1-2
SGT. FURY VOLS. 1-4
THE SILVER SURFER VOLS. 1-2
THE SUB-MARINER VOLS. 1-5
THE MIGHTY THOR VOLS. 1-12
WARLOCK VOLS. 1-2
THE X-MEN VOLS. 1-8
THE UNCANNY X-MEN VOLS. 1-8

THE GOLDEN AGE

As the Great Depression wore on and the specter of war hung over the heads of all Americans, a new entertaining escape from the newspapers' horrifying realities was born: the comic book. Within their four-color pages, larger-than-life super heroes could make short work of America's foes, giving readers of all ages hope for victory against the real-life enemies that faced the United States.

At the forefront of this new medium was Timely Comics, a young company staffed by such legendary talents as Carl Burgos, Bill Everett, Joe Simon, Jack Kirby and Stan Lee. These skilled writers and artists created a vast array of characters that would give rise to the Marvel Universe!

GOLDEN AGE ALL-WINNERS VOLS. 1-4
GOLDEN AGE CAPTAIN AMERICA VOLS. 1-6
GOLDEN AGE DARING MYSTERY VOLS. 1-2
GOLDEN AGE HUMAN TORCH VOLS. 1-3
GOLDEN AGE MARVEL COMICS VOLS. 1-7
GOLDEN AGE MYSTIC COMICS VOL. 1
GOLDEN AGE SUB-MARINER VOLS. 1-3
GOLDEN AGE U.S.A. COMICS VOLS. 1-2
GOLDEN AGE YOUNG ALLIES VOLS. 1-2

THE ATLAS ERA

Seeing super heroes waning, Timely Comics evolved into Atlas Comics and took on a vast new range of genres: science-fiction tales of outer space adventures and unimaginable monsters; realistic war comics; buxom jungle heroines; horror comics that would become the center of a moral panic that rocked the industry; and romance comics for the emerging teen audience. Even the classic costumed heroes of the '40s retooled to take on the threat of Communism. From Western gunfighters to crime to horror, Atlas had it all!

ATLAS ERA BATTLEFIELD VOL. 1
ATLAS ERA BLACK KNIGHT/YELLOW CLAW VOL. 1
ATLAS ERA HEROES VOLS. 1-3
ATLAS ERA JOURNEY INTO MYSTERY VOLS. 1-4
ATLAS ERA JUNGLE ADVENTURE VOLS. 1-3
ATLAS ERA MENACE VOL. 1
ATLAS ERA STRANGE TALES VOLS. 1-6
ATLAS ERA TALES TO ASTONISH VOLS. 1-4
ATLAS ERA TALES OF SUSPENSE VOLS. 1-4
ATLAS ERA VENUS VOL. 1